HARVARD ECONOMIC STUDIES

HARVARD UNIVERSITY PRESS
CAMBRIDGE, MASS., U.S.A.

HARVARD ECONOMIC STUDIES

PUBLISHED UNDER THE DIRECTION OF
THE DEPARTMENT OF ECONOMICS

VOL. XXVIII

LONDON : HUMPHREY MILFORD

OXFORD UNIVERSITY PRESS

THE THEORY OF
INTERNATIONAL PRICES

History, Criticism and Restatement

BY

JAMES W. ANGELL, Ph. D.

ASSOCIATE PROFESSOR OF ECONOMICS IN COLUMBIA UNIVERSITY

AWARDED THE DAVID A. WELLS PRIZE FOR
THE YEAR 1924–25 AND PUBLISHED FROM
THE INCOME OF THE DAVID A. WELLS FUND

CAMBRIDGE
HARVARD UNIVERSITY PRESS
1926

215.

PRINTED AT THE HARVARD UNIVERSITY PRESS
CAMBRIDGE, MASS., U. S. A.

To

J. N. G.

PREFACE

THE World War and its aftermath have given the problems of international trade and finance a greater importance in the United States than they have enjoyed since the middle of the last century. The urgent needs of the war itself, and the almost equally urgent needs of the first phase of reconstruction, created an enormous foreign demand for the products of American farms and factories. The total inadequacy of the world's mercantile marine similarly led to a dramatic boom in American shipping. Finally, the collapse of European commerce enabled the United States to secure for a time an unequalled place in the world markets. In the last three or four years, however, the tide has begun to set the other way. The recovery of Europe is steadily increasing the severity of the competition that American producers encounter abroad, the shipping boom disappeared almost over night, and the future of our foreign trade does not seem as glowing as it did in 1919. On the other hand, the United States, for almost a century a heavy borrower from the older countries, has now become Europe's investment banker. Such marked changes in the world's commercial and financial situation have inevitably drawn an increasing amount of general attention to international exchange, and to the conditions that govern its terms.

The present study is directed to one aspect of these conditions. It reviews the history of the doctrines and investigations dealing with international price relationships, in various European countries and in the United States, and then seeks to combine the conclusions reached into a general theory of international prices themselves. The study was conducted under the direction of Professors F. W. Taussig and Allyn

A. Young, of Harvard University. It was originally undertaken at the suggestion of Professor Taussig, but later seemed to fall particularly within the province of Professor Young, to whom I am indebted for detailed suggestions and criticisms at every point. To both Professor Taussig and Professor Young I acknowledge the profound and happy obligation which springs from the cherished relations of student to teacher.

I am also indebted for assistance of various sorts to Professors Charles Rist and Bertrand Nogaro, of the University of Paris, and to Professor F. Sauvaire-Jourdain, of the University of Aix-en-Provence; to Professors Luigi Einaudi and Pascale Jannacone, of the Royal University of Turin; to Professor Joseph Redlich, of the University of Vienna, and to Dr. Ludwig von Mises, of the Vienna Chamber of Commerce and Industry. The charts and diagrams were drawn by Mrs. Alice F. Stryker.

My wife has given me the benefit of her criticisms on many debated questions, and has read the proofs.

JAMES W. ANGELL

NEW YORK CITY
November 25, 1925

CONTENTS

PART I

THE HISTORY OF ENGLISH THOUGHT

PART II

THE HISTORY OF CONTINENTAL THOUGHT

PART III

A RESTATEMENT OF THE THEORY OF
INTERNATIONAL PRICES

PART I

THE HISTORY OF ENGLISH
THOUGHT

CHAPTER I

INTRODUCTION

1. The economic relationships between the leading countries of the world are extraordinarily close, and extraordinarily deep-rooted. They pass through every sort of geographic and racial obstacle, and are rapidly becoming one of the most characteristic features of modern life. Long-standing political antagonisms have little effect upon them, while the dramatic episodes of military conflict seem able to interrupt their development only temporarily.

These international economic relationships are of various kinds, some of them long familiar but some a product of the last few decades alone. The most important, of course, is foreign commerce. The foreign trade of antiquity was a relatively simple affair. It turned primarily on the movement of commodities to regions where there was no local production of the particular article, or where the local output was physically inadequate to meet the demand. The foreign trade of to-day, however, is far more complicated. In part, it still rests on the shipment of goods to countries in which there is little or no domestic production, but much of it now involves a direct competition between foreign and domestic manufacturers. This competition has become increasingly severe since the beginning of the nineteenth century. A second type of relationship, in large part the historical outgrowth of the needs of commerce itself, is that between the principal financial centers. The national markets for short-time funds, for short-time loans, have been intimately connected for well over a century, and since about 1850 the markets for long-term investment have entered on a similar though less rapid development. Finally, there is a vast number of less important economic links between one country and another. They originate in the international movement of populations, the operations of transportation and communication and insurance, and indeed from most of the diversified activities of modern civilization.

These various forms of international relationship bind the economic life of each country to that of every other, although the degrees of intimacy are not always the same. No large economic change, whether commercial or industrial or financial, can take place in any one region without sooner or later producing an effect upon the rest of the world. If Japan has a banking crisis, the repercussions are felt in New York and London and Paris. If American prices sag, all Europe is aware of the fact. If Argentina suffers from a drought, the Russian peasant derives an unconscious benefit. Whatever the political boundaries, whatever the linguistic and social barriers, the more advanced nations of the world form a single economic organism. They are different districts in a world economy, not independent isolated entities.

2. The theory of international prices deals with one aspect of these relationships. It undertakes to explain the connections between the various national price structures. In the first instance at least, it is therefore concerned only with the prices of the commodities that actually enter foreign commerce, with their determination and with the causes and effects of their fluctuation. The number of factors that can influence the course of international exchange, however, is very large. Before a complete explanation of such prices themselves can be given, it is necessary to take account of almost every phase of the complex economic relations between countries, and of many others which at first sight seem purely domestic. From the mechanistic point of view, the theory of international prices is thus one of the most involved branches of general economic doctrine.

It must answer some four principal questions. First, how are the levels of "international" prices determined, relative to the levels of other prices in each country? Second, what governs the levels of the money prices of any one type of article in *different* countries? How is the international scale of such prices set up, and how closely do actual price quotations adhere to it? Third, what is the process by which the scale is maintained or altered, after it has once been established? Finally, how are the ratios of intercommodity exchange between countries fixed, and what controls their variations?

To solve these problems, two elements of doctrine are necessary. One is evidently a theory that will explain the levels of general prices within any one country. The other, less easily defined, is a theory of the determinants and mechanisms of international exchange itself, and of the character of the general price relationships *between* countries. Given these two elements, which are to some extent interdependent, a comprehensive theory of international prices can be erected.

3. The purpose of the present study is to trace the historical development and synthesis of these subsidiary doctrines in the more important literatures, to make an examination of the results reached by other writers, and finally to draw up a positive formulation of the central theory itself. The study is thus divided into two major sections, one historical and critical, the other more constructive. Part I deals with the growth of the English doctrine. It begins with the more characteristic aspects of Mercantilism. It then follows the gradual evolution of ideas through the classical and post-classical school, and ends with the conclusions reached by English and American writers in the last few years. Part II, also descriptive, is concerned with the principal Continental literatures — the French, Italian, German and Austrian. Except in the case of France, however, it has not seemed profitable to push the study further back than the middle of the last century. These literatures are less closely knit than the English, and it is not as easy to find lines of continuous development. Part III, finally, undertakes to make that necessary combination of ideas from which the theory of international prices itself must be built. Grounds will be submitted for rejecting considerable portions of the characteristically English teaching, and an alternative position will be presented. This alternative position rests at one point on the general methodology employed by the mathematical school, but chiefly on an attempt to take account of recent data bearing on the conditions and relationships of international economic life.

The field of inquiry thus defined is evidently of limited extent. Little will be said in the following pages of the question of the tariff; of the nature and distribution of the benefits arising from foreign trade; of the consumers' surpluses presumably involved; nor of the recently-agitated "real ratio" of international exchange. It is not the aim here to present a review of the theory of international trade in all its branches. We shall be concerned primarily with problems of mechanisms and price relationships alone. These relationships and mechanisms, conceptually if not always statistically, can be expressed very largely in quantitative terms.

4. Certain peculiarities in the existing literature, and in the present status of the problem itself, may be pointed out in advance.

In the first place, paradoxical though it sounds, a complete theory of international prices does not yet exist. Although the analysis of the relations between money and internal prices is one of the oldest elements in the economic thought of to-day, and although quite comprehensive theories of international exchange as a whole were developed at least as far back as the later Mercantilists, the two bodies of doctrine have almost never been brought together in any very real and intimate sense. In writer after writer we shall see them adequately worked out, yet kept separate. A direct and explicit combined statement is rarely given. Even in the leading discussions of the English classical school it can be found only by inference, and then by inference from propositions which are to some extent contradictory. This repeated defect makes difficult a consecutive description of the growth of the ideas involved.

In the second place, the history of the theory of international prices is very largely the history of English doctrines, of their development and of their fortunes on foreign soils. The significant independent contributions made by the writers of other countries have been few, at least until recent years. Nor has a complete alternative system ever been set up in any country, although a partial exception should be made for the teachings of the mathematical school.

Just why the theories of international exchange have found their principal home in England, and why English thought has dominated other literatures, it is not easy to say. Historical conditions have undoubtedly played an important part. England was among the first countries to develop a substantial external trade, and a reasonably uniform currency different from that of foreign centers; her geographic homogeneity, because of her insular position, is greater than that of any Continental nation; and her political unity has never been disturbed. The British Isles have not been subjected to serious invasion in modern history, and they have escaped the dominance of foreign powers. In the other countries of Europe, on the contrary, the continuity of historical and economic development has been relatively slight. The racial and territorial divisions around which a realistic theory of foreign trade must be built have undergone unceasing change in their physical composition, and in their political allegiance. The disruptions produced by the great war are only the latest episodes in a long history. It is therefore not unreasonable to regard this instability as one of the principal causes for the small interest most Continental economists have taken in any but the most immediate and practical problems of international exchange. Where the raw materials of theory undergo constant alteration, study of the theory itself must seem rather futile.

Whether these perhaps debatable generalizations be accepted or not, however, the fact nevertheless remains that the greatest part of the history of the doctrines in which we are here interested has been the history of English (and recently American) hypothesis and investigation. During the Mercantilist period, it is true, the Continental thought was active and independent, and in some ways surpassed the English. But for fifty years after the disappearance of Mercantilism it was absolutely stagnant. When a slow revival at last began, it followed in the main the paths already blazed by English writers.

The last matter to which it is desired to call attention here is the present alignment of the problems at issue. The general economic growth of the last twenty or thirty years, together with the upheavals consequent on the Great War, has produced a marked shift in emphasis. The question of the ratios of inter-commodity exchange between countries, once quite widely agitated, has ceased to concern the majority of writers. Discussion of the relation between money and internal prices has also rather dropped into the background, and is giving way to analyses based on the phenomena of the business cycle. The principal problems to-day turn on, first, the character of the concrete mechanisms of international exchange (interpreting the term mechanism rather broadly), and the means by which they can be controlled; and second, the international aspects of the phenomena attending the progress and correction of monetary depreciation. Since 1914, indeed, the latter question has dominated all others.

This particular distribution of emphasis, however, is by no means characteristic of the whole period that we shall have under review. At given times current events have brought one question especially to the fore, at others a quite different one. It necessarily follows that certain of the controversies and investigations of the past, as viewed from the standpoint of present conditions and present interests, will seem devoid of real practical significance, and academic to a degree. But later generations will undoubtedly pass a similar judgment on much of the work that is being done to-day.

5. One other observation must be made. In the chapters that follow, it will be impossible to avoid a difficulty which generalized economic analysis encounters at every turn. This is the difficulty inherent in the concept of "causation." Physical science teaches that the term should be applied, if used at all, only to definitely established and recurring sequences of events. In the complex field of international exchange, however, it is frequently far from easy to determine the actual order of even a single series of phenomena, and still less easy to show that the sequence is really recurrent. This is especially true of the peculiar conditions appearing under a régime of inconvertible paper. It will therefore often be necessary, if we are to make any progress towards a description of past facts and theories, to employ the idea of causation in a much looser sense than the canons of precise reasoning would seem to permit.

CHAPTER II

ENGLISH THOUGHT BEFORE THE NINETEENTH CENTURY

1. The formulation of a theory of international prices is, in strict logic, the result of combining a (national) theory of money and prices with a theory of international exchange. Historically, however, its origins have been somewhat simpler. If we look back over its development, we find it beginning to emerge whenever an acceptance of the quantity theory of money is combined with a recognition of the fact that continued adverse balances of trade produce compensating flows of specie. This second combination, until the nineteenth century at least, provides a sufficient criterion of the *possibility* of the existence of a theory of international prices. Although the theory does not always appear even in scantiest form when the combination is made, a lack of the combination invariably acts to prevent the slightest suggestion of its emergence. At the present day, when so many means other than specie exist for satisfying an adverse trade balance, the criterion would be wholly inadequate. But for the period before the beginning of the last century, when foreign trade was made up almost entirely of commodity movements, and when the international transfer of capital in any form other than goods and specie was negligible, it can be used with safety.

The application of this criterion serves to establish fairly definitely, in English thought at least, the point at which the history of the theory of international prices begins. In the earlier Mercantilists even the raw materials of the theory are sometimes lacking, and at best they are set forth rather clumsily. Only at the end of the seventeenth century, at the hands of North, Locke, and Clement, is their combination at all clearly suggested; and only with Hume (and perhaps Vanderlint) is it at last explicitly made. Yet even Hume did not elaborate his ideas into a very exact theory of international *prices*. Not until Ricardo can we talk of such a doctrine with confidence.

It is with these early and somewhat scattered origins, primarily Mercantilistic, that the present chapter is concerned. We shall begin with the doctrines of Malynes, to show the general state of thought in the earlier part of the seventeenth century; then turn to the more liberal and reasoned views of Mun and Petty; and from them to the relatively advanced analyses made by North, Locke, and Clement, at the close of the century. The next important stage in the earlier development is presented by the propositions of Hume, who in a few brief paragraphs overthrew the Mercantilist position, and laid the effective foundations of the classical theory of international trade. Finally, we have the contradictory statements of Steuart, the qualified doctrines of the mid-eighteenth century Mercantilists, and the completion of Hume's destructive work by Smith — without, however, any radical additions of a positive character.

No attempt will be made to present a complete account of each writer's views, nor of the teachings of each school. I have tried to select only the high lights in the picture, and to show only those larger steps in the progress of the theory of international prices which mark an important advance over preceding stages. The general character of the thought of the periods concerned is well enough known to all students to make repetition unnecessary. This is especially true of Mercantilism. No distinction will be made here between the various phases of Mercantilist doctrine, except in so far as the approach to the theory of international prices is directly affected.

2. It is impossible to understand Mercantilism, or to make a fair estimate of its value, without some knowledge of the general political and economic premises from which the Mercantilists departed. In the opening years of the seventeenth century England, and to a less extent some of the other European countries, was entering on the full flood of a period of aggressive and irritable nationalism. England herself was only just beginning to emerge as a unified and self-conscious state. She was constantly involved in military and economic warfare, and the problems of over-seas colonies and trading companies were rapidy gaining in importance. Under these conditions, which were both cause and result, it was inevitable that her leaders should come to regard the national welfare as the highest possible good in the state, and dominance over other and rival nations as the surest guarantee of that welfare. The teachings of individualism and *laissez faire*, with which we are now so familiar, were at that time almost unheard of. The nationalistic ideal was supreme. Furthermore, the resulting concept of national or collective prosperity was placed apart from, and above, the concept of individual prosperity. To the thorough-going Mercantilist, a condition of poverty among the majority of the population was in no way necessarily inconsistent with the prosperity of the State itself, and indeed might often be the essential condition of the latter.[1]

It was thought that national prosperity could best be obtained by maximizing the national wealth; and at this point the more characteristic Mercantilistic doctrines impinge upon the conditions and problems of international trade. The Mercantilist teaching, at least in its earlier phases, regarded the precious metals as the best and truest form of wealth, and devoted every effort to their accumulation from abroad.[2] The various forms of the balance-of-trade theory, which need not be elaborated,

[1] See E. S. Furniss, *The Position of the Laborer in a System of Nationalism* (New York, 1920), pp. 1–8 and following, from which this summary is largely drawn. It is the most illuminating recent study of Mercantilism that I know of. It also contains an excellent bibliography.

Also see, as well as the standard histories of economic thought, W. Cunningham, *Growth of English Industry and Commerce in Modern Times* (4th ed., Cambridge, 1905–1907; 2 vols., paged continuously), pp. 177, 264 n., and especially pp. 395–401. The nationalistic character of Mercantilism, and especially the consequent contrast between its *external* policies of restriction and its *internal* policies of free trade, are clearly brought out in G. Unwin, *Industrial Organization in the Sixteenth and Seventeenth Centuries* (Oxford, 1904), ch. 7; especially pp. 189, 190, 194, 195. For an interesting description of a similar antithesis upon the Continent, see A. P. Usher, *The History of the Grain Trade in France, 1400–1710* (Cambridge, 1913), especially Part II, ch. 5.

Reference may also be made to Sir W. J. Ashley, *The Tory Origin of Free Trade Policy* (11 Quarterly Journal of Economics, 1897); to L. B. Packard, *International Rivalry and Free Trade Origins, 1660–1678* (in the same Journal, for 1923); and to E. Cossa, *L'Interpretazione Scientifica del Mercantilismo* (Messina, 1907).

[2] This view was not quite so naïve as it now seems. The frequent emergency of war made an ample supply of the precious metals a powerful national asset; and, in a period when most commodity markets were but little developed, specie was often the *only* form in which "wealth" could be kept truly liquid.

were the result.[1] It was held that, at whatever cost, the national holdings of specie should be built up, and those of other countries be impaired. Even when the predilection for the precious metals began to be abandoned, after the end of the eighteenth century, the aggressive advocacy of a "favorable" balance of trade continued quite unabated, though it was based on somewhat different grounds.[2]

This violent economic nationalism oriented the views of every Mercantilist, however clear-headed and subtle he might otherwise be. It gave to the Mercantilist doctrines a peculiar twist which, if we examine them only in the light of *laissez-faire* premises, makes them almost unintelligible. The twist is especially apparent in the first two writers to be considered here, Malynes and Mun. Indeed no English writer before Smith, unless it be Hume, was entirely free from it.

3. Gerard Malynes, writing in 1622, was on the whole a thorough-going bullionist.[3] He deplores the exportation of specie, on the familiar ground that it is causing a scarcity of money in England, and is thus ruining her trade. To stop the flow he proposes

---

[1] From this doctrine, as it was gradually expanded and refined, an interesting corollary was also derived: the proposition that imports should consist as far as possible of raw materials, and exports of manufactured articles, so as to maximize the balance of specie payments due. This proposition was based on the fact that manufactures are evidently worth more than raw materials, *per unit of raw materials*. See Furniss, *op. cit.*, pp. 10–12 and following.

[2] It began to be held that "the wealth of the country consists in the supply of its labor industriously employed" (Furniss, *op. cit.*, pp. 60–72), and every effort was therefore made to increase this employment. Condemnation of purchases of foreign substitutes for domestic products, and other make-work fallacies, inevitably followed. An unfavorable balance of trade was regarded as evidence that foreign products were displacing the domestic, in the country's markets; and that the field of employment for domestic labor was in consequence being reduced.

The writings of Charles Davenant afford one of the first clear examples of this new position, among the orthodox Mercantilists. See for example his *Essay on the Probable Methods of making a People Gainers in the Balance of Trade* (London, 1699), p. 192; also pp. 12, 50.

[3] Gerard Malynes, *The Maintenance of Free Trade* (London, 1622). Strictly speaking, Malynes belongs not so much to the crude bullionist school itself as to the "balance of bargains" school, but the general trend of his argument, on the points of interest to us, is of the familiar bullionist order. See L. Cossa, *Histoire des doctrines économiques* (translated by A. Bonnet, from the third Italian edition; Paris, 1899), pp. 212–226.

that a par rate of exchange with each place, based on the relative weight and fineness of the respective coins, be established by the king; and that merchants be prohibited from handling bills of exchange except at rates near this par.[1] He also advocates the export of "surplus" commodities alone. In other words, starting with the familiar concept that money and wealth are identical, Malynes regards any export of money as harmful to the nation, and not necessary to the processes of foreign trade.

Yet much of his analysis of the actual operations of foreign trade is inconsistent with these practical policies. He understands clearly enough the necessity of bullion exports to meet adverse trade balances, for he says that "nothing causes merchants to export more money out of the kingdom than they bring in, but only the bringing in of more commodities into the realm than they carried out." [2] He sees that debasing or raising the value of coins will affect the foreign exchanges in proportion; [3] and he further declares that if coins are overvalued in exchange, the exchange rates will rise, the prices of commodity imports will increase, and as a consequence it will become necessary to make larger payments to foreign merchants.[4] But he conceives of money as having an "intrinsic" value based on its bullion content; he thinks of the value of this bullion as being itself unalterable;[5] and he has no clear idea of the quantity theory of money.[6] In consequence, he sees no contradiction between the advocacy of an accumulation of specie and the recognition that an adverse balance of trade leads to specie exports. The connecting link, a change in prices, was missing.

While, therefore, Malynes had a not inaccurate conception of the mechanism of international exchange, his lack of any form of the quantity theory led him into numerous errors, and prevented him from trying to evolve a theory of international prices. In-

---

[1] Malynes, *op. cit.*, pp. 84 ff.

[2] *Ibid.*, p. 61. The spelling and typographic forms are modernized. The same practice will be followed throughout this study.

[3] *Ibid.*, pp. 14, 15.   [4] *Ibid.*, p. 23.   [5] *Ibid.*, pp. 9, 62.

[6] When, as on page 3 and elsewhere, he seems to speak of the value of money as changing with demand and supply, he has in mind loanable capital; the "value" being measured not by commodity prices, but by interest and exchange rates.

deed, the best thing he gives on that head is a quotation from another book, by an anonymous author: "It is not the rate of exchange, but the values of monies, here low, elsewhere high, which causes their exportation; nor do the exchanges, but the plenty and scarcity of money, cause their values." [1] This writer, at least, seems to have been ahead of his times. Malynes was not, nor was he self-consistent. He knew that adverse trade balances must be met in specie, yet he sought by direct legal prohibition to stop specie exports.

Thomas Mun, on the other hand, belonged to the balance-of-trade school of Mercantilism, and was probably the first English protagonist of that school to put his views in print.[2] He wrote at about the same time as Malynes, but was much ahead of him in the clarity and the comprehensiveness of his thought. Like nearly all Mercantilists, he identified money with wealth. Unlike the bullionists, however, he sought to increase the amount of money in the country not by prohibiting the export of bullion, but by securing a favorable balance of commodity exports. Indeed, he finds that the export of bullion may actually be advantageous, since money begets trade, and this a further increase in money:[3] "The ordinary means . . . to increase our wealth and treasure is by *foreign trade*, wherein we must ever observe this rule; to sell more to strangers yearly than we consume of theirs in value." [4] And "the over or under balance of our trade doth effectually cause the plenty or scarcity of money." [5] That is, when commodity exports exceed commodity imports, bullion is imported.

In other words, Mun sees clearly enough that there must be an equality of some sort between the various aggregates of goods and

---

[1] Malynes, *op, cit.*, p. 62. The quotation is from *The Modern Merchant of Hackney: A Treatise of Free Trade*. Malynes does not give any further reference, and I have been unable to find the book.

[2] Mun's *Discourse of Trade* was published in 1621. *England's Treasure by Foreign Trade* was published by his son in 1664, but appears to have been written some thirty years or more before that. Both works are reprinted in *Early English Tracts on Commerce* (London, 1856), edited by J. R. MacCulloch.

[3] *England's Treasure by Foreign Trade*. I have used the reprint given in *Early English Tracts on Commerce*. The reference here is to page 134.

[4] *Ibid.*, p. 125.

[5] *Ibid.*, p. 159.

money entering foreign trade, and he recognizes the necessity of flows of bullion to meet adverse commodity balances. One more step, the correlation of the quantity theory of money with these doctrines, would have given him a tenable position not far from modern views. But of the quantity theory itself he had no clear grasp. In one place, it is true, he says that "plenty or scarcity of money do make the exchange high or low,"[1] but the context shows that he is referring, like Malynes, to the demand and supply of bills of exchange — ultimately, that is, to the demand and supply of loanable capital. With him, as with Malynes, the analysis of international exchange was still in a primitive and incomplete stage.

Another small step forward was taken by the authors of a report of the Council of Trade, published in 1660.[2] The report declares that exports and imports of bullion depend principally upon the balance of trade, and says that if upon the balance money is due abroad, the strictest of laws cannot stop its export. It even holds that such prohibitions defeat their object. They cannot prevent the export of bullion, whereas the risk attached to a subsequent attempt at exportation actually hinders its import. Accordingly, a removal of the current restrictions on the exportation of bullion is recommended. This is interesting, for it shows one explicit case where theory had gotten far ahead of practice. The actual English policy was still flatly bullionist.

In Sir William Petty, on the other hand, we find views which do not represent any marked advance over those propounded by Mun fifty years before. Petty sees that the prohibition of bullion exports is futile, and shows that either goods or money will be exported, depending on their relative prices abroad. Nor will the country necessarily be impoverished by the export of bullion.[3] Yet he retains to its fullest the Mercantilist predilection in favor

---

[1] *England's Treasure by Foreign Trade*, p. 159.

[2] H. M. Council of Trade: *Advice Concerning the Exportation of Gold and Silver* (1660). Reprinted in *Tracts on Money* (London, 1856), edited by J. R. MacCulloch. See especially p. 145.

[3] *The Economic Writings of Sir William Petty*, edited by C. H. Hull (Cambridge, 1899). This work is in two volumes, but is paged continuously. The reference here is to p. 440. (*Quantulumcunque concerning Money:* 1682.)

of money. "The great and ultimate effect of trade is not wealth at large, but particularly abundance of silver, gold, and jewels, which are not perishable, nor so mutable as other commodities, but are wealth at all times, and all places. . . . The following of such trade, which does store the country with them, . . . is profitable before others. But the labour of seamen, and the freight of ships, is always of the nature of an exported commodity, the overplus whereof, above what is imported, brings home money . . . ," etc.[1] And so elsewhere: his desideratum is a favorable balance of trade, which shall bring in money. It is interesting, in passing, to note the inclusion of freight charges in the balance of international payments, and at a later point the proceeds from lands sold to foreigners.[2] The recognition of what are now called "invisible items" was not common at that time.

In the field of money, however, Petty is less definite. He shows that raising the denomination of coins, without changing their bullion content, will not increase the value of money, and will simply raise prices in proportion.[3] But this is not a quantity theory of money, and indeed Petty has no very clear conception of that principle. Nor has he anything approaching a theory of international prices.

4. The work of the first three quarters of the seventeenth century, which the writings of Malynes, Mun and Petty serve simply to exemplify, had thus firmly established the intimate relation between specie flows and the commodity balance of trade, and had gone at least a certain distance toward analyzing the connection between money and prices. In the last decade of the century, the theory of international exchange made another great stride forward. A comparatively modern doctrine of the causes governing the world distribution of money appeared, and the theory of international prices itself received for the first time something approaching a definite form of statement. These advances were developed in the writings of North, Locke, and Clement, and to a less extent of Barbon. All four men, relative to the state of general opinion at the time, were "liberal," and even "radical."

[1] Petty, *loc. cit.*, pp. 259, 260. (*Political Arithmetic:* ca. 1671.)
[2] *Ibid.*, p. 313.   [3] *Ibid.*, pp. 87, 88. (*Treatise of Taxes:* 1662.)

They were protesting against the older and cruder forms of Mercantilism, and especially against its restrictive character. But their liberalism was in large degree only relative. When they are measured by the standards of to-day, they seem distinctly reactionary. North's "free-trade" policies turn out, on examination, to be of limited scope; and Locke, despite a brilliant theoretical analysis, relapses into flagrant Mercantilism whenever he touches on practical policies. Clement alone has some success in steering clear of these reefs.

North's free-trade doctrines we may omit here. His views on the distribution of money, however, are extremely interesting. He says in part: "In the course of trade, gold and silver are in no sort different from other commodities, but are taken from them who have plenty, and carried to them who want, or desire them, with as good profit as other merchandise. So that an active prudent nation groweth rich, and the sluggish drones grow poor; and there cannot be any policy other than this, which . . . shall avail to increase trade and riches." [1] North goes on to show that the prohibition of exportation defeats its own end, by making men unwilling to import specie; and he observes that "silver and gold, like other commodities, have their ebbings and flowings." [2] Then he comes to the world distribution of money itself. He concludes that:

There is required for carrying on the trade of the nation, a determinate sum of specific money [i. e., cash], which varies, and is sometimes more, sometimes less, as the circumstances require. . . . This ebbing and flowing of money supplies and accommodates itself, without any aid of politicians. For when money grows scarce, and begins to be hoarded, then forthwith the mint works, till the occasion be filled up again. And on the other side, when peace brings out the hoards and money abounds, the mint not only ceaseth, but the overplus of money will presently be melted down, either to supply the home trade, or for transportation abroad. Thus the buckets work alternately; when money is scarce, bullion is coined; when bullion is scarce, money is melted down. [3]

---

[1] Dudley North, *Discourses of Trade*, 1691. Reprinted in *Early English Tracts on Commerce*, edited by J. R. MacCulloch (London, 1856). The quotation is from p. 527 of MacCulloch's edition. (The essay is, *A Discourse of Coined Money*.)

[2] *Ibid.*, p. 532.

[3] *Ibid.*, pp. 538, 539. (Essay entitled *Postscript*.) It should be borne in mind, however, that North's contemporary influence was slight. His work did not begin

It is fair to observe, however, that North did not tie up this automatic theory of the adjustment of the supply of metallic money with commodity price movements. Nor did he say much of the actual intermediary mechanisms. These tasks were left for Hume.

Locke went much farther than North both in the breadth of his views, and in their profundity. He had the common intellectual heritage of his time, the doctrine that excess commodity balances of trade must be met by the movement of specie; he had a clear grasp of the quantity theory of money; and finally we find in him a theory of international prices which, while incomplete and not logically self-supporting, is nevertheless far ahead of the doctrines of his predecessors. Yet Locke retained much of the Mercantilist bias, and in his practical policies in foreign trade was quite inconsistent with his theoretic reasoning. At the end of a really brilliant discussion of the mechanisms of foreign trade, he reverts to a vehement balance-of-trade position, and deplores an unfavorable balance as the beginning of the national ruin! [1]

In the field of money Locke gets away from the older doctrine, held for example by Malynes, that there is something absolute and unchanging about the value of money. He declares that its "intrinsic value" is "not natural, but is only the opinion of men consenting to it." [2] He then goes on — apparently the first Englishman to do so — to develop a clear-cut statement of the quantity theory: "The *measure* of the value of money, in proportion to anything purchasable by it, is the quantity of the ready money we have, in comparison with the *quantity* of that thing and its *vent*." That is, "the *value of money* in respect of those [other articles] . . . depends only on the plenty or scarcity of money in proportion to the plenty or scarcity of those things." [3] Moreover,

to be seriously studied until the opening of the nineteenth century. See J. H. Hollander's introduction to North's *Discourses,* in his *Reprint of Economic Tracts* (Baltimore, 1903–1914).

[1] John Locke, *Consequences of the Lowering of Interest,* etc. (London, 1691; edition of 1692 used), pp. 177–179. Locke's principal economic doctrines are contained in this work, which is really a general treatise on political economy, and I have therefore not given references to his other publications.

See Furniss, *op. cit.,* p. 63, for an interpretation of Locke's views different from that expressed here.

[2] Locke, *op. cit.,* p. 30.   [3] *Ibid.,* p. 44.

the amount or proportion of money needed to support trade "depends not barely [i. e., not merely] on the quantity of money, but on the quickness of its circulation."[1] Independent use is not made, however, of this last element.

Locke had thus made a distinct advance over his predecessors in the field of monetary theory, both in the accuracy and in the range of his statements. His advance in the field of international trade was even more clearly marked. He recognizes, like Mun, the fact that an adverse commodity balance of trade must be met by exports of specie;[2] he gives at various points remarkable analyses of the foreign exchange mechanisms; and then he presents the first outline that I have discovered of a theory of international prices. He says:

> In a country that has open commerce with the rest of the world, and uses money made of the same materials as their neighbours', any quantity of that money will not serve to drive any quantity of trade, but . . . there must be a certain proportion between money and trade. The reason whereof is this, because to keep your trade going without loss, your commodities amongst you must keep an equal, or at least near the price, of the same species of commodities in the neighbour countries, which they cannot do, if your money be far less than in other countries. For then, either your commodities must be sold very cheap, or a great part of your trade must stand still; there not being money enough in the country to pay for them . . . at that high price which the plenty, and consequently less value of money makes them at in another country.[3]

Handicraftsmen will emigrate, and general distress ensue.

Here, then, we have the first partial theory of international prices themselves, and a suggestion of a theory of the world distribution of money. Yet it is not complete. Nothing is said of the more or less automatic adjustment which, through the mediation of the flows of goods and of specie, keeps world prices in substantial harmony. Locke had all the materials to hand, but he failed,

---

[1] Locke, *op. cit.*, p. 47. Unlike his Italian contemporary Montanari, however, he neglects to limit his statements to money and goods *in circulation*. (See ch. viii, sect. 2, below.) These qualifications first appear in the English literature with Hume.

It may be remarked that Locke, in his anxiety to get away from the idea of an "intrinsic" value in money, here comes very close to present-day nominalism. But elsewhere his position, though not too clearly stated, is more like that of the commodity-theorists.

[2] *Ibid.*, p. 14.   [3] *Ibid.*, pp. 75–78.

by a very narrow margin, of attaining the goal. He had a clear enough grasp of the quantity theory to perceive that a relative deficiency of money would lower prices in the country, in comparison with those elsewhere. He was unable to take the further step, however, and see that that situation contains its own correctives: that specie and goods will flow until the balance is restored. Instead, he concluded that trade must simply dwindle. Nor did he think that money, despite its distribution in a definite proportion to trade, keeps a uniform value throughout the world, for he says that "money . . . is of most worth in that country where there is the least money, in proportion to its trade." [1]

One or two other points deserve mention. Locke saw that international loans have the same effect upon the exchange rates as commodity movements:

> For though lending to foreigners upon use [i. e., at interest] does not at all alter the balance of trade, . . . yet it does alter the exchange for so much as is lent, by not calling away the money that should follow the over-balance of trade; . . . all one as if the balance of trade were so much altered.[2]

The quantitative importance of this he finds, however, to be small. As to the exchange rates themselves, he declares that they are the resultant both of monetary conditions and of economic conditions in general. The exchanges may be above par *either* because of the trade balance, *or* because of the richness of the country and the consequent plenty of money.[3] Then he modifies this last proposition:

> I think the overbalance of trade is that which chiefly raises the exchange in any country, and that plenty of money . . . does it only for so much of the money as is transferred either to be let out to use, or to be spent there [i. e., in foreign countries].[4]

This ingenious and not wholly incorrect suggestion again shows, however, the common partial confusion of money and capital.

Finally, he gives an interesting account of the probable effects of a compulsory lowering of interest rates. He thinks that the

---

[1] Locke *op. cit.*, p. 78. This passage presumably refers to the value of money as measured by interest rates. But since no clear distinction was made between this value and that taken in terms of commodities, an international inequality in the one would naturally seem to require an inequality in the other.

[2] *Ibid.*, p. 81.   [3] *Ibid.*, pp. 79, 80.   [4] *Ibid.*, p. 81.

country will gain only so far as the diminution in interest payments to foreigners exceeds the loss arising from the discouragement to trade. Lowering the interest rates would, if effective, either lower commodity prices or check commerce.[1] A change in interest rates may also alter the value of money in time, with reference to commodities, by inducing an export or an import of money or commodities, and thus changing the proportion between them. The reasoning here, however, is confused.

5. The third writer in the quartet which distinguished the closing years of the seventeenth century was Clement. The scope of Clement's investigations was less wide than Locke's, but in certain directions he went distinctly further.

Clement's principal contributions were an analysis of the relation between the exchange rates and the price of bullion, and an exposition of the "specie point" mechanism. This is the earliest clear statement of the latter process that I have found. He begins with the general observation that the value of money depends on its scarcity or plenty.[2] Then, after commenting on the use of bills of exchange in making unnecessary the transport of bullion, he says:

> But whenever the demand for bills to any place is greater than that those exchangers can find other remittances to reimburse their correspondents, they are then necessitated to transport so much in bullion as will make the balance. And . . . they are not to have regard to the computations of their own money, but to the value that the foreign nation puts upon its weight. . . . The exchanger also takes such a consideration from the remitter as may not only pay his charge and hazard, but also redound to his profit. Yet this *praemio*, or advance on the exchanges, cannot be great, unless . . . upon some extraordinary emergencies, because people would then rather choose to send their own bullion to answer their particular occasions.[3]

He thus gives a clear statement of the doctrine of the payment of surpluses in bullion, which was not new; and of the essence of the specie-point mechanism, which was. He further recognizes

---

[1] Locke, *op. cit.*, pp. 17, 18.

[2] S. Clement, *The General Notions of Money, Trade, and Exchanges, . . . etc.* (London, 1695), p. 7. I have used the first edition, in the British Museum. Despite the able and sometimes brilliant character of Clement's work, it attracted little attention from his contemporaries, and is to-day almost unknown.

[3] *Ibid.*, p. 9.

the nature of the relationship between the exchange rates and the price of bullion, saying that "bullion is capable of a small rising and falling of price. Exchanges are also reciprocally subject to the same alteration; the one being commonly influenced by the other."[1] That is, the relationship is as a rule causal in both directions.

Clement then examines the effect of a specie premium on the course of trade and on prices. In times of emergency, he declares that commodity imports may so greatly exceed exports as to require large bullion exports to settle the balance.

And as this will first cause the exchanges to rise extravagantly, so the necessity of purchasing bullion to export for the satisfying of the overbalance of . . . trade will of consequence cause an advance upon the price of bullion.[2]

Nor will debasing the coinage, or raising its denomination, reduce the amount that must be sent out. If such an alteration is undertaken,

the exchange will infallibly rise proportionable to the same alteration they shall make in their coins; because . . . foreigners will only respect the weight of the bullion,

not its denomination.[3]

If domestic prices should at first fail to rise after this alteration, bullion will flow in, since prices *in bullion* are lower; and exports can be increased. But the export of domestic goods will soon glut the foreign markets, result in a general readjustment, and prevent a further increase in exports. Meanwhile the bullion cost of *imports* will be the same as before, that is, *higher* in terms of the altered money.[4]

But Clement does not push his discussion farther. He takes little or no account of money as a separate factor, and he has nothing to say, other than what is given in the preceding paragraphs, of the adjustment of prices between one country and another. Nor does he attempt to apply the quantity theory of money *beyond* the limits of any one country. Indeed, his grasp of the quantity theory itself sometimes seems rather uncertain. For all these

---

[1] Clement, *op. cit.*, p. 10.   [3] *Ibid.*, p. 11.
[2] *Ibid.*, pp. 10, 11.   [4] *Ibid.*, p. 30.

things we must turn to Hume. Nevertheless Clement marks the beginning of the new era, and we shall find his ideas recurring in the doctrines of a much later period.

The last writer of importance in the seventeenth century was Barbon. Barbon's works are in general much inferior to those of his three contemporaries, but certain points deserve mention. Although an advocate of a system of partial protection, he refuted the theoretical basis of the whole restrictive structure by showing that the importation of foreign goods necessarily evokes a corresponding exportation of national products.[1] This seems to have been the first time that the correlation between imports and exports was stated in just that form.

At another point in his essay Barbon joined violent issue with Locke. Locke had protested against the proposal to "raise" the value of money by decreasing its bullion content, arguing that since the balance of all foreign accounts must be paid in money, and since this money passes only according to the metal it contains, raising its value is futile. To this argument Barbon, anticipating some of the propositions of a much later generation, made various objections. First, he declared that there is no such thing as a general "balance" of accounts, since the operations of international trade are conducted by individuals, not by the nation, and are settled currently.[2] Second, he denied that a "favorable" balance (even if such a balance exists) is necessarily of no advantage, whether paid in gold and silver or not. These too are but commodities, and "the only way to know what sort of goods are most profitable to a nation is, by examining which sort of goods employ most hands by importing and manufacturing."[3] Third, "the balance of trade (if there be one) is not the cause of sending away the money out of a nation. . . . That proceeds from the difference of the value of bullion in several countries, and from the profit that the merchant makes by sending it away, more than by bills of exchange."[4] That is, bullion need *not* flow because of the

---

[1] See L. Cossa, *Histoire des doctrines économiques* (cited above), p. 261. The reference is to N. Barbon, *A Discourse of Trade*, 1690.

[2] N. Barbon, *A Discourse Concerning Coining* (London, 1696), pp. 35, 36. I have used the first edition, in the British Museum.

[3] *Ibid.*, pp. 40, 41.   [4] *Ibid.*, pp. 59, 60.

state of the balance of payments; and, conversely, it *may* flow without a prior adverse balance of debts.[1] Barbon is thus divorcing specie movements from any necessary connection with the state of the balance of payments. This point was rather lost from sight in the rigidly simplified mechanisms of the classical writers.

6. By the end of the seventeenth century the generalized analysis of international exchange was thus taking on a definite and quite modern form, although practical policy still lagged far behind. The principal elements recognized, however incompletely, were the connection between specie flows and the balance of trade; the limits set by the specie point mechanism on the fluctuations of the foreign exchanges; the relations between money and internal prices; the world distribution of the precious metals; and the perception that the levels of prices in different countries are not arbitrarily established, but bear a certain relationship (not very clearly worked out) to one another. No one writer had yet presented all of these various elements, however, and they had not been combined into a self-consistent doctrine.

That task remained undone for nearly fifty years. Then in 1741 David Hume published the short, driving essays which wrecked one system of thought dealing with the theory of international exchange, and which founded another. Hume was the first to apply the quantity theory explicitly and successfully not to one country alone, but to the universe of countries having commercial dealings with one another. In little more than a single paragraph, as lucid as it was brief, he overthrew the theoretical basis of the lingering Mercantilist predilection for gold and silver as the best form of wealth, and in another such paragraph he destroyed the logical support for the doctrines and policies centering around the balance of trade. In their place he set the propositions which afterwards became the cornerstones of the classical English doctrine of international trade, and incidentally presented the first self-consistent attempt at a complete theory of international prices. Yet without in any way impugning the genuineness of Hume's achievements, it must not be forgotten that most of the elements for his work had long lain ready to hand: the quantity

---

[1] Barbon, *op. cit,*. pp. 57, 58.

theory of money; the recognition that excess trade balances tend to produce specie flows; the doctrine that the world's supply of specie is distributed more or less automatically; the doctrine of the effect of exchange rate movements upon prices; and indeed all of the more important parts of the theoretical analysis of the machinery of international trade. Hume's rôle was simply to combine these elements, hitherto kept more or less separated, into a self-consistent whole, and, by relating the complex phenomena of trade to a few simple principles, to put the breath of actual life into the extant scattered propositions dealing with them. If the classical writers were here his intellectual descendants, the Mercantilists and their earlier critics were his forbears.

First, Hume's doctrines on money. He says: "If we consider any one kingdom by itself, it is evident, that the greater or less plenty of money is of no consequence; since the prices of commodities are always proportioned to the plenty of money."[1] Money is "none of the wheels of trade;" it is simply a method of numeration, a set of counters. In foreign trade it is, rather, a disadvantage, for much of it results in a higher price of labor. An increase in the quantity of money will raise prices in proportion, but an interval of time is required for these changes to work themselves out. "It is only in this interval . . . that the increasing quantity of gold and silver is favorable to industry." Industry is temporarily able to pay higher money wages, which for the time being are also higher real wages, and thus get more work done. But when the effects finally spread back to commodities, the gain disappears. Things resume their previous relationships, except that more counters are used.[2]

Furthermore, "prices do not so much depend on the absolute quantity of commodities . . . and money which are in a nation, as on that of the commodities which come *or may come* to market, and of the money which circulates."[3] If hoarded, the two never

---

[1] David Hume, *Essays Moral, Political, and Literary* (edited by Sir J. Lubbock, London, 1894; first edition 1741), p. 167. (*Essay of Money.*)

[2] *Ibid.*, p. 170.

[3] *Ibid.*, p. 172. (Italics mine.) This was Montanari's qualification, which Locke had overlooked.

meet, and cannot affect one another. Finally, Hume denies the
existence of any connection between the quantity of money and
interest rates. The quantity of money, in lending operations, is
simply a representative of labor and goods. "By receiving *five per
cent* you always receive proportional labour and commodities,
however represented, whether by yellow or white coin, whether by
a pound or an ounce." [1]

In the field of international trade, Hume applied the quantity
theory beyond the limits of any one country, and at a single stroke
wrecked the balance-of-trade theory. The passage, though familiar, is well worth quoting.

> Suppose four fifths of all the money in Great Britain to be annihilated in
> one night . . . what would be the consequence? Must not the price of all
> labour and commodities sink in proportion . . . ? What nation could then
> dispute with us in any foreign market, or pretend to navigate or to sell manu-
> factures at the same price, which to us would afford sufficient profit? In how
> little time, therefore, must this bring back the money which we had lost and
> raise us to the level of all the neighbouring nations? Where, after we have
> arrived, we immediately lose the advantage of the cheapness of labour and
> commodities; and the farther flowing in of money is stopped by our fulness
> and repletion.[2]

This is of course the now commonplace analysis of the automatic mechanism of specie flows, and of the consequent readjustment of prices; an analysis resulting from a synthesis for which

---

[1] Hume, *op. cit.*, pp. 176, 177. (*Essay of Interest.*) But compare Professor Irving
Fisher's familiar doctrine concerning appreciation and interest.

[2] *Ibid.*, pp. 185, 186. (*Essay of the Balance of Trade.*)

It can be claimed, with a certain show of reason, that the intellectual credit for
the first statement of this principle belongs rather to Hume's contemporary, Jacob
Vanderlint, who made a quite similar analysis some years before Hume's work appeared. The reasons for assigning the intellectual as well as the effective credit to
Hume are these. First, Vanderlint did not push his analysis through to the point
reached by Hume — to the restoration of equilibrium. Second, unlike Hume, he did
not incorporate his ideas here into the general body of his economic thinking. He
remained essentially a Mercantilist, though of an advanced type. Finally, he does
not seem to have exerted any considerable influence either on his contemporaries or
on later thought. Hume's propositions, though ignored at the time, were subsequently studied very carefully.

The passage in question, which is too long to quote, occurs in Vanderlint's tract,
Money Answers All Things (London, 1734; edited by J. H. Hollander, in his *Reprint
of Economic Tracts*, Baltimore, 1903 ff.), p. 15. Hume does not seem to have been
familiar with it.

many others had had the materials, but which no one had before entirely achieved.

Hume then goes on to the question of the world distribution of the supply of money:

It is evident, that the same causes which would correct these exorbitant inequalities . . . must prevent their happening in the common course of nature, and must forever, in all neighbouring nations, preserve money nearly proportionable to the art and industry of each nation.[1]

Finally, he adds one other influence which checks adverse trade balances, though it is of course more limited in its effects than are the specie flows.

When we import more goods than we export, the exchange turns against us, and this becomes a new encouragement to export; as much as the charge of carriage and insurance of the money which becomes due would amount to. For the exchange can never rise but a little higher than the sum.[2]

This last doctrine, though crudely put, is of course the familiar analysis of the operation of the specie points, first clearly presented by Clement some fifty years before.

From these passages it is evident that we have in Hume all of the essential elements of the later full-blown classical theory of international prices, so far as concerns trade under a common specie standard. These elements are, first, the quantity theory of money; second, the automatic adjustment of international prices and of the value of money itself, through the effects of specie flows on prices; third, the corrective effect upon commodity prices of the movement of the exchange rates; and fourth, the limitation imposed by the specie-point mechanism upon fluctuations of the exchanges — and the corollary fact that specie will move when the exchanges reach the specie point. The contributions made by Ricardo and Mill, and by later writers, consisted either in a refinement of the details of these theories; or in an application of them, as far as possible, to other sorts of monetary conditions; or,

---

[1] Hume, *op. cit.*, p. 186. Compare this with Ricardo's doctrine that money will be so distributed as to allow the terms of trade to be the same as those under barter. Hume's doctrine has the merit of being more comprehensive; it tells us more of the probable absolute quantities of money.

[2] *Ibid.*, p. 186 note.

finally, in an analysis of the underlying causes which give rise to international trade itself, and that govern its terms.

7. The writers of the eighteenth century who came after Hume, so far as their doctrines concern us, were principally occupied either in filling in the interstices of a structure of which Hume had raised the framework and much of the walls, or in trying to overthrow the building itself.[1] Of these we need consider only three: Harris, Steuart, and Adam Smith.[2]

Harris' doctrines seem at all essential points to be a reflection of Hume, though I find no acknowledgment of an intellectual debt, nor even a reference to Hume's work. They offer various interesting features, however, and while it is unnecessary to undertake a complete survey of Harris' views, the improvements on Hume are worth listing. First, Harris presents some minor changes in the form of statement of the quantity theory, which we need not review.[3] Second, he observes that the prices of commodities have

[1] Two interesting American fragments which appeared in the middle of the century, but which are quite out of the main English current, may be mentioned here. One, by William Douglass, is entitled *Currencies of the British Plantations in North America* (Boston, 1740); reprinted in *Tracts on Paper Currency and Banking* (London, 1857), edited by J. R. MacCulloch. (Also reprinted by other editors later.) Among other things, it attempts to show that under inconvertible paper the balance of trade determines the value of money. The suggestion is valuable, and far ahead of most contemporary thought in England. (See MacCulloch, p. 50.) The other is an essay by Benjamin Franklin, in which he declares that the unfavorable balance of trade has drained away the colonies' metallic money, and that the consequent lack of media of circulation has *caused* the issue of paper money. He also denies, unlike his more consistent predecessor, that there has been a general depreciation of money. See, in Jared Sparks' edition of Franklin's *Works* (Boston, 1836), vol. 2, the essay entitled *Remarks and Facts relative to the American Paper Money;* especially pp. 341, 342, 350, 351.

[2] It will be observed that no place is assigned here to the writings of Richard Cantillon. It has seemed to me more appropriate to examine them in connection with the development of French thought, because although the origins of Cantillon's peculiar doctrines were English, their effects were almost entirely confined to France. They are discussed in ch. viii, sect. 4, below.

The work of his cousin Philip Cantillon, *The Analysis of Trade* (London, 1759), is in every respect an inferior production, partly a poor copy of Richard Cantillon himself, and partly a reversion to a crude Mercantilism.

[3] W. Harris, *Essay upon Money and Coins* (London, 1757–1758: 2 vols.). I have used here the reprint of this work given in *Tracts on Money* (London, 1856), edited by J. R. MacCulloch. It is there described as the work of an anonymous writer,

not risen in proportion to the increase in money which was consequent on the discovery of America. This he finds is due partly to the increase in commodities themselves, partly to improvements in the arts, and partly to the fact that much bullion has been sent to the East Indies, and has thus passed completely out of the European commercial system.[1] Third, he gives a fuller exposition than Hume of the effects of specie flows upon various sorts of prices. In that connection he remarks that, while the demand for bills may force the price of bullion much *above* the value of coined money, the price can never go *below* that value as long as the mints are kept open.[2] Fourth, he shows that a permanent adverse balance of trade may be due to permanent bullion exports, as in the case of a mining country, and will therefore have no special significance relative to exchange rates or commodity prices.[3] Foreign debts are likewise equivalent, in their effects here, to an adverse balance of trade.[4] Fifth, the proportion of the world's supply of money which each country shall have is settled by the daily operations of commerce, and is proportioned to the whole wealth and traffic of that country, but this proportion is constantly changing.[5] Finally, the range between the upper and the lower points at which specie will move is different between different places. It varies with the cost of transporting bullion.[6]

These various observations need no specific comment. They are not all original with Harris, and none of them presents any very radical departure. But they are interesting as an indication of the nature of the process by which a rough path, blazed through the wilderness by a pioneer thinker, is slowly built up piece after piece by his successors, until it at last becomes a broad paved highroad.

The next important work to appear, Sir James D. Steuart's "Principles of Political Economy," [7] is a curious production. In

but the same book is in the British Museum, under the authorship of W. Harris., The reference is to pp. 396, 397.

[1] Harris, *op. cit.*, p. 398.

[2] *Ibid.*, pp. 405–407, pp. 424, 425.   [3] *Ibid.*, p. 426.

[4] *Ibid.*, p. 427.   [5] *Ibid.*, p. 407.   [6] *Ibid.*, p. 427.

[7] Published in London, 1767; 2 vols. I have used the first edition, in the British Museum.

many ways it is one of the great works in economic literature, yet much of its force is destroyed by curious inconsistencies and even outright blunders. This is especially true of the various discussions bearing on international trade. In that field Steuart presents a number of doctrines which are partly or wholly right, and which are real contributions to theory; yet he flatly rejects the most vital parts of Hume's teachings. He denies Hume's statement that there can be no such thing as an enduring balance of trade on one side or the other; he denies that money tends always to seek its own level throughout the channels of the world's commerce; and finally, relapsing into flagrant Mercantilism, he insists upon the maintenance of a favorable balance of trade, as being the one sure way of augmenting the national wealth.[1] Nor does the quantity theory of money ever seem to have become an integral part of his intellectual equipment. At certain points, indeed, he explicitly rejects it, though at others he seems to accept it.

Yet, despite these almost fatal errors, much of what he has to say is good. He gives a fair discussion of the components of price, tracing profits to a demand in excess of costs, and showing that if in foreign trade excessively high profits become incorporated in costs, trade will cease: prices become too high to permit of export.[2] Had he carried this a little farther, we should perhaps have had one of the first discussions of elasticity of demand. He also has some faint idea of the principle of comparative advantage, basing it primarily on the industriousness and sobriety of the population;[3] and he gives a novel analysis of the effects of the introduction of foreign trade into a new country.[4]

Later on in the book Steuart offers a theory, excellent as far as it goes, of the determination of international prices. It takes no account of monetary phenomena, however, and is therefore not capable of standing alone. He declares that within any one country prices are dependent, first, on competition among consumers, which tends to raise prices; and, second, on competition among merchants, which tends to lower them. This second form of com-

---

[1] Steuart, *op. cit.*, vol. i, p. 416, and elsewhere. See especially p. 96, in connection with the fishing industry.

[2] *Ibid.*, vol. i, p. 182.   [3] *Ibid.*, vol. i, pp. 184–188. See also pp. 273–275.

[4] *Ibid.*, vol. i, p. 208.

petition is determinate, though the first is not. Its limit is reached when profits are reduced to the minimum, to the exact "physical necessary" of the workman — which is used as equivalent to cost. In foreign trade, however, the demanders are not consumers, but still other merchants, whose price offers are regulated by profits. Hence competition on *either* side of the exchange situation will cease when profits are reduced to the minimum. "The degree, therefore, of foreign competition will alone regulate the prices of . . . exportable commodities, and of consequence the profits of such as are employed in them." [1] At another point, he refers to this method of price determination as one of "reciprocal demand," [2] although the term does not carry here the meaning assigned to it in the later classical theory.

He also speaks, somewhat less intelligibly, of a balance between "work" and "demand," the balance being of such a character that "if . . . there be found too many hands for the demand, work will fall too low for workmen to be able to live; or, if there be too few, work will rise, and manufactures will not be exported." [3] This proposition contains possibilities of a quite modern theory of the relationships between international trade and the distribution of national productive power, but in view of the obscurity of the context it is safer to regard it as a random venture, and to ignore it. [4]

Steuart's views on the relations between national productive power and international trade, and between wages and prices, were in part a reflection of — and in part an improvement upon — a type of doctrine which was common to many Mercantilists

---

[1] Steuart, *op. cit.*, vol. ii, p. 12.   [2] *Ibid.*, vol. i, pp. 184–188 *passim.*

[3] *Ibid.*, vol. i, p. 224.

[4] For example, Steuart regards the ultimate collapse of this balance as inevitable in every commercial state, and thinks that the collapse must entail the destruction of national prosperity. See also p. 276.

In speaking of seignorage on the coining of money, he says that seignorage ought to keep the value of the coin above that of bullion. A "wrong" balance of trade, however, will raise the price of bullion to that of coin — though it cannot go higher, since coin would then be exported too. And commodity prices ought to go up in like degree; that is, *bullion* prices will stay the same, but *coin* prices will rise, as the artificial differential disappears (vol. ii, p. 5). Yet it is interesting to note that, in his view, this "normal" adjustment may be obstructed by the operations of traders, to whom a power over the exchanges is tacitly ascribed (vol. ii, p. 6).

of the eighteenth century. The doctrine was never worked out
very accurately, however; and the writers in whom it is to be
found, usually in fragmentary form, are not of sufficient importance in the general English literature to be treated separately
here. The interested reader will find a full discussion in Professor
Furniss's work, already referred to.[1]

The essence of the position is this. First, it was held that wages-
cost determines the cost of production of goods in the export
trade. At a time when the dominant English export was still
cloth, when the cost of the raw materials was roughly the same
throughout western Europe, and when knowledge of the more important trade secrets was widely diffused,[2] this conclusion was not
unreasonable. Second, it was held that wages tend constantly to
approach the subsistence level, and to fluctuate with the prices of
the necessaries of life; and that the reduction of these prices is
advantageous to the nation, because, through the consequent
reduction in wages, it conduces to superiority in the export trade.
Proceeding from these two elements of doctrine,—a subsistence-
theory of wages and a wages-cost theory of export prices,—a
number of writers hinted rather vaguely at a real labor-cost theory
of international values. But only Cantillon, whose influence was
largely confined to France, took the final step of attempting to
proportion the selling price of goods to the amount of labor used
in their production.[3] And even Cantillon failed to apply this idea
to the determination of the course and terms of international trade
— an application which would have led him to an anticipation of
Ricardo's classical doctrine. The other contemporary English
writers employed their subsistence-theories only to justify the paying of still lower wages to the laborers in the export industries.[4]

[1] Furniss, op. cit., ch. 7; especially pp. 162–172.

[2] Ibid., p. 172.   [3] See ch. viii, sect. 4, below.

[4] The principal writers in this group, and some of their more characteristic pas-
sages, are: Charles Davenant, An Essay upon the Probable Methods of making a
People gainers in the Balance of Trade (London, 1699 and ff.), pp. 144, 145; Jacob
Vanderlint, Money Answers All Things (London, 1734; reprinted by J. H. Hol-
lander), pp. 9, 16, 17, 23, 24; Sir W. Mildmay, The Laws and Policies of England
(London, 1765), pp. 22, 23; and a number of Josiah Tucker's works. On Tucker see
W. E. Clark, Josiah Tucker, Economist (New York, 1903), pp. 144 ff. For other
similar writers. see Furniss, op. cit., ch. 7.

Steuart seems to have started from similar theories of wages and prices, but he pushed the analysis one step farther by his attempt to take account of the conditions and fluctuations of demand in the *importing* countries. His discussion, it is true, is confused and incomplete; and he never undertakes to reconcile the theory of *export* prices, as determined by demand, with the subsistence- and wages-cost theory of *internal* prices. Yet it is possible to find in Steuart more than a glimmering of that "equation of international demand" which Mill, confronted with a similar problem, was to work out some seventy-five years later.

8. The last important writer of the eighteenth century is Adam Smith, whose influence far exceeded that of any of his contemporaries. Smith's talent, however, so far as it was directed toward foreign trade, lay primarily in the direction of practical policy. His rôle was not so much to evolve new theories as to select the usable portions of old ones, to fill inert and often merely academic doctrine with the cogent breath of life. To him more than to any other one man belongs the credit for the overthrow of the maze of Mercantilist policies, yet the essence of the propositions on which he based his forceful arguments, in so far as they were concerned with the actual mechanisms of exchange, is taken straight from Hume. Smith is the first to admit the debt. We therefore find no radical new departures in his formulations of theory. He presents simply a continuation of that process of refinement and elaboration of which the inception has already been traced.

In the field of money it is difficult to pin Smith down to any exact generalized statement, and still more difficult to make his various observations consistent with one another. At times he seems a sincere quantity theorist of the less doctrinaire type. For example, he says at one point that

the discovery of the abundant mines of America seems to have been the sole cause of this diminution [1570–1640] in the value of silver in proportion to that of corn. It is accounted for in the same manner by everybody, and there never has been any dispute either about the fact or about the cause of it.[1]

---

[1] Adam Smith, *The Wealth of Nations* (edited by Edwin Cannan: third edition, London, 1922), vol. i, p. 175. Also see vol. i, pp. 172, 188, 311, 312. The passage on p. 172, dealing with the maximum and minimum prices of the precious metals, sounds curiously like Mill's more concise theorems of the next century.

In the following pages, I have not given separate references to Smith's *Lectures*

Yet elsewhere, in discussing the effects of issuing (convertible) paper money, Smith adopts what seems to be the exact antithesis of the quantity-theory view.[1] He declares that such an issue simply leads to the exportation of an equal amount of gold and silver, and that the total volume of paper which can be kept in circulation can never exceed the amount of the specie which it displaces. Such a doctrine must necessarily presuppose *fixity* of prices, for the time being at least. It conceives of the "channel of circulation" as being confined within rigid price walls, and assumes that its flow, "the commerce being supposed the same," can never exceed the normal magnitude. Conversely an increase in the demand for silver, resulting from an expansion of industry and trade, will likewise cause no change in prices. The purchase of more bullion in other countries, to supply the deficiency, will be the sole result.[2]

But Smith has still a third doctrine. He says that

the proportion between the value of gold and silver and that of goods of any other kind, depends . . . upon the proportion between the quantity of labour which is necessary in order to bring a certain quantity of gold and silver to market, and that which is necessary to bring thither a certain quantity of any other sort of goods.[3]

Here, the determining factor is nothing other than labor costs of production.

We thus find Smith holding at least three different and to some extent mutually contradictory positions, with respect to the value of money. I think that a considered view of the general trend and character of his reasoning must lead, in the first place, to the conclusion that nothing which can properly be called a quantity theory is to be found in his writings. In discussing the effects of the American discoveries, he simply drew attention to the his-

---

(edited by Edwin Cannan: Oxford, 1896). On the points of interest here, Smith's ideas were in the main much less clearly and completely formulated in the *Lectures* than in the *Wealth of Nations*, and the *Lectures* do not reveal important differences.

[1] For example, see *Wealth of Nations*, vol. i, pp. 277, 283. Also see vol. i, pp. 307 ff., 322, 323, 406, 407.

[2] See *ibid.*, vol. i, pp. 188 and 322. As applied to *inconvertible* paper, this whole position is evidently erroneous: specie will be neither driven out nor attracted.

[3] *Ibid.*, vol. i, pp. 311, 312.

torical fact that, in the past, an increase in the supply of silver *had* at one time led to a decrease in its value. He did not intend to present this fact as a general theoretical proposition. On the other hand, he did not adopt an explicitly anti-quantitative position. In his discussion of the effects of issuing paper money, just referred to, he was again simply stating the results of his concrete observations, without attempting to draw up a necessarily universal conclusion as to theory. There remains the labor-cost doctrine. In this is to be found the real key to Smith's ideas, at least with respect to the precious metals. He regards labor-cost, operating through quantitative relationships only in so far as is consistent with his own version of the general labor-cost doctrine, as being the explanation and source of the relative value of gold and silver in terms of other kinds of commodities.[1] It is to labor cost that he appeals whenever he faces the issue squarely. Yet it must be admitted that even this position is by no means consistently held.

In the field of international trade proper, as distinct from the field of money, Smith's chief concern was with the overthrow of practical Mercantilist policy. The arguments by which he sought to attain this goal, — the mutual advantages of the division of labor, the futility of accumulating the precious metals for their own sake, the self-defeating effects of restrictions upon industry and commerce,— are now almost commonplace, to English and American students at least, and need not be reviewed. The history of the success of these arguments, of the replacement of Mercantilism by *laissez faire*, is almost equally commonplace. It might perhaps have been expected that Smith's practical

---

[1] The value of *inconvertible* paper money was regarded as being governed by the degree of confidence in its redeemability. See for example *Wealth of Nations*, vol. i, p. 308. It does not appear, however, that Smith ever contemplated the case of complete inconvertibility as we now know it. Rather, he was thinking of various degrees of difficulty in securing conversion.

Smith also presented, at one point, what would now be called a "dynamic" formulation of the quantity theory, in which the element of growth was included: see *ibid.*, vol. i, pp. 176, 177. But his argument here is rather parenthetical, and was never incorporated into his general reasoning on monetary problems. In view of the slight attention paid to it by later writers, it cannot be regarded as especially significant.

conclusions would prove to be based on some new and striking type of theoretical analysis. But such is not the case. The novelty of his work here lay in its simple and convincing presentation of old ideas, not in its doctrinal basis. All of his tools, painfully manufactured by Hume and the liberal Mercantilists, lay ready to hand. Indeed, Smith never worked out very accurately the theories underlying his own doctrines, and his presentation of them, far from improving upon that of his predecessors, is in many respects inferior.

His principal contribution to the theory of the subject — though it was not original with him — was his repeated demonstration of the reciprocal advantages arising from the international division of labor;[1] a doctrine with which Ricardo later started, in formulating the principle of comparative costs. Yet Smith quite misunderstands the very nature of the benefit itself, at least at certain points. He says that

between whatever places foreign trade is carried on, they all of them derive two distinct benefits from it. It carries out that surplus part of the produce of their land and labor for which there is no demand among them, and brings back in return for it something else for which there is a demand.[2]

Why an unwanted "surplus" should ever have been produced at all, is not indicated.

With respect to the problems that enter more directly into the theory of international prices, Smith is even less satisfactory. He adopts, it is true, the practical conclusions of Hume's price-specie flow analysis, and repeatedly declares that no action of the government can increase or maintain the amount of gold and silver in the country beyond the needs of commerce. But the only agent of adjustment to which he refers is the somewhat vaguely-defined element, "effectual demand." Changes in prices — the one essential factor in the situation — are not even mentioned.[3] Prices are regarded, rather, as being fixed elements; and specie flows, far from being assigned any causal relationship to price

[1] Especially, in *Wealth of Nations*, vol. i, pp. 413, 453. The underlying idea is found in a number of Smith's predecessors.

[2] *Ibid.*, vol. i, p. 413. See also the curious proposition (vol. i, p. 348) that capital employed in foreign trade replaces *two* capitals, one at home and one abroad.

[3] See for example *ibid.*, vol. i, p. 402.

changes, are made dependent on the changing needs of trade and the changing proportion of paper money. From this came the familiar but misleading idea of a "redundant" currency. Moreover, we have already seen that his conception of the effects of paper money upon foreign trade was incomplete; a conception which involved, incidentally, a confusion between convertible and inconvertible conditions.[1] In general, Smith accepted the *fact* of a world distribution of the precious metals, but gave little concern to the theoretical explanation. He was content with the circular proposition that each country needs, and obtains, simply the amount requisite to circulate the annual produce of its land and labor — the distribution being accomplished through the working of "effectual demands."[2] He neither accepted Hume's analysis entirely, nor concurred in Steuart's opposition.[3]

In a word, Smith quite failed to combine the various elements of doctrine which were available to him into a single theory of international prices. It would have been entirely possible for him to have done so. In addition to the teachings of Hume, with which he was of course familiar, he had all his own miscellaneous observations in the fields of money and of foreign trade to draw upon. But he was not especially interested, nor especially adept, in constructing formulations of theory, and his ideas on these questions in the main failed to become incorporated into the doctrines of the nineteenth-century schools of English thought. The latter were derived, rather, directly from Hume. Even Smith's principal contribution, the demonstration of the benefits of the in ernational division of labor, was based on an idea which was ar from original with him.

[1] Such a confusion also seems to be implicit in the discussions of vol. i, pp. 285 ff. and 306 ff.

[2] See *Wealth of Nations*, vol. i, pp. 322, 352; vol. ii, pp. 10 ff.

[3] For a similar conclusion see J. H. Hollander, *The Development of the Theory of Money from Adam Smith to David Ricardo* (25 Quarterly Journal of Economics, 1911), p. 439.

A similar indifference to theoretical exactness appears in Smith's discussions of the world value of money. At some points he seems to suggest that it tends to equality in all civilized countries, though the intermediary mechanism is not clearly indicated, while at others he explicitly denies any such equalization. See *ibid.*, vol. i, pp. 172, 190, 216, 402.

If we desire a theory of international prices from him, we must get it by implication and inference, by reading between the lines. But the task is not difficult. Smith was eminently familiar with Hume's work, and Hume's conclusions were here an integral part of his own mental equipment. To get Smith's probable doctrine, therefore, we need only take the theory as it left the hands of Hume, and append to it those elaborations and refinements which Smith worked out in the field of monetary phenomena: principally, a formulation of the less rigid theory of money, and those qualifications in the theory of the foreign exchanges required by the recognition of relatively disordered monetary conditions. But we must be chary of attributing too much force to any such revised statement. It would be hypothetical at best; a statement of what Smith *might* have said, not of what he *did* say. And, as we shall see later, the more novel terms in this presumptive statement wholly failed to become incorporated in the theories and concrete doctrines of the subsequent schools of English thought. These last were derived, rather, directly from Hume.

9. The seventeenth and eighteenth centuries had thus witnessed the gradual emergence and combination of two of the more important elements in the theory of international prices: the recognition of the fact that continued excess trade balances tend to produce specie flows, and the acceptance of a workable form of a national theory of money and prices. The two are found in various Mercantilistic writers, but they do not begin to converge until Locke and Clement, and they are not explicitly combined until the time of Vanderlint and Hume. A third element in the general theory, the automatic distribution of the world's supply of specie, had also been clearly suggested by North, though the proposition was given logical support and significance only by Hume. These three elements, however, are the total of the major contributions of the pre-Ricardian era to the theory of international prices, unless a partial exception be made for the wages-cost theories of export prices found in some of the later Mercantilists. From them alone, it is not possible to build a complete position. The most important element of all is missing, an explanation of the determination of the actual ratios of international exchange. The filling in of this gap was one of the principal achievements of the classical English writers on international trade. Their solution of the problem was long the only significant one in existence. It was not until comparatively recent years that a partial alternative answer began to assume importance at the hands of Continental economists of the mathematical school.

A word may be added, in retrospect, as to the general character of English Mercantilism. With regard to the theory of international exchange, Mercantilism contained one great and fundamental fallacy. This was its failure to take account of the apparent contradiction between an acceptance of the quantity theory and the advocacy of the accumulation of the precious metals. The general practical policies of Mercantilism, both relative to the supremacy of the precious metals and relative to the restrictive system, had begun to be questioned and combatted in England well before the end of the seventeenth century, but its essential *logical* error seems never to have been suspected there until Hume suddenly revealed it, and thereby made possible Smith's later demolition of the whole system. Once presented, however, the adequacy of the argument was never put in debate.

The history of English Mercantilism, regarded as a theory, thus presents only two principal stages, one of slow growth and florescence, the other of almost instantaneous and unnoticed disappearance. It will be shown later that this history is in marked contrast to the course of events upon the Continent, especially in France. There not two stages but three appeared. Several sincere and far from unconvincing efforts were made to reconcile the accumulation of the precious metals with the quantity theory, and thus to justify a retention of the main parts of the Mercantilist teachings. The destruction of the Mercantilist strongholds in France was correspondingly slow, and indeed the task was not completed until the end of the eighteenth century.

CHAPTER III

THE BULLION CONTROVERSY AND THE EARLY
CLASSICAL WRITERS

1. For nearly twenty-five years after the appearance of the "Wealth of Nations," English speculation on the theory of international trade and on the theory of money seems to have lain dormant. Not until the beginning of the nineteenth century do we find any publications worthy of especial comment. Shortly after the year 1800, however, a thin trickle of more or less polemical pamphlets and tracts began to appear. The trickle grew slowly at first, but by 1810 had become a veritable torrent of controversy, and continued with slowly-diminishing force throughout the next decade. Much of what was written was not worth the cost of printing, and has passed into deserved oblivion. An important fraction, however, was of high merit, and succeeded in carrying current thinking upon monetary questions to a level of clarity and precision hitherto unapproached.

The ultimate source of this sustained discussion, conveniently known as the Bullion Controversy, is to be found in the conditions arising out of the contemporary wars upon the Continent.[1] For a year or two after their inception, in 1793, British commerce and finance were not seriously affected. But by 1795 the foreign exchanges had become definitely unfavorable, and large quantities of specie began to be taken from the Bank of England for export. At the same time the general fear of raids upon the coast, and the consequent desire to convert property into cash, led to runs on

---

[1] More detailed descriptions of the course of events during this period are given in R. G. Hawtrey, *Currency and Credit* (London, 1919; 2 ed., 1923), ch. 16; E. Cannan, *The Paper Pound of 1797–1821* (London, 1919), Introduction; N. J. Silberling, *British Prices and Business Cycles, 1779–1850* (Review of Economic Statistics, 1923), pp. 237, 238; and idem., *Financial and Monetary Policy of Great Britain during the Napoleonic Wars* (38 Quarterly Journal of Economics, 1924), *passim*. Also see H. S. Foxwell's preface to A. Andréadès's *History of the Bank of England* (London, 1909; 2 ed., 1924).

some of the country banks. The burden of these internal and external specie drains, which were accompanied by a growing demand for extensions of credit to the market and to the government, was too heavy for the Bank to bear. After a period of panic, it suspended specie payments in 1797. Its notes were not declared to be full legal tender until 1812, but by general consent they immediately became such in effect.

The subsequent course of events is presented in detail in a statistical Appendix at the end of the present volume. The outstanding features were these. Prices, which had been climbing steadily since 1794, reached an initial high point in 1801; then, after several years of fluctuation, began rising again after 1807, with a pause in 1810–1811, and attained their maximum in 1814. Thereafter they fell rapidly until 1816; recovered a little in 1817 and 1818; and then declined again until well after the end of the Restriction period. The foreign exchanges and the specie premium, moving closely together, reached a peak in 1800–1801, fell back until 1808, and then climbed rapidly — a rise which was the signal for a new outburst of controversy, both in the pamphlet press and in Parliament. The exchanges reached their highest point (144) in 1811, and the silver premium in 1813 (138). They then declined to par in 1816, and thereafter remained at or near it. The volume of Bank of England notes in circulation increased slowly but steadily until 1817, when the notes were at roughly two and one half times the quantity in 1792, and then decreased somewhat more rapidly. The country-bank issues, finally, fluctuated violently in volume, but showed no single definite maximum.

These were the principal facts accessible to contemporary writers. All agreed that the situation was abnormal, even dangerous, and all agreed that corrective measures should be undertaken at the earliest opportunity. But radical differences of opinion as to the source of the trouble quickly appeared, and even greater differences as to the remedy to be applied. The more conspicuous though numerically smaller group interpreted the premium on bullion as an evidence of the depreciation of the currency. It attributed this depreciation to gross over-issue on the part of the Bank of England, and saw in the contraction of the

Bank's circulation the panacea for all contemporary troubles. These were the Bullionist writers, of whom Ricardo eventually became the leading spirit. They reached the height of their influence in the years just before and just after 1810. The second group, far less compact in both composition and doctrine, contented themselves with attempted refutations of the Bullionist conclusions. They declared that the country banks were at least as responsible as the Bank for credit and currency inflation; pleaded that contraction of the Bank's issues would ruin both the Bank and the government; and in some cases even denied the fact of depreciation itself. This group, representative of the majority of the business and banking interests, and of the government then in power, wrote and argued far less convincingly than the Bullionists. But when the critical tests came their views prevailed. The recommendations of the Bullion Report of 1810, drafted partly under Ricardo's guidance, were uncompromisingly rejected (as had been the proposals to terminate the Restriction in 1802–1803). When the question of contraction and resumption was again agitated, some seven years later, the situation had entirely changed. The Napoleonic wars were over, the national danger had passed, and all parties could unite in seeking a sound monetary system. The conflict between Bullionist and anti-Bullionist explanations and policies no longer had practical significance.

Recent investigations, and the painstaking compilation of new materials, have made it possible to place still another and perhaps more realistic interpretation upon the course of events during the Restriction period. This interpretation is based upon data largely unavailable to contemporary writers, that deal with various aspects of government financing, with the money-market operations of the Bank, and with the balance of international payments. It now appears that the Bank of England, in so far as it was allowed to control its own extensions of credit, was *not* primarily responsible for inflation. The chief sources of inflation were, rather, the constant pressure of the government on the Bank to assist in its war-time financing, and the operations of the horde of largely unregulated country banks. Furthermore, the depreciation of the exchanges and the premium on specie were not directly related to the issues of Bank paper at all, nor to the course of prices. They were, on the contrary, intimately controlled by the varying pressure of the government to make remittances to the Continent for military purposes; and to some extent, perhaps, by Continental efforts to restore a metallic currency. These questions, however, are too intricate to examine here. A fuller discussion is given in the Appendix already referred to.

2. The Bullion Controversy freed the larger part of monetary theory of the remnants of its Mercantilist trappings, and established it firmly on its present-day foundations. Many details still remained to be worked out, but from that time on the existence of *a* relation of sorts between prices and at least the major fluctuations in the volume of currency and credit was rarely questioned. Moreover, as a rather incidental result, the analysis of the processes of international exchange was carried very much farther forward on its monetary and financial side. The theory of international prices began to emerge as a real though still fragmentary part of economic doctrine. The writings of the Restriction period contain elaborate expositions of the world distribution of the precious metals; of the international equalization of prices; of the relations between inconvertible currencies; and even of the recently-received purchasing-power-parity doctrine itself. The advance beyond the ideas of Hume and Smith was prodigious. Yet in examining all of these discussions, one caution must be observed. Very few of the writers — not even Ricardo himself — kept the fundamental distinction between convertible and inconvertible conditions clearly defined. Only Horner, and perhaps Malthus, seem to be quite free from this confusion. Another peculiarity of the literature is that, in the great majority of cases, the point of departure was not Smith but Hume. The product, however, was probably all the better for that reason. The loss of Smith's realism was more than made up by the clarity in theoretical statement derived from Hume.

Of the innumerable writers who took part in the Bullion Controversy, we need consider only those who made especial additions to the theory of international prices: Boyd, Thornton,

Horner, Lord King, and Wheatley; Ricardo, and at one point Malthus. No attempt will be made to determine the general importance of these men, either in the growth of economic thought at large or in the history of the period.

The first contribution in the new direction was made by Walter Boyd, a London banker and a leading financier of his day. Boyd, in his "Letter to Pitt," [1] stated for the first time the substance of the theories which ultimately became orthodox Bullionist doctrine. It was a period of agricultural dearth, and of unusually high prices — of provisions, of the precious metals, and of foreign exchange. In these last conditions Boyd saw evidence of an excessive currency. The excess he traced to the Bank of England, and blamed on its Directors. With the requirement of convertibility in abeyance, he regarded them as free to expand their credits unscrupulously in whatever way would profit them most.[2] This was of course the view so cogently urged, a few years later, by Ricardo. The country banks, on the other hand, were ardently defended. Boyd held that since they had not been relieved from making cash payments, increases in their issues could come only from increases in trade, *or* from an increase in those Bank of England notes which they used as reserve. And these reserves could be increased only on the initiative of the Bank, not of the country institutions. That is, Boyd conceived of the Bank-country situation as being a unilateral relationship, with the Bank alone responsible for changes.[3] This view soon became very common, and led to much confused theorizing.

He then turns to a more explicit analysis of the relation be-

---

[1] W. Boyd, *A Letter to the Right Honorable William Pitt, on the . . . Stoppage of Issues in Specie, etc.* (London, 1801).

[2] *Ibid.*, pp. 3, 28, 60, and elsewhere. Professor Silberling has suggested that his animus against the Bank was due to its failure to help him when he was caught with a large amount of government loans on an adverse market: N. J. Silberling, *Financial and Monetary Policy (loc. cit.)*, p. 404.

Boyd quite left out of account the effects on the exchanges of the large and continuous government remittances to the Continent; effects which, as a foreign-exchange expert, he could not help but be aware of.

[3] For a strenuous but logically rather weak criticism of Boyd's conclusions, by a defender of the Bank, see Sir Francis Baring, *Observations on the Publication of Walter Boyd* (London, 1810).

tween money and prices. He finds that an increase in the quantity of (presumably inconvertible) money in circulation will lead to a "depreciation" of the currency. By this, however, he does not ordinarily mean a rise in prices. Rather, as was also true of the later Bullionists, he means that metallic money will go to a premium in terms of the paper currency. He distinguishes between "a positive degradation of the standard" and a rise in prices produced by such a degradation; the degradation being itself caused by the increase in money. In other words, to the familiar quantity-theory relation between money and prices is added an intermediate step, degradation. The sequence is not increase in money — rise in prices, but increase in money — degradation — rise in prices.[1] Nothing is said, however, to show whether the rise in prices is proportional to the degradation, or whether either is proportional to the increase in money. An understanding of this chain of reasoning is important because it provides the only satisfactory key to the contradictory pronouncements upon monetary theory of the later writers, even those of Ricardo.

Boyd also examined the effects of increasing the supply of a purely metallic currency. Here too he concluded that the consequence will be a rise in prices, but that the surplus money will be exported to other countries "to seek that employment which it could not readily have found in this."[2] This proposition, in summary form, is of course the same as Hume's theory of the world distribution of the precious metals, though the subsequent *fall* in prices, and the restoration of equilibrium, are not given. Boyd then remarks that bank notes, on the other hand, are not exportable, and that their increase must therefore cause a (permanent) rise in prices. This dictum is presented without qualification, and applied to all bank notes indiscriminately. It shows that confusion, to become so familiar in the later literature, which has already been commented on: the confusion, namely, between convertible and inconvertible conditions.

[1] Boyd, *op. cit.*, p. 65. At another point, however, he comes closer to the ordinary quantity-theory view: see *ibid.*, p. 52.

[2] *Ibid.*, pp. 8, 9.

Finally — an isolated fragment of theory that has appeared again only in comparatively recent years — he finds that a rise in internal prices, if *less rapid* than the depreciation of the exchanges, will stimulate exportation. The stimulus arises "in consequence of the diminished value of British money abroad." With respect to imports, however, the volume of movement will not be affected.[1] Unfortunately Boyd did not pursue the topic farther, but he was evidently well on the way towards present-day theories of the effect of depreciation on the course of foreign trade.

3. Boyd's work, which was widely read and which exerted a great contemporary influence, traced out the main lines along which the subsequent controversy was to develop. In very large degree, later writers simply carried his analysis into more detail, or else undertook to refute the conclusions which he had first clearly presented. To understand Boyd is to understand much, if not quite all, of the subsequent Restriction period polemic. This is conspicuously true of the next publication to appear, Thornton's classical essay on paper credit.[2]

Thornton at once took up the thread of Boyd's discussion. Like Boyd, he was sympathetic to the country banks.[3] But, unlike Boyd, he was a Director of the Bank of England, and hence a staunch defender of its policy. When his theoretical analysis would in another step or two have led him into a condemnation of its action, he usually evaded the issue, or sought a makeshift explanation in some other direction.

Thornton started with Boyd's unilateral conception that the Bank was the basis and the controlling element in the country's credit circulation. He held that a country-bank expansion will simply lead to increased country purchases in London, a drain of notes and drafts to meet the London debts, and a contraction in country reserves and note issues. (London prices were assumed to be unaffected by the remitted country notes.) On the other hand, if the Bank of England increases its issues and its credits granted

---

[1] Boyd, *op. cit.*, pp. 36, 37. The stimulus to exportation, he finds, will incidentally lead to higher wages.

[2] Henry Thornton, *An Inquiry into the Nature and Effects of the Paper Credit of Great Britain* (London, 1802).   [3] *Ibid.*, ch. 4, *passim.*

to London houses, this will lead to a direct increase in country reserves, and therefore in country issues.[1] Having gone this far, however, Thornton refrained from drawing the natural inference with respect to contemporary conditions. He admitted the possibility of inflation from the action of the Bank, but denied that it actually existed at the time. Unlike Boyd, therefore, he also denied that the Bank's policy had been wrong. Instead, he called attention to the bad harvests and to the heavy government payments abroad, as the explanation of the flight of gold.[2]

Thornton then turned from these practical considerations to a more theoretical aspect of the problem. In developing his analysis of the London-country relationships Thornton, like Boyd, had been led to the conception of an equilibrium in the value of money as between different areas within any one country, and he now applied the same idea to the relationships *between* commercially connected countries. With respect to the conditions under metallic currencies, he adopted the price-specie flow doctrine worked out by Hume some sixty years earlier. That is, he held that the precious metals are distributed among the various countries by means of the effects of currency expansion and contraction on the levels of commodity prices, and on the balance of trade. This doctrine in turn led him to the conception of a world level in the purchasing power of gold, the level being maintained by specie flows.[3] Yet even he, like Boyd, failed to observe the essential distinction here between convertible and inconvertible conditions, for he frequently implied that an excessive quantity of an *inconvertible* paper currency can be the cause of an exportation of gold.[4]

Thornton also, however, turned the price-specie flow analysis in a new direction. He applied it not only to the correction of rela-

---

[1] Thornton, *op. cit.*, chs. 7, 8.

[2] *Ibid.*, pp. 217–229. See also the excellent summary in Silberling, *Financial and Monetary Policy* (*loc. cit.*), pp. 407, 408.

[3] Thornton, *op. cit.*, chs. 4, 5, 8; especially pp. 120 ff. and 209 ff. At the latter point he takes Smith severely to task for not showing how the import and export of gold is brought about; that is, by means of price changes.

It will be observed, however, that Thornton himself does not explain how the "equalized" value of money is to be measured. It remained for Wheatley, a year later, to express the equalization in terms of commodity prices.

[4] See, for example, *ibid.*, pp. 133, 200, 201.

tive excesses of metallic money, but also to the adjustment of deficits in the balance of trade that originate on the commodity side. To illustrate his argument, he assumes that a failure of the harvest has led to a very unfavorable balance of trade.[1] He further assumes that the debtor country either cannot at once supply a sufficient amount of goods in payment, or, more probably, that those which it can supply are not in sufficient demand abroad to yield a reasonable price. The creditor country, therefore,

being in a certain degree eager for payment, but not in immediate want of all that supply of goods which would be necessary to pay the balance, prefers gold as part, at least, of the payment; for gold can always be turned to a more beneficial use than a very great overplus of any other commodity.[2]

Here, then, we have gold flows appearing as the *result* of the position of the balance of trade, not only as its *cause*. This conclusion, soon attacked by Ricardo, was subsequently adopted by Mill, and became the orthodox classical doctrine.[3] It must indeed be pointed out that Thornton did not explicitly carry his argument through to the subsequent price changes, and to the restoration of equilibrium. But this last step can safely be credited to him, in view of his pronouncements elsewhere. The omission was one of negligence rather than of incapacity.

With respect to the situation under inconvertible currencies, finally, Thornton made an excellent analysis of the way in which an increase in inconvertible paper money raises prices, and depresses the exchanges. He finds that such an increase leads to greater facility in borrowing at the Bank, an increase in the scale of trading operations, and a general tendency to buy rather than to sell. It thus conduces to higher prices.[4] The higher prices, in

[1] He held that the country's total imports and exports must always tend toward equality, for otherwise the accumulation of debts would become impossibly large; or else an export of gold, of equally impossible magnitude, would take place (Thornton, *op. cit.*, p. 116). This dictum of course takes no account of the "invisible items," if applied to the balance of *trade* alone.   [2] *Ibid.*, p. 131.

[3] For a more elaborate study of the differences here between Thornton, Malthus, and Mill, on the one hand, and Ricardo on the other, see J. Viner, *Canada's Balance of International Indebtedness* (Cambridge, 1924), pp. 191–202. Also see sect. 5, below.

[4] Thornton, *op. cit.*, pp. 261–279. See especially pp. 263, 264. That the rise in prices will be *proportional* to the increase of money, however, is explicitly denied.

turn, lead to increased imports, to an excess demand for bills in the exchange market, to attempts to buy gold for export, and to a consequent rise in the market price of bullion above the mint price. But the exchange rates will also fall, and this readjustment will "in a great degree" offset the effects on the balance of trade of the increase in prices.[1] Here, at least, bullion is clearly separated from paper money, and the convertible — inconvertible confusion is absent. In consequence, Thornton must be credited with developing at least half of the present-day "purchasing-power-parity" doctrine, for he explicitly declares that a rise in paper prices will produce a substantially equivalent rise in the exchanges, and thus restore the balance of trade. But nothing is said about *foreign* prices. This last step was left for Wheatley.

Thornton's book attracted a great deal of attention, and was examined at length by Francis Horner in the newly-launched Edinburgh Review.[2] Horner first pointed out the fact that Thornton had frequently confused the effects of convertible and inconvertible paper, and then substituted a much clearer statement of his own. He declared that a rise in inconvertible-paper prices will not cause a rise in the *bullion* prices of commodities, for bullion will rise as well, in terms of paper. It will therefore fail to cause an outflow of gold. It *will* affect the exchanges, but the balance of trade will not be altered, except in so far as the exchanges lag behind prices:

When an excessive issue of [inconvertible] paper-money produces a nominal rise of prices, a nominal fall of the foreign exchange will always take place, and is a *consequence* of that steady excess of the market price of gold above its mint price, which originated immediately in the excessive issue of paper.[3]

Except for the omission — as in Thornton — of price changes in the foreign country, this is as good a statement of the purchasing-

Like most of the Bullionists, Thornton was a quantity-theorist only in a very loose sense: the sense in which the quantity theory is true of all commodities. He placed quite as much stress on the varying conditions of demand as on mere changes in the volume of the currency. (See *ibid.*, pp. 222 ff.)

[1] Thornton, *op. cit.*, pp. 198, 200, 201. The passages are too long to quote.

[2] Francis Horner, *An Inquiry into the Nature and Effects of the Paper Credit of Great Britain. By Henry Thornton, M.P.* (Edinburgh Review, 1802). The review was unsigned.   [3] *Ibid.*, p. 184.

power-parity doctrine as one could desire. Incidentally, it affords the first clear example of that distinction between "real" and "nominal" exchange rates which Blake was later to make so much of.

Finally, Horner says that he is in a state of "unaffected doubt" with respect to the alleged dependence of the current state of prices upon the current state of the circulation — an interesting admission from one of the future authors of the Bullion Report. He shrewdly observes, however, that this dependence would be established beyond question if the rise in prices should continue *despite* the restoration of a permanently favorable balance of trade.[1]

4. In the same year that Thornton and Horner wrote, 1802, the signing of the Peace of Amiens terminated the first French war. A new controversy broke out at once over the continuance of the Restriction, but did not become very wide-spread. Confined chiefly to the chambers of Parliament, it was soon closed by the passage of an act renewing the suspension of specie payments. Most of the debates were of mediocre quality, and some were merely superficial.[2] To this there was, however, one important exception: the speech of Lord King. King afterwards systematized his remarks, added a good deal to them, and published them in a work that was extensively read.[3] In it he followed the path already marked out by Boyd and Thornton, although with most of the latter's qualifications thrown overboard. Despite the suggestions made by Thornton and Horner, the connection between the Bank's position and the carrying on of the war apparently escaped him, as did that between government remittances to the Continent and the exchanges. The book was of importance in the history of the period, but contains few theoretical elements that are new.

[1] Horner, *op. cit.*, p. 200.

[2] See Hansard's Parliamentary Debates, April 9 and 21, 1802 (Commons); February 7 and 12, 1803 (Commons), and February 22, 1803 (Lords). The principal speakers were Peel, Thornton, Fox, and Lord King.

[3] Lord Peter King, *Thoughts on the Restriction of Payments in Specie, etc.* (London, 1803; 2 ed., 1804). Also see Horner's review of the book (Edinburgh Review, 1803).

Just the opposite was true of a striking work that appeared at about the same time as King's. Wheatley's "Remarks on Currency and Commerce," like his later "Essay on the Theory of Money," [1] exerted comparatively little contemporary influence, and virtually none later, yet its positive contributions to the theory of the subject were great. Wheatley began with the assertion that an increase in the quantity of money will produce a proportional decrease in its value, a decrease which is synonymous with a rise in prices.[2] By this simple statement he refuted Boyd's erroneous conception — a confusion found even in Ricardo — of "degradation" or "depreciation" as something necessarily apart from, and a *cause* of, a rise in prices. Wheatley also denied that the increase in money will act as a stimulus to industry, on the ground that wages will rise in proportion.[3] He thus gave the quantity theory the most rigid formulation that it had received since the days of Hume. He next presented Hume's own price-specie flow analysis in full, and from this passed to a genuine doctrine of price equalization, both within and between countries. The doctrine is simply a development of Thornton's position, already examined. But whereas Thornton had stopped short, like Hume, with the concept of an international equalization in the value of gold, Wheatley pushed on to the equalization of commodity prices at large. He says that "the facility with which the reciprocal communication of nations is carried on, has a necessary influence on the markets of all, and approximates the price of their produce to a general level." [4] This levelling is effected through the price-specie flow mechanism. A similar statement is made later: "The markets of the various nations of the world

---

[1] John Wheatley, *Remarks on Currency and Commerce* (London, 1803); *An Essay on the Theory of Money and Principles of Commerce* (vol. 1: London, 1807). The first work was a preliminary study for the second.

[2] *Remarks*, pp. 1–18, 180, 181. (In the *Essay*, see p. 40.)

[3] *Ibid.*, pp. 18, 19.

[4] *Ibid.*, p. 26. (In the *Essay*, see pp. 43–47.) Wheatley even declares that, within any one country, *wages* will be brought to an approximate level. The argument is the same as for commodities: a higher wage will attract a greater supply of labor, and thus cause the wage to fall. (*Remarks*, p. 22.) The implicit assumption — perfect internal mobility of labor and international immobility — is one of those on which the classical theory of comparative costs was later based.

have a reciprocal action on each other to maintain the general equilibrium of money." [1] Wheatley was the first writer to develop so explicit a doctrine of price equalization, and for many decades was the only one. We shall find it neither in Ricardo nor in Mill.

All this analysis had of course been concerned with metallic or convertible currencies. Elsewhere Wheatley turned to the problem of inconvertible currencies, and at once formulated the purchasing-power-parity doctrine in its entirety. He declared that "the course of exchange is the exclusive criterion [of] how far the currency of one [country] is increased beyond the currency of another." [2] The possible influence of the balance of payments was almost entirely ruled out, and the relative quantity of money, operating through prices, was made the sole determinant.[3] Even the most extreme present-day adherents of the doctrine could hardly do better. Yet it must be pointed out that Wheatley's reasoning was not always quite consistent with this proposition. At one place he applies it, rather questionably, to metallic currencies as well — neglecting the effects of the specie points;[4] at another point he finds that a fall in *paper* prices will alter the balance of trade favorably;[5] and at still a third he attributes the contemporary disappearance of gold primarily to the excessive (*inconvertible*) paper currency.[6]

Finally, he undertook an examination of Great Britain's contemporary monetary difficulties. This examination led him into clear-cut opposition at certain points to the familiar Bullionist teaching, for he exonerated the Bank of England, and attacked the country banks as the chief sources of the current difficulty. As long as the Bank of England had had the *sole* power to issue

---

[1] Wheatley, *Remarks*, p. 186.

[2] *Ibid.*, p. 207. Also see pp. 70 ff., 85–92, 122, 123; and, in the *Essay*, pp. 60–65, 68 ff., and 84–86.

[3] *Remarks*, pp. 70 ff.   [4] *Essay*, pp. 60–65.   [5] *Remarks*, p. 222.

[6] *Ibid.*, pp. 70 ff. This reveals once more the familiar confusion between convertible and inconvertible conditions. Indeed, one sometimes doubts that Wheatley realized that the English currency *was* inconvertible; or at least that he realized the actual, as well as the theoretical, implications and consequences of inconvertibility. The same doubt arises with respect to nearly all the writers of the period, even Ricardo; Horner and perhaps Malthus alone excepted.

notes, he found that its regulation of the currency (with the exchange rates as index, and the discount rate as tool) had been unexceptionable. But now the country-bank notes were allowed to circulate too. They had increased more than in proportion in times of security, thus inflating the currency and forcing up prices, while in time of stress they had weakened so badly that their burden was thrown on the Bank of England in addition to its own.[1] Wheatley was almost the only writer of his day to advance this view — to show that the London-country relationship was not unilateral, and that the country banks were also at fault. It is interesting to observe that, uncelebrated though he has been, recent research has confirmed his view rather than that of the Bullionists.[2] With respect to the immediate cause of the disappearance of gold, however, his position was more like that of other writers of the time. Denying virtually all effect from the government's foreign remittances, he attributed it, erroneously, to the adverse balance of trade caused by an excessive (inconvertible) currency and by its concomitant, high prices.[3]

The other important conclusion as to contemporary conditions to which his theory led him was the still more debatable proposition that the French wars could have been financed on a convertible basis, and without the loss of the precious metals. Wheatley thought that by keeping prices low enough (by means of a contracted currency), a sufficient export surplus could be acquired to take care of the government's foreign remittances in this way alone.[4] This is an unusually rigid application of pure theory to the complications of a major war, and although an interesting suggestion, can hardly be regarded as workable. Wheatley seems to have taken it over from Adam Smith.[5]

5. With the exception of Wheatley's second work, the years from 1803 until 1809 were not marked by the appearance of any publication of especial consequence.[6] The period was one of com-

---

[1] Wheatley, *Remarks*, pp. 209–221; *Essay*, pp. 336 ff.

[2] See Appendix A, below.

[3] *Remarks*, pp. 70 ff.   [4] *Essay*, pp. 175–181 and ff.

[5] See Silberling, *Financial and Monetary Policy* (*loc. cit.*), p. 416. The passage in Smith is in vol. i, p. 408, of Cannan's edition of the *Wealth of Nations* (cited above).

[6] An exception should perhaps be made for Lord Liverpool's *Treatise on the Coins of the Realm* (London, 1805). This work was chiefly concerned with another set of

parative tranquillity in domestic affairs, and there was little reason
for controversy. The exchanges and the specie premium stood at
moderate figures (under 110); the Bank circulation was nearly
stationary; and though prices were high — the index was over
150, with 1790 taken as 100 — they had ceased their precipitate
rise. But in 1808 this calm was abruptly broken. The government began to make very much larger remittances to the Continent, and to borrow heavily; the country note circulation soared,
followed more slowly by the Bank issues; prices resumed their
upward movement; and for the first time the exchange depreciation and the premium on specie threatened to become really
acute. The consequence was a new storm of controversy, in
which Ricardo soon became the leading figure. Ricardo himself
wrote at considerable length on the question, and, what was even
more important, he instigated the undertaking of a Parliamentary inquiry. The result was the formation of the celebrated Bullion Committee, whose Report he so strongly influenced. The Report was presented in 1810. In the following year, however, its
recommendations were happily rejected, and thereafter the Bullion Controversy, as such, rather died down. Men continued to
write at length on monetary questions, and indeed the crisis was
not passed until after 1814, but the essential inexpediency of sudden contraction in the midst of war-time finance had come to be
generally appreciated.

problems, but it is interesting to notice that Lord Liverpool, unlike most of his contemporaries, adopted Adam Smith's idea that the total volume of paper money can
never exceed that of the gold and silver which would *otherwise* have been in circulation.   (See the *Treatise*, pp. 227–229.)

Attention should also be called to an interesting inquiry made in this period by
another writer, Torrens, into the benefits from international trade. In it he corrected Smith's doctrine on that head. He found that the benefit consists in the increased production resulting from the international division of employment — thus
anticipating Ricardo. And whereas Ricardo confined the benefit to one country
alone, with respect to any one article (regarding it as equal to the whole difference in
the comparative cost), Torrens more accurately held that it is divided between both
countries, in a variable proportion. It does not appear, however, that his views attracted any considerable attention, either then or later. See R. Torrens, *The Economists Refuted* (London, 1808), especially ch. 5; and the preface to the second edition
of his essay on *The Principles and Practical Operation of Sir Robert Peel's Act* (London, 1857), pp. xiv–xvi. This second edition contains a reprint of the earlier tract.
The first edition, which does not, was published in 1848.

Of the many writers in this second phase of the Bullion Controversy, I propose to deal at any length only with Ricardo. Substantially all of the important doctrines of the period had already been worked out, between 1801 and 1803. Comparatively little new material was added in the fields of especial interest to us. Indeed, Ricardo himself would not merit more than brief comment here had he not exerted so powerful an influence over both the contemporary and the later literature, and had he not been so widely misinterpreted. Until the appearance of his "Principles of Political Economy" in 1817 (and with a partial exception for his "Proposals for an Economical Currency," of 1816), Ricardo cannot be regarded as an originator either in the field of monetary theory, or of international exchange. He was simply the expositor — and often a confused, though forceful, expositor — of the body of post-Smithian speculations that lay ready to his hand.[1]

Ricardo's principal publications at this time were his "Letters to the Morning Chronicle," in 1809,[2] his essay on "The High Price of Bullion," in 1810, and his "Reply to Bosanquet," in 1811.[3] Inasmuch as many points are discussed over and over in two or more of them, it will be convenient to treat them in the order of their principles, rather than chronologically.

Ricardo's general position is well known, and can be summarized in a word. He attacks the Bank of England bitterly, as being the exclusive cause of the currency depreciation and of the expulsion of specie, while the country banks are held blameless. The currency depreciation is taken as being revealed through, and as measured by, the premium on specie and the depreciation of

---

[1] For a view similar in some respects, see J. H. Hollander, *The Development of the Theory of Money from Adam Smith to David Ricardo* (25 Quarterly Journal of Economics, 1911), pp. 431, 432, 469, 470.

[2] D. Ricardo, *Three Letters on the Price of Gold* (republished in J. H. Hollander, *A Reprint of Economic Tracts*, Baltimore, 1903). The references here are to this reprint. The letters originally appeared in the issues of the Morning Chronicle (London), for August 29, September 20, and November 23, 1809.

[3] D. Ricardo, *The High Price of Bullion* (1810; 4 ed., 1811); and *Reply to Mr. Bosanquet's Practical Observations* (1811.) Both tracts are reprinted in E. C. K. Gonner, *Economic Essays by David Ricardo* (London, 1923). The references here are to Gonner's edition. Gonner uses the fourth edition of *The High Price of Bullion*.

the exchanges.[1] The remedy for the situation is held to be a contraction of the Bank issues, for he declares that a reduction of two to three million pounds is sufficient to induce the importation of gold [2] — a tacit approach to Wheatley's conclusion, with respect to the financing of the war on a convertible basis. All of this is of course orthodox Bullionist doctrine. The logical foundation on which it rests is for the most part almost equally familiar: namely, the theory of the effects of an "excess" of currency under convertible and inconvertible conditions, and of the adjustment of disequilibria in international exchange.

With respect to the situation under a convertible currency, Ricardo's doctrine is simply that the precious metals are distributed among the various countries according to their relative effective needs. The distribution is secured through specie flows, themselves produced by a relative redundancy of the currency. The result is that "the currency of any one country can never be much more valuable, as far as equal quantities of the precious metals are concerned, than that of another." [3] This sounds entirely like Thornton, and like Wheatley. But Ricardo goes on to limit his doctrine of international adjustments very narrowly. In explicit opposition to Thornton, he declares that

the temptation to export money in exchange for goods, or what is termed an unfavorable balance of trade, never arises but from a redundant currency.

---

[1] Only once is the level of prices made a test. See the *Three Letters* (*loc. cit.*), p. 16.

[2] *Ibid.*, pp. 11, 14; *Reply to Bosanquet* (*loc. cit.*), p. 94; and *The High Price of Bullion* (*loc. cit.*), pp. 26, 27.

Ricardo's hostility to the Bank is explained by Professor Silberling on grounds of personal interest and pecuniary gain: that Ricardo was a consistent bear of the public loans, and had suffered from the Bank's liberality to other traders. The only direct evidence adduced for this view, however, is a single obscure pamphlet, and it must therefore be regarded as somewhat questionable. See Silberling, *Financial and Monetary Policy* (*loc. cit.*), pp. 427–429.

It is interesting to note that by 1819, when he had become a landed proprietor, Ricardo had quite changed his views. He then recommended resumption only because the specie premium had become small. Had it been large, he would have advised devaluation. (See Silberling, *loc. cit.*, pp. 437, 438; and Ricardo's evidence before the Commons committee of 1819, on the resumption of specie payments.)

[3] *The High Price of Bullion* (*loc. cit.*), p. 6.

. . . The exportation of the coin is caused by its cheapness, and is not the effect but the *cause* of an unfavorable balance.[1]

These passages do not appear to have been taken into account adequately in certain more recent interpretations of Ricardo. Ricardo did, it is true, subscribe to the doctrine of the price-specie flow mechanism when it is applied to the adjustment of a relatively redundant currency. This doctrine had come down, with reputable support, from the time of Hume or earlier. But he explicitly denied the further doctrine, also ordinarily described as "classical" and "Ricardian," which explains the adjustment of original disequilibria in international trade in terms of the resultant specie flows. That doctrine is found in Thornton, and, as we shall see later, in Mill. Both writers held that an unfavorable shift in the balance of trade, due for example to a crop failure, will be corrected by specie flows and by a *subsequent* change in prices. It is most emphatically wrong, however, to attribute such a view to Ricardo. His was an exclusively "unilateral" doctrine.[2]

On the other hand, it is equally true that Ricardo worked out no tenable alternative explanation. He contented himself with a mere denial of Thornton's position, and with the implication that a change in relative demands would take place. This omission Malthus, siding with Thornton, was at pains to point out.[3]

---

[1] *The High Price of Bullion* (*loc. cit.*) pp. 9, 10. (Italics mine.) Also see the *Reply to Bosanquet* (*loc. cit.*), p. 94.

[2] Also see sect. 7, below, with respect to Ricardo's similar position in the *Principles*. Ricardo took over Hume's doctrine, and confined it *only* to those limits that Hume had tentatively marked out, whereas the adherents of the "bilateral" view applied it to a much wider range of conditions. Polemics aside, however, the two seem to come to much the same thing so far as the balance of international payments is concerned, except quantitatively. A high level of prices due to excessive currency, or a crop failure, or international lending, all produce qualitatively similar results: an excess demand for foreign bills. The differences between the cases are largely ones of degree alone, except in so far as the high general level of prices due to too much money produces such wide effects that specie drains become necessary — whereas in the other cases they do not. But an empirical line would be hard to draw.

In recent discussions these questions have been raised more especially in connection with the analysis of international borrowing operations.

[3] T. R. Malthus, *Publications on the Depreciation of Paper Currency* (Edinburgh Review, 1811), pp. 342, 343. The review was unsigned. For a fuller development of the criticisms of Ricardo suggested above, see J. Viner, *Canada's Balance of In-*

With respect to the situation under inconvertible paper, Ricardo is guilty of confusion and even of outright error. In the first place, like Boyd and other writers, he undertakes to distinguish between "depreciation" and that rise in prices of which depreciation is regarded as a partial cause. The test of "depreciation" is made the state of the exchanges and the specie premium, and its source the excessive issue of paper money. Thus he says that "the effect produced on prices by the depreciation has been most accurately defined, and amounts to the difference between the market and the Mint price of gold."[1] This use of the term depreciation is of course perfectly permissible, but to make depreciation the *cause* of the rise in prices is then wrong. In the second place, he more than once refers to the increase in (*inconvertible*) paper money as the cause of the disappearance of bullion;[2] while on the other hand, as we have already seen, he regards its contraction as a sure stimulus to importation. This too is an error taken over from the earlier literature. Finally — quite inconsistently with these last propositions — Ricardo seems to come close to the purchasing-power-parity doctrine. He states it, however, in terms not of prices but of "depreciation." He says that when the currency consists of depreciated paper, the exchange "necessarily will fall according to the degree of the depreciation. The exchange will, therefore, be a tolerably accurate criterion by which we may judge of the debasement of the currency." And he quotes a passage from Steuart with approval, to the effect that a change in the value of a given currency is best ascertained by comparing it with the value of some other currency that has remained stable.[3] This is not the genuine purchas-

ternational Indebtedness, pp. 191–202. Viner seems to be the only recent writer who has noted the difference between Ricardo's position and Mill's.

On the other hand, however, in a private letter written at this time Ricardo admitted that a discrepancy in the balance (of payments) would stimulate exportation by moving the exchanges to a lower level; and that important quantities of goods would move *before* specie flows took place. This view he never put into print. See the *Letters of Ricardo to Malthus* (edited by J. Bonar, Oxford, 1887), pp. 20–23. The letter is dated December 22, 1811.

[1] *Reply to Bosanquet* (*loc. cit.*), pp. 134, 135.

[2] *Ibid.*, pp. 94, 109–111.

[3] *The High Price of Bullion* (*loc. cit.*), pp. 19, 20. Also see the *Letters of Ricardo to Malthus*, p. 15. The letter is dated July 17, 1811.

ing-power-parity doctrine, however. It amounts simply to the evident proposition that the exchanges and the specie premium move fairly closely together.[1]

Ricardo's analysis of the situation under inconvertible paper was thus both incomplete and erroneous; incomplete because of the virtual omission of commodity prices, and erroneous because of its frequent confusion between convertible and inconvertible conditions. Nevertheless it exerted great influence both in private circles and in Parliament, and has constantly been referred to since as the orthodox and correct exposition.

One other point in Ricardo's theory requires comment: his conception of the relation between the quantity of money and prices. Ricardo is often, and perhaps usually, regarded as a straight-forward quantity theorist. I think that a study of his writings *other* than the "Principles," confused and contradictory though they sometimes are, will lead to a somewhat different view. It must be enough here, however, simply to summarize his apparent position. With respect to metallic currencies, Ricardo emphatically denies that there is any proportional relationship between money and prices,[2] and develops what seems to be primarily a labor theory of the value of money, as had Adam Smith.[3] Yet this conclusion is not altogether certain. Elsewhere in the same work he appears to hold, by implicit if not by explicit statement, a fairly loose quantity theory,[4] especially with respect to a *convertible* paper currency.[5] It is doubtful, however, if he meant this in any sense other than that in which quantity determines the value of *all* commodities.[6] We are then thrown back upon his gen-

---

[1] But see sect. 7, below, for the somewhat different view that Ricardo later expressed at one point in his *Principles*.

[2] See the *Letters of Ricardo to Malthus*, pp. 3, 5. Written in March, 1810.

[3] In *The High Price of Bullion* (*loc. cit.*), p. 3, he says that "gold and silver, like other commodities, have an intrinsic value, which is not arbitrary, but is dependent on their scarcity, the quantity of labor bestowed in procuring them, and the value of the capital employed in the mines which produce them."

[4] *Ibid.*, pp. 3, 34.   [5] *Ibid.*, p. 5.

[6] In a speech in the House on June 12, 1822, he asserted that "quantity regulates the value of everything. This is true of corn, of currency, and of every other commodity, and more, perhaps, of currency than of anything else." So see Hansard, *Parliamentary Debates*, New Series, vol. 7, column 946. Also see columns 938, 939.

eral theory of value itself. If a summary statement may be ventured, it can be said that Ricardo explained the long-run determination of the value of metallic money primarily by a labor theory, as did Smith, and the short-run determination by those quantitative relationships which he postulated of commodities in general. He did *not* have a "quantity theory" of money, at least in the ordinary sense of the term.

Ricardo's position with respect to inconvertible currency, however, is somewhat clearer. It has been suggested several times in the course of the preceding discussion. Ricardo held a "quantity theory" with respect to the relation between the quantity of money and the premium on specie, but that was absolutely all, except that the premium on specie and the fall of the exchanges were regarded as substantially equivalent indices. He talked about commodity prices, as such, comparatively rarely. When he did, it was only to ascribe their rise to the intermediary element "depreciation," not directly to the quantity of money. Any rise in prices *beyond* the level of depreciation did not appear to interest him; he left it to the reader to choose between bad harvests, heavy taxes and other disturbances as the explanation.[1] At the risk of repetition, it may be pointed out that this was precisely the fallacy which had been started nearly a decade earlier by Boyd.

6. In the same year that "The High Price of Bullion" was published, 1810, the Bullion Committee was formed — largely at Ricardo's instigation — and drew up its celebrated Report.[2] This

---

[1] *Reply to Bosanquet* (*loc. cit.*), pp. 134, 135; *The High Price of Bullion* (*loc. cit.*), pp. 24–26; etc. For a similar interpretation see Silberling, *Financial and Monetary policy* (*loc. cit.*), pp. 421–426. It is borne out, also, by many passages in Ricardo's letters to Malthus, MacCulloch, and Trower.

On the other hand, in 1819 Ricardo had apparently become a quantity-theory convert, for the time being at least. Speaking of inconvertible paper, he said: "Relative prices are determined by the relative value or quantity of currencies. . . . Double the quantity of currency in England and commodities will rise to double their former price in England." But this was probably only an experimental formulation. It was never published by Ricardo, and is not consonant with his general reasoning. The passage occurs in a memorandum, reprinted in the *Letters of Ricardo to MacCulloch, 1816–1823* (Publications of the American Economic Association, 1895), p. 36.

[2] The Report has recently been reprinted and edited, in the main uncritically

Report embodied the most extreme Bullionist views, as we have traced them in the preceding pages. The Committee quite disregarded the greater part of the evidence presented before it.[1] Proceeding largely on the basis of its own theoretical preconceptions, it recommended a policy of severe contraction, and advocated resumption within two years. Most of its witnesses had declared that the current situation was the inevitable and natural consequence of war-time conditions and of war-time finance, and had predicted disaster should contraction be enforced. But the Committee went calmly ahead on its own path. It made an analysis of the relations between the quantity of money and international trade which, correct enough when applied to a convertible currency, was hopelessly fallacious with respect to the contemporary *inconvertible* conditions. Its practical recommendations, drawn from this analysis, were of the rashest character. One would hardly suspect from reading them that a major war was in progress. Sudden contraction would probably have ruined the Bank, would have hampered the government very badly, and would perhaps have lost the war. Parliament, more sane than the Committee, fortunately rejected its conclusions,[2] but the mere threat of immediate deflation brought on the acute crisis of 1810–1811.[3] Far from being the inspired production of advanced thinkers who were combating vulgar error, the Bullion Report, under the circumstances, was a short-sighted and dangerous document, written at least five years too soon. It is high time that the Bullion-Committee myth was dissipated.

The other writers of the period require only passing attention. Blake, also in 1810, wrote a treatise on the exchanges which would

by Professor Cannan: *The Paper Pound of 1797–1821* (London, 1919). The principal drafters of the Report were Horner (chairman), Thornton, and Huskisson.

[1] For a similar view see H. S. Foxwell's preface to Andréadès's *History of the Bank of England* (2 ed., 1924; cited above), especially pp. xvii and xx; and Silberling, *Financial and Monetary Policy* (*loc. cit.*), pp. 430–434. Silberling holds that much of the statistical evidence which the Committee brought forward in support of its more critical findings of fact (see the Appendices to the Report), was hopelessly inaccurate.

[2] See Hansard's *Parliamentary Debates* for 1811, *passim*. The principal opponents of the Report in Parliament were Rose, Vansittart, and Lord Castlereagh.

[3] Silberling, *op. cit.*, p. 437.

have been a remarkable performance had it been published ten years earlier.[1] As it was, however, Blake presents practically no new elements of theory. Apart from its lucidity, the book is chiefly noteworthy for its avoidance of the more extreme Bullionist errors on contemporary questions. In 1811, Bosanquet presented the best of the anti-Bullionist essays,[2] but this too contains little that is new. It undertakes to deny the Bullionist assertions of fact, but beyond calling attention to the sins of the country banks it does not offer any alternative explanation of the current situation. The position of the balance of international payments, for example, and the effects of government war financing, are quite passed by.

This deficiency was in part made up by Torrens, who in 1812 accounted for the depreciation of the currency by alarm, the excessive issue of paper money, and the balance of international payments.[3] But with respect to this last point Torrens, like so many of his contemporaries, fell into the old confusion between convertible and inconvertible conditions.[4] His principal contribution was, rather, the new concept of an ordered series of articles, which can be successively called on to meet deficits in the balance of international payments. He finds that when a deficit appears each available article is exported in turn, until its rising price in the domestic market, and its fall abroad, threatens to wipe out the ordinary profit of the merchant *with respect to those surplus imports which had caused the deficit* — as of wheat in times of crop failure. Thus an article may be exported, though its price be higher at home than abroad, if the price is not *enough* higher to wipe out the profit on the antecedent importing operation. But if it is too high, then the next most available article will be called on.[5] These last propositions are unrealistic, of course, but the

---

[1] W. Blake, *Observations on the Principles which Regulate the Course of Exchange* (London, 1810). The book remained for many years, however, the best non-controversial work on the theory of the exchanges. Blake followed Thornton rather than Ricardo in the matter of specie flows. See Blake, *op. cit.*, pp. 4 ff.

[2] C. Bosanquet, *Practical Observations on the Report of the Bullion Committee* (London, 1810).

[3] R. Torrens, *An Essay on Money and Paper Currency* (London, 1812), p. 102.

[4] *Ibid.*, pp. 193–209 ff.

[5] *Ibid.*, pp. 2–9. Torrens gave a much better version of this doctrine in a later

fundamental idea of a hierarchy of successively less attractive alternatives is perfectly sound. It represents a further development of Thornton's propositions, denied by Ricardo but appearing again in Mill, concerning the causes of deficits in the balance of payments and the means by which such deficits are met.[1]

The other participants in the Bullion Controversy proper do not require comment,[2] and from 1812 to 1817, when Ricardo's "Principles" appeared, little was published that was significant. We may therefore pause to summarize here the chief developments of theory to which that controversy had led — bearing always in mind, however, the fact that this post-Smithian literature took its departure primarily not from the doctrines of Smith himself, but from those of Hume and his predecessors.

First, with respect to conditions under a convertible currency a number of writers from Boyd down had followed in Hume's footsteps, and had worked out theories of the world distribution of the precious metals; of the world equilibrium in the value of money; and even, in Wheatley, of an equalization in world prices. As the mechanism by which all this was made effective, they had fallen back upon the price-specie flow analysis. With respect to the nature of that mechanism, however, differences in opinion

work. See his *Comparative Estimate* (London, 1819), pp. 4–12, and especially p. 8. Torrens here brought out more clearly the concept of a series of points of equilibrium, successively reached as the pressure for remittances becomes heavier. These doctrines were original with Torrens, but unfortunately they dropped from sight in the subsequent literature — only to be revived independently by quite recent writers.

[1] One other interesting point in Torrens should not escape attention. He declares that the general remedy for the current distress is convertibility. Yet he also finds that this requirement, as applied to the issue of bank paper, may lead to stringency and collapse, for under it the Bank cannot issue more than a certain amount of currency. Elasticity in the conversion-requirement is therefore necessary. (*Essay on Money*, pp. 112–116 ff.) The solution, he says, lies in "limiting the issues of bank paper to the discounting of solid mercantile bills, payable at a fixed and moderate date." (*Ibid.*, p. 125.) This is a striking anticipation of the "banking principle" evolved some thirty years later.

[2] The principal writers are Huskisson, Sinclair (the first opponent of the Bullion Report), Smith, Trotter, Mushet, and Lauderdale. The more important works are listed in the Bibliography at the end of the present study. See also Hansard's *Parliamentary Debates* for 1811, and the evidence given before the Bullion Committee.

soon appeared. Thornton attempted to make it bilateral; to proceed, that is, not only *from* the state of the currency *to* the balance of trade (via specie flows), but also from the state of the balance of trade to the volume of currency and the level of prices. In this he was supported by Malthus, and at Mill's hands Thornton's conclusion later became the orthodox classical doctrine. Ricardo, however, made the mechanism unilateral alone. He explicitly confined it to the adjustment of an initial excess or deficiency in the volume of currency, and made specie flows exclusively the cause — never the effect — of changes in the balance of trade. It is therefore quite erroneous to attribute the origin of the price-specie flow analysis to Ricardo. In the bilateral sense it was originated by Thornton, and *rejected* by Ricardo, while in the unilateral sense it had first been worked out by Hume many years before. The common description of the price-specie flow mechanism as "Ricardian" rests on another myth.[1]

The question of the direct relation between prices and the quantity of a convertible currency was rather slighted by all of these writers. A loose quantity theory is presumably implicit in most of them, in virtue of their adoption of the price-specie flow analysis. Ricardo, however, regarded the quantity theory as valid with respect to metallic money only in the general and short-time sense in which it is valid for all commodities. He held, rather, a primarily *labor* theory of the value of metallic money; a view taken over directly from Smith.

Second, with respect to conditions under an inconvertible currency all of the writers of the period except Horner (and perhaps Malthus) fell into a fundamental error at the outset. They attempted to apply the principles that had been worked out for convertible currencies to the *inconvertible* situation. The contemporary exports of gold were attributed to the excess of the (incon-

---

[1] The reason why the non-orthodox "bilateral" analysis is ordinarily described as Ricardian probably lies in the fact that Mill subsequently adopted the bilateral view and, failing to see any difference between this and Ricardo's position, credited Ricardo with the whole doctrine — instead of attributing the two parts, respectively, to Hume and Thornton. (See ch. iv, sect. 3, below.) But, as already suggested, it is hard to find an essential distinction between the two, except in the degree of their effects.

vertible) paper money, while contraction was regarded as the one sure method of inducing gold imports. Further, the effects of the increased currency were usually measured by the specie premium and the exchanges, rather than by the level of prices. A third element, "degradation" or "depreciation," was erroneously made to intervene between money and prices. The rise in prices was regarded as being in large part the immediate result of the "depreciation," not directly of the increase in money. The depreciation itself, however, *was* thought to be causally and proportionately related to the increase in money. To this extent the quantity theory can be credited to the corresponding writers, notably to Boyd and to Ricardo. Finally, though inconsistently with their other views on inconvertible currencies, a number of men developed part or all of the recently-revived purchasing-power-parity doctrine. In Thornton and Horner, for example, half of it is given, while to Wheatley belongs the credit for its first complete statement. Ricardo also suggested it, though rather equivocally.[1]

The Bullion Controversy literature had thus carried the theory of international prices a long distance forward, but the advance had been primarily on the monetary side alone. Moreover, the first systematic treatise on economic theory to appear after the Bullion Controversy had passed its height, Ricardo's "Principles," was written by a professed Bullionist, who made little or no use of the positive doctrines of his opponents. Some of the most interesting and most valuable of these doctrines, therefore, failed to become incorporated into the general literature of economics until a much later date.

---

[1] It may be pointed out that the principal errors and omissions of the Bullionist writers proper, from Boyd to Ricardo himself, seem to have been, first, the attack upon the Bank of England as the sole source of fluctuations in the volume of currency and credit; second, the attribution of the specie premium and the exchange depreciation to excessive currency alone; third, the failure to consider the effect of the balance of international payments upon the exchanges (indeed, that the balance had exerted *any* effect was usually denied), and of government wartime financing; and, fourth, the conclusion that a contraction of the (inconvertible) paper currency would lead to gold imports, thus providing a panacea for England's monetary difficulties. A demonstration of the essential practical fallacy of these doctrines will be found in Appendix A, below.

7. Ricardo's "Principles of Political Economy" appeared in 1817.[1] As just indicated, it summarized in compact and masterly fashion the leading conclusions of the Bullionist school, but Ricardo here added little or nothing to his own earlier pronouncements — nor, indeed, to the doctrines of his immediate predecessors. The great contribution of the "Principles" to the theory of international prices was, rather, its development of a doctrine that had been conspicuously lacking in all the earlier literature: namely, a tenable explanation of the ratios or rates of inter-commodity exchange in international trade. This Ricardo accomplished through the formulation of the principle of comparative costs.

The general character of the principle of comparative costs is sufficiently familiar to make a detailed exposition unnecessary.[2] It is asserted that whereas in internal trade the course of exchange is governed by *absolute* differences in costs, the immobility of labor and capital as between countries makes this determination invalid for international trade. The determinants therefore become *comparative* differences in costs. If a country produces both of two commodities at less cost than a second country, but if its advantage is smaller for one of the two commodities than for the other, it will pay the country to import that commodity, and to export the other in payment. The possible fluctuations in the ratio of the exchange between the two are limited by the ratios between their costs in the one country and the other.

These costs, it is true, are taken as being measured in terms of labor. They are "human" costs. But Ricardo's labor theory of value permitted an easy transition from such costs to the relative money prices which govern the operations of the actual market. The relation between given quantities of labor and the magnitudes of the corresponding money prices was of course not regarded as being necessarily the same in different countries, but a comparative advantage in terms of the one was held to yield an equivalent comparative advantage in terms of the other.[3] A

---

[1] D. Ricardo, *Principles of Political Economy and Taxation* (London, 1817). I have used here the convenient edition published in the Everyman series, 1912.

[2] *Ibid.*, ch. 7, *passim*.

[3] In a later chapter, we shall find the mathematical economists suggesting a

limited zone was thus defined by costs (and prices) in the one country and in the other, within which a profitable exchange could take place. The benefit, however, was regarded as confined to one country alone with respect to any given commodity. It remained for Mill to try to develop an *a priori* determination of a single precise ratio of exchange, and to show conclusively that the benefit was reciprocal.[1]

I shall reserve any discussion of this doctrine, the validity of which has almost never been seriously questioned by the later English economists, until another chapter.[2] It should be remarked, however, that Ricardo's claim to striking originality here seems beyond debate. It is true that possible logical bases for the doctrine can be found, on the one hand, in the doctrine of the mutual advantages of the division of labor so forcefully summarized by Adam Smith; and on the other hand in the later Mercantilistic suggestions of an international labor theory of value.[3] But in the first place, there is no internal evidence that Ricardo was consciously borrowing from any previous writer, and in the second place, it is a far cry indeed from these scattered fragments to the complete theory itself. The formulation of the principle of comparative costs was an intellectual *tour de force* of unusual brilliance.[4]

The second major contribution of the "Principles" to the theory of international prices was its analysis of the relations be-

somewhat different method of bridging the gap between human costs and money prices.

[1] Torrens had previously concluded, in 1808, that the benefit is divided. See the reference in sect. 5, above.

[2] See ch. xiv, sect. 3, below.

[3] See ch. ii, sect. 6, above. It should be pointed out that in 1803 Wheatley had called attention to the internal *mobility*, and international *immobility*, of labor, and Ricardo undoubtedly used this idea as one of his points of departure. See sect. 4, above.

[4] I cannot agree with Mill's dictum that Torrens is entitled to share the credit for originality with Ricardo. Torrens' tract, *The Economists Refuted* (1808), established the real nature of the gain from international trade before any work of Ricardo's appeared in print (see sect. 5, above), and the principle of comparative costs was perhaps latent in his demonstration. But Torrens himself did not state the principle in recognizable form at that time. (See J. S. Mill, *Principles of Political Economy*, Bk. III, ch. 17, sect. 2; in W. J. Ashley's edition, London, 1920, p. 476, second footnote.)

tween money prices in different countries, under convertible conditions. Here, too, as in connection with the price-specie flow mechanism, I think that later writers have frequently misinterpreted Ricardo.[1] It has often been implied, and sometimes explicitly stated, that Ricardo held a doctrine of international price equalization, and of the maintenance of equilibrium in international trade through the corresponding price movements. But this is not quite Ricardo's position. He found that the world values of the various monetary units, *in terms of gold or silver*, are always kept substantially equal (translated at the prevailing rates of exchange) through the operation of the foreign exchange mechanism itself. But he denied outright that they are or can be kept equal in terms of *commodities:* "When each country has precisely the quantity of money which it ought to have, money will not indeed be of the same value in each, for with respect to many commodities it may differ 5, 10, or even 20 per cent, but the exchange will be at par. One hundred pounds in England, or the silver which is in £100, will purchase a bill of £100, or an equal quantity of silver in France, Spain, or Holland." [2]

What then determines the amount of money that a country "ought" to have? Under metallic standards, the answer turns on the cost of transportation of the country's exports, and of its imported gold (assuming it not to be a mining country). The value of gold will be low — the general level of prices will be high — if a country enjoys a relative superiority in manufactures, thus exporting articles of high value and small bulk; and if it is relatively near the point from which the gold comes.[3] Each of these

[1] A very good statement of the alternative type of interpretation adopted here has recently been presented by Professor Gustav Cassel, in his work on *Money and Foreign Exchange after 1914* (New York, 1923). See especially p. 173.

[2] Ricardo, *Principles*, p. 91. Also see, for example, p. 88.

[3] *Ibid.*, p. 89. An improvement in the production of the precious metals, making their labor cost lower, would lead to the same effect. The effect of taxation is simply to disturb the actual or potential equilibrium, as is that of any other restriction on free movement and exchange. See *ibid.*, pp. 90, 91, and also pp. 150, 151.

It may be remarked that Ricardo also uses these two elements, superiority in manufactures and distance from the mines, to provide the criterion of a country's general benefit from foreign trade.

conditions will make the corresponding costs of transportation relatively low. Since such costs are ordinarily different for different countries, the consequence necessarily must be that the relative amounts of gold and silver that constitute the proper quantity for each country will likewise be different, and the levels of their commodity prices hence not the same.[1] This doctrine of permanent price *difference* is then extended even to those articles "which are common to most countries,"[2] but without any qualification for the actual fact of price equality with respect to articles that are actively traded. We are thus left with the implicit conclusion that within considerable limits there is no necessary relationship at all between the price structures of different countries, under metallic standards. Permanent (though presumably variable) price differences exist, the differences being determined by the comparative labor costs of obtaining the precious metals.[3] The world value of money, in other words, is to be fitted into the comparative-cost doctrine itself.

It follows as a corollary that the only short-time "equilibrium" which can be postulated in Ricardo's analysis is the equilibrium

[1] The way in which Ricardo thought that this automatic distribution of the precious metals is effected has already been examined above. The famous classical dictum, that the terms of international trade will be the same under money as under barter, follows as a natural corollary.

[2] *Ibid.*, p. 88. See also p. 92.

[3] Ricardo has little to say here about conditions under an *inconvertible* currency. For that we must turn to his earlier pamphlet writings and to his various letters, already examined above. So see, for example, the summary propositions on p. 91 of the *Principles*.

It is true that, in a quite different connection, Ricardo presented unequivocally what is now called the purchasing-power-parity doctrine. He said: "If a country used paper money not exchangeable for specie, and, therefore, not regulated by any fixed standard, the exchanges in that country might deviate from par in the same proportion as its money might be multiplied beyond that quantity which would have been allotted to it by general commerce, if . . . the precious metals had been used." (*Principles*, ch. xvi, p. 151.) Certain present-day writers have therefore concluded, without going farther, that this passage fairly represents Ricardo's position. If we remember, however, that it is placed in the middle of a discussion bearing on another problem (taxes on wages); that the doctrine is not to be found in that chapter explicitly devoted to foreign trade and the foreign exchanges; and that Ricardo developed a quite different view in his earlier writings (see sect. 5, above), we are then justified, I think, in attaching no very great importance to it. It is a suggestive but rather incidental fragment.

of the exchanges and of the balance of international payments, not of prices or of commodity trade.[1] Yet on the question of how the equilibrium of the balance of payments is maintained, Ricardo says surprisingly little in the "Principles." We have already seen that, in his earlier pamphlet writings, he confined the price-specie flow mechanism to the adjustment of relative redundancies or deficiencies in the currency, explicitly denying that specie flows could be the *consequence* of initial deficits in the balance of payments. Here, it is true, he seems to contradict this position by declaring that a premium on foreign exchange which is itself the consequence of the state of the current balance will alter the balance of *trade*, and lead to an export of specie.[2] But a reconciliation between the two views can be effected, by regarding that state of relative prices which brought about the deficit in the balance of payments as being itself symptomatic of a relative redundancy or deficiency in the currencies. Such, I think, is the correct interpretation of the passage.

This leaves us, however, with still another contradiction, for which a solution cannot be found so easily. If the doctrine of disequality in prices as between countries be accepted, how does the automatic distribution of the precious metals work itself out? How can any such distribution be effected, *except* through the agency of some fairly definite normative tendency in relative prices; and what other criterion can there be of a relatively redundant or a relatively deficient currency? A possible answer, that the distributive mechanism was assumed to operate only through the actively-traded "international" commodities, seems to be ruled out by the specific inclusion in the category of price-differences of those articles which "are common to most countries." The explanation must apparently be simply that Ricardo never thought his own theorems completely through.[3]

---

[1] It is probably true that Ricardo also had in mind an underlying equilibrium based on comparative labor costs, and on that stability in the general course of trade to which the stability of labor costs presumably gives rise. But the idea does not appear very definitely.

[2] *Ibid.*, pp. 85, 86. See also a similar apparent contradiction in Ricardo's letter to Malthus of December 22, 1811 (see above, sect. 5.)

[3] We shall find a not dissimilar confusion in Mill.

As an exercise in logic we can, it is true, conceive of a situation in which the commodity-price systems of the various countries are largely independent; and in which the precious metals are distributed through the attractive or repellent effects of slight variations in the market prices of these metals from the ratios between the various mint pars. This was probably the sort of situation that Ricardo had in mind when he made his specie-flow mechanism exclusively "unilateral," though he never defined it in such unequivocal terms.[1] That is, he held that specie is distributed not by the differences in its market price in terms of *commodities*, in the one country and the other, but by the differences in its price *in terms of the respective currency units*. These last are reduced to equivalents at the ratio between the mint pars, plus or minus the percentage needed to reach the import or export points for specie.

The argument would be entirely tenable if specie were the only commodity exchanged between countries. But under actual conditions, of course, a great many other articles also enter the situation. It is therefore inevitable that comparisons should be made between the values of specie in terms of *them* in different countries, as well as in terms of the various currency units. Moreover, such comparisons will affect the world movements of gold. The consequence must be that the prices of at least certain kinds of commodities — "international" commodities — will tend to maintain an approximate equivalence. The doctrine of price inequality then becomes erroneous with respect to such commodities. In other words Ricardo's position, if not indeed inconsistent with itself, is incompatible with the apparent facts of international trade.

Such seems to be the explanation of this confused and often misinterpreted part of Ricardo's doctrine.

8. In the decade after the appearance of Ricardo's "Principles," a number of works were published which are of consider-

---

[1] At least not in the *Principles*. But see the passage in *The High Price of Bullion*, p. 6, already quoted in section 5, above: "the currency of any one country can never be much more valuable, *as far as equal quantities of the precious metals are concerned*, than that of another." (Italics mine.)

able importance in the general development of economic thought. But in the main they contain little new material that is relevant to the theory of international prices.[1] The only contributions to which attention should be drawn are Torrens' development of the new conception of "lags" in economic relationships,[2] and Tooke's most suggestive analysis of short-time fluctuations in prices, credit and business. Tooke dwelt especially on the normal fluctuations produced by speculation and by the seasons, and came close to a cyclical theory.[3] His discussion was realistic and detailed, and contains the germs of many more modern doctrines.

With Nassau Senior, however, the theory of international trade itself took a new departure, both in concreteness of formulation and in content. Senior's lecture on the transmission of the preci-

[1] See especially James Mill, *Elements of Political Economy* (London, 1821); T. R. Malthus, *The Measure of Value* (London, 1823); W. Blake, *The Effects Produced by the Expenditure of Government* (London, 1823); and J. R. MacCulloch, *Principles of Political Economy* (London, 1825.) So far as these works touched upon money and international trade at all, they were in the main content with a repetition or a simplification of the Ricardian doctrines, and with a review of the Restriction-period experience as seen through Bullionist eyes.

[2] R. Torrens, *Essay on the Production of Wealth* (London, 1821), especially pp. 404 ff. Torrens is here examining the repercussions of a shortage or a glut in the supply of an article upon its price, the incomes of its producers, their purchases of *other* articles, and consequently upon *all* commodities. There is also a good discussion of interest rates (pp. 422 ff.), of the relation between wages and prices (pp. 324 ff.), and of the social effects of changes in the value of money (pp. 324–339). These all involve some use of the concept of lags, and even of a *cyclical* lag (as see p. 416). Torrens did not tie these ideas up directly with international trade, but the concept of lags has become so important in modern economic literature that it is worth while to call attention to what seems to have been its first explicit appearance.

[3] Thomas Tooke, *Considerations on the State of the Currency* (London, 1826), especially pp. 62 ff. Tooke also shows here, I think for the first time, that the Bank rate can be used as a *deliberate* method of correcting an excessive circulation; the symptom of an excess being, under convertible conditions, the tendency of the precious metals to leave the country. At a later point, he stresses the delay that must appear before even a radical change in general conditions will affect the balance of trade, the delay being due to lack of information. Gold movements will therefore be necessary for a time.

Reference should also be made to Tooke's earlier work, *Thoughts and Details on the High and Low Prices of the Last Thirty Years* (London, 1823), in which he undertook a thorough and on the whole convincing refutation of the orthodox Bullionist interpretation; convincing, at least, relative to the data at his disposal. See for example pp. 61, 62, 177, 200–203; and in the *Considerations*, just cited, pp. 2, 3.

ous metals,[1] it is true, was simply an orthodox exposition of the price-specie flow mechanism and the foreign-exchange process. Its chief merit for our purposes lies in its demonstration that the "real" exchanges can be permanently unfavorable only in the case of a mining country exporting the precious metals. His lecture on the cost of obtaining money,[2] on the other hand, offers a quite new type of analysis.

Senior comments on the wide discrepancies observable in the wages of labor, as between different countries,[3] and accounts for it in this way.[4] First, in non-mining countries the wages of the labor which is engaged in the production of exportable commodities are dependent on the efficiency of the labor itself, relative to that in other countries. The greater the efficiency of this labor, the greater will be the quantity of gold and silver received for its (exported) products. Second, the wages of labor in the export industries regulate the wages of all other labor in the same country. The *relative* scale of wages is of course what it otherwise would have been,[5] but the *absolute* scale, the levels of *money* wages, is governed by the wages of that labor in return for whose products money first comes into the country. These two propositions are then applied, by an easy transition, to the determination of commodity prices. Senior states his conclusion — which becomes involved in his theory of value, not itself relevant here — as follows. In a non-mining country, the gold-and-silver prices of all commodities not the subject of monopoly depend on

the gold and silver which can be obtained by exporting the result of a given quantity of labor, [on] the current rate of profit, and, in each individual case, [on] the amount of the wages which have been paid, and [on] the time for which they have been advanced.

Finally, "in the mining countries all prices ultimately depend on the cost of producing the precious metals." The relative scale is

---

[1] Nassau Senior, *Three Lectures, on the Transmission of the Precious Metals ... and the Mercantile Theory of Wealth* (London, 1827).

[2] *Three Lectures on the Cost of Obtaining Money, and on Some Effects of Private and Government Paper Money* (London, 1830).

[3] *Ibid.*, pp. 1–10.

[4] *Ibid.*, pp. 11–15.

[5] Based, apparently, on relative sacrifice. See *Ibid.*, p. 15.

again what it otherwise would be, but the absolute levels are derived from the miners' rewards, and are based thereon.

From this it follows that "the amount of the income in money of each individual depends on the prosperity of our foreign commerce."[1] Assume, in a non-mining country such as England, that an improvement in machinery has doubled the value of English manufactures in the foreign market. If the wages of the corresponding laborers are likewise raised, the effect would be the same as if, in a mining country, the cost of producing silver were cut in half. Other wages would also increase, to maintain their former proportion; most prices would rise; and the internal purchasing power of money incomes would eventually be as before. But the general power of purchasing those domestic goods in which the improvement has taken place, and of purchasing *foreign* labor and commodities, would be raised in proportion to the improvement.[2] Moreover, the benefit to one country from such an improvement may be another's loss. If, as a result of an invention in France, England were cut out of the world market for cottons, England would find it easier to obtain cottons, but more difficult to import everything else. The value of her exports having fallen, the cost of obtaining the precious metals would rise for her, and fall for France.

We need not enter into a detailed criticism of these propositions. It is sufficient to point out the nature of Senior's contribution. Like Ricardo, he bases his theory of international prices upon the comparative cost of obtaining the precious metals. But whereas Ricardo made his principal criterion a relative superiority in manufactures, operating through costs of transportation, Senior adopts the more exact test of the relative efficiency of labor in the export industries.[3] And he goes much beyond Ricardo in working out a complete if somewhat lightly sketched system of the levels of prices and money incomes, as between

[1] Senior, *Three Lectures*, p. 16.   [2] *Ibid.*, pp. 18, 19.

[3] Senior's criterion does not differ from Ricardo's as much as might at first glance appear, since the factors contributing to superiority in manufactures and to a relatively high efficiency of labor are at bottom much the same. The difference is one of emphasis, and of the objective index used. Senior's advance over Ricardo lay, rather, in the wider use he made of the general principle.

countries. Ricardo had much the same elements of theory at his disposal, and indeed the germs of Senior's reasoning here can be found very largely in his writings, but he failed to combine them into a doctrine of anything like the same breadth and reality. Senior was the first to make a complete study of this sort; a study which proceeded primarily from the monetary point of view alone, and which was in large part divested of all furniture taken over from an *a priori* theory of value.

9. After the publication of Senior's lectures, nothing of importance appeared until 1844. In that year the long-smouldering controversy over the best form of organization of the Bank of England came to a head, and gave rise to a new stream of polemical literature. The practical question involved was that of whether the Bank's note circulation should be treated like the issues of any private bank, and be allowed to fluctuate without limit as long as convertibility was maintained — the "banking principle"; or be treated as a simple substitute for a pure metallic currency, and therefore be required to fluctuate as such a currency would if left to itself — the "currency principle." The legislative issue was soon solved by the passage of Sir Robert Peel's Bank Charter Act in 1844, itself a compromise between the two extreme positions, but the general merits and demerits of the act continued to be agitated for a number of years.

The theoretical foundations of the alternative views just outlined have an important bearing on the problem of international prices. They involve certain definite assumptions as to the relations between the course of international trade, the volume of the internal currency, and commodity prices. The doctrine of the currency-principle adherents is already familiar to us. It turned essentially on the type of price-specie flow analysis found in Ricardo, though with certain modifications to allow for changes in the volume of bank credit. The doctrine of the banking-principle adherents, however, is more novel. Of this doctrine the best-known contemporary exponent was probably Tooke, but for our purposes the quite similar analysis made by Fullarton is better. It will suffice to summarize the latter's position.

In the first place, Fullarton declares that drains of specie are due exclusively to the state of the balance of international payments, and not at all to the state of internal prices or to the relative excess of the convertible paper currency.[1] Ricardo is criticized for holding the opposite view too rigidly. In the second place, he finds that the level of internal prices is itself determined by the volume of bank credit, not by the amount of money in circulation.[2] In consequence, it is useless to try to correct specie drains by contracting the *currency*. What is necessary is a contraction of *bank credit*. But the possible rôle of the Bank of England in deliberately inducing such a contraction is limited. The action of the Bank can be effective only if "some degree of commercial difficulty and a low state of private credit, *rendering the community more than usually dependent on the Bank of England*, should be concurrent with the commencement of the drain, which by no means always occurs." [3]

Finally, these specie drains themselves do not necessarily come from the country's monetary *circulation*, and hence need not affect internal prices at all. Under a pure metallic currency, they come largely from various types of private "hoards"; under a mixed currency such as England's, from the Bank of England re-

---

[1] John Fullarton, *On the Regulation of Currencies* (2 ed., London, 1845), pp. 130, 131. The first edition appeared in 1844. The weakness in Fullarton's position is that he fails to explain why, *apart* from the state of relative prices, the balance of payments should have been in disequilibrium.

[2] The proposition that there can never be an excess or a deficit in the volume of the bank note circulation relative to the needs of trade, as long as convertibility is maintained, follows as a corollary of these doctrines. (See *ibid.*, ch. 3, *passim*.) If, however, prices are determined by the volume of bank credit, and this by trade needs, we seem to be involved in a circle. The escape lies in the requirement of convertibility, but the operation of this requirement, in the last analysis, ultimately affects internal conditions only through international trade (in a non-mining country). We are thus thrown back on that doctrine, of changes in *relative* prices as between countries and of specie flows produced by them, which Fullarton explicitly rejects.

A position similar to Fullarton's was adopted by Tooke in his *Inquiry into the Currency Principle* (London, 1844), pp. 65–76, 123, 124.

[3] Fullarton, *op. cit.*, p. 137. (Italics mine.) Also see p. 150. This vital limitation on the effectiveness of the Bank's discount policy has been too often neglected. It is on the other hand true, however, that "psychological" factors give this policy more than a merely mechanical control over the market.

serves in which the private hoards are concentrated.[1] Moreover, most varieties of specie drain are self-terminating. There is no one sure corrective that will work before they have reached their natural limit. The Bank, therefore, can only try to accumulate sufficient reserves to enable it to hold out until the reflux of specie begins of itself.[2] If it attempts to apply pressure, and by the coincidence just mentioned is successful in stopping the drain, it will only precipitate a crisis, and all to secure a result that in any event would usually have appeared in due course.

It is thus evident that Fullarton and the other advocates of the banking principle, despite various logical weaknesses in their position, made a very real contribution. They established tenable grounds for attacking and rejecting the whole price-specie flow mechanism, at least within considerable limits, by their doctrines of the elasticity of a country's bullion reserves and of the lack of a direct connection between money and prices; and Fullarton, at least, pointed out the essentially qualified character of the Bank's control over prices and the market. These were the first clear voices that had been raised against Hume's type of analysis since the time of Steuart. The theory of international prices has been much the loser, as has the theory of international trade in general, in that their ideas were never made a really integral part of the generally-accepted doctrine.[3]

10. The first third of the nineteenth century, taken as a whole, had thus witnessed a series of remarkable advances in the various elements that enter into the theory of international prices, and that theory itself had begun to emerge for the first time as a definite entity. Perhaps the most striking development was

---

[1] Fullarton, *op cit.*, pp. 140–143 and ff. Tooke similarly declared that gold flows up to five or six million pounds could take place without affecting the value of money or the level of internal prices. See his *Currency Principle* (cited above), pp. 121, 122, and elsewhere.

[2] Fullarton, *op. cit.*, pp. 151–153.

[3] It may be remarked that in the United States a literature not dissimilar to that produced in England by the Bank Charter controversy appeared in the years after 1825–1830. See H. E. Miller, *Earlier Theories of Crises and Cycles in the United States* (38 Quarterly Journal of Economics, 1924), for an excellent description of this literature.

Ricardo's construction of a consistent explanation of the terms of inter-commodity exchange in international trade, by the invention of the principle of comparative costs. But the analyses of the relations between money prices in different countries, successively worked out by Thornton, Horner and Wheatley, as well as by Ricardo himself, were of at least equal importance. They involved an attempt to make Hume's rather rigid doctrine of the world distribution of the precious metals more realistic. They thereby led to the new concept of a world equilibrium, not only as between currencies but also in the normal course of international trade itself. Some writers, particularly Wheatley, even pushed this last idea through to a perhaps naïve doctrine of international price equalization. Ricardo, in opposition, concluded that permanent price *differences* existed. He was in consequence compelled to limit his theory of international equilibrium to terms of the balance of payments and the exchanges. Senior went beyond even Ricardo in revealing the conditions that determine such permanent differences, both in prices and in money incomes. Senior, indeed, was the first to develop a consistent explanation of the relations between *all* the classes of prices and incomes in one country, and all classes in another. On the other hand, certain writers of the Bank Charter controversy were later able to bring forward forceful criticisms of those supposed relations between money, prices and international trade, on which the whole Hume-Ricardo-Senior doctrine was based.

Finally, the Bullion Controversy itself led to really remarkable progress in the practical knowledge and theoretical explanation of what takes place under a régime of inconvertible paper. Some of the ideas advanced were quite erroneous as applied to then-contemporary conditions, but others, such as the purchasing-power-parity doctrine, have now been made the explanation of events since 1914. And although the purely domestic theory of money and prices was not carried through by the Bullion Controversy writers to a form that is altogether acceptable at the present day, the path was nevertheless well cleared of obstructions. The later Bank Charter controversy accomplished much of the fundamental work that remained to be done.

It is therefore true in a very real sense that the great foundations of the theory of international prices were laid, however incompletely, well before John Stuart Mill ever wrote. A domestic theory of money and prices; a theory of international ratios of inter-commodity exchange; theories of the relations between money prices in different countries, under both convertible and inconvertible conditions; a theory of the foreign exchanges; and a doctrine of general equilibrium in international trade — these are the elements which were now definitely established. The later writers have added no fundamentally new ones. Their rôle has been, rather, to modify the traditional doctrines in such fashion as to make them more accurate descriptions of actual events; to incorporate into them the frequently valuable suggestions of their critics; and — what no one had yet done — to strive to draw all of these scattered fragments together into one comprehensive and self-consistent theory.

CHAPTER IV

THE GENERAL THEORY OF INTERNATIONAL TRADE
AFTER RICARDO

1. Ricardo's exposition of the theory of international trade opened up a new field of inquiry in English economic thought, and one which is without adequate counterpart in the literatures of other countries. It gave the problem a fresh and characteristic form that has never been lost. But Ricardo did more than this. He also had the privilege, rarely enjoyed by the originators of new systems, of marking out virtually all of the main lines in the subsequent development of his own ideas. The task of the later classical and post-classical writers has after all been, at bottom, one of refinement and elaboration alone. They have not added essentially new elements of importance, nor have they turned the current of inquiry into essentially new channels.

Of these later modifications, only four are of major significance: Mill's attempt to establish a more exact *a priori* determination of the ratios of international exchange, by the use of the "Equation of International Demand"; Cairnes' refinement of this last analysis, especially with respect to non-competing groups; the realistic effort, made in part by Mill but chiefly by Bastable, to allow for variability in supply and demand schedules; and finally Professor Taussig's reasoned exposition of the determination of the scales of prices and money incomes as between countries. To the foregoing elements, however, should perhaps be added certain miscellaneous discussions of the effects of tariffs upon international trade and prices, especially those of Bastable and Marshall. The present chapter will be concerned with the propositions of these various writers.

John Stuart Mill's doctrines, like those of Ricardo, are too familiar to make a detailed exposition necessary, and indeed we have already examined most of their important features in the works of other writers. Mill, despite the originality of some of his ideas, was essentially an eclectic, a systematizer and expounder of the scattered theories of other men. He wove together into a single fabric the best elements in Hume, Steuart and Smith, in Thornton and Wheatley, in Ricardo, Torrens and Senior, but his own contributions were not numerous. In chief, they consisted of the Equation of International Demand itself, and of his refinements upon Ricardo's doctrine of the determination of the world value of money. The principle of comparative costs, the analysis of the world distribution of the precious metals, the general theory of foreign trade under disordered monetary conditions, the theory of the exchanges, and most of the rest of Mill's positive teachings, were taken over from earlier writers with little substantial alteration.

Moreover, by a curious irony of fate Mill's own most original theories were largely anticipated by another writer, at least in the actual date of their publication. The first draft of his ideas upon the laws of international exchange was presented in his "Essays upon Some Unsettled Questions," brought out in 1844.[1] The particular essay in question was written, Mill tells us, in 1829–1830, but had never been published before. It is here that the irony appears, for earlier in the same year, 1844, Col. Torrens published his treatise upon the budget,[2] and in the introduction laid down principles which, however hastily sketched in, were at bottom like those advanced by Mill. The resemblance was at some points so close, indeed, that Mill felt constrained to explain that his own work had actually been done fifteen years earlier, and that he had not plagiarized from Torrens.[3] It would be interesting to compare the two works in detail, but the more valuable elements in each were presented four years later, in far better form, in Mill's "Political Economy."[4] To this work, therefore, we may now turn.

2. The portions of Mill's argument which are of greatest in-

[1] J. S. Mill, *Essays on Some Unsettled Questions of Political Economy* (London, 1844), Essay I.

[2] R. Torrens, *The Budget* (London, 1844).

[3] Mill, *op. cit., Preface.*

[4] J. S. Mill, *Principles of Political Economy* (London, 1848). I have used the edition prepared by W. J. Ashley (London, 1909 and 1920).

terest to the theory of international prices are those which deal with the ratio of international exchange itself. Mill took over without comment Ricardo's principle of comparative costs, and elaborated it into the more usable form with which we are now familiar. But the principle of comparative costs, evidently, does not define *a* single ratio of exchange; it simply indicates a zone, within whose limits any ratio whatsoever will be advantageous to the countries concerned.[1] This lack of exactness Mill sought to correct by his Equation of International Demand. He tried to find an *a priori* criterion which should establish one and only one ratio, within the limits set by the extant comparative costs. The general line of the analysis is as follows:

"The value of a thing in any place depends on the cost of its acquisition in that place; which, in the case of an imported article, means the cost of the thing which is exported to pay for it."[2] That is, the values of foreign commodities depend on the terms of international exchange; on the quantity of a country's exports which, at a given price, will just offset the quantity and price of its imports. These terms are in turn dependent on the Equation of International Demand.[3] The outside limits, beyond which the fluctuating values of the traded commodities cannot go, are fixed at the points at which it would be as cheap to manufacture the article within the given country as to import it. Within those limits — assuming for convenience only two countries and two commodities — the particular rate at which the exchange will take place is dependent on the relative strength of the demand of each country for the other's product. Equilibrium is reached when the rate is such that the imports one country requires will exactly pay for the imports the other requires, *provided* that the given quantity of each of the two commodities exactly satisfies the extant demand at the given prices. That is, "the demand on each side is [then] precisely sufficient to carry off the supply on the other."[4] Or, put more elaborately,

---

[1] For a criticism of the principle, see ch. xiv, sect. 3, below.
[2] Mill, *Principles*, p. 583.
[3] *Ibid.*, p. 584.
[4] *Ibid.*, pp. 585, 586.

when two countries trade together in two commodities, the exchange value of those commodities relatively to each other will adjust itself to the inclinations and circumstances of the consumers on both sides, in such manner that the quantities required by each country, of the articles which it imports from its neighbor, shall be exactly sufficient to pay for one another.[1]

This, then, is what is meant by the statement that the terms of international exchange are determined within the indicated limits by the Equation of International Demand. Mill goes on to tie all this up with the comparative efficiency of labor as between countries, and says:

Every country gets its imports at less cost, in proportion to the general efficiency of its labor.[2] . . . What [a country's] imports cost to her is a function of two variables; the quantity of her own commodities which she gives for them, and the cost of those commodities. Of these, the last alone depends on the efficiency of her labor. The first depends on the law of international values; that is, on the intensity and extensibility of the foreign demand for her commodities, compared with her demand for foreign commodities.[3]

In other words, the cost of imports is determined by (1) the *quantity* of the corresponding exports, which is dependent on the Equation of International Demand; and by (2) the *cost* of those exports, which is dependent on the relative efficiency of labor. This latter cost, it should be noticed, is taken as measured in terms of quantities of labor. The efficiency of labor itself has no share in determining the *money price* of imports.

This is the argument as it originally appeared. But various critics, especially Thornton, soon pointed out the fact that more than one rate might satisfy the Equation of International Demand. The determination of the ratios of exchange was therefore still not exact. Mill attempted to escape the difficulty, in later editions, by throwing the ultimate determination of the rate of exchange back upon potential demand and cost schedules, and upon the possible alternative distribution of productive forces. He tried to show that "the whole of the commodities which the

---

[1] Mill, *Principles*, p. 587.

[2] Mill credits Senior with the first statement of this proposition, but says that Senior confined it to imports of the precious metals; a criticism which seems to me hardly justified. Thus see Senior's lecture, cited above, on *The Cost of Obtaining Money*, pp. 11, 12.

[3] Mill, *Principles*, pp. 605, 606.

two countries can respectively make for exportation, with the labor and capital thrown out of employment by importation, will [just] exchange against one another." [1] But, even if it could be granted that this condition would produce a single ratio of exchange, there is evidently no *a priori* reason for holding that the products of the displaced labor and capital will enter foreign trade rather than domestic. Various Continental critics have also observed that the displaced productive power itself may in large part be lost outright, not merely diverted into other channels. It may be incapable of finding equally remunerative employment in other directions, and the assumed transfer may therefore itself be physically impossible. On the whole, it is probably better to disregard Mill's attempt to secure a more exact determination, and to rest content with the partial truths [2] contained in his original statement. His emendations mar the symmetry of the general argument, while they impair its convincingness more than they improve it.

It may be added that Mill, like Ricardo, conducts all of this discussion of ratios of exchange under the hypothesis that the trade is one of barter. But whereas Ricardo contents himself with little more than a mere statement of the assumption, Mill later attempts a formal proof of the proposition that the terms of trade under barter and under money are the same. The proof consists in the demonstration that a lack of equilibrium in foreign trade, under money, will result in specie flows, changes in general prices, changes in the balance of trade, and a re-establishment of equilibrium at a different ratio of exchange. It is asserted that this last is precisely what will happen under barter.[3] Criticism of the argument must be reserved for a later chapter, but it may be pointed out here that it is, to say the least, incomplete. There is no proof that the ratios of exchange necessarily change in like degree in the two cases. Nor is allowance made for permanent alterations in *relative* prices produced by an alteration in *absolute* prices.

3. Before proceeding farther with Mill's argument, it will be useful to present his own theory of money and prices, or at least

---

[1] Mill, *Principles*, p. 600.   [2] For a fuller discussion, see ch. xiv, sect. 2, below.
[3] Mill, *Principles*, pp. 619–621, 629, 630.

its more important outlines. Mill distinguishes carefully between the proximate and the ultimate determination of the value of money. For the proximate determination, he makes use of a form of the quantity theory essentially the same as that employed by his immediate predecessors.[1] Velocity of circulation is taken into account somewhat more fully, however, and the influence of credit is more adequately allowed for. Its use is held to make the connection between prices and the amount of money much less intimate, and to necessitate a more complex mode of formulation.[2] But at bottom his theory seems to have been of the familiar "static" character. It makes little real allowance for the element of growth in economic life, or for the somewhat bewildering phenomena of the transition periods. Price readjustments, for example, are apparently regarded as fundamentally frictionless, and money is at bottom treated as a merely passive transmitter of inter-commodity values.[3] In other words, Mill quite passes over the actual events and the mechanisms involved in short-time fluctuations, and gives only an analysis of what may be called the "normal" or "normative" short-run tendencies. In this respect, at least, he is distinctly inferior to his less well-known contemporaries, such as Torrens, Fullarton and Tooke.

With respect to the ultimate determination of the value of metallic or convertible money, Mill further distinguishes between countries that do and those that do not mine the precious metals. In mining countries, the value of money is ultimately dependent upon costs of production at the worst mine which it is necessary to work in order to obtain the required supply.[4] But this state-

---

[1] Mill, *Principles*, pp. 483–498. See also pp. 542–544 and 634, 635.

[2] *Ibid.*, pp. 495, 523.

[3] These criticisms may at first glance seem quite unjustified. At one point (pp. 490–492) Mill traces the mechanics of the effects of an increase in the quantity of money, and shows that a change in the distribution of the national income and productive power may result. He even admits a possible permanent change in *relative* prices. And later (p. 497) he gives more than a hint of the operation of the effects of long-time growth. But these ideas seem never to have become genuinely incorporated into his own general thinking. When he applies the quantity theory to international trade, he uses it in its most unmistakably "static" form; elaborately qualified, it is true, but still essentially frictionless and direct-acting.

[4] *Ibid.*, p. 502.

ment must be qualified for the effects of government regulation and for the expenses of coinage, which may raise the value of the coin above that of its bullion content;[1] and also for the fact that, because of the large extant supply of gold and silver relative to the current production, a change in the cost of production will operate only very slowly upon the value of money.[2] Finally, the two determinations of the value of money, by cost of production and by demand and supply, are tied together with respect to mining countries by the statement that "alterations . . . in the cost of production of the precious metals do not act upon the value of money except just in proportion as they increase or diminish its quantity."[3] It should perhaps be added that the measure of this cost of production, which includes "labor and expense," and risk, seems to be somewhat uncertain. [4]

In non-mining countries, the situation is somewhat different. There, the value of money is in part still ultimately dependent on cost of production at the mines. But in part, also, it is dependent on the Equation of International Demand. The value of money is lowest in those countries for whose exports there is the greatest foreign demand, and which themselves have the least demand for foreign commodities.[5] Anything upsetting the Equation will thus alter the value of money in one country or in both, by compelling its offer or surrender on cheaper terms to reëstablish the Equation.[6] And a further qualification is made, which is reminiscent of Ricardo. The cost of obtaining bullion is declared to be governed in part by the cost of transportation both of the bullion itself, and of the goods with which it is purchased. In consequence, those countries tend to get bullion most cheaply which are nearest the mines, and which themselves export articles of high value and small bulk.[7]

Taken as a whole, Mill's theory is thus an ingenious attempt to combine the determination of the value of money by demand and supply with a determination by cost of production — and, in the case of non-mining countries, by the terms of international ex-

[1] Mill, *Principles*, p. 501.   [2] *Ibid.*, pp. 502–504.
[3] *Ibid.*, p. 504.   [4] See p. 502, and elsewhere.
[5] *Ibid.*, p. 609.   [6] *Ibid.*, p. 610.   [7] *Ibid.*, p. 609.

change. This dual or even treble basis, which Continental economists have frequently (though I think erroneously) criticized as inconsistent, was evidently the result of fusing the doctrines of Ricardo with those of Senior. But Mill carried the earlier analyses one step farther; and he deserves credit for evolving from them the first really complete explanation of the world value of money, both short-time and long. The short-time basis is supply and demand, the long-time, cost of production — a familiar dualism which runs through nearly all of the classical economics.[1]

Mill then turns to the world distribution of the precious metals, and at once presents the price-specie flow analysis.[2] The general character of this analysis is already sufficiently familiar to make repetition unnecessary, but two points in Mill's formulation should not escape comment. In the first place, whereas all previous writers had regarded specie flows as the only means of correcting a permanent disequilibrium in trade which is due to the state of general prices, Mill declared, on at least one occasion, that the correction might also be made by an equivalent annihilation of *credit* in one of the two countries. This last proposition is the first attempt of the orthodox classical writers to link international trade directly with the state of credit; of credit, that is, taken as a separate element.[3] In the second place, the sort of price-specie flow mechanism which Mill described was what we have elsewhere called the "bilateral" type. That is, he applied it not only to the correction of a disequilibrium due to the state of prices, as Ricardo had done, but also to the correction of an original disequilibrium in the balance of payments, such as results from an improvement in the manufacture of an export. Mill thus

---

[1] The foregoing analysis was of course confined to metallic or convertible currencies. With respect to inconvertible currencies, Mill adopts substantially the Bullionist position outlined in the preceding chapter. Although he avoids the more flagrant Bullionist errors, he makes "depreciation" and the premium on specie equivalent — a view which may be quite misleading. And, like Ricardo, he also finds that the new "par" of the exchanges will be determined by the degree of this depreciation: a modified purchasing-power-parity doctrine. See *Principles*, pp. 542–544, and especially pp. 634, 635.

[2] *Ibid.*, especially pp. 620–625, 629, 630.

[3] *Ibid.*, pp. 617, 618. It will be remembered, however, that Fullarton presented the same idea much more elaborately in 1844. See ch. iii, sect. 9, above.

followed Thornton, not Ricardo. Yet he seems to have been conscious of no difference between his position and Ricardo's, despite the latter's vigorous rejection of the bilateral view, and indeed he refers to Ricardo here in terms of the highest approval. It is doubtless this merging of the two doctrines by Mill that has led later writers to describe the bilateral analysis, erroneously, as "Ricardian." [1]

There remains, finally, the question of the tendency of prices themselves to a world equality. Ricardo, it will be remembered, had given answers to this question which, while somewhat inconsistent, were in the main negative. Price equality was not made a necessary condition of his conception of equilibrium. Mill's position is even less precise, but he too seems to recognize permanent differences. Thus in speaking of a prolonged drain of specie and its correction, he says:

> The efflux would continue until the currencies of all countries had come to a level; by which I do not mean, until money became of the same value everywhere, but until the differences were only those which existed before, and which corresponded to permanent differences in the cost of obtaining it.[2]

Mill also took over Ricardo's general analysis of mechanisms, and his general conception of equilibrium, without essential alterations. This equilibrium was stated only in terms of the balance of payments and the foreign exchanges (and ultimately, perhaps, in terms of comparative costs). It therefore seems probable that Mill, like Ricardo, regarded the value of gold as being the same in different countries in terms of *currencies* (translated at the established rates of exchange), but as being permanently different in terms of *commodities;* the differences being determined by relative differences in the comparative (labor) costs of obtaining the

---

[1] See ch. iii, sect. 5, above; also sect. 7. It was there suggested that the difference between the two views is at most one of degree: they reduce to much the same thing, in terms of the mechanisms of the market. The question has recently been raised again in connection with the analysis of international borrowing operations. For a review of the literature of this last topic see J. Viner, *Canada's Balance of International Indebtedness*, pp. 191–206.

Mill's position here is also discussed in sect. 6, below, in connection with Bastable's corrections.

[2] Mill, *op. cit.*, p. 631.

precious metals themselves.[1] But it is only fair to point out that Mill, like Ricardo, did not carry this doctrine through to an explicit formulation made integral with the rest of his position. He never demonstrated quite what meaning is to be attached to the conception of a "world equality," or a "world inequality," in the value of money and of commodities.

It necessarily follows, too, that Mill's theory of international prices was itself incomplete. Indeed, as of Ricardo, such a theory can be ascribed to him only by inference. He did not himself make an explicit statement. The major elements would be somewhat as follows. First, a theory of the actual ratios of international exchange, turning on the principle of comparative costs, and within its limits on the Equation of International Demand; second, the Ricardian doctrine of equilibrium in trade, based primarily on the balance of payments; third, a dual (short- and long-time) theory of money and prices; fourth, the Ricardian analysis of the world distribution of the precious metals; fifth, the Bullionist exposition of the phenomena of trade under disordered monetary conditions; and finally, the Ricardo-Senior theory of the comparative levels of prices and money incomes in different countries — though Mill somewhat neglected the question of money incomes. But these elements were never drawn compactly together. The uncertainty of Mill's position with respect to the world equality of commodity prices and the value of money makes them in any event incomplete.

4. Until after the middle of the nineteenth century, the succession of writers upon the general theory of international exchange had kept its component parts fairly well integrated. Their doctrines of the mechanisms of foreign trade were closely bound up with their doctrines of the relations between money and prices, and their monetary theory usually took some account of international conditions. After the appearance of Mill's work, however, the paths of development of the various elements became in large degree separated. The theory of money and prices, now evolved into a quite independent department of thought and

---

[1] See ch. iii, sect. 7, above, for a fuller discussion of Ricardo's position. Its logical inconsistency is there suggested.

controversy, came to deal more and more with primarily *intra-national* phenomena. Its international aspects were usually slighted, and often disregarded entirely. At the same time the theory of international trade proper, subjected to less violent attacks and to less searching attention, was carried through a slow process of refinement and elaboration that took but little account of the development of (intra-national) monetary theory. Finally, the theory of international price *adjustments*, dealing especially with trade under disordered monetary conditions, became still another and separate department. The more recent history of this last body of thought, and also of the general theory of money and prices, must therefore be reserved for separate treatment at another point. The balance of the present chapter will be devoted to the development of the theory of international trade alone, from Cairnes to the present day.

Cairnes, who has advanced the general theory of international trade farther than any writer since Mill, started from the Ricardo-Mill doctrine of comparative costs. He took these costs as being measured in terms of sacrifice, of labor and abstinence. He regarded them as human costs, not money costs. Like Ricardo, however, Cairnes saw clearly enough that the proximate motive to international trade is not these *human* costs, but prices expressed in money.[1] Ricardo had escaped the difficulty by using the labor theory of value. Granted that theory, it follows that since prices in each country are governed by labor costs, a comparative difference between countries with respect to the one implies a corresponding comparative difference with respect to the other. In other words money prices and human costs move together, maintain the same relationship, and can therefore be regarded as equivalent. One can be taken as a relative measure of the other. On that basis Ricardo had evolved his familiar cost of production theory.

To this Cairnes, however, took forceful exception; an exception based on his own theory of value. He held that *within* any one area of effective competition costs of production, it is true, deter-

---

[1] J. E. Cairnes, *Leading Principles of Political Economy* (London, 1874), pp. 382–386.

mine prices. But as *between* "non-competing groups" the determination by costs of production breaks down, and is replaced by Reciprocal Demand. That is, the prices of the articles exchanged between such groups are governed solely by the relative strength of the demands of each group for the other's products. This condition of incomplete competition he thought was very largely characteristic of the trade between countries. His conclusion was therefore this. In international trade, the *proximate* determinant of that trade is comparative money prices. The *ultimate* determinant, where there is effective competition, is costs of production — human costs, reflected in money prices. Where competition is lacking, on the other hand, the ultimate determinant is not costs of production, but Reciprocal Demand between non-competing groups; that is, between countries. Here, costs of production simply set certain outside limits within which Reciprocal Demand works.[1]

This theory of international values is in the first instance an attempt at a reconciliation of Mill's and Ricardo's positions, a mediation between the determination by cost of production and the determination by the Equation of International Demand. But it is more than that, for it offers an application of the doctrine of non-competing groups to international trade and to international values. The general conception was of course not original with Cairnes, and in other fields he failed to see its social significance as clearly as did Mill, but he was the first to make it an integral part of the mechanism of international exchange. In his hands, and in those of later writers, it proved a tool of great power.

Cairnes next turns to the forces governing the range of a country's prices and money incomes, and gives a doctrine quite like Senior's proposition of nearly fifty years before.

The rate of wages prevailing in a country and the character and course of its external trade . . . are coördinate effects of a common cause, that cause being the degree and direction in which a nation's industry happens to be productive. Whatever be the articles with respect to which the industry of a nation is especially productive, these are the articles which will form the

---

[1] Cairnes, *op. cit.*, pp. 386–388. See also pp. 418–424. He also refers to monopoly in international trade as a case in which cost of production very clearly controls the "aberrations of value."

staple of its external trade, and, *measured in these*, the wages of labor will be high. If wages are high, measured in money, this will indicate either rich mines of gold or silver, or a high productiveness of industry in some commodities in large demand abroad, with which gold and silver may be purchased on favorable terms. . . . Thus the commodities, whatever they are, measured in terms of which wages are high, will either form the staples of the country's foreign trade, or will be such as may be obtained at small cost through those staples.[1]

High money wages, that is, are the result of the country's efficiency in getting gold, either from mining or from the export industries.[2]

A similar sort of analysis is then applied to the problem of the general range of money prices.

The range of prices that actually prevails in a country is, broadly speaking, the resultant of two conditions — the cost at which that country produces or obtains its gold, and the cost at which it produces or obtains commodities.

---

[1] Cairnes, *op. cit.*, p. 407. He makes the further interesting observation that in a state of equilibrium in the trade between any countries, the two *aggregates* of money wages and profits are equal; that is, the two totals of money costs. He employs this statement — true, of course, only if the "invisible items" be regarded as non-existent — to show that, since the levels of money incomes are notoriously dissimilar as between countries, the rate at which human costs are remunerated in money must also be unequal. The argument is somewhat involved, and not very conclusive. See *ibid.*, pp. 413, 414. He also tries to explain the differences between countries in the relative scales of money wages in another way. He finds that such differences indicate the degree to which the exchange values of the products *fail* to be in proportion to the human costs of production involved. (Pp. 416, 417.) This explanation is quite different from the one which can be inferred from the quotation given in the text above, and Cairnes does not offer a reconciliation. He is trying, of course, to get behind the *fact* of differences in relative efficiency in getting gold, and to reduce that fact to terms of human costs, not of money prices and incomes; but his analysis stops short of the goal.

[2] It is interesting to see how he applies the non-competing group concept here. He declares that within any given country it makes no difference whether wages are high or low, since no redistribution of productive powers is involved. But a particular part of the country's labor may be in a non-competing group, relative to the rest, and in this event the corresponding industry and foreign trade may turn entirely on the question of wages in that group. If they are relatively low, the industry will have an advantage in foreign and domestic trade greater than that to which it is apparently entitled. Its competitive prices will be below the "normal." Cairnes cites the case of the Polynesian laborers in the Queensland sugar fields, who worked at a rate of wages far below that of white labor in the rest of the colony. And so elsewhere. Partial and limited movements in particular wage rates, that is, may affect the corresponding prices, but a *general* change will not. Nor will it affect international trade. (See *ibid.*, pp. 387–406.)

Fluctuating and disturbing causes apart, the gold and the commodities will exchange for each other in proportion to their costs; and cheap gold, therefore, will be the concomitant of high prices, only so far as the cheapness incident to the gold is not shared by the other products of industry.[1]

Thus a nation which gets its gold *relatively* cheaply will get all imported commodities at a relatively low cost. In purely domestic transactions, of course, there will be no permanent gain from cheaper gold. More counters will be used, but relative prices will not change.

This leads Cairnes directly to the question of the test of benefit from international trade. He declares, in opposition to some of the preceding writers, that a nation gains not from having its prices high, but from getting its gold cheaply. The cheapness is to be measured in terms of human cost, however, not value: of ease and comfort, or of sacrifice. Usually cheap gold (in this sense) and high prices go together, but not necessarily. If the cost of getting or producing goods other than gold is also low, then both they and gold will be cheap.[2]

His subsequent analysis of the factors governing the range of money wages, as far as it goes, would probably be accepted by most writers at the present day. It amounts to saying that money wages are relatively high in countries where the effectiveness of labor in the export industries is high ("effectiveness" being relative both to costs of production, and to international demand); and that wages in the export industries set the pace for wages in domestic industries — though this last is implicit, rather than explicitly stated. But his argument concerning the range of money prices is more open to objection. His attempt to distinguish between money prices and human costs is not always successful, and not always self-consistent. Had he based his reasoning here simply upon the relative effectiveness of labor, as he did in dealing with money incomes, he would have been far more convincing. So too with respect to the test of benefit in international trade.

[1] Cairnes, *op. cit.*, p. 494.
[2] *Ibid.*, pp. 493–498. Although a different index is used, this test of benefit reduces to much the same thing as those of Senior and Mill, and even — though less clearly — of Ricardo: namely, the relative effectiveness of labor, and the relative intensities of demands.

We would doubtless agree that the benefit arises from getting imports more cheaply, but we would seek the immediate criterion of that cheapness in the relatively high level of money incomes, not in the cheapness of gold (measured in terms of human costs). Had Cairnes abandoned the human-cost concept, in favor of the effectiveness of labor, he would himself have arrived at that result. Nevertheless the value of his work here was great, although due as much to the mere fact that he recalled attention to the problem as to the profundity of his analysis.

Cairnes made one other major contribution to the theory of international trade, which was perhaps of greater permanent merit than any of his doctrines hitherto considered.[1] This was his analysis of the stages in international borrowing, and of its effects on the equilibrium of international trade. It was quite original with him, and had peculiar significance because of the manner in which his theoretical conclusions and predictions were subsequently verified — especially in the trade between the United States and Europe, from 1862 to 1879 and in later years. His argument is too familiar, however, to require more than a brief recapitulation. He distinguishes three stages in the borrowing operation.[2] In the first period, when the principal of the loan is being sent out, the lender begins with an excess of exports, both of goods and of gold. The flow of gold raises prices in the borrowing country, lowers them in the lending country, and thus eventually, because of the effects of changes in the levels of relative prices, allows the loan to be paid in goods alone. In the second period, when the growing interest payments begin to offset the further exports of new capital, these influences are gradually counteracted. The stimulus to the lender's export trade is slowly removed, and transferred to that of the borrower, until at last the two sets of changes balance. In the third period, fresh loans have virtually ceased, and the interest payments are no longer offset by the lender's obligations. The sequence of events then becomes the reverse of that in the first period. This opposite situation, an

[1] His striking analysis of the effects of the Californian and Australian gold discoveries is examined below, in ch. vi, sects. 1 and 3.

[2] Cairnes, *op. cit.*, pp. 431–437.

excess of exportation by the borrower, continues either until the original debt is paid, or until the original borrower, by virtue of economic growth, itself becomes a lender to other countries.

5. Until the last quarter of the nineteenth century, the ascendancy of the classical theory of international trade as a whole had never been seriously challenged in England. Even Thornton's comments on the Equation of International Demand seem to have been designed more to improve the accuracy of Mill's statements than to overthrow the doctrine itself. At about the time of the appearance of Cairnes' "Leading Principles," however, a number of scattered criticisms of the whole position began to appear. To these we shall now turn. But we must be cautious of attaching too much importance to them, or even to the mere fact of their existence, for they seem to have exercised virtually no influence upon the thought of the "orthodox" post-classical writers. Indeed, their quality was usually not such as to merit very elaborate attention. Their chief interest lies in the fact that they constitute virtually the only body of actively hostile opinion which has as yet been advanced in either the English or the American literature of the subject.

The first suggestions of dissent came from the pen of Macleod, who here allowed his anti-classical animosities to lead him into shallowness.[1] His general line of attack consisted in denying that there can be one economic law for internal trade, and another for international trade. Such a distinction violates one of the principles of Natural Philosophy, the Law of Continuity, and must therefore be untenable. This is especially true of Mill's use of a cost of production theory of value for internal trade, and of the law of demand and supply for international exchange. Macleod also branded as absurd the proposition that the value of a foreign commodity, in any country, depends on the quantity of home produce which must be given in exchange for it. He found that the imported article is simply worth what it will *sell* for. Finally, he declared that the essential fallacy in the Ricardo-Mill system arises from a confusion of *value* with *cost*.

---

[1] H. D. Macleod, *The Principles of Economical Philosophy* (2 ed., London, 1872–1875), vol. ii, part i, pp. 282–286.

A little later Musgrave criticized the whole classical economics for its colorless treatment of money, and for its neglect of the fact that money is itself an article of exchange.[1] Thus he attacks the proposition, implicit in Mill, that a direct exchange of two articles for one another produces the same result as an intermediary exchange through some third article itself having an intrinsic value. Musgrave asserts that in foreign trade, for example, the movement of gold permits the transfer of purchasing power, and may thus result in a gain from the ultimate inter-commodity exchange greater than that proceeding from the direct exchange of the articles themselves.[2] With respect to the principle of comparative costs, he objects that under barter there is no necessary gain in total production from the pursuit of comparative advantages, while under a money economy *both* commodities cannot be cheaper in one country if trade is to take place. Thus the principle of comparative costs, as distinct from a law of comparative money *prices*, loses any especial significance.[3] Indeed, the whole "barter assumption" itself is rejected, although somewhat unconvincingly.[4] Finally, Musgrave objects to the doctrine of the maintenance of equilibrium in trade by price movements and specie flows. Even if specie should flow because of disequilibrium, he declares that there is nothing to prevent its proceeding at once from the receiving country to still another one, without affecting prices in the former and without exerting the assumed corrective upon the course of trade.[5]

Shadwell, on the other hand, adopted the greater part of the classical doctrine — the principle of comparative costs, the price-specie flow analysis, the theory of the foreign exchanges, and so on.[6] He takes exception only to Mill's theory of international values, to the Equation of International Demand.[7] He finds that Mill "has not really explained the subject, but has merely restated the problem in a different way." Mill's proposition was

---

[1] A. Musgrave, *Studies in Political Economy* (London, 1875), pp. vi, vii.

[2] *Ibid.*, pp. 138, 140, 141.   [3] *Ibid.*, especially pp. 136, 137.

[4] *Ibid.*, pp. 165, 171.   [5] *Ibid.*, pp. 160, 161, 172, 173.

[6] J. L. Shadwell, *A System of Political Economy* (London, 1877), pp. 388-391, 400-405.

[7] The following quotations are from *ibid.*, pp. 406, 407.

that "the produce of a country exchanges for the produce of other countries at such values as are required, in order that the whole of her exports may exactly pay for the whole of her imports." But Shadwell objects that this is essentially nothing but the statement of an identity. "The fact that the exports pay for the imports implies that the two exchange for one another, and to say that the ratio is that in which the two exchange, is to say that the ratio determines itself." Mill, in other words, does not explain *why* the given quantities and ratios appear, — why, for example, some other quantity of exports was not equated with the given quantity of imports, and a different ratio thus secured. In this criticism there seems to me to be a great deal of force. As was suggested earlier in the present chapter, it is difficult to see how Mill's Equation can be made to yield *one*, and only one, ratio of exchange.[1] Shadwell's own solution is suggestive. He says: "By referring to the cost of production in one country, and to the comparative efficiency of labor in the other, the value of any foreign commodity can be explained; and if these particulars are known in the case of two commodities, a comparison of them will explain the ratio in which the two will exchange for each other." The attempt to reduce the demand side of the problem to terms of costs of production, however, cannot be regarded as altogether successful.

Leslie developed still another line of attack, designed to overthrow the classical theory of value in all its branches. He says:

The distinction which Mr. Mill has drawn between international trade and home trade, in respect of the transferability of labour and capital and the equalization of wages and profit, if it once had some foundation when trade at home was simpler and better known, and when foreign countries were almost wholly unknown, cannot now be sustained. Not that the doctrine of the equality of profits and of the determination of comparative prices by comparative cost of production is now applicable to both, but that it is applicable to neither.[2]

---

[1] Also see ch. xiv, sect. 2 and following, below; and later chapters.

[2] T. E. C. Leslie, *The Known and the Unknown in the Economic World* (Fortnightly Review, 1879), p. 942.

Precisely the opposite view was developed twenty-five years later by J. A. Hobson in his *International Trade* (London, 1904). The question will be taken up again in ch. xiv, below.

He then dwells at some length on the general lack of information as to economic conditions, with its consequent discrepancies in actual incomes and prices. He does not, however, go into more detail with respect to the classical theory of international trade itself.

Finally, Professor Sidgwick advanced still another type of criticism of Mill's formulation of the laws of international values. He declared that the peculiarity of the determination of international values rests not on the imperfect mobility of labor, but on the fact of distance, which renders international exchange costly. He finds that the difference in the aggregates of utility obtainable by similar sacrifices in different localities is not much greater than can be accounted for by the costs of transportation between them. Any substantially greater difference will be annihilated by corresponding movements of the population. The problem therefore lies in the determination of the conditions governing the division of costs of transportation. The combined laws of demand of the different wares exchanged tend to determine how much of the double cost of carriage (that is, of the given export and of the corresponding import) is to be added to the "real price" of each article when sold, and thus effectively establish the levels of international values.[1] Sidgwick grants that the immobility of labor and capital will influence the situation, since if wages and interest are appreciably higher in one country than in another because of that immobility, it may pay to import things which would otherwise be produced at home. But the actual international values themselves are dependent on the fact of costs of transportation, not on the fact of immobility.[2] They are determined by reciprocal demand within the two limits set by home costs of production with *double* costs of transportation added, and home costs with *no* costs of transportation added.[3]

Sidgwick's argument has a certain plausibility, and it could conceivably be put so as to contain a very considerable degree of truth. If it be taken as he presents it, however, it is not capable

[1] Henry Sidgwick, *Principles of Political Economy* (London, 1883). I have used the third edition, edited by J. N. Keynes (London, 1901). The reference is to pp. 212–214.

[2] *Ibid.*, p. 214.   [3] *Ibid.*, pp. 218, 219.

of standing alone. Sidgwick becomes involved in a confused use of terms, especially in connection with "cost of production" and "real price," which makes it either meaningless or invalid. A more significant criticism of his ideas, however, is that made by Professor Bastable.[1] Bastable shows that Sidgwick confines his attention simply to the question of the division of costs of transportation, and that his problem is therefore unlike Mill's. Mill had dealt with the division of the *gain* from international trade, and considered costs of transportation as only one of several diminutions to that gain. Sidgwick's conception of the problem of international values is in consequence far narrower, and his answer is correspondingly less adequate. At best, it deals with only a part of the question.

6. Professor Bastable's own contributions to the general theory of international trade take in the main the form of an elaboration and a refinement of Mill.[2] He begins with a discussion of international values, and of the principle of comparative advantage. Finding that, in the simplest cases of trade between countries, the terms of exchange depend on comparative intensity of demand, he then introduces various qualifications appropriate to more complex situations. These qualifications it will suffice to enumerate.[3] First, a qualification for varying elasticity of demand. Here he is simply carrying Ricardo and Mill farther, and putting their familiar reasoning in more complete form. Second, a qualification for diminishing or increasing returns in the various sorts of production. Ricardo and Mill had virtually assumed constant returns. Bastable, by taking account of all three of the possibilities here — increasing and decreasing, as well as constant, returns — arrives at a more complete statement. The presence of increasing or diminishing returns causes those limits to vary (set up by comparative costs of production), within which the

---

[1] C. F. Bastable, *The Theory of International Trade* (4 ed., London, 1903), pp. 176–179.

[2] Cairnes' positive contributions here he somewhat slights.

Reference should also be made to the briefer discussions of general theory found in Professor Bastable's *Commerce of Nations* (London, 1891; 5 ed., 1911), especially in ch. iii.

[3] Bastable, *Theory of International Trade*, pp. 22–48.

relative intensity of demand determines international values. Furthermore, the presence of *diminishing* returns results in the production of the same article in more than one country, quite apart from costs of transportation or other impediments.[1] Finally, Bastable qualifies his propositions more elaborately than Mill with respect to hindrances to competition, and for other sorts of obstructions to completely free exchange. He also gives an illuminating analysis of the conditions governing the distribution of the corresponding burden (and, conversely, of the benefits from trade), in the light of the first two general qualifications given above: variable returns, and varying elasticities of demand. In essence, these qualifications consist simply in applying our more recent knowledge of the nature of markets and production to the theory of international values, but nevertheless they constitute an important advance. They make the theory seem far more real, and far more accurate.

Professor Bastable also made, a few years before, some improvements and corrections in Mill's analysis of international payments not originating in commerce. Take, for example, the case of a foreign loan. Mill's argument [2] would have been that, commerce being previously in a state of equilibrium, the first payments (i. e., in the hypothesis that Bastable sets up, the repayments of the original loan) are necessarily made in money. This flow of specie will result in higher prices in the creditor country, and lower prices in the debtor; an increase in the debtor's exports; and a decrease in its imports. When the excess of exports equals the sums annually due from the debtor country, the flows of bullion will cease. Imports and exports will not balance, but payments will, and the exchanges will be at par. But the paying (debtor) country will suffer a double loss, and the creditor a double gain, for the latter gets the payment itself, and also gets all the exportable produce of the debtor country at a lower price.

---

[1] A short time before Professor Simon N. Patten had also called attention to the effects of variable costs, in his essay on the *Economic Basis of Protection* (Philadelphia, 1890). His treatment, however, is rather summary, and is concerned chiefly with the question of the benefits from foreign trade.

[2] Cf. Mill's *Principles*, Bk. III, ch. 21, sect. 4. (In W. J. Ashley's edition, pp. 627, 628.)

With this conclusion, however, Bastable to some extent disagrees. Call the paying (debtor) country A, and the receiving (creditor) country B. B's "sum of incomes" is higher than before, since she has got the payments from A without cost. She is better able to purchase than before, and she may wish to take from A new goods, beyond that excess of A's exports over imports represented by the payment. In so far as this happens, the terms of exchange will be *against* B, and A's loss will be counteracted.[1]

Bastable further disagrees with Mill's analysis of the processes that would be involved in such a repayment. He does not think that money will necessarily move from A to B, or that prices will necessarily be affected. Money *incomes* will be altered; but in B, for example, the increased incomes will simply mean that more goods will be bought at the *same* price, — thus securing the necessary excess of A's exports over imports.[2] On the basis of this reasoning, also, he finds that debt payments are disadvantageous only under certain conditions, and that even then the loss is trifling. Country A will lose only to the extent that country B's "demand for foreign products *through the use of her exports* is reduced by this application of her claim, and the terms of exchange are thereby rendered more favorable to her." That is, B gains (and A loses) only in so far as the debt payments turn the exchange in B's favor. In view of the narrow limits of the exchange fluctuations under a metallic standard, however, this is factually unimportant.[3]

---

[1] C. F. Bastable, *Some Applications of the Theory of International Trade* (4 Quarterly Journal of Economics, 1889), pp. 14, 15. He points out, however, that Mill notices this point elsewhere, in connection with the proof that the richest countries gain least from trade. See Mill's *Principles*, Bk. III, ch. 18, sect. 8. (In W. J. Ashley's edition, p. 604.)

[2] Bastable, *op. cit.*, pp. 16, 17. This is one of the first applications of the concept of *aggregates* of income to international trade, and it is only to be regretted that Bastable did not make fuller use of it. Cairnes had employed the term, but took little advantage of its possibilities. (See above, sect. 4.)

It is evident that in this analysis of the adjustment of relatively permanent disturbances in trade Bastable sides with Ricardo rather than with Thornton and Mill, for he finds that the correction will come about automatically through changes in relative demands, rather than through the effects of specie flows. See ch. iii, sects. 5 and 7, above; also ch. vi, sect. 7, below.

[3] Bastable, *op. cit.*, p. 16.

Professor Bastable's argument here is more significant than might appear at first glance, and it is rather surprising that it has not attracted wider comment. Had he applied a similar chain of reasoning to his general theory of the exchange process in foreign trade, he would have come out with something quite unlike that orthodox gold-flow-price mechanism which he elsewhere accepts. For he here declares that, in this particular case of an excess balance of payments due between countries, specie will *not* necessarily flow, and prices will *not* necessarily be affected — changes which are of the very essence of the classical analysis! Bastable considers, rather, the changes in aggregate incomes, and in them finds the motivation of the process. His argument is not complete, however, for he says little or nothing of the actual mechanisms involved, nor of the ways in which, under this reasoning, equilibrium will or will not be restored. Indeed, the whole discussion rather disappears from view elsewhere in his work. It is perhaps best regarded as another case of that familiar phenomenon, "compartment thinking."

7. The next writer of importance for our purposes [1] is Professor Nicholson. Nicholson's work here was not, in the main, an attempt to improve upon the classical theory of international trade

[1] I have omitted from treatment in the text Professor Edgeworth's three articles upon *The Theory of International Values*, in the Economic Journal for 1894, on the ground that they are somewhat aside from the main problems here held in mind. They are concerned chiefly with general aspects of the benefit or loss arising from international trade under various conditions, rather than with questions of prices and price adjustments and market mechanisms. In the first named field, they are a remarkable and learned contribution. It may be added that they have recently been reprinted, in revised form, in their author's collected *Papers* (London, 1925), vol. 2.

Professor Edgeworth's principal addition to the subject, I think, was the conclusive demonstration that completely unrestricted trade, because of the effects of the action of private individuals seeking private profit alone, *may* result in a loss to one country greater than the gain to the other. In this connection he rather subtly applies the conditions of variable costs, which Professor Bastable had elaborated, to the problem of producers' and consumers' "surpluses" — a step Bastable had not taken. He further shows that international trade will not necessarily cease even though comparative costs become equal; and suggests an interesting analogy between the problem of international trade and that of (intra-national) distribution.

See also Bastable's criticisms, in his *Theory of International Trade* (edition cited above), especially pp. 181–187; the controversy carried on by Bastable, Edgeworth and Loria in the Economic Journal for 1901; and Francis Walker, *Increasing and Diminishing Costs in International Trade* (Yale Review, 1903).

itself. He was trying, rather, to alter the method of its statement by expressing it in terms of money, not of intercommodity values and physical quantities of labor. He took exception to the "barter" theory — to the accepted practise of regarding foreign trade as being essentially the barter of commodities — and introduced prices and money wages at the outset of his exposition.[1] We can feel much sympathy for the object he had in view, but the methods he adopted for attaining that object were not very fortunate. In the particular case that he set up as an example, as Professor Bastable has pointed out,[2] the commodity that will first move between the two countries is neither wheat nor cloth, but gold;[3] a consideration which Nicholson apparently passed by. Nicholson also makes the character of the international price adjustments, and the distribution of the subsequent gain or loss, dependent upon the relative size of the trading countries. If one country is relatively large, and the other relatively small, he finds that the larger country will dominate the situation. The prices of the smaller country will have to adjust themselves to those of the larger one, and the gain or loss from the adjustment will be chiefly, if not exclusively, confined to the smaller country. This theory is tenable as far as it goes, but its importance as a description of the actual trade between the leading commercial nations of the present day is obviously limited. For most traded commodities, prices are fixed in the "world" market resulting from the existence of a considerable number of producing and consuming countries.[4]

In general, the goal Professor Nicholson had in mind must seem laudable. The monetary or pecuniary approach is novel and re-

---

[1] J. S. Nicholson, *Principles of Political Economy*, vol. ii (London, 1897), p. 298. A similar type of approach is offered in A. W. Flux, *Economic Principles* (London, 1904, 2 ed., 1923).

[2] Bastable, *The Theory of International Trade*, p. 182. Bastable's more general criticism of Nicholson's "monetary" approach, however, seems to me less acceptable.

[3] Nicholson, *op. cit.*, pp. 301–304.

[4] Nicholson neglects an important qualification here. If the disparity in size between the countries is actually great, the adjustments in the smaller country will tend to be much quicker than in the larger, other things being equal, and a secondary train of repercussions upon the terms of exchange will appear.

freshing, and promises quite as close an approximation to the realities of the problem as the "commodity" approach of classical theory. But we must inevitably be somewhat critical of the results actually attained in the attempt to apply the monetary method. Professor Nicholson's exposition is complicated rather than simplified by the use he makes of money. It is obscure, and it is not always self-consistent.

8. The most recent important refinements in the theory of international trade have been those introduced by Professor Taussig. Professor Taussig's general position is that of the classical school, and requires no comment — unless to observe that he finds that, under actual conditions, international trade most commonly rests largely on *absolute* differences in cost. Where it rests on comparative differences, their presence is to be explained by the immobility of labor and capital as between countries.[1] Professor Taussig's principal contributions lie, rather, in the stress he places upon money *incomes* in international trade; in his penetrating analysis of the forces governing the general range of prices and money incomes as between countries; and in his general emphasis upon human rather than merely physical factors.

He employs money incomes to give the criterion of the benefit derived from international trade. His statement is that that country benefits in which the range of money incomes is high relative to other countries. The gain arises simply with respect to foreign-trade articles, and comes from the fact that a country with relatively high money incomes gets its imports *relatively* cheaply; cheaply, that is, in terms of "real" cost. High incomes are not necessarily an impediment to foreign trade. They are perfectly compatible with low money prices, if the relative effectiveness of labor is great.[2] Finally, the extent of the gain depends on the interplay of international demand, and on the effectiveness of labor in producing exported commodities.[3]

The elaboration of these propositions leads him at once to the

[1] F. W. Taussig, *Principles of Economics* (3 ed., New York, 1922; 2 vols.), vol. i, pp. 487–490.

[2] *Ibid.*, pp. 500–502. Also see Professor Taussig's article on *Wages and Prices in International Trade* (20 Quarterly Journal of Economics, 1906), pp. 497–501.

[3] *Principles of Economics*, vol. i, pp. 502, 503.

question of relative scales of money incomes and prices. First, what causes high money wages? Professor Taussig finds that "those countries have high money wages whose labor is efficient in producing exported commodities, and whose exported commodities command a good price in the world's markets." [1] That is, "those countries whose exports are in most urgent demand will have the greatest *possibility* of high money incomes. Whether they will have high incomes in fact, depends on the labor cost of their exports." [2] Thus, following Senior and Mill, he makes the range of money incomes dependent first on the terms of international demand; and second, on the relative effectiveness of labor. One vital qualification is necessary here, however: "It is to be assumed that the exporting industry does not partake of the character of a monopoly within the country." Where monopoly occurs, high effectiveness of labor may fail to result in high wages.[3]

Second, with respect to "domestic" goods, which are not exported or imported, Professor Taussig finds that "the range of domestic prices within a country, as compared with the range of prices of the same things in other countries, depends on the efficiency of labor in producing commodities that do not enter international trade." [4] The range is "high in so far as the efficiency of labor in domestic commodities is small, low so far as the efficiency of labor in domestic commodities is great." [5]

Finally, these two lines of reasoning are tied together.

The determining cause of the general rate of money incomes and wages in a country is to be found in the exporting industries. These set the pace; not for real wages, but for money wages. Whatever is yielded by them tends to become, under the influence of competition, the ruling rate in the country at large, — in other industries, as well as in those exporting.

In non-exporting industries, the rate of money wages is, relatively, a matter of indifference. Prices there will rise and fall with wages and incomes, as in the export industries. Imports alone do not reflect these changes. From this fact arises the gain in international trade resulting from high money incomes. The higher incomes lead to a lower *real* price of imports.[6]

---

[1] *Wages and Prices in International Trade, loc. cit.*, p. 510.
[2] *Ibid.*, p. 511. (Italics mine.)   [3] *Ibid.*, p. 512.   [4] *Ibid.*, p. 502.
[5] *Ibid.*, p. 510.   [6] *Principles of Economics*, vol. i, p. 503.

The mechanism of the process is this. Suppose that a change in international demands results in a higher price for the given country's exports. The increased prices of exports will then be reflected in higher money incomes in the exporting industries; this, under the influence of competition, will lead to higher money incomes in the purely domestic industries; and these, to higher domestic prices.[1] "In the exporting industries the higher wages will be the result of higher prices; but in other industries the higher prices will be as much a result as a cause of higher wages."[2] The latter process is thus to some extent one of reciprocal causation.

All this argument, however, is based on the assumption that in domestic exchanges values and prices depend on sacrifice, on labor; that where labor cost is relatively low, for example, prices will also be low, and that there will hence be an inducement to export. But do value and price, in point of fact, depend upon labor cost? Are there not non-competing groups, the existence of which destroys the validity of the foregoing analysis; and is not *utility* the permanent regulator of value? Professor Taussig's answer is twofold. First, there is probably more competition among laborers than the bare assumption of non-competing groups admits. There is not a complete equalization of reward, but on the other hand the barriers are not impassable. The greater the difference in reward, the greater is the number of those who will surmount them. Labor cost, sacrifice, is hence always in the background, not dominating but controlling. The greater the deviation of value from it, the less likely is the deviation to persist.[3]

Second, goods are made not by one, but by a number, of grades of workers. Therefore,

if the relations of the different grades to each other are the same in different countries, and if the same combinations of labor are used for any one article, the conditions of competition between countries are precisely the same as if within each country labor cost alone determined value.[4]

Professor Taussig points out that this absolute identity of course does not exist in fact. A particular non-competing group may be in greater demand in one country than in another, or vice versa.

---

[1] *Wages and Prices in Relation to International Trade*, pp. 513, 514.
[2] *Ibid.*, p. 514.   [3] *Ibid.*, p. 519.   [4] *Ibid.*, pp. 519, 520.

Its wages, and the prices of the corresponding products, will then be relatively high, or relatively low.[1] But it is a fair inference from his argument, though he does not specifically make the statement, that the general tendency is toward a correspondence between labor cost and value; a correspondence close enough so that the earlier analysis is substantially valid.

It is in this manner, then, that Professor Taussig determines the criterion of the benefit from international trade, and analyzes the forces governing the range of prices and money incomes. His criterion of benefit is simply arrived at, and to my mind is not open to question. Proximately, it is relatively high money incomes; ultimately, it is the relative effectiveness of labor in the export industries, on the one hand, and the degree of the foreign demand for the products of those industries on the other. At bottom, therefore, the factors involved are precisely the same as those on which Ricardo, Senior, Mill, and Cairnes had more or less explicitly rested their criteria. The difference lies simply in the choice of the index by which the operation of these factors is to be measured. The greater accuracy and significance of the index selected by Professor Taussig, however, is self-evident.

The analysis of the conditions determining the *range* of prices and money incomes, again, derives its force not so much from any essential novelty in the elements on which the determination is based as from the precision of its statement, and from its elaboration of a specific chain of sequences. That the range of prices and incomes was in some way dependent upon the effectiveness of labor, and upon the state of international demand, had been clearly recognized by Senior. Professor Taussig's contribution consists in the clear light that he has cast upon the actual mechanisms involved. We may be permitted a certain skepticism as to whether the process is really so frictionless and clearly defined as Taussig's analysis, despite his qualifications in theory and in fact, would suggest. But that its general character is such as he indicates can hardly be denied.[2] And his application of the doctrine

---

[1] Taussig, *Wages and Prices*, pp. 520–523.

[2] An attempt to carry the analysis somewhat farther in certain directions is made in ch. xv, sect. 4, below, and the difficulties latent in the concept of the "effectiveness" of labor are pointed out.

of non-competing groups to the problem is extremely suggestive. It outlines a field of inquiry of fundamental social significance, the surface of which has as yet hardly been touched.

9. Since the war another American writer, Professor Graham, has subjected certain portions of the general classical theory of international trade to a searching and not always friendly examination. From this examination three conclusions emerge which are of especial interest here.

One is the proposition that the operation of the principle of comparative advantage, in the trade between two countries — the development of an international specialization — may lead to the production of a combined output *smaller* than that which would result if trade had not been opened up. This condition will appear when one country's exports are produced under diminishing returns, the other's under increasing returns; provided, however, that the increase in the one case is less in terms of total money values than the decrease in the other.[1] This criticism of the Ricardian theorem, we shall find later, was first suggested by Pareto in 1906, though with less detail and without explicit reference to diminishing returns.[2]

The second proposition is addressed to Mill's Equation of International Demand. Mill had concluded that, except under unusual conditions, the play of demand will cause the terms of international exchange between any two traded commodities to settle somewhere *inside* the limits set by comparative costs of production. Graham, on the contrary, concludes that Mill's exception is really the normal situation. Ordinarily the trading countries are not of equal size, nor are the two commodities (of a given selected pair) of equal economic importance in the one country and the other. It therefore follows that the market for country A's exports in country B will usually be greater than that for B's exports in A, or vice versa. The two demands will not balance (measured in terms of total money values), and the ratio of exchange between the two commodities involved will be forced to

---

[1] F. D. Graham, *Some Aspects of Protection Further Considered* (37 Quarterly Journal of Economics, 1923), pp. 199–211.

[2] See ch. x, sect. 3, below. A somewhat similar conclusion was reached by Edgeworth in 1894. See a note in sect. 7, above.

one or the other of the limits set by comparative costs. The appearance of a balance *inside* these limits could only be a fortuitous coincidence.[1]

Finally, Professor Graham points out that the segregation of only two commodities and only two countries is unrealistic, and often entirely misleading. His demonstration turns primarily on the question of relative benefits from foreign trade, rather than on the establishment of the terms of international exchange; a topic beyond our province here. It may be pointed out, however, that his hypothetical tables show the terms of exchange in these more complicated cases to be unpredictable as a rule, in so far as anything at all can be inferred from comparative costs alone.[2]

Taken as a whole, Graham's conclusions do not impair the classical theory itself, but they suggest that important qualifications are necessary. Granted the general classical premises and the general classical method of formulating the problem, they are undoubtedly sound. On the other hand — and at the risk of anticipating the argument of later chapters — it can fairly be asked if this approach, this formulation, is really the one most useful under modern conditions. Graham, like Mill on such questions, says little or nothing of money prices, of the function of money, or of the other market mechanisms involved in the determination of actual ratios of exchange between countries. These omissions require a more convincing defense than has hitherto been advanced.

In the same year that Graham's articles appeared Professor Marshall brought out his last book, and in it presented the substance of his unpublished essay (privately printed in 1879) on the pure theory of foreign trade.[3] The essay was for many years unique in the English literature, but it has a number of later copies or analogues in the writings of economists of the mathema-

---

[1] F. D. Graham, *The Theory of International Values Re-Examined* (38 Quarterly Journal of Economics, 1923), pp. 55 ff. He also points out, what few writers of the classical school have seen, that the line between national comparative advantage and disadvantage is a moving one: that within considerable limits given articles pass back and forth unpredictably between the export and import categories. On this also, see ch. xv, sect. 2, below.

[2] Graham, *loc. cit.*, pp. 60–67 ff. Also see ch. xiv, sect. 3, below.

[3] A. Marshall, *Money Credit and Commerce* (London, 1923), Appendix J: pp. 330–360.

tical school. Its more important features were first publicly reproduced by Pantaleoni in 1889, and a discussion of its contents may therefore be reserved for the later chapter on Italian thought. This postponement is warranted both by the demands of chronology, and by the more natural place which the essay takes in the development of Continental doctrines. In England, except for the work of Professor Edgeworth,[1] its direct influence has been slight. One observation may be made at this point, however, for future reference. In the body of the book itself, Marshall's discussion of the general theory of international trade follows the orthodox Ricardo-Mill line of analysis: it runs in terms of days (or quantities) of labor.[2] But in this Appendix, the argument throughout deals with quantities of *goods*, and with the ratios of exchange between them. That there might be a contradiction between the two methods of approach, or at least a hiatus which requires filling up, is not a possibility which seems to have been considered.[3]

10. It remains to give some account of one other body of theory not taken into consideration in the preceding parts of this chapter: those doctrines which deal with the incidence and effects of import duties. Import duties of course simply offer an impediment to international trade. They modify international values, and change international prices, but they do not alter the fundamental processes that govern the determination of the values and prices themselves. They are subsequent, rather than antecedent, phenomena. For that reason they have been omitted from the more general treatments of theory hitherto presented. Nevertheless their effects on international prices, and on the terms of exchange, are often very great, and in view of their quantitative importance it is rather surprising that they have been assigned so small a part in the discussions of general theory. I propose to give here, however, only the most cursory summary of the development after Mill of certain doctrines dealing with them. In the space available, it is not possible to give an outline of

---

[1] See his articles in the Economic Journal for 1894, referred to in sect. 7, above.

[2] Marshall, *op. cit.*, pp. 10, 11, 157–165 ff.; also Appendix H, pp. 321–329.

[3] Yet the point seems to me vital to the whole theory of international trade. See ch. xiv, sect. 3, below; also ch. xviii, sect. 6.

even the "scientific" literature of the protectionist controversy itself.

Professor Bastable, in an address before the British Association,[1] declared that the incidence of import duties depends on four things.[2] First, on the conditions of demand *within* the imposing country. If the quantity of the taxed goods imported falls off, in consequence of the duty, not all of the burden falls on the domestic consumer. Second, on the extent of the demand for the taxed commodities *outside* the imposing country. Foreign producers will not submit to the decreased prices consequent on decreased (quantitative) demand if it is possible to escape, and will seek other markets, either domestic or foreign. If the taxing country controls the bulk of the demand, however, escape may be difficult: some part of the duty may be shifted on to the foreign producers. Third, on the existence of untaxed substitutes for the dutiable articles. This also will lead to an attempt to escape from the tax, but the escape may obviously be avoided by taxing the substitutes themselves. Fourth, on whether the duty be for revenue or for protection. A revenue duty differs from a protective duty in that the latter leaves the native source of supply untaxed, and thus limits the rise in price of the imported article — just as does the existence of an untaxed substitute.

As to the net effects upon foreign trade, Bastable concludes that,

speaking generally, values (or their simplest index, prices) will not be much lowered, but trade will be limited, a smaller amount of the taxed articles being imported at nearly the same price (duty apart) as before the introduction of the tax.[3]

Or, to put this into the terminology to be used in later chapters, the *total money values* of the taxed imports will be reduced; not by a decrease in price, but by a decrease in quantity. Bastable also examines the probable effects of the duty upon the country that

[1] C. F. Bastable, *The Incidence and Effects of Import and Export Duties*, in the Report of the British Association for 1889.

[2] *Ibid.*, pp. 441, 442.

[3] *Ibid.*, p. 442. Evidently this assumes either constant costs and a unitary elasticity of demand, or else offsetting variations from these conditions.

exports the taxed commodities.[1] The argument here is more obvious, and need not be repeated in detail. It turns on the possible decrease of investment in the export industries, on the lowering of the corresponding wages and profits, and, as in Mill, on the resulting redistribution of the world's supply of money. Prices will be raised in the taxing country, and the exporting country will also suffer in so far as it is the consumer of the former's exports. Bastable adds, however, that with modern credit facilities the change can be effected with little or no actual transfer of bullion.

Nearly twenty years later, Professor Marshall made an analysis which was in essence a refinement upon Bastable's.[2] He found that, *prima facie*, the incidence of the tax is upon the consumer.[3] But conditions may arise under which an important fraction of the burden can be shifted. First, the taxing country, A, can throw much of it on the exporting country or countries, B, if the conditions of international demand are such that A can dispense with a great part of the goods imported from B; and if at the same time B can *not* dispense with any large fraction of the goods received from A.[4] Second, assuming somewhat different conditions, the situation is still further altered if countries A, C, D, E, etc., all concurrently put a heavy tax on one of B's exports. B must then either very much diminish her export of the taxed article, or else bear a large part of the burden of the duty.[5] And if, finally, A, C,

---

[1] C. F. Bastable, *op. cit.*, pp. 442, 443.

[2] A. Marshall, *The Fiscal Policy of International Trade* (Memorandum to the House of Commons; ordered to be printed, November 11, 1908).

The contemporary American counterpart of Marshall's work here is the really brilliant paper by Francis Walker, already referred to, on *Increasing and Diminishing Costs in International Trade* (Yale Review, 1903). Walker, who developed an argument for the "scientific" protection of industries with increasing costs, was perhaps not so successful as Marshall in dealing with price movements and the other intermediary mechanisms. But he went distinctly farther in showing the effects of variable costs upon producers' and consumers' surpluses. In this respect he resembles Edgeworth more closely. See also the earlier and not altogether dissimilar study of Professor Simon Patten, *The Economic Basis of Protection* (Philadelphia, 1890).

A doctrine which is in essence like Walker's has been elaborated in more detail by Professor F. D. Graham, *Some Aspects of Protection Further Considered* (37 Quarterly Journal of Economics, 1923), especially pp. 199–211.

Marshall, *op. cit.*, p. 3.   [4] *Ibid.*, p. 4.   [5] *Ibid.*, pp. 18, 19.

D, E, etc., all put heavy duties on *all* of B's exports, B is almost certain to bear much of the burden. The foreign duties, that is, will enter into the real cost to her of whatever *net* imports she requires. She may concentrate on domestic production for domestic consumption, but she is almost certain to need at least some imports, and to that extent will suffer. This effect is decreased, however, in so far as B's corresponding exports are in great demand abroad, and have a partial monopoly value.[1]

Marshall introduces two further qualifications, however, which are not found in Bastable's reasoning, nor to be derived from it. First, if a country has a comprehensive system of fairly heavy tariff duties, the level of prices will be raised, and the purchasing power of gold — an untaxed import — will fall. In so far as this occurs, the burden of the duties on the domestic consumer will be correspondingly diminished. The effects of this change in the international distribution of gold must be allowed for in any attempt to measure the burden of the duty by the change in price levels.[2] Second, improvements in production and transportation are constantly raising money incomes, relative to prices. If a tariff is imposed, or raised, the rise in prices may therefore be considerable, yet the real burden be much less than the price move-

---

[1] A. Marshall, *op. cit.*, p. 19. It may be added that the quantitative degree of the effects, in these various cases, depends in part on whether the duty is specific or *ad valorem*. If it is *ad valorem*, the absolute amount by which prices are raised to the home consumer will vary with the variations in price, in the *exporting* country, of the taxed imports. An *ad valorem* duty is hence a greater stimulus to economies in production in the exporting country (designed, by lowering prices, to make possible a partial retention of the market) than is a specific duty.

[2] *Ibid.*, pp. 3, 18. Just what the mechanics of this rise of prices is, however, is not stated.

In connection with the question of the relation between tariff duties and the world distribution of gold, see also Marshall's evidence before the Indian Currency Committee of 1898 (Part II; 1899 Parliamentary Papers, XXXI), *Question 11,828*. Marshall there holds that the immediate effect of import duties is to raise prices, and thus make necessary an increased supply of gold. Then the import of gold stops, and equilibrium is restored. But the imposing country's financial "feelers" in other countries are decreased, in consequence of the diminished volume of trade resulting from the tariff; and it is therefore less able to stand unexpected foreign drains without exporting gold. Hence, once equilibrium is reached, a tariff operates against rather than in favor of the retention of gold.

ment alone would indicate.[1] This last, however, I take to be intended as a long-time rather than an immediate qualification.

Finally, reference should also be made to a paper by Professor H. C. Emery, on the tariff and its possible incidence.[2] Emery draws attention to the wide "spread" between producers' and consumers' prices, especially under American distributive conditions, and to the extreme irregularity of their movements relative to one another. Not only is the gap between them great, but their fluctuations often, if not always, bear no sort of automatic and necessary relation to one another.[3] He therefore thinks that it would be possible to arrange a tariff in such fashion that producers' prices would be raised while consumers' prices remain unaffected, the result being obtained by decreasing the spread between the two.[4] Comment on this proposal may be reserved until later, but it undeniably presents some interesting possibilities.

[1] *Fiscal Policy*, p. 4. The elaboration of the argument here may be omitted. It turns on the elasticity of demand (as in the text above); the changing relations between money incomes, money prices and the real cost of exports and imports; changes in the distribution of productive forces; etc.

[2] H. C. Emery, *The Tariff and the Ultimate Consumer* (American Economic Review, 1915).

[3] *Ibid.*, pp. 534–536.

[4] *Ibid.*, p. 541. In the next few pages of the article Professor Emery gives specific examples of this wide spread, and attempts to show just how and where his plan could be adopted.

See also the criticism by H. A. Wooster, under the same title (American Economic Review, 1916); and Emery's *Note in Rejoinder*, in the same issue.

Reference should also be made to an earlier article by T. N. Carver, *Some Theoretical Possibilities of a Protective Tariff*, in the Publications of the American Economic Association, 1901. Professor Carver's problem, however, is somewhat different from that which we are concerned with here.

For a more general theoretical discussion of the effects of tariff duties on international trade, see F. W. Taussig, *Some Aspects of the Tariff Question* (Cambridge, 1915), chs. 1–3; and, by the same author, *Free Trade, the Tariff, and Reciprocity* (New York, 1920), chs. 1, 3, 4. (Chapter 4 is a reprint of his article on *Wages and Prices in Relation to International Trade*, cited above). Chapter 3, dealing with the manner in which the tariff affects wages, shows that the tariff is not in itself a cause of high wages, but in those competing industries where the effectiveness of labor is not high the tariff will keep wages up.

Finally, Professor Graham has recently advanced a partial defense of permanent protection, especially where a comparative advantage exists for an article produced under increasing costs. See F. D. Graham, *Some Aspects of Protection Further Considered* (cited above).

This completes our survey of the development of the general theory of international trade after Ricardo. In that development, the principal new features have been the attempt to secure a determination of international values more exact than that provided by the principle of comparative costs; the introduction of detailed qualifications for variability in cost and demand schedules; and the elaboration of a workable explanation of the scales of prices and money incomes as between countries.

Our next task is to trace the growth down to 1914 of the second main element in the general theory of international prices: namely, the various intra-national doctrines of money and prices. To that the following chapter will be devoted. We shall then turn to certain general theories dealing with international price adjustments, especially under disordered monetary conditions; and finally, to complete the history of the English and American thought, shall give some consideration to the facts and speculations presented since 1914.

CHAPTER V

THE THEORY OF MONEY AND PRICES, 1848-1914

1. In the years between the appearance of Mill's work and the outbreak of the Great War, the development of the theory of money and prices in English and American thought proceeded along two distinct and in the main quite independent lines. In England, a succession of writers attempted to break away from the type of approach established by Hume, Ricardo and Mill. Following, rather, the precedents set by such writers as Fullarton and Tooke,[1] they sought the explanation of the short-run relations between money and prices in the influence exerted by changes in bank reserves and in discount rates. In the United States, on the other hand, Mill's formulation of the so-called quantity theory was retained as the starting point of nearly all analysis, both short-time and long. A protracted and wearisome controversy was carried on for many years, and culminated at last in two striking attempts to verify the quantity theory itself by statistical methods. These two schools of thought have paid surprisingly little attention to one another. The American writers seem, until very recently at least, to have had almost no knowledge of the conclusions reached by the English theorists; and while some of the English writers remained faithful to the older classical method, their work was with a few exceptions conducted quite independently of the American investigations.[2] The two resulting bodies of theory are not, however, to be regarded as essentially opposed or contradictory. They are mutually complementary. One

---

[1] The ideas here involved first began to develop at the time of the Bank Charter controversy, before and after 1844. See ch. iii, sect. 9, above.

I have not thought it worth while to undertake here a separate study of this controversy. The more valuable conclusions to which it led were incorporated, in the main, in the doctrines of later writers.

[2] In the last few years, however, American writers have begun to pay some attention to Professor Marshall's work, while Professor Fisher's attempt to verify the quantity theory inductively has aroused quite wide interest in England.

has concerned itself primarily with the quantitative relationships between certain elements in the general price situation, which are taken to be significant indices of the size and direction of the fundamentally determinant forces. The other has dealt with the detail of the actual processes through which those forces make themselves felt. And while one has been very largely content with discussing the immediate short-time relationships involved, the other has also sought to examine their ultimate bases. The difference, at bottom, is not so much one of principle as of emphasis.

It would be irrelevant to our purposes here, however, to examine the growth of the two bodies of doctrine in any very great detail. We require only a sufficient knowledge of them to explain the monetary presuppositions of those theories, of the relations between money and international trade and of the adjustments of international prices, which form the subject of the two following chapters. Among the English writers we need consider only Sidgwick, Giffen, Nicholson, and Marshall; among the American, principally Taussig, Mitchell, Laughlin, and Fisher. Since we are interested in the more important constructive advances in the theory of money and prices alone, most of the primarily controversial discussion in the United States can be passed by.

2. Sidgwick, in his "Principles of Political Economy," [1] makes the first systematic attempt in the English literature at interpreting the short-run relations between money and prices in terms of the changes in bank reserves and in discount rates. His analysis is the result of an examination of the presumable effects of an influx or efflux of gold. He finds that an increase in the amount of gold, unaccompanied by a parallel increase in the amount of work to be done by it, will eventually lower the purchasing power of money relative to commodities in general. But in the *first stage* of the process the increment of coin (or, in England, of notes representing new gold in the Issue Department of the Bank of England), must pass through the hands of the bank-

---

[1] Henry Sidgwick, *Principles of Political Economy* (London, 1883). I have used, as before, the third edition (edited by J. N. Keynes: London, 1901). The passages here referred to are textually the same in the first and third editions.

ers.[1] It will thus increase the amount of the general medium of exchange that they have to lend. The price paid for the use of money (interest and discount rates) will therefore tend to fall. This fall, in turn, will tend to increase borrowing, and hence to increase the use of the medium of exchange. The consequent rise in general prices will gradually draw most of the new coin or notes into ordinary circulation. "Thus the fall in the *purchasing power* of money, consequent on an influx of gold, will normally establish itself through an antecedent and connected fall in the value of the *use* of money." [2] Conversely, too, when gold has to leave a country, it will come chiefly from the reserves of the banks. This necessitates a restriction in loans outstanding, and hence tends to raise the rate of discount. The effect of such an efflux of gold is usually greater, the smaller the ratio between the aggregate metallic reserve and the media of exchange supplied by the banks. England is an extreme example.

Comment on this chain of reasoning, which is usually traced only to Marshall, may be reserved until a later point. It is at once apparent, however, that we have here something quite new in English theory. The analysis was latent in a number of preceding writers,[3] it is true, and Macleod's work came quite close to it, but the credit for giving it complete and unequivocal form seems to belong to Sidgwick.

The analysis was almost immediately pushed a step farther by Giffen. A few years before, in his work on stock exchange securities,[4] Giffen had introduced various illuminating qualifications

[1] No particular proof is offered to show why this is necessarily so. What we should now call the "direct" effects of influxes of gold are rather passed by; that is, the effects proceeding from outlays by the gold importers themselves, other than through the mediation of the banks.

For Sidgwick's interesting but less novel analysis of the value of money in general, see *op. cit.*, pp. 238–253.

[2] Sidgwick, *op. cit.*, p. 255. (Italics mine.)

[3] In addition to the English writers at the time of the Bank Charter controversy, already referred to, several American writers such as Raguet and C. F. Adams presented, between 1840 and 1860, some quite remarkable "anticipations" of the so-called Marshallian doctrine. See H. E. Miller, *Earlier Theories of Crises and Cycles in the United States* (38 Quarterly Journal of Economics, 1924).

[4] R. Giffen, *Stock Exchange Securities* (London, 1877).

into the discussion of the connection between the quantity of money and prices. These dealt especially with the effects of the use of money substitutes, when money itself is scarce; of the effects on prices of different sorts of methods in business; of the limitations on the fluctuations of security prices and commodity prices; and of the cyclical relation between these price groups and the volume of credit. But the ends Giffen had in view in his work here were such that it is difficult to apply his somewhat fragmentary conclusions to strictly monetary theory, and a detailed discussion would not be especially pertinent at this point. His principal contributions lay, rather, in his later analysis of the connection between the gold supply and prices, and in his attempt to give a "dynamic" formulation to the quantity theory. These contributions were made in his "Essays in Finance." [1]

Giffen's main proposition is that the gold supply is intimately connected both with prices and, through the size of bank reserves, with the rate of discount. Furthermore, prices and the rate of discount are themselves directly connected with one another. With reference to this last thesis, he says that

a change in the level of prices affects the money market. A rise tends to make "money" [i. e., short-time loans] in demand, and to raise discount rates; a fall, to make "money" abundant and to lower rates. At the same time, a change in the discount rates acts on prices. A rise tends to lower prices; a fall to raise them. Prices in turn react on discount rates. There is incessant action and reaction.[2]

Then, after an examination of the factors affecting the short-loan market, he declares that a change in the general state of credit will also affect prices. Suppose an increase in lending to appear, especially in the short-loan market. Prices will tend to rise, for borrowers borrow either in order to purchase, or to avoid having to sell. "Nominal" capital, especially that represented by loans and bank deposits, will be increased. In consequence wages will rise, the need for small change will grow, and there will be a drain from bank reserves.[3]

---

[1] R. Giffen, *Essays in Finance*, Second Series (London, 1886). I have used the third edition (London, 1890). The references are to the second essay: *Gold Supply; the Rate of Discount, and Prices*.

[2] *Essays in Finance*, Second Series, pp. 38, 39.   [3] *Ibid.*, p. 49.

To this point Giffen's analysis, though more elaborate, is essentially like Sidgwick's. But he then carries it another step forward. He finds that this drain of cash from the banks and into circulation, by decreasing reserves, will *of itself* check the other wise cumulative process of expansion. It will compel bankers, faced by increasing liabilities and dwindling reserves, to raise their rates of discount, and thus to decrease the volume of current borrowing.[1] Giffen's analysis here is none too clear, and he does not make much use of it, but his conclusion — his indication of the automatic check to the reciprocally causal increases in prices and in bank loans — is important in the extreme.

Then, after a fairly detailed attempt at a statistical verification of these propositions, he examines the presumable sequence in time of some of the phenomena. He finds that low prices, for example,

rather succeed the high discount rates, than exactly correspond, which is what we should expect. The high rates cause sales by borrowers, discredit is apt to attend them, and so there is a fall. Similarly it is rather at the end of a period of low rates of discount that prices rise than at the beginning.[2]

Security prices, however, are affected more immediately than commodity prices.

This whole mechanism may be described as "indirect" in its operation. Giffen also, however, ascribes to prices a "direct" and even more important connection with the quantity of gold, and likewise to wages and profits; a connection, that is, which is distinct from the one running through bank reserves and the discount rate.[3] But the argument and the analysis of processes are much briefer, more nebulous, and less convincing than the discussion of the indirect connection. It is enough to point out that Giffen recognizes it. It turns, of course, on the effects of outlays by the actual producers or importers of gold other than the banks, and on the effects of exports made by them.

Finally, Giffen gives the first comprehensive statement since Adam Smith of what we may call the "dynamic" form of the quantity theory. The term "dynamic" is employed here in part to distinguish this statement from the direct-acting, almost fric-

[1] R. Giffen, *Essays in Finance,* pp. 49, 51–53.

[2] *Ibid.,* p. 72.   [3] *Ibid.,* pp. 54–56.

tionless and short-time form adopted by Hume and Mill; but in part, also, because Giffen's argument deals with *rates* of change, not merely with the absolute changes themselves. His remarks are worth quoting at some length. He says:

> One year with another, other things being equal, the population of gold-using countries increases in numbers, and commodities are multiplied in even greater proportion. Given the same range of prices and the same rates of wages and money incomes as before, and a continuance of the same general conditions of business, this means that one year with another a banker's deposits and liabilities will increase, or rather the aggregate deposits and liabilities of a given banking system will increase, and consequently a larger and larger reserve will be required. If no such reserve is forthcoming, then equilibrium can only be restored by a decline in nominal values, which must be brought about, if necessary, by a raising of the rates of discount. For similar reasons a steady increase in numbers and wealth, other things being equal, implies a larger and larger requirement for cash as small change. If no such cash is forthcoming, then it is quite impossible for the increased and richer population to effect their transactions. To effect them they must trench on bank reserves, necessitating the same rise of discount rates and fall of nominal values which would in any case become inevitable from the decline in the proportion of the banking reserves to liabilities. The two effects are produced *pari passu*, and they contribute in turn to the same result. To maintain equilibrium in the complex system, therefore, a steady addition to the stock of cash is required.[1]

This argument requires no particular comment. It is simply a translation into the field of long-time phenomena of the general process whose workings have already been examined in the short-time field. It is interesting to notice, however, that whereas in the short-time period direct and indirect effects were kept separate, here they are fused. Both discount rates and money in circulation are made to exert their influence on prices through, or because of, the changes in bank reserves.

3. Professor Nicholson, writing a few years later, presents both the Sidgwick-Giffen chain of reasoning on the relation between money and prices, and the Hume-Mill line. After finding that the superstructure of credit rests fundamentally upon the quantity of metallic money,[2] and after examining the causes affecting the demand and supply of gold for coinage,[3] he declares that a relative

[1] R. Giffen, *Essays in Finance*, p. 53.
[2] J. S. Nicholson, *Treatise on Money* (5 ed., London, 1901), pp. 337, 338. (First edition: 1888.)   [3] *Ibid.*, pp. 339–341.

scarcity in the supply of gold may cause a general fall in prices in either of two ways.[1] It may result in putting pressure on bank reserves, and thus, by means of rising discount rates and decreasing loans, cause a fall in prices. Or it may cause a contraction of the currency. This Nicholson regards as being the "more fundamental method of reducing prices." But just what the process is, how the contraction is supposed to be brought about and how it actually causes a fall in prices, he does not quite say. He regards the forces affecting the demand and supply of gold as the "*verae causae*" of changes in the levels of prices,[2] but he seems to take the intervening mechanism for granted.

Indeed, Nicholson's general position is none too clear. He asserts that "relative values will be adjusted, when they are reckoned in money, just as they would be if money did not intervene "[3] This statement, made without any particular proof, shows no advance over the earlier classical theory. He also has another doctrine, presented more clearly in his "Principles of Political Economy," which is open to severe criticism. He retains the distinction between value and price (without indicating quite what it is), and then says that

whatever disturbances due to causes affecting money may take place in general prices, if time is allowed for them to exercise their full effect, relative prices will be adjusted to relative values. In other words, a change from one level to another in general prices (owing to currency changes) must, when equilibrium is restored, leave relative values unaffected, excepting always the relative value of the standard itself.[4]

He takes some slight account of temporary changes in these relative values, but adds that when such alterations arise, "at once all the forces of industrial and commercial competition are called into play to bring about a readjustment." [5] Were "other things," the commodity side, always equal and unchanging, these proposi-

---

[1] J. S. Nicholson, *Treatise on Money*, p. 342.

[2] *Ibid.*, p. 349. Improvements in production and transportation, changes in the distribution of wealth, and so on, are similarly regarded either as indeterminate, or as being of minor importance. See pp. 344–348.

[3] *Ibid.*, p. 341.

[4] Nicholson, *Principles of Political Economy*, vol. ii (London, 1897), p. 16.

[5] *Ibid.*, p. 17. See also pp. 118–124.

tions might be true, at least in theory. But under the highly dynamic conditions of modern economic life, they have little significance. Perhaps the most characteristic single feature of the general money-price situation to-day is the universal presence of friction. Lags in time, maladjustments, and the failure of effects to have the same quantitative importance as their supposedly corresponding causes, are almost universal phenomena. Mill, who realized that purely monetary changes could alter the distribution of the national productive forces, was here far ahead of Nicholson.

4. Professor Marshall, whose testimony before the Gold and Silver Commission of 1888 is so familiar to English students, is usually credited with the first statement of the "indirect" chain of effects that connect money and prices. In point of fact, however, we have already seen that his analysis was anticipated in its essential features by Sidgwick in 1883, and by Giffen in 1886. Marshall's contribution consisted, rather, in his elaboration of the mechanisms presumably involved, and in his stress upon certain quite different elements.[1]

His presentation of the chain of indirect effects is enough like those of Sidgwick and Giffen to make only the briefest summary necessary. He finds that an absolute increase in the currency (where it is supposed to come from, however, is not stated) will result in increased bank reserves, this in a lower discount rate, and this in increased "speculation." By the latter term he apparently means an increase in all the types of financial operations which go to make up "Lombard Street": not only speculation in the strict sense, but also all the other activities of the primarily short-time money market. The increase in "speculation" raises prices; in consequence people need more money for cash transactions; and the initial increment in the currency, called into circu-

---

[1] At least, Sidgwick anticipated Marshall in the announcement of the doctrine to the general public. But Marshall had worked out most of his ideas a number of years before; and it is not unlikely, in view of the intimacy between the two men, that something in the nature of a joint intellectual authorship was involved — with Marshall's rôle quite surely the dominant one. Compare J. M. Keynes, *Alfred Marshall, 1842–1924* (Economic Journal, 1924), p. 337 and note; also pp. 316 ff. and 327.

lation to meet this need, now *supports* the rise in prices.[1] Or if there is more gold in circulation than people want — what we may call a *relative* increase in the currency — the surplus will be turned back to the banks, and by a process similar to that just outlined will induce a sufficient rise in prices to draw the excess back into circulation again.[2]

Marshall makes certain qualifications in this analysis, however, which are even more interesting than the analysis itself, though they are less clearly defined. In general, he declares that changes in the "other things" which are usually assumed "equal," in the customary statement that prices fluctuate with the volume of metallic currency, are often and perhaps generally more important than changes in the volume of currency itself.[3] More specifically, he comments, first, upon the large and (at that time) as yet unmeasured effects upon prices of the methods of doing business. This is especially true, for example, of the proportion of bank reserves to loans; of the extent to which the banks pool their reserves, directly or indirectly; and of the proportion of their money that people choose to keep in their pockets.[4] Second, he says that an accumulation of bank reserves beyond what is needed to establish the banks' credit will not affect prices [5] — an obvious case where the "methods of doing business" have a positive effect, though here a nullifying one. Third, he declares that there might be a sensible increase or diminution in the quantity of currency, without its being true that a sensible increase or decrease would necessarily follow in prices; while if there is a sufficient change in the methods of doing business, a great rise of prices is possible *without* any change in the supplies of gold and

[1] Gold and Silver Commission of 1888, *Final Report, Minutes of Evidence* (1888 Parliamentary Papers, XLV), *Questions 9640–9644*, and *9649–9650*. See also *Questions 9633, 9639*, and *9661*. The gist of Marshall's conclusions here has at last been brought together, in somewhat different form, in his *Money Credit and Commerce* (London, 1923), especially Bk. I, chs. 4–6.

[2] Gold and Silver Commission, *Minutes of Evidence, Question 9650*.

[3] *Ibid., Questions 9629, 9630*.

[4] *Ibid., Questions 9638, 9643, 9644*. See also Giffen's *Stock Exchange Securities*, cited above, to which Marshall refers.

[5] Gold and Silver Commission, *Minutes of Evidence, Question 9639*.

silver.[1] It is only regrettable that the argument here is not worked out more fully. It concerns actual and presumably not uncommon changes in certain of those "other things" which later writers, notably Fisher, have arbitrarily assumed to be "equal." Finally, Marshall shows that while in the immediate sense the supply of gold and the discount rate are connected, and move inversely, as regards long-run results they are not. In the long run, the discount rate is dependent on the average rate of interest, and this on the profitableness of business. The influx of gold simply causes a temporary downward "flutter" of the discount rate.[2]

If we take Marshall's position as a whole, therefore, we find in it two things. The first is an analysis of the chain of "indirect" effects that connects money and prices by way of bank reserves and the discount rate — an analysis which Marshall himself declares to be valid only if a fairly large number of conditions be given. The second is the clear inference that the quantity of currency itself is only one of a variety of factors which jointly determine the levels of prices, and probably not the most important one. Logically carried out, this second conclusion would make most of the wordy controversies of the last thirty years seem useless and beside the point. How far it is sound, will be considered in a later chapter.

Two other writers may be mentioned here, who have contributed along not dissimilar lines to the body of opinion brought together by the Gold and Silver Commission of 1888. They are Professor Lexis of Göttingen, and H. D. Macleod. Professor Lexis, in his reply to a questionnaire sent out by the Commission,[3] declares that an increase in the quantity of metallic money does not necessarily lead to a rise in prices, nor a decrease to a fall; and that a rise in prices may take place without any increase in the cash reserve of a country, or even with a decrease. In support of these propositions, he gives examples drawn from the monetary history of the United States and of various European

---

[1] Gold and Silver Commission, *Minutes of Evidence, Question 9648.*

[2] *Ibid., Questions 9651, 9662.*

[3] W. Lexis, *Answer to Questionnaire*, in Gold and Silver Commission of 1888, *Second Report* (1888 Parliamentary Papers, XLV), p. 267, col. 2.

countries between 1872 and 1887. The dependence of prices is, rather, on causes other than metallic money: notably, upon "a general upward movement of the economic conditions of life caused by great speculative activity or rapid business advance." And, like Marshall, he finds that an increase in metallic reserves may provide a surer basis for credit expansion, but will not of itself act as the cause of such an expansion. That is, there is no necessary and fixed relation between an increase in the quantity of the precious metals and extensions of credit. Thus he finds that the movements in the Bank of England discount rate, and in the volume of its loans, are not immediately produced by the movement of gold, but depend upon causes which ensue from the Bank Act.

With this Macleod agreed, declaring that there is no necessary connection between the quantity of money, the quantity of goods, and prices.[1] Macleod also stressed the importance of "methods of doing business" as a factor governing prices.

5. After 1888, no general advances important enough to require attention were made in England until the war and post-war periods. Writers in the main followed the Marshallian train of reasoning,[2] and indeed the whole question of the theory of money and prices rather dropped from sight.

In the United States, however, a long controversy has been carried on for the past thirty years, and still flares up at intervals. With this controversy itself I do not propose to deal. Its general character was indicated at the beginning of the present chapter.

[1] Gold and Silver Commission, *Second Report, Minutes of Evidence* (1888 Parliamentary Papers, XLV), *Questions 7224–7226.* See also *Questions 7227–7231,* and 7177.

[2] The theories of W. W. Carlile are the principal exception. See following note.
Reference should also be made, however, to a chapter on the variability of the value of money, in A. C. Pigou's *Wealth and Welfare* (London, 1912: Pt. IV, ch. 4). Professor Pigou finds the principal determinants to be (1) the variability in the demand for money; (2) the elasticity of the supply; (3) the variability of the supply; and, (4) the interaction of the demand and supply schedules. The factors in turn affecting and controlling each of these determinants are examined at length. The analysis is suggestive, and offers one of the best formulations that I have found of the "dynamic" theory of money and prices — dealing with changes and rates of change. It is to be regretted that the complexity and occasional obscurity of the argument renders it somewhat inaccessible to the general student.

It turns on the attempt to verify or disprove, by statistics and by *a priori* reasoning, the so-called quantity theory of money. The formulation of the theory which has been taken as the starting point by both defenders and antagonists is the one given it by Mill, or else some modification of Mill's doctrine. The resulting literature, both in book form and in periodicals, is very large, and most of it seems singularly futile at this range. Little or no attempt has been made, as a rule, to examine the character and operation of the mechanisms involved, and the results obtained by English writers, primarily theoretical though they were, passed quite unnoticed. Furthermore, it was rarely recognized that the character of the asserted relationships may be modified by the general cyclical movement of business. Yet the existence of this movement, if not its details, has been familiar for over a century. The various arguments involved, tacitly assuming a "normal" or "static" condition of affairs, have usually proceeded directly from money to prices, or from prices to money. When divested of their polemic verbiage, they appear to have turned very largely on the meaning and use of terms. Misinterpretation and obscurity, rather than any very radical differences in opinion as to the essentials of the problem, lay at the bottom of most of the debate. In proportion to the quantity of paper and ink consumed, the results attained have been meager. We therefore need undertake only two things: first, a recapitulation of some miscellaneous theoretic conclusions, relevant to general monetary theory, that certain writers have derived from studies of actual monetary conditions; and second, a brief examination of the attempts made by Professor Kemmerer and Professor Fisher to verify the quantity theory inductively.[1]

---

[1] The following is a partial list of the more important books and articles, other than those referred to in the text, in the general development of the quantity-theory controversy. The arrangement is chronological.

F. A. Walker, *Money* (New York, 1878); idem., *Value of Money* (8 Quarterly Journal of Economics, 1893); idem., *The Quantity Theory of Money* (vol. 9 of that Journal, for 1895); S. McL. Hardy, *The Quantity of Money and Prices, 1860–1891* (Journal of Political Economy, 1895); W. C. Mitchell, *The Quantity Theory of the Value of Money* (Journal of Political Economy, 1896); H. P. Willis, *Credit Devices and the Quantity Theory* (in *ibid.*); W. A. Scott, *The Quantity Theory of Money* (Am. Econ. Assoc., Economic Studies, vol. 2, Supplement); idem., *Money and*

In 1892 Professor Taussig, reviewing the history of silver in the United States from 1878 to 1892,[1] drew one conclusion at variance with general expectations. He found that

the expansion of the silver currency [i. e., after 1878] has followed, and not preceded, the rise in prices, the speculative activity and the other phenomena which are associated with an increase in the supply of money. . . . The increase of our silver currency seems to have been effect, not cause. When it was first issued, in 1878, at a time of quietude in business operations, it caused no expansion or inflation; on the contrary, the Treasury was unable to get the silver into circulation. When the general revival set in during 1880–1881, it went into circulation rapidly and in large amounts; but the movement of silver followed, and did not precede, the general industrial change. When the period of depression began in 1884, the Treasury went through another period of short circulation, and the regular issue of silver money had not the slightest effect in checking the tendency to depression and falling prices. The attempt to get out the silver money simply led to embarrassment; it flowed back to the Treasury in tax receipts. The phenomenon repeated itself in 1890–1892. The attempt to put forth more silver had the same effect as it had in 1885; it caused a back-flow into the Treasury. For an easy and ready circulation of the new issues, — if that is to come at all [written in 1892], — we must await a revival of general industrial activity.[2]

These generalizations are much more closely analogous to the English line of reasoning than to the then-contemporary body of American doctrine, and had sufficient attention been paid to them, much of the subsequent quantity-theory controversy might have been avoided. They show that the quantity of money in circulation was, immediately at least, much more a result of prices than a cause. Indeed, price changes themselves seem to have been

Banking (New York, 1903); J. L. Laughlin, *Principles of Money* (New York, 1903); W. C. Mitchell, *The Real Issues in the Quantity-Theory Controversy* (Journal of Political Economy, 1904); D. Kinley, *Money* (New York, 1904); idem, *The Relation of the Credit System to the Value of Money* (Publications of the American Economic Association, 1905); A. P. Andrew, *Credit and the Value of Money* (in *ibid.*); J. L. Laughlin, *Gold and Prices, 1890–1907* (Journal of Political Economy, 1909); and J. D. Magee, *Money and Prices* (in that Journal for 1913).

The English literature bearing on this controversy as such is naturally rather scanty. See, however, Baron T. H. Farrar, *Studies in Currency* (London, 1898), especially the fifth essay; W. W. Carlile, *The Evolution of Modern Money* (London, 1903); idem, *Monetary Economics* (London, 1912); and J. A. Hobson, *Gold, Prices, and Wages* (London, 1913).

[1] F. W. Taussig, *The Silver Situation in the United States* (New York, 1892). I have used the second edition (New York, 1893).

[2] *Ibid.*, pp. 72, 73.

at least as much a consequence of the general state of business as of purely monetary conditions. But the argument is in a sense logically incomplete. It deals with only a part of the total quantity of currency, and it says nothing of the crucial relations between the phenomena it examines, on the one hand, and bank reserves on the other. Professor Taussig goes on, however, to formulate a more general conclusion, which is put in illuminating fashion:

> The true way to state the conditions on which, in our own day, the general range of prices depends, is to compare the quantity of commodities offered for sale with the total volume of *purchasing power in terms of money*. In this volume of purchasing power the largest item consists in our day not of actual money, but of credit in various forms. . . . In such a state of things the increase of other forms of currency can have, in itself, only a minor effect.[1]

Ten years later Professor Mitchell made an elaborate statistical study of conditions in the United States during the period of depreciated paper currency, 1862–1879,[2] and among other perhaps more important results secured what can be interpreted as a moderately good *post facto* verification of the quantity theory, in its simplest and least assailable form. It must be admitted, however, that Mitchell did not himself regard his results as being especially in the nature of a verification of the quantity theory. Rather, he took the opposite view. He was particularly interested in "lags," not in direct non-lag correlations; and his general position, as evidenced in other writings, is at most that of a "metallist." Mitchell also finds that, under depreciated paper, the premium on gold and the index of wholesale commodity prices do not coincide by any means closely in their movements. The gold premium is

---

[1] Taussig, *The Silver Situation in the United States*, pp. 74, 75. See also Professor Taussig's very suggestive discussion of the relation between the value of the precious metals and their costs of production. He finds that, as a consequence of the tenuous character of this relationship, the value of gold may over considerable periods determine what shall be the marginal sources of supply. Only in a rather ultimate sense do the marginal sources govern value. See similarly his *Principles of Economics* (3 ed., New York, 1922), vol. i, pp. 249–251, 259, 260; and also, in connection with the effects of the Californian and Australian gold discoveries, — which were to some extent an apparent contradiction of theory, — *ibid.*, pp. 232–235.

[2] W. C. Mitchell, *History of the Greenbacks* (Chicago, 1903). See also his *Gold, Prices and Wages Under the Greenback Standard*.

much the more variable. Its major fluctuations are always reflected in prices in less degree and with a lag, but it would be inaccurate to take the depreciation of paper in terms of gold as
measuring the depreciation in terms of goods at all exactly.[1]

At about the same time I. A. Hourwich investigated, with the
aid of the reports of the Director of the U. S. Mint, the production
and consumption of the precious metals.[2] One result that he secured is of especial interest for our purposes. He found that while
the total production of gold in the United States, from 1884 to
1899, increased some 50 per cent, the industrial consumption increased by only 9 per cent; and the proportion of industrial consumption to total production fell from 24 to 18.5 per cent. In
other words the industrial consumption, in *absolute* terms, was
nearly constant. All the new gold mined, and even some secured
from imports and from melting down extant stocks, was used for
coinage.[3] A comparison with Soetbeer's figures indicates that
somewhat similar conditions have prevailed with respect to the
supply of the whole world since the Californian and Australian
gold discoveries. The industrial consumption is not over 25 per
cent of the total. This casts some little light on the proposition
that the value of metallic money is primarily based on its "commodity value." The tail seems to be wagging the dog.

Finally, in 1904 Professor Sprague made a study of the distribution of money in the United States from 1893 to 1903,[4] and
in consequence secured results, partly theoretical but to a large

---

[1] *History of the Greenbacks*, especially p. 277, chart.

[2] I. A. Hourwich, *The Production and Consumption of the Precious Metals*
(Journal of Political Economy, 1902, 1903).

[3] *Ibid.*, 1902, pp. 601–610, and especially the tables, pp. 601–604. Similar results
were secured for silver (see *ibid.*, 1903, pp. 503–539), though the industrial consumption of silver relative to the total production was somewhat larger. See also
R. A. Lehfeldt, *Gold, Prices and the Witwatersrand* (London, 1919), for data since
1841. Lehfeldt also makes an interesting estimate of the world's annual need for
gold since 1850, and compares the actual with the theoretically required supply.
He finds that the level of general prices has fluctuated very closely with the changing
ratio between the two — a most significant verification of the loosely stated quantity theory, so far as the data on which it is based are adequate. See especially pp.
22–37.

[4] O. M. W. Sprague, *The Distribution of Money between the Banks and the People
since 1893* (18 Quarterly Journal of Economics, 1904).

degree statistical, that confirm the now familiar English analysis of the money—bank reserves—commodity price relationship. His discussion is vigorous and fresh; and had its principal conclusions not already been presented in an earlier part of this chapter, in connection with the work of Marshall and his predecessors, it would be well worth giving in detail. Sprague begins by assuming the existence of a loan expansion. He then traces its effects, starting with the necessarily concomitant increase in general business activity, through more regular employment; an increase in general purchasing power (at first simply from the greater frequency of income receipts, later from a higher rate as well); a rise in prices, and a later rise in the general rate of money incomes (chiefly profits and wages); a consequently increased need among people at large for more money with which to make cash payments; a drain from bank reserves; and so to the eventual check to the initial loan expansion: that is, a rise in discount rates, inaugurated to protect the dwindling reserves.[1] The process thus returns upon itself, and ultimately provides its own automatic limit.

6. It remains to comment briefly on the two attempts at a statistical verification of the quantity theory. One was made by Professor Kemmerer in 1905,[2] the other by Professor Fisher in 1911.[3] Fisher's book, however, is in its essentials an elaboration of Kemmerer's work, and offers the same general type of analysis, though it of course differs in many points of detail. The latter, therefore, we need not examine, though it deserves all credit as the first essay in a new and fruitful field of investigation.

The general trend of Fisher's argument is well known. He selects five elements, which he declares to be the immediate agents in the determination of the level of prices. They are the quantity of money, the volume of bank deposits, the velocity of circulation of money, the velocity of circulation of deposits, and the volume of trade. These elements are combined into the famil-

---

[1] Sprague, *op. cit.*, pp. 521–528.

[2] E. W. Kemmerer, *Money and Prices* (New York, 1907). The second edition is better known (New York, 1909).

[3] Irving Fisher, *The Purchasing Power of Money* (New York, 1911).

iar "Equation of Exchange," $MV + M^1V^1 = PT$.   Fisher then determines the statistical values of the five elements in the United States over a period of years, by methods which, especially with respect to the measures of velocities of circulation, are extremely ingenious. He thus secures what may be called a "theoretical" price level, the one which the various measured changes in the determining elements apparently ought to have produced. This he compares with the actual course of prices over the same period, as indicated by index numbers. The correlation of the actual with the theoretical results is found to be extremely close, and Fisher takes this high correlation as a substantial proof of the correctness of the quantity theory of money.

That Professor Fisher has made an important contribution to monetary science by his exhaustive and painstaking investigation, cannot be denied. He assembled a vast amount of new material; he enormously clarified the discussion of money and prices, and brought it back to earth; and he resumed the various forces supposed to be at work into a compact and intelligible formula, which carries conviction by its very clarity. But that his results prove quite what they appear to prove at first sight, is more open to question. The Equation of Exchange is valid as a *post facto* description, as a résumé or cross-section of particular elements at a particular instant or period, but it is not a sufficient proof of *causation*, of a particular sequence between the phenomena. Even granting the assumptions on which it is based, it is at best an identity, as Fisher himself points out. It amounts simply to the declaration that what is paid is equal to what is received. Obviously the average price times the total quantity of goods exchanged *must* equal the total volume of money payments — the absolute amount of money and credit, times the rapidity of its circulation. There is force, too, in Anderson's further criticism that both sides of the equation are stated in terms of money. The contrast between the "money side" and the "goods side" is only apparent.[1]

A more fundamental objection must be made, however, not only to the equation of exchange but also to the method as a

[1] B. M. Anderson, *The Value of Money* (New York, 1917), pp. 161, 162.

whole. At bottom, this method proceeds directly from money to prices. It supposes that an increase in money can find its main outlet only in a rise of prices: that velocities of circulation and the volume of trade will not be affected, because they depend on "technical" conditions, and bear no necessary relation to the quantity of money in circulation.[1] The argument therefore takes no account whatsoever of the type of reasoning, just examined in connection with the development of English thought, which makes the effects on prices of an increase in the quantity of money depend primarily on the conditions of business at the given time, and on the character of business methods. Further, it deals wholly with money in active circulation. Yet if the Sidgwick-Giffen-Marshall line of approach is correct, the significant element is not this at all, but money in bank reserves. Changes in *that* element lead to price changes, and these in turn produce changes in money in circulation — which is thus not a cause, but a result. Not only is Fisher's order of sequences open to objection, therefore, but it also entirely omits one of the most important elements. Finally, Fisher makes little or no attempt to examine the actual mechanisms involved — to discover, for example, just how money really does get at prices, and how it alters them.[2] Had he made such an examination the grounds for many of these criticisms would have been removed.

It is only fair to state, however, that Professor Fisher himself is commendably cautious in deducing any necessary causal sequence from his results. The foregoing criticisms must therefore be taken as directed against the general type of position that he exemplifies, rather than against his own views. Moreover, Fisher declares that "the strictly proportional effect on prices of an increase in M [i. e., in the quantity of money] is only the *normal* or *ultimate* effect, after transition periods are over."[3] But this qualification proves to be in point of fact a very minor one, with

[1] Fisher, *op. cit.*, especially pp. 152–155.

[2] On pp. 153, 154, and elsewhere, he speaks of an increase in money unaccompanied by rising prices as resulting in a "plethora" of money, which can be gotten rid of only by increasing prices. That it might flow back into the bank reserves, without necessarily affecting credit, is apparently considered impossible.

[3] *Ibid.*, p. 159.

respect to the general trend of his argument, for the actual variations from the equation of exchange are asserted to be quantitatively slight. And the transition periods are held to be truly
"transitional." That is, they are something between two "nor-
mals" which represent the more usual state of affairs. Fisher's
primary concern is either with long-time or with "normal"
periods (which, it is not always easy to say); and, in those periods,
with certain quantitative relationships which it seems to me can
be regarded as accurate only in the descriptive, *post facto* sense.
They are not correct when regarded as *a priori* statements of
necessary causal sequence, valid for the future as well as for the
past.[1]

Indeed, I think that this type of criticism can fairly be
brought against nearly all of the pre-war American discussions of
monetary theory, and against many of the English. In the United
States, with but few exceptions, the very formulation of the problem itself has ordinarily continued to follow the rather unreal conception definitively established by Mill. It has been made to run
in terms of an assumed "normal" or "static" condition of affairs,
usually without even the saving recognition that such an assumption was being made. In this static analysis any consideration of
the actual short-time mechanisms of operation has as a rule been
left out. Moreover, as was suggested earlier in the present chapter,
the essential qualification imposed on all monetary theory by the
cyclical movement of business has been almost entirely passed by.[2]
In England the question of intermediary mechanisms, it is true,
has been given elaborate attention, and in this way some of the
weaknesses of the more rigid proportional-quantitative doctrine
have been avoided. But here too the cyclical element has been
largely ignored. Nevertheless this element radically alters, at
different points in the cycle itself, both the time sequence and the
presumable "causal" relationships of the factors involved. With

---

[1] See O. M. W. Sprague, *Fisher's Purchasing Power of Money* (26 Quarterly Journal of Economics, 1911), for a more favorable criticism.

[2] Detailed statistical studies of the business cycle are of course a matter of the
last few years alone. But the *existence* of recurrent and more or less periodic fluctuations has been recognized for over a century.

our rapidly increasing knowledge of the quantitative aspects of the business cycle, it should no longer be possible to state and ostensibly solve the price-money problem in quite the old terms. A different formulation, as yet unmade, is urgently called for.[1]

---

[1] The post-war discussions of monetary theory have by no means solved the problem, but they have undoubtedly steered clear of some of the more objectionable features of the older analysis. See ch. vii, sects. 2 and 3, below.

CHAPTER VI

INTERNATIONAL PRICE ADJUSTMENTS: THEORIES AND INVESTIGATIONS, 1848–1914

1. It has been remarked elsewhere that the more recent literature dealing with the theory of international prices and its component elements centers, in general, around three principal problems. The chapters immediately preceding have indicated the solutions offered for two of these problems — the domestic theory of money and prices, and the general theory of international trade. The third problem is essentially one of mechanisms: the problem of *how* international price adjustments are in point of fact effected, under various sorts of conditions. With this question the present chapter is concerned. The first part of the chapter reviews the general deductive analyses of the processes of adjustment, chiefly under metallic standards, which have been advanced by a succession of writers already familiar in these pages. The concluding sections will deal with three recent inductive examinations of the conditions of trade before 1914, under common metallic standards and under depreciated paper.

A word may be added as to the relations of this third principal division of the literature to the other two. In the main, it has been worked out without especial reference to their later developments. The writers concerned have usually taken the older form of the classical theory of international inter-commodity values for granted, and have at most discussed the subsequent more or less temporary changes imposed on the course of commodity trade by monetary disturbances. At the same time, they have assumed that the price adjustments are those which would result from the operation of a rather simple quantity theory. The post-classical elaborations in the theory of international trade, turning on the variability of cost and demand schedules and on the world organization of price and money income scales, have rarely been taken into account adequately. Similarly, those qualifications in the theory of money and prices which turn on the delayed and often unpredictable effects on prices of changes in the currency have usually been quite passed by.

Attention should be called first to two fragmentary but interesting contributions to the general theory, one made by Cairnes and the other by Macleod. In 1854, Cairnes presented an extremely able examination of the effects of the Bank Act of 1844.[1] He found that its operation had concentrated practically all of the country's metallic reserve in the Bank itself. In consequence the volume of the English currency in circulation, which was very largely paper, fluctuated directly with the flows of gold in international trade (except for the uncovered issue, of approximately fourteen million pounds). It was therefore very much more variable than a purely metallic currency would have been.[2] These considerations led Cairnes to examine the causes of the movements of the precious metals themselves. He concluded that the effects of money in circulation had been given quite undue importance. The then-accepted doctrine, making the movement of specie and of goods dependent on price levels and the latter on money in circulation, he found to be correct as far as it goes, but incomplete.

It is not true that the motives to importation and exportation depend on prices alone; and should the fall [*e. g.*] in prices be very sudden and violent, I conceive its effect on the whole would be rather unfavorable than otherwise on the exportation of commodities.

For while the state of exports and imports depends in part on the state of prices, as compared to those elsewhere,

the quantity of foreign goods . . . which we import from foreign countries does not depend solely on the prices at which these commodities are to be purchased; it depends quite as much upon the means at the disposal of people in this country for the procurement of such articles.[3]

This follows from the fact that any circumstance which renders industry less profitable, or which diminishes the general wealth of the country, will curtail the purchasing power available for

---

[1] J. E. Cairnes, *The Principles of Currency involved in the Bank Charter Act of 1844* (London, 1854).

[2] *Ibid.*, pp. 12–15.   [3] *Ibid.*, p. 34. Also pp. 33, 36, 37.

foreign goods. It will thus decrease the volume of importation *without* any necessary prior change in prices. Examples are provided by the case of bad harvests, industrial stagnation, and so forth.

How far we can agree with Cairnes that prices will not necessarily be affected, is doubtful. The antecedent conditions he has in mind are usually accompanied in actuality by a falling movement. But his effort to go *behind* prices for the real determinants of even the most immediate movements of goods and specie — an approach quite neglected in his later work — is interesting.

He finds a confirmation of his conclusions in the English crisis of 1847. There was at that time an acute shortage of bank accommodation, and because of general hoarding, a scarcity of even legal tender. The currency in circulation was greatly contracted, and prices fell. But exports, far from being stimulated, were checked and indeed almost ceased. Foreign trade virtually came to a standstill. The explanation lay in the extraordinary difficulty in discounting bills. Here again the determinant of trade was not the price-money situation, but banking and commercial conditions.[1]

A year or two later Macleod published his treatise on banking.[2] The bulk of Macleod's propositions and conclusions are not relevant in the present connection, but one point deserves mention. Macleod was, as far as I know, the first writer to see that the discount rate is one of the *primary* determinants of the foreign exchange rates, and that it may be manipulated in such fashion as to correct the exchanges. Credit for the observation is usually given to Goschen, who did not bring out his study for another half dozen years. Thus at one place Macleod says that the major causes of a drain of specie are the indebtedness of the country; a depreciated paper currency; and *a difference in the rate of discount*, between any two countries, more than great enough to pay the cost of transporting bullion.[3] Elsewhere he declares that the two ways of correcting an adverse exchange, if the currencies

---

[1] Cairnes, *op. cit.*, pp. 44–57.

[2] H. D. Macleod, *The Theory and Practise of Banking* (London, 1855–1856). I have used here the fourth edition (2 vols., London, 1883).

[3] *Ibid.*, vol. ii, p. 344.

are not depreciated, are an export of produce and a rise in the rate of discount. The latter movement will attract bullion, and increase the foreign demand for bills on the given country.[1] Beyond that, however, his analysis does not go.

2. The first comprehensive treatment of international price adjustments to appear in the period after Mill was presented in Goschen's famous essay on the Foreign Exchanges.[2] The book, a worthy successor to Blake's classical work, is in part a description of the mere mechanics of commercial transactions in the exchange market. A large portion of it, however, is devoted to the theory of the exchanges themselves, and to an analysis of their operation under various sorts of monetary conditions. Goschen was not consciously trying to do anything new, and indeed most of his theoretical ideas can be found in one form or another in earlier writers, especially in Blake and in Mill. But he put his propositions so clearly and so convincingly that much of the credit for original discovery has, not without a certain justification, been subsequently assigned to him.

Goschen first examines, more comprehensively than Macleod, the elements in the fluctuations of the exchange rates. Currency disturbances apart, they are: (1) the balance of indebtedness, which, however, will cause fluctuations only within the specie points, (2) the relative rate of interest in the two countries, (3) the state of credit in each, and (4) political disturbances; or some combination of the four.[3] Of these, the first two usually operate simultaneously, but in opposite directions. Money will be dear (that is, interest rates will be relatively high) in that country which owes much to foreign creditors, and relatively cheap in that country which has exported much. But, at the same time, high interest rates will be *attracting* money (i. e., short-time capital) to

---

[1] See Macleod, *op. cit.*, vol. i, pp. 381–432. Macleod also asserts that the rate of discount is "the true supreme power of controlling the exchanges and the Paper Currency" (*ibid.*, vol. ii, p. 365), a suggestion which compares favorably with certain more recent conclusions on the subject. The particular way in which Macleod connects discount rates with gold movements is, however, more open to criticism.

[2] Viscount G. J. Goschen, *Foreign Exchanges* (London, 1861). I have used here the reprint of the third edition published by Wilson (London, 1901).

[3] *Ibid.*, pp. 49–54.

precisely that country from which specie is flowing out in payment of foreign debts.[1]

As to the width of the fluctuations of the exchanges, this depends in part upon the particular kind of bill involved. The fluctuations of sight bills are primarily limited by the specie points. They cannot exceed these points except for short periods, and then only when the countries are so far apart that specie cannot be sent rapidly, and when immediate returns are of importance; that is, only under rather unusual circumstances. The fluctuations in the rates for long bills, however, are without any such limit. They are co-extensive with changes in interest rates in the accepting country, and with the degree of trust or distrust in the solvency of the names on the bills.[2] They are also, of course, somewhat more susceptible than sight bills to the effects of anticipated political disturbances.

Finally, Goschen discusses the factors affecting the balance of payments, and also the exchange rate–premium–gold flow mechanism. This last he makes turn on the prices of *bills;* not, as in the Ricardo-Mill statement, on the prices of *commodities.*[3] He finds that the principal direct corrective of specie flows lies in their effects upon discount rates, not upon prices. These emendations were made without conscious intention of altering the Ricardo-Mill explanation of the adjustments. Yet it is evident that while retaining the general frame-work, they distinctly change its emphasis. The critical factor in the maintenance of an international equilibrium, and in the correction of its aberrations, becomes the

---

[1] Goschen, *op. cit.*, p. 127 *et seq.* While he finds that speculation can modify, and hasten or retard, the operation of these four elements, he declares that speculation cannot itself be a primary and determining element in the fluctuations. It is "dependent." (See p. 117.) This proposition has at best only a rather long-time validity, however, with respect to such conditions as those witnessed since 1914.

With respect to specie movements and the prices of bills, also, he says elsewhere that "it is the price of short bills, not of those which have some time to run, which determines the course of bullion shipments" (pp. 88, 89). This obvious distinction between the effects of changes in the two sorts of exchange rates is often lost sight of in discussions of the exchange rate–gold flow mechanism.

[2] *Ibid.*, p. 55.

[3] *Ibid.*, pp. 41–46.

money market; that is, discount and exchange rates, not commodity markets and commodity prices.[1]

Goschen then turns to the more complicated problems of trade under depreciated currencies. He distinguishes three principal types of situation: trade when bullion exports are not prohibited, but are difficult; trade when bullion exports are impossible; and trade between two countries, one of which is on a silver standard and one under gold. They may be examined in order.

First, if one of the countries has an inconvertible paper currency with no bullion, or if bullion can be obtained only at an enormous premium, or if its export be prohibited, then the limits on the fluctuations of the exchanges are apparently entirely removed. But as long as there is any gold left, a check of sorts is still in operation: namely, the amount of the premium on gold, in terms of the (depreciated) domestic currency.[2] The price of foreign bills within the country will rise to the same extent that the prices of all purchasable articles, bullion included, are raised by the depreciation.[3] Beyond that it will not go, as long as any gold is left. If it did, then despite the premium it would be less expensive to ship gold than to buy bills. With respect to the distribution of the effects of depreciation, however, he finds that this depends on the particular case. As between a transaction completed before the depreciation and one completed afterward, providing no further depreciation takes place, Goschen declares that there is neither gain nor loss. The gain to the paper-country exporter from falling exchanges is offset by the rise in paper prices. If, however, the transaction takes place during the process of depreciation, the paper-country exporters lose and the foreign importers gain, since the purchasing power of the paper payment originally contracted for will have fallen.[4]

In other words, Goschen is here treating the premium on gold and the rise in general prices as equivalent measures of the depreciation of paper, and is using either or both to indicate the

---

[1] For a fuller discussion, see especially M. Ansiaux, *Principes de la politique regulatrice des changes* (Brussels and Paris, 1910), pp. 48–53.

[2] Goschen, *op. cit.*, pp. 60–63.

[3] *Ibid.*, p. 104.   [4] *Ibid.*, pp. 65–69.

limit of the depreciation in the exchanges. To this, however, we must take exception. The movement of the exchange rate, it is true, is under these conditions very closely related to the movement of the gold premium. As long as any of it is left, gold is the most nearly universal common denominator in international exchanges, and its price will govern their course. But the premium on gold by no means necessarily coincides with the rise in *general* paper prices. It is an international, not merely a domestic, currency.[1] A similar sort of criticism may be made of Goschen's discussion of the origin and distribution of the gain or loss from depreciation. The principal source usually lies not in changes in the value of the currency during the period of the transaction, but in the failure of purely domestic prices to move exactly with the prices of international commodities, *including* gold. This point, too, will be elaborated later. Finally, the distribution of the gain or loss with respect to any particular transaction also depends on how the shipment of goods is invoiced. If payment is called for in the stable currency, then the loss from the exchange fluctuation is very largely removed — though the effects of changes in prices, as measured in the depreciated currency, of course remain.

In the second case, where bullion exports are absolutely impossible, Goschen finds that the fluctuations of the exchanges are subject to no limitation whatsoever. The prices of bills are determined by their demand and supply alone.[2] If there were an equality of imports and exports — an equilibrium in trade — the value of the depreciated currency within the given country would be equivalent to its value in terms of the foreign exchanges, and a stable basis for trade might ultimately be secured. But such an equality does not in fact appear, under these conditions.[3] Under a depreciated currency, and with bullion exports prohibited, imports are more likely to *exceed* exports.

It is a little difficult to discover just what chain of reasoning underlies this proposition, which has been more criticized than almost any other doctrine in the book. Goschen contents himself

---

[1] At a later point Goschen himself equates the exchange depreciation to the premium on gold alone, without, however, suggesting that his earlier use of the general price level might be inaccurate. (See *ibid.*, pp. 104, 105.)

[2] *Ibid.*, pp. 70–72.   [3] *Ibid.*, pp. 75, 76.

with a very negative sort of proof. He says only that if the opposite situation were to prevail, if exports exceeded imports, then bullion would flow into the paper country, since other countries would pay part of their debts in gold. The export of bullion would therefore no longer be impossible.[1] This is of course hardly definitive. It amounts simply to saying that when a country is under a depreciated currency and has no gold, it can be inferred that the trade balance is against that country, for otherwise it would not be lacking gold, and might even not have a depreciated currency.[2] Rather, it will be shown later that although under certain conditions Goschen's conclusion is correct, — as in the case of Germany in 1921,— the explanation is quite different; and under other conditions the conclusion itself is wrong.

In the third case, of trade between a gold-standard and a silver-standard country, he declares that the par of exchange is established by the market ratio between the metals themselves. Since this ratio obviously changes constantly one of the two metals, when regarded as a currency, is nearly always appreciated relative to the (fixed) mint ratio. The limit to the exchange fluctuations is then set by the premium on that metal.[3] The argument is self-evident, and need not detain us. In the case of trade between a country with a single standard and one under bimetallism, the par of exchange is determined by the metal which is common to both countries. The exchange fluctuations are limited by the specie points on either side of the par.[4] It is interesting to notice, incidentally, that in both of these cases Goschen's argument on the exchanges runs wholly in terms of the premiums on the precious metals. His earlier predilection for the general price level as the index of depreciation seems to have been abandoned.

Goschen's general position is now sufficiently clear to make further elaboration unnecessary, and his work in other parts of the subject is not relevant here. Nor is any more specific criticism required. To his argument as a whole, to its main trend, we can-

---

[1] Goschen, *op. cit.*, pp. 72, 73.

[2] He goes so far as to suggest at several points that the excess of imports, by causing a continued drain of specie, may itself be the cause of the country's being forced on to a paper standard. See especially pp. 14, 72.

[3] *Ibid.*, pp. 76–80.   [4] *Ibid.*, p. 81.

not but accord high praise. It was by far the clearest and most accurate analysis of the adjustments of international prices, especially under disturbed monetary conditions, that had been made to that time, and it still has great value. Exception must be taken, however, to many of its details. The primarily "domestic" aspects of the processes of adjustment, at the present day at least, are often quite unlike those which Goschen had in mind. Furthermore, various factors of which he took no account may enter the exchange situation, and may entirely alter it. These propositions will be supported more elaborately in later pages, however, and need not be amplified at this point.

3. A year or two before Goschen's work appeared, Cairnes had published in periodical form his remarkable discussions of the effects of the Californian and Australian gold discoveries. They do not seem to have attracted much attention at the time, and it was not until they were reprinted in his "Essays," in 1873,[1] that their value began to be recognized. For that reason they are placed here rather than earlier in the present chapter, where in strict chronology they properly belong.

Cairnes was not, in the main, attempting any venture into the fields of theoretical speculation in these studies. He was undertaking a description of the bare facts in so far as they were then available. Only at certain points did he relate them to the established theory of international trade. This description, primarily concerned with the Australian discoveries, may be summarized briefly.[2]

He found that the discoveries had led at once to a great initial increase in general money wages in Australia, because of the high level of earnings at the mines. Prices soon followed suit, and settled semi-permanently at the new level, though their initial rise was delayed at first by the lack of a mint.[3] But the effect on

---

[1] J. E. Cairnes, *Essays in Political Economy* (London, 1873).

[2] Essay I, *The Australian Episode.* (First published in 1860.) The principal discoveries were made in 1851 and the years immediately following.

[3] There was no mint for about a year after the first discoveries had been made. In consequence the reduced cost of producing gold, and the extraordinary increase in its quantity, were for a time unable to affect the actual coin circulation, and the value of the currency was held above its "natural cost level." In Australia the diver-

the commercial world at large, in the first eight or nine years after the discoveries (Cairnes was writing in 1860), was small. The proportion of the Australian emigration to the total business of the world, and of the new gold to the vast extant supplies, was not great enough to produce much immediate change. In consequence, a remarkable divergence between the Australian level of prices and the world level soon developed. Furthermore, all Australian industries other than gold mining suffered severely from the effects of the discoveries. They were totally unable to meet the high standard of money incomes set by the mines; much of their labor was diverted; and the net result was that while Australia exported gold, she imported, despite heavy costs of transportation, almost everything else. Cairnes points out that this situation affords an excellent illustration of the law of comparative cost, since Australian labor was also more efficient than the world average in several products other than gold, but was far less efficient in them than in the production of gold itself.[1] Finally, the high level of money incomes had made domestic products dear, but had also made all foreign goods cheap. Australia's gain, however, was the world's loss. The discoveries did not in themselves increase the world's wealth. They only redistributed it.

In the next Essay, Cairnes examines in greater detail the mechanism of the price changes caused by the discoveries, and the processes by which the new gold is gradually spread throughout other countries.[2] He finds that the effects of an increase in gold production on general prices and on the value of gold itself are of three sorts. (1) Directly, the new gold will raise prices by increas-

gence was brief, but Cairnes finds that a similar type of argument holds for the world as a whole. The world's currencies are so large that they can be increased only slowly; and a fall in the cost of obtaining gold will not affect their values, through an increase in quantity, for a considerable period. It may require thirty or forty years for all the effects to become apparent. In the interim, the value of gold is "too high." (*Essays*, pp. 41, 42, and 56).

[1] Cairnes comments on the contrast between this situation and that in California at about the same time. Certain of the California industries, notably those producing food, were not seriously hurt by the gold discoveries and the consequent general flood of imports, because California's advantage over other countries in these industries was, up to a certain point, as great as that which she enjoyed in producing gold.

[2] Essay II, *The Course of Depreciation*. (First published in 1858.)

ing the money demand of those into whose hands it first comes. This will cause a temporary rise in prices, increased production, and a subsequent return of prices to their old level.[1] (2) Indirectly, it will raise prices by curtailing the supply of those articles that do not come within the range of the new demand. This will follow on the rise of wages in the industries which *are* directly affected, for the rise will be communicated to industry at large, and will lead to decreased profits. This in turn will result in decreased production, a rise in prices, and eventually a return to the old level of production. (3) Finally, these various consequences are themselves qualified by the character of the particular currency into which the new gold is received. If the currency is purely metallic, the effect will simply be proportional to the relative size of the increase. If it is partly a credit currency, however, the effect may be much more than in proportion to the increase. A wide divergence between countries, with respect to the prices of the articles produced in each, is therefore almost inevitable. The divergence, however, will be checked to some extent by the competition in neutral markets of different countries producing the same article, and to a less extent by the reciprocal demands of different countries for one another's products.

Indeed, despite modern improvements in trade, transportation, and commerce, Cairnes admits that the effects of the gold discoveries can proceed from commodity to commodity, from class to class, and from country to country, only with very considerable intervals. The total elapsed time may be as long as thirty or forty years. The inequalities in price relationships resulting from

---

[1] Cairnes makes an interesting statement as to the order in which the prices of the articles coming under the new range of expenditure will be affected. Articles consumed by the laboring and artisan class will rise first. Of these manufactures may lead, but they cannot continue long ahead of other sorts, since their supply can be expanded rapidly. On the other hand, that supply is not easily contracted, and the prices of manufactures may therefore fall temporarily below the general level. Raw materials will follow next, and since their supply is not easily extensible their prices may remain above the average for some time. Finally, those articles not directly in the range of new expenditure will be affected last, and only indirectly. (See *Essays*, pp. 64, 65.)

This hierarchy of classes of commodities, based on the sensitivity of the movements of their prices, is an interesting anticipation of parts of certain more recent doctrines dealing with commodities and the business cycle.

the great and uneven disturbances to world currencies may not find their correction until the very end of the period of depreciation and transition. During this period itself the action of the new gold will be partial, not uniform. Certain classes of commodities and services will be affected much more powerfully than others. Prices in general will rise, but with unequal steps.

This analysis of the effects of the gold discoveries was the first systematic attempt that had been made, at least in the English literature, to examine the actual process by which an increase in the quantity of gold really gets at world prices. It deserves great credit for its originality, and it deserves credit, too, for its content. At the present day we should perhaps lay more stress on the chain of results that proceeds from changes in bank reserves, and somewhat less on that series of "direct" effects with which Cairnes is chiefly concerned, but the value of the results obtained cannot be denied. Subsequent writers have elaborated Cairnes's work, and have greatly improved upon it, but they have not impaired the substantial validity of his general conclusions as far as they went. Nor have they impaired the accuracy of his verification of various parts of the general theory of international trade.

4. No attempt to revise the Mill-Cairnes-Goschen explanations of the adjustment of world prices was made until nearly thirty years after Cairnes's essays first appeared. Between 1888 and 1893, however, Nicholson, Marshall and Bastable all undertook a partial re-examination of the problem, concerning themselves primarily with the peculiar form given to it by the existence of currency dissimilarities. These discussions were provoked by the disruption of foreign trade and the foreign exchanges, in many countries, to which the abandonment of bimetallism and the fall in the value of silver had led.

Nicholson adopts, as we have seen elsewhere, a rather loose and general form of the quantity theory, based exclusively on the quantity of metallic money. The quantity of credit is taken as being reduced to a certain minimum proportion to the metallic reserves. A loose theory of international commodity-price equalization is also presented, and the causes that produce changes in general prices, both in and between countries, are worked out with marked subtlety.[1] Then Nicholson turns to the determination of prices in the trade between gold-standard countries on the one hand, and those under a silver standard on the other. He finds that if the commercial ratio between gold and silver changes in the same proportion as the general levels of gold prices and silver prices, there will be no disturbance to trade. Should a discrepancy appear, it will eventually be removed by the flow of gold or of silver, and by the movement of goods.[2] This stimulus or check to imports and exports, indeed, is especially stressed, and is eventually made the principal agent in the restoration of equilibrium. But the stimulus is regarded as arising simply from the temporary discrepancy between the commercial gold-silver ratio and the gold price silver price ratio. The possible lag of domestic costs of production does not seem to be considered.[3] Finally, Nicholson offers the characteristic statement that "after sufficient time to make the adjustment, the *relative values* of commodities generally must . . . eventually be unaffected." [4]

Nicholson makes his analysis of these adjustments turn on changes in the relative value of gold and silver themselves — in the gold-silver ratio. This view he sets up in explicit antithesis to the Ricardo-Mill type of reasoning, which makes the precious metals "colorless," and disregards their possible independent effects.[5] He also shows that the gold-silver ratio itself may change before and apart from general trade conditions; and may thus be the *cause* of alterations in these last.[6] Such, for example, was the effect of the great increase in the quantity of silver offered in the market after its demonetization. Finally, he makes an interesting criticism of Mill. Mill had found that a stimulus to exports due to purely monetary causes will bring counteracting forces into play, and will tend to be converted into some change in silver prices or gold prices or in the ratio of gold to silver. Nicholson's objection is that the process of adjustment takes time, and

---

[1] J. S. Nicholson, *Treatise on Money* (5 ed., London, 1901), pp. 342–357. (First edition: 1888.)

[2] *Ibid.*, pp. 359–362.

[3] *Ibid.*, pp. 370, 371.

[4] *Ibid.*, p. 363.

[5] *Ibid.*, pp. 371, 372.

[6] *Ibid.*, pp. 374, 375.

that before one disturbance is corrected another may therefore begin to operate.[1] Money, in other words, may remain an independent source of disturbance.[2]

The views of Professor Marshall are more comprehensive. They are contained chiefly in a Memorandum he submitted to the Gold and Silver Commission of 1888, but certain amplifications are also to be found in his evidence before the Indian Currency Commission of 1898. It will be most convenient to treat the two bodies of material together. Marshall first accepts the familiar analysis of the price-gold flow mechanism, as developed by Mill, Goschen and others, and agrees that, with allowance for double cost of carriage, prices at the seaboard tend to equality. He next makes a brief examination, entirely along classical lines, of the limits of exchange-rate fluctuations under a gold standard, and of the character of the balance of payments.[3] Having thus cleared the ground, he then turns to the problem more particularly in hand.

First, the trade between two countries of which one is on a gold standard, and the other under inconvertible paper. Marshall finds that when trade is in equilibrium, the exchange rate will precisely reflect the ratio of gold prices to paper prices. In case the equilibrium is disturbed a readjustment will take place, through the agency of a temporary resulting bounty to exports and tax on imports. The bounty will go to the exporters of that country whose currency is undervalued in foreign exchange (undervalued, that is, relative to the ratio of commodity prices). The tax will be felt

---

[1] Nicholson, *op. cit.*, p. 366.

[2] See T. N. Whitelaw, *Professor Nicholson on "The Causes of Movements in General Prices"* (Economic Journal, 1894), for a detailed criticism. For an application of Nicholson's theories to the Indian currency problem, see the latter's own article on *The Effects of the Depreciation of Silver*, in the same volume of that journal.

Reference may also be made here to Nicholson's later treatment of the course of international trade under inconvertible paper, and of the causes of gold flows. These last he finds to be dependent not on commodity prices, but on interest rates. See his *Principles of Political Economy*, vol. ii (London, 1897), pp. 282–285.

[3] A. Marshall, *Memorandum as to the effects which differences between the currencies of different nations have on international trade*, in Gold and Silver Commission, *Final Report* (1888 Parliamentary Papers, XLV), p. 47, col. 2, and p. 48, col. 1.

See also the brief recapitulation of Marshall's views in his *Money Credit and Commerce* (London, 1923), Appendix G.

by the importers of this same country, for they will lose if their bills are sold at the current rates. Exporters' bills will therefore be left without a market, at the new exchange rate. Their value will fall, and the old equilibrium will be restored. Thus a change in the exchange rate, unless accompanied or preceded by changes in prices, can give no *permanent* stimulus to exportation, for the rate must "almost instantaneously" accommodate itself to the gold-paper commodity price ratio.[1]

With respect to the trade between a gold-standard and a silver-standard country, a similar type of reasoning is used. Marshall holds that the exchange rate will be adjusted to the ratio between gold prices and silver prices. The adjustment in the case of a disturbance here, however, will be slower than in the case of gold-paper trade. Silver is exportable, and can move between countries, whereas paper money cannot. The paper country exporters could use their bills only to buy foreign commodities, but those of the silver country can use them to buy silver as well. If silver is undervalued in the gold country, relative to the gold-silver commodity price ratio, silver will therefore flow into the silver country until the price ratio is readjusted. Until equilibrium is thus restored, the silver-country exporters will receive a bounty.[2]

Finally, Marshall examines along classical lines the world distribution of the precious metals, and the determinants of their demand and supply. His analysis under the second head is interesting, but not very novel. Under the first head, he declares that

the precious metals are so distributed throughout the world, that independently of the demand for them for the purposes of hoarding and of the arts, each country has just that aggregate amount of the two metals which corresponds in value to the volume of that part of her business which the habits of her people cause her to transact by payments in coin, account being taken of the rapidity of circulation of coin, and of the absorption of some quantity of the precious metals to act as the basis of a paper currency.[3]

This proposition, in effect simply a "modernization" of Ricardo, is then elaborated, but its essential features are not changed.

---

[1] *Memorandum*, p. 48, cols. 1, 2.
[2] *Ibid.*, p. 49, col. 1.
[3] *Ibid.*, p. 49, col. 2.

In the evidence given in 1899[1] Marshall substantially reaffirmed these various doctrines, due allowance being made for factual differences in the subject matter. He introduced, however, one or two important qualifications. First, in connection with the trade between a gold country and a silver country, he now says that the exchange rate indicates the ratio between gold prices and silver prices *at the ports* — not simply, as seems to be implied in the detail of the earlier argument, between prices at large in the two countries. He further shows that inland prices, in India as in the United States, are far less influenced by exchange fluctuations and foreign prices than are prices at the seaboard.[2] The pitfalls inevitable in the use here of the concept of a "general price level" are thus at last avoided. Second, he adds one quite new element to his earlier analysis. He repeats the proposition that a *depreciating* currency will give a temporary bounty to exporters. But he now also declares that it will give an equal bounty to any *other* manufacturer. The bounty arises not from the fact of export, but from the lag of wages and other costs of production behind prices. It is not a bounty, however, in the sense that it will permanently increase exports relative to imports. Except in the case of international borrowing operations (either with respect to the initial loan, or to its repayment), any such stimulus to exports will be followed and compensated by an exactly equal falling off of the exports themselves, relative to imports. The initial excess of exports gives rise to an excess of exporters' bills, and this at once results in a bounty to imports. The bounty is exerted through the rate of discount for bills, and through imports of the precious metals and other commodities.[3]

I do not propose to attempt any detailed criticism of these various doctrines here. The questions involved must in the main be reserved for the later chapters that will deal with them alone. It

---

[1] A. Marshall, in Indian Currency Commission, 1898: *Evidence,* Part II (1899 Parliamentary Papers, XXXI).

[2] *Ibid., Question 11,788.*

[3] *Ibid., Question 11,792.* See also *Question 11,824,* in connection with the world distribution of the precious metals and the readjustment, after a disturbance, in international price levels. The exchange rates are regarded as being simply the *agent* in the process.

will be convenient, however, to summarize the essential features of Marshall's position.

First, he adopts the general classical view of the exchange rate – gold flow – price mechanism: that world (gold) prices are kept in substantial harmony by the effects of exchange-rate premiums, and, when necessary, by gold flows that themselves correct prices. After what has been said of this doctrine in earlier pages, it is perhaps unnecessary to repeat that while its validity can perhaps be granted in the long-run sense, it is far from accurate or complete with respect to those short-time phenomena with which Marshall was presumably dealing here. Marshall's own theories on money and prices, examined in the preceding chapter, are a sufficient proof of this. He had himself dwelt at length elsewhere upon the frequent uncertainty of the effects of changes in the metallic currency, upon the delay in their appearance, and upon the perhaps minor importance, in the process of price determination, of changes in the mere quantity of the currency itself. In other words the gold flow mechanism, so far as its effects upon prices are concerned, is by no means so certain and direct-acting as the classical analysis would indicate. Yet Marshall, having clearly seen this with respect to prices *within* any one country, quite forgets it with respect to prices as *between* countries.

Second, he gives a refined statement of the classical doctrine concerning the world distribution of the precious metals. This statement is not especially novel, of course, nor does it seem to me especially significant. It amounts to little more than a declaration that each country has as much of the precious metals as it needs, — or needs as much as it has, — and it casts no very real light upon the conditions that govern the determination of the relative and the absolute shares of each country. Third, he offers a clearly-put theory of the factor which determines the exchange rate between countries with dissimilar currencies: namely, the ratio between commodity prices in the one country and the other. In its earlier form, this proposition bore a close resemblance to the theory underlying Professor Cassel's "purchasing-power-parity" doctrine, to be examined in another chapter. Marshall's later statement, however, confines the term "prices" to prices at the ports. With this formulation, as far as it goes, we can probably agree.[1] Fourth, and finally, he makes an analysis of the process of international exchange rate and price adjustment, again under dissimilar currencies. Here his earlier statement was essentially like that of Goschen, as far as the mechanisms involved are concerned. His later doctrines, however, brought in the question of the divergence between domestic costs of production and international prices. It is in this that his most important and most novel contribution in the general field consists, and to it we may accord unreserved praise. The ground for disagreeing with him here, if there be any at all, lies in his constant implication that after any given disturbance matters must inevitably revert to the *status quo ante;* a "static" view of trade conditions which cannot be altogether acceptable.

5. The last important English writer in this period was Professor Bastable, who between 1889 and 1893 published two significant articles, and brought out his well-known general treatise.[2] His views on the theory of international trade itself are essentially an elaboration of the earlier classical position, and have been examined in another chapter. It remains to consider his conclusions as to the rôle of money in international trade, and as to the adjustment of international prices. Here, however, his work was less important, and offers little that is not contained in the writings of one or another of the men whom we have already discussed. Its value lies more in the clarity of its statement than in its essential novelty. Bastable concurs in the Ricardian doctrine of the distribution of the precious metals as for a barter trade. Like the post-Ricardian writers, he shows that the distribution itself is the result of the state of international exchange and of the range of general prices. He also repeats the familiar analysis of the process of adjustment under a common metallic standard, by means of

---

[1] Though see ch. xvii, *passim*, below.

[2] C. F. Bastable, *On Some Applications of the Theory of International Trade* (4 Quarterly Journal of Economics, 1889), especially pp. 1–8; *The Incidence and Effects of Import and Export Duties*, in the Report of the British Association for 1889, especially pp. 442–445; *The Theory of International Trade* (London, 1893). In the fourth edition of this last work (1903) see pp. 51–71; and pp. 85–89 and following.

specie flows and price changes. Comparative prices themselves are held to be so adjusted, by a more or less automatic process, as to reflect the operation of the principle of comparative advantage, and also of that of reciprocal demand. Money is thus regarded as being relatively passive in its action, and almost frictionless.

Where the currencies involved are dissimilar, the readjustment is secured by a change in the ratio between them. Bastable's statement of the actual process involved here, however, is none too complete. He sees that the operation of the classical mechanism is retarded by these differences in currencies themselves, and by the effects of custom in holding prices rigid, but the resulting qualifications are not regarded as in the least impairing or altering the general analysis. At one point, it is true, Bastable questions the conclusion that a movement of the precious metals or an alteration of the hitherto-prevailing ratios between different currencies will really cause a change in prices.[1]   For a moment, we are in hopes that he may try to introduce into his analysis the now-familiar theory of the inconstant and *uncertain* connection between money and prices (by way of bank reserves), but he proves to be thinking again only of the retarding effects of custom.[2]

We have now examined at sufficient length the more important bodies of theory that attempt to erect a single unified and comprehensive doctrinal structure with respect to international price adjustments. It remains to consider certain later and more fragmentary contributions.

---

[1] Cf. ch. iv, sect. 6, above.

[2] There are of course many other points of detail which are of interest. See especially, in his *Theory of International Trade* (4 ed., pp. 85–87), the statement that the exchanges may go below the specie point, even under an unrestricted metallic standard, when a stringent money market is coincident with a favorable exchange. So too, less commonly, when in a new country there is an excess of exports, combined with difficulty in getting coined money, as in Australia in 1852–1853. (This is the case cited by Cairnes, and referred to above.) These propositions contrast with Goschen's declaration that in the absence of depreciation or political disturbances, under a gold standard, the rate for sight bills can never pass beyond the specie points.

Bastable also concludes that a disturbance in the equation of international demand may arise from an alteration in conditions which are primarily monetary, as well as from a change in the trade situation. See his article, *On Some Applications of the Theory of International Trade* (cited above), pp. 7–8.

In 1895 Professor Lexis, of Göttingen, published an article in the Economic Journal which re-opened the problem of the effects of dissimilar and depreciating currencies on international prices.[1] Lexis observes that most business men had held that a premium on gold, whether in terms of a paper or of a silver currency, acts as a bounty on export and a duty on import. This was the conclusion which Professor Wagner, making an examination of the Russian situation, had reached as early as 1868.[2] On the other hand many writers, among them Marshall, Pierson, and Levasseur, had disagreed.[3] Lexis himself sides in the main with the dissidents. He declares that no such permanent divergence in world prices as a real bounty on exports would require can ever occur, in view of the rapid transportation and almost instantaneous communication of to-day. Temporary deviations may appear during the period of actual depreciation, it is true, but they tend to produce their own correctives.

Lexis then elaborates this last proposition in an interesting analysis of the processes of adjustment. Under a paper standard, he finds that a fall in the foreign exchange on gold countries, by increasing the premium on gold, tends to stimulate exportation. The gold prices of the paper-country exports abroad will fall (paper prices remaining the same), and the volume taken will therefore presumably increase. Similarly importation will be checked, since the internal (paper) prices of all imports have risen. The stimulus to exports can be effective only if the *general* value of paper money fails to decline within the country to the same extent that it declines relative to gold; but in point of fact this condition is usually realized. The internal value of the paper money at first remains unchanged, and the volume of exports is therefore increased.[4] The excess of exports, however, will produce its own corrective. It leads to a subsequent *rise* in the (gold) value of paper, by improving the exchange quotation and thus decreasing the gold premium. The rise in the value of

---

[1] W. Lexis, *The Agio on Gold and International Trade* (Economic Journal, 1895).

[2] See ch. xiii, sect. 5, below. Wagner's book, *Die russische Papierwährung*, was published in 1868.

[3] Lexis, *loc. cit.*, pp. 532, 533.

[4] *Ibid.*, p. 547.

paper will then tend to decrease exports and increase imports, and in this way will prevent the bounty to exports from becoming permanent.[1] Lexis adds that it is by just such a process as this that a paper money country must meet an adverse balance of international payments. His argument here, however, is less convincing. The adjustment he finds will be attained by a fall in the *gold* value of the paper currency (not, of course, in its internal value), which leads to a surplus of exports. Both conditions continue until the necessary payments are made.[2]

Under a silver standard, however, the process of adjustment is somewhat different. There, given free coinage, exportation may increase considerably without causing a rise in the gold value of silver. This value is determined by the general world market, quite independently of the circumstances of the particular country. The corrective to excess exportation, present in the case of a paper country, is therefore delayed or lacking here.[3] Beyond this, however, Lexis does not carry his analysis, and just what the process of ultimate adjustment is supposed to be is not stated. Presumably we are to fall back on an explanation running in terms of the adjustment of the country's various sorts of prices to the world ratio between gold and silver.

He also offers a certain amount of statistical evidence to support the two chains of reasoning, and arrives at this general conclusion: Whether it be silver or paper, a fall in the value of the given currency relative to gold is accompanied by a continuously-acting relative advantage [4] to exportation from the paper or silver

[1] Lexis, *op. cit.*, p. 536.

[2] *Ibid.*, pp. 547, 548. Lexis makes the interesting and valuable suggestion that this excess is secured quite as much by a decrease of imports as by an increase in exports. (See also *ibid.*, pp. 540–542.) We shall find further confirmation for this view in the Argentine case, discussed below.

[3] *Ibid.*, p. 536.

[4] The term "relative," as suggested above, implies not that exporters necessarily gain in absolute terms, but that they *lose less* than the importers from the depreciation; or that their position remains unchanged, while that of the importers suffers. Thus in the first phase of the depreciation of a paper currency, the exporters were assumed to receive the *same* paper price for their products. They gained only from the increased volume of trade consequent on a fall in *gold* prices. But the importers suffered in both ways: from a decreased volume of trade, and — since the gold price of their imports remained the same — from *higher* paper prices.

country to the gold country, and by a check to importation. The situation, however, is frequently concealed by other sorts of influences, and its effects may in practise fail to be recognizable. Further, the relative advantage to export produced by a falling exchange indicates that the rate of exchange between native and foreign labor is unfavorable. That is, although particular private interests may profit, the country as a whole is at a disadvantage in international trade.[1]

Professor Lexis' analysis is in general closely allied to the trains of reasoning that we have already examined in Goschen and Marshall; closely enough so that we meet it without any marked feeling of unfamiliarity. None the less it is different in several respects. Perhaps its most important feature is the attempt to show that there is a limit of sorts to the depreciation of the exchange on a paper-standard country, or at least that a strong corrective force is at work. This tendency to a correction arises both from the divergence between the paper price of gold and the paper price of goods at large, and from the tendency of the prices of primarily international goods to regain the general internal level. As far as it goes, the point seems to me well taken, though it does not offer a complete mechanism by which, granted internal monetary stability, the exchange rates may be kept near some given point. It provides only for the partial return of the rates after a fall. This stress on the divergence between internal prices and gold prices incidentally brings Lexis close to Marshall's later explanation, examined above, of the temporary bounty created by the divergence between foreign trade prices and domestic costs of production. He misses this last step by very little.

6. A number of years later an American writer, Professor Whitaker, made a further contribution to the general theory of money and international trade.[2] Professor Whitaker's concern

---

[1] Lexis, *op. cit.*, pp. 548, 549.

[2] A. C. Whitaker, *The Ricardian Theory of Gold Movements and Professor Laughlin's Views of Money* (18 Quarterly Journal of Economics, 1904).

The title of the paper is somewhat misleading in its reference to the "Ricardian" theory. The second type of specie movement listed by Professor Whitaker would not have been admitted by Ricardo. "Mill's" theory would have been more correct.

was not with those problems of price adjustments under dissimilar currencies to which the immediately preceding pages have been largely devoted, but with the question of the world distribution of gold.

He first discusses the various types of specie movements. These types, which it is nevertheless often impossible to distinguish in practise, are: (1) producers' shipments, which frequently neither create nor discharge debts, and to that extent do not affect the exchange rates; (2) commercial shipments, which are made to discharge balances of debt, and which are therefore a result of the position of the exchanges; and (3) financial shipments, which are caused by differences between countries in the rate of discount.[1] These last do not discharge debts but *create* them, and are therefore usually followed by a later return movement of gold. They may take either of two forms. They may be direct loans of gold, presumably made upon collateral, which are sent to the center with the higher discount rates in order to benefit by their employment there. (Or, more commonly, to relieve financial strain — in which case the transactions are usually effected between the central banks or Treasuries.) Or they may be made in payment for the purchase of floating international securities. These securities tend to move away from the market having a high discount rate. Gold therefore again moves toward the latter market, but for a different reason. Thus the movement of securities may be only one of several means by which the force of the discount rate is brought to bear on the movements of specie. It may also, however, be due not to financial operations but to genuine long-time international investment. Here too a gold flow would result, but of the "commercial" rather than the "financial" type.

Whitaker then comes to the "national quota" of each country in the world distribution of gold. His general theory here offers nothing very novel, but he undertakes a statistical demonstration that the *relative* quotas of the important commercial nations have tended to remain substantially the same over a period of years.[2]

---

[1] Whitaker, *op. cit.*, pp. 221–226.   [2] *Ibid.*, pp. 226–229.

The proof is not altogether conclusive, perhaps,[1] but it is suggestive in the extreme. These relative quantities, shown to be comparatively constant, seem to have been quite independent of the
accidents of international trade and of the absence or presence of
domestic production of gold. To explain the situation Whitaker
turns to the trade in commodities, and to the adjustment of international prices. Declaring that the gold is distributed almost entirely to make payment for commodities bought in the course of
trade (in other words, that commercial shipments are by far the
most important type of transfers), and that gold tends always to
go to those places where its exchange value is highest, he concludes
that the national quotas of gold are maintained by movements of
the general price levels in the countries concerned.[2] This conclusion he also links up with the balance of international indebtedness. Minor inequalities in the balance may be settled by security
movements or by other palliative devices, but a fundamental disturbance can be corrected only by means of gold flows, price
changes, and an alteration in the commodity balance of trade.[3]
To these doctrines, which are intended simply as an elaboration
of the classical position, the only important objection is the one
which we have made frequently in the preceding pages, in dealing
with other writers — that they are stated in terms of the general
price level, of commodities at large. Had Whitaker here confined
his statement primarily to *international* prices, it would have been
open to much less question.[4]

[1] See Spurgeon Bell, *A Statistical Point in Ricardian Theory of Gold Movements*
[sic] (Journal of Political Economy, 1907). Bell holds that Professor Whitaker's
data do more to cast doubt upon the Ricardian theory than to verify it.

[2] Whitaker, *loc. cit.*, pp. 229, 230.

[3] *Ibid.*, pp. 231, 232. See also H. G. Brown, *International Trade and Exchange*
(New York, 1914), p. 119. Professor Brown is here dealing with the effects on international trade of movements of the exchange rates. He admits that a low rate tends
to stimulate importation, and a high rate exportation, but he declares that the exchange fluctuations are too narrow in range to have a determining influence. It is
"quite likely" that an excess of purchases abroad will not be checked, or give rise to
corresponding purchases by foreigners, until a flow of gold has changed the relative
price levels.

[4] This qualification he introduced some seventeen years later, in his book on
Foreign Exchange (New York, 1921), p. 622. He there says that the "natural" share
of gold belonging to each country, the "national quota," is the quantity which "will

A word may be added as to certain anti-quantitative views of the general process of international price adjustment. The question at issue is the accuracy of the classical price-specie flow analysis, which the writers hitherto discussed had accepted without especial comment. That analysis of course rests on one form or another of the quantity theory, and it has therefore provided an obvious point of attack for the critics of the latter doctrine. Professor Laughlin, for example, bases his rejection of the classical theorem primarily on the declaration that imports of specie cannot affect prices because the specie all goes into bank reserves. An increase in reserves, though making more loans *possible*, does not of itself lead to increased loans.[1] Professor Kinley has concluded that the value of the precious metals is not the same throughout the world, that price changes are not necessarily followed by movements of specie, and that the actual working of the classical theorem is much modified by economic friction.[2] Finally, Dr. Anderson finds that international gold movements are the result of changes in particular prices alone, not in the general level. He even goes so far as to say that changes in most prices do not affect the movement at all, and that the rise in certain sorts of prices will *attract* gold instead of repelling it.[3] To these various views we may accord a certain measure of agreement, for there is clearly no such direct and immediate connection between gold flows and prices as the strict classical proposition implies. The whole question, however, will be examined again in a later chapter.[4]

7. The great majority of the writers hitherto discussed have

make the general price level of the group of *internationally movable* commodities the same here as abroad." (Italics mine.)

[1] J. L. Laughlin, *Principles of Money* (New York, 1903), ch. 10, especially p. 387. This chapter is substantially a reprint of his earlier article on *Prices and the International Movement of Specie* (Journal of Political Economy, 1902). See also Professor Laughlin's recent book, *Money and Prices* (New York, 1919), especially pp. 24–26. For a detailed criticism and statistical refutation of his views see the latter part of Professor Whitaker's article, cited above.

[2] D. Kinley, *Money* (New York, 1904), especially pp. 78–98.

[3] B. M. Anderson, *The Value of Money* (New York, 1917), especially pp. 315–319.

[4] See ch. xvi, sects. 5 and 6, below; and ch. xvii.

approached the problems of international price adjustments from
an essentially deductive standpoint. They have taken over the
theories of Ricardo or of Mill without much hesitation, and have
expanded them or criticized them, in large part, with the aid of
a priori reasoning alone. Within the past five or six years, however, three American writers have made elaborate studies of the
actual mechanisms of such adjustments. Two of the studies deal
with the conditions of trade under depreciated currencies; the
third, with large-scale international borrowing under the gold
standard. They are included in the present chapter, although it is
confined to the years before 1914, because the subject matter of
each of them is found in the earlier period, and because the doctrinal conclusions drawn from them belong in the main to the pre-
war type of analysis. We shall find, in a subsequent chapter, that
the reasoning based on the post-war experience is in many respects
of a quite different order, and concerned with different problems.

Of the studies of trade under depreciated currencies one, by
Professor Graham, deals with the commerce between the United
States and Europe from 1862 to 1879, during the greenback
period; the other, by Professor J. H. Williams, with Argentine
international trade from 1880 to 1900, when Argentina was un-
dergoing a protracted series of monetary upheavals.

Professor Graham's investigation was undertaken as a verification of the conclusions originally put forward by Professor Taussig in 1917, in his paper on international trade under depreciated
paper.[1] Taussig's main thesis had been that in the trade between
a gold country and a country under depreciated paper, inequalities in the balance of international payments will be settled by
changes in the commodity side of the price situation — in the
commodity balance of trade; and that while the final results
will be the same as though both countries were under gold, the
intermediate price movements will be just opposite. These propositions Graham tested by the use of statistical data. In all essentials he found them to be correct: the theory was in the main

---

[1] F. W. Taussig, *International Trade under Depreciated Paper* (31 Quarterly Journal of Economics, 1917). See also the criticism by J. H. Hollander, under the same
title, in vol. 32 of the Journal (1918), and the rejoinder by Professor Taussig.

verified.[1] It would be interesting to present Professor Taussig's argument separately, but the subsequent repetition would be needless. We may therefore turn at once to Graham's work. It must be remembered, however, that while the verification is Graham's, the theoretical analysis itself was Professor Taussig's, and to him belongs the original credit. His work has stood the test of subsequent statistical investigation in all important particulars.

During the period held in view, from 1862 to 1879, the United States was under a régime of inconvertible paper currency consequent on the financial exigencies of the Civil War. After the cessation of hostilities the volume of paper outstanding was gradually reduced, but the paper was never entirely withdrawn, and when resumption was finally achieved in 1879 an important fraction was re-issued. In the earlier part of this period, also, the United States was borrowing heavily and constantly from various European countries, especially England. The crisis of 1873, however, virtually brought an end to the flotation of loans abroad, and from that time on the repayment of interest and principal greatly exceeded the infrequent new borrowings.

Such is the general setting of the problem Graham set out to examine. His principal conclusions as to the nature and results of the processes involved were these. First, he found that the commodity balance of trade (including gold and silver) moved very closely with the course of international borrowing. Exports were slightly in excess of imports prior to the war, and until 1864; but from 1864 to 1873, when the heaviest borrowing was going on, imports were considerably in excess (with the exception of one year). After 1873, on the other hand, when fresh lending had practically ceased, exports were very much in excess. In other words, the purely commodity trade was dominated by these loan operations.[2]

---

[1] F. D. Graham, *International Trade under Depreciated Paper: The United States, 1862–1879* (36 Quarterly Journal of Economics, 1922). Graham's conclusions were first presented in 1919, in his thesis for the Ph.D. degree in Harvard University. See Appendix B, below, for the more important statistics. A manuscript copy can be found in the Harvard University Library.

[2] Graham, *loc. cit.*, pp. 225–234. Graham finds that the "invisible items" either tended to cancel or were quantitatively negligible (p. 226).

Second, the price of gold in terms of the depreciated paper currency also moved closely with the shifts in international borrowing. During the period of active lending, the gold premium was below the general index of wholesale commodity price expressed in paper. After that, it was usually above. The explanation lies in the fact that the price of gold tended to move in sympathy with the rate of sterling exchange, which was of course relatively low (in dollars) while the series of original loans was being transmitted, and relatively high when the repayment operations became dominant. Gold, become under paper a merchandise commodity, was for the purposes of foreign trade equivalent to sterling exchange.[1] Furthermore, in the period of active borrowing the value of gold in terms of paper tended always to rise whenever the rate of borrowing became at all constant. This Graham, like Taussig, attributes to the general increase of commodities in the country consequent on the receipt of the proceeds from the original loans. A further depreciation in the value of gold ensued only when the rate of borrowing was accelerated. These, however, are "long-range" forces, and the effect of their operation was often so delayed as never to appear with real definiteness.[2]

Third, the movements of prices were substantially those which the theory at issue would expect. They were the opposite of those which would appear under a gold standard, but quite similar in their effects.[3] In the period of heavy borrowing as we have just seen, the transmission of the loans caused the gold premium to fall below the general level of wholesale paper prices. But the *gold* prices of American exports and imports, which were set abroad, of course experienced no such change. Their *paper* prices therefore fell relative to the general level of paper prices, because of the decline in the gold premium. (In absolute terms, both sets of prices sometimes rose and sometimes fell, depending on the general state

---

[1] Graham, *op. cit.*, pp. 235–245.

[2] *Ibid.*, p. 241.

[3] Graham's price data are based in the main on quarterly quotations, and the critic may therefore reasonably object if too finely drawn conclusions are derived from them — especially in regard to the delicate question of precedence in time. The validity of the more general inferences that they seem to warrant, however, is not impaired by this consideration.

of the paper currency.) The fall led to increased imports, decreased exports, and to an unfavorable commodity balance of trade. In this way the balance of international *payments*, into which the loans of course entered, was kept in equilibrium. Two qualifications, however, are necessary. First, in so far as competition failed to be effective in foreign markets the gold prices of American exports tended to rise there and their paper prices in the United States to be gradually increased. Second, import and export prices did not fall (relative to the general level, that is) with equal rapidity. At first, the fall in the gold premium simply gave a bounty to American importers, since the conditions of demand had not changed and since they secured the same paper price as before. But competition soon brought these prices down. Export prices, on the other hand, fell at once — though with a slight tendency to recover later, in so far as their gold prices abroad could later be raised.

In the period of repayment, the price of gold was relatively high. Gold prices abroad remained fairly constant. The paper prices of exports were therefore also high, and exportation was stimulated. The paper prices of imports likewise rose, though more gradually (since this rise could be accomplished only at the expense of diminished sales, demand remaining the same), and importation was checked. The commodity balance of trade then became favorable, and the balance of payments was again restored to equilibrium. In the first period, the original transmission of the loans had depressed the exchanges and the gold premium, *lowered* the paper prices of international goods relative to other paper prices in America, and thus so changed the commodity balance of trade that the loans could be made almost entirely in commodities. In this second period, the repayments led to a relative *rise* in the gold premium and in the paper prices of international goods, an overturn of the balance of trade in America's favor, and a repayment again primarily in commodities. The *effects* were precisely those which would appear under gold, but the intervening price changes were thus just the opposite. In the usually accepted theory, for example, the first stage in the initial transmission of a loan would be a flow of gold, a *rise* in prices, and an excess of imports into the borrowing country consequent on the higher price level.[1]

Fourth, the course of the price movements in England, which is taken as typical of the lending, gold-standard countries, was substantially opposite to the movements in the United States. In the borrowing period the prices of British exports tended to be relatively high, for they commanded the same paper prices as before in the United States. Since the gold premium had fallen, this meant higher prices in gold. But under the influence of competition the high prices tended to be forced down. The prices of imports also rose. The gold received by the American exporter now yielded, with a lower premium, less paper money than before, and except in so far as England was able to import similar products from other countries, the price *to her* of the American exports therefore tended to be increased.[2] Thus the necessary excess of English exports over imports was secured. In the more nearly long-run period, also, there was a *general* rise of prices in England, consequent on the relative diminution of commodities and on the relative increase in the amount of money. In the period of repayment the opposite series of changes appeared, and general prices fell.[3]

Fifth, and finally, the course of wages in the United States reflected these various changes in the manner which theory demands. We should ordinarily expect the export industries to be unprosperous during the period of borrowing, relative to those producing for domestic consumption, and we should expect the opposite conditions to prevail in the period of repayment. The best obtainable test of this prosperity or distress is probably rela-

---

[1] Graham, *op. cit.*, pp. 248–252. For the statistical verification, see pp. 252–258. It should be explained that the price movements outlined in the text above are what Graham calls immediate or "transitional" effects. The "long-range" effects tend to compensate and neutralize the transitional effects, but before they can work out, they are usually superseded by a new disturbance and a new set of transitional phenomena.

[2] Graham is guilty of some slight inconsistency here, with respect to the supposed distribution of the gain or loss between American and English traders. In discussing American conditions he regarded the foreign (gold) price as relatively constant, and the paper price as varying. Here, he seems to make the paper price the base. In fact, of course, both will usually vary somewhat.

[3] *Ibid.*, pp. 258–260. For the statistical verification, see pp. 260–265.

tive wage rates, and their actual course in the American case supports the theoretical conclusion. In the first period wages in the export industries were low, relative to the general level of wages; in the second period, they were high.[1]

It is evident that we have here a type of analysis which is quite new not only in its wealth of objective detail, but also in its content. Heretofore the few writers who had given much attention to the problems of trade under depreciated paper had contented themselves, in the main, with more or less dogmatic theoretical statements as to the character of the forces at work, and as to the nature of certain general relationships. Here, on the contrary, we find an elaborate examination of the particular mechanisms involved, and a series of specific propositions dealing with the processes of international price adjustments under disordered monetary conditions. Furthermore, these propositions are supported at each point by statistical evidence drawn from a concrete and well-known case of disturbance. It is a type of investigation which had never before been undertaken on any comprehensive scale, and it has carried the general theory of the subject much beyond its previous level. This is especially true of the discussions of the causes and effects of price movements. It is likewise true of the careful distinction between the various sorts of prices. Earlier writers had in the main tended to speak of "prices in general," or had at most admitted a difference between international and domestic prices. Of the analysis itself, first made deductively by Professor Taussig and then substantially verified by Professor Graham, I shall attempt no criticism. Such a criticism would deal only with certain details which are after all comparatively unimportant. The general conclusions to which the analysis leads do not seem to me to be open to question.

It will not be unprofitable, however, to draw attention to two perhaps minor points which bear on the theoretical interpretation of such cases in general, and which limit the range of applicability of these conclusions. The points concern two assumptions which underlay Professor Taussig's *a priori* reasoning, and one of which, at least, was unstated. In the first place, Professor Taussig de-

[1] Graham, *op. cit.*, pp. 265–272.

liberately supposes that the amount of money in the borrowing country — here the United States — either remains constant, or at the least is not the chief source of disturbance in prices and trade. But conditions may evidently exist, such as those prevailing since 1918, under which the effects of the borrowing operations are completely engulfed by the effects of purely *internal* monetary disturbances. It may then become necessary to include factors other than those hitherto considered, in the explanation of the way in which the capital transfers are effected.

In the second place, Professor Taussig's discussion seems to carry with it an adherence to the purchasing-power-parity doctrine, since exchange rates and the gold premium are regarded as being "high" or "low" according to the relation they bear to presumptive price parities. In the American case, however, the prices of *international* commodities were consistently lower than the prices of domestic articles until well after the new borrowing had ceased — when they moved *above* domestic prices. This seems to indicate that it is in general the movements of international prices (including the price of gold) relative to domestic prices, rather than the movements of the exchanges and the gold premium relative to the price parities, that are the significant feature in the situation. While the second class of movements will not necessarily alter the ratio between exportation and importation, the first clearly does. The price parities, that is, can be disregarded. This point will be elaborated later.

8. The second empirical investigation of international trade under depreciated paper, made by Professor Williams, presents a somewhat different sort of case.[1] It is concerned with the payment balances of Argentina from 1880 to 1900. Argentina was under a paper régime in the period selected, and, like the United States in the case just examined, was engaged in heavy and continuous borrowing operations. But whereas in the United States the foreign exchanges were badly dislocated, in Argentina they were not. Throughout the years of depreciation, a gold exchange was

---

[1] J. H. Williams, *Argentine International Trade, 1880–1900* (Cambridge, 1920). It may be remarked that this study, like Graham's, was carried out under Professor Taussig's guidance. The principal data are given in Appendix B, below.

maintained with Europe. The exchanges did not depreciate, a gold par and the corresponding specie points continued effective, and while gold of course could not enter the local currency, it was very far from being driven out of the country. There were in effect not one but *two* currencies in circulation. Gold was used for international transactions, while paper was used for internal transactions and for the purchase of gold within the country. An Argentine importer who had remittances to make abroad bought gold with his paper money, and with the gold bought foreign exchange, while an exporter would buy gold with his bill and then convert the gold into paper. The Argentine gold peso itself continued to be bought and sold in large quantities on the stock exchange. The gold par, which was genuinely operative throughout the entire period of depreciation, was the ordinary par between this gold peso and the foreign moneys. That is, the depreciation itself did not affect the exchanges.[1] Gold of course stood, however, at a premium in terms of paper.

The general character of the price movements in the Argentine case, and the adjustments of international prices themselves, were substantially like those in the American case, and need not be restated. The remittance of the original payments of the Argentine loans led to a fall in the gold premium and in the paper prices of international goods; to a large excess of imports; and to the consequent transmission of the bulk of the loans in the form of commodities. The distinguishing feature of the situation arose, rather, in connection with the part played by gold in this process, and with its direct effect upon the value of the local paper money.

The value of gold in terms of paper was a resultant of two conditions. First, it depended upon the quantity of paper money out-

---

[1] Williams, *op. cit.*, pp. 17–20. It is not easy to account for this somewhat unusual situation. It was presumably made possible by the borrowing operations, and by the consequent tendency to a favorable commodity balance of trade, which in the earlier years prevented any marked drain of gold into other countries. But that is not of itself an adequate explanation. The answer is probably to be found in the economic backwardness and lack of homogeneity of Argentina at the time. From the monetary and financial point of view, she was not an economic unit. It would therefore be possible for the foreign-trade centers to use gold as a second currency, *without* having the gold become diffused into the paper-using interior — where it would have disappeared either from hoarding, or from unnoticed foreign drains.

standing. This controlled the value of paper itself in terms of the various sorts of commodities. Second, it depended upon the balance of international payments. The balance of payments governed the fluctuating volume of the imports of international goods, and hence their value in paper. Gold, unlike its rôle in the American situation, *continued* to be one such commercial import. The premium on gold, therefore, depended both on the (commodity) value of paper money and on the supply of gold as determined by the conditions of international trade.[1] Of these the latter seems to have been somewhat the more important, since during a period of at least five years (1891–1896) there appears to have been no correspondence whatever between the amount of paper money in circulation and the premium.[2] It also followed that an inflow of gold had an effect on prices precisely opposite to that which would usually be expected under a gold standard. Gold could enter the *country*, but not the *currency*. Its influx therefore produced a decrease in the premium on gold in terms of paper, and a fall in the gold prices of international goods.[3] It should be added, however, that this result is in no wise different from that produced by the inflow of any other commodity whatsoever, with respect to the value of that commodity in terms of paper money. It is only because gold is an international currency that its behavior is singled out for especial attention.

The chain of events therefore seems to have been this. The heavy and continued foreign borrowings of Argentina dominated the balance of its international payments, and made necessary a continuous flow of remittances from Europe. The exchanges, which remained upon a gold basis, fell to the gold import point. International commodities, including gold, then flowed in. The premium on gold diminished, and the gold prices of international commodities likewise fell. Exports reacted quickly. Their paper prices were lowered, and their volume lessened. Imports followed suit more slowly, but their volume was soon increased. The commodity balance of trade was thus so adjusted that the major part of the loans could be remitted simply in commodities. In a later period, when the process of repayment had gotten under way,

---

[1] Williams, *op. cit.*, pp. 9, 10, 17, 18.   [2] *Ibid.*, pp. 145, 146.   [3] *Ibid.*, p. 21.

these effects were gradually reversed, and the commodity balance was overturned. This last change was accomplished in part by an actual stimulus to exports, arising from the divergence between international prices and domestic costs of production (a point to which Marshall had called attention). But Professor Williams finds that the principal cause of the overturn was not an increase in exports but a *decrease in imports*, consequent on that rising premium on gold to which the repayment operations had led. The increased premium, of course, entailed a fall in the paper prices of imports. If the conditions of demand be supposed not to have changed materially, the former level of import prices could therefore have been regained only by a decrease in the volume of goods imported.[1] The statistical proof of this proposition, although somewhat weakened by the difficulty in securing adequate data, seems fairly definite.

9. The third and most recent study of the processes by which international trade and international prices are adjusted to prolonged disturbances, made by Professor Viner, is free from the complexities introduced by the presence of monetary depreciation. It deals with the history of Canadian foreign borrowing in the decade and a half before the war, and can be taken as a fair sample of the first phase of a borrowing operation under "normal" conditions. The loans dominated the course of Canadian foreign trade in these years, and were one of the principal factors controlling the internal growth of Canada. The case reveals with especial clarity the nature of the more characteristic changes involved.

Throughout the period from 1900 to 1913 Canada was borrowing heavily and at a rapidly increasing rate from various foreign countries, of which the chief was England. The purpose of Professor Viner's investigation[2] is to discover just how the loans were transmitted, what the process of adjustment in international trade must have been, and whether or not the corresponding part of the deductive classical theory of international trade is verified by the resulting data. It will be remembered that that theory, in

[1] Williams, *op. cit.*, pp. 253, 256.

[2] J. Viner, *Canada's Balance of International Indebtedness, 1900–1913* (Cambridge, 1924). The statistics especially relevant here are presented in Appendix B, below.

the form imparted by Mill, holds that the attempt to transmit the loans will lead to specie flows; this to price changes in the lending and in the borrowing countries; and this to a shift in the commodity balance of trade, of such a character that the bulk of the loan is transferred in the form of commodities.[1]

This theory Viner concludes is effectively verified by the facts in the Canadian experience, though with certain modifications. In consequence of the borrowing operations, the Canadian banks acquired an increasing amount of gold. Bank deposits and purely "domestic" prices rose steadily, whereas export prices rose somewhat less and import prices very little.[2] Finally, the commodity balance of trade became permanently "unfavorable" after 1902.[3] It thus became possible to transfer a large part of the loan in commodities. If Viner's data be examined more closely, however, it will be found that for the period as a whole only 49 per cent of the loans can be accounted for by the excess of imports over exports. Of the balance, 7 per cent was accounted for by a debit excess of freight charges, 2 per cent in other ways, and the biggest fraction, 42 per cent, by Canadian interest payments on *prior* loans in each given year (and by a small volume of new lending by Canada).[4] These percentages are interesting, for they show how rapidly interest charges begin to catch up with even a large volume of new foreign investment, and how transitory any one shift

---

[1] It will also be remembered that Mill's version of the process of adjustment, taken over from Thornton, differed materially from Ricardo's. Ricardo held that an automatic shift in relative demands would take place. (See ch. iii, sects. 5 and 7, above.) Bastable, however, had rather hesitantly sided with Ricardo (see sect. 5, above). The difference between the two positions is elaborately and clearly discussed by Viner: *op. cit.*, pp. 191–206.

Mill himself did not apply his conclusions to the problem of borrowing. He was discussing subsidies, tributes, and other non-commercial remittances. (See Mill's *Principles*, Bk. III, ch. 21, sect. 4.)

[2] Viner, *op. cit.*, p. 230. With 1900 = 100, the wholesale price indices were: domestic 161.7; export 133.9; import 114.1.

[3] *Ibid.*, p. 95.

[4] *Ibid.*, pp. 95, 101. Viner does not compute these percentages himself.

The correction in the trade balance was secured by a triangular adjustment. With England, whence most of the loans came, Canada had an *export* surplus. But with the United States, from whom she borrowed comparatively little, she had a large *import* surplus; a surplus more than twice the size of the American loans, on the average. See p. 281.

in the balance of trade must be. The situation, except momentarily, is constantly changing. Cairnes's doctrine, setting up some three distinct phases in the borrowing operation, is apparently useful chiefly as a conceptual aid alone.

The more difficult part of the analysis, however, turns on the question of how these changes in the commodity balance were brought about. The situation was peculiar, for the financial operations involved in the transmission of the loans were triangular. Instead of being effected directly between London and Montreal, they were effected through New York. Viner concludes that

the fluctuations in the outside reserves of the Canadian banks [chiefly deposits in New York] operate to adjust the Canadian balance of payments to capital borrowings in the manner attributed to gold movements in the generally accepted explanation of the mechanism of international trade.[1]

That is, in so far as the increasingly unfavorable balance of trade *failed* to keep pace with the new borrowings, it was to be expected that the outside reserves would be built up, and that this would correct the trade situation — as the orthodox theory assumed that gold flows would do — by inducing a rise in Canadian prices.[2]

But, although Viner's verification of the general theory seems to me conclusive on other points, I think that it breaks down on this question of the intermediary financial mechanisms. Neither the statistical data submitted [3] nor the reasoning based upon them show any clear sequence *from* the outside reserves *to* credit and price conditions within Canada itself. Outside reserves moved closely with bank deposits in Canada, and showed no independent relationship to prices. Rather, the sequence must have been that which Viner himself rather hesitantly suggests at another point.[4] The Canadian borrowers, having sterling funds at their disposal, deposited them with the Canadian banks (except in so far as the loans were spent in England). These funds, thus converted into Canadian currency and credit, were spent in Canada and induced a rise in prices; a rise which roughly adjusted the commodity balance of trade to the volume of new borrowings.[5] The

---

[1] Viner, *op. cit.*, p. 178.
[2] Cf. p. 184.
[3] For example, on pp. 161, 165–167.
[4] *Ibid.*, pp. 177–181.
[5] A *net* increase in deposits ensued, however, only in so far as the shift in the balance of trade did not keep up with the *increase* in the annual volume of borrowings;

Canadian banks recouped themselves by selling the sterling funds in New York, the proceeds being left there or taken back to Canada as needed. It does not appear from the data, however, that these changes in the *New York* balances had any direct and independent effect upon conditions within Canada. By providing potential additional metallic reserves, their increase made a Canadian credit expansion *possible*, but there is no convincing evidence, inductive or deductive, to show that it provided the initial stimulus to expansion. The stimulus came, rather, from the original increase in bank deposits within Canada itself.[1] With respect to gold flows, finally, Viner himself shows that they played an altogether minor and dependent part. Those from New York to Montreal were the result of the prior expansion of Canadian bank deposits. Those from London to New York, so far as they were dependent on the Canadian loans, were the result of the state of the balance of payments.

I do not intend by this to deny the general classical theory of the adjustment of international trade to protracted disturbances. The movements of prices in the Canadian case, and the shift in the trade balance, were substantially those which it would lead us

and vice versa. When it did keep up no change appeared, in total deposits or in prices, that was traceable to the borrowing operations. These propositions can be deduced from the data on pp. 103, 166, 186, and 220 of Professor Viner's book. A more elaborate statistical defense of them will be found in Appendix B, below.

[1] These conclusions will be defended at greater length in Appendix B, below, on the international transfer of capital. What seems to me to be the correct explanation of the process of adjustment in the balance of payments, which it is possible to outline only very summarily here, is elaborated in ch. xvi, especially sect. 3, below.

The crux of the explanation is the proposition that the importation of capital increases the supply of bills offered in the local exchange market for discount relative to the demand, thus increasing the bank's average holdings of such bills. A corresponding increase in the volume of bank deposits results, and if it is on a large scale produces the indicated effects on prices and the commodity balance of trade.

What really affects prices, of course, is not simply changes in bank deposits but changes in the *total* volume of purchasing power in circulation. Of the latter bank deposits are not an accurate index in short periods, because the distribution of currency itself, between reserves and active circulation, changes materially. But in longer periods (the data here are annual only) those fluctuations in money in circulation which do not correspond to the general movements of bank deposits tend to be smoothed over. Deposits can therefore be used as an index in such periods without serious distortion.

to expect. But I think that Professor Viner's data warrant the inference — despite the opposite conclusion which he himself draws — that the classical theory is erroneous with respect to the rôle of gold flows, under modern conditions. The correction of the maladjustment in trade produced by the loans did not come from the effects of the gold flows, or of changes in the outside bank balances. It came from the effects of the original (and prior) increase in Canadian bank deposits. This conclusion, if it be accepted, evidently has an important bearing on the whole problem of the correction of large disturbances in trade. It deprives gold flows of any effective causal connection with price movements and shifts in the balance of trade, and makes them simply a function of exchange market conditions or of the need for metallic bank reserves. The initial and significant changes, when the disturbance is great enough to require a correction in prices and the trade balance, are rather those in bank deposits. The connection between such changes and general prices is direct and immediate.[1] This point will be elaborated, however, in a later chapter.

10. We may now recapitulate the principal conclusions suggested by this review of the theories of international price adjustments.

The more general and primarily deductive speculations with which we were concerned earlier in the chapter have proved to be somewhat indefinite in their results. The classical price-specie flow theorem has emerged with an overwhelming weight of opinion in its favor, but certain inconsistencies with the (intra-national) monetary theories of the various writers concerned apparently exist. The post-classical statements of the theorem are correspondingly impaired by their failure to take full account

[1] In the case of a protracted import "excess," relative to current commercial and financial conditions, a *decrease* in total deposits will appear, and a consequent fall in prices. The necessary debit international payments will be effected through temporary transfers of bank balances, securities, and even gold, until the commodity balance of trade has shifted sufficiently. One or more other countries and financial centers will usually be involved in the adjustment.

Evidently any such analysis, however, must also be conditioned by the position of the countries in their respective business cycles. It can be made in unqualified form only with respect to periods longer than the cycle.

of the recent refinements in these doctrines. On the other hand, Cairnes's descriptive work confirmed rather than weakened the classical analysis of the way in which large price movements are transmitted from country to country, and Goschen, by shifting the emphasis from commodity prices and movements to the foreign exchanges and discount rates, added greatly to the realistic character of the propositions dealing with the creation and maintenance of equilibria in foreign trade. Finally, for the case of international borrowings at least, Viner's work has convincingly verified the general theory of the way in which large and enduring disturbances in foreign trade are corrected — that is, through price changes and the consequent shifts in the balance of trade. Grounds were suggested, however, for questioning Viner's conclusions as to the nature of the intermediary financial mechanisms, and indeed for rejecting the whole classical explanation of the rôle of gold flows.

In the field of trade under dissimilar and fluctuating currencies, certain propositions have met with general approval. It has been agreed that no permanent stimulus or check to trade can arise from a mere alteration in the value of the currency, but a temporary influence is admitted. Both the source and the duration of this influence, however, are debated. Professor Nicholson makes it long, and traces it to a discrepancy between the inter-currency and the inter-price ratio. Professor Marshall makes it shorter, and explains it by the lag of internal costs of production behind prices. With respect to the general cause of the disorder, recourse is usually had to some form of the quantity theory. The depreciation of the exchanges, that is, is explained in terms of a prior depreciation of the currency itself. Only Goschen, who thereby provided the point of departure for many Continental theorists, suggests that the initial cause of the disturbance may be a continued excess of imports. Finally, the doctrine of a world equalization of prices, as far as countries under *dissimilar* currencies are concerned, has in growing degree been confined to the prices of actively traded commodities and to quotations at the seaports. No other general conclusions, however, seem to have emerged. Nor has any comprehensive deductive study of the theory of foreign trade under dissimilar and fluctuating currencies been attempted. That task has been left to Continental writers.

The results secured by the two statistical examinations of the actual conditions of trade under disordered currencies have been much more definite and convincing. First, and by far the most important, they have provided an elaborate explanation of the causes, character and effects of the various price movements produced by a radical disturbance in the general conditions of trade. The investigations agree as to the essential features of these movements. The effects themselves are found to be the same as those which would appear under a gold standard, but the direction of the various changes is precisely the opposite. Second, they have shown that the three major groups of prices — import, export, and domestic — move in quite different ways, and without any very immediate connection between the first two groups and the last. The adjustment of the commodity balance of trade and of the balance of payments, far from operating by means of general changes in commodity prices as a whole, seems to depend for its effectiveness very largely upon the results of *differences* between the direction and degree of the various sorts of price movements. Further, the premium on gold — become under paper simply one of a number of international commodities — necessarily follows more or less closely the fluctuations of international prices at large, especially those of the exchange rates. To these points we shall have occasion to return in a later chapter. Third, Professor Williams's work has brought out the fact that there is no *necessary* connection between a depreciation of the currency and the position of the exchange rates. Under certain conditions, the monetary disturbance may completely fail to find reflection in a dislocation of the exchanges. Finally, it also shows that the overturn of the trade balance consequent on a rising premium on gold may be due not so much to the stimulus to exports, as to the discouragement of *imports*. This aspect of the question earlier writers had rather neglected.

We have now completed our survey of the development, in the pre-war English and American literatures, of the three principal elements that enter into the theory of international prices. These elements are the domestic theory of money and prices, the theory of ratios of inter-commodity exchange in foreign trade, and the various analyses of international price adjustments under similar and dissimilar monetary conditions. It remains to give some account of the frequently chaotic body of doctrines that have emerged since the war. In the main, these doctrines are oriented by the unprecedented economic upheavals that the war itself brought about. It will therefore not seem unnatural if their conclusions, and even the very problems which they attempt to solve, prove to be of a somewhat different order from those with which we have hitherto been occupied. The link with the past literature, if not actually severed, has at the least become tenuous.

CHAPTER VII

THEORIES OF PRICES AND THE EXCHANGES SINCE 1914

1. The dramatic and almost incredible course of events since 1914 has necessarily led to various changes in the doctrinal elements that enter the theory of international prices, and to various additions to its content. It is true that these changes and additions have on the whole been on lines already long marked out. In the English and American literatures at least, no radically new types of thought have been developed. But a further chapter has been added to the world's history of depreciation, a chapter containing the record of monetary upheavals of hitherto unprecedented severity and scope. Before the war the doctrines intended to explain such upheavals were based largely on depreciations that would now be regarded as comparatively moderate. From these the more recent experiences have differed, in the first instance, only in degree. The quantitative difference has in some cases been so great, however, as to be really qualitative as well. It has become necessary to take account of forces and conditions which had previously failed to assume a dominating rôle, or even to be recognized. Of these perhaps the most conspicuous is the effect of widespread anticipation on the movements of prices, the foreign exchanges and the quantity of money in circulation.

The theory of money and prices as such, treated without reference to the special problem of depreciation, has also received a certain amount of attention. It will be convenient to review the discussions in this field first, in order to secure as complete a picture as possible of the general monetary conceptions from which discussions of the question of disordered currencies and exchanges have ordinarily started.

2. The quantity theory of money, in the general form made familiar by Professor Fisher, has been examined by a number of writers in the past ten years, and important modifications have been suggested. Various criticisms, some of them already referred to in an earlier chapter, have been offered by Anderson,[1] Davies,[2] and again by Laughlin.[3] Pigou, on the other hand, has set up a formula which is unlike Fisher's, but which agrees with it as to what the essentials are.[4] Pigou makes no attempt, however, to establish a particular sequence of events. He specifically declares that his formula is simply designed as a summary, in compact and orderly form, of the principal factors in the situation. The analysis also turns on the demand and supply of *titles* to legal tender, rather than of currency itself.

Keynes has offered a still different approach,[5] which nevertheless retains most of the elements in Fisher's Equation (although they are divided somewhat differently), and which is not inconsistent with it. He selects four elements. They are the number of monetary units in circulation, the reserve ratio of the banks, the amount of "real balances" or consumption-units (based on standard articles of expenditure) that the public chooses to keep in cash, and the amount kept in the banks. If these items be designated respectively by the letters n, r, k, k^1, and prices by p, then:

$$n = p(k + rk^1)$$

Such a formula as this, when actual data are substituted as far as possible for the letters, is of evident use in the problem of controlling price fluctuations, for it shows where pressure can be

---

[1] B. M. Anderson, *The Value of Money* (New York, 1917). Also see the criticism of this work by Walter Stewart: *Social Value and the Theory of Money* (Journal of Political Economy, 1917). Dr. Anderson has been a frequent critic of the quantity theory, and has recently arraigned it vigorously in another connection. See his essay, *The Gold Standard versus "A Managed Currency"* (Chase Economic Bulletin, March 23, 1923).

[2] J. M. Davies, *The Quantity Theory and Recent Statistical Studies* (Journal of Political Economy, 1921).

[3] J. L. Laughlin, *Money and Prices* (New York, 1919); *The Quantity-Theory of Money* (Journal of Political Economy, 1924).

[4] A. C. Pigou, *The Value of Money* (32 Quarterly Journal of Economics, 1917).

[5] J. M. Keynes, *Monetary Reform* (American edition: New York, 1924), pp. 81–92. Keynes's ideas here are adapted in the first instance from Marshall and Pigou, but they also suggest something of Hawtrey's characteristic approach—as see below.

Something will be said at a later point with respect to Keynes's observations on the conditions in a period of severe and progressive depreciation.

applied most effectively. The question can fairly be asked, however whether it will do this at the critical time — in *advance* of actual price changes. Moreover, it is so stated that it conceals the changes in three other highly important and partly independent variables in the price situation. These are the levels of money incomes, the volume of transactions, and the velocity of circulation of money and bank deposits. Keynes's "real balance" includes too much. We also need to know something of the movements of each of these last elements taken separately.[1]

Fisher's Equation of Exchange itself has been reviewed by several writers. Professor Working, on the basis of a statistical study of the period 1890–1916, has concluded that both it and the "causal" formulation of the quantity theory are substantially correct.[2] He starts from the interesting premise, apparently borne out by the facts, that the relation between V and T (velocity of circulation and volume of transactions) *changes* at a fairly uniform rate. Disturbances in the rate of change are corrected through the effects of changes in prices. That is, the relation can be expressed as a constant of the second order, changes in one of the two factors being accompanied by a corresponding change in the other. Another recent writer, Mr. Carl Snyder of the New York Federal Reserve Bank, has also worked over a considerable mass of data that go back to 1875, and on the basis of ingenious indices has shown that the velocity of circulation of bank deposits is both a dominant and a highly variable factor in the price situation.[3] His results fit into Fisher's formula, however, and can

---

[1] A more comprehensive formulation of this sort was suggested by Professor Schumpeter in 1918. See ch. xiii, sect. 2, below. Also see the discussions of Hawtrey's ideas later in the present chapter.

[2] H. Working, *Prices and the Quantity of Circulating Medium* (37 Quarterly Journal of Economics, 1923). Professor Working also takes his results as showing the possibility of *predicting*, roughly one year in advance, the changes in prices. No complete explanation is given, however, for the existence of an interval of this length. Moreover, in the 27 years examined 12 show a *coincidence* of the actual and calculated price levels, not a precedence, and 2 indicate a lack of definite relationship. Only 13 show an unmistakable annual precedence. This proportion is not large enough to be convincing. Finally, the possible cyclical approach is entirely omitted.

[3] See especially his articles, *New Measures in the Equation of Exchange* (American Economic Review, 1924); *A New Index of Business Activity* (Journal of the Ameri-

in general be taken as a confirmation of the quantity-theory approach.

Reference must also be made to the growing number of studies of the business cycle.[1] It is true that these studies, although based on exhaustive data and on most elaborate statistical methods, have not yet led to general conclusions that are widely accepted. Nor has any detailed attempt been made to relate them to the problems and doctrines of the theory of money and prices itself. But that such a relationship must exist is self-evident. It is therefore both legitimate and even necessary to include such investigations under the head of contributions to this theory, inadequately defined though the nature of the contribution still is. Until more positive results are reached, however, it is sufficient to call attention to the further problems that the literature raises.

3. In England, as in the United States, the recent development of monetary theory has in general followed along the lines laid down before the war. The work of Pigou and Keynes, just commented on, ultimately derives in large part from the formulation of J. S. Mill. The complementary type of analysis usually associated with the name of the late Professor Marshall, perhaps more characteristic of present-day English thinking, has been elaborately restated at the hands of Hawtrey, and later by Marshall himself. Hawtrey, indeed, has pushed it through to striking conclusions that are far beyond the scope of the original doctrine. Various other writers, notably Professor Cannan, have also made contributions at special points. The only systematic and comprehensive treatments of the subject not already discussed, however, have been those of Marshall and Hawtrey.

can Statistical Association, 1924); and *A New Index of the General Price Level from 1875* (in the same volume of that Journal).

Reference should likewise be made to an article by W. R. Burgess, also of the New York Federal Reserve Bank: *The Velocity of Bank Deposits* (Journal of the American Statistical Association, 1923). I take it that Burgess's and Snyder's results were worked out more or less together.

[1] It is of course impossible to review the literature of the subject here. The best-known American investigations have been W. C. Mitchell's *Business Cycles* (1914); and W. M. Persons's *Indices of General Business Conditions* (Review of Economic Statistics, 1919), and subsequent articles.

Professor Marshall's book [1] is in large part a compilation and codification of his earlier scattered writings in the field, drawn from his essays, from the "Principles," and from his evidence before various government commissions. It is really a formalization of ideas that, especially through his university teaching, have been familiar to students of these questions for many years past.[2] It inevitably seems lacking in novelty, for the very reason that its doctrines have so long been an unquestioned part of the mental equipment of most English economists, and of not a few American. On matters of monetary theory, and of the mechanisms of international exchange relationships, it contains little of which some account has not been given in earlier chapters. That very fact, which makes further comment here unnecessary, is itself an adequate tribute to the magnitude of Professor Marshall's achievement.

Hawtrey's book is of a quite different order.[3] It is probably the most important single contribution to abstract monetary theory that has been made since before the great war. Yet the frequent obscurity of the exposition makes its comprehension difficult, and criticism sometimes impossible.

The striking aspect of the study lies not so much in its analyses of specific mechanisms as in its general point of view, and in its method of approach. Hawtrey manages to get almost entirely away from that too-familiar terminology and logical apparatus, which constant repetition in the long series of post-classical treatises has made so monotonous and so lifeless. In the first place, he selects as the logical (if not the historical) point of departure, for his examination of the general monetary economy, the conception of debts, not the conception of money. He finds that dealing in debts, the operations of the banker, are the phenomena of pri-

---

[1] A. Marshall, *Money Credit and Commerce* (London, 1923).

[2] Cf. J. M. Keynes, *Alfred Marshall, 1842-1924* (Economic Journal, 1924), p. 327, and p. 337, note. See ch. v, sect. 4, and ch. vi, sect. 4, above.

[3] R. G. Hawtrey, *Currency and Credit* (London, 1919; 2 ed. 1923). For an enlightening review and criticism see A. A. Young, *Hawtrey, Currency and Credit; Fisher, Stabilizing the Dollar* (34 Quarterly Journal of Economics, 1920). I have drawn heavily on this article here, and still more heavily on Professor Young's discussions of the book in his class in Harvard University during the spring of 1921.

mary importance, while the exchange of (legal) money itself plays but a secondary rôle.[1] This view evidently leads to the nominalistic position. In the second place, Hawtrey concentrates the greater part of his attention on consumers' income, consumers' outlay, and the effects of changes in the difference between them.[2] The older machinery, of quantities of money and goods and transactions, is thus put into the background at the outset. We hear little of it in the subsequent discussion.

The emphasis placed on these last factors provides the key to Hawtrey's whole argument. To put this argument into a single phrase, he finds that the changing difference between consumers' income and consumers' outlay is the principal factor governing the course of prices. This difference is called the "unspent margin." It can be equated to all the money in circulation, plus all the bank credit outstanding.[3] A change in its size, as from an expansion of bank credit or from an importation of specie, will produce a substantially corresponding change in the unspent margin, and hence in prices.[4]

These, however, are rather general conceptions. Hawtrey therefore turns next to the actual mechanisms involved, and at once reveals his kinship with Marshall. In a period of credit expansion, the successive steps are held to be these: increased activity of business, a consequent augmentation of consumers' incomes, a forcing up of prices, a gradual drain of money from bank reserves into circulation, accompanied by rising discount rates; and eventually, as a result of this last, the initiation of

[1] Hawtrey, *op. cit.*, 1 ed., pp. 4, 5, 17.

[2] *Ibid.*, pp. 10–13, and *passim*.

[3] *Ibid.*, pp. 34, 35, 39.

[4] *Ibid.*, pp. 44–46. In a static condition of affairs the correspondence will be exact, and the quantity theory, in this form, rigidly true.

Hawtrey's own conception of the quantity theory, however, is far from satisfactory. See for example the confused statement on p. 48, in which he declares that "it is better to limit the rigorous quantity theory [by neglecting total money transactions and velocity of circulation] to the bare arithmetical relation between the unit of value and the quantities measured by it, and to approach the more complex problem presented by the variation of economic conditions from the standpoint of the influences which may affect balances of cash or credit." This seems to leave very little of the theory itself for working purposes.

effective contraction in bank credit and in consumers' outlays.[1] The critical features in the sequence of events are: first, the changing relation between consumers' incomes and consumers' outlay; and second, what Hawtrey calls "latent" demands. These latent demands arise from the initial lag of outlays behind income, and from the fact that new orders to manufacturers are not immediately reflected in increased demands for bank credit — not until after extant orders have been filled. It therefore follows that the original expansion of bank credit does not *at once* bring a restraining pressure to bear on the banks. They do not begin to experience the drain from their reserves, and the simultaneous burden imposed by a growing deposit structure, until after a certain interval has elapsed. In this fact lies the danger of the situation, for evidently the expansion may get entirely out of hand before its existence is generally perceived. Moreover, the measures taken by the banks to enforce contraction will likewise not be immediately effective. For some little time after the elevation of the discount rate, the latent demands will continue to be felt, and will further imperil the position of the banking system.[2]

In case this analysis seems to the reader obscure, it may be pointed out that the "unspent margin" of course actually affects prices only by *being spent.* If the rate at which it is being used up is increasing, or even merely constant, prices may continue to rise in the face of a decline in the rate at which bank credit is being created; in the face, that is, of a decline in the quantity of media of exchange in circulation. It should also be borne in mind that Hawtrey's theories are essentially short-time throughout. His interest is in business crises and cycles, in their analysis and their control.

Finally, Hawtrey comes to the international aspects of his prob-

[1] Hawtrey, *op. cit.*, pp. 61–66; also pp. 86, 91 ff. The effects of a crop failure, and of international borrowing, are submitted here to a similar analysis. In the latter case, however, the mechanism of the international relationships which Hawtrey outlines is fragmentary.

[2] *Ibid.*, p. 86. How long the time intervals of the analysis outlined in this paragraph are supposed to be, however, is not clear. On p. 89 Hawtrey speaks of a drain of cash resulting from a too lavish credit creation that occurred "long before," but this may mean almost anything.

lem. He stresses the interdependence of the principal financial centers, and propounds a theory of world-wide credit and price movements.[1] The essence of the doctrine is simply that a credit expansion in one country leads to rising prices, relatively increased imports, and drains of specie, which in turn serve in the receiving countries as the basis for new credit expansions there. A credit contraction produces opposite and even more clearly accentuated effects. It must be remarked, however, that such data as we have by no means conclusively establish the fact of simultaneity in the cyclical fluctuations of credit and prices in different countries. There is at least a certain amount of evidence to show that they move in opposite directions.

If we take Hawtrey's position as a whole, it is evident that it offers something quite new, something which previous writers never expressed and rarely hinted at. Yet, to repeat an earlier observation, the importance of Hawtrey's work lies in its general point of view and in its qualitative stress on certain neglected elements in the situation, rather than in the content of the specific doctrines advanced. The discussions of the concrete mechanisms involved in the domestic expansion and contraction of credit are, it is true, of the greatest value, but with respect to the problems of international exchange (so far as it is distinct from these last matters) comparatively little that is conclusive has been added. Moreover, the theory of the "unspent margin" is extremely difficult to reduce to terms of daily experience. I do not deny for a moment the value and even the accuracy of the concept itself, but I question its significance as a usable description of actual market phenomena. The addition of the formula drawn up by Keynes, however, can perhaps be regarded as a key to the solution of this difficulty.[2] Finally, Hawtrey leaves one in considerable doubt as to just what he really conceives the relationship between money,

---

[1] See Hawtrey, *op. cit.*, chs. 6, 9, 10, *passim;* especially, for example, pp. 137, 162. The argument, however, is scattered.

Attention may also be called to Hawtrey's more detailed discussion of the relations between credit expansions or contractions and the international movements of goods and capital, as on pp. 91–95; and of the relations between the total consumers' outlay of a country and its share in the products of the world market (pp. 66–68).

[2] See sect. 2, above.

credit and prices to be. The older form of quantity theory is taken away, but the character of the substitute is not quite clear. Unlike Marshall, he does not offer even the proportion of change in bank reserves as a possible loose index of future changes in prices and credit. Nor does the frequent shift in the basis of the argument, from the gold standard to paper and back again, help to diminish the reader's uncertainty.

4. The monetary theories hitherto considered have in the first instance been based largely on the assumption that the currency standard was either stable, or at least not subject to great and sudden fluctuations.[1] Such fluctuations introduce elements that are incapable of quantitative treatment. Indeed, in the more extreme cases at least, they make any form of designedly mechanistic analysis seem rather beside the point. Even where the disturbance is comparatively moderate, one factor must be accounted for which the older forms of price-money theory entirely ignored. This is the effects of movements in the foreign exchanges. It therefore follows that when we turn to the doctrines that have been explicitly based on the actual experience of the past few years, we find a somewhat different range of facts and problems coming up for explanation and solution. Money, prices, the foreign exchanges and the course of international trade all become simply different aspects of one central phenomenon, depreciation.

In England and the United States, the discussion of these questions has turned very largely on the purchasing-power-parity theory. The majority of writers have found in it the key to the complex relationships which history and statistics have revealed, while those who have adhered to some other doctrine have in the main presented their evidence in terms of a refutation of its propositions.

The purchasing-power-parity theory was first developed over a century ago, it will be remembered, at the time of the Bullion Controversy in England.[2] Revived during the war by Professor

---

[1] This assertion is of course not true of Keynes's formulation, and not altogether of Hawtrey's. But it is entirely valid with respect to those "causal" statements of the quantity theory that are patterned on Professor Fisher's Equation of Exchange, and also with respect to Hawtrey's analyses of specific *sequences* of events.

[2] By Wheatley. See ch. iii, sect. 4, above.

Cassel, it has attracted a great deal of attention, and is sufficiently familiar to make any very detailed presentation of its tenets unnecessary. Its earlier form of statement was as follows.[1] The rate of foreign exchange is regarded as being an expression of the value put upon the money of one country in terms of the money of another country. From this it is inferred that the rate of exchange between any two countries is fundamentally determined by the ratio between their general levels of prices. That is, it is determined by the ratio between the purchasing powers against goods of the two currencies. This ratio, or quotient, constitutes the "purchasing power parity" at each given moment. Any deviation of the exchanges from the parity, barring interference, will be automatically corrected through the effects of variations in the commodity balance of trade. Finally, these ideas are combined with the acceptance of a definitely quantitative theory of money. It is held that changes in general prices, and therefore in the parity, will be substantially proportional to the degree of change in the volume of money in circulation. The exchange rates are therefore really governed by the relative degrees of inflation in the various monetary systems. In other words, the theory not only asserts that price parities and exchanges will move together, but also undertakes to set up a causal relationship between them. The sequence of changes is held to be money (and deposits) in circulation – general prices – foreign exchanges.

5. Such was the rather unqualified doctrine originally propounded in 1916 and 1917. But the subsequent course of events compelled the introduction of a number of modifications, of such scope that it may fairly be questioned if the theory itself has really been left very much practical significance.

In the first place, some very wide and enduring discrepancies soon appeared between the market rates of exchange and the calculated price parities. To account for them, Professor Cassel adopted the explanatory device of "temporary deviations" from

---

[1] I shall not try to indicate in detail the successive stages in the development of Professor Cassel's ideas. His first article, in English at least, was published in the *Economic Journal* for 1916. One or two of his later publications will be referred to in the following pages, and a list of the more important ones is given in the Bibliography at the end of the present volume.

the parity. Such deviations he declared may be due to one-sided restrictions on trade; to distrust in the future of the monetary standard; to the export of capital; to the failure of export prices to reflect the *general* price level closely; and to other factors of a similar order. But it was his view that such disturbances will not endure long, and that permanent alterations in the level of the exchanges can come only from a prior change in the price parity itself.[1] It is evident, however, that these qualifications deprive price-parity theory of much of its value as a practical explanation of the state of affairs at any one time, or in the immediate short-run future. The controlling elements become largely incapable of measurement or prediction, and also not in the first instance especially germane to a theory ostensibly turning on *price* relationships.

In the second place, and perhaps of greater importance, the history of the more severe depreciations in the years after the war seems to show conclusively that in certain cases the sequence of events predicated by the theory is exactly the opposite of that witnessed in actuality. The *first* step has often been the collapse of the exchanges. A rise in internal prices then followed, and only at the end did an increase in the quantity of money in circulation appear. On this question Cassel himself has been rather non-committal, and at certain points even self-contradictory. His principal English adherent, however, — J. M. Keynes, — has frankly admitted the difficulty. He takes refuge in the new proposition that the price-parities should be regarded as the comparatively long-time norm of the exchanges, rather than as their immediate determinants. With this doctrine Cassel appears to agree. But neither writer has given an entirely satisfactory account of the mechanism of adjustment, and indeed Keynes on occasion holds

[1] More recently, Cassel has stressed those psychological factors that can be regarded as leading to under- or over-estimations of the value of a currency in the exchange market. (See his *Money and Foreign Exchange since 1914*, London, 1923: pp. 149, 150.) The exchanges then tend to coincide not with the actual but with the anticipated *future* price parity. (Cf. Bordes, *The Austrian Crown*, London, 1924: pp. 198, 199.) But to concede this is to throw away the whole position, as far as immediate short-time relationships are concerned. The motivating agent in exchange fluctuations then becomes the balance of international payments, with prices left to follow along as best they can.

that under certain conditions the exchanges will alter the price parities themselves. The explanation of this apparent confusion is, of course, that no one short formula can be made to embrace all of the complications of the post-war phenomena.[1]

Finally, a protracted scrutiny of the logical basis of the doctrine has revealed one other fundamental defect. The doctrine is of course compelled in practice to use price indices of some sort, in order to determine the price parities in question. But these indices must rest on a base year or period. Now if the prices of internationally traded commodities were always to keep a given place in the various national price structures, no difficulty would arise. The *relative* changes in the national aggregates of prices would be accompanied by equivalent changes in the international groups. But this has by no means always been what has actually happened. The international group, in many countries, has changed its position in the corresponding national price structures. In consequence, the exchange rates and the calculated price parities (based on general price indices that include purely domestic as well as international prices) have often swung apart, yet without giving rise to any corrective movement. In other words, the price parities ceased to present the true state of affairs, for the relative positions of the *general* price indices no longer reflected the relative positions of the prices of the articles actually exchanged between countries. The influence which the position of the price parities should apparently have exerted on the commodity balance of trade has therefore frequently failed to appear.

The attempt to escape from this difficulty has resulted in giving the theory what is really a new form, in which it is treated as the

---

[1] See J. M. Keynes, *Monetary Reform* (American edition: New York, 1924), pp. 105–116; and G. Cassel, *Money and Foreign Exchanges since 1914* (London, 1923), pp. 143, 144, 184, 185. At one point Keynes makes the *monetary policy* of the country the ultimate determinant of the internal and external purchasing power of its currency. This doctrine was first set forth by Professor Rist (see ch. xi, sect. 9, below).

In an earlier work, Keynes had placed an at least equal stress on the balance of international payments, rather than on any direct influence exerted by the state of relative prices, and with respect to immediate (not long-run) conditions had emphasized the effect of speculation. See *A Revision of the Treaty* (London, 1922), pp. 92, 93. On the short-time immobility of labor and capital and business organization, and the consequent losses arising from a disturbance, see *ibid.*, pp. 154, 155, 166.

source of only rather long-run influences, and in which much of its distinctive force is lost. It has become more convincing, but also less significant. The price parities are now calculated not directly from current price indices themselves, but in terms of the degree of deviation from a prior state of assumed equilibrium in foreign trade, such as the condition in 1913. In this way it is possible to allow for costs of transportation, tariffs, and the like, and also to take account of goods and services that do not enter international trade themselves. Moreover, the price parities are now no longer distorted by changes of the place of international prices in the various national price structures, *provided* that these changes are of equal degree in each country.[1]

But even this solution is only partial. If the price parities are to be valid as thus calculated, certain conditions must be fulfilled. The changes in prices must be due to monetary causes alone; labor and capital must be mobile as between the export industries and the domestic; and the "equation of exchange" in international trade, the "real" terms at which a country gets its imports, must either remain unaltered, or at least change to an equivalent extent in the countries concerned. Otherwise the relative position of international prices will cease to be the same in the various national structures, and the calculated price parities will again become inaccurate.

Evidently these conditions are impossible of practical fulfillment, however, except in rather brief periods of time — in which it is no longer claimed that the theory is necessarily valid.[2] Furthermore, any doctrine resting even partially on an (inter-commodity) "equation of exchange" must necessarily neglect international loans, as well as the other invisible items in the balance of payments. Yet they are important, and at times dominant.[3]

---

[1] Cf. Cassel, *op. cit.*, pp. 155–158; Keynes, *Monetary Reform*, pp. 105 ff.

[2] Granted budget equilibrium and a reasonably sane banking system, the current price parities will inevitably establish a working (long-time) norm of the exchanges. But in the absence of these conditions the price parities are ineffective, and indeed themselves become liable to indefinite alteration *in consequence* of the fluctuations of the exchanges.

[3] The "equation of exchange" has come in for an increasing amount of attention in recent years. See for example Professor Taussig's most suggestive article, *The Change in Great Britain's Foreign Terms after 1900* (Economic Journal, 1925), and

On the whole, it seems fairer to disregard these latest modifications in the price-parity theory, and to adopt the simpler form at which both Cassel and Keynes finally arrive. Thus Keynes declares that the essence of the theory is (now) to be found "in its regarding internal purchasing power as being in the long-run a more trustworthy indicator of a currency's value than the market rates of exchange, because internal purchasing power quickly reflects the monetary policy of the country, which is the final determinant." [1] The price parity, like the gold parity before the war, provides the equilibrium point about which the short-period movements of the exchanges fluctuate. In the absence of a persisting change in the basic economic relationships between countries, the parity is itself governed by *internal* money and credit and price conditions.

This doctrine is convincing. It is evidently far removed, however, from the dogmatic assertions Professor Cassel made in 1916. The theory is now primarily a long-time affair; and it says little or nothing about the detail of the quantitative relationships presumably involved.[2]

6. The history of the price-parity doctrine at the hands of other English and American economists can be indicated briefly.

the antecedent literature there referred to. The questions at issue are beside our main purpose here, however, since they center around the character and measure of the benefit derived from foreign trade.

As a conceptual device the "equation of exchange" is obviously very useful, but as a practical tool its significance is less clearly established. Some of the difficulties involved have been indicated in the text above. The actual exchanges between countries consist of more than commodity transactions alone; and there is as yet no way of measuring the thing which it is at bottom sought to get at — the relation between the "real cost" of a country's imports and their "real value" to her. On the other hand, it must in fairness be pointed out that Professor Taussig's results seem to show that shifts in the equation of exchange, even when measured in terms of commodities alone, help to explain general movements in the level of the country's money incomes. But I believe that he regards these conclusions as only tentative.

See also ch. xv, sect. 5, below, and Appendix B, sect. 4.

[1] Keynes, *Monetary Reform*, p. 105. With respect to the last proposition in this quotation, it must be pointed out that the exchanges usually respond far more quickly than internal prices. Why Keynes overlooks this familiar fact here is not clear.

[2] A more elaborate criticism of this and other theories will be presented in ch. xvii, below.

In England it has met with wide and in the main quite uncritical acceptance.[1] Professor Pigou, it is true, has questioned parts of it, but he admits its most important tenet, the assertion that the "norm" of the exchange rates tends to move with, and to be governed by, the quotient between relative general prices.[2] In the United States, on the other hand, the majority of writers have opposed it. Dr. Anderson, in particular, has criticized it at almost every point.[3] He attacks it for its use of the concept of a "general" price level, and for its use of the quantity theory; for its neglect of the rôle of the discount rates and of the balance of trade in the determination of the exchanges; and for its disregard of the asserted fact that the value of paper money is primarily governed by the prospect of eventual conversion. He also denies that real "parities" of any sort whatsoever can exist under paper. Finally, citing the experience of the United States between 1862 and 1879, he declares that commodity prices follow the exchanges, instead of governing them. This proposition is now generally admitted to be true in certain cases. Somewhat similar

---

[1] For example, at the hands of Professor Edwin Cannan, in a symposium entitled *The World's Monetary Problem* (Annals of the Academy of Political and Social Science, 1920), p. 283; T. E. Gregory, *Foreign Exchange* (Oxford, 1921), pp. 81–83; and D. H. Robertson, *Money* (American edition: New York, 1922), p. 137. In the English journals only the Dutch writer, Miss Van Dorp, has explicitly criticized it (in the Economic Journal for 1919 and 1920).

[2] A. C. Pigou, *Some Problems of Foreign Exchange* (Economic Journal, 1920), pp. 462, 463; and *The Foreign Exchanges* (37 Quarterly Journal of Economics, 1922), pp. 62–67. In the earlier paper Pigou shows that Cassel's doctrine is of course not necessarily true for articles not entering international trade, but in the second paper he decides (I think erroneously) that there is no general reason why the prices of such articles should change in a different proportion from those which are traded — although no equilibrium rate of exchange can be postulated with respect to such articles as *between* countries. He substantially rejects, however, what he calls the "positive" aspect of Cassel's doctrine. This is the proposition that the equilibrium rate of exchange is necessarily that one which makes internal and external purchasing powers equal.

Attention may also be called to Professor Pigou's precise theoretical study, in the second of the two articles, of the conditions of equilibrium in foreign trade. With the exceptions already noted, it is essentially a refinement — and a most illuminating one — on the same general theory as Cassel's.

[3] B. M. Anderson, in the symposium on *The World's Monetary Problem* (referred to above), pp. 268–273.

objections have been advanced by Scott and Hepburn,[1] and by Williams.[2] Williams cites the conditions in the Argentine from 1883 to 1888, and in Germany after 1920, for proof that the state of the balance of payments often governs the exchanges and the value of the local currency. Only Professor Fisher,[3] and perhaps Dr. Chandler,[4] have supported the price-parity doctrine at all unreservedly.

If we seek to judge the doctrine fairly, however, we must examine it quite as much with respect to its attempted application to recent monetary problems in Europe as with respect to its strict theoretical accuracy. At a time when the grossest inflationism and the crudest balance of trade theories were rife, especially on the Continent, Professor Cassel's writings rendered a service which was far from small. They called attention to the fundamental fact that there is a definite relationship of sorts between excessive issues of paper money, the depreciation of the exchanges, and the rise in prices; and they thus helped to restore some semblance of sanity in the general chaos. It is only to be regretted that in Germany and Austria, where a sincere adoption of this simple teaching would have been of the greatest value, it was in point of fact least influential. In the other countries of western Europe, it added weight to those more conservative forces which struggled to keep the threatened monetary cataclysm within bounds.

7. In addition to the literature centering directly around the price-parity theory, a number of other statistical and doctrinal studies have sought to cast light upon the tangled facts and problems of recent experience.[5]

---

[1] In *The World's Monetary Problem*, pp. 277, 281, 282.

[2] J. H. Williams, *Foreign Exchange under Depreciated Paper* (Journal of the American Bankers' Association, 1922), pp. 493, 494.

[3] Irving Fisher, in *The World's Monetary Problem* (cited above), p. 276.

[4] H. A. E. Chandler, *Discussion of Some Fundamental Factors in Foreign Exchange Fluctuations* (Commerce Monthly, 1921).

[5] No attempt will be made here to discuss the views of Professor Marshall on the question of international trade under depreciated currencies, recently restated in his *Money Credit and Commerce* (London, 1923). His earlier conclusions have been examined at another point (see ch. vi, sect. 4, above), and no substantial additions seem to have been undertaken. Little reference is made to the course of events since 1914.

Professor Williams, as far back as 1920, called attention to the fact that heavy commodity imports into Europe had taken place from 1914 to 1919 in the face of depreciating currencies and exchanges. This was an apparent contradiction of the classical theory on the point.[1] The explanation lay in the tremendous contemporary borrowing abroad of the European countries, for military purposes. Similarly in post-war Germany, from May to November, 1921, imports increased in the face of a tumultuous and growing exchange depreciation.[2] Here, however, the explanation was different. It was to be found partly in the restrictive control over exports exerted by the government; and partly in the fact that, because of the character of German foreign trade, an increase in exports (chiefly manufactures) required a preceding increase of imports (chiefly raw materials). But the principal reason was the fact that the German public had suddenly become panic-stricken, and had lost all confidence in the mark. This led to a wave of home buying, which by increasing the competition for domestic products aggravated the decline in commodity exportation.

In this article Williams makes one or two other observations of interest. He shows that although depreciation has in point of fact usually stimulated commodity exportation, as the classical analysis would expect, nevertheless a *violent* fall in the exchanges may *retard* it. Such a fall precipitates a buyer's panic, as it did in Germany, and confuses all trade relationships. Moreover, the stimulus to exports operates only when the shipments are invoiced in the foreign currency. This results from the fact that time contracts drawn in the domestic money become hazardous, and as far as possible will be avoided. Finally, Williams concludes that the source of the German collapse of 1921 lay neither in the excessive issue of paper money nor in budget deficits, in the first

---

[1] J. H. Williams, *Foreign Exchange, Prices, and International Trade* (Annals, American Academy of Political and Social Science, 1920), pp. 201–209. In connection with the controlling influence of the balance of payments on the exchanges see his earlier paper, *Latin American Foreign Exchanges and International Balances during the War* (33 Quarterly Journal of Economics, 1919), pp. 423–425.

[2] J. H. Williams, *German Foreign Trade and the Reparations Payments* (37 Quarterly Journal of Economics, 1922), pp. 487–493.

instance, but in the pressure of reparations payments upon the exchanges. The sequence of events apparently was this: reparations payments, depreciating exchanges, rising import and export prices, rising domestic prices, consequent budgetary deficits, and at the same time an increased demand for bank credit (in terms of numbers of marks); and finally increased note issue.[1]

The reality of this last type of analysis, which runs *from* the balance of payments and the exchanges *to* general prices and the increased issue of paper, seems to be definitely established, and is now admitted by adherents of the ostensibly opposed price-parity theory. The chief defect in Professor Williams's exposition is that he does not stress sufficiently the effects of speculation and anticipation, especially within the country. This is one of the most important factors in the short-time movement of prices and the foreign exchanges, under a régime of severe and rapidly growing depreciation.

The significance of speculation (in a wide sense of the term) has recently been presented with especial force by Professor Young.[2] Professor Young concludes that the characteristic sequence of events in post-war Europe has not been inflation — unbalanced budgets — disordered exchanges, but unbalanced budgets — disordered exchanges — inflation. The lack of budgetary equilibrium has itself been primarily the result of the pressure of war-time debts, both internal and external. The connecting link between government debts and the status of the paper currencies is found in foreign and domestic "speculation" with respect to the future course of the currency unit — or, since that term usually has a limited technical sense, in what may be called widespread "anticipation." An obvious illustration is provided by the history of the German mark after the adverse North Silesian decision in the autumn of 1921, and after the failure of the attempt at stabilization in December of that year. The result was a collapse in the first half of 1922. All faith in the future of the mark was abandoned, both at home and abroad; the currency

[1] *German Foreign Trade and the Reparations Payments*, pp. 502, 503.

[2] A. A. Young, *War Debts, External and Internal* (Foreign Affairs, 1924), especially pp. 402–405.

market turned bear; and the process of depreciation became fatally cumulative. Yet before that time general confidence had kept the mark too *high*. This last was an illustration of the working of psychological factors in the opposite direction.

8. The most important investigation in the group now under consideration, however, is de Bordes's study of the Austrian crown. It is the only detailed history of the complete cycle of depreciation and eventual stabilization that has yet been published in English, and is a remarkable contribution to the subject.[1] On matters of general principle de Bordes reaches two sets of conclusions, one dealing with the theory of money and prices, the other with the theory of the foreign exchanges.

With respect to the first, he undertakes to examine the applicability of Professor Fisher's formula ($MV + M^1 V^1 = PT$), in order to discover which of its elements was cause in the Austrian experience, and which effect.[2] In Austria, the typical quantity-theory explanation was definitely borne out in 1914 and 1915. The quantity of money increased first, and the level of prices reacted only somewhat later. But between 1916 and 1923, at the end of the period examined, prices rose far beyond the circulation, and in the middle of 1923 reached an index some seven times as high. At one time the physical shortage of commodities adequately accounted for this divergence, but in the latter part of 1921, and in 1922, the reason was quite different. It lay chiefly in the terrific increase in the velocity of circulation of money.[3] Every one unfortunate enough to possess money dashed off to buy goods with it, lest it depreciate still farther in their pockets.[4]

---

[1] J. van Walré de Bordes, *The Austrian Crown* (London, 1924). Conclusions somewhat similar were reached by J. H. Penson with respect to the history of Poland in 1921: *The Polish Mark in 1921* (Economic Journal, 1922), especially pp. 167–170.

Reference may also be made to A. Rasin's more summary account of the Czecho-Slovakian experience to the end of 1921: *Financial Policy of Czecho-Slovakia* (Oxford, 1923); and to D. B. Copland, *Currency Inflation and Price Movements in Australia* (Economic Journal, 1920).

[2] Bordes, *op. cit.*, pp. 159, 162 ff.

[3] To some extent, also, in the influx of foreign currency, which made unnecessary a corresponding amount of increase in the domestic circulation. The size of this influx could not be measured statistically.

[4] Cf. Keynes, *Monetary Reform*, pp. 47–69.

This made it possible to get on with a far smaller total gold value of the currency than usual, and permitted a comparatively moderate quantity of money to support an exorbitantly high price level. The increase in money followed, and indeed was often the obvious result of, the increase in prices. Here the quantity theory, at least in its simpler and commoner form, evidently breaks down.

With respect to the theory of the foreign exchanges, de Bordes does not commit himself to any one definite position. He declares, however, that in periods of severe depreciation prices come to be fixed in terms of some foreign money, not in terms of the fluctuating and collapsing local currency.[1] Under these conditions the price level is in the most literal sense the result of the foreign exchange movements. Such was the situation in Austria from the beginning of 1921 until the stabilization, late in 1922. Similar episodes, it may be added, have frequently been observed in Germany, Poland and Russia since the war. The rate of exchange itself, finally, was governed partly by the international movement of capital, but chiefly by speculation in the market. While the demand and supply of the other elements in the balance of payments — goods and services — is comparatively inelastic, and insensitive to immediate fluctuations, the movements of capital and the pressure of speculation are subject to no such limitations. The greater the prospect of further depreciation, the stronger does the bear tendency become. It thus brings on and exaggerates that fall which it is itself attempting to discount in advance. The process, that is, becomes viciously cumulative. Prices are carried along on the flood of the exchange cataclysm.

These definitely established facts seem to run directly counter to the tenets of the price-parity theory. De Bordes, however, refrains from drawing too general an inference from what is after all but one phase in the cycle of depreciation. He concludes that the exchanges and the price parities tend to coincide in their movements, but that, depending on the particular situation, *either* one may be the stronger factor, and thus draw the other to it.[2] This interpretation, which seems to me the only one possible as a universal formulation, is finding increasingly wide acceptance.

[1] Bordes, *op. cit.*, pp. 172 ff.   [2] *Ibid.*, p. 199.

In the period of stabilization, finally, the process was begun with the exchanges, not with prices. The stability of the exchanges, however, led at once to stability of prices. This situation was maintained in face of the apparently impossible fact that the note circulation increased nearly seven fold. The explanation is that the increase in the quantity of money merely offset the rapid decline in the velocity of circulation from its previous high level, and was actually necessary in order to prevent a severe crisis from a currency *shortage*. Furthermore, the stabilization led to such an influx of capital that for a time there was grave danger of a disastrous *appreciation* of the exchanges. This fact too is not easily fitted into the price-parity theory, when it is viewed as a strictly short-time analysis.

9. Such has been the development of the theory of money and prices, and of international exchange relationships, since the war. The propositions advanced have in the main been concerned with the phenomena of currency depreciations which were of unprecedented range and severity. In the field of monetary doctrine, the older form of the quantity theory has been carried through a process of further refinement, while the Marshallian type of analysis has been restated and broadened. But each of these methods of approach finds logically incontestable and unqualified application only to conditions of comparative general stability in prices and currencies. In periods of violent upheaval it is sometimes possible to make use of them, but at other times it clearly is not. To account for the events of such periods, therefore, it has been necessary to search for some other approach, and to find an explanation that can include within its terms the evidently intimate relationship between money and prices and the foreign exchanges.

The first solution tried was the price-parity theory. Experience soon showed, however, that the earlier forms of statement contained many defects, and the price parities have now been relegated to a rather long-run, normative position. Although no complete alternative theory has yet been worked out, the tendency in recent years has been to admit the dominance of the balance of payments and the exchange rates in the field of *short-time* fluctuations, and to seek the common origin of both price and exchange movements in some antecedent general condition. The condition selected usually reduces, in the last analysis, to the state of the national finances. A general anticipation, both at home and abroad, of future stability or instability of the budget finds swift reflection in the internal and external values placed upon the local currency.

It is not proposed, however, to undertake further criticisms of these various doctrines at this point. That task is reserved for later chapters, in which a revaluation and restatement of the whole theory of international exchange will be presented.

10. We have now traced the origin and development of the more characteristic English theories of international exchange from the time of the Mercantilists down, and have followed out their elaboration in the recent English and American literatures. These theories, it is true, have not as yet been welded into a single doctrine of international *prices*. But the principal elements have been adequately worked out, and it is not difficult to derive a satisfactory synthesis from them. The elements are a theory of the ratios of inter-commodity exchange in foreign trade; a domestic theory of money and prices; a theory of the relationships between price structures and income structures in different countries; and a theory of the actual mechanisms of international trade under various sorts of monetary conditions.

In Part II, we shall review the changing fortunes of these theories upon the Continent. With the exception of the mathematical school, it will be found that the Continental economists have in the main followed the line of approach laid down by the English classical writers. But whereas in England and the United States the orthodox doctrines have in general been accepted without serious criticism, on the Continent the characteristic attitude has usually been one of disagreement, and on certain points of agnostic neglect.

PART II

THE HISTORY OF CONTINENTAL THOUGHT

CHAPTER VIII

FRENCH MERCANTILISM AND THE ANTI-MERCANTILIST REACTION, TO 1776

1. The general body of French thinking upon the problems which are bound up in the theory of international prices is divided, chronologically, into two quite distinct periods. One is the period of Mercantilistic thought and of the anti-Mercantilist reaction, which may be taken as lasting until 1776. The second is the period since 1776, and especially since the beginning of the nineteenth century. The thought of this second period, except in so far as it is concerned with monetary theory, is to an extraordinary degree independent of, and detached from, the thought of the preceding era. That continuous and closely integrated development of ideas through a number of centuries, which may fairly be described as characteristic of English doctrine, is notably absent in France. The lack of cohesion between the two periods is in part explainable upon historical grounds. The fall of the old empire, the Revolution, and the Napoleonic wars so completely altered the intellectual and social character of France as to make it in many ways a quite different nation, only tenuously connected with its own past. But the same discreteness of thought appears also in the period since the beginning of the nineteenth century. Far more than the English, the successive French economists of even the last hundred years seem quite commonly to have written in comparative ignorance of the work that had been done but a short time before in their own country. The tracing of continuous lines of development is therefore always difficult, and sometimes impossible.

The other outstanding characteristic that distinguishes the French thought of both periods from the English is the relatively large part played in the former by foreign influences. In the earlier Mercantilist period the foreign element was chiefly Italian, thereafter chiefly English. In the nineteenth century, indeed, —

a point of which more will be made later, — French discussions of the theoretical problems of international trade can be interpreted almost entirely in terms of the elaboration or criticism of antecedent English doctrines. The only really new ideas of a constructive character to be advanced by French writers, until recent years, have been those expounded by Cournot; yet upon many points Cournot himself adopted methods and conclusions not materially different from those of the English economists. It may be added further, however, that whereas the English themselves have not as yet presented any very comprehensive and generally accepted criticisms of the so-called classical theory of international trade, the French have gone far in that direction, and have brought radical objections against it that must eventually be fully recognized.

The history of French thought may for convenience in presentation be grouped into four sections, which will constitute the present and the next three chapters. The topics involved are most easily indicated by repeating the corresponding chapter headings, as follows: French Mercantilism and the Anti-Mercantilist Reaction, to 1776; The Theory of International Exchange in France, 1776–1880: English Doctrine and Early French Critics; The Theory of International Exchange in France after 1880: Partial Adaptations and Radical Criticism; and finally, Recent French Theories of International Trade under Depreciated Currencies. First, French Mercantilism.

2. The period of French Mercantilism and of the anti-Mercantilistic reaction shows a number of distinct currents, some of which are similar to those already examined in the history of English thought, and some of which are not. The parallelism is close enough, however, and the general political situation was sufficiently similar, so that the present chapter can be regarded as substantially a supplement to the earlier chapter on English Mercantilism. In French Mercantilism itself, which was based on a nationalism somewhat less aggressive and less irritable than the English, we find the development of the quantity theory of money; the doctrine of the supremacy of the precious metals as the best or the most expedient form of wealth; the advancement

of successive practical policies by which national stocks of the precious metals might be increased; and, finally, a self-consistent and reasoned attempt to reconcile these policies with an acceptance of the quantity theory itself. All of these ideas, except the last, were presented even more elaborately by the English writers than by the French. It is true that, in the period of the French anti-Mercantilist reaction, the quantity theory does not seem to have been criticized, whereas it was explicitly rejected by at least one or two of the English writers. But the attack on other features of Mercantilist doctrine closely resembles the English. The supremacy of the precious metals was denied; the specific contradiction between the quantity theory and the policy of accumulating the precious metals was pointed out, though not always on quite the grounds adopted in England; agrarian and industrial interests were set up as of paramount importance to the welfare of the State, in the place of commercial interests; and finally doctrines of economic liberty, based ultimately on the concepts of natural law, were advanced in opposition to all policies of governmental interference and restriction. These various currents of thought will be examined in order, beginning with the development of the theory of money and prices.

In England, the quantity theory of money cannot be said to have appeared definitely until the time of Locke. It was hinted at by a number of the antecedent Mercantilist writers, but rarely in any very complete form. In France it was definitely formulated at an early date by Jean Bodin,[1] and from then on it was an integral part of French economic thinking. Bodin's conclusions were the direct product of contemporary monetary conditions. Between 1500 and 1675 there was an enormous influx of the precious metals into Europe, and a rise in prices to perhaps three times the former level.[2] The second phenomenon, especially, attracted great attention, and drew forth various partial explana-

---

[1] I have chosen, perhaps arbitrarily, to disregard the partial formulations of the Scholastic and Canonist periods. On these writers see E. Bridrey, *La théorie de la monnaie au XIV ème siècle* (Paris, 1906). Oresme, for example, does not seem to have had any very definite doctrine as to the *value* of money.

[2] A. Dubois, *Précis de l'histoire des doctrines économiques* (Paris, 1903), vol. i, p. 125.

tions. It was not until Bodin wrote, however, that the rise in prices was associated with the increase in the precious metals, and it was left for him to make the one fact the principal explanation of the other. After proving that the rise was "real," and that the actual contemporary debasements of the currency could account for only a small part of it, Bodin showed that it was for the most part attributable to the increased quantity of gold and silver in Europe — the rise being greatest in those countries, such as Spain and Italy, which had received the largest part of the increase.[1] The argument is quite clear, and turns simply on the idea that the increase in the quantity of the precious metals causes their value to fall, just as does the abundance of anything else, and thus makes prices go up. Bodin found that other factors, such as monopolies, the scarcity of goods, extravagance and waste, and so on, had also contributed to the current situation, but that their importance was much less than that of the increase in the precious metals.[2] His doctrine, skilfully supported by rigorous reasoning and elaborate factual corroboration, found general acceptance in the next two centuries in both France and England, and aroused almost no opposition.[3]

A few years later, in 1588, the Italian Davanzati gave the quantity theory a much more rigid form, in which prices were made to depend upon the quantity of money alone, and in which a direct proportional relationship was asserted.[4] This formulation had great influence in France as well as in Italy, and although its dogmatic character laid it open to easy attack, it did perhaps more than Bodin's realistic but less definitive statements to clarify sub-

---

[1] Jean Bodin, *Réponses aux Paradoxes du Sieur de Malestroit*, . . . etc. (1568). I have used the edition (contained in the Bibliothèque Nationale), published at Lyon in 1593, by Vincent. The volume also contains *Les Six Livres de la Republique* (1576); the *Apologie de René Herpin pour la Republique de J. Bodin;* and the original *Paradoxes du Seigneur de Malestroit, sur le faict des monnoyes*. The reference here is to p. 59 of the *Réponses*.

[2] *Réponses*, pp. 52, 53 ff. See also Dubois, *op. cit.*, pp. 181–187; and R. Gonnard, *Histoire des doctrines économiques* (Paris, 1921–1922: 3 vols.), vol. i, pp. 153–156.

[3] Arias has observed, however, — and I think correctly, — that Bodin gives no actual definition of the value of money, and no real theory of value. Davanzati was the first to do that. See G. Arias, *Les précurseurs de l'économie monétaire en Italie* (Revue d'économie politique, 1922), pp. 734, 735.

[4] Dubois, *op. cit.*, pp. 185–187.

sequent thought upon monetary questions. Finally Montchrétien, in 1615, repeated Bodin's proposition that the great quantity
of gold and silver which had been brought to Europe from the
American mines had made the prices of all commodities rise, but
he added that they had not always risen *in proportion* to the increase in the amount of money.[1] This important and necessary
qualification was often lost sight of in later writers.

After Montchrétien no substantial modification was introduced
into the formulation of the quantity theory in France[2] until the
time of Cantillon, in the middle of the eighteenth century. Cantillon added another element, the rapidity of circulation of
money, to the earlier statements.[3] He also gave the first detailed
explanation of the mechanism by which a rise in prices, consequent
on an increase in the quantity of money, is actually effected. He
concluded that the rise is initiated by the increased outlays of the
producers or importers of the precious metals. This results in an
increase in the prices of the objects upon which the outlays are
spent, and that increase is then communicated in turn to wages
and prices at large, through a general expansion of consumption.[4]
That is, Cantillon is here giving what is now sometimes called the
"direct" chain of sequences, between changes in the quantity of

[1] Antoyne de Montchrétien, *Traicté de l'oeconomie politique*, 1615 (edited by
Funck-Brentano: Paris, 1889), p. 257.

[2] So Montesquieu, in Bk. XXII of the *Esprit des Lois* (1748), bases the change in
prices on the quantity of money alone.

It should nevertheless be pointed out that the Italian Montanari, writing in
1680, added another important qualification which subsequently became incorporated in the French thought. He confined his formulation of the quantity theory
to money and goods *in circulation*. On this see A. E. Monroe, *Monetary Theory before Adam Smith* (Cambridge, 1923), pp. 108–110.

[3] Locke had called attention to it, in England, more than half a century before.
See ch. ii, sect. 4, above.

[4] Richard Cantillon, *Essai sur la nature du commerce en générale* (printed in Paris,
1755; reprinted for Harvard University, Boston, 1892), pp. 179–196, and pp. 215–
231. Also see Dubois, *op. cit.*, p. 187.

Cantillon was an Irish banker, living in Paris. The Essay was originally written
in English, in 1734, but was never printed. It was translated into French by Cantillon himself, and published in 1755. (See the prefatory note to the Harvard University reprint.) It is therefore a fair question as to whether Cantillon should be
placed with the history of French thought or with the English. For the purpose in
hand, however, it has seemed to me better to place him with the French, leaving to

money and changes in prices. He omits to say here, however, whether or not this increase will be permanent, and also what will be its effects upon the volume of production. The point will come up again later, in connection with his propositions dealing with the balance of trade.[1]

Some years later François Forbonnais presented a doctrine which, if not an outright refutation of the quantity theory, was at least a very important modification of it.[2] His view was that a *gradual* increase in the amount of money stimulates production, thus offsetting the tendency of prices to rise, and that in this way it is highly beneficial to the nation. The argument is tied up with his defense of the balance-of-trade theory, given below,[3] but part of it may be repeated here.

> Under certain circumstances, where the increase in the amount of money has been sudden and great, the prices of commodities have changed rapidly from their ordinary proportion, because production could not adjust itself; and wages have followed the same path. . . . Yet . . . it is undeniably very advantageous that they [i. e., prices] should rise gradually, in so far as this increase can stimulate work and production. But it is this *transition* which is stimulating, not the greater or less quantity of gold that each commodity unit receives in exchange.[4]

Of the two types of change in the amount of money, the second is held to be the more probable under actual conditions. For,

the English the imitation of his work published by his relative, Philip Cantillon (*The Analysis of Trade*, 1759; see *supra*, ch. ii, sect. 7). While Cantillon followed Hume chronologically in England, and was hence at best distinctly behind the times there, in France his rôle was much more important. In the history of French doctrine he was a precursoi of the Physiocrats, for his formulation of the balance-of-trade theory presaged the advent of a system in which the first place should be given to agriculture. (See Dubois, *op. cit.*, pp. 242–244.) Yet it must not be forgotten that this agrarian bias was probably drawn to a considerable extent from the Englishman Sir William Petty, as well as from such earlier French writers as Boisguilbert and Melon. See for example an article by W. S. Jevons, the first "discoverer" of Cantillon: *Richard Cantillon and the Nationality of Political Economy* (Contemporary Review, January, 1881).   [1] See *infra*, sect. 4.

[2] François V. de Forbonnais, *Principes Économiques* (Amsterdam, 1767). I have used the reprint given in the *Collection des Principaux Économistes* (edited by E. Daire, Paris, 1843–1847: 15 vols.), Mélanges, vol. i.

[3] *Infra*, sect. 5.

[4] Forbonnais, *loc. cit.*, p. 226 (ch. 5, sect. 5). Hume, with whose work Forbonnais was probably familiar, had made a similar observation concerning the stimulus in the transition period. See ch. ii, sect. 5, above.

the quantity of silver which can annually enter from the mines being limited, and distributed among various countries, it follows that in no society is the increase great enough at any one time to effect a considerable rise in the prices of [all] commodities; but some being raised to greater advantage [than others], the profit from their production increases.[1]

This idea, that an increase in money will stimulate production and thus prevent a rise in prices, was not original with Forbonnais. It is found in Law, and also in Melon. But Forbonnais gave it the most concrete and convincing form of expression that it had till then received; a form which, at the end of the next century, was to provide the only line of attack upon the quantity theory which is logically unassailable. It may be remarked, finally, that he added the interest-rate factor to his analysis. He found that interest rates tend to fall with an increase in the amount of money, but that this tendency may in part be offset by the resulting increase in production and by the consequent increased competition for capital advances.[2]

Finally Condillac, in 1776, made a remarkable analysis of the actual paths or channels of the circulation of money — of its continued movement of distribution and reflux through many little canals, from and to the central reservoirs. These reservoirs are the farmers, the great proprietors, the dealers and the artisans; especially the last two, since money circulates but little in the country. In other words the reservoirs are, in effect, primarily the cities. Condillac was also the first writer to take account of business methods as a factor influencing prices. He declares that if accounts are settled twice as often, only half as much silver will be needed. If the former quantity of silver remains in circulation, prices will then rise. Further, he allows for the function and rôle of credit, which is able to replace silver to a large extent. Finally, he concludes that under given conditions prices are approximately proportional to the quantity of money, though not precisely.[3]

---

[1] Forbonnais, *loc. cit.*, p. 227 (ch. 5, sect. 6). How this world distribution of the precious metals is effected, however, is not indicated; the price-gold flow mechanism of English theory is absent.

[2] *Ibid.*, p. 225 (ch. 5, sect. 5).

[3] Étienne B. de Condillac, *Le commerce et le gouvernement* (Paris, 1776). I have used the reprint given in the *Collection des Principaux Économistes*, Mélanges, vol. i. The reference is to pp. 294–299.

Such, in brief outline, was the development of the theory of money and prices from Bodin to the beginning of the modern period. The theory takes two forms, one asserting a direct and proportional relationship, the other introducing qualifications that make the relationship less definite. One or the other of these forms was adopted by every French Mercantilist after the time of Bodin, as well as by the opponents of Mercantilism, but the essential contradiction between the quantity theory and the Mercantilist doctrines concerning the precious metals does not seem to have been appreciated until late in the eighteenth century.

3. Our examination of English Mercantilism in an earlier chapter makes unnecessary any detailed discussion of the French Mercantilist doctrines themselves, since the two bodies of thought are not very dissimilar with respect to the questions that concern us. Sully and Montchrétien afford examples of early seventeenth century bullionism.[1] Laffemas,[2] who wrote a considerable number of memoirs and opuscules at about the same time, was apparently the first French protagonist of the balance-of-trade theory, as distinct from crude bullionism itself. He saw that the prohibition of the exportation of the precious metals is futile, and urged their accumulation, instead, through a favorable balance of trade.[3] The Italian Serra also combined the dogmatic assertion of the importance of an abundance of money with the realization that it is impossible to prevent exports of gold and silver.[4] But at this time, in the seventeenth century, the balance-of-trade theory proper found its principal adherents in England, not in France. The French thought of the period was quite as much concerned with the ways of encouraging one or more of the principal branches of economic activity as with trying to increase the national wealth directly by an accumulation of the precious metals.

---

[1] Sully, *Économies royales*, 1598 and ff.; Montchrétien, *Traicté de l'oeconomie politique*, 1615 (cited above). On Sully, see A. Dubois, *op. cit.*, pp. 226-228.

[2] See especially his treatise on *Comme l'on doit permettre la liberté du transport de l'or*, . . . etc., 1602. (In the Bibliothèque Nationale, at Paris.)

[3] See L. Cossa, *Histoire des doctrines économiques* (translated from the second Italian edition by A. Bonnet: Paris, 1899), p. 213.

[4] *Ibid.*, pp. 193-195; and also G. Arias, *Les idées économiques d'Antonio Serra* (Journal des Économistes, 1922).

In the eighteenth century, however, there was a revival of interest in the more typically English variety of Mercantilism. Between 1749 and 1760 the works of a considerable number of the English writers, such as Petty, Gee, Tucker, Child, and others, were translated into French.[1] At the same time Cantillon reaffirmed the proposition that the precious metals are the best form of wealth, and advanced an elaborately qualified balance-of-trade theory to prove his case (see below). Finally Forbonnais, in 1767, gave the Mercantilist doctrine the least assailable form of statement that it has ever received. These last two writers, however, belong to that more sophisticated school of quasi-Mercantilism which sought to reconcile Mercantilist policy with the quantity theory of money. Their theories must therefore be examined under the latter head, rather than under that of "pure" Mercantilism.

4. It has always been puzzling to students of the history of economic theory that the apparently fatal flaw in the Mercantilist position should have remained so long unnoticed: that so many successive generations of writers could have advocated the accumulation of the precious metals without limit, while at the same time subscribing to a perfectly workable form of the quantity theory. The explanation of the contradiction lies partly in the failure of the Mercantilists to keep the entire economic system of the country in mind at the same time. It also lies partly in the fact that, under the then-extant organization of economic society, such changes in prices as resulted from the operations of foreign trade did not produce counter-flows of specie large enough to attract general attention — large enough, that is, to make inevitable their being attributed to the prior fact of (relatively) high prices. But whatever the explanation, the reality of the inconsistency remains. In England no effort was ever made to reconcile the two conflicting doctrines. They were held more or less concurrently until Hume emphatically pointed out the contradiction. Thereafter the advocacy of an accumulation of the precious metals simply disappeared from English economic writing, with a few exceptions. On the Continent, however, — in France and

---

[1] See F. Sauvaire-Jourdain, *Isaac de Bacalan* (Paris, 1903), p. 48, n. 1.

to some extent in Italy, — a rather subtle attempt was made at reconciling the two. The attempt turned in general on the idea that an increase in the amount of money will stimulate production, make a rise in prices impossible, and thus prevent any counter-drain of specie.

Law had held the first half of this theory, for much of his famous system turns on the idea that an increase in money provokes increased economic activity, and thus offsets the tendency of prices to rise. He did not, however, apply this idea to international trade, and indeed threw the balance-of-trade doctrine entirely overboard. Melon, writing in 1731, took over many of Law's theories, and used them to provide at least a suggestion of a possible solution of the Mercantilist dilemma.[1] Cantillon saw the solution clearly, though in his writings it is obscured by other doctrines, and Forbonnais presented it in its most unequivocal form. The Italian Verri also outlined it in 1771. With Law and Melon we need not be concerned here, but the ideas of Cantillon and Forbonnais merit attention.

Cantillon's doctrines on international trade are almost inextricably bound up with his theory of value. It is impossible to appreciate his analysis of quasi-monetary mechanisms without at the same time taking some account of this theory. He finds that exchange value is the product of the varying combination of two factors: a certain amount of soil, which in one form or another provides the raw material, and a certain amount of labor. Applying this concept to international exchange, he then declares that a country should seek to export articles having as little as possible of the products of the soil in them, and to import those having as much as possible. A net excess of those imports that consist in products of the soil constitutes a "favorable" balance of trade.[2]

---

[1] On Law and Melon, see Dubois, *op. cit.*, pp. 258–262. Also see sect. 2, above.

[2] Richard Cantillon, *Essai sur la nature de la commerce en générale* (cited above), pp. 297–307. See also, on Cantillon's views here, Dubois, *op. cit.*, pp. 242–244 and 262, 263; and also Gonnard, *op. cit.*, pp. 280–285.

Cantillon distinguishes between *market* value, determined by demand and supply, and *intrinsic* value, the source of which is land and labor. Under normal conditions and in the long run, the former will tend to be equal to the latter. He also goes some distance toward developing a labor-cost theory of value, based on the combination of a subsistence-wage theory with a wages-cost theory of costs of production.

When a country has more of these products it can maintain a larger population, which means increased national strength and prosperity. The increased population, supported by foreign products of the soil and itself manufacturing articles in which the proportion of labor to soil is high, in turn produces more "value" (i. e., in terms of products of the soil) than it consumes. This follows because the foreigner who buys its products, unable to pay for them all with products of the earth, must send gold and silver, which are the "reserve corps" of the state.[1] A large population is thus not only a cause, but also an effect, of increased wealth.

This leads Cantillon from the more abstract aspects of value to the concrete mechanisms involved. Here he makes his famous attempt to reconcile the balance-of-trade theory with the quantity theory of money. He finds that an increase in the precious metals may be due, first, simply to an exploitation of the mines. Such an increase, however, will result only in the national ruin. Prices will rise; this will give a margin of profit to foreign producers, who are still working on the basis of the former money costs of production; the national manufacturers will be slowly destroyed by importation; and, finally, the excess money from the mines will drain off into other countries to pay for the imported goods.[2]

But the increase may also be due to a favorable balance of trade. Here the results may, for a time at least, be quite different, and the destructive consequences of that increase which comes from the exploitation of the mines may be avoided. It is with this

So see E. S. Furniss, *The Position of the Laborer in a System of Nationalism* (New York, 1920), pp. 162, 163. In this Cantillon was in agreement with the trend of contemporary English Mercantilism. See ch. ii, sect. 6, above.

His labor-cost theory, however, must presumably be confined to those articles which are chiefly not products of the soil. Nevertheless, had Cantillon applied it to the determination of *international* trade he might well have anticipated Ricardo's classical doctrine of comparative (labor) costs.

[1] This is one of a number of points at which Cantillon's presentation of the detail of how the process actually works is obscure. Here, he fails to show just how these non-monetary "values" get at the money prices of the real market, and hence how the monetary balance of trade is affected. The comprehension of the argument requires the granting of a number of debatable assumptions.

[2] Cantillon, *op. cit.*, pp. 215–220. See also Gonnard, *op. cit.*, pp. 282–285. It will at once strike the reader that this analysis contains the entire argument and proof of

alternative that Cantillon's "reconciliation" of the quantity theory and the balance-of-trade theory is alone concerned. He makes an abundance of the precious metals the effect of a favorable balance of trade, as did other Mercantilists. But he also declares that it is within limits the *cause* of the favorable balance, and hence of an increase in the national welfare. We are at once tempted to accuse him of a vulgar Mercantilist error, but the charge would be unjust. He understood quite as clearly as his contemporary Hume that a relative increase in the amount of money in the country will lead to a rise in prices, and hence to an *unfavorable* balance of trade. What he had in mind was the period between the beginning of the rise in prices and the overturn in the trade balance. Moreover, when he speaks of the balance as being "favorable" he does not mean the trade balance in the usual sense, but that other balance, between exports and imports of the products of the soil, which is "favorable" when *imports* are in excess.

Put into modern phraseology, Cantillon's argument was substantially this. Take the period in which prices are rising, in consequence of the abundance of the precious metals, but in which the changes in prices have not yet altered the volume of importation and exportation. During this period the country sells relatively dearly, and buys relatively cheaply. Hence, since the balance in terms of *money* always tends to equilibrium, the country either gives less of the products of labor for more (in terms of "real" value, that is), and thus lives better without impoverishing itself; or it gives a lesser quantity of the products of the earth for a larger, and thus enriches and strengthens itself.[1]

But, as just remarked, Cantillon saw that this beneficial rising movement of prices cannot continue indefinitely. The rise in

Hume's price-specie flow doctrine. It seems unlikely that Cantillon borrowed from Hume, however, for while he published his book three years after Hume's work appeared, it was presumably written nearly twenty years before. Both men were probably indebted to Locke, and may find their common ground only in him. But in justice to Hume it should be added that Cantillon does not make anything more of the idea than has been indicated in the text. It drops from sight later, and it is doubtful if Cantillon appreciated its real significance.

[1] Cantillon, *op. cit.*, pp. 307–313. See also pp. 249–252, and pp. 220–225.

prices will eventually reduce exportation, increase importation, and thus induce a series of changes precisely opposite to those just outlined.[1] The excess quantity of money will then leave the country. Yet if the state is on a sound basis, and if its leaders intervene at the proper time, some part of the excess may be retained, and the balance will later become favorable again. The nominal rise in prices causes only temporary retrogressions, which do not prevent the country's opulence from making a new advance with each national tide.[2] These ideas, however, lead Cantillon into his theory of alternating periods of national prosperity and depression,[3] with which we are not further concerned here.

He is thus brought back, by a devious route, to what are in effect the cardinal points of the Mercantilist doctrines upon international exchange. He finds that an accumulation of the precious metals is desirable, not so much because these metals are the best form of wealth as because they are the symptom of national prosperity, and within certain limits its cause. He also advocates the seeking of a favorable balance of trade, in order to secure such an accumulation. But it is at once evident that his position here, ostensibly like the ordinary Mercantilist teaching, is in point of fact quite different. First, the "balance" involved is not the ordinary trade balance at all, but one based on the products of the soil, and it is "favorable" when imports are in excess. This theory does not seem to have been fully worked out, however, and it contains various gaps, already commented on, in its logical sequence. It becomes more intelligible to us if gold and silver are specifically included among the imports of "soil," although Cantillon himself seems to separate them. Second, the fact that even this form of favorable balance cannot endure is recognized, and a reconciliation of sorts with the quantity theory is thus effected. In this he again differs from most Mercantilists, who recognized no such

---

[1] There is a certain obscurity here as to just why this decline, this cycle of prosperity and depression, should take place. We may grant the *fact*, explaining it on other grounds, but just how it is to be explained on the peculiar grounds adopted by Cantillon is not altogether clear.

[2] Cantillon, *op. cit.*, pp. 249–252. See also F. Sauvaire-Jourdain, *Isaac de Bacalan*, p. 13, n. 2.

[3] Cantillon, *op. cit.*, pp. 241–247.

limitation on their doctrines. Nevertheless Cantillon retains something of the pure Mercantilist bias, for he declares that properly-timed state intervention can enable the country to retain at least a part of the money which the automatic specie-flow mechanism would otherwise carry off.[1]

The mechanism by which this balance was supposed to work is too intangible, and too much obscured by Cantillon's peculiar theory of value, to make any further discussion of its details profitable. Nevertheless the general significance of the analysis in the theory of international prices in France is great. The connection between those specie flows which are *consequent on the operations of foreign trade* and the rise in prices was clearly stated for the first time in the French literature; and the fact that such a rise in prices must sooner or later produce a counter-flow of specie itself — the automatic character of the process — was pointed out for the first time in *any* literature. While Cantillon's work was not published till 1755, three years after Hume's essays had appeared, it was presumably written some twenty years before, and the credit must therefore be divided between them.[2]

5. A few years after Cantillon's work was published the contradiction between the balance-of-trade doctrine and the quantity theory was again resolved, in more objective and convincing fashion, by Forbonnais.[3] Forbonnais followed the line of attack directly deducible from Law's theories. In his general policies, he was a thorough-going Mercantilist. He advocated protection, he sought an increase in the quantity of precious metals in the country by means of a favorable balance of trade, and he resisted the liberalist tendencies of his generation with intransigeant vigor. Yet his analyses of money, commented on above, are unusually good, and the grounds on which he based his conclusions are not easy to attack.

Forbonnais advocates an increase in the quantity of the precious metals not so much because of the peculiar character of the metals themselves, as because of their beneficial effects upon

---

[1] Cantillon, *op. cit.*, pp. 323–340, and elsewhere.

[2] See on this a note earlier in the present section.

[3] François V. de Forbonnais, *Principes Économiques* (Amsterdam, 1767). I have used the reprint given in the *Collection des Principaux Économistes*, cited above.

economic activity. Unlike most Mercantilists, he does not seem to have any particular preference for the precious metals as such, and does not regard them as being necessarily the "best" form of wealth, for he admits that a greater or less quantity simply means more or fewer counters in exchange.[1] But he finds it highly important, when once a given quantity has been put into circulation, that it should not be decreased. The levels of wages and prices become, after a time, a sort of tacit convention. A reduction in the amount of money therefore means not lower prices and wages, but less business, unemployment and suffering.[2] Indeed, he finds that a gradual increase is beneficial:

> When an important amount of silver, that was not there before, enters into the circulation of commodities, it is inevitable that after a time the prices of these commodities should rise. The increase in the profitableness of labor increases the number of workers and the quantity of production, and the new competition offsets, by the diminution in profits as well as by the lowering of interest rates, the rise in prices.[3]

Then he shows how the increase in the amount of money is brought about by the balance of trade, and in so doing incidentally explains the determination of export prices:

> Since, in countries which have no mines, silver can enter the circulation only through commerce, its increase first benefits those commodities which have contributed to its introduction. Those who have produced these commodities will increase their consumption, in consequence of the benefit, and thus give rise to new production.

A rise in prices is thereby prevented. The increase in the quantity of money works out its effects on production and consumption alone.

Finally, Forbonnais gives the more elaborate argument that we have already examined in connection with the quantity theory.[4] He repeats that it is not the absolute *size* of the quantity of money which is advantageous, but the *transition* from a lesser quantity to a greater.

He thus presents a number of ideas which are lacking in other writers, or at best incompletely put. He develops the one line of

---

[1] Forbonnais, *loc. cit.*, p. 223 (ch. 5, sect. 5).
[2] *Ibid.*, p. 224 (ch. 5, sect. 5).　　　　[3] *Ibid.*, p. 225.
[4] *Supra*, sect. 2; Forbonnais, *loc. cit.*, pp. 226, 227 (ch. 5, sects. 5, 6).

attack upon the quantity theory which, on *a priori* grounds, is logically unassailable; he analyzes the price-phenomena of the important "transitional" period; he explains the mechanism by which, through specie flows and *export* prices, an increase in the amount of money alters prices in general; and he combines these elements to provide a forceful justification for the balance-of-trade theory — a justification which, granted the premises, cannot be overthrown. Account is not explicitly taken, it is true, of Hume's argument concerning the counter-flow of specie consequent on a rise in prices, but in so far as Forbonnais's position is correct this argument is irrelevant. It is one of the ironies of fate that the best defense of Mercantilism ever advanced, a defense based on elements of theory acceptable at the present day, should have been written at a time when the main current of thought had already begun to turn with irresistible force in another direction. The many fresh and valuable suggestions in Forbonnais's writings simply dropped from sight. The good was condemned along with the bad.

How far Forbonnais was indebted to earlier writers it is hard to say. The contemporary practice of not troubling to acknowledge such intellectual obligations makes any statement dangerous. The general mechanisms of international exchange, and especially the use of specie to settle the balance of payments, are of course found in many of his predecessors. The refutation of the quantity theory, or at least its raw materials, is given in Law and Melon. Moreover, the general character of Forbonnais's reasoning and the goal at which it was aimed makes it seem highly probable that he was familiar with Hume's radical criticisms of Mercantilism, which had been translated into French some thirteen years earlier. But the reconciliation of the balance-of-trade theory with the quantity theory on purely monetary grounds was distinctly Forbonnais's own, and we cannot but admire him for it.[1] Cantillon's much less conclusive reconciliation had been oriented on a quite different line of approach.

[1] A similar solution was advanced four years later by Verri, in his *Meditazione sull' economia politica* (1771; French translation, 1773). So see Dubois, *op. cit.*, pp. 258–262. Dubois does not, however, make any reference to Forbonnais in this connection.

6. Even at its height, in the late seventeenth and early eighteenth centuries, a general reaction against Mercantilism had begun to set in. The supremacy of the precious metals, found open to suspicion as far back as Bodin,[1] was flatly controverted by Boisguilbert [2] and by Melon. It was presented in qualified terms by Cantillon, and before the combined effects of the influence of Hume's thought [3] and the development of Physiocratic theory it entirely disappeared from French thinking. The promotion of commerce, on the ground that it is the chief source of national prosperity, was opposed even in the early seventeenth century by the industrialism of the Italian Serra (1613) and of Montchrétien (1615), and later by the agrarianism of Boisguilbert, Melon, Cantillon, and the Physiocrats themselves. Protests against the contemporary restrictive policies had appeared as early as Bodin; and, based more and more upon the concept of natural law, they rapidly grew in power. With the liberalism of D'Argenson,[4] Montesquieu, the Physiocrats, and Adam Smith, the whole structure of interference was finally swept away.

Until the middle of the eighteenth century, however, the non-Mercantilist French writers had not added much to the theory of international prices, and even then their doctrines were chiefly reflections of Hume. Two isolated fragments of the earlier theory alone require comment.

First, Professor Martin's researches [5] have recently shown that

---

[1] See, for example, Bk. VI, ch. 3, of *The Republic*, cited above.

[2] Pierre de Boisguilbert, *Factum de la France* (1707), ch. 3. See also his *Détail de la France* (1697), Part II, ch. 18. Both works are reprinted in the *Collection des Principaux Économistes* (cited above), as are also some of his shorter memoirs. It should be added, however, that in this same chapter of the *Détail* Boisguilbert shows a lingering fondness for the precious metals, despite his well-thought-out arguments against attaching any especial value to them. So see this not untypical proposition: "Money, not being consumed by being used, produces utility without end or limits in the countries to which it is brought." (*Détail*, edition cited, p. 211.)

[3] Between 1754 and 1767 four partial translations were made of Hume's *Essays;* and Hume's own prolonged residence in France (1763-1766) did much to increase his influence, especially upon the Physiocratic writers. See Sauvaire-Jourdain, *Isaac de Bacalan*, p. 36.

[4] See Sauvaire-Jourdain, *Isaac de Bacalan*, pp. 27-29.

[5] G. Martin, *La monnaie et le crédit privé en France au XVIe et XVIIe siècles; les faits et les théories, 1550-1664* (*Revue d'histoire des doctrines économiques et sociales*, 1909).

some of the officers of the French Cour des Monnaies, in the period from 1550 to 1650, held very modern views on the mechanisms of the foreign exchanges. This is indicated by an essay of François la Begue, "Traicté et advis sur les désordres des Monnaies" (Paris, 1600), and especially by an anonymous writer's work, "Le Traité de monnayes, par un conseiller d'État" (Paris, 1621). The passages which Martin quotes[1] are too long to give here, but they may be summarized briefly. It is held that in a country with depreciated money the consequently unfavorable exchanges act as a stimulus to exports, and a check to imports. But this stimulus can at best be temporary. The rise in the exchange rates will eventually result in a rise in the internal prices of the country's imports. This rise will soon spread to other articles, and eventually to wages. The greater the quantity of money that is then issued to meet the stringency in the supply of money itself, the worse will the situation become, until at last trade will almost cease.

It would not be easy to improve upon this argument at the present day. The analysis deserves further praise in that it is probably the first definite attempt to examine one of those fundamental problems of mechanism with which the theory of international prices is particularly concerned: namely, the problem of how a movement in the exchange rate and in international prices actually gets at, and alters, the general body of prices and money incomes in any one country. Had it been specifically extended to include export prices, and prices in the non-depreciated country, nothing more could have been added.

Second, at the end of the seventeenth century, Boisguilbert showed that the precious metals extracted from the mines of the new world must for the most part be taken to the countries from which goods have gone to the mining regions.[2] He then gives an outline of the changes that these metals will produce in the countries which receive them. Just how the distribution is effected, however, is not explicitly stated. The proximate connection between the movements of the precious metals and the balance of

[1] Martin, *loc. cit.*, pp. 28–30.
[2] Boisguilbert, *Détail* (cited above), Part II, ch. 18.

payments, and the ultimate connection between them and the relative state of prices, is hinted at clearly. Some such mechanism is obviously in Boisguilbert's mind, but an actual description of the process is not given.

7. It was not until the middle of the eighteenth century that the anti-Mercantilist writers made any further contributions to the theory of international prices. The new developments were incidental to an attempt to show the inconsistency between the Mercantilist balance-of-trade theory and the quantity theory. They are largely traceable to English inspiration, notably to Hume. As already remarked, Hume's Essays were translated into French within two years of their publication in English, though incompletely, and Hume's own residence in France from 1763 to 1766 did much to give his ideas a wide currency.[1] His general influence was greatest among the Physiocratic writers, but his analysis of the mechanisms of international trade found its chief reflection in the little-known manuscripts of De Bacalan.

The Physiocrats, as was inevitable from the very character of their fundamental doctrine, were not primarily interested in international trade or in its problems. Mercier de la Rivière, for example, considered that international trade is at best a "pis aller." Its existence presupposes that a nation lacks within itself a sufficient number of consumers to yield its products a good price, and that it is therefore compelled to seek foreign markets. It follows, also, that the benefit from international trade arises not from the fact of trade itself, but from the manner in which it is conducted. Foreign trade can be harmful, just as it can be useful. Its usefulness consists entirely in that utility to whose "reproduction" it serves — that is, in the reproduction of foodstuffs and raw materials.[2] This theory is quite similar to Cantillon's.

One or two more constructive ideas, however, are worth noting. The Physiocrats were "free traders" in a sense, but chiefly with

---

[1] Sauvaire-Jourdain, *Isaac de Bacalan*, p. 36. Hume's complete works were not translated until 1788, although four partial translations of his essays had been made before that time.

[2] Mercier de la Rivière, *L'Ordre naturel et essentiel des sociétés politiques* (London and Paris, 1767). I have used the reprint given in the *Collection des Principaux Économistes* (cited above), volume Physiocrates. The reference is to p. 547 (ch. ii).

respect to the export trade in agricultural products (the importation of which was not possible under contemporary conditions).[1] The ground for this partial liberalism was the belief that freedom of trade brings *high* prices, not low prices. Thus Quesnay, in his nineteenth "Maxim," held that low prices were disadvantageous because "a low price of foodstuffs lowers the wages of the common people, decreases their comfort, gives them less work and lucrative employment, and destroys the revenue of the nation." [2] Similarly in the preceding Maxim he advocates the prevention of a lowering of prices, for "the reciprocal trade with foreign countries would then become disadvantageous." The grounds for this assertion, however, are not given. Quesnay also takes exception to the monetary aspects of Mercantilism. He declares that that nation may often lose, instead of profiting, which receives a surplus in money.

The attack was carried much farther by Mercier de la Rivière. He first showed that money is not itself wealth. Wealth in the form of money is only the result of wealth in products.[3] Then he indicated clearly that an excess of money, received from the state of the balance of trade, will either (1) remain unused, and hence be useless; or (2) will be carried out of the country by its owners; or (3) will raise prices and thus be expelled.[4] This is not Hume's price-specie flow theory, however, for by "carried out by its owners" is simply meant that the owners are compelled to emigrate, because the rise in prices makes it unprofitable for them to stay. Yet Rivière came very near this theory. He declared that an artificial increase in the quantity of money will decrease its value and increase prices, decrease exports, and increase imports.[5]

---

[1] Gide and Rist, *Histoire des doctrines économiques* (4 ed., Paris, 1922), p. 34.

[2] F. Quesnay, *Maximes Générales du gouvernement économique d'un royaume agricole* (1760). Reprinted, with the rest of Quesnay's works, in the *Collection des Principaux Économistes*, volume Physiocrates. See also *Maxims Twenty-Four and Twenty-Five*, and the appended *First Economic Problem*.

[3] Rivière, *L'Ordre naturel* (cited above), pp. 568–574 (ch. 14).

[4] *Ibid.*, pp. 575–585 (ch. 15).

[5] *Ibid.*, p. 583. It may be added that Rivière gives the doctrine which was later advanced by J.-B. Say, with so many fanfares, as the "loi des débouchés": that all buyers are sellers, and all sellers buyers; that the totals of the two operations must be equal; and that sales, even in money, are only exchanges of equal values.

He lacked only the corrective supplied by the counter-flow of specie. He found also that the annual increase in the precious metals must "necessarily" be distributed among the various countries, though what the actual process is he does not say.

8. From this summary sketch, it is apparent that while Hume's practical policies in international exchange had exerted a considerable influence upon Physiocratic doctrine, his theories themselves had wholly failed to take root. It remained for a little-known writer of the same period, Isaac de Bacalan, to appropriate these theories and to give them a form which, while showing clearly the debt to Hume, was original and convincing. De Bacalan formulated the more important of the ideas which later formed the dogmas of the liberal school with respect to international trade, and he anticipated at least some of the theoretical propositions of the rigid classical analysis. Yet we must be chary of attaching too great importance to his place in the history of thought. Nothing that he wrote was published, and his influence was exerted almost entirely through his functions as an administrator of the French kingdom.[1]

De Bacalan bases his free-trade doctrines on four principal propositions.[2] They are as follows. (1) International commerce

The importance of the "law" — which, in so far as it has any significance, is little more than a truism—has been greatly exaggerated. See Rivière, *loc. cit.*, pp. 537–543 (ch. 10).

[1] De Bacalan's work was first made known to the general economic world through the brochure of F. Sauvaire-Jourdain, already cited frequently: *Isaac de Bacalan et les idées libre-echangistes en France vers le milieu du dix-huitième siècle* (Paris, 1903). The brochure contains (1) an essay by Professor Sauvaire-Jourdain, on the liberal predecessors of De Bacalan in French thought; (2) the text of De Bacalan's principal work, hitherto unpublished, entitled "*Paradoxes philosophiques sur la liberté du commerce entre les nations*" (1764); (3) notes by Professor Sauvaire-Jourdain on the text of the *Paradoxes*. The three parts, taken together, form a most illuminating critical study of French economic thought in the first two thirds of the eighteenth century. The preliminary essay was published separately, under the same title, in the *Revue d'économie politique* for 1903.

See also A. Dubois, *Un rapport d'Isaac de Bacalan, intendant du commerce* (1768) (1908 *Revue d'histoire des doctrines économiques et sociales*). The article contains, besides commentary, a reprint of a manuscript entitled "*Observations faites par M. de Bacalan, Intendant de Commerce, dans son voyage en Picardie, Artois, Haynaut et Flandre, l'an 1768.*"

[2] Cf. Sauvaire-Jourdain, *loc. cit.*, pp. 9–12.

reduces to an exchange of commodities. A surplus balance of money is therefore of no advantage, since this surplus must itself be exchanged for goods. (2) The importation of money is limited, for such imports result in an increase in prices and in a consequent reëxport of money. This is Hume's price-gold flow mechanism. (3) A country benefits from the progress of other countries. This is the idea of economic solidarity. (4) A country gains from free trade, even though other countries maintain protective systems. Of these ideas, the second is the one of particular interest here.

In the actual text of his "Paradoxes" De Bacalan first shows, on negative grounds, the futility of the Mercantilist advocacy of an accumulation of the precious metals. Suppose a balance of payments to be received in money. It then follows that

even this is only an exchange. Either the money is considered only as a symbol, and hence has no real value; or else it is considered as a commodity, in which case the trade has only resulted in an exchange [of commodities], and the balance is still even.[1]

But the argument also has a positive side. Suppose a single state to furnish to all others more than it takes, and to receive the balance in money.

Can it be believed that this situation would be permanent, and that the state would slowly absorb all the money in the world? Without a doubt, no. The increase in the quantity of money would decrease its price, luxury would increase, and with it the consumption both of domestic and of foreign commodities. The result would be that this state would transport a smaller quantity of commodities to the others, and would take a greater quantity from them. These it would in turn be obliged to pay for in money, and the circulation would be re-established.[2]

This formulation is adequate, but it is less good than Hume's. It lacks the perhaps deceptive precision and clarity of Hume's statement, it does not bring out the *opposite* movement of prices in any two selected countries, and it does not contain so concrete and convincing a discussion of actual market phenomena and of

[1] Sauvaire-Jourdain, *loc. cit.*, p. 43.

[2] *Ibid.* It may be remarked further that De Bacalan also adopts Hume's views on the determination of the rate of interest: he finds the rate to be not the cause, but the effect, of commercial conditions, though his statement is less definite than Hume's. (*Ibid.*, p. 39.) He is thus in disagreement with the then-current Mercantilist doctrine, that interest rates are governed by changes in the quantity of money.

the rôle of the exchange rates. On the other hand, it has the merit of drawing attention to changes in consumption, an aspect of the situation that is much dwelt upon at the present day. It is chiefly noteworthy for our purposes, however, because it presents the only explicit statement in the French literature until less than a hundred years ago of the equilibrium tendency inherent in the working of the price-gold flow mechanism. The price-gold flow analysis as such is to be found in various writers, especially Cantillon and Forbonnais, but it is always either associated with the idea that the surplus of money consequent on a favorable balance of trade can in some way be retained, or else, as in the Physiocrats, it is presented and then simply neglected.[1] Nevertheless little importance in the history of French thought can be attached to De Bacalan's discussion, or to that proposition of Hume's on which it is based. Neither doctrine seems to have attracted especial attention at the time, and when they appeared again in the nineteenth century, under the influence of the classical English school, they had all the force of new ideas.

9. The contributions of the Mercantilist and anti-Mercantilist thought in France to the theory of international prices can be summarized as follows.

The first contribution was the quantity theory of money—a field in which the Italian influence was marked. This theory, laid down in qualified form by Bodin and more rigidly by Davanzati, was confined by Montanari to money and goods in actual circulation. It was then modified by Cantillon to include the velocity of circulation of money, and was further modified by Forbonnais (and by Verri) to allow for the possibility of an offsetting increase in production, consequent on an increase in the quantity of money. The second was the various isolated analyses of the interconnections of the price structure, and of the actual mechanisms through which price changes are effected and disseminated. These analyses are found in one or two manuscripts of officers of the Cour des Monnaies, to some ex-

---

[1] Condillac gives the first half of the price-specie flow mechanism, but the second half, the restoration of equilibrium, is lacking. See Condillac, *Le commerce et le gouvernement*, Part II, ch. 2. (In the edition already cited, reprinted in the *Collection des Principaux Économistes*, Mélanges, vol. i: pp. 382, 383.)

tent in Boisguilbert, in Cantillon and Forbonnais, in De Bacalan, and in Condillac. The third was the price-specie flow mechanism, presented more or less completely by such writers of the middle eighteenth century as Cantillon, Forbonnais, De Bacalan, and to some extent by the Physiocrats. The fourth was the recognition that the distribution of the precious metals tends, through the agency of price movements, to seek an equilibrium of sorts. This proposition is found only in the translations of Hume, and in De Bacalan. Finally, the observation was made that price changes in a given country can affect the volume of its foreign trade. This idea, which is in a sense almost a truism, is probably latent in most of the writers whom we have had in mind, yet it finds explicit expression in almost none. Cantillon, some of the Physiocrats, and De Bacalan are the principal exceptions. For the idea, while simple enough in itself, must almost inevitably carry with it a comprehensive grasp of the character and mechanisms of international exchange. Such a grasp can be provided only by a theory like Hume's.

Of these various doctrines the first, the quantity theory, has held its place without a break until the present day. The others disappeared completely with the fall of the old Empire, and when a few isolated writers began to present them again, toward the middle of the last century, it was necessary to break the ground afresh. For all the direct effect it has had upon modern French thought, the older body of ideas and investigations into the principles of international exchange might as well have never existed.

CHAPTER IX

THE THEORY OF INTERNATIONAL EXCHANGE IN FRANCE
1776–1880
ENGLISH DOCTRINE AND EARLY FRENCH CRITICS

1. The history of the theory of international exchange in France during the last hundred years or more is very largely the history of the changing fortunes of English doctrine upon French soil. There has been no such continuous and uninterrupted development of ideas, running through a number of centuries, as is found in England. With the rise of the Physiocratic doctrine to preëminence, French economic thought turned to domestic problems almost exclusively. The upheavals of the Revolution and of the Napoleonic era only served to strengthen the diversion of interest. When, more than half a century later, French economists again began to examine the theoretical aspects of international exchange seriously, the new movement was in considerable part not spontaneous. It was due to the stimulus of English thought, and to the desire to verify or disprove the conclusions of English writers. The theory of international exchange, as distinct from the theory of purely internal commerce, has never regained the position which it held in the pre-Physiocratic literature. Even at the present day the great majority of the general French treatises on economics content themselves with discussions of tariff policies and of the exchange-market mechanisms, finding nothing in the theory of international value and prices, as such, to make it essentially different from the theory of values and prices in general.

Nevertheless it is far from true that the general theory of international trade, in the English interpretation of the term, has been entirely neglected in France or on the Continent at large. The not uncommon statements to that effect are quite erroneous. Nor is the assertion that French writers are in the main indebted to English inspiration to be taken as meaning that they have produced no original and worth-while ideas of their own. But these ideas, whether constructive or destructive, have almost always been of such character that they fit into the general framework of the doctrines already advanced by English theorists. No fundamentally different line of constructive approach to the problem has been laid down by the French, except by Cournot. And even Cournot, although he arrived at a theory of the determination and the effects of international exchange which was radically unlike the English teaching, exercised so slight an influence that from the point of view of the development of French theory his work can almost be ignored.

It is possible to distinguish some five phases in the history of the adoption and criticism of English doctrines by French writers, phases which in point of fact correspond to the principal stages in the development of French thought itself upon the theory of international exchange. They are as follows: first, the early positive reflections of the English ideas, presented in the middle of the nineteenth century by Chevalier, Cherbuliez, De Laveleye, Juglar, and others; second, the mathematical studies of Cournot, which led him to formulate the problem in somewhat different terms, and which provide the first real criticisms of the classical line of thought; third, the more recent partial adoptions of English theories, especially at the hands of the Italian mathematical economist Pareto, and also certain isolated attempts at an empirical verification; fourth, the radical criticisms advanced since the beginning of the present century by Professor Nogaro, and in some degree by other writers, which turn largely on the validity of the classical price-gold flow analysis; and finally, a number of miscellaneous studies made in the past twenty years of the actual processes of currency depreciation, and of the effects of such depreciations upon the course of international trade. Of these phases the first two, covering the period to 1880, are treated in the present chapter. The third and fourth will be examined in the following chapter, and the fifth, together with the recent history of French monetary theory, in the chapter next succeeding.

2. It is first necessary, however, to outline briefly the history of the direct introduction of English ideas into France through the translation or paraphrase of English works. Of these, the book which has had by far the greatest influence upon French thought in general is Adam Smith's "Wealth of Nations." Four different translations appeared between 1779 and 1802.[1] Then in 1803 J.-B. Say published his famous treatise, which was inspired by and in considerable degree based on the "Wealth of Nations."[2] Say enormously increased Smith's influences on the Continent. This influence, however, was of course exerted primarily in the field of practical governmental policies in international trade. Smith's ideas seem to have had but little effect upon the general theory of the subject in France, and indeed Smith's own interest, as we have seen in another chapter, did not lie in that direction. Nor did Say's additions provide any material contribution to the theory. The celebrated "Loi des Débouchés" proves, on examination, to be little more than a truism, and his other doctrines here are of minor importance.[3] In the field of the more abstract analysis, it is necessary to turn to other writers to find the real beginnings of the active English influence.

[1] Gide and Rist, op. cit., p. 123.

[2] J.-B. Say, Traité d'économie politique (Paris, 1803: 2 vols.). Subsequent editions appeared in 1814, 1817, 1819, and 1826. A sixth edition, in one volume, was edited and published by his son, H. Say, in 1841. See also J.-B. Say's Cours complet d'économie politique pratique (Paris, 1828–1829; 6 vols.; 2 ed., 1840: 2 vols.; with notes by H. Say).

[3] The Loi des Débouchés, or "law of outlets" (see the Traité, 6 ed., 1841, pp. 141 ff.), reduces simply to the proposition that the production of an article provides de facto an "outlet," or opportunity for sale, to some other article, since in the last analysis products must exchange for products. The "law" was advanced primarily to break up the inherited predilection in favor of money as such, by showing that money is not in itself wealth, but only the means of attaining wealth. Say and his followers applied it to international trade to prove that the fact of importation carries with it, as a necessary corollary, the fact of an equivalent exportation; and further to show that the absolute amount of money in a country is not important (ibid., pp. 145, 146). But a little reflection makes it clear that this proposition does not help materially toward an understanding of the determination, or of the mechanisms, of foreign exchange. It takes no account of the price-specie flow mechanism (which is not explicitly given by Say: see ibid., p. 140); and it affords no explanation of the significance of specie flows in the actual world of affairs. See the references, later in this chapter, to De Laveleye's Le marché monétaire; and Sauvaires Jourdain's translation of Bastable (also cited below), p. x. Yet only recently it wa-

The so-called classical theory of international trade was first definitely formulated by Ricardo, and inasmuch as a translation of his "Principles" appeared in 1819 (and of his complete works in 1847),[1] we might well expect to find an early reflection of this theory in France. But the passages dealing with the world distribution of the precious metals were badly rendered, and the general Ricardian theory of international trade itself seems to have entirely escaped the attention of contemporary French commentators.[2] Only after the appearance of Mill's work did the classical doctrine began to take real root in France, and even then the process was slow. Chevalier reproduced fragments of it in 1850, and again in 1866, but it was not until 1862 that Cherbuliez presented a complete copy. Courcelle-Seneuil's "Traité," published in 1857, was in general a paraphrase of Mill, but the theory of foreign trade was left out. Courcelle-Seneuil denied that there was a separate place for such a theory. Mill's work itself was not actually translated until 1873.[3] Before that time his doctrines on international trade exerted a direct influence only upon those few French economists who had read them in English.

announced that this "law" gives the "real characteristic" of economic life. See Guyot and Raffalovich, *Inflation et Déflation* (Paris, 1921), p. 41.

Elsewhere Say refutes the balance-of-trade theory, but only by showing that an increase in the quantity of money does not of itself cause an increase in wealth (*op. cit.*, pp. 162–174). The essential contradiction between this theory and the quantity theory of money is not specifically pointed out.

In the field of money, he presents views not much different from those of Smith. He adopts the convenient Smithian idea of a total of non-monetary values, to which the value of the monetary unit itself is adjusted according to the extant quantity of money (*ibid.*, pp. 162, 248–257); and he asserts that when the quantity of money is inadequate for the volume of business it soon increases, because money is a commodity, and every kind of commodity seeks the place where there is need of it (*ibid.*, p. 140). But just what the process is, he does not show. Finally, like Forbonnais, Say suggests that a gradual increase in the quantity of money, and a consequent gradual fall in its value, is favorable to industry (*ibid.*, p. 271, note 1).

[1] D. Ricardo, *Des principes de l'économie politique et de l'impôt* (translated by S. S. Constancio, Paris, 1819; 2 vols.); Constancio and Fonteyraud, *Oeuvres complètes de David Ricardo* (Paris, 1847). The latter is contained in the *Collection des Principaux Économistes* (cited above).

[2] Cf. the *Oeuvres*, p. 107, note, and p. 117, note. Also see Sauvaire-Jourdain, *Isaac de Bacalan* (cited above), pp. 54, 55, note 15.

[3] J. S.-Mill, *Principes de l'économie politique*, translated by Dussard and Courcelle-Seneuil, from the third English edition (Paris, 1873; 2 vols.).

Finally, mention must be made of translations of four other English works, which have had an important place in the later development of French thought. They are the "Report of the Bullion Committee of 1810" (1865);[1] Goschen's "Foreign Exchanges" (1866);[2] Clare's "English Money Market" (1894);[3] and Bastable's "Theory of International Trade" (1900).[4] But it must be pointed out that these translations, like the works of Mill and Ricardo, have owed their general currency among French students chiefly to the light they cast upon the problems of market mechanisms, of the foreign exchanges, and to some extent of tariff policies. The serious study of the abstract classical theory of international trade itself has remained the province of a comparatively small number of economists. The great body of French treatises upon general economic theory, and the great majority of French writers upon the more specialized problems of international exchange, have taken no account of it at all.

3. The direct reflections of the English theory of international exchange, those works which were designed to copy part or all of the English doctrine or to improve upon it constructively, were far from numerous in the period before 1880. They consist chiefly in the writings of Chevalier, Cherbuliez, De Laveleye and Juglar. To these, however, may be added Bastiat's presentation of the free-trade argument,[5] and also Wolowski's discussion of the foreign exchanges — which was based very largely on Goschen.

[1] The translation is contained in Coullet et Juglar, *Extraits des enquêtes parlementaires anglaises, 1810-1858* (Paris, 1865; 8 vols.), vol. i.

[2] G. J. G. Goschen, *Théorie des changes étrangers*, translated by Léon Say from the fifth English edition (Paris, 1866); 2 ed., 1875; 3 ed., 1892; 4 ed., 1896. The second and following editions also contain Say's report on the French indemnity-payment operations after the war of 1870.

[3] George Clare, *Le marché monétaire anglais et la clef des changes*, translated by G. Giraud from the second English edition (Paris, 1894).

[4] C. F. Bastable, *La théorie du commerce international*, translated by F. Sauvaire-Jourdain from the second English edition (Paris, 1900); with an Introduction by the translator).

[5] Bastiat, whose *Harmonies Économiques* was published in 1850, was a free-trader of the "mono-lateral" Ricardian type. He held that a country gains from the abolition of protection even though its neighbors maintain tariff-walls against it. His doctrines are not especially relevant here, and no further mention will be made of them. For a convenient summary, however, see Paul Cauwès, *Précis de cours d'économie politique* (Paris, 1878-1880; 2 vols.), vol. i, pp. 619-621.

Chevalier's theory of international trade was the result of a curious blend of Say's "Loi des Débouchés" and the classical price-specie flow analysis.[1] He found it to be true that, over a period of years, international commodity transactions tend to balance, so that products exchange for products alone. This was Say's "law." But at any one time this balance may fail to appear. The exchange rate will then move in response. The consequent premium will act as a check to exports and a stimulus to imports, or vice versa. Gold may also flow, and thus lend its influence to the correction of the balance of payments.[2] A large and sudden movement of the precious metals, however, will produce a commercial disaster. Domestic producers will be compelled to liquidate their resources, and to sell abroad at a loss if necessary; and the decreased value of public loans will attract capital from abroad — a result also attainable by raising the discount rate. Thus the specie flow will be stopped, and the crisis ended.[3]

But this is as far as Chevalier goes. The more smooth-working mechanism which Ricardo and Mill had in mind is not reproduced, nor is the supposedly opposite and compensating movement of prices in the two selected countries examined. Further, the equilibrium-tendency of the classical theory is presented very incompletely, and then only with respect to the exchange markets and the balance of money payments. Finally, the classical theory of international (non-monetary) values is entirely neglected.

Chevalier, from the point of view of the theory of international trade, is thus at best a quasi-classicist. He is not an opponent or a critic, but he is very far from being a thorough-going supporter. His contemporary Cherbuliez, however, gives a quite unexceptionable presentation of Mill's position — the first, indeed, in

---

[1] Michel Chevalier, *Cours d'économie politique* (Paris, 1841–1850: 3 vols.; 2 ed., 1855–1866).

[2] Chevalier, *op. cit.*, 2 ed., vol. iii (1866), pp. 677–684. I have been unable to obtain access to the first edition of volume iii (published in 1850), and cannot say how far it differs from the second. One ground for thinking that the difference is probably slight, however, lies in the complete lack of any clear reflection of Mill's doctrines, as distinct from Ricardo's, in the second edition.

[3] *Ibid.*, pp. 695–704.

France.[1] His reproduction is so perfect that it is unnecessary to do more than indicate its principal heads.[2] These are the classical assumption that the immobility of labor and capital, as between countries, makes the determination of value in international trade unlike their determination in internal trade; the further assumption that the introduction of money does not necessitate any modification in the theoretical analysis of these values; the principles of comparative and of absolute advantage; the determination of international values themselves by comparative intensities of demand, within the limits set by comparative costs; the equation of international demands; and finally the price-specie flow mechanism, and the doctrine of the consequent tendency to an equilibrium. The analysis of the world distribution of the precious metals, however, does not seem to be given separate consideration. The "equilibrium" in question is that of the exchange market and the balance of international payments alone.

Two points alone require further comment. The first is the curious fact that, while Cherbuliez avowedly based his propositions on Mill, they were taken not from Mill's "Principles" but from his "Unsettled Questions," published four years before the "Principles." [3] What the explanation is, is not clear. The second point is this. Despite the clarity and force of his exposition, Cherbuliez's doctrines apparently failed absolutely to make any impression upon his contemporaries or upon his successors. Somewhat like most of Cournot's writings on economic subjects, his work stands out like an isolated island in a sea of indifference and neglect. When, some fifteen or twenty years later, the general body of French economists began to take partial account of the classical theory of international trade, the references are almost always directly to the English writers themselves. For any indication that they give, Cherbuliez might as well have never written.

---

[1] A. E. Cherbuliez, *Précis de la Science Économique* (Paris, 1862; 2 vols.). Cherbuliez was a Swiss, but the fact that he wrote in French, and that his principal audience was found in France, justifies the usual practice of including him among the French writers.

[2] *Ibid.*, vol. i, pp. 375-391.

[3] *Ibid.*, p. 375.

4. At about the same time, in 1865 and 1868 respectively, De Laveleye and Juglar began to introduce more constructive modifications into the classical theory. The term "modification," however, is perhaps misleading. Neither man was writing to attack or to defend the classical theory as such. Each was dealing, at the points that interest us, simply with the *mechanisms* of the international money markets. Their conclusions, which were in point of fact emendations of classical doctrine, therefore affect only the analysis of the price-specie flow mechanism.

De Laveleye's concern was with the money market, and with the explanation of its crises.[1] His general theory, now familiar under various forms, was that such crises are caused by the drain of specie into international trade. These drains result in a decrease in the available media of exchange, this compels liquidation, and prices fall both at home and abroad. The situation persists until the return of gold at last restores general confidence and ends the crisis.[2] The detail of the process by which these changes in the quantity of gold are supposed to affect commodity prices is interesting in the extreme, and will be examined in the next chapter. It is in effect an anticipation of the so-called "Marshallian" analysis, which first clearly appeared in English thought with the publication of Sidgwick's work in 1883. The point of especial interest here, however, is De Laveleye's discussion of the exchange-market mechanisms and of their tendency to equilibrium. The discussion is based on Goschen's familiar propositions, but it is so compactly and so clearly put that it is worth repeating.

When a country has imported more than it has exported, . . . there are many bills in the foreign market payable in this country, and as they are offered they fall in price. They fall to the point at which it is more profitable to the foreign creditors to import gold than to sell bills. Then a drain of the precious metal begins. But as soon as the rise in interest rates [consequent on the drain of specie], followed by the fall in prices, attracts foreign capitalists, these last begin to seek those same bills which were but recently disdained, in order to make their remittances. The [original] creditors, able to sell their bills advantageously, will give up importing specie. The rate of ex-

---

[1] Émile de Laveleye, *Le marché monétaire et ses crises* (Paris, 1866). De Laveleye was a Belgian, but is included in the history of French thought by the same license that permits the inclusion of the Swiss Cherbuliez.

[2] *Ibid.*, pp. 125–128.

change will improve, will tend to regain parity, and the exportation of gold from the debtor country will in consequence stop. . . . Independently of these purchases of goods and securities, which make gold flow back to the countries where interest rates are high, there are also other operations which will have the same effect. It is advantageous to employ money for discount where interest rates are high. Those who have loanable money will therefore send it to the market where it is possible to get 7 or 8 per cent by discounting good paper, instead of getting only 3 or 4 per cent at home.[1]

De Laveleye then goes on to summarize Goschen's explanation, in his "excellent study," of how this is done — of how an increase in discount rates results in correcting the exchanges.[2]

In other words De Laveleye gives here, perhaps more clearly than Goschen himself, an analysis of specie flows which is based in the first instance on the phenomena of the money market. It is based, that is, on the discount rate and the volume of credit. The subsequent effect on commodity prices is recognized,[3] but it is made secondary in the actual order of events to the antecedent changes in credit. Nor is the tendency to equilibrium neglected, but it is regarded as operating only through the foreign exchanges and the discount rates. The rigid classical theory had proceeded directly from commodity prices to specie flows, and had paid only passing attention to the exchange market. De Laveleye, on the contrary, makes the exchange market the principal element, with commodity prices treated (from this point of view) as minor and consequent factors. Moreover, whereas the classical theory had rested its analysis of the corrective influence of gold flows and of the resulting equilibrium-tendency directly on the prices of *commodities*, De Laveleye bases these movements primarily on the prices of *bills*.[4] His discussion can-

[1] De Laveleye, *op. cit.*, pp. 175, 176.

[2] This seems to be the first definite recognition in French literature of the connection between the discount rate and the exchanges; a recognition due, like so large a proportion of the French ideas upon international exchange and monetary phenomena, to English inspiration. The second edition of Chevalier's *Cours*, which appeared in 1866 (cited above), also makes some reference to it, but assigns it a rôle of much less importance.

[3] See the passages just quoted, and pp. 138-144.

[4] Léon Say, in the Introduction to his translation of Goschen (cited above), goes so far as to assert that this readjustment of the balance of payments by specie flows, operating through the discount rate, is the principal factor maintaining the "necessary" amount of money in each country.

not be said to be less comprehensive than that of the English writers, for it considers not only all of the factors they dealt with, but also some others as well. Furthermore, it emphasizes an aspect of which the classical theory never took adequate account. De Laveleye drew his ideas, of course, primarily from Goschen, but he made far more of them than Goschen did himself, and tied them up more convincingly with general monetary theory.

Finally, De Laveleye concludes that the absolute quantity of money in a country is very far from being a matter of indifference. The teachings of abstract theory make it seem as though a change in the amount of money means nothing more than a change in the number of counters used. But that is not true, proximately at least. Such a change will influence discount rates, affect the volume of credit, and possibly precipitate (or, conversely, prevent) a crisis. This fact De Laveleye finds to be the explanation of the great importance attached by the business world to specie flows. He calls attention, also, to the antithesis between this view and J.-B. Say's "Loi des Débouchés." Say regarded such flows as being of no particular significance, since "products must after all exchange for products." [1]

Three years later, Juglar published a book which despite the difference in title had much in common with De Laveleye's work, and which likewise drew heavily from English sources.[2] For our purposes its chief interest lies in its monetary theories, to be examined later. It may be remarked here, however, that Juglar gives (without explicit acknowledgment) what is sub-

[1] De Laveleye, *op. cit.*, pp. 128–138 and following. Also see his *La monnaie et la bimétallisme internationale* (Paris, 1891), pp. 41–51, for a more specific attack on Say.

In 1857 De Laveleye had published a booklet in which he took over, without criticism and apparently without too profound comprehension, Mill's doctrines on international values, on the price-specie flow mechanism, and so on. See *La liberté du commerce international* (Paris, 1857), pp. 66–71. The book is not of much value, and it apparently exerted no perceptible influence, except upon a few isolated French free-traders.

[2] Clement Juglar, *Du change et de la liberté d'émission* (Paris, 1868). Juglar is somewhat indebted to Goschen, but he drew most heavily from such English writers upon money and banking as Tooke and Lord Overstone, and from the reports of the various English committees on these questions.

stantially the Ricardian doctrine of the world distribution of the precious metals. He makes this distribution turn on the fact that when a country's prices are relatively high, gold becomes the cheapest way of effecting remittances.[1] He also, like De Laveleye, connects specie flows with the discount rate, though his discussion seems to take no account of a possible automatic tendency to equilibrium.[2] Finally, he makes an interesting though summary attempt to tie up gold flows with *cyclical* price movements. He finds that as prices rise, specie drains out. The flow cannot be stopped until a few big liquidations bring on a crisis, and thus turn the price trend downward again.[3]

These various explanations of the exchange-market mechanisms, and of the rôle of the precious metals in foreign trade, were at bottom derived largely from Goschen. They contain much that is valuable, and had they been applied rigorously they might have led to a revision of at least the form, if not the essential content, of the classical theory of international trade.[4] They might well, also, have provided the starting point for an independent and highly realistic school of thought in France itself. But little attention was paid to them at the time, and I have not found more than a few scattered references to them in all the succeeding body of the French literature.

5. The English classical doctrines, in the period before 1875, had thus exerted a marked influence on the works of Chevalier, De Laveleye and Juglar, and had been reproduced almost entire by Cherbuliez. It remains to give some account of two writers who held somewhat different views: Courcelle-Seneuil, and Cour-

---

[1] Juglar, *op. cit.*, p. 271.

[2] *Ibid.*, p. 275. A similar reflection of Goschen is to be found in L. Wolowski, *Le change et la circulation* (Paris, 1869), pp. 143 ff. Indeed, Wolowski's whole treatment of the exchanges is taken very largely from Goschen — with occasional references, in connection with the phenomena of depreciation, to the Bullion Report of 1810 (see p. 102 ff.).

[3] Juglar, *op. cit.*, pp. 469, 470.

[4] The same observation, it will be remembered, was made concerning the neglect by the later classical writers themselves of the work of Goschen, and of the successive advances made in monetary theory. I do not see that these matters can be ruled out as irrelevant in any theory of international exchange which undertakes to deal with things as they actually work. The principle cannot be divorced from the mechanism through which it operates without leading to sterility.

not. Courcelle-Seneuil [1] can be dismissed with a word. He denied that there is a genuine difference between internal and international commerce, and held that those inequalities in productive powers as between countries, on which the separate theory of international trade had been built, arise equally *within* any one country. In consequence, he refused to admit that there is any place or justification for such a theory:

> All those observations to which the phenomena of the largest market give rise can properly be applied to the smallest market. . . . There is no scientific distinction between the two sorts of commerce. Everything that is true of one is true of the other, and can be applied to it.[2]

No especial proof is given for these rather dogmatic statements, but they must not be allowed to go unnoticed on that account. They represent a point of view characteristic of the majority of French economists even to the present day.

Cournot's writings are of a quite different caliber.[3] Cournot, in the first instance a mathematician and a philosopher, presents as an economist the not uncommon case of a genius who perhaps only because of the obscurity of his style, or because of the difficulty of his argument, quite failed to secure the recognition which he deserved. His work in economics is brilliant and suggestive at almost every point, and is one of the first serious attempts to apply the mathematical method to social problems. Cournot began writing in 1838, published a second book in 1863, and a third (in which the mathematical method is omitted) in 1877. Yet with the exception of a few economists of the isolated mathematical school, no general attention seems to have been paid to him until less than forty years ago, and then the "discoverer" was an Englishman, Professor Jevons.[4] In France, no serious

---

[1] J. G. Courcelle-Seneuil, *Traité théorique et pratique d'économie politique* (Paris, 1857; 2 vols.).

[2] Courcelle-Seneuil, *op. cit.*, 3 ed. (1891), vol. i, p. 268.

[3] A. C. Cournot, *Recherches sur les principes mathématiques de la théorie des richesses* (Paris, 1838); *Principes de la théorie des richesses* (Paris, 1863); *Revue sommaire des doctrines économiques* (Paris, 1877).

[4] See K. H. Hagen, *Die Nothwendigkeit der Handelsfreiheit für das Nationaleinkommen mathematisch nachgeweisen* (Königsberg, 1844), pp. 30–32; L. Walras, *Élémens d'économie politique pure* (Lausanne, 1874), pp. 202–207; and W. S. Jevons, *The Theory of Political Economy*, 2 ed. (London, 1879), Preface. A brief review of the

study of his doctrines appeared until 1912. While Cournot's ideas are of the greatest interest to us as students of economic theory, care must therefore be taken not to assign them too large a place in the history of French doctrine. They are almost completely detached from the contemporary literature, and have been devoid of any material influence upon the main body of later thought.

In the field of the theory of international exchange, Cournot deserves credit for working out a method of approach which was quite different from the English, and which was in the first instance independent of it. In his "Principes" and in the "Revue Sommaire," published in 1863 and 1877 respectively, he speaks at length of the English doctrine, and attempts to demonstrate some of its fallacies. But the essential features of his own ideas are all contained in his "Recherches," published in 1838. In this book he shows no knowledge of the then-extant English theory, as formulated by Ricardo and Senior.

Cournot is sometimes represented as being in effect simply a critic of the English teaching. That proposition, however, is not altogether correct. He was much more than a mere critic. He was concerned with problems which at some points were the same as those with which the English writers chiefly dealt, but which at other points were quite different. It therefore follows that his apparent criticisms have often, in point of fact, no true common ground with the propositions of English theory. It is probably more accurate to think of Cournot's ideas and the English as forming two independent systems of thought, which are not rivals so much by original construction as by later interpreta-

inception and growth of Cournot's influence is given in Irving Fisher, *Cournot and Mathematical Economics* (12 Quarterly Journal of Economics, 1898), pp. 133–136.

Hagen's criticisms, which are almost too summary to be of use, turn partly on Cournot's measurement of various magnitudes, and partly on his refusal to regard the total productive power of the country as necessarily limited. Hagen, on the contrary, holds that a greater outlay at one point means a corresponding diminution at another.

Also see Professor Edgeworth's comments on Hagen and Cournot, in his articles in the Economic Journal for 1894. That Cournot was acutely conscious of the indifference with which his work was in general received, is shown clearly in the preface of the *Principes*.

tion. They are opposed only in so far as they chance to deal with similar questions. It is but fair to add, however, that Cournot's doctrines are far from being as comprehensive in their scope as the English. They provide an explanation of only certain parts of the processes of international exchange, not of that exchange in its entirety.

The pure classical theory may be taken as turning on three cardinal questions.[1] (1) What determines the movements of foreign trade? (2) What are the effects of this trade on the countries concerned? (3) Is there a tendency to an equilibrium? Of these questions, the classical writers concentrated their attention chiefly on the first. They asserted that the principles governing international trade are different from those governing internal trade. To explain the course of international trade, they worked out the principle of comparative costs and the various later refinements of the theory of international values. The second question they dealt with rather perfunctorily. They found that the benefit from foreign trade arises primarily in connection with imports alone, the measure lying in the ratio of exchange between such imports and the corresponding exports. In consequence they kept in mind only the interest of the consumers, and neglected that of the producers. This procedure they justified by the assumption that productive forces, when displaced by importation, can be turned without loss to other lines of economic activity. To the third question they answered that there is undoubtedly a genuine tendency to equilibrium in foreign trade. The argument here was worked out on familiar lines.

Cournot accepted the third of these propositions without modification and almost without comment, for the equilibrium concept is inherent in all his theory of prices and values.[2] But on the

[1] I have taken this classification from the excellent study of Cournot made by H. E. Barrault: *Les doctrines de Cournot sur le commerce international* (Revue d'histoire des doctrines économiques et sociales, 1912), pp. 110, 111. Somewhat different classifications are used at other points in the present study, but this one is especially convenient here.

[2] So see Cournot's *Recherches*, pp. 29, 30 and following, and parallel passages in the other two books. It should be added, however, that the equilibrium is stated in terms of international debts and credits as expressed in terms of money — with a rôle of major importance assigned to the actual foreign exchange rate of the market.

other two he adopted positions which, both from the theoretical
and from the practical point of view, were diametrically opposed
to those of the classicists. With respect to the first proposition,
the determination of international exchanges, he concludes that
these exchanges are governed by precisely the same conditions as
purely internal transactions; namely, by differences in prices,
after allowance has been made for costs of transportation and for
the state of the foreign exchanges. Thus in the "Principes" he
begins his discussion by saying that

it is clear that any article capable of being transported must flow from the
market where its value is less to that where its value is greater, until a point
is reached at which the difference in value, as between one market and the
other, is no greater than the cost of transportation.[1]

These values are of course translated at the current rate of (foreign) exchange. In the earlier "Recherches" especially, this general thesis is worked out by mathematical symbols and equations
to show the conditions and rates of exchange between any selected
number of markets, *whether these be in the same or in different
countries*.[2]

A little later, in connection with his criticisms of Mill, Cournot
carries the attack much farther. He discards the principle of
comparative costs without particular comment, and for it substitutes an explanation running in terms of ratios of exchange.[3]
He takes two articles, each produced in both of two countries,
which have definite ratios of exchange as between one another in
each country. Neglecting costs of transportation (and assuming
the trade to be possible at all), he finds that the two articles will
be exchanged in international commerce at some intermediate

It therefore differs in form if not in substance from the classical statement, and
carries with it somewhat different implications. The fact of specie flows to meet a
deficit in the balance of payments is explicitly recognized, but their effects outside
of the exchange markets, on prices at large, are not elaborated. See the *Recherches*,
pp. 30–45.

[1] *Principes*, p. 311. See also the *Recherches*, pp. 134–136.

[2] *Recherches*, pp. 29–45. It is interesting to note that Walras here took over
bodily, with acknowledgments, Cournot's methods, conclusions, and even notations,
with an additional reference to Goschen's analysis of the elements in the balance
of international payments. See L. Walras, *Élémens d'économie politique pure*
(Lausanne, 1874), pp. 202–207.

[3] *Principes*, pp. 338–340.

ratio lying between the extremes set by the previous ratios within the one country and the other. Further, as in the classical theory, he finds that a point of equilibrium will be reached in this exchange. This point is determined by the laws of consumption and production in each country.[1] Having made these statements, however, Cournot stops. He fails to find anything in the determination of international values, barring the fact of a variable exchange rate, which in any way distinguishes it at bottom from the exchange between two separated markets in the same country.

It is at once apparent that these theories are unlike the classical doctrine. Cournot recognizes no essential difference between international and internal exchange, unless it be the somewhat greater complexity of the former, and he applies precisely the same apparatus of exchange ratios and equilibria to the one that he does to the other. The classical theory of international values is thus entirely discarded, but more by substitution than by direct attack. Cournot does not seem to assign it a place of its own in his criticisms, and it may be questioned whether he appreciated its full intended significance. Whether Cournot was right, whether or not international values can in point of fact be treated satisfactorily through the agency of prices and made indistinguishable from other values, will be considered in another chapter.[2] The danger in the method lies in the obscuring of that condition of imperfect competition, arising from the assumed international immobility of labor and capital, which is held to separate international from internal commerce. Cournot's presentation, however, has two distinct advantages. It runs in terms of prices, which are usable phenomena of actual experience; and it emphasizes not only the possibility but the certainty that a limit will be reached on the profitable exchange of any one article — a condition ignored by the classical theory. Finally, Cournot agrees with the classicists in holding that the presence or absence of

---

[1] This leads him into an obscure discussion of plural equilibria, and of Mill's unsatisfactory solution of the dilemma.

[2] Ch. xviii, below. The attempt to interpret international trade in terms of prices alone was not made again until Professor Nicholson's *Principles* appeared. See ch. iv, sect. 7, above.

money does not make necessary any essential modification in the general analysis.[1]

6. It is Cournot's doctrines on the second classical proposition, the effects of foreign trade upon the countries concerned, which have in recent years been made the principal object of attack.[2] His statements dealing with "asymmetrical" markets were advanced in that connection; statements which have been much misinterpreted, and which, granted Cournot's premises, are not unreasonable. Cournot starts with the fundamental idea that the mobility of the productive forces in any given country is relatively slight. In consequence, he holds that when a domestic industry is partly or wholly driven out of business by the importation of foreign products, the wealth tied up in this industry is in large part lost. This proposition, which is in direct contradiction to the comparatively perfect internal mobility assumed by the classicists, is latent throughout Cournot's argument. Yet it never seems to have found explicit and specific expression. The failure to recognize it accounts in large part for the failure of various recent critics to do Cournot entire justice. The essence of the argument, which is supported by elaborate though hypothetical arithmetic examples, is this.

Cournot has in mind a single article M, produced in both of two countries, and produced, also, under increasing costs. Suppose the export of this article, as from country A to country B, to have been previously prohibited. Then suppose the prohibition to be removed, while all other conditions of communication between the two markets remain the same. If a given quantity of the com-

---

[1] So see especially the *Recherches*, p. 189, and the *Revue Sommaire*, pp. 208, 209.

[2] See C. F. Bastable, *Theory of International Trade* (4 ed., London, 1903), pp. 173–175; F. Y. Edgeworth, *The Theory of International Values* (4 Economic Journal), pp. 152, 625; and Irving Fisher, *Cournot and Mathematical Economics* (12 Quarterly Journal of Economics, 1898), p. 129. Fisher's concern here was to show that Cournot's conclusions in defense of protection are explained by a careless error in his mathematical procedure, and that a correction of the error would have led him to the free-trade position. Reference should also be made to the short but able criticism in A. Landry, *Manuel d'économique* (Paris, 1908), p. 839.

For a reasoned examination and refutation of most of these criticisms see Barrault's article on Cournot, already cited, especially pp. 119–124.

modity M is imported into B from A, an equal money value must be imported directly or indirectly into A from B. But this necessary increase in the foreign demand for B's product is more than offset, in B, by two sources of loss. One is the impoverishment of B's producers of M — the assumption being, as just indicated, that the displaced productive force is in large part lost, and does not find equally profitable employment in other fields. The other is the reduction in the total funds that B's nationals can apply to their total demands for the commodities in B, *other* than the import. The reduction is consequent on the decreased or entirely discontinued total return from the manufacture, in B, of the article M. In country A, however, the opposite changes take place. There the diversion to foreign commodities of a part of the funds previously devoted to national products is more than offset by two sources of gain. One is the enriching of A's producers of the article M, in consequence of its exportation. The other is the increase in the total funds that A's nationals can apply to commodities *other* than M. The increase results from the increased total return from the production of M itself. Country A, then, gains from the removal of the former barrier to trade, while B loses. With respect to this single commodity, and under the assumption of increasing costs, the two markets are therefore "asymmetrical." That is, the effects of the opening up of exchange between them are dissimilar.[1]

Such is this now well-known argument, summarily put. It was intended simply as an analysis of a particular situation, with respect to a particular commodity and under given hypotheses. It is of course equally valid, if the conditions are reversed, for an export from B into A. In that case not A but B would benefit. With respect to two articles, one an export and one an import, *both* countries may hence gain, but relative to different commodities. With respect to either article alone, the condition of "asym-

---

[1] The argument is presented in the *Recherches*, pp. 187–198; in the *Principes*, pp. 316–324; and more briefly in the *Revue Sommaire*, pp. 204–208. It is supported by arbitrarily selected arithmetical examples. These, however, it has not seemed to me worth while to examine here in detail.

It should be added that Cournot's theory is essentially "short-time." He did not concern himself with the long-run aspects of the problem.

metry" still prevails.[1] Later critics to the contrary notwithstanding, Cournot's conclusion was not intended as a generalized proposition giving the explanation of any and all international exchange. His own presentation specifically confines it to a particular type of situation. I think that Professor Bastable is simply in error when he says that Cournot's main thesis is the implied proposition that a country gains by exportation, and loses by importation.[2] This is not Cournot's main thesis; and it is explicitly presented. As to the soundness of the argument itself, that may be left to the reader's judgment. Granted Cournot's hypotheses, however; granted the unstated premise as to the probable loss from a displacement of domestic industry; and remembering always that it assumes increasing costs, the analysis seems to me to be substantially valid, independently of the correctness or incorrectness of the arithmetic examples by which it is illustrated.

7. Cournot also made, in his "Principes," a quite elaborate examination and criticism of the classical barter assumption.[3] This criticism starts out promisingly, but it resolves in large part into a demonstration that when a considerable number of articles enter the exchange, the assumption of a trade of barter is not the simplest method of presenting the situation. The simplest method consists in a resort to the actual common measure, money. Indeed, reasoning on the barter assumption is held to be permissible, in strict logic, only when the countries concerned actually have some such measure in common. Cournot does not, however, use these objections as a weapon for further attacks upon the fundamental classical position itself.

One other isolated point in his doctrines may be mentioned. This is his formulation of the price-gold flow theorem.[4] He finds that if one market, N, pays its debt to the other market, M, in the precious metals, then the annual flow "will end by raising the prices of all articles in the market M, and lowering them in the

---

[1] So see Cournot's specific statements in the *Principes*, pp. 325–328; and also Barrault, *loc. cit.*, pp. 111-116.

[2] Bastable, *The Theory of International Trade* (4 ed.), p. 173.

[3] *Principes*, pp. 339–350; *Revue Sommaire*, pp. 209–213.

[4] *Revue Sommaire*, p. 209.

market N, to the point where some other article can be found which can be shipped with profit from N to M." This proposition, held to be equally true whether the two markets are in the same or in different countries, is one of the earliest suggestions that the total of the articles in a country can be grouped to form a series of alternatives, which will or will not move in international trade according to the state of prices. In combination with his statement referred to elsewhere, that there is a limit on the profitable exchange of any one commodity, this gives us the basis for a sort of "continuum" conception of the process of international exchange. That is, it gives us the conception of a number of articles in each country which may or may not enter foreign trade, depending on the state of prices, and each of which in any event ultimately reaches the limit of profitable exchange.[1]

Cournot's general position in the history of the theory of international prices, and his contributions to that theory, may be summarized as follows:

First, he denied that there is any essential distinction between international and internal exchange. He then applied his already-developed analysis of prices and price-equilibria to international trade, and thus secured a determination of the course of that trade which was based on the objective phenomenon of market price, on actual ratios of exchange. Cournot's doctrine here, however, is not a complete substitute for the classical theory of international values as determined within the limits set by comparative costs, although it provides a possible point of departure for such a substitution. His argument, which turns on ratios of exchange, runs largely in terms of the demand side of the problem alone. Despite the great emphasis elsewhere placed on the effects of foreign trade upon production, supply is here treated primarily as a variable physical quantity alone. The influence of money costs of production, and their possible rôle in providing ultimate limits to the determination of exchange ratios, are on the whole passed by. Cournot's apparatus consists only in the utilization of current ratios of exchange, in the one market (or country) and the

---

[1] The first statement of this proposition, which failed to attract attention at the time, had been made by Torrens in 1812. See ch. iii, sect. 6, above.

other; in a demonstration that the possibility or impossibility of an inter-market exchange depends on these ratios; and in an analysis of the effects on the ratios of changes in demands and physical quantities. There is no attempt, other than this, to explain the actual rates themselves at which two or more commodities produced in *different* markets will exchange for one another — a problem which was at the heart of the classical theory.

Second, he gave the germs of a sort of "continuum" conception of the products of any one country, which may be set up in contrast to that separation of "international" from "domestic" products which is implicit in most of the classical literature. Third, he drew attention to certain effects of foreign trade, upon the importing and exporting industries themselves, which the classical doctrine had slighted. In so doing, he tried to show that foreign trade is not necessarily and always a source of gain — that the importing country may suffer a net loss. This proposition also led him into a partial justification of protection under certain conditions.

On the other hand, it must be remembered that Cournot's writings belong primarily to the negative and critical side of the history of the theory of international exchange. He himself had no such international theory, as distinguished from a theory of the exchange between any two different markets in the *same* country, and he did not see that there is any place for one. Finally, an earlier caution may properly be repeated here. This is the caution with respect to the almost negligible direct influence exerted by Cournot upon subsequent French thought, exception being always made for the mathematical economists.

CHAPTER X

THE THEORY OF INTERNATIONAL EXCHANGE IN FRANCE AFTER 1880: PARTIAL ADAPTATIONS AND RADICAL CRITICISMS

1. In the period after 1880, the general classical theory of international trade almost entirely dropped from sight in France. Professor Sauvaire-Jourdain translated Bastable's "Theory of International Trade" in 1900, and thereby presumably committed himself to the classical position, while a few years later Professor Landry explicitly adopted its principal conclusions, but they are the only recent French writers who have done so unequivocally. The Italian economist, Pareto, also made a detailed examination of parts of the doctrine in 1897, and again in 1909; and finally Professor Nogaro, between 1904 and 1911, subjected it to a number of searching criticisms. With the writings of these four men, however, the list of serious studies of the classical theory as a whole is complete. The influence of their work, while far from negligible, has not been great enough to give the more characteristic English ideas anything which can be described as a real foothold in France. Professor Sauvaire-Jourdain's translation, for example, is often cited as an authoritative source in current discussions, but the references are almost invariably to passages dealing with the exchanges or with specie flows. The classical theory of international values itself has been entirely ignored by the great majority of French students. Nevertheless, this is far from meaning that the French thought of the past fifty years has contributed nothing to the theory of international *prices*, in which we are here primarily interested. It has made contributions of very considerable value, but along lines somewhat different from those pursued by the corresponding English investigations.[1]

[1] For an excellent though brief summary of the general position of the classical doctrine in France to 1900, see Professor Sauvaire-Jourdain's translation of Bas-

The abstract theory of the process of international exchange has not been of paramount interest to the majority of the recent French writers. They have been concerned, rather, with the explanation and solution of the concrete problems of the moment. These problems, in the field of international economic relationships, have been of two principal types. One, turning on the free-trade–protectionist controversy, is not especially relevant here, and the corresponding literature therefore need not be examined. The other involves the monetary mechanisms and processes of international exchange in general, and their control. The key to this part of the French literature is to be found in the character of the questions raised by international financial and monetary conditions in the years before the great war. Of these the more important were the general fall in the value of silver after 1875, the appearance of depreciated and fluctuating silver or paper currencies in many of the countries with which France has had commercial relations, and the frequent common fear of a protracted drain of specie consequent on an "adverse" balance of international payments. It is to these latter questions and their solution, by bimetallism or compensating tariffs or "bank policies," that French writers in the field of international exchange have turned their principal attention. As a consequence, the controversies in which they have from time to time engaged have been, for the most part, controversies over the explanation of particular concrete phenomena or over the effectiveness of particular practical policies. The defense or criticism of general theories, English or otherwise, has had but little place in their work.

Nevertheless, whether consciously or unconsciously, the English doctrine has provided the point of departure for nearly all of the French studies, and it can fairly be said that this part of the classical teaching has had not only an important but even a dominant place in recent French thought. But the direct derivation of ideas proves, on examination, to be primarily from Goschen. Ricardo and Mill have had an admitted influence only in so far as

table's *Theory of International Trade*, cited frequently elsewhere, Introduction of the Translator, pp. ii–iv. The Introduction itself may be recommended to all students for its survey of the fundamental tenets of the classical theory.

their doctrines found reflection in Goschen's work. It follows that
the propositions which are found in most of the French literature
are essentially refinements on him alone. His theories of the foreign exchanges and of the mechanisms of the exchange market appear time and time again, and are rarely questioned. But the
classical price-specie flow analysis is almost never reproduced,
and when the essentially Ricardian concept of an equilibrium in
international exchange is presented, it is usually stated in terms
of exchange rates and international debts, not in terms of commodity prices and movements.

In view of our earlier discussions of the antecedent English
works, it is unnecessary to review the bulk of this literature in any
detail. Its principal interest lies in the investigations it contains
of those questions, dealing with depreciated currencies and international trade, which have been reserved for another chapter.
The more important French texts upon political economy as a
whole have all adopted Goschen's exchange-market analyses,
with minor modifications. One or two, notably Gide's "Principles," also adopt the Hume-Ricardo idea of a self-restoring
equilibrium,[1] while Cauwès arrives at the opposite view, and
dwells upon the dangers of a protracted drain of specie.[2] Nearly
all of these writers, except Gide, are also moderate protectionists.
But with a single important exception none of them has anything
to say of the classical theory of international values in general, and
only in Colson do we find even the principle of comparative advantage.[3] The exception is Professor Landry, who took over

[1] Charles Gide, *Principes d'économie politique* (Paris, 1884; 12 ed., 1909); continued in subsequent editions with the title, *Cours d'économie politique* (Paris, 1909
ff.). The reference here is to the *Principes*, 12 ed., pp. 291–295. Also see *ibid.*,
pp. 354–362; and the *Cours*, 2 ed. (1911), pp. 363–366.

See also the excellent explanation, on Ricardian lines, of the world distribution of
the precious metals and of the equilibrium tendency, given in Paul Leroy-Beaulieu,
Traité théorique et pratique d'économie politique, 3 ed. (Paris, 1900: 4 vols.), vol. iv,
pp. 123–135.

[2] Paul Cauwès, *Précis du cours d'économie politique* (Paris, 1878–1880: 2 vols.;
2 ed., 1881–1882). The third and following editions bear the title, *Cours d'économie
politique*. The reference is to the *Cours*, 3 ed. (1893), vol. ii, pp. 528–532.

[3] C. Colson, *Cours d'économie politique* (Paris, 1901–1907: 3 vols.; 2 ed., 1907–
1910; 3 ed., 1910–1921: 6 vols.). The reference is to the first edition, vol. ii (1903),
Bk. IV, ch. 5, especially pp. 618–624.

virtually the entire English position as it left the hands of Mill.[1] Landry's very able account, however, does not seem to have obtained the attention which it deserves, and it cannot be regarded as typical of any very large fraction of current French opinion. The principal general texts and monographs upon the theory of the exchanges themselves it will suffice to list in a footnote.[2] The more specialized investigations will be referred to later.

The balance of the present chapter, therefore, will be devoted to the few studies of the general classical theory of international trade that have appeared in France since 1880. Of these only two groups, the writings of Pareto and those of Nogaro, are of major importance, and they alone need be examined in any detail. Mention has already been made of the work of Landry and Sauvaire-Jourdain. But Professor Landry's treatment was brief, and undertook no radically new departure. Professor Sauvaire-Jourdain's rôle as the translator of Bastable's work of course prevented him from making any comprehensive emendation then of the doctrines there expounded, and as far as I know he has not undertaken a reëxamination of them since.[3] There have been, it is true, other more or less isolated adherents of parts of the classical theory,[4] especially with respect to the price-specie flow an-

---

[1] A. Landry, *Manuel d'économique* (Paris, 1908), pp. 831–836.

With respect to the principle of comparative costs, Landry makes a suggestion which seems to me very important. He concludes that the principle does not explain the origin and general development of the commerce between countries, but simply "indicates how it is determined *when the monetary equilibrium [between these countries] is established.*" That is, the phenomena and interrelationships of prices and the consequent readjustment in terms of money comes *first*. When this adjustment has been made, *then* it will be found that importation and exportation are being governed by comparative labor costs. But the mere initial existence of a difference between these costs is not enough, of itself alone, to set up and determine a trade between countries. This view is in substantial agreement with the propositions that will be advanced later in the present study. (See ch. xiv, sect. 3, below.)

[2] M. Bourguin, *La mesure de la valeur et la monnaie* (Paris, 1896); Paul Reboud, *Essai sur les changes étrangers* (Paris, 1900); A. Arnauné, *La monnaie, le crédit, et le change* (Paris, 1902; 6 ed., 1922); Maurice Ansiaux, *Principes de la politique regulatrice des changes* (Paris, 1910); Jules Decamps, *Les changes étrangers* (Paris, 1922).

[3] See, however, his brochure on Isaac de Bacalan, cited frequently elsewhere.

[4] So see L. Walras, *Théorie du libre échange* (*Revue d'économie politique*, 1897); A. Pinard, *Ricardo* (*Journal des Économistes*, 1901); Jacques Pallain, *Des rapports entre les variations de change et les prix* (Paris, 1905); and others. Pallain makes an

alysis. That analysis itself, divorced from the general classical doctrine, has also been subjected to various scattered attacks.[1] But great care must be taken not to ascribe too much importance in the general history of French thought to these reflections and criticisms of English teaching. The most convincing and far-reaching attack on the English position of which I know, that formulated by Professor Nogaro, has quite failed to attract general attention of any sort in France, favorable or unfavorable. Professor Landry's exposition has hardly been more fortunate. French students as a whole have accepted almost without question Block's famous and summary dictum that "the Continental economists have done well in leaving 'the theory of international value' on the other side of the Channel." [2] They have been primarily interested in the classical theory of the foreign exchanges alone, and to a certain extent in the various sorts of specie flow analysis.

With these preliminary observations, we may now turn to the writings of Pareto and Nogaro.

2. Professor Pareto, though an Italian, wrote his first general treatise in French. His second work, in a revised and elaborated form, has been made familiar to French students through Bonnet's excellent translation.[3] Pareto's widest following is found in Italy, but he has enjoyed a marked influence in France. The ori-

extremely interesting attempt to verify certain parts of the classical theory of international trade by the use of statistics; notably the parts dealing with the equilibrium of the exchanges. His data, however, are in the main yearly; no especial attempt is made at obtaining a refined statistical correlation; and the nature of the material makes inevitable certain gaps in the effort to build a chain of sequences on statistical bases alone. The same criticism must be made here that is made of the statistical side of Nogaro's work, later in the present chapter. The degree of conviction carried by the study depends more upon the preconceptions of the reader than upon any unmistakable testimony in the data themselves. From the point of view of statistical method, they are not conclusive one way or the other.

[1] So see the reference to Cauwès, earlier in this section; also Reboud, *op. cit.*, pp. 159, 160; and Dubois, *Histoire des doctrines économiques*, p. 265.

[2] M. Block, *Les progrès de la science économique* (Paris, 1890: 2 vols.). The quotation is taken from the second edition (1897), vol. ii, p. 171. For a somewhat more specific criticism of various classical writers, which, however, is still too summary to be of much value, see *ibid.*, pp. 26-30.

[3] Vilfredo Pareto, *Cours d'économie politique* (Lausanne, 1896-1897: 2 vols.); *Manuel d'économie politique* (translated by A. Bonnet, Paris, 1909).

gins of his ideas are so distinctly French — and French Swiss — as to justify his inclusion in the present chapter. His general position is derived from the combination of an adherence to the mathematical method of Cournot and Walras with an acceptance of at least some parts of the classical theory of international trade. At certain points, however, and especially in connection with the theory of international values, he makes partial criticisms which would have constituted an effective revision of the classical doctrine itself if they had been carried through to their logical conclusion.

Pareto first gives, without much detail of mechanism, the Hume-Ricardo analysis of the world distribution of money — the doctrine that if a country acquires too much or too little currency relative to the position of equilibrium the surplus or deficit will be adjusted by means of price changes.[1] Then he presents a mathematical demonstration, in terms of relative *money* costs, of the principle of comparative costs as between markets which are

---

[1] Pareto, *Cours d'économie politique*, vol. i, pp. 186–191 ff. The "position of equilibrium," however, is in the first instance interpreted in terms of "ophelimity," which has substantially the same meaning as the "utility" and "dis-utility" of the English economists. Thus Pareto finds that, under a régime of free competition, prices are established in such fashion as to secure to each exchanger the maximum of ophelimity. This position is one of stable self-restoring equilibrium (*ibid.*, pp. 3–5, 27, 28). The transition from the equilibrium of what we may call "psychic" values, to the market-equilibrium of money values, is made possible by the assumption that, under competition, the one set of values reflects the *maximum* values or ophelimities of the other set, and changes in proportion to it — though the argument is put with greater subtlety and sophistication than this summary statement can indicate.

In the appendix to his *Manuel*, it is true that Pareto passed beyond the conception of "ophelimities" to the more general conception of "lines of indifference," and of "function-indices" designed to show the direction of movement of the consumer's choice (see especially pp. 659–661 ff.). He did not, however, qualify his exposition of the theory of international trade for this addition, and I shall therefore continue to use the term "ophelimity" in the present discussion. For the purposes here in mind, I think — subject to correction by those more skilled in the mathematical apparatus — that one can pass from it to the "function-index" and back without serious difficulty. The first refers to quantities of pleasure; the second, to changes in the *relation between* such quantities, as derived from the one article and the other.

Also see Pareto's article on *Économie mathématique*, in the *Encyclopédie des sciences mathématiques* (Paris, 1911–), t. I, vol. 4, fasc. 4, especially pp. 596–599.

in free competition with other markets, but only with respect to certain products and capitals.[1] He finds that this principle cannot be enunciated with precision by economists who do not use the mathematical method, because they do not distinguish clearly enough between costs as expressed in different currencies, and costs in terms of sacrifice — in terms of what he calls "ophelimity." Mill had considered only the quantities of labor necessary to produce the commodities concerned, and had seemed to hold that the exchanges depend on the relations between those quantities. "In that form," Pareto declares, "the proposition is wholly erroneous. But probably Mill was thinking of a certain cost of production that included wages and 'profits,' and merely expressed himself badly."[2] Cairnes, also, would compare costs in terms of the sacrifices necessary for production (that is, Pareto says, in terms of ophelimity), not in terms of money. Cairnes found that as long as the question is only one of *relationships* the two give the same results, since the first type of costs is proportional to the second. Pareto points out, however, that Cairnes seems to be thinking of the sacrifices made by a certain person called "society." But society is in point of fact made up of many different individuals, whose costs in terms of sacrifice are subjective, dissimilar, and incapable of being summated. Pareto himself declares that sacrifices or ophelimities — i. e., "psychic" values — are only proportional to prices when *maximum* ophelimities are involved. When, as in the case of an alternative use of a given article, the ophelimity is less than the maximum, the necessary correspondence between psychic or subjective values on the one hand, and monetary values on the other, breaks down.

Pareto shows that the classical, non-mathematical formulation of the principle of comparative costs has other defects.[3] It usually neglects costs of transportation, insurance, and so forth entirely; yet these may be a very important part of the import price of goods that have a small value per unit of bulk. Further, the Ricardian formulation of the principle cannot work if *all* money costs in country A are lower than in country B. He concludes,

[1] *Cours d'économie politique*, vol. ii, pp. 208–215.
[2] *Ibid.*, vol. ii, p. 211.   [3] *Ibid.*, vol. ii, pp. 215–219.

however, that this last condition will as a rule be transitory.[1] Money will flow from B to A, and commodities from A to B, until the resulting changes in prices have restored an equilibrium. Prices in A will rise, rapidly for those goods that it produces with the greatest difficulty, slowly for those produced more easily. The first class will soon reach the limit at which exportation ceases,[2] but the second will not. The latter will therefore continue to move after equilibrium is reached. The opposite course of events will take place in B, and when equilibrium is attained the two countries will be left exporting the things they produce most easily. This reasoning is then worked out, in more precise mathematical terms, by formulae of equality and inequality.[3]

3. In the "Manuel," published twelve years later, Pareto somewhat modified his own propositions. He takes two "collectivities," one of which produces article A and gets B by exchange, while the other produces B and gets A by exchange. He disregards the movements of money, since they restore equilibrium when it is temporarily upset but in the long run substantially balance, and considers only commodities and capitals. From the mere fact of the exchange itself, Pareto says that

we can deduce only that the first collectivity finds it more advantageous to produce A for its own consumption, and to obtain B by exchange, than to produce both A and B for its own consumption; and so, *mutatis mutandis*, for the second collectivity. We cannot conclude from this that B is produced more easily by the second collectivity than by the first, and that A is produced more easily by the first collectivity than by the second. This is what Ricardo's theory of comparative costs comes to at bottom. . . . Moreover, nothing of what has just been said is especially precise. It is not easy to know what is meant by saying that one thing is produced *more easily* than

---

[1] Pareto makes an exception in the case where B mines the metals of which money is made, but the presumably consequent modifications of the theory are not elaborated.

[2] It will be remembered that this idea, of a definite limit to profitable exchange, is also found in Cournot — who, however, makes much more of it than does Pareto. The classical theory concerned itself with setting up the limiting costs within which exchange is possible, and with showing how the actual ratio of exchange within those limiting costs will be determined. But it did not emphasize the fact that there is also a limit on the exchangeable *quantity* of each article, beyond which that quantity cannot be increased profitably. This second type of limit is perhaps only less important than the first.

[3] *Cours d'économie politique*, vol. ii, sect. 856, note 1.

another. Professor Bastable informs us that the comparison between the costs of A and B relate not to prices but to *sacrifices*, but he does not say, and he could not, precisely what these *sacrifices* consist in. In point of fact, this theory can be rigorously set forth only with the aid of mathematics.[1]

Pareto goes on to examine the Ricardian example of two workers, one of whom makes both of two commodities better than the other worker, but who gets a greater advantage by producing the one in which his superiority is greatest, and then procuring the other by exchange. He finds, by the use of hypothetical arithmetic examples, that the Ricardian conclusion is not true under all conditions. Specialization does not lead to a total output which is necessarily greater than that secured from the production of both articles by both workers.[2] It follows that the principle is not universal in its application, and may involve a *non sequitur*. Having gone this far, however, Pareto fails to add more constructive criticisms. He works out a general formula for the conditions under which the total product in one of two selected periods may be made greater than in the other,[3] but he does not carry his arithmetical demonstration through to show just what the maximizing conditions in point of fact are. Nor does he go any farther toward working out a restatement of the Ricardian formulation.

Pareto also has something to say of the rôle of money in foreign trade. He finds that trade under money is not altogether like trade under a barter economy, because the degrees and rates of change under money are uneven. He therefore refuses to take over the classical barter assumption in its entirety.[4]

[1] *Manuel d'économie politique*, pp. 506, 507.

[2] *Ibid.*, pp. 507–514. The illustrations are too elaborate to present here, but they offer no especial difficulty. The reader can easily devise their analogues. When the exchange is between two commodities alone, a greater total output of one article results from specialization, but a smaller output of the other. This conclusion can of course be drawn directly from Ricardo's own examples. When money is introduced into the situation, a perfectly permissible manipulation of the prices assigned the two articles will cause the total money value of the combined outputs to appear smaller under specialization than with unspecialized production.

This doctrine has recently been elaborated, with specific reference to diminishing returns, by Professor F. D. Graham. See ch. iv, sect. 9, above.

[3] *Manuel d'économie politique*, p. 509, note 1. See also pp. 365–367, on price equilibria in international commerce. No essential modification of doctrines is indicated here, however.

[4] *Cours d'économie politique*, vol. ii, p. 216.

The use of money is the thing which complicates international exchange. It is necessary to consider a transition-state, and subsequently that static state which terminates it. In other words, the static problem is complicated by a dynamic problem.[1]

Then, by another hypothetical example, Pareto shows how the introduction of money into a primitive state of international trade will at once cause a nominal modification of prices and wages; and how, during a period of transition, *real* prices and wages will be altered because of the unequal facility and rapidity of their movements. But again he stops short, and does not attempt to push these ideas to a further conclusion.

Pareto thus offered a number of well-grounded criticisms of the form of statement of the classical doctrine, and even of its content. He demonstrated with great skill its weakness at several important points, and went a certain distance in indicating the remedy. This is especially true of his criticisms of the classical method of traversing the gap between labor costs or sacrifices and money costs in the market, and with respect to the possible *non sequitur* he revealed in the principle of comparative costs itself. He showed, too, the dangers involved in the use of the classical assumption that the effects of money can be substantially ignored. But on the constructive side Pareto did not go so far. While pointing out the fallacies of the classical position, and while suggesting that the remedy lies in the use of the mathematical apparatus, he did not present an alternative system himself, nor even a positive form of revised statement. He also failed to say anything at all of the classical theory of international values as determined *within* the limits set by costs of production — that is, of Mill's "equation of international demand." His own theory, presumably, would run in terms of that apparatus of maximum ophelimities and price-equilibria with which he resolves the determination of values in general, in those cases where the "markets" in question are "open" with respect to *certain alone* of their total products and capitals.

[1] These propositions are then qualified more elaborately for the diversity of the actual conditions of trade, but without altering the essential argument. See, especially, the attempt to work out a mathematical determination of the quantities that will be exchanged (*Cours d'économie politique*, vol. ii, pp. 219–241).

Yet a fundamental difficulty still remains. Even granting for the moment that prices in each country are on the whole "proportional" to "maximum ophelimities," we are left in the dark as to the determination of international prices themselves — prices which at least tend to an absolute equality in terms of money. A maximum ophelimity in one country is not necessarily the same as a maximum ophelimity in another, and — especially since the hypothetical ratios involved will quite certainly be different — the money prices which are proportional to them therefore need not be equal. Given the actual *fact* of a known exchange, we can proceed from money prices to the corresponding ophelimities in each country, and even draw up a system of relative price and money income scales for each on the basis of the asserted "proportionality" in the particular market. But, given only a knowledge of ophelimities, we cannot proceed from them to the prospective terms of an inter-market or inter-country exchange, or to the determination of international prices. They do not provide an adequate *a priori* basis.[1]

Two other criticisms may also be brought against Pareto, somewhat similar to those brought against Cournot elsewhere.[2] First, the influence of money costs of production in limiting and determining the actual ratios of exchange — money prices — is distinctly neglected. Second, no clear-cut theory is provided for determining the exchange ratios between two or more commodities themselves produced in different countries. The argument deals primarily with commodity values *within* any one market, rather than as *between* markets. In general, then, while it is possible to use Pareto's position as a starting point for constructive criticism of the classical theory, that position does not in itself offer a complete alternative solution.

A not dissimilar type of mathematical approach was worked out at about this time by Aupetit, who used Walras's technical apparatus.[3] Aupetit declares that

[1] For a similar type of criticism of the principle of comparative costs in general, see ch. xiv, sect. 3, below.

[2] See ch. ix, sect. 7, above.

[3] A. Aupetit, *Théorie générale de la monnaie* (Paris, 1901). For still another quite similar mathematical exposition of the theory of international exchange, see the

in international trade, the condition of maximum utility suffices to determine the quantity of each commodity that will be exchanged, and also the rate of exchange.[1] . . . When the exchanges between two distinct markets are in a state of equilibrium, the ratio of the averages of the prices in the two markets is equal to the reciprocal of the price of the money of the one, in the money of the other.[2]

This is an interesting statement of the theorem which Professor Cassel has recently renamed the "purchasing power parity" doctrine. Aupetit then qualifies these unequivocal propositions with respect to the slowness of adjustment that characterizes actual conditions, and with respect to disturbances from secondary causes. The main force of his argument, however, turns on the existence of those presumably dominant equilibria which are to be regarded as the "usual" thing.[3]

4. An entirely different line of approach, turning largely on a fusion of monetary theory with the theory of international exchange itself, was developed a few years later in the writings of Professor Bertrand Nogaro.[4] Professor Nogaro, in his thesis for the doctorate and in subsequent articles, has made the most thorough examination of the entire classical theory of international trade that has yet appeared in France, and has formulated the most comprehensive and radical criticisms of this theory that I have found in any country. His work seems to have attracted little attention in France, and still less abroad. Yet it is of such striking character and such broad scope that the adherents of the classical theory cannot well remain content simply to ignore it. In so far as it is valid, it makes necessary a radical revision in the form of statement of the classical doctrine, and perhaps in its essential content. Before we turn to it, however, one observation

---

work of the two Austrians, Auspitz and Lieben, *Recherches sur la théorie du prix* (translated by L. Suret: Paris, 1914), pp. 267–280. See ch. xiii, sect. 7, below.

[1] Aupetit, *op. cit.*, p. 118.   [2] *Ibid.*, p. 119.

[3] *Ibid.*, pp. 119, 120. See also pp. 156–166, and pp. 201–215.

[4] Those publications of Professor Nogaro which bear especially upon the general theory of international trade are the following: *Le rôle de la monnaie dans le commerce international* (Paris, 1904); *Contribution à une théorie réaliste de la monnaie* (*Revue d'économie politique*, 1906); and *Le problème national des échanges avec l'extérieur* (*Revue économique international*, 1911). His other articles will be examined in the next chapter.

must be made. Nogaro's destructive criticism is far-reaching, but he offers little or nothing in the place of the doctrines which he attacks. It would perhaps be unjust to say that on the positive side he is content merely with an analytic description of objective mechanisms and relationships. But such general theoretical explanations of the processes of international exchange as he subscribes to must be credited to him more by inference than from his own direct statements. On the other hand, he has what is for our purposes the supreme merit of making his monetary theory an integral part of his discussions of the theory of international trade; a merit to which but few of the English writers can lay even partial claim.

Nogaro adopts two general lines of attack upon the classical position, each of which leads to a rejection of the characteristic classical doctrines of equilibrium. One, which runs through nearly all of his writings in this field, consists in an elaborate criticism of the classical price-specie flow analysis. The bases of the criticism lie partly in his rejection of the quantity theory of money in its usual form of statement, and partly in his belief that the actual workings of the exchange market, the various means by which the balance of payments is actually kept in equilibrium, are not always those which the classical theorem necessarily presupposes. Indeed, Nogaro tries to show that the "equilibrium," in this sense of the word, has no necessary existence at all. He denies that an excess or a deficit of money will be inevitably corrected by price changes, or a specie drain be automatically stopped. The other line of attack, which is less clear-cut, appears only in Nogaro's first work. It is concerned with the theory of international values, and consists in the proposition that the introduction of money destroys the necessary correspondence between particular purchases and particular sales in international trade. This in turn destroys the basis on which Mill's theory itself is essentially built, and makes the "equation of international demands" meaningless. These latter propositions may conveniently be examined first.

The criticisms of Mill's theory of international values are not very well-ordered, and our difficulty in grasping them is sometimes increased by the feeling that Nogaro's interpretation of Mill

is not always correct. The argument is in general this. Nogaro
takes Mill's position to consist in two propositions. The first is
the "equation of international demands" — the theorem that
imports and exports tend to equilibrium, abstraction being made
from the rôle of money. The second is the conclusion that the
determinants and terms of the international exchange can be
deduced from the mere existence of this equilibrium. To the
first proposition, Nogaro objects that it begs the question. Mill,
in his discussion of trade under barter,

assumes that his two commodities *are exchanged for one another*. (They must
be exchanged for one another if they are to have the same ratio of exchange
in the two countries, and if he is to try to determine this ratio.) He assumes
that they must *necessarily pay for one another*, for he declares that *the only
means* by which a country may acquire a greater quantity of foreign commodities is to offer a greater number of its own products. It is on this idea of
exchange, this necessity of paying for the total of importations by the total of
exportations, that his so-called demonstration of equilibrium is based. But in
point of fact a country would have no need to alter the ratio of exchange to
its own disadvantage in order to stimulate foreign demand, if it were not
obliged to pay for the commodities it receives with other commodities — if
the equivalence of importations and exportations were not necessary. The
demonstration of an equilibrium rests upon an hypothesis which contains
the equilibrium by definition. All this argumentation is therefore a mere
begging of the question. It can only indicate the causes which may affect the
determination of the ratio of exchange when the fact of an exchange itself is
given, as it is in effect in the hypothesis. Between this processus and that
based upon the properties of money, there is hence not a logical connection,
but only a rough similarity.[1]

Nogaro finds that Mill's error resulted from a confusion between trade without money, and trade under barter. The latter
sort of trade tends to carry with it an implication of equality as
between purchases and sales, and this equality Mill unconsciously
assumed in his attempts to prove its existence.[2] The error is
brought out still more clearly when we turn from trade under barter to trade under money. Under money the necessary equivalence between a given purchase of commodities and a given sale
entirely disappears. The failure of this equivalence to appear will
not be necessarily corrected by a change in the ratio of exchange
between the commodities themselves. Money is itself sufficient

[1] Nogaro, *Le rôle de la monnaie*, pp. 28, 29.   [2] *Ibid.*, pp. 31–37.

to meet any "unsatisfied demand" arising, for example, from an excess of importation, and its flow will readjust the balance of payments without any necessary alteration in the ratio of inter-commodity exchange. Mill's hypothesis is hence not realized.[1] With the necessary equality of international intercommodity demands disproved, his argument becomes simply a repetition of the law of demand and supply. It ceases to have especial reference to international trade, whether under money or otherwise.[2]

Nogaro then turns to the second proposition in Mill's doctrine. He declares that even were it proved that imports and exports tend to equilibrium, nevertheless a theory of international values cannot be deduced from this equilibrium itself. In a state of barter, certain definite and limited categories of commodities in one country are exchanged for certain similar categories in the other country. There is a double demand, and a double supply. Before the actual exchange takes place, it is true, there is a preliminary evaluation of the commodities offered, by each party, and the ratio of exchange finally determined upon is then in a sense the product of the relative intensities of demand. Mill's theory of international trade is based on this sort of conception. For the sake of argument, its validity under barter can perhaps be granted.[3]

But the conception, Nogaro finds, is absolutely inapplicable to trade under money. Under money, the exchange is no longer confined to definite categories of commodities; the necessary equivalence between commodity-purchase and commodity-sale disappears; and the ratios of exchange cease to be determined by the relative intensities of the demands for one commodity and the other. Money creates a universal market, which includes and fuses the operations of internal and of international commerce. It places all producers in the presence of all consumers. The importers and exporters of each country, under money, are absolutely ignorant of the nature and volume of the total goods to be

---

[1] Nogaro, *op. cit.*, pp. 49–54. This argument turns in part on a denial of the necessary connection between specie flows and price changes, an argument which is examined below.

[2] *Ibid.*, pp. 29, 30.   [3] *Ibid.*, pp. 56, 57.

sold. It is impossible to know or even to conceive of the sale, in one country, which is the counterpart of a given sale in another country, and the *psychological* process involved in an exchange between commodities cannot be realized. Moreover, a commodity may be bought not with another commodity, but with money itself. The exchange, with respect to commodities, is then unilateral. It follows that the determination of exchange ratios according to the relative intensity of the demands for commodities ceases to be effective. Mill's formula of international value, conceivably applicable to trade under barter, thus absolutely fails to be valid for trade under money.[1]

Finally, Nogaro brings certain criticisms to bear upon the doctrine of comparative costs, and upon the general rôle assigned to costs of production in the classical theory.[2] His remarks here, however, are less convincing and less fresh than at other points, and they are subordinate to the main trend of the criticisms just presented.

To this argument, the line of reply which would be adopted by adherents of the classical theory as it is formulated in Mill's writings is obvious. They would presumably concede without hesitation Nogaro's assertion that the introduction of money fuses individual exports and imports into a single aggregate of exportation and importation. They would also agree that the "psychological process" of an intercommodity exchange, the necessary equivalence between a given commodity purchase and a given commodity sale, quite disappears under modern conditions. But they would fall back on the price-specie flow analysis, and on the strength of that analysis would flatly refuse to surrender

[1] Nogaro, *op. cit.*, pp. 54, 55, 58–60.

[2] *Ibid.*, pp. 67–74. The criticism turns on the proposition that the principle of comparative advantage is operative only where *money* costs and prices are already such as to secure similar results. The "principle," that is, tells us nothing new. See ch. xiv, sect. 3, below, for a similar type of comment. Nogaro also criticizes Mill for refusing to think in terms of money prices themselves.

It may be added that he here accepts the classical dictum that the peculiarity of international as distinct from internal trade lies in the international immobility of labor and capital. In a later publication, as we shall see, he rejects the dictum itself. At this point, however, he was content to deny the conclusions as to the determination of international values which are drawn from it.

their views as to the erection of international values. If a flow of specie entails a necessary and corresponding change in prices, the movements of money *in effect* produce their own neutralization. Money becomes a colorless intermediary, and the terms of international exchange become substantially those which would obtain were money not present. They are, in other words, the terms that would obtain under barter. International values are hence determined, as before, by the relative intensities of the demand of each country for the others' products. The only difference is that the process is more complicated, less direct, than under barter. But it is precisely against the price-specie flow analysis, which is the effective pivot of the classical theory of international trade as applied to money economies, that Nogaro brings his most strenuous and most detailed objections.

5. In advancing this second group of criticisms, Nogaro shifts his attention from Mill to Ricardo himself. Whether his rigid distinction between the two writers is altogether tenable is perhaps open to question, but the grounds on which it is based are interesting. He summarizes his review of Mill in these striking phrases:

All this effort of Stuart Mill to give the Ricardian theory a wider basis, by founding it *not on the mechanisms of exchange but on the fundamental conditions of the exchange* [*itself*], *is hence futile.* There is nothing worth preserving . . . in this paradoxical conception, the converse of a literal interpretation of Ricardo, in which the function of money consists in neutralizing the effects of its own existence, and in making international trade as much like barter as though [money] itself did not exist.[1]

In other words, Nogaro concludes that the "fundamental conditions" of exchange itself do not justify a belief in an equilibrium of the international exchanges; and he rejects Mill's demonstration. His next problem is therefore to discover whether or not an equilibrium can result from the mechanism through which these exchanges are in point of fact conducted; that is, from the intervention of money. From this point on, it may be added, the theory of international *values* rather drops from sight in Nogaro's argument. His primary interest now lies in the correctness or incorrectness of certain postulated mechanisms, and in the rôle assigned to money.

[1] Nogaro, *op. cit.*, p. 74.

One other comment must also be ˪made in advance. Throughout his discussion Nogaro, like most contemporary writers, assumes that Ricardo held what has elsewhere been called the "bilateral" theory of equilibrium in international exchange. This is the doctrine that the necessary adjustments may proceed not only from money and prices *to* the commodity balance of trade and the balance of payments, but also *from* the balance of payments to prices. Nogaro's criticisms are chiefly concerned with the latter sequence. It was one of the chief purposes of an earlier chapter in the present study, however, to show that this interpretation of Ricardo is only partly correct. The first half of the theorem Ricardo subscribed to completely. The second half he did not. Indeed, he devoted much effort to the attempt to prove it fallacious. It was the property of Thornton, and later of Mill, but not of Ricardo himself.[1] But this observation does not impair the correctness of Nogaro's argument *per se*. It merely shifts the onus of his attack from Ricardo to certain other men.

The classical demonstration of the mechanism by which equilibrium is maintained in the balance of payments depends on the validity of the price-specie flow analysis. It is held that an excess of imports, for example, results in an export of money; this in a decrease in the national stock of money; this in an increase in the *value* of money, and a corresponding fall in prices; and this in a stimulus to exports, through which the balance of payments is reëstablished. Thus that movement of gold, which results from the destruction of the equilibrium of payments, itself restores the equilibrium automatically. In this analysis, Nogaro finds that relations of cause and effect are implied between three pairs of terms: (1) between the balance of payments and movements of metallic money; (2) between the movements of metallic money and prices; (3) between prices and the course of international trade.[2] After a general discussion of the weaknesses of the quantity theory of money,[3] he examines these three relationships in order. His aim is to show, by inductive and deductive argu-

---

[1] See ch. iii, sect. 5, above; also sect. 7.

[2] *Le rôle de la monnaie*, pp. 75, 76.

[3] *Ibid.*, pp. 76–86. Professor Nogaro's various attacks upon the quantity theory will be examined more specifically in the next chapter.

ment, that no one of them is necessarily valid, and that the demonstration of the existence of an equilibrium in international trade is therefore inexact.

(1) The balance of payments and movements of metallic money. The first term cannot be measured statistically. By a theoretical analysis of the actual mechanisms of the exchange market, however, Nogaro shows that metallic currency is not always and necessarily put into movement when the balance fails to be in equilibrium. In part, at least, securities may be substituted. While their function in settling international balances is the same as that of money, their properties and their effects upon the national economy may be quite different. It therefore follows that the relation between the first and second terms above is not necessarily constant. A disturbance in the equilibrium does not necessarily give rise to movements of specie.[1]

(2) Movements of the precious metals and prices. Here Nogaro makes three distinct objections to the classical theory, which it will suffice to enumerate. First, that theory takes account only of changes in the *supply* of money, as measured by the current stock, and proceeds directly from fluctuations in the stock to fluctuations in prices. Nothing is said of changes in *demand*. But the really significant thing, with respect to prices, is neither demand nor supply. It is the changing relationship between them.[2] Second, the metallic stock and the actual monetary circulation are not, of course, coincident, and Nogaro finds that except within certain maximum limits the proportion between them is not constant. With regard to the effect of specie flows upon the rate of discount, he questions the quantitative importance of the initial decrease in the metallic basis of the outstanding volume of credit produced by specie flows in foreign trade. He therefore doubts the significance of the supposed effect upon that volume. On both counts, he concludes that the effect of movements of the precious

---

[1] *Le rôle de la monnaie*, pp. 87-89, 96-99. On the function of securities as an international money, see *ibid.*, pp. 97-116.

[2] *Ibid.*, pp. 117-119. The classical assumption that "other things remain equal" provides a logical escape, but not one which is in itself of much use in a study of the changing conditions of actuality. It is a scaffolding which must later be removed.

metals is uncertain.[1] Finally, he declares that because of these and other considerations "the relation which actually exists between variations in the monetary stock and prices is too complex and too uncertain to be reduced to the single conception of the Ricardian [i. e., classical] theory."[2] This argument is in part bound up with his denial of the universal validity of the quantity theory, to be examined later, but in part it stands on the grounds just outlined. It will be observed, however, that Nogaro does not say that the classical doctrine is absolutely incorrect. He only asserts that it is not always and necessarily valid: that it is "inexact."[3]

(3) The movement of prices and the movement of foreign trade. Here again he denies the *necessity* of a connection, between the two phenomena, of that type prescribed by classical theory. He denies that a decrease in prices will necessarily mean that the corresponding commodities are more desired by the foreign country, and further denies that the increase in demand (in the market sense of the term) will be so great that the total value of the exportation will be increased. It may in point of fact be increased. But it may also remain unchanged, or even be diminished, and the net effect upon the balance of payments, as far as this source of change goes, may be just opposite to the one postulated.[4]

Nogaro then offers a statistical study of these three sets of supposed relationships.[5] It is rather rudimentary in method, however, and like most statistical studies in this field depends for its convincingness more upon the preconceptions of the reader than upon any unmistakable testimony in the data presented. Nogaro's conclusion, however, is interesting in the extreme. He finds that

the only factor which the Ricardian [i. e., classical] theory takes into account — that is, the action which variations in the metallic stock, under the influence of the balance of payments, exert upon prices — is certainly not preponderant. Hence this factor, which is not the only nor even the dominating agent, can in no way explain the conditions of equilibrium in international trade.[6]

---

[1] The argument is contained in *Le rôle de la monnaie*, pp. 120–142.

[2] *Ibid.*, p. 152.   [3] See *ibid.*, pp. 142–152, and elsewhere.

[4] *Ibid.*, pp. 153–156; also see pp. 156–158.   [5] *Ibid.*, pp. 159–191.

[6] *Ibid.*, p. 191. This passage is printed in italics, omitted here.

Even if the correctness of the quantity theory be conceded (which Nogaro is very far from doing), the relationship between variations in the metallic stock and prices, under the influence of the balance of payments, is extremely indefinite. Nor can it be concluded that the latter relationship determines the conditions of equilibrium in international trade, for metallic money does not always intervene when the state of the balance requires the making of foreign payments. Securities may be employed instead. Even when it does intervene other factors may affect prices in the given country, or these combined influences may be neutralized by an offsetting movement of prices in the other country. Moreover, the whole processus is in considerable degree independent of the conditions of international trade itself. The law of the tendency of the balance of payments to equilibrium, when it is based upon the quantity theory, is not absolute. It is in no way demonstrated, and it has little scientific value.[1]

Then, reviewing his study as a whole, Nogaro repeats the statement that he has been led to reject any belief in a natural equilibrium of the balance of payments based upon the fundamental fact of exchange. Nor has he been able to find that such an equilibrium results from the rôle that the quantity theory — or at least the application made of it in the classical doctrine — assigns to metallic money. The exchange rates give evidence of the existence of this equilibrium, and lengthen the periods during which it can manifest itself, but they do not create it.[2]

Hence there is no natural regulator of the balance of payments in the concrete mechanism by which international exchanges are actually affected, any more than in the fundamental fact of exchange itself.

Consequently there is no equilibrium.[3]

[1] *Le rôle de la monnaie*, pp. 193–195. For a review of Nogaro's objections to the classical theory, as well as of his criticisms of other antiquantitative writers, see an article by H. E. Barrault, *Le sens et la portée des théories antiquantitatives de la monnaie* (*Revue d'histoire des doctrines économiques et sociales*, 1910), pp. 391–397; also, with reference to trade under depreciated currencies, pp. 397–402.

[2] Nogaro, *loc. cit.*, p. 200.

[3] *Ibid.*, p. 201. Nogaro admits an equilibrium of sorts with respect to international securities, but it is one which is based simply on arbitrage operations in these securities, and which has no necessary connection whatsoever with the trade balance. See *ibid.*, p. 110.

This concluding proposition leads him into a brief defense of the view that an "adverse" balance of payments may continue indefinitely, and that the consequent steady drain of specie, being without a natural and automatic corrective, may bring about the ruin of the given country. Thus

a country which no longer has a superiority, in some branches of production, great enough to assure the equilibrium of its exchanges with foreign countries, and which in consequence becomes more a consumer than a producer, will see its currency drain out, while certain domestic producers, driven from the market by foreign competition, will be reduced to emigrate *en masse.* Such, at least, is the formula by which we may express the problem which presents itself.[1]

From this arises the possible need for tariff policies, fiscal policies, bank policies, and the other familiar paraphernalia. No criticism of these propositions will be attempted here. It may be remarked, however, that they give an excellent picture of a type of thought which is characteristic of many, if not of most, of the Continental economists. They are logically tenable only if the Hume-Ricardo-Mill analysis be rejected, and only if any necessary equilibrium tendency be flatly denied.[2]

6. In his later writings Nogaro has reaffirmed his position frequently, and has expanded it at certain points. Two years after his first book appeared he published an extremely interesting study of various monetary conditions in Australia.[3] In the course of this article he again criticized the classical theory of the world distribution of the precious metals. Gold, he says, is essentially an international money, and it therefore flows naturally from the debtor countries to the creditor countries. Its distribution hence rests on the balance of payments. But, if the classical theory here is to be believed, the production of gold acts upon the balance in such fashion as to bring about its equitable distribution among the

---

[1] Nogaro, *op. cit.*, p. 204. See also pp. 4, 5.

[2] Similar doctrines have been advanced by various writers referred to in the preceding pages. So see De Laveleye, *Le marché monétaire et ses crises, passim;* Cauwès, *Cours d'économie politique*, 3 ed., vol. ii, p. 531; Ansiaux, *Principes de la politique régulatrice des changes*, pp. 34–36; and other works of less importance. Ansiaux's general position, though much less fully worked out, is quite similar to Nogaro's. See Ansiaux, *op. cit.*, pp. 1–40.

[3] *Contribution à une théorie réaliste de la monnaie (Revue d'économie politique,* 1906).

nations automatically. It provokes, first of all in the producing countries, a rise in prices which checks exportations, destroys the equilibrium of the balance of payments, and causes an outward flow of the precious metals.

Such is the classical doctrine, especially in the form made familiar by Cairnes. But Nogaro presents the results of a statistical study of conditions in Australia — a mining country — in the decade before 1905, and concludes that it is incorrect. First, the production of gold did not seem to exert the anticipated initial influence in the producing country. Australian prices themselves were not especially affected. Second, there was no assignable statistical connection between this production and the prices of exports. Third, the volume of exports was *increasing*. This apparently upsets the theoretical attribution of the drain of gold to a diminution in this volume. Fourth, the exports of gold were more than twice the excess of Australia's commodity imports, and were hence largely due to the "invisible" items alone.[1]

Nogaro concludes that "an examination of the facts prevents our believing in a relation, between the production of gold and its exportation, *based on the rise of prices*." [2] Such a relationship exists, but it rests on two factors quite different from price changes. One is the actual deficit of exportable commodities *other* than gold in a gold-mining country which is new and sparsely populated, for mining itself draws labor from other industries. The second is the fact that, in a new country, the capital necessary for mining operations is in large part raised in other countries, and the dividends on this capital must therefore also go abroad. For example in Australia, from 1894 to 1898, commodity imports much exceeded the total exports of goods and gold combined, the deficit coming from foreign borrowings; but after 1898 imports were much below the combined total, because of interest payments on the earlier loans. This type of situation, however, does not usually appear in countries that have already attained a marked economic development.[3]

---

[1] *Contribution à une théorie réaliste de la monnaie* (*Revue d'économie politique*, 1906), pp. 709–711.

[2] *Ibid.*, p. 712.   [3] *Ibid.*, pp. 712–714.

He further declares that,

in effect, the exportation of gold does depend upon the balance of payments. This sometimes tends to reach equilibrium automatically, as a consequence of certain arbitrages in securities, but sometimes certain states contrive, by floating loans abroad, to divert a part of the production of gold to themselves. Nevertheless it does not appear, when the problem is examined closely, that there is a necessary equilibrium in the distribution of gold. In fact, at the present day the great nations, always creditors of foreign countries, . . . absorb most of the production of a few new countries.

The absorption does not necessarily take place by means of *commodity* price changes.[1] It is made effective, in the first instance, by means of the balance of payments and the *exchange* markets, which are capable of being radically affected by influences quite independent of commodity prices. Such are, notably, the international transfer of securities and the relative state of the discount rates.

For these various propositions of Nogaro's there is a great deal to be said, although their correctness in the particular case at issue can be verified only by a more protracted reëxamination of the statistics than is here possible. The general question involved will be considered in greater detail at another point.

In a later article, in connection with the measurement of the benefit from international trade, Nogaro returned to his attack upon the strict Ricardian analysis.[2] But he added nothing to his earlier argument, and his discussion of the point may be omitted here. He did, however, embark on a brief review of the fundamental assumptions of the general classical theory. He declares, first, that the mobility of labor and capital is not great even within a given country; second, that when national productive forces are displaced by importation they may fail to find more advantageous employment in other directions; and third, that "contrary to the essential postulates of the classical doctrine, the production of a country is not a determinate quantity, and the conditions that govern [international] exchanges are not necessarily natural conditions."[3] That is, they may be acquired by a judicious com-

---

[1] *Contribution à une théorie réaliste de la monnaie*, p. 714.

[2] *Le problème national des échanges avec l'extérieur* (*Revue économique internationale*, February, 1911), p. 289.   [3] *Ibid.*, pp. 295–297.

mercial policy. This argument, which is strongly reminiscent of some of Cournot's doctrines, leads Nogaro into a defense of moderate protection to "maintain national economies," stimulate production, and so forth.[1] In effect, it is a denial of the postulate of economic solidarity. Similarly, in his first book his closing words had been of "the conflicts between the national economy and the world economy, to which international exchange gives birth." [2]

7. Professor Nogaro's general position can be summarized in a single sentence. It consists in a flat denial of the classical doctrine that there is a necessary tendency in international trade to a self-restoring equilibrium. If, as he declares is done in Mill's writings, the proof of the existence of this supposed equilibrium be based on the antecedent general conditions of exchange itself, the proof can be shown to be not valid. There is no necessary equivalence between commodity-purchase and commodity-sale, under a money economy at least, and a deficit in the balance of payments can be met by the movement of money itself, without any necessary alteration in the exchange ratios between commodities. If on the other hand the proof be based on the actual mechanisms of international exchange, it too can be overthrown. None of the three pairs of causal relationships implied — those between the balance of payments, movements of specie, prices, and the course of foreign trade — are definite, nor do they necessarily exist at all. Finally, it should be added that Nogaro has also criticized the principle of comparative advantage and the rôle assigned to costs of production in classical theory, as well as some of the fundamental classical presuppositions. The foregoing propositions, however, are his two main theses.

It is evident that this whole edifice of criticism, of destruction and of subsequent partial reërection, rests very largely on a single foundation. That foundation is a rejection of the quantity theory of money, in any sense of that theory rigid enough to be of practical significance. Nogaro's own fear of specie drains, and his advocacy of protection and of other sorts of governmental inter-

---

[1] *Le problème national des échanges avec l'extérieur*, pp. 297–302.
[2] *Le rôle de la monnaie*, p. 205.

ference, are deduced primarily from this negative postulate. His denial of the Ricardian equilibrium-analysis is based on it directly, and his attack on Mill's theory of international values, so far as these values are assumed to be governed by relative intensities of demand, depends upon it chiefly if not exclusively. The ground for the rejection of the quantity theory itself, and the question of whether or not the rejection is justified, are matters which will be discussed in other chapters. It is of especial interest here, however, to observe that Nogaro makes his own analysis of the process of international exchange integrally and inseparably dependent upon his theory of money and prices. Having started with an anti-classical doctrine on the one question, he arrives inevitably at an anti-classical doctrine on the other.

He thus differs at the very start from almost all of the more recent English and American writers on international trade. As we have already seen, these writers tend nearly always to keep their two bodies of theory in separate compartments, and fail to consider the vital and unavoidable interfiliations between them. In Ricardo and Mill, it is true, the two were kept closely together. But the later adherents of the classical theory of international trade have for the most part ignored the post-classical refinements in the theory of money and prices, and have not sought to discover whether the advances made by the one theory make necessary an alteration in the other. The principal exception is found in the writings of Professor Laughlin, from whom Nogaro drew heavily at certain points, though Laughlin has not gone so far in demonstrating the international implications of his monetary doctrines. Whether we agree with Nogaro's conclusions or not, the theory of international prices is indebted to him in two important respects: first, for his searching criticisms of the classical doctrine, of which that doctrine must eventually take account; and second, for demonstrating more clearly than almost any other writer the essential dependence of the theory of international prices upon the theory of money, in the widest sense of the latter term. Avoiding the dangerous tendency to a separation of doctrinal elements, Nogaro has returned to the more realistic methodology of the early English economists.

CHAPTER XI

RECENT FRENCH THEORIES OF INTERNATIONAL TRADE UNDER DEPRECIATED CURRENCIES

1. The two preceding chapters have been concerned with the development of French theories dealing with international trade under stable monetary conditions. In the present chapter we shall examine various recent investigations of the course of international exchange under depreciated and fluctuating currencies. Quantitatively, these investigations comprise by far the largest division in the French literature upon international exchange, unless it be the parts dealing with the tariff controversy, but their value is uneven. They often fail to reward detailed study, and only a few need be considered at any length.

Before embarking on this discussion, however, it will be convenient to outline briefly the general development of French monetary theory in the last fifty or sixty years. The intrinsic merit of some portions of it is great. Moreover, many of the studies of trade under disordered monetary conditions can be understood only in terms of their sometimes unconscious preconceptions in the field of monetary theory.

The history of the theory of money and prices in France, like its history in other countries, shows two distinct and opposed trends. One group of writers has supported the quantity theory of money in some form or other, while a second group has rejected it. But whereas in England and the United States the opponents of the quantity theory have been distinctly inferior to its supporters in both numbers and influence, in France the balance has been much more nearly even. Since the opening of the present century, indeed, the anti-quantitative position has been the more characteristic one. And whereas abstract deductive reasoning has on the whole played the larger part among English and American students, among the French the rôles have been reversed. As in all that branch of economic thought with which we have been concerned in these pages, their tendency has been to seek their ultimate criteria in statistics and in other empirical data.

The literature of the French theory does not become important as a whole, either in size or in general interest, until the last decade of the nineteenth century. Before that period, however, three writers referred to in an earlier chapter had formulated ideas of which it is necessary to give some account: namely, Cournot, De Laveleye, and Juglar. Their work here seems to have been unknown to the great majority of French students, if one can judge from the subsequent literature, and their influence has therefore been almost negligible. Yet the value of certain of their doctrines is considerable. Both De Laveleye and Juglar, for example, anticipated most of the so-called "Marshallian" explanation of the relation between money and prices.

In 1863 Cournot gave a quasi-"dynamic" formulation of the determination of the value of money.[1] He based it chiefly on the quantity of wealth, industry, and business, on the size of the population, and on the annual *rate* of production of the precious metals. The velocity of circulation of money, however, seems to be omitted. He held that, other things remaining equal, an increase in the annual production of the money-metal will lower its value. If rapid, the fall will produce phenomena like those of a commercial crisis, since holders of the metal will seek to get rid of it, and thus bid up prices and wages. For a time, production will therefore be stimulated. But if the fall in money be the only change, the increased production will soon become merely a source of encumbrance. It will subside, and in due course, though inevitably with individual losses, a new equilibrium will be established. The rise in prices will be the only enduring change, except in so far as the temporary stimulus may have resulted in some permanent progress in production. If the increase in the quantity of money is slow, on the other hand, there will be no crisis. The only disturbances caused by the gradual fall in the value of money will be those in fixed incomes. Conversely, an increase in factors

[1] Cournot, *Principes*, Bk. II, ch. 5, especially pp. 220–222.

other than the quantity of money will raise its value, while if both groups change together some sort of balance will be struck.

Cournot thus comes out with what is essentially the familiar quantity-theory position. De Laveleye's ideas, however, were somewhat different. De Laveleye's principal concern, as we have already seen, was to explain crises in the money market by the drain of specie into foreign trade. The elaboration of this thesis led him to make various propositions that are of interest. In a preliminary analysis, he finds that the drain of specie into international trade will cause a rise in interest rates; this in turn will cause a decrease in the outstanding media of exchange; prices will fall; and a general depression will ensue.[1] An influx will produce the opposite effects. A few pages later he elaborates and qualifies this analysis as follows.[2] He finds that an increase in the amount of money in a given district may simply be spent directly on commodities. It will then raise prices, but will produce no other change. It may instead, however, be advanced to the entrepreneurs of industry. In that event it will at once act upon the money market, and will lower interest rates. Later, and secondarily, it will also raise prices. But each of these conclusions is true only if "other things" remain equal. The new money, loaned to industry and diffused throughout the district, may instead have the effect of stimulating enterprise, increasing production, and thus multiplying the number of transactions. Interest rates, instead of falling, will then rise in consequence of the increased demand for capital advances; and prices will fall instead of rising. This he declares to be the explanation of the phenomena that accompanied the California and Australia gold discoveries. Despite the opposite opinion of many economists, up to a certain point an increase in the quantity of money really does stimulate the development of industry. It produces this stimulus as long as it does not exceed the "needs of circulation," for it facilitates exchanges, and lowers interest rates without raising prices. Beyond that point, however, it raises prices without lowering interest rates.

[1] De Laveleye, *Le marché monétaire* (Paris, 1865), pp. 128–132.
[2] *Ibid.*, p. 141, note 1, and pp. 143, 144.

We need not try to disentangle the truth from the fallacy in these propositions. It is enough to point out here that this type of analysis, which at some points is reminiscent of Law, Forbonnais, and Verri, anticipates in most essentials the later so-called "Marshallian" explanation. It falls short in failing to indicate where the additional metallic money actually comes from, — that is, from bank reserves, — and in failing to show specifically how an increase in the volume of credit media consequent on an increase in reserves will of itself call the increased supply of metal into active circulation. But while these propositions were not formally stated by De Laveleye, it is probably not going too far to say that they are implicit in his reasoning. Without them or something similar, he could hardly have been led to the conclusions finally reached.[1]

Three years later Juglar advanced propositions substantially similar to De Laveleye's.[2] He held that if the quantity of the precious metals increases in greater proportion than the total quantity of products, prices will undoubtedly tend to rise. But the increase in money itself facilitates exchanges, stimulates the undertaking of new enterprises, and thus, by an increase in wealth, offsets the rising movement. Prices then tend to remain the same. Indeed, Juglar attaches much more importance in the determination of prices to these last factors, the degree of economic activity and changes in wealth, than to changes in money. He also concludes that changes in the quantity of money affect interest rates, and ascribes the effects of the former upon prices only to their intermediary effects upon the volume of credit.

---

[1] At another point (see *Le marché monétaire*, pp. 135–138), De Laveleye asserts that money *as money* is unlike other commodities because changes in its value affect all articles, and because of its legal tender quality. He also finds that while, if scarce, money will float more exchanges in the long run, this is distinctly not true of the immediate effects.

In a later book he again questions the classical formulation of the quantity theory, suggesting that the fact that in actuality "other things" are not "equal" upsets it. So in connection with the question of the velocity of circulation of money, the use of credit substitutes, and the fact that if production is stimulated by an increase in money, prices will rise less than in proportion. See his *La monnaie et le bimétallisme international* (Paris, 1891), pp. 38–40.

[2] Juglar, *Du change et de la liberté d'émission* (1868), pp. 27–39.

Finally, it should be observed that while De Laveleye seems to base his ideas chiefly on an expansion of Goschen, Juglar was familiar with most of the literature of the mid-nineteenth century banking controversy in England. He derived many of his views from these English sources, especially from Tooke.

2. After De Laveleye's and Juglar's books had appeared, the theory of money and prices was for a time forced into the background by the imperative claims of the bimetallic controversy. This controversy left as a heritage, however, a revived interest in general monetary problems, and in the last thirty-five years they have been subjected to constantly increasing attention. It would be interesting to review the resulting literature in some detail, but its general trend and conclusions are enough like those of the parallel English and American writings to make such a study unnecessary. The point at issue has been primarily the quantity theory of money, usually in the form given it by Mill. Little or no attempt has been made at such analyses of specific processes and mechanisms as were undertaken by De Laveleye and Juglar, and indeed this earlier work has been almost entirely neglected. The quantity theory has had no irreconcilable defenders in France, but more or less elaborately qualified versions have found favor with a number of writers. Of these Bourguin, whose remarkable work is still a classic, and Dolléans are sufficient examples.[1] Colson has adopted an intermediate position, and holds that the simplistic quantity theory is not so much erroneous as inexact. He finds that the tendency of prices to stable equilibrium is being constantly modified by the new production of the precious metals, the use of metallic-money substitutes, industrial consumption, the activity of business, and so on. Of these only the "activity of business" is a "short-time" influence. It is therefore the principal cause of large and rapid changes in prices.[2] The quantity

---

[1] M. Bourguin, *La mesure de la valeur et la monnaie* (Paris, 1896), especially p. 71 and pp. 131–133; E. Dolléans, *La monnaie et les prix* (the first essay in a symposium entitled, *Questions monétaires contemporaines*, Paris, 1905), especially pp. 120–124. This essay has been reprinted separately. Also see L. Dechesne, *Influence de la monnaie et du crédit sur les prix* (*Revue d'économie politique*, 1904), and a later article, *Pour la théorie quantitative de la monnaie et du crédit* (*ibid.*, 1914).

[2] Colson, *Cours* (1 ed.), vol. ii, Bk. IV, ch. 2, especially pp. 375–379.

theory has also found supporters among the mathematical economists, of whom Aupetit here provides the best instance.[1] In the period since the war the analysis of monetary problems has necessarily been bound up in large part with the question of the foreign exchanges. Discussion of this literature may therefore be postponed until we come to the exchanges themselves. Attention should be called, however, to one study which was oriented on the older line of approach. This is Mourre's interesting attempt to eliminate the velocity of circulation of money as an independent element, on the ground that it fluctuates directly with the volume of exchanges.[2] As applied to periods of large and abrupt changes, however, — such as a time of intensive currency depreciation, — this conclusion is hardly accurate. Velocity of circulation is more apt to move with prices and the exchanges; or rather, with the degree of the depreciation and the prospects for its termination.

The anti-quantitative position has had a large and growing number of supporters. Mongin, at the end of the last century, advanced "nominalist" views of the most extreme variety, and denied that there is any fixed or determinate connection whatsoever between money and prices.[3] De Foville, on the basis of a statistical investigation of the period 1848–1894, likewise concluded that there was no necessary correlation, and found that the qualifications requisite to make the quantity theory accurate

---

[1] A. Aupetit, *Théorie générale de la monnaie*, pp. 98–131. See also Pareto, *Cours*, pp. 177–179; Auspitz and Lieben, *Recherches sur la théorie des prix* (translated by L. Suret), *passim;* and others. Auspitz and Lieben were Austrians, but the translation of their work has had a large enough influence in France to warrant its being mentioned here.

Reference may also be made to an interesting though perhaps naïve attempt to measure the velocity of circulation of bank credit: P. des Essars, *La vitesse de la circulation de la monnaie* (*Académie des sciences morales et politiques, Comptes-Rendus*, 1895, vol. i).

[2] Baron Charles Mourre, *Les causes de la hausse des prix* (*Revue d'économie politique*, 1919). See also the article by M. Barré, *La circulation fiduciare* (*ibid.*, 1918).

[3] Marcel Mongin, *Des changements de valeur de la monnaie* (*Revue d'économie politique*, 1887); *De l'abondance de la monnaie métallique* (*ibid.*, 1888); *La monnaie et la mesure des valeurs* (*ibid.*, 1897). See also, for a refutation of the first article, Jules Aubry, *Quelques observations sur la valeur de la monnaie* (*ibid.*, 1887).

were so numerous as to leave little or nothing of the theory itself.[1] Nogaro has elaborated this last thesis, and has also taken over much of Laughlin's familiar doctrine. He has not, however, added anything here that is very novel.[2] Pupin has also recently made a rather unfair attack on the more rigid form of the quantity theory.[3] Finally, a number of the studies of foreign trade under depreciated currency have expressed views which are in effect anti-quantitative, as will be demonstrated below.[4] Indeed, it is only in such studies that the anti-quantitative position continues to be explicitly reaffirmed — not that it is being abandoned, but that it is too firmly entrenched in France to require frequent defense.

If we take the discussion of the quantity theory as a whole, however, it appears to be open to the same general criticism that has been brought against most of the corresponding English and American literatures, at least of the pre-war period. It is not especially convincing one way or the other, for much of it is quite divorced from contact with actual conditions, and the empirical evidence advanced has to be subjected to so many qualifications that its force is often largely dissipated. The principal exceptions to this generalization are provided by the various investigations of the conditions of international exchange under depreciated currencies which have been made in the last thirty-odd years. To these we may now turn.

3. The more recent French literature dealing with the conditions of international trade under depreciated currencies has at least three principal divisions. First, there is a body of writings

---

[1] A. de Foville, La théorie quantitative et les prix (L'Économiste français, 1896, vol. i).

[2] B. Nogaro, Le rôle de la monnaie (cited above), especially pp. 142–152. See also his Contribution à une théorie réaliste de la monnaie (Revue d'économie politique, 1906); and his article on L'expérience bimétalliste du XIX siècle et la théorie générale de la monnaie (ibid., 1908), especially pp. 665–668.

[3] R. Pupin, L'Or, les prix, et la guerre (Journal des Économistes, 1917).

[4] An excellent and exhaustive survey of the various trends of anti-quantitative doctrine is given in an article by H. E. Barrault, Le sens et la portée des théories anti-quantitatives de la monnaie (Revue d'histoire des doctrines économiques et sociales, 1910). A somewhat more summary, though illuminating, review of the general body of the theories of money and prices is presented in A. Mawas, Le système monétaire et le change anglais depuis la guerre (Paris, 1921), pp. 87–114.

which, perhaps concerned more with propaganda and political issues than with scientific analysis, has tried to show that depreciated exchanges abroad necessitate the erection of compensating tariff barriers in the stable-money countries. Second, there is a large group of studies which start from a general acceptance of the quantity theory and of the classical English type of analysis here, and then trace the depreciation of the exchanges to an antecedent depreciation of the currency. In this group should also be included two or three investigations, made in the period since the war, which have been primarily concerned to show the actual statistical correlations between price movements and fluctuations of the foreign exchanges. They have also cast much light on the mechanisms involved, and on the character of the general price-structure in any given country. Finally, there is a group which has taken just the opposite position, and which, starting from an anti-quantitative conception, has concluded that the depreciation of the exchanges is usually the cause rather than the effect of monetary depreciation. These three divisions are themselves bisected by the war, however, and indeed the last two have so drawn together that it is not always easy to distinguish one from the other.

The first group of doctrines has been of not inconsiderable importance in the history of French politics, but its theoretical interest is slight. The argument at issue is simple. It is held that a depreciation of the foreign exchanges acts like a protective tariff against the exports of stable-currency countries, and places a bounty upon their imports from the depreciated countries. In consequence, the industries of the stable-money countries must soon be ruined by foreign competition at home, and by the cutting off of their foreign markets, unless a compensating tariff wall is erected to protect them. The mixture of truth and fallacy in these propositions is self-evident. Apart from the practical difficulty in constantly adjusting the tariff to changing foreign conditions, the theoretical argument is of course valid only in so far as prices in the depreciated country fail to rise in proportion to the depreciation of the exchanges. This lack of coincidence usually appears, on any important scale, only for comparatively short periods of time (at least, such was generally the case before 1914). Moreover, when the exchanges are improving rather than depreciating just the opposite condition tends to prevail. Nevertheless these doctrines, which owe their appearance to the fluctuating trade conditions consequent on the general fall of silver after 1873, had a considerable vogue in France in the period from 1885 or 1890 to about 1910. They were waved particularly before the eyes of alarmed agriculturists, in further defense of the protectionist thesis. Their principal protagonists have been Allard,[1] coiner of the famous phrase "the exchanges, grave-diggers of free trade," and later E. Théry, the distinguished editor of "L'Economiste Européen."[2] They have also found a certain currency with the writers of general economic texts, notably Cauwès.[3] Since the war, however, the change in the general foreign-exchange position of France has deprived them of most of their significance.

4. The second group of writings is of much greater interest for our purposes. Approaching the problem of trade under depreciated currencies from a more scientific point of view, it has on the whole explained the depreciation of the exchanges by the antecedent depreciation of the currency, and has tried to work out some of the consequences of this situation — especially with respect to the relations between prices and the exchange rates. The type of analysis is essentially that of the classical English school. Its starting points have been an acceptance of some form of the quantity theory, and an adoption of much of the Mill-Goschen type of theory of the exchange rates and market mechanisms.

The first important work in this field, and in many ways still the best, was Bourguin's "La Mesure de la Valeur et la Monnaie," pub-

---

[1] Alphonse Allard, *La crise, la baisse des prix, la monnaie* (2 ed., Brussels, 1885); *Étude sur la crise en Angleterre* (Brussels, 1888); *Les changes fossoyeurs du libre-échange* (Paris, 1890).

[2] See especially Théry's book, *La crise des changes* (4 ed., Paris, 1894), pp. 253–261. The same thesis runs through much of Théry's work; a thesis which he reconciles with his general free-trade position by asserting that, under these peculiar conditions, free or fair trade can really be secured only by compensating duties.

[3] Cauwès, *Cours* (3 ed., 1893), vol. ii, pp. 528–532, and elsewhere. Also see E. Viollet, *Le problème de l'argent et l'etalon d'or au Mexique* (Paris, 1907). At a number of points, Viollet stresses the protective effect of a depreciating currency. See also the discussion of Bourguin's views in the next section of the present study.

lished in 1896.[1] Bourguin, after a long preliminary discussion of other matters, first gives the familiar argument that under a common metallic standard, with free coinage, a stable parity of the exchange rates will appear. The actual fluctuations around this parity are governed wholly by the balance of payments and by the relative rates of discount. The former is much more important, with respect to the prices of sight bills. Under dissimilar metallic standards, on the other hand, the parity is variable, and the exchange rates are therefore determined primarily by the depreciation of one currency in terms of the other. But at any one time, provided coinage be unlimited, the dissimilar standards are in effect equivalent to a single standard. The fluctuations of the exchanges around the current par are determined as in this latter case. If the coinage be restricted, however, the ratio between the two metals will diverge from their commercial value, and some other unpredictable parity will result.[2]

Bourguin next turns to the effects on international trade of the depreciation of one of the two metals, say silver. He finds that the fall in silver usually acts as a premium to the exports of the silver countries, and as a check to their imports. The check or stimulus is due to the fall in the commercial value of silver, as reflected in the foreign exchanges. It tends constantly, however, to be offset by the fall in the value of silver *within* the silver countries. But the actual phenomenon of a steady gradual decline in the latter value has often kept the fall of silver in terms of domestic prices in the silver countries somewhat less than its fall in terms of gold.

In the gold countries, on the other hand, the fall in the prices of many if not all exports has usually been injurious to producers, though beneficial to consumers.[3]

These conclusions, which Bourguin supports with elaborate references to historical examples, must be somewhat modified when they are applied to countries in which the coinage of silver is limited. Such was the case in Spain, for example, especially

---

[1] The book is a liberal education in the methodology of price-money theory. It is regrettable that it is so little known to English and American students.

[2] Bourguin, *La mesure de la valeur*, pp. 153–158.

[3] *Ibid.*, pp. 158–163.

after 1891. Here the depreciation of the exchanges was the consequence *not* of the depreciation of metallic silver (which was prevented from finding full expression in the exchanges by the limitation on coinage), but of an adverse balance of international payments. For, while the Spanish money was held above the value of metallic silver within Spain by the limitation on its coinage, no especial provision was made to keep it at any particular ratio to gold in *international* exchange.[1] Its external value — the exchange-rate quotation — therefore became primarily dependent on the balance of payments, except in so far as a possible ultimate limit on the depreciation was set by the export-point of metallic silver. There was hence no true parity, even a moving one. When the balance was adverse, the exchange depreciation and the premium on gold increased (that is, on gold for foreign payments. Gold had no circulation within Spain in the form of money). When it was favorable they diminished.[2]

Finally, Bourguin examines the case of trade between a country on an inconvertible paper standard and one under gold. Here there is no limit whatsoever to the possible depreciation of the exchanges. The course of the exchange-rate fluctuations, and the premium on gold, are determined almost wholly by the state of the balance of payments. The premium on gold fails to provide even a temporary parity, for this premium is itself governed by the state of the exchanges. Gold has no internal circulation, and its quoted value in the paper country arises only from its function as a medium of international payments. Such was the situation in Russia at various times, and also in Argentina.[3] Here, as in the case of the silver countries, the paper country benefits from the depreciation only in so far as the paper currency loses its domestic purchasing power *less rapidly* than it loses purchasing power with respect to gold. Some slight advantage of this sort usually does

---

[1] Later, however, an attempt was made to enforce such a provision. See the investigations of Mitjavile, Nogaro, and Roux, cited below.

[2] Bourguin, *op. cit.*, pp. 172–174. For a brief discussion of the case of India, see pp. 175–177. On this last see also, especially with reference to the earlier history of the gold exchange standard, A. Arnauné, *Le bimétallisme français et le bimétallisme indien* (*Académie des sciences morales et politiques, Comptes-Rendus*, 1903, vol. ii).

[3] Bourguin, *op. cit.*, pp. 177–179.

appear in actuality. But whereas prices seem on the whole to have remained relatively stable in the silver countries, in the paper countries they did not. The depreciation of paper in terms of commodities at large followed almost inevitably, as a rule, its depreciation in terms of gold. The gain to producers from depreciation is therefore small, and at best temporary. It arises principally from the lag of such costs of production as taxes, wages, rentals, and costs of transportation.[1]

It should perhaps be added that there seems to be a certain gap in Bourguin's reasoning on the situation under paper. He does not show explicitly the connection between the quantity of paper currency and its internal value, on the one hand, and the balance of payments and the external value of the paper currency on the other. But the bridging of the gap is easy enough. The whole trend of Bourguin's argument is such as to make the quantity of paper money and its fluctuating internal value the starting points of the general disturbance. The changes in the balance of payments and in the exchange rates follow from them, with the premium on gold in turn following the exchanges. The general position is essentially like that of the Mill-Goschen-Marshall school.

Substantially similar views have been advanced by a number of other writers. Colson declared that while under a paper standard the internal value of the currency depends on the quantity issued, the external value depends on the balance of payments. He then goes on to fill, in part, the gap in Bourguin's argument, and shows that the depreciation of paper from excessive issue is itself the cause of the fall of the exchanges. He concludes from this, incidentally, that there is no gain from the depreciation of paper except to speculators.[2] There have also been four or five

---

[1] Bourguin, *op. cit.*, pp. 179–181. Bourguin, as we have seen in an earlier chapter, also takes issue here with Goschen's dictum that, where the rise in prices and the depreciation of paper in terms of gold are simultaneous and equivalent, the rise in prices encourages importation and discourages exportation. Goschen had based his argument on the idea that a paper-money country is necessarily a debtor to foreign countries, since otherwise gold would come back and end the paper régime. Bourguin shows that such a country may perfectly well be a debtor, without having an excess of imports. See especially *ibid.*, p. 180, note 1.

[2] Colson, *Cours* (1 ed.), vol. ii, pp. 443–452, and pp. 468–471 (Bk. IV, ch. 2). See also Ansiaux, *Principes de la politique regulatrice des changes*, especially pp. 79–104,

more specialized studies, along these lines, of exchange and currency conditions in particular countries, but these need not detain us here.[1]

5. Shortly after the war, a translation of Professor Subercaseaux's essay on paper money was brought out in France. Although based entirely on the history of depreciations that occurred before 1914 — the Spanish original was published in 1912 — the excellence of the book at once gave it a wide and growing influence. Its aim was not so much to prove or disprove particular theories by particular cases, as to examine the inductive evidences of a relationship between prices and the exchanges, and between various groups of prices themselves. In general, however, it follows the fundamentally pro-quantitative method of approach established in France by Goschen and Bourguin. Both this fact and the more evident limitation imposed by the character of the material treated require, therefore, that it be placed with the pre-war studies.

Subercaseaux's chief concern is with the general internal history and theory of inconvertible paper money,[2] but he also has

for a modification of these doctrines. Ansiaux, while not abandoning the classical position, goes some little distance with Nogaro (see below), and assigns the primary rôle in the determination of the balance of payments to financial and commercial factors, rather than to the monetary influence alone.

[1] On Greece: J. A. Valaoritis, *Notes, tableaux, et graphiques relatifs à la question du cours forcé et du change en Grece* (Athens, 1902–1903: 2 vols.); C. J. Damiris, *Le système monétaire grec et le change* (Paris, 1920: 3 vols.). On Spain: H. Mitjavile, *La crise du change en Espagne* (Bordeaux, 1904); G. Roux, *Le change espagnol et son amélioration actuelle* (Montpellier, 1911). Mitjavile explains the Spanish depreciation largely by budgetary deficits, which led to issues of paper and to large loans. The collapse of various attempts at improvement aggravated the disorder. Roux adopts an intermediary position somewhat like Ansiaux's, indicated in the preceding footnote.

See also Pallain, *Des rapports entre les variations du change et les prix*, and Viollet, *Le problème de l'argent et l'etalon d'or au Mexique*, both cited in earlier pages; and R. Théry, *Rapports des changes avariés et des règlements extérieurs* (Paris, 1912). Théry advances (*loc. cit.*, pp. 270, 271) the idea that a depreciation of the exchanges will induce a revival in economic activity capable of influencing the balance of payments favorably, and that on this basis timely and forceful government intervention may make possible a restoration of monetary stability. The doctrine has been revived in recent years in connection with the payment of German Reparations. Evidently it may involve great dangers.

[2] G. Subercaseaux, *Le papier-monnaie* (Paris, 1920; translator not given). Sub-

much to say of its international aspects. He begins with the Bullion Report dictum that an increase in the quantity of money in a country, if this money be of such character that it cannot drain out into foreign trade, will produce approximately proportional increases in prices, the gold premium, and the exchanges. Statistical evidence is then offered, however, to show that in point of fact the depreciation of paper relative to gold is often much less than proportional to the increase in its quantity. The explanation lies in the fact that large issues of paper can frequently be absorbed without affecting the foreign-exchange market, although excessive changes in the quantity of the currency will almost certainly alter the premium.[1]

A little later in his book Subercaseaux presents one of the few attempts that have been made in any literature, except the English and American, to trace the mechanism of the actual process whereby, under inconvertible paper, fluctuations in the exchange rates affect prices. He also distinguishes carefully between the various sorts of prices themselves. First, wholesale prices.[2] He finds that the wholesale prices of those imports which are only produced abroad are directly influenced by exchange-rate fluctuations, though if the extant stocks are large, the effect on prices may be less than in proportion to the change in the gold premium — which is taken as synonymous with the depreciation of the exchanges. If the imported commodities are also produced in the paper country, however, the case is somewhat different. Here the gold premium acts as a sort of protective duty, and gives the domestic manufacturer some advantage, since domestic costs of production do not fluctuate directly with the exchanges. The effect is felt most clearly at the beginning of the period of premium, and tends to disappear as purely domestic prices and costs of production rise to the level of the exchange depreciation. This group of imports therefore follows fluctuations in the premium less closely than the first group.

ercaseaux, it may be added, is a professor at the University of Chili. The original work bore the title *El Papel Moneda* (Santiago, 1912).

[1] *Le papier monnaie*, pp. 134–159.

[2] *Ibid.*, pp. 208–211.

Wholesale *export* prices, on the other hand, are without distinction affected proportionately by the movements of the exchanges. Export prices are received in gold, and competition tends to make them follow the premium closely. Further, a depreciating exchange acts as a stimulus to export, because of the lag of domestic costs and prices.

Finally, the wholesale prices of purely "domestic" commodities, which are both produced and consumed within the country, are subjected to no direct influence from the exchange-rate fluctuations at all. Some of these commodities are wholly devoid of any relationship. For others such a relationship arises only because they are the raw materials of international commodities, or from the fact that they are possible substitutes for such commodities; or *vice versa* in both cases. Thus the exchanges *tend* to have an influence of sorts on the body of purely domestic wholesale prices, but one of indefinite extent and rapidity of effect. Other forces, such as inadequate communication or ineffective competition, may break down even this partial connection.

Then Subercaseaux examines the course of retail prices and wages. He finds that retail prices respond much less quickly to changes than the corresponding groups of wholesale prices.[1] Wages are still slower in their movement, and usually rise in a smaller proportion than prices in general.[2] To support these propositions he refers constantly to the available statistical data, especially to W. C. Mitchell's investigations.[3]

His general conclusion is that the rise in the gold premium — the depreciation of the exchanges — exercises an influence which tends of itself to raise the general price level.[4] The rise begins with exported and imported goods, and spreads from them to other groups with greater or less rapidity. The tendency to a rise thus becomes general. But certain classes of prices are extremely stable, and move either not at all or only slightly. Finally, it may be added that Subercaseaux gives an analysis much like Bour-

---

[1] *Le papier monnaie*, pp. 214–216.

[2] *Ibid.*, pp. 216–222.

[3] Especially to Mitchell's *History of the Greenbacks*, and to his *Gold, Prices, and Wages*.

[4] Subercaseaux, *op. cit.*, pp. 222–225.

guin's of the effects of a rise or fall in the gold premium, in stimulating or discouraging the export and import industries.[1]

Subercaseaux's analysis of the interfiliations of the price-
structure, and of the way in which different parts of this structure
are affected by exchange-rate fluctuations under a paper standard,
is thus unique in the history of French thought. It is far more
broadly based, both with respect to the use of statistical data and
with respect to the use of other works, than can be indicated here.
As far as it goes, it is quite on a par with the best English and
American work. From the point of view of the theory of international prices, however, two criticisms of omission can be
brought against it. First, little suggestion is given of what we
have called the "continuum" in international exchange — of the
process by which, under the influence of changing price and exchange-rate conditions, particular articles pass in and out of the
international sphere. Second, the analysis of the price-exchange
rate relationship is not begun far enough back, and perhaps not
carried far enough through. Subercaseaux takes his departure
only from the *fact* of a depreciation of the exchanges. The depreciation is presumably regarded as due to the presence of an
excessive quantity of inconvertible paper money, but the mechanism of the procession from one phenomenon to the other is not
worked out in any detail. The antecedent changes in prices, and
in the balance of payments, are matters which still require a certain illumination. Nor has he anything to say of the subsequent
repercussions upon the balance of payments and upon the exchange rates, which result from price movements themselves
consequent on the fluctuations of the exchanges.

6. The work of Bourguin and Subercaseaux and their followers
rested at bottom on an acceptance of the characteristic English
teaching, and therefore involved also an acceptance of some form
of the quantity theory of money. But the dominant doctrine in
France, at least in the decades before the war, was based on a non-
quantitative or even an explicitly anti-quantitative interpretation
of the international-exchange relationships appearing under dissimilar and depreciating currencies, and was set up in ostensible

---

[1] Subercaseaux, *op. cit.*, pp. 234–249.

opposition to the English view.[1] If disproportionately little space is given to this doctrine here, it is simply because the detail of the works in which it is presented contains less of interest for our purposes than does the other group of writings, historically less important though the latter are.

The general character of the non-quantitative doctrine has already been indicated. It holds that the origin of the disturbance in monetary and commercial conditions ordinarily lies not in an initial internal depreciation of the currency, but in an adverse balance of international payments. This adverse balance then produces a depreciation of the exchanges. Simultaneously a premium appears on gold, since gold is the standard medium of international payment. From gold the rise in prices spreads to other international commodities, and perhaps to "domestic" articles as well. That any *general* and uniform rise in prices can result from this single source of disturbance, however, is regarded as impossible. Should a partial internal depreciation of the currency nevertheless follow the depreciation of the exchanges, it is still denied that any one definite relationship between the two can be assigned.

This theory seems to have been first advanced seriously in France by Milet, who drew upon the monetary disorders of Brazil for his evidence.[2] It is also suggested, though little is made of it, by Reboud,[3] and is presented by Roux as a partial explanation of the Spanish depreciation.[4] But by far the most important and most elaborate exposition is to be found in the earlier writings of Professor Nogaro.[5] Nogaro, it will be remembered, has also been

---

[1] It will be shown later in the present chapter that the two are not, in point of fact, necessarily inconsistent with one another.

[2] H. A. Milet, *D'un aphorisme orthodoxe mais inexact sur la monnaie* (*Revue d'économie politique*, 1890).

[3] Paul Reboud, *Essai sur les changes étrangers* (Paris, 1900).

[4] Georges Roux, *Le change espagnol et son amélioration actuelle* (Montpellier, 1911).

[5] B. Nogaro, *Contribution à une théorie réaliste de la monnaie* (*Revue d'économie politique*, 1906), especially pp. 718-722; *Les dernières expériences monétaires et la théorie de la dépréciation* (*Revue économique internationale*, 1908), especially pp. 493-500; *Le problème du change espagnol* (*ibid.*, 1910), especially pp. 65-70. His more recent work will be examined later.

one of the leading French critics of the quantity theory itself.
His views in the latter field have inevitably brought him to a
typically non-quantitative doctrine of the conditions of international exchange under depreciated currencies.[1] Criticism of
these views, however, may be postponed until after the modifications more recently placed upon them have been indicated.
These are the modifications evoked by the course of events since
1914.

7. The war opened a chapter in the history of monetary depreciation that the economists of fifteen years ago would have
regarded as purest fiction. Both the extraordinary severity of the
depreciation and the range of countries in which it appeared have
far surpassed anything hitherto experienced. The distinction between the events of the past ten or twelve years and parallel
episodes in earlier decades has in the first instance been only
quantitative, it is true, but the differences in degree were so great
in certain cases as to constitute real differences in kind as well.
This change in the actual subject-matter of general reasoning has
necessarily been reflected, to a certain extent, in a change in the
character of the reasoning itself.

In France the shift in the emphasis and content of the corresponding doctrines has been quite as pronounced as in England or
the United States. It is possible to distinguish three principal divisions in these doctrines, the last of which has no adequate counterpart in the English literature. One, of relatively small actual
importance, has followed the general classical tradition — rather
loosely interpreted — and has come out at the purchasing power
parity theory. A second, finding its chief expression in the writings of Professor Nogaro, has adhered to the ostensibly opposed
anti-quantitative position. But under the pressure of recognized
historical events its rigidity has been greatly moderated, and its
real antithesis to the first theory is by no means so clear as before
the war. The third division, finally, adopts a middle ground. On
the whole, it is the most convincing of the three. It starts with

---

[1] For an excellent summary and criticism of the anti-quantitative position here,
see H. E. Barrault, *Le sens et la portée des théories antiquantitatives de la monnaie*
(frequently cited above), especially pp. 391–402.

neither the quantity of money nor the balance of international payments as the exclusive source of disturbance, but attempts to go behind both, and to find an antecedent explanation in the general state of the national finances. Its principal exponent has been Professor Rist.

Of these groups the first can be dismissed rather briefly. The purchasing power parity theory has found singularly few avowed advocates in France, and indeed was allowed to pass quite without comment for a considerable time. In 1923 Professor Cassel's book on "Money and Foreign Exchanges" was translated into French by Lachapelle,[1] but it does not seem to have secured much support.

In the previous year Olivier made a study, along similar lines, of the statistical relationships between price and exchange-rate fluctuations in 1920 and 1921.[2] He concluded, from data for a dozen different countries, that there is a very close correlation between the course of actual prices and the theoretical price indices calculated from foreign-exchange rates. The correlation is closer, the less the depreciation. He further observes that where the exchange depreciation is slight, the internal purchasing power of the currency is usually somewhat *below* its external purchasing power, while where the depreciation is great it is *above*. The latter fact is attributed to over-confidence in the currency at home, and to under-confidence abroad.

But these two writers are the only ones who have recently committed themselves at all definitely, as far as I know, to the price-parity analysis.[3] Olivier, indeed, says little about the *doctrine* as such, although the general relationships he endeavors to establish are of course those which it postulates.

8. The majority of the French economists who have examined

---

[1] G. Cassel, *La monnaie et le change depuis 1914* (trad. G. Lachapelle, Paris, 1923). The translator's preface to this work has also been reprinted separately under the title, *Les théories du Professeur Cassel sur la monnaie et le change* (*Revue d'économie politique*, 1923).

[2] M. Olivier, *Le change et les prix* (*Revue d'économie politique*, 1922).

[3] It was adopted by certain French economists, without especial comment, at the time of the Brussels Conference of 1920. But this rather tacit approval seems to have been subsequently withdrawn.

Professor Cassel's theory in any detail, and even they are not numerous, have on the contrary been opposed to it. They have preferred that type of analysis which treats the balance of payments and the foreign exchanges as the starting-point in the general disturbance, and which regards internal price fluctuations as results rather than causes. It may be remarked in passing that the latter doctrine has in point of fact usually been defended in France by men who hold an anti-quantitative position with respect to the theory of money and prices, whereas the few pro-quantitative theorists have been inclined rather towards Cassel's view. But this division is to some extent a coincidence, or at least an historical development, and not a logical necessity. The proposition that exchange movements precede internal price movements is not inconsistent with the less rigid forms of the quantity theory. It is possible to hold that actual or prospective inflation simply produces its effects on the exchanges, through the agency of speculation and general anticipation, *before* it disturbs internal prices materially. The point will be elaborated in a later chapter.[1]

In this group the two most important writers[2] have been Aftalion and Nogaro. Aftalion has contented himself with a criticism of Cassel. Nogaro goes farther, and advances doctrines of a more positive character.

Aftalion concludes, on the basis of a detailed statistical investigation, that the facts of recent history show the price-parity theory to be largely erroneous.[3] He selects for study the period 1922–1923, when the war-time influences had largely subsided and when most of the exchanges were no longer controlled. In three countries, Germany, Austria, and Poland, he finds that prices and the exchanges remained fairly constant in this period, despite great increases in the circulation. In France, Belgium, and Denmark they rose, on the other hand, but without the prior existence of any real inflation. In England, Czecho-Slovakia, and

---

[1] Ch. xvii, below.

[2] See also, however, the rather summary review by Yves Guyot, *Le professeur Cassel et la dépréciation systématique de la monnaie* (*Révue économique internationale*, 1923).

[3] A. Aftalion, *La circulation, les changes, et les prix* (*Revue économique internationale*, 1924).

Finland, finally, they fell heavily, yet without serious *deflation*. In other words, prices did not follow the fluctuations in the circulation, and *did* follow those of the exchanges. Aftalion himself points out that the discrepancy between prices and the circulation is accounted for, by some writers, in terms of changes in the velocity of circulation of money, but he does not attach great importance to this alternative explanation.

In general, he admits that price parities and the exchanges do tend definitely to coincide, but he denies that more rigid formulation which makes changes in the quantity of money the source, through price movements, of fluctuations in the exchanges. Money and the exchanges have often moved not together, but in opposite directions. This does not indicate that money never governs the exchanges, but it does show that money is not the exclusive source of their fluctuations, nor of those in prices. Aftalion refrains from giving a complete alternative theory of his own, but he evidently leans strongly towards a "psychological" explanation running in terms of the anticipation of the future.[1] He is also quite definite in holding that any program for stabilization should begin with the exchanges rather than with the currency.

The most important criticisms of Cassel's theory, however, and the most important elaborations of the historically alternative doctrine, have come from the pen of Professor Nogaro. Nogaro, who has set forth his views in several recent books and articles,[2] starts in general from that anti-quantitative position which we have already encountered in the pre-war period. He so modifies

[1] Reference should also be made to a more recent article by Aftalion, *Les variations du change en France tiennent-elles aux cycles économiques?* (*Revue économique internationale*, 1925). Here he concludes that cyclical forces are on the whole playing an increasing part in the fluctuations of the post-war exchanges, these forces themselves resting ultimately in the general credit cycle. I cannot help but feel, however, that the concept of "cycles" here implied is rather primitive. Except for the exchanges themselves, the data employed are all annual, and the period treated is of necessity brief.

[2] B. Nogaro, *Réparations, dettes interalliées, et restauration monétaire* (Paris, 1922); *La monnaie* (Paris, 1924). See also his article, *La signification de l'expérience monétaire Tchèco-Slovaque* (*Revue économique internationale*, 1924).

Reference may be made to an article by the present writer, *Monetary Theory and Monetary Policy* (39 Quarterly Journal of Economics, 1925), in which *La monnaie* is reviewed at length.

it, however, that the barrier between it and the price-parity theory no longer seems unscalable.

In all of his earlier publications Professor Nogaro had been an irreconcilable opponent of the quantity theory of money. But he now admits that when the initial increase in the quantity of money is too great and too sudden to be offset by any possible increase in production, then the quantity-theory conclusion is substantially valid. Prices, that is, will be forced up in proportion to the excess increase in the circulation. He continues to hold, however, that small and slow changes are taken up by changes in the volume of production,[1] and thus retains at least a part of the ostensibly anti-quantitative view.

His position with respect to the foreign exchanges is similarly, and commendably, lacking in doctrinaire rigidity. He admits that if an initial and rapid increase appears in the quantity of money, then this increase may itself be the cause of a depreciation of the exchanges. He finds, however, that ordinarily the sequence of events has run the other way. The exchange depreciation has come first, the internal depreciation second, and the increase in money in circulation has been a distinctly later consequence. Here, the immediate explanation of the initial exchange depreciation is to be found in the state of the balance of payments. But this in turn depends, at least in part, on "psychological" factors of a non-mechanical character, such as speculation, the anticipation of political or monetary changes, and so forth.[2]

These propositions Nogaro then illustrates from the post-war history of various countries.[3] In France, he declares that bill

---

[1] *La monnaie*, pp. 170–172, 202–204. This last proposition was used by Forbonnais as a leading defense of Mercantilism. See ch. viii. sect. 5, above.

[2] *La monnaie*, pp. 174–195. In the earlier book, *Réparations*, his position was more dogmatic, and resembled that which he held before the war. See for example pp. 10–15 in that work.

With respect to the monetary history of the nineteenth century, Nogaro makes an interesting attempt to explain both the protracted stability of the gold-silver ratio, and its eventual collapse, in terms of the balance of payments between gold-standard, bimetallic, and silver-standard countries. So far as the data available permit a critical judgment, this seems to offer a clear case for the balance-of-payments theory of the exchanges (as versus the price-money theory).

[3] *La monnaie*, pp. 86–133.

speculation long held the exchanges above the level to which they would otherwise have fallen. In Germany the larger stages in the exchange depreciation corresponded to the course of general political events, while the more immediate fluctuations were governed by the flight of capital and the degree of budget disequilibrium. Prices moved with the exchanges themselves, though usually not so far, and the quantity of money in circulation was largely the *result* of the price level. In England, the gradual fall in prices and the exchanges was the consequence of the discount-rate policy, rather than of changes in the circulation (though the relation between prices and exchanges themselves has been uncertain). In Czecho-Slovakia and Austria, finally, price stabilization was the result of exchange stabilization, rather than the reverse, and in the latter case was effected in the face of a great increase in the quantity of money. The Czecho-Slovak stabilization itself is explained by foreign bull movements, and by government intervention; the Austrian, by government intervention and by foreign loans.

Nogaro then turns to the purchasing power parity theory, and in examining it brings his own views still more clearly into relief. To this theory he makes detailed objections.[1] First, as already indicated, he holds that changes in circulation are usually the result, not the cause, of fluctuations in the exchanges. Second, although price parities and exchanges usually do tend to move substantially together, it does not follow from the mere fact of this coincidence that either can be regarded as necessarily dominating and controlling the other. The price parities may often determine the level of the exchanges, but there is also an abundance of evidence to show that, in particular cases, these parities may be altered without necessary limit by the fluctuations of the exchanges themselves. The history of Germany, Russia, and Czecho-Slovakia provides frequent examples. Finally, the maintenance of equilibrium in international exchange cannot be explained in terms of price and commodity movements alone.

---

[1] *La monnaie*, pp. 206–216. Cf. *Réparations*, pp. 108–120, in which the mechanics of the process by which an exchange depreciation actually operates on general internal prices are worked out in more detail.

The explanation must run, rather, in terms of the international flow of capital, and of the manipulation of discount rates — the latter being used to attract such capital movements and to minimize gold flows. Nor can any one statement whatsoever be complete which deals only with quantitative factors, and which neglects those "psychological" elements already referred to.

Such is Professor Nogaro's general analytical position. Its chief characteristic is its insistence that the exchanges, rather than money and prices, are the initial source of disturbance. The contrast to the familiar price-parity position, however, is evidently far less marked than that of the pre-war doctrines of the anti-quantitative school, and indeed less marked than Nogaro would on occasion lead us to infer. Nogaro now admits that a rapid increase in money will force up prices and the exchanges· while the leading adherents of the price-parity doctrine acknowledge the fact that under certain conditions exchange movements themselves precede changes in prices and in the quantity of money.[1] Similar considerations apply, in greater or less degree, to most of the other points of difference. We may already begin to suspect — what will be demonstrated at length elsewhere — that the apparent antithesis is not so much a matter of underlying principle as of emphasis, of the particular point selected for departure and of the particular cases held in mind.

9. There remains, finally, a third view which is intermediate between the price-parity theory and the type of doctrine emphasized by Nogaro. This view does not seek to make either the quantity of money or the exchanges and the balance of payments the exclusive source of disturbance. Rather, it regards the exchanges and internal prices as being in a relation of interdependence, reacting upon one another indiscriminately, and each taking in turn the rôle of prime mover in the sequence of changes. Furthermore, it attempts to go behind price and exchange fluctuations, and to discover the nature of the conditions which govern them both.

This approach to the problem was first tentatively suggested as far back as 1921 by Dr. Mawas, who published in that year a

[1] See ch. vii, sects. 4 and 5, above.

study of English financial conditions since the war.[1] The study is an illuminating piece of work, and is remarkable for that relatively early stage in the history of the post-war depreciations. But the earliness of its appearance also necessarily restricts the range of the results reached, and the argument is not pushed through to a complete analysis of the conditions which are antecedent to movements in prices and the exchanges. It is therefore unnecessary to review it in more detail.

The chief advocate of the position, which is really a separate doctrine in itself, has been Professor Rist.[2] Unlike the great majority of French writers in this field, Professor Rist has been able to base his conclusions on a survey of groups of continuous data, and has drawn from them a lucid and convincing interpretation. Incidentally, he has managed to make even smaller the real antithesis between the views of Professor Cassel and those typified by Professor Nogaro.

Cassel and Keynes, it was shown in another chapter, started their analysis in the main from the extant *fact* of inflation, and of increased prices; Nogaro, with exchange depreciation. Rist, on the contrary, is primarily concerned with those more fundamental and antecedent disturbances from which the fluctuations of both prices and the exchanges themselves take their rise. His general thesis is that the underlying explanation of the facts of inflation and depreciation lies in the budget situation, and that the very possibility of *deflation*[3] is dependent on the establishment of

[1] A. Mawas, *Le système monétaire et le change anglais depuis la guerre* (Paris, 1921). Dr. Mawas is an Egyptian, and I believe is now in the civil administration of his country.

Mawas works out in some detail the process by which the three magnitudes — money (and deposits) in circulation, price levels, and the exchanges — reciprocally affect one another (pp. 58–62, 115 ff.; also see pp. 80–86, 277–281). Certain criticisms must be made, however, of the statistical methods used. No especial allowance is made for the element of "lag"; the effects of purely monetary depreciation on the exchanges are not separated from those of the balance of payments; and many of the figures submitted are based on a lumping together of the data for some five different countries. This last procedure makes accurate interpretation difficult, and verification impossible.

[2] C. Rist, *La déflation en pratique* (Paris, 1924). Reference may again be made to the present writer's article, *Monetary Theory and Monetary Policy*, for a more detailed review.

[3] The reader's attention is invited to the careful and valuable distinction (*La

budget equilibrium. Granted such an equilibrium, an improvement in the exchanges will follow of itself, as will a fall in prices. The amount of money is here strictly a resultant. During a period of inflation, on the other hand, an increase in the mount of money and credit in circulation is usually the first step in the collapse, with price and exchange depreciation as common results. When the depreciation has become severe, however, and is steadily growing worse, the sequence may be reversed.

These conclusions Rist derives from a painstaking study of four countries in the period since 1919. The cases at issue are presumably familiar to the interested reader, however, and a brief reference is sufficient. In England he finds that the fall in prices and the exchanges after 1920 was due primarily to the gradual recovery of British finance, and especially to the definite arresting of further new inflation. No strictly mechanical explanation of the improvement can be adequate, for the decrease in money and deposits in circulation was far too small (only 7 per cent from 1920 to 1922) to account for it. Nor did the exchanges show any definite relation either to prices or to the circulation. In the United States, financial and credit deflations were similarly accomplished through the Federal Reserve discount policy and the resulting crisis, while there was no monetary deflation at all. In France, on the other hand, a crisis led to financial and credit deflation, but the government's inability to balance the budget prevented a permanent *monetary* deflation. A new period of inflation then ensued. In Czecho-Slovakia, finally, it proved impossible to stabilize prices and the exchanges until after a budget equilibrium had been secured. But once this had been accomplished, the mere fact of an equilibrium, together with general confidence that it would be maintained, induced a heavy importation of capital. The exchanges improved in consequence, while prices fell with them, and the amount of money in circulation steadily declined.[1]

déflation, pp. 1–10) between the various types of deflation: monetary, credit, and financial. The latter term refers, of course, to the *public* finances.

[1] Rist also makes two other observations of interest. First, when inflation is definitely stopped the resulting stability of prices resists any further exchange depreciation, because of the repercussions on the balance of trade and of payments (as under a gold standard). But such resistance to rising exchanges also increases the

It requires no demonstration that this type of interpretation of recent monetary history draws very closely together the price-parity theory, on the one hand, and that doctrine which Professor Nogaro has concerned himself to defend on the other. Rist finds that under certain conditions exchange movements preceded internal price movements, while under other conditions the price movements, in response to initial internal inflation, themselves came first. But the focus of the central problem is evidently shifted entirely away from the selection of one or the other of these two alternatives, and comes to rest on conditions which are antecedent to them both. These conditions are the state of the national finances, and the prospects for their future. This shift in emphasis is the largest single step forward, in the theoretical analysis of severe depreciations, that has been taken since the war.

On the other hand, it must be remembered that Professor Rist's doctrine ceases to apply *after* the national finances are once definitely, and presumably permanently, established on a sound footing. Should a régime of inconvertible paper still continue under these conditions, we should then be thrown back on one or the other of the two alternative theories for an explanation of the movements of prices and the exchanges.

A word may be added as to Rist's interpretation of the relation between money and prices. The propositions just outlined suggest that he is opposed to the quantity theory, or at least indifferent to it. Such is not the fact: he is at pains to establish himself as a defender. But whereas he finds that the effect of an increase in the amount of money upon prices is rapid, the effect of a decrease is asserted to be slow. An increase first operates on raw materials, wages, and necessities of life, and from them is quickly transmitted to the whole market. A decrease, on the contrary, is first felt in articles of luxury and in other goods at the periphery of the market structure, and penetrates only slowly to its interior.[1]

demand for money, and if the government is not strong may induce a new inflation. This happened frequently in Germany (C. Rist, *La déflation en pratique*, pp. 96–101). Second, under these conditions capital movements are at least as important as transfers of commodities and services in maintaining exchange equilibrium. Though far smaller in amount, they are also far more elastic (*ibid.*, pp. 120, 121). Nogaro has a similar doctrine.

[1] *Ibid.*, pp. 115–117. See also pp. 96–99, 128–130.

Whether this can be accepted as legitimate quantity-theory doctrine, however, is evidently debatable. In any event, it is regarded as applying primarily to the major phases of price movements alone, rather than to short-time fluctuations.

10. We may properly conclude these chapters on the history of French thought with a review of the general position of the theory of international exchange in France during the last seventy-five years, and of the contributions of French economists to this theory. The point of departure has nearly always been the body of ideas developed by the succession of English economists, especially by Mill and Goschen. The English doctrine itself, however, is divisible into two principal sections, one dealing with the (non-monetary) theory of international values and the other with the more concrete phenomena of prices, specie flows, and exchange rates. Of these, it is the latter to which the lion's share of attention has been paid.

Nevertheless, the classical theory of international values has not been wholly ignored. It has had a few defenders, and it has evoked far more trenchant criticism than was ever directed against it in England. This criticism took two principal forms. One, developed by certain mathematical economists, turns at bottom on the proposition that there is no essential difference between the determination of values in international exchange and their determination in internal exchange. The problem of international trade is therefore stated primarily in terms of money prices, rather than in terms of labor costs, and conclusions quite different from those of the classical theory are reached as to the determinants and the effects of such trade. Of this position the principal expositors have been Cournot and Pareto, although neither has presented a complete statement. The other line of criticism, advanced only by Professor Nogaro, deals more with Mill's modifications than with the Ricardian principle of comparative costs itself. It finds that the rôle of money in international exchange is such that international values cannot be regarded as being determined, in any significant sense of the term, by an "equation" of international values. Individual exchanges become merged in the total of international payments. Money, far from being a colorless transmitting medium, is capable of producing variations in the situation independently of other factors, and any doctrine which ignores it must necessarily be erroneous. Each of these two groups of criticisms, which the pro-classical theorists have in large measure neglected, contains many elements of permanent value.

The English analyses of prices, specie flows, and the exchanges, and of the various exchange mechanisms, have been much more widely studied in France than the theory of international values. The price-specie flow theorem has been accepted by certain writers, and vehemently rejected by a number of others, notably Professor Nogaro. The essential ground of the rejection is usually a denial of the validity of the quantity theory. The conception of a self-restoring equilibrium in international trade, on the other hand, has been quite generally adopted. But it is Goschen's formulation of this equilibrium tendency to which French economists have in the main turned, rather than to Ricardo's and Mill's. Moreover, the tendency is ordinarily stated in terms of the prices of bills of exchange, and of money-market mechanisms, rather than in terms of commodity prices and commodity markets.

Finally, the French literature of foreign trade under depreciated currencies contains various elements not found in other countries. Bourguin has presented an essentially pro-quantitative explanation, Nogaro the anti-quantitative view, and Subercaseaux a non-doctrinaire analysis of the mechanical relations between various groups of prices and the exchanges. In the period since the war the study of objective data has been pushed steadily forward, while the contrast between the two extreme theoretical positions has been diminished. This last process of reconciliation may be regarded as having culminated in Rist's thesis, which moves the fundamental emphasis entirely away from prices and the exchange rates as such, and places it on the (logically antecedent) condition of the national budgets and the national finances at large. We shall return to these doctrines, as well as to the French criticisms of the theory of international values, in later chapters.

CHAPTER XII

RECENT ITALIAN THOUGHT

1. The general body of recent Italian thought [1] upon those problems which enter into the theory of international prices is of a character quite different from the French. In both, the main lines of approach have resembled those laid down by earlier English writers, but whereas in the one case the reaction to English teaching has been characteristically critical and even destructive, in the other the criticisms have been few, and the typical attitude one of acceptance. The majority of the Italian economists have taken over the classical theories bodily, premises and conclusions alike. Only at certain rather isolated points have they attempted any important modifications, and then with somewhat indifferent success. Moreover, at each given time the reflections of English doctrine have usually been based not on *current* English ideas, but on the ideas of a generation before. In consequence, to students already familiar with its antecedent originals the Italian literature must necessarily seem lacking in vigor and freshness.[2]

---

[1] No attempt will be made here to examine the literature of Italian Mercantilism. Certain of the writers and doctrines involved have already been referred to in the corresponding chapter on French thought. The novelty of the additional material to be found in the Italian literature is not great enough, to the best of my knowledge, to justify the laborious study that would be required. Nevertheless it must not be forgotten that many of the typical propositions of Mercantilism, especially in the earlier period, were Italian in their origin.

The first half of the nineteenth century offers little that is worth while for our purposes.

[2] It is an interesting question as to why the classical English teaching, not only on international trade but in general, has met with such wide acceptance in Italy, whereas in the other Continental countries it has had but indifferent success. Much of the explanation undoubtedly lies in the intimate and sympathetic relationship, at the beginning of the second half of the nineteenth century, between English liberalism and the new political and social movement in Italy. But a part of it, also, is probably to be found in the formative influence of Professor Francesco Ferrara, the leading Italian economist of the last generation, and a great admirer of the English school. Professor Ferrara also began the publication of the *Biblioteca dell' Economista* (Turin, 1850–), in which most of the important English works have

Even the writers of the mathematical school, which has had a larger following in Italy than in any other country, have not explicitly tried to overthrow the classical theory itself. Rather, they have sought only to modify it, and to restate its propositions in accordance with their own characteristic views on general economic theory and methodology.

This lack of doctrinal novelty in the larger part of the Italian literature makes the task of description correspondingly easier, and justifies a rather summary treatment of most of its aspects. Four principal problems are involved: the general theory of international trade itself; the theory of money and prices; the relations between money and international trade under common metallic standards; and finally, the explanation of the course and terms of trade under inconvertible paper.

2. With respect to the first problem, the general theory of international trade, the chief interest of the Italian thought lies in its occasional criticisms or modifications of English doctrine. The majority of the works that enter the field seem to have accepted the entire classical position, often only in the form given it by Mill, without especial comment. When we have mentioned the fact itself, we have done them sufficient justice. Following the corresponding English theorists with a "lag" of a generation or more, as a rule, the orthodox Italian economists have made but little attempt to add anything new.[1] The members of the mathe-

found a place. Smith's *Wealth of Nations* was translated in this series in 1851, as was Mill's *Principles;* Ricardo's *Principles* in 1856; Cairnes's *Leading Principles* in 1878; and Goschen's *Foreign Exchanges* in 1899.

Whatever the explanation, the English influence has undeniably been very great. In consequence the general economic theory of Italy to-day, taken as a whole, is a curious blend of English doctrine, the methodology of the Lausanne mathematical school, and the practical teachings of socialism — primarily of the German cathedral variety. With respect to this last, and the influence of German thought in general, see A. Graziani, *Sulle relazioni fra gli studi economici in Italia e in Germania nel secolo XIX*, in G. Schmoller, *Die Entwicklung der deutschen Volkswirtschaftslehre im 19. Jahrhunderts* (Leipzig, 1908), vol. i, Essay 17.

[1] See especially: U. Buzzetti, *Teoria del commercio internazionale* (Milan, 1877); E. Lorini, *La moneta e il principio del costo comparativo* (Turin and Rome, 1896); C. Supino, *Principii di economia politica* (2 ed., Naples, 1905), Bk. II, ch. xiii; A. Graziani, *Istituzioni di economia politica* (Turin, 1904). In the latter work, see especially the third edition (1917), pp. 350–365. Cairnes's theory of non-competing

matical school, it is true, have developed a quite different method of approach, but of the non-mathematical writers only Professor Loria has undertaken a criticism which is at all searching.[1] His observations are put in an illuminating way, and deserve comment.

Professor Loria adopts the classical position in general, but he brings against Mill's theory of the determination of international values a criticism which we have met elsewhere. He finds that Mill's formula does not give a *definite* determination, and that his later attempt at escape is inadequate.[2] This objection, as far as it goes, is well founded, but Loria's own solution is less easy to justify. He seems to hold that international values will be fixed midway between the two points of maximum and minimum gain, for the one country and the other.[3] This can perhaps be regarded, however, as a legitimate deduction from the principle of comparative costs.

In a later work, Loria also advanced the interesting proposition that, while under money a fall in the cost of production of a given article will be reflected in the ratio of international exchange, in a state of barter it need not be.

When the international exchange is effected in kind, the foreign consumer and the domestic consumer give two different articles in exchange for that one, of which the cost is reduced. When the quantity of goods given by the

---

groups is also found in E. Leone, *Lineamenti di economia politica* (Rome, 1914), pp. 414 ff., though Leone adopts, in general, the mathematical position.

I have as yet been unable to obtain a copy of Professor G. Del Vecchio's recent essay, *Teoria del commercio internazionale* (Padua, 1923).

[1] See, however, L. Fontana-Russo, *Traité de politique commerciale* (Paris, 1908; translated from the Italian edition of 1906 by L. Poli), pp. 28–35 ff. Fontana-Russo accepts the classical theory of international values, though himself ending up with full-fledged protectionism. He concludes, however, that the classical assumptions as to the internal mobility and external immobility of labor and capital are badly exaggerated. The first is far greater, and the second far less, than the classical writers thought.

His composite comparative-cost curves (pp. 38 ff.) seem to me entirely erroneous.

[2] A. Loria, *Studi sul valore della moneta* (Turin, 1891), pp. 54–58. Nevertheless, in his *Economic Synthesis* Professor Loria threatens to make reciprocal demand into a general law of value.

Also see his interesting though somewhat involved criticisms of Cournot's theories: *Studi*, p. 61, note 1.

[3] *Ibid.*, pp. 60 ff.

second consumer alone diminishes, from a fall in the costs of production, that given by the first may remain the same, without his having any means of helping himself. When, on the other hand, the international exchange is effected by the use of money, the foreign consumer and the domestic give the same commodity, money, in exchange for that product whose cost is reduced. Consequently, if the quantity of this commodity given by the second consumer diminishes, that given by the first must also fall in equal degree. Otherwise he would not hesitate to acquire the product concerned, through the agency of a domestic consumer.[1]

It is regrettable that Loria did not work out the further conclusions which these propositions suggest, for they might have cast much light upon the significance and validity of the classical theory of international trade. This theory explicitly assumes that the terms and conditions of trade will be the *same* under barter as under a money economy.

The most important modifications and partial criticisms of the classical theory, however, have come from the mathematical writers. The doctrines of the mathematical school itself have taken two distinct forms, one advanced by Pantaleoni, the other by Pareto and his followers. First, Professor Pantaleoni's doctrines. In general, Pantaleoni starts from a quasi-hedonistic position. This is the view that all exchanges tend to be determined at the point of maximum satisfaction, and that costs of production tend to be identical with the final degree of utility. These ideas he then applies to international exchange, making use of the mathematical and graphical apparatus first employed by Marshall in his privately printed essay, "The Pure Theory of International Values," and taking over its more important conclusions without question.[2] The general law governing such exchanges he finds to be this. Given two non-competing or closed markets, and full competition within each, then under normal

---

[1] A. Loria, *Il valore della moneta* (Turin, 1905), p. 27. In Loria's general text, however, these ideas fail to appear. He gives only the usual classical theory, briefly and without especial comment: *Corso completo di economia politica* (Turin, 1910), pp. 434–442.

[2] M. Pantaleoni, *Pure Economics* (translated by T. B. Bruce, London, 1898), pp. 197–209. The Italian original bore the title, *Principii di economia pura* (Florence, 1889). Professor Marshall's essay was first published in 1879. Marshall himself has also recently presented its substance to the general public in his latest work, *Money Credit and Commerce* (London, 1922), Appendix H. (See ch. iv, sect. 9, above.)

conditions an increase in exports will result in a fall in export prices. But the fall will not be great enough to decrease the aggregate mass — or total money value — of the corresponding imports. Rather, "an increase of exports determines an increase of imports, but at a rate of interchange less favorable to the market in question."[1] An initial increase in imports produces the opposite results.

To this general law, however, there are two principal exceptions. A decrease in exports may produce such a rise in foreign prices as to cause an actual *increase* in imports; and an increase in the output of exported articles, by reducing domestic expenses of production, may cause a fall in their domestic value greater than the fall abroad, and thus decrease the total imports.

These basic propositions, and others less significant, he proceeds to demonstrate by means of that type of curve — or rather, of pairs of curves — now familiar in nearly all of the more recent mathematical economics.[2] Both curves start from the intersection of the two axes, the geometric origin, and normally move upward and to the right. They may be so constituted that they move increasingly away from one another from the origin, being convex on adjacent sides. In this case the proposed exchange is evidently impossible. If they are not mutually exclusive from the start, however, they will eventually intersect. Exchanges can then take place within the limits defined by the enclosed area. Curves of a "normal" type will meet only once. Their intersection then provides the point of stable equilibrium, which actual ratios of exchange necessarily tend to approach. In the abnormal cases of "exceptional" demand, however, the curves may turn back toward one axis or the other.[3] In that event their intersections may or may not be points of stable equilibrium, depending on their character.

It is evident that, when stripped of its peculiarities of apparatus, this theory is essentially the familiar law of normal equilibria established by or at the points of intersection of the curves of demand and supply. It is qualified, however, for differences in the

[1] Pantaleoni, *Pure Economics*, p. 198.
[2] *Ibid.*, pp. 199–203. For a fuller discussion and partial criticism of this type of curve, see ch. xviii, sects. 2 ff., below.   [3] *Ibid.*, pp. 204–209.

rate of variation, as quantities change, of costs of production and elasticities of demand. It is not set up in direct and intentional antithesis to the older classical theory of international trade. Indeed, Pantaleoni explicitly subscribes to the law of comparative costs, though with the observation that it can be satisfactorily expressed only by the use of the mathematical apparatus.[1] But the classical theory of international values, in the form worked out by Mill, is not presented or referred to. Indeed, the whole method of approach seems to me quite inconsistent with the classical method. Both cannot be altogether correct. This question, however, will be examined in more detail at another point.[2]

The other principal type of mathematical approach found in the Italian literature is that developed by Professor Pareto and his followers. Pareto's work, however, has been discussed at sufficient length in an earlier chapter.[3] Despite the differences in apparatus and terminology, and the much greater refinement in the doctrinal scheme, Pareto's own method of approach and positive doctrine are not far from those of Marshall and Pantaleoni. The principal difference, for our purposes, lies in the way in which Pareto has resolved the apparent logical hiatus resulting from the application of the principle of comparative costs to price economies. As we have seen elsewhere, he finds that since money prices are under competition proportional to maximum "ophelimities," a comparative advantage in terms of sacrifice is also a comparative advantage in terms of money price.[4] This possible hiatus seems to have quite escaped Professor Pantaleoni's attention.

Pareto's followers in Italy do not appear to have made any really substantial modifications in his doctrines, at least in the field of international exchange.[5]

3. A general theory of international exchange is one of the two

---

[1] Pantaleoni, *op. cit.*, p. 197.   [2] Ch. xviii, sect. 6, below, and ch. xiv, sect. 3.

[3] Ch. x, sects. 2 and 3, above. Reference was made there to Pareto's *Cours*, and to his later *Manuel*. In addition, see two of his articles: *Teoria matematica dei cambi forestri* (*Giornale degli Economisti*, 1894), and *Teoria matematica del commercio internazionale* (*ibid.*, 1895). The latter article contains an interesting criticism of Professor Edgeworth's articles on *International Values* (*Economic Journal*, 1894).

[4] Ch. x, sect. 2, above.

[5] See especially E. Barone, *Principi di economia politica* (Rome, 1908), pp. 78–97; E. Leone, *Lineamenti di economia* (Rome, 1914), pp. 414–420, 452–455.

primary elements from which any theory of international prices must be built. A domestic theory of money and prices is the other. To this, as it has been developed in the recent Italian literature, we may now turn. The connection between the two elements has been no closer in Italy than in other countries, it is true, but a definite link nevertheless necessarily exists.

In monetary theory, as in other departments of Italian thought, the classical English influence has clearly been dominant, if not exclusive. Only one important writer, Berardi, who drew much of his inspiration from Professor Laughlin's works, has been flatly opposed to the quantity theory.[1] The mathematical school, under Pareto's leadership, has of course also criticized the theory, along lines now familiar, and has confined its rigid application to the case of an inconvertible paper circulation. But the employment of the apparatus of marginal utilities or ophelimities and stable equilibria to metallic money, theoretical subtleties aside, seems to lead to general results that would not be unacceptable to most pro-quantitative economists.[2] The defect of the mathematical method here, as at other points, lies in its inability to describe concrete mechanisms significantly, and to deal adequately with the phenomena of continuous change.

The theory of the value of money, in the double form given it by Mill, has found quite wide acceptance. Even at the present day, writers frequently content themselves with distinguishing between "normal" value, as determined by the cost of production or of importation, and "current" value, as determined by demand and supply, using both terms only in the sense given them by Mill.[3] A few writers, on the other hand, have explicitly rejected

---

[1] D. Berardi, *La moneta nei suoi rapporti quantitativi* (Turin, 1912), especially pp. 98–113.

[2] The references to Pareto's works were given in sect. 2, above, and in ch. x, sects. 2 and 3. See also Leone, *op. cit.*, pp. 294–299 ff. Leone differs from most of the mathematical economists in the greater attention he pays to the theoretical analysis of the intermediary phenomena between given equilibria. He tends also to agree with Giffen's theory that the quantity of metallic money is the result rather than the cause of the level of prices — that is, the result of the need for a circulating medium. His analysis of the actual mechanisms, however, is necessarily limited.

[3] Of the earlier writers, a good example is afforded by L. Cossa, *Primi elementi di economia sociale* (13 ed., by Graziani: Milan, 1914), pp. 101 ff. (First edition:

the distinction. Professor Loria, for example, declares that Mill's attempt to reconcile the two views is logically untenable. Yet Loria himself, while admitting that any precise statement is impossible, concludes that the cost of production of metallic money determines its long-time value, and that this value in turn governs the quantity which can remain in circulation.[1]

Most of the Italian economists, however, have been chiefly concerned with the immediate, demand-and-supply side of the problem; that is, with the quantity theory as it is usually understood. They have as a rule tied up the value of money with their general theory of value, but Professor Fisher's formulation of the "equation of exchange" has also recently received a fair amount of attention. Fanno, in particular, has accepted it without especial comment,[2] while Supino has criticized it adversely.[3] Supino declares that Fisher much exaggerates the importance of the monetary element, and neglects the forces that arise from changes in the values and costs of goods themselves. He himself makes the "movement of business" the critical factor for changes in both prices and the quantity of money. This theory he bases largely on conclusions drawn from Professor Mitchell's "Business Cycles." In general, however, the characteristic tendency of the Italians has been towards a quite uncritical acceptance of a rather rigid form of the quantity theory, which is in turn made to depend on a doctrine of general value. The long controversies waged in the United States and France, and to a less extent in England, have found but little reflection in their writings.[4]

1875.) More recently, see Supino, *Principi* (cited above), pp. 211–226; and Graziani, *Istituzioni* (cited above), pp. 722–732. In other works, however, both of these last two writers have advanced somewhat more detailed theories, especially in connection with the rôle of discount rates. See Graziani, *La moneta nei pagamenti internazionali (Riforma Sociale,* 1906), especially pp. 434–436; and Supino, *Moneta e prezzi (ibid.,* 1917), pp. 442–443.

[1] A. Loria, *Il valore della moneta,* pp. 11, 12.

[2] M. Fanno, *Inflazione monetaria e corso dei cambi* (a series of articles in the *Giornale degli Economisti* for 1922 and 1923). The reference is to the *Giornale* for 1922, p. 343.

[3] C. Supino, *Moneta e prezzi (Riforma Sociale,* 1917), pp. 433–443.

[4] For a general review of the recent development of monetary theory in Europe, and for an application of the marginal-utility theory to the problem of the value of money, the reader may be referred to the series of articles by G. Del Vecchio, pub-

Some account should also be given of a more recent examination of the relations between discount rates and prices. In 1916, Bresciani-Turroni made two statistical studies that have yielded some curious results. Using monthly averages based on reliable English and American sources, he worked out the correlation between price movements and discount-rate movements by means of a double-frequency table. The correlation he found to be only + 0.02. He concluded, from this and other data, that

oscillations of brief duration, in the discount rate, cannot influence the prices of commodities. They only induce movements, in the opposite direction, in the prices of securities. It is necessary, in order that even these prices should be modified, that the . . . fall in the discount rate be prolonged for a certain period.[1]

In another article, he turned to the problem of long-time relationships, and put through a similar series of correlations. These, however, were based not on monthly but on annual data. He found here that the *long-run* correlation between prices and discount rates is on the whole very close.[2]

These results are interesting, and, if they can be accepted, have an important bearing on the interpretation of international price-determinations. But, while I am not competent to judge of their technical validity from the data submitted, they nevertheless seem to me to be open to serious question. The Pearsonian coefficient was not used here, and the significance of a frequency table for correlations of this sort seems to me doubtful. Nor does any test seem to have been made for different intervals of lag.

lished in the *Giornale degli Economisti* from 1909 to 1917. See especially, *I principii della teoria economica della moneta* (issue for 1909); and *Questioni fondamentali sul valore della moneta* (issue for 1917).

An early and authoritative formulation of the quantity theory, from which many Italian writers have since taken their departure, is given in A. De Viti De Marco's excellent work, *Moneta e pressi* (Citta di Castella, 1885), pp. 1–15. See also M. Fanno, *La moneta* (Turin, 1908), especially p. 3. A considerable number of other works which present the orthodox quantity theory (turning on the quantity of money, its velocity, and the "movement of affairs," or volume of business) might also be cited, but these references are sufficient for the purpose.

[1] C. Bresciani-Turroni, *Oscillazioni dello sconto e dei prezzi* (*Giornale degli Economisti*, 1916), pp. 331, 332. Italics omitted.

[2] Bresciani-Turroni, *Relazioni fra sconto e prezzi durante i cicli economici* (*Giornale degli Economisti*, 1916), pp. 372–380 ff.

Yet on *a priori* grounds we should certainly expect a lag of some sort to appear. In the absence of such tests, therefore, the value of the results obtained must be regarded as uncertain.

4. For our purposes, however, the most interesting studies of the mechanisms of international exchange that have been made by Italian economists have been undertaken to show the relations between money, discount rates, and the course of foreign trade. A number of Italian writers have adopted the older classical position with respect to the world distribution of money, and have regarded money as being essentially colorless. Thus Pantaleoni gives, briefly and without especial comment, the classical theory of gold movements, which turns on price changes and the balance of payments.[1] Loria has a slightly qualified form of the same doctrine, and, far from admitting that the international flow of the precious metals can affect international values, he asserts that this flow is itself governed by the conditions of reciprocal demand.[2] Supino's position is similar.[3] The mathematical economist, Leone, even goes so far as to say that the presence of money, coupled with the operation of the price-specie flow mechanism, makes the marginal utility of money the same throughout the world. Money can therefore have no effect on the determination of international values.[4] Only Berardi, arguing from the general position already familiar to English and American students in the works of Professor Laughlin, flatly attacks the classical theory.[5]

A few writers have also, however, attempted to go somewhat farther in the analysis of actual mechanisms, especially with respect to the part played by the discount rate. In 1885, De Viti De Marco gave a brief but excellent summary of the effects of the mass of metallic money upon the exchange rates. The intermediary factors are the rate of discount and the balance of trade.[6]

---

[1] Pantaleoni, *op. cit.*, pp. 276–278.

[2] Loria, *Studi sul valore della moneta*, pp. 53–74, especially pp. 73, 74; *Il valore della moneta*, pp. 24–34, 50, 51.

[3] Supino, *Principii*, pp. 323–327.

[4] Leone, *Lineamenti*, pp. 421–430 and 452–455. Leone thus carries Pareto's line of attack farther than Pareto himself. See ch. x, sects. 2 and 3, above.

[5] Berardi, *La moneta*, pp. 116–122.

[6] De Viti De Marco, *Moneta e pressi*, pp. 110–115. On the general determination of the levels of the exchanges, see pp. 103–134.

His argument, drawn in large measure from English doctrines of the Goschen-Bagehot type, has had great influence upon later Italian students. In 1906 Graziani, for example, also concluded that variations in the discount rate may change the volume of commodity imports and exports, and may directly affect the entry or exit of the precious metals themselves. He went on to relate world specie movements not only to the rate of discount, but also to the general conditions of the markets for long-time and for short-time loanable capital, and to the composition of the given country's monetary circulation.[1] This argument, likewise taken primarily from Goschen and Bagehot, is of a familiar order, and regards the specie movements as essentially automatic. It differs chiefly from the English writers mentioned in attaching greater importance to the commodity-price movements as such. It is thus a partial reversion to the older classical doctrine.

Fanno, a year or two later, presented an interesting modification of the classical theorem, in an attempt to show what the actual mechanism of the process in point of fact is by which gold moves from a mining country to a non-mining country. He takes as his example the case of England and the Transvaal. Starting with a "scarcity" of circulating media in England, he finds the sequence to be as follows: high discount rates in England; a depression of English prices, including the prices of those articles used in gold mining; a consequently increased rate of profit from gold mining itself, in the Transvaal; a flow of goods from England to the Transvaal; and a counter-flow of gold from the Transvaal to England, due to the relatively high state of prices in the former country, and their relatively low state in the latter.[2] The argument thus turns on the prices of goods actually used in mining — not, as in most of the classical writers, on the prices of goods in general. It can hardly be accepted without a number of revisions and amplifications, but it is worth bearing in mind.

[1] A. Graziani, *La moneta nei pagamenti internazionali* (*Riforma Sociale*, 1906), especially pp. 434–436. Graziani also criticizes the common French view, advanced especially by Gide, that specie flows are not necessarily self-corrective, and that interference by the government or the banks is necessary to prevent the possible monetary ruin of the country.

[2] Fanno, *La moneta*, pp. 23, 24.

Still more recently, Del Vecchio has advanced a proposition in which the older classical doctrine, as to the means by which equilibrium is maintained in international trade, is largely lost sight of. He finds that the movements of the discount rates and of the exchange rates, not commodity price changes, are the most important correctives of dis-equilibrium in international trade. Not only do they support the correction due to price changes, but they "have so great a rapidity and efficiency, in comparison with the limited and slow movements of prices, that they obscure these last, if indeed they [i. e., the movements of prices] exist at all." [1] This proposition is advanced in explicit opposition to the early classical view, in which the fall of prices consequent on monetary contraction is regarded as the chief cause of the return of international trade to equilibrium. Del Vecchio holds that if a country has an excess of imports, a fall in prices *may* ensue, but it need not follow necessarily. If it does appear, it may *or may not* depend on an antecedent monetary contraction. Such a contraction, and such price changes, are not the conditions on which equilibrium depends. The first sign of dis-equilibrium, such as would result from an excess of imports, is a stringency in the exchanges and in the discount rates. This stringency usually exerts a sufficient corrective in itself. Price changes, if indeed they appear at all, are a secondary consequence. Nor need gold flows ever be called upon. They take place only when the exchanges are forced to the gold points. Further, while the excess of imports here assumed may not be adjusted by price changes, in the long run it is directly self-corrective because of its effect on the reciprocal international demand for commodities. How this form of correction can take place *apart* from price-changes, however, is not explained. Finally, the international movement of capital must be allowed for. Such movements complicate the general theory of the process, but they make the practical restoration of equilibrium much easier, since the discount rate has a greater effect on the flow of loans than on the flow of goods.[2]

[1] G. Del Vecchio, *Contributi alle dottrine della circulazione* (*Giornale degli Economisti*, 1914), p. 123.

[2] *Ibid.*, pp. 124–125. See also his article, *Teoria dell' esportazione del capitale* (*Giornale degli Economisti*, 1910).

Evidently Del Vecchio is here following Goschen's line of approach rather than that of the orthodox classical writers. He gives a theory of international equilibrium which runs, not in terms of commodity imports and exports, but simply in terms of the balance of payments. It finds its corrective machinery in exchange-rate and discount-rate movements, not in price changes. If, in advancing it, Del Vecchio has not gone beyond present-day writers in England and America, at least he has got clearly away from that literal adherence to the older classical doctrine which still characterizes many of the Italian writers. He is not trying to establish an equilibrium in the commercial balance of *trade*, nor is he concerned to show that international exchange tends to reduce simply to a commodity barter. Indeed, the possibility that an excess in the commodity balance (relative to some previous level) may exist for at least a considerable period, without evoking any necessary tendency to correction, is clearly recognized.

Finally, Bresciani-Turroni has recently made a statistical study of the exchanges and the discount rates which offers some interesting results. Taking the London – New York exchanges in the period 1899–1908, and applying the Pearsonian coefficient to monthly averages of the exchanges and of the discount rates in the two cities, he finds that the course of the Anglo-American exchanges was regulated by the difference between the rates of discount in the markets of New York and London. This proposition, which he sets up in opposition to opinions prevalent in America, he explains by the effects of finance bills on the exchanges. The international movements of such bills is, of course, especially sensitive to discount rate fluctuations.[1] He also finds that the relation between the excess importation or exportation of gold and the course of the discount rate is much less intimate than is usually supposed. The correlation for New York is only -0.18 ± 0.04.[2] The significance of these results, if they can be accepted as statistically correct, is evidently great.

[1] C. Bresciani-Turroni, *Oscillazioni dello sconto e dei prezzi* (*Giornale degli Economisti*, 1916), pp. 318, ff.

Ibid., p. 327.

5. The theoretical problems presented by the phenomena of international trade under inconvertible paper have, on the whole, attracted surprisingly little attention. Most of the writers have been content to repeat the older English doctrines, especially those of Goschen, without any especial attempt at elaboration or revision.[1] Since 1914, it is true, a number of articles have been published in the Italian journals that deal with the disordered conditions induced by the war, but they have been concerned more with the description of specific phenomena than with their theoretic interpretation and explanation. Even Professor Cassel's doctrines have evoked detailed study, as far as I can discover, from only one writer — who accepts them without criticism.[2] This whole branch of economic theory seems to have been of indifferent interest to the majority of the Italian economists, and their work in it lacks originality.

To this generalization, however, there is one important exception: Professor Jannacone's recent study of Italian foreign trade and monetary conditions between 1871 and 1913.[3] His arguments and conclusions are worth presenting in some detail, for although explicitly confined to the given country and period, they contain a more general significance. They are supported by an imposing

---

[1] See, for example, Supino, *Principii*, pp. 280–283, and Fanno, *La moneta*, pp. 65–108. Reference should also be made to the various studies of disordered monetary conditions in particular countries, made by Professor Lorini between 1893 and 1904. (See the Bibliography, below.) These studies are primarily descriptive, however. They attempt little in the field of theory.

[2] M. Fanno, *Inflazione monetaria e corso dei cambi* (*Giornale degli Economisti*, 1922 and 1923), in vol. 2 for 1922, p. 352. Also see, however, G. U. Papi, *Prestiti esteri e commercio internazionale* (Rome, 1923). Although based chiefly on the work of Professors Taussig, Graham, and Williams, the latter study makes a brief examination (pp. 140–145) of Cassel's doctrine.

On the war period see A. Loria, *Le peripezie monetarie della guerra* (Milan, 1920); and L. Einaudi, *Corso dei cambi, sbilancio commerciale, e circolazione cartacea* (*Riforma Sociale*, 1918). Professor Einaudi's study, based on Italian conditions from 1915 to 1917, is designed to show that the effect of the commercial balance of trade on the exchange rates may, for a time at least, be almost wholly obliterated by the effects of foreign loans. Bresciani-Turroni has also made a useful investigation of recent conditions in Germany and Austria: *Considerazione su alcune recenti esperienze monetarie* (*Giornale degli Economisti*, 1925).

[3] P. Jannacone, *Relazioni fra commercio internazionale cambi esteri, e circolazione monetaria in Italia nel quarantennio 1871–1913* (*Riforma Sociale*, 1918).

array of statistical data, laboriously compiled and manipulated, and by citations from many competent authorities, especially English and American. One caution, however, is necessary at the outset. The statistical data are all based on yearly averages. The entire lack of monthly figures necessarily limits the scope and refinement of the resulting conclusions.

Professor Jannacone's problem is the relationships between three pairs of factors from 1871 to 1913, when Italy was under a paper standard, and the explanation of their intimate connection. The pairs of factors are the commercial balance of trade and the exchanges on Paris, the exchanges on Paris and the paper circulation, and the paper circulation and the balance of trade.

First, the relation between the balance of trade and the Paris exchanges. The Italian commodity balance of trade was more or less heavily adverse throughout the entire period considered. The exchanges, with a few isolated exceptions, were also steadily unfavorable, and during much of the time distinctly exceeded the nominal gold points. An application of the Pearsonian coefficient of correlation to the two forty-three year series of annual averages, variously manipulated, yielded the following results: [1] (1) For the absolute values of the excess of the exchanges above par and the excess of imports, $r = -0.51 \pm 0.08$; (2) for eleven-year moving averages, $r = -0.77 \pm 0.05$; (3) for the values as calculated by Cauchy's method of interpolation (fourth degree), $r = -0.62 \pm 0.06$; (4) for the *annual percentage excess*, of the balance of trade and of the exchanges, $r = -0.53 \pm 0.07$; (5) for eleven-year moving averages of the percentage excesses, $r = -0.90 \pm 0.02$. From this Jannacone concludes that the negative correlation of the two phenomena, on which the series are based, is highest when short-time oscillations are most successfully ruled out. This is further supported by the fact that the coefficient for the *differences* in annual effective values is $+0.10 \pm 0.12$; and for the deviations from the interpolated values (Cauchy's method), -0.09 ± 0.10. There is hence

---

[1] Jannacone, *op. cit.*, pp. 521, 522. Jannacone further illustrates the character of these various manipulated series by an elaborate set of curves. So also in the other sections of his study.

almost no correlation between the annual oscillations.[1] Finally, an inspection of the plotted curves shows that both series run in cycles of 22 to 23 years, composed of 11-year phases. Moreover, in three out of four cases the maximum or minimum of the exchanges preceded, by 4 to 5 years, the (inversely) corresponding minimum or maximum of the balance of trade.[2]

Second, the Paris exchanges and the paper circulation. In order to obtain significant conclusions here, Jannacone finds it necessary to distinguish between the "sufficient" and the "excess" circulation at each given time. He determines the depreciation of the circulating medium not by reference to the absolute quantity of money, but by its excess above a certain variable limit which would presumably be "sufficient" for the needs of business.[3] As a roughly proportional measure of the changing "sufficient" circulation, Jannacone selects the volume of commerce, and as a convenient index of this volume he takes the total value of Italian commodity imports and exports at each given time. The ground for the choice of that particular index is that it is simple, and that a large part of the raw materials of Italian industry are secured from abroad. The variations in the volume of foreign trade are therefore assumed to be nearly proportional to those in the total commerce of the country.[4] Yet the logical dangers of this procedure are great, and the charge of circular reasoning must be entertained. An *independent* criterion cannot result from it. The volume of foreign trade is measured by its total money value *in Italy* — that is, in terms of the very currency whose depreciation and excessive quantity it is designed to reveal. Moreover, the volume of this trade is necessarily in a certain relation of dependence or interdependence upon the other two elements, the exchanges and the balance of trade. Nevertheless Jannacone's results are interesting, for he finds a very high positive correlation, both short-time and long-time, between the

---

[1] Jannacone, *op. cit.*, p. 522.   [2] *Ibid.*, pp. 517, 518.

[3] *Ibid.*, pp. 525, 526. The idea, which goes back at least to Smith, is clear enough, but it carries with it various rather vital implications as to the international price structure and as to international monetary relationships; implications which Jannacone, presumably starting from the orthodox classical position, quite neglects.

[4] *Ibid.*, pp. 532, 533.

excess circulation and the exchanges.[1] Here again the exchange rates appear to precede changes in the excess circulation by 4 to 5 years. That is, their maxima and minima occur that much in advance of the corresponding maxima and minima of the excess circulation.[2]

Finally, there is the relation between the excess circulation and the commercial balance. Here the maxima and minima show a close inverse correspondence, and the Pearsonian coefficients of correlation are also high. This is especially true of the 11-year moving averages, which show a coefficient of − 0.86 ± 0.03.[3]

6. Jannacone then comes to the problem of making a consecutive explanation of the intimate relationships between these various elements. He disposes at once of the theory that a steadily adverse balance of trade can, by its effects on the balance of payments, cause a permanently unfavorable rate of exchange. The resulting rise of the exchange rate (i. e., as quoted in the domestic currency) is self-corrective. It tends, as far as its own influence goes, to produce a decrease in imports and an increase in exports, and thus to restore the balance.[4] Nor is it correct to say that the depreciation of the currency creates a *less unfavorable* balance of trade, since the consequent premium on exports, and the stimulus to economic activity in general, can at best be only temporary.[5] Instead of these partial theories Jannacone advances the proposition that all three sets of fluctuations, in the exchanges, the balance of trade, and the excess circulation, are common products of a single cause. This cause is the cyclical variations in general prices, and the periodic alternations of general prosperity and general depression. Allowance must be made, however, for the fact that the exchange rates themselves are also influenced by the relative movements of gold prices and paper prices; that is, in the Italian case, of world prices and national prices.[6]

Such is the essence of Jannacone's argument. A more detailed

---

[1] Jannacone, *op. cit.*, pp. 538, 539. Five correlation coefficients are worked out, running from + 0.62 ± 0.07 to + 0.99 ± 0.02. How far the closeness of the correlation is due to the peculiar character of the measure of the excess circulation is a problem which, after what has just been said in the text, may be left to the reader's judgment.

[2] *Ibid.*, pp. 542–544. [3] *Ibid.*, pp. 544, 545. [4] *Ibid.*, p. 516. See also p. 545.
[5] *Ibid.*, pp. 545–548. [6] *Ibid.*, pp. 550–562.

presentation would add little. A certain amount of independent statistical verification is offered, but it is much less convincing than that presented in the earlier parts of the study. Reliance for proof is placed in the main upon the theories and data of other writers, especially those of Giffen and W. C. Mitchell. Jannacone finds himself handicapped at the start by the lack of any very complete body of data on cyclical price fluctuations, in Italy itself, with which to compare his own results. Even with due allowance for this handicap, however, he has overlooked an important alternative explanation. It is evidently possible that the cyclical movements of domestic prices may themselves have been *results*, rather than causes, of the movements in the balance of payments. A verification of this proposition, however, would presumably require data having a smaller time-interval than those actually available.

Professor Jannacone makes one other extremely interesting application of his theory, which merits attention. Italian international trade, especially between 1902 and 1912, had presented the apparent paradox of a large adverse balance of trade, an increasingly excessive paper circulation, and an exchange rate near par, all appearing steadily together. Jannacone explains the paradox in this way. The period in question was one of rising prices and general national prosperity. Italy, characteristically a borrower in the international market, further increased her borrowings. The loans took the form of goods, very largely, and the balance of trade hence became increasingly "adverse." At the same time the necessity of remitting the proceeds of the loans to Italy from foreign countries tended to make the exchange rates more favorable. Further, this movement of the exchanges caused the gold prices received for Italian exports to fall in terms of paper, and thus diminished their volume. This condition made the trade balance still more unfavorable,[1] and thus aggravated the apparent paradox. Jannacone also points out, however, that in a *lending* country which is also on a metallic monetary standard the opposite situation would appear. Prosperity and rising prices would tend to make the balance of trade increasingly favorable, while the exchanges would move adversely.

[1] Jannacone, *op. cit.*, pp. 562–565.

Such is the main argument of Jannacone's study, and such its principal conclusions. It is a suggestive and able analysis, developed along novel lines, and some parts of it can be accepted without further comment. But certain criticisms must also be entertained, both as to method and as to theory. The principal difficulties as to the method used have already been indicated. They proceed from the failure to secure a logically independent measure of the "sufficient" quantity of money, and from the fact that, for an accurate analysis of at least the more immediate mechanisms, conclusions based only on yearly data must necessarily be of limited scope.

On grounds of theory, the following further criticisms can be made. First, the concept of a "sufficient" quantity of money is of course perfectly admissible, but only with rather elaborate qualifications as to the implied monetary relationships between the countries concerned. These qualifications Jannacone does not present. Second, the significance of the so-called tendency of the exchanges to precede changes in the balance of trade and in the excess paper circulation by 4 to 5 years is very uncertain; and it is difficult to explain so great an interval in terms of any of the mechanisms of the market. There is ground for regarding it as largely fortuitous. The proof of the existence of the tendency, moreover, is based largely on the location of the points at which, with respect to eleven-year periods, the various series reach maxima and minima. This is hardly a conclusive demonstration. Third, no especial account is taken of possible variations in the quantity of paper money appearing *independently* of price cycles and trade conditions. Such are the variations due to the state of the public finances. Had a large issue of paper money been made in the period in question simply to meet a budget deficit, Jannacone's whole theory would be distorted. Finally, and partly in continuation of this last objection, the problem of the rôle of money itself in international exchange seems to be slighted. This is especially true of the theory of cyclical fluctuations. There is little in Jannacone's argument to show why the gradually increasing amount of money might not itself have been the cause of the long period of prosperity, and therefore have been the real starting-point of that whole series of phenomena which he tries to explain by the cyclical theory. To this suggestion he offers at one or two points a summary denial, but neither his theoretical argument nor his statistics actually disprove it. As already suggested, the sequence of events may equally well be interpreted as running *from* the balance of payments and the exchanges *to* the movements of domestic prices. Of this alternative possibility Jannacone takes no adequate account.

7. From this review of the recent Italian literature, it is evident that only two trends of thought have attained to major importance. One is the post-classical trend, the other the mathematical. The contributions of the mathematical school to the general theory of international prices have been largely confined to the problem of international values. To their typical ideas, as to the similar propositions advanced by the writers of this school in other countries, we shall return later. The principal contributions of the post-classical economists, on the other hand, have not lain in the domain of general theory. They have in the main been content to follow the English writers of a preceding generation, and they are therefore open to much the same criticisms that, in earlier chapters, have been brought against their teachers. Their most interesting suggestions have been advanced, rather, in the field of the actual mechanisms of foreign trade under dissimilar monetary conditions. This is especially true of the conclusions of Del Vecchio with respect to the foreign exchanges, discount rates, and the maintenance of equilibrium in international exchange; of the more specialized studies of Bresciani-Turroni on the discount rate; and finally, of Jannacone's elaborate analysis of certain aspects of trade under inconvertible paper.

Taken as a whole, however, the recent Italian literature is much less vigorous and original than the corresponding studies in England and France and the United States, and — though this is of course not necessarily a defect — its quantity is small. The Italian writers have been excellent scholars, and painstaking students of foreign doctrines, but few of them, at least in this department of economic inquiry, have attempted to develop really new lines of investigation.

CHAPTER XIII

GERMAN AND AUSTRIAN THOUGHT SINCE 1860

1. When we turn from Italy to Germany and Austria, we are confronted with a style of thought which is different in both its method and its problems. Recent French and Italian economists, in their treatment of the questions that enter into the theory of international prices, have in the main followed the general lines of investigation laid down by preceding English writers, although the former were critics rather than disciples. In Germany and Austria, on the other hand, the direct English influence has been relatively slight, and the scope of independent investigation and speculation has been correspondingly wider. This is especially true in the field of monetary theory, but it is also characteristic in some degree of other departments.

The general problem of the theory of international prices presents at least two principal aspects, which are quite distinct. One is essentially a problem of mechanisms. It begins with a theory of the determination of prices and price structures within any one country; and passes from this, by way of a theory of the foreign exchanges, to price relationships *between* countries. The other, essentially a problem of inter-commodity ratios of exchange, likewise proceeds from a general theory of the determination of such ratios within each country to their determination as between countries; that is, to a theory of international ratios of exchange. As a corollary, it has something to say of the establishment of international scales of relative money incomes. In the more recent literatures that we have thus far examined, these two problems have often been kept separate to an amazing degree, and have been treated as though they really did not belong to the same universe of inquiry. A similar separation is on the whole characteristic of German and Austrian thought. In discussing the corresponding literature we shall therefore be concerned with the recent development, along lines mutually rather isolated, of some four principal bodies of theory.[1] They are, first, the quantitative or dynamic aspects of the various theories dealing with the value of money; second, theories of international trade under depreciated currencies; third, the general theory of international trade itself; and finally, certain analyses of cost-structures and price-structures. These elements, however, have never been drawn together into a unified synthesis. In consequence no complete theory of international prices has ever been built, in Germany or in Austria, from the raw materials which they provide.

2. What may be described as the dominant and most characteristic aspect of German and Austrian monetary theory, in recent years, is an aspect which has been without an important counterpart in the literatures of other countries. This is the so-called "qualitative" aspect.[2] The qualitative theories have become involved in what might almost be called the metaphysics of money. They have been concerned with its character, its function, its composition, and above all with the origin (both logical and historical) of its value. A large body of writings has resulted, often intensely polemical, and containing much that is of great interest to students of general monetary theory. This literature is not in itself, however, directly relevant to the problem of international prices, since it has nothing to say of specific mechanisms and processes. For them we must turn to those parts of the German and Austrian doctrine, perhaps less peculiarly characteristic

[1] By "recent" development is to be understood here a period running back not more than fifty or sixty years at most. It may at once be admitted that the delimitation of a definite time-period, however, is rather arbitrary, and has been in considerable part dictated by the usability of the material apparently available. The difficulty is similar to that encountered in connection with the Italian literature. No attempt will be made here to examine the literature before the nineteenth century.

[2] An excellent though brief history of German monetary theory in the nineteenth century is given in S. P. Altmann, *Zur deutschen Geldlehre des 19. Jahrhunderts*, in G. Schmoller, *Die Entwicklung der deutschen Volkswirtschaftslehre* (Leipzig, 1908), vol. 1, Essay 6. The convenient distinction between "qualitative" and "quantitative-dynamic" theories, used above, is taken from it. On the period since 1905, see H. Döring, *Die Geldtheorien seit Knapp* (2 ed., Griefswald, 1922). On the doctrines of the last few years, see R. Kerschagl, *Überblick über das Schriftum des Geldwesens von 1914 bis 1920* (*Zeitschrift für Volkswirtschaft und Sozialpolitik*, 1920). For a more exhaustive but less illuminating outline of the general history of monetary theory, see F. Hoffman, *Kritische Dogmengeschichte der Geldwerttheorien* (Leipzig, 1907).

but none the less important, which deal with the quantitative aspects of money, with problems of change.

In other countries, writers upon the quantitative or dynamic aspects of monetary theory have placed themselves in one or the other of two main categories. One group has subscribed to the quantity theory in some form, while the other has rejected it. These categories have also found representation in Germany and Austria, although the explicit and uncompromising anti-quantitative position has not obtained many adherents. In recent years, however, a third category has appeared, and has secured an extraordinarily wide following. This is the "agnostic" position initially derived, in large part, from Knapp's so-called "state" theory or "political" theory of money. The theory is of course essentially nominalistic, but it seems to have led to practical conclusions not usually derived from nominalism in other literatures. It will be worth while to say something of the content of each of the three bodies of doctrine, since they provide much of the background for the various analyses of international prices.

The pro-quantitative writers, while admitting a direct relationship between the quantity of money and its value, have as a whole adopted a much less rigid and extreme position than the classical English economists. They have admitted, and even strenuously declared, that a one-to-one proportionality need not and usually cannot exist; they have by no means confined attention to the "money" side of the situation, as distinct from the "commodity" side; and they have usually come out with a formulation which, while pro- rather than anti-quantitative, is very loose indeed. Among these writers two groups are clearly distinguishable. One, starting from a selected doctrine of general value, has attempted to apply this doctrine to the problem of money, and has been led to a non-proportional theory of the relation between the amount of money and its value. The other group, composed of only two or three writers, has denied the applicability of general value-theory to money, and, confining its attention to mechanisms, has made a *caeteris paribus* assertion of proportionality.

Of these groups the first, in view of our previous survey of other monetary literatures, does not offer a great deal which is novel, or which requires much comment. The two writers who have exerted the greatest influence on German economic thought since the latter part of the nineteenth century, Schmoller and Wagner, have presented rather obscure doctrines of the value of money based on eclectic theories of general value, and have also advanced loose non-proportional forms of the quantity theory. Lexis has given a similar somewhat inconclusive doctrine.[1] In all of these writers the stress on concrete mechanisms is very weak; so much so, indeed, that it is rather difficult to place them definitely on either side of the quantity-theory fence.[2] Certain theories have also been based on doctrines of objective value. An example is provided by the labor-value theory of the Marxian Socialists.[3]

Finally, and especially in Austria, a number of theories have been advanced which are derived from a *subjective* doctrine of value. These theories all deny the rigid Ricardian formulation. They assert the entire lack of any necessary proportionality between the amount of money and its value, and tend to stress the "commodity" side of the complex of factors which alter that value. Of the writers in this school, it is sufficient to name Menger, Wieser, Philippovich, and Mises.[4] Wieser and Mises give,

---

[1] For example, see G. Schmoller, *Grundriss der Allgemeinen Volkswirtschaftslehre* (revised edition by L. Schmoller, Leipzig, 1920: 2 vols.), vol. 2, pp. 163 ff.; A. Wagner, *Theoretische Sozialökonomik* (Leipzig, 1907–1909: 2 vols.), vol. 2, pp. 211 ff.; W. Lexis, *Allgemeine Volkswirtschaftslehre* (Berlin, 1910), pp. 101, 102, 127. For a brief review of these theories, see Altmann, *op. cit.*, pp. 43–49; and Döring, *op. cit.*, pp. 193–209. It may be added that in a much earlier work, *Die russische Papierwährung* (Riga, 1868), Wagner presented a mild form of the anti-quantitative position (see sect. 5, below).

[2] Lexis, for example, seems in another work to be more inclined to oppose even a loose form of the quantity theory than to support it, though again the position is rather inconclusive. See his article, *Papiergeld* (*Handwörterbuch der Staatswissenschaften*, 3 ed., 1909–1911, vol. 6), p. 992. And so see the flat rejection by Wagner, many years before, of *any* strict formulation of the quantity theory: *Die russische Papierwährung*, pp. 85, 86, 94, 97–99, et al.

[3] For instance, R. Hilferding, *Das Finanzkapital* (Vienna, 1910), *passim*. See also Döring, *op. cit.*, pp. 179–193.

[4] E. von Philippovich, *Grundriss der politischen Oekonomie* (8 ed., Tübingen, 1909), vol. i, sects. 94, 96; C. Menger, article *Geld* (*Handwörterbuch der Staatswis-*

too, what has at another point been called the "direct" chain of effects produced by an increase in the quantity of money. That is, they begin with the augmented purchasing power of those who first receive the new increment of money, and show how this purchasing power, gradually diffused throughout the given society, leads to an irregular rise in general prices.[1] Wieser also makes an interesting attempt to state the problem of the value of money in terms of the relation between real and money incomes. A change in this relationship from either or both sides is regarded as finding expression, through the mechanisms of the market, in a change in the value of money.[2] The method of approach is extremely suggestive, and it is only to be regretted that Wieser did not work it out into more usable form. It might well have led him into a theory of cyclical fluctuations of money incomes, such as that suggested by the apparent phenomena of the business cycle. As it is, however, neither he nor the other exponents of the subjective theory have advanced propositions which offer much that is new to students of English theory.

The last division of the essentially pro-quantitative theories is provided by those writers who, while refusing to apply a general theory of value to the problem of the value of money, have nevertheless maintained a doctrine of proportionality based on the

senschaften, 3 ed., 1909–1911, vol. 4), pp. 592, 593; F. von Wieser, *Der Geldwert und seiner Veränderungen* (*Schriften des Vereins für Sozialpolitik*, vol. 132, Leipzig, 1910), pp. 514–530; Idem, *Theorie der gesellschaftlichen Wirtschaft* (in *Grundriss der Sozialökonomik*, by a symposium: vol. 1, Tübingen, 1914), pp. 322–327; L. von Mises, *Theorie des Geldes und der Umlaufsmittel* (Munich and Leipzig, 1912), especially pp. 149–166.

A convenient statement of some of the objections to the Austrian theory of value, as applied to the problem of money, is given in K. Helfferich, *Das Geld* (2 ed., Leipzig, 1910), pp. 543, 544. Helfferich's own position, however, seems quite inconclusive. See for instance *ibid.*, pp. 546–552.

[1] Wieser, *Der Geldwert und seiner Veränderungen*, pp. 523–526; Mises, *loc. cit.*
[2] Wieser, *Der Geldwert und seiner Veränderungen*, especially pp. 516, 520–523. He rejects velocity of circulation as an independently-operating source of changes in the value of money, because "it can never lead to a change in the relation between money incomes and real incomes. Money always receives its velocity of circulation from commodities." That is, the velocity follows the greater or less need for circulating media, consequent on the production of more or of fewer commodities (*ibid.*, pp. 522, 523).

objective mechanisms themselves.[1] The general type of thought is that made familiar by Professor Irving Fisher's studies. In the Austro-German literature, the most original and clear exposition of this essentially mechanistic method of approach is contained in a recent article by Dr. Schumpeter.[2] It is impossible here to do more than indicate the general outline of his position, but it is too interesting to pass by wholly without comment. Schumpeter's general stress, like Wieser's, is not on commodities but on incomes. He regards the "value" of money as being simply the purchasing power of the given *income-unit*.[3] Starting from this proposition, an examination of the general relationships of the (supposedly isolated) money economy as a whole leads him to lay down a law of "fundamental equality" (Grundgleichung) in these relationships. He finds that, in a state of stationary equilibrium, the price totals of all the *consumption* goods produced in a given period are equal to the price totals of all the *production* goods produced, and that each is equal to the total of all money incomes.[4] From this proposition a general formula is deduced, summarizing the relationships between the total of money incomes, the quantity and velocity of circulation of money, and the prices and quantities of consumption goods.[5] The general conclusion reached is

[1] Cf. Döring, *op. cit.*, p. 143.

[2] J. Schumpeter, *Das Sozialprodukt und die Rechenpfennige* (*Archiv für Sozialwissenschaften*, 1917–1918). Schumpeter, here setting forth a nominalist view of the general character of money, completely reverses his position of ten years earlier. Then, he had been a commodity-theorist, and had *denied* that proportionality which he now maintains. See his *Das Wesen und der Hauptinhalt der Theoretischen Nationalökonomie* (Leipzig, 1908), pp. 286–297.

Until recently Schumpeter's propositions seem to have evoked little printed comment. In 1924 and 1925, however, Haberler, Marschak and Schönfeld all made critical examinations of them. The corresponding titles are given in the Bibliography of the present study.

[3] Schumpeter, *Das Sozialprodukt*, p. 651.

[4] *Ibid.*, pp. 634, 635.

[5] The formula, given in *ibid.*, p. 675, is this. Let E be the total of private and public money incomes, M the money in circulation, U its average velocity, m and p the quantities and prices of particular consumers' goods. Then:

$$E = M \times U = p_1 m_1 + p_2 m_2 + p_3 m_3 + \ldots + p_n m_n$$

This formula differs from Professor Fisher's more familiar "equation of exchange" in various respects. It measures velocity not by the number of times the given piece of money changes hands in the selected period, but by the number of

that changes in either the commodity side or the money side will, other things equal, produce a proportional change in the other factors. But it is pointed out that a change in the quantity of money, for example, will change only the price *totals* in proportion, not necessarily prices alone. Theoretically, at least, the whole effect may be concentrated on quantities of commodities, without affecting prices themselves.[1] The possible bearing of these propositions on the problem of international price mechanisms is evident, though Schumpeter does not work them out.

3. The explicitly anti-quantitative view of the value of money has also had a certain number of adherents, of whom Hildebrand provides perhaps the best example. In general, he denies that the quantity of gold in circulation influences the general level of prices. The denial is based partly on the asserted difficulty of allowing for credit and other non-metallic substitutes, and partly on the proposition that prices do not depend on the mere quantity of coin. He holds that they are governed primarily by the inclinations, the psychology, of the buyers and sellers. In presenting this view, he cites Sir James Steuart with approval.[2]

The most important and most characteristic non-quantitative writers of recent years, however, have not specifically opposed the quantity theory itself at all. They have tended, rather, to evade that whole problem of mechanisms and dynamics which the quantity theory has in mind. These are the various writers who have espoused doctrines of the "state" theory type.[3] The "state" theory, or "political" theory (*staatliche theorie*) of money was

times it enters consumers' incomes; that is, by the number of times it flows through the circle from consumers to producers and back again. Further, the term "goods" is confined to consumption goods alone. Finally, the dominant stress is laid upon the fundamental equality of the "social product" (the right side of the formula, equivalent to Marshall's "national dividend") and the total of money incomes.

Three corollary laws, in which some of the details of the supposed mechanism are worked out, are derived from the formula, but are too long to present here. They are given, respectively, in Schumpeter, *Das Sozialprodukt*, pp. 676, 677, 681, 697.

[1] See *ibid.*, pp. 697–700.

[2] R. Hildebrand, *Die Theorie des Geldes* (Jena, 1883), pp. 108–110 ff., and elsewhere.

[3] That nominalism and non-quantitative views do not necessarily go together is shown in the case of Schumpeter's recent theory, just examined. The two are more usually found associated, however, in the Austro-German literature.

originally set forth by Knapp, in 1905. Its essence consists simply in the proposition that money is the creation of the state. The state by its ordinance establishes a particular and "nominal" value-unit, already developed historically, as the one in terms of which money values shall be expressed, and to which they shall be referred.[1] This theory is set up in direct antithesis to the older commodity-value theory of money. It is nominalistic to an extreme, and denies that the particular unit used as money need have, in itself, any value whatsoever. The underlying concept is essentially juristic, and the theory itself therefore has great difficulty in finding common ground with doctrines of a more peculiarly economic character.[2]

Aside from the questionable validity, either in history or in logic, of this derivation of the value of money,[3] it is evident that the political theory is quite unable to cast light upon questions of purchasing power and its changes, or indeed upon the whole dynamic problem. Its very essence involves the denial of *any* specific relation between the value of money and the incidental fact, its quantity.[4] Nevertheless its adherents, who have grown rapidly in number, especially in Germany, have not hesitated to apply conclusions inferred from it to the monetary problems induced by the war. The results, in so far as these conclusions have been allowed to find expression in practical policies, have not been happy. Since the value of money depends, in this view, not on the character or the quantity of money itself but on the (antecedent) value-unit to which the action of the state attaches it,

---

[1] G. F. Knapp, *Staatliche Theorie des Geldes* (3 ed., Munich, 1921), especially pp. 1–20. (The first edition appeared in 1905.)

See also the recent review by J. Bonar, *Knapp's Theory of Money* (*Economic Journal*, 1922).

[2] Reference should also be made to F. Bendixen's work. Bendixen, while adopting the general state-theory position, presents a far from unoriginal version. His combination of the state theory with his own assignment (*Anweisung*) theory leads, however, to practical conclusions essentially like Knapp's. See, for example, Bendixen's *Das Wesen des Geldes* (3 ed., Munich, 1922), pp. 9 ff. For a brief survey of the other more important writers in this group see Döring, *op. cit.*, pp. 135 ff.

[3] See for example Wieser, *Theorie der gesellschaftlichen Wirtschaft*, p. 321.

[4] See L. von Mises, *Zur Klassification der Geldtheorien* (*Archiv für Sozialwissenschaft*, 1917–1918), pp. 202–204, and Döring, *op. cit.*, pp. 2, 130–135.

these writers concluded that the changes in prices must have arisen from the commodity side of the situation alone, not from anything that has to do with the quantity of money. They therefore declared that there had been no "inflation" after the war, and that still further quantities of paper money could be issued without entailing disastrous consequences to the country.[1] The teachings of experience seemed to have no success in dissipating these not always insincere illusions.

From this brief survey, it is evident that recent German and Austrian monetary theory has not reached conclusions which cast much light upon the problem of international prices. Its dominant trends have been non-quantitative. Even those writers who have not opposed or disregarded the quantity theory itself have, with few exceptions, presented a formulation so loose as to be almost without value. Furthermore, in the general discussions both of money and of banking the primarily international aspects of monetary phenomena have been rather slighted. There has been much good descriptive work, and many elaborations of supposedly desirable policies of state interference, but, as will be shown again later, the attempts to develop a comprehensive and self-consistent system of doctrines in this field have been few.

With this outline in mind as the essential background, we now come to the second principal division in the general theory of international exchange in Germany and Austria. This division turns on the questions raised by monetary depreciation.

4. The theories and investigations dealing with the problems of foreign trade under depreciated currencies offer, in the main, comparatively few theoretical conclusions of which we have not already found examples in the corresponding English and French literatures. Each writer's description and explanation of the phenomenon of depreciation, and of its international repercussions, is very largely conditioned by his preconceptions of the relations between the quantity of money and its value. The pro-

---

[1] A typical example of the latter part of this argument, unfortunately only one of many, is afforded by K. Diehl's study, *Über Fragen des Geldwesens und der Valuta* (Jena, 1921), especially pp. 59 ff. He assigns to changes in the quantity of money only a "secondary" rôle in the determination of the general level of prices; a rôle which on examination proves to be very secondary indeed.

quantitative writers find that the first step in the mechanics of the process of depreciation is an excess of a non-metallic currency. The subsequent position of the balance of payments, the depreciation of the exchanges, and the character of the resulting differentials in price movements, are then explained by a cause-and-effect relationship to this initial excess. The anti-quantitative and non-quantitative writers, on the other hand, usually begin with an "unfavorable" balance of payments, or even of trade, and proceed from this to a depreciation of the exchanges, a drain of metallic money, the replacement of this metal by paper, and an eventual depreciation of the internal currency itself. The necessity and even the existence of the last phenomenon, however, is sometimes denied. In the German and Austrian literature both of these diametrically opposed views have found wide adherence, yet with few exceptions — and those rather recent ones — no serious attempt has been made to point out their mutual inconsistency, and to select one of them as exclusively correct. The violent polemics of other fields do not appear here.

In the last third of the nineteenth century, the more or less chronic monetary difficulties of Austria-Hungary and of Russia provided the occasion for a number of studies along pro-quantitative lines. Földes, in 1877, made an ambitious statistical investigation of the relations between the premium on silver in Austria and the course of foreign trade, in the period 1852–1876.[1] He found that the initial effect of the introduction of a paper régime was to increase imports. At first, the supply of money exceeded the demand. The rise in prices was therefore not only apparent but, relative to the depreciation of the exchanges, real. This situation, however, was only temporary, and was soon reversed.[2] In reaching this last conclusion Földes apparently missed the possible lag of domestic costs of production behind commodity prices. He based the stimulus to exports or imports, as the premium rises or falls, simply on the success of dealers in buying at a low premium and selling at a high one — that is, on speculative factors. He

---

[1] B. Földes, *Der Einfluss des Agio's auf den Aussenhandel* (Vienna, 1877). It may be added that Földes was a Hungarian, though at the time, I believe, resident in Vienna.

[2] Földes, *op. cit.*, p. 3.

also makes, however, an interesting distinction. He finds that the prices of those articles which are "necessary" to production or consumption usually follow the premium closely, and that changes in the premium therefore do not affect the volume of commodity importation and exportation. But in so far as the demand for the articles is "mobile," not unqualified and necessary, their volume may be very appreciably altered.[1] In confirmation of these propositions he presents a series of annual statistical data. The most striking fact which they reveal is that the total volume of foreign trade was greatest when the premium was high, and vice versa.[2] A satisfactory explanation, however, is not given.

At about the same time Hertzka, in a series of able books, presented essentially the classical English theory of mechanisms. He stressed the proposition that the position of the balance of payments is *not* the antecedent condition that forces a country on to a régime of inconvertible paper money, but is itself an effect.[3] Grunzel, in a somewhat obscure study, also advanced "orthodox" views. He added the observation that where the depreciated country's exports dominate the foreign market, prices in the latter will tend to fall.[4] Otherwise they will not, and domestic production will for a time be stimulated by the relatively high prices received in the domestic currency. Philippovich has likewise made a brief but excellent analysis of the problem, in which the influence of the lag of domestic costs of production behind prices is clearly brought out. He concludes that exports are stimulated, and imports checked, in proportion to the magnitude of this lag. The depressing effect of depreciation upon those countries which have maintained stable currencies is also emphasized.[5] Finally, a num-

---

[1] Földes, *op. cit.*, p. 18.

[2] *Ibid.*, p. 5. See also a later article, *Ursachen und Wirkungen des Agios* (*Jahrb. für Nationaloekonomie*, 1882).

[3] T. Hertzka, *Die Gesetze der Handels- und Sozialpolitik* (Leipzig, 1880), vol. 1, pp. 44, 45; *Weckselkurs und Agio* (Vienna, 1894), pp. 6–12, 26–28. Others of Hertzka's works will be cited later in this chapter.

[4] J. Grunzel, *Der Internationale Wirtschaftsverkehr und seine Bilanz* (Leipzig, 1896), pp. 174, 175.

[5] E. von Philippovich, *Grundriss der Politischen Oekonomie*, vol. 1 (8 ed., Tübingen, 1909), sect. 96. (First edition, 1893.) K. Helfferich is another writer who on the whole follows here a line of reasoning analogous to that of the classical English

ber of other studies of particular monetary reforms were made in the last decade of the nineteenth century, and cast light on the international aspects of the situation. They too are oriented along the classical lines, however, and it is sufficient to list a few of them.[1]

More recently, Hennicke has made a very good statistical study of the monetary history of Spain from 1868 to 1906.[2] The general character of the problem is already familiar from the various French investigations which we have examined elsewhere. It will therefore be sufficient to list some of Hennicke's more important conclusions. First, he found that the chief cause of the depreciation had been the disordered and sometimes perilous state of the public finances. An initial increase in the silver coinage had caused an export of gold. The further financial difficulties of the government then led to an issue of Bank notes and of government bonds, and the net result was a depreciation of the internal currency itself. This depreciation was especially conspicuous in the period 1895–1898, during the Cuban revolution and the Spanish-American war.[3] Second, general confidence in the country's political stability or instability and the play of speculation were two factors of major importance in the determination of the fluctuating levels of the exchanges.[4] Third, the theory that depreciation was due to a prior unfavorable balance of trade, or of payments, finds support neither in logic nor in the historical facts of the case.[5] Fourth, the doctrine that an increased premium on specie promotes commodity exportation is on the whole verified. The stimulus arises from the lag of costs of production, and disappears

---

writers, though his arguments do not go into much detail. See, for example, his essay on *Aussenhandel und Valutaschwankungen*, reprinted in his *Studien über Geld-und Bankwesen* (Berlin, 1900), especially pp. 84–93; and *Das Geld* (2 ed., Leipzig, 1910), pp. 441–462. For a brief but excellent presentation of the "orthodox" position, see also L. Petritsch, *Die Theorie von der sogenanten günstigen und ungünstigen Handelsbilanz* (Graz, 1902), pp. 133, 134 (referred to again later in this chapter).

[1] See, more especially, C. Menger, *Beiträge zur Währungsfrage in Österreich-Ungarn* (Jena, 1892); Idem, *Die Valutaregulierung in Österreich-Ungarn* (*Jahrb. für Nationaloekonomie*, 1892); and L. Sachs, *Die italienische Valutaregulierung* (in *ibid.*, 1892).

[2] A. Hennicke, *Die Entwicklung der spanischen Währung (1868–1906)* (Stuttgart and Berlin, 1907).

[3] *Ibid.*, p. 49.   [4] *Ibid.*, p. 63.   [5] *Ibid.*, pp. 66 ff.

as soon as the internal depreciation catches up with the external.[1] (The distinction between a *high* and a *rising* premium, or exchange rate, is however missed.) Fifth, Spain's foreign trade was comparatively large and active in the period examined, and the effects of exchange fluctuations on purely *internal* prices therefore tended to be correspondingly great.[2] Finally, the fact that the foreign-exchange value of the peseta was steadily *above* its metallic value, in the decade before 1906, is explained by the limitation on the coinage of silver. Although the exchanges were below the ostensible gold-coin par, they were higher than the level to which, under free coinage, the world depreciation of silver would have brought them.[3]

Hennicke also stresses the close relationships between the exchanges, the premium and the international money market. The various issues, sales and repurchases of the Spanish government securities, and the changing regulations governing interest and principal payments, had a great and immediate effect upon the exchanges and the premium.[4] Indeed, the effect was so pronounced that the premium, the exchanges and the foreign price of these securities nearly always moved very closely together. Any one of them could be taken as a substantially accurate measure of the others.

5. In the last decade or two, however, and especially since the war, the dominant theories of foreign trade under depreciated currencies have with a few important exceptions [5] been based on the anti- or the non-quantitative teachings. To these, therefore, we may now turn.

In the literature of the last generation a mild form of the non-quantitative position was presented in Adolph Wagner's well-

---

[1] Hennicke, *op. cit.*, pp. 73, 74. A qualification is made, however, for the case of foreign-owned enterprises. These benefit only from the lag of wages. The Spanish mining industries were a partial case in point (*ibid.*, pp. 74–78).

[2] *Ibid.*, pp. 118, 119.

[3] *Ibid.*, pp. 116–118.

[4] *Ibid.*, pp. 18–60, *passim.*

[5] See especially the excellent article by Professor von Mises, *Zahlungsbilanz und Devisenkurse* (*Mitteilungen des Verbandes österreichen Banken und Bankiers*, 1919). Professor Mises's general treatise, as we have already seen, is also pro-quantitative (*Theorie des Geldes und der Umlaufsmittel*).

known study of Russian monetary conditions.[1] Wagner, under Tooke's influence,[2] rejected all rigid formulations of the quantity theory. In consequence, he denied the existence of any simple or necessary relationship between the amount of paper money, the specie premium and commodity prices. He found that the specie premium — which, within the limits set by the double cost of transporting specie itself, he regarded as identical with the depreciation of the foreign exchanges[3] — is determined not by the amount of paper money as such, but by the demand and supply of the precious metals. This demand and supply, in turn, are governed partly by the needs of industry, and partly by the need for specie to make international payments. But above all they are governed by the "psychological" factor: that is, by confidence in the country's economic and political stability, and by the prospect of resumption. The element of confidence or distrust takes effect on the premium through credit operations of all sorts, especially through speculative transactions in the precious metals themselves. The *quantity* of paper money affects its value only in so far as changes in this quantity affect the intermediate factor of confidence, or in so far as they alter the supply of purchasing power available for the buying of specie.[4] Usually, their influence is obscured by the effects of other more important disturbances, of which political events are among the chief. In "anomalous" or abnormal periods of economic or political crisis, the direct demand for specie itself is the principal determinant of the premium. Here, the premium governs the balance of payments and the exchanges, and these in turn exert an aggravating reaction upon the premium itself.[5] In "normal" times, however, confidence and credit are the chief factors. The balance of payments governs the exchanges, and these in turn govern the premium.[6]

[1] A. Wagner, *Die russische Papierwährung* (Riga, 1868). For a convenient and fairly complete summary of the theoretical aspects of this work, see S. P. Altmann, *Zur deutschen Geldlehre des 19. Jahrhunderts* (cited above), pp. 41–43.

[2] Wagner, *op. cit.*, pp. 85, 86.

[3] *Ibid.*, p. 89.   [4] *Ibid.*, pp. 86–88.

[5] *Ibid.*, pp. 89, 90. This "direct" demand arises partly from the need for specie to make international payments, and partly from the desire of paper-money holders to convert their paper into metallic currency of more stable value.

[6] *Ibid.*, pp. 92, 93.

The balance of payments itself is also affected, to some extent, by the quantity of paper money. The forces tending to an international equalization of prices operate to alter the balance in so far as the paper régime has altered paper prices — as translated, of course, through the exchanges. A reciprocal action thus develops, not only from the premium to prices but also from prices to the premium. Indeed, a certain tendency to an automatic and reciprocal correction appears.[1] But Wagner does not dwell on this suggestion. Rather, he concludes that since the factors of credit and confidence are in point of fact never stable, no real equilibrium can actually exist between prices, the premium and the amount of paper money.[2]

These considerations lead him to the question of price determination itself; that is, to the forces governing the value of the paper money in terms of goods and services, not of specie alone. His general position is of a familiar order, for he holds that a change in the amount of paper money will in the first instance affect only the prices of those articles directly concerned, such as the objects of public expenditure. But in so far as these articles, or ones like them, enter into the production of *other* articles, the prices of the latter will be affected by the alteration in their costs of production. The changes are then passed on to other goods in turn. The whole process of diffusion, however, is extremely irregular. It lacks uniformity and proportionality, and is conditioned by the degree of economic organization and the adequacy of internal communications.[3]

Not content with this, however, Wagner distinguishes in detail between three principal classes of commodities, and between the effects of the specie premium on each. (1) Imports. If the imports consist of "necessary" articles not produced in the paper country, their prices will in general follow the premium closely.[4] If they are also produced in important amounts within the country, the premium acts as a protective tariff checking imports, *in so far and as long as* the premium exceeds the rise in paper prices (and eventually in so far as it exceeds the rise in costs of produc-

---

[1] Wagner, *op. cit.*, p. 93.   [3] *Ibid.*, pp. 94, 97–99, 111, 112.
[2] *Ibid.*, p. 96.   [4] *Ibid.*, pp. 100–103.

tion).[1] (2) Exports. For these the premium, under a similar argument, acts as a bounty, and tends to increase their volume.[2] (3) Articles of primarily domestic production and consumption alone. Here, as in the case of an increase in the quantity of money itself, the effects of the premium on prices are irregular, and lack uniformity.[3]

Finally, Wagner submits these deductive conclusions to statistical proof, based on data taken from the history of Russia in the period 1851–1867. The figures are in the main annual averages, and hence cannot be regarded as entirely conclusive, but some of the results may be listed. First, no close relation is found between the amount of money, the amount of the specie cover, the foreign exchanges, and the premium. But the influence of political events, on the last two items especially, is very marked.[4] Second, the total money value of the Russian exports in terms of foreign currencies remained nearly constant throughout the period, despite all political and economic disturbances. This Wagner accounts for partly by the industrial stagnation within Russia at the time; partly by the contemporary fall in world prices, which prevented the premium from exerting its full influence as a bounty; and partly by the lag of paper prices behind the premium, which enabled foreign buyers to pay less *in paper* than they would otherwise have found necessary.[5] Finally, he attributes the fall in the exchanges from 1861 to 1866 to the unfavorable state of the balance of international payments. Crises in central and western Europe, and the competition of American paper, had led to the return of many outstanding Russian securities, while Russian exports had also declined.[6]

Wagner's general position thus hinges on a rigid distinction between the depreciation of paper money in terms of specie on the one hand, taken as measured by the premium, and the depreciation in terms of goods and services on the other, as measured by the rise in prices. Indeed, the distinction is so rigid that the two

[1] Wagner, *op. cit.*, pp. 103–106.   [2] *Ibid.*, pp. 106 ff.   [3] *Ibid.*, pp. 109–111.
[4] *Ibid.*, p. 141. See also the table giving all these items, p. 122.
[5] *Ibid.*, pp. 163 ff.   Tables on pp. 159–162.
[6] *Ibid.*, p. 178.

sides of the position are never really brought together in complete form. Wagner bases the level of the premium itself primarily on the degree of general confidence in political and economic stability, and in the prospects for resumption. Starting from the initial fact of a (varying) premium, he makes an analysis of its effects on import and export prices. To this analysis exception can hardly be taken. It is a brilliant and original piece of work. But with respect to the origin of the movements of other classes of prices, his discussion is at the least less convincing. Some influence is granted to the quantity of paper money, just as some is granted to the premium itself, but no definite relationship is presented. Indeed, the agnostic view may be the only one justified by the facts, for Wagner was dealing with a country having a comparatively low degree of economic organization and coherence. It was therefore not unnatural that general changes should appear to work themselves out very slowly and incompletely. Even granting the agnostic view, however, we are left with a certain feeling of inadequacy. The place of domestic prices in the *general* system of the phenomena of depreciation is not clearly assigned.

One other matter may also be mentioned. Wagner adopts, at certain points, that anti-quantitative view which makes the exchanges (and therefore presumably the premium) dependent on the balance of payments, but at other points he makes the premium itself govern the exchanges and therefore the balance. It is possible to hold both views without inconsistency, according to varying conditions, but only after an exact analysis of the mechanisms and relationships involved. This analysis, despite many partial essays, Wagner never quite achieves, and his position is therefore not complete.

After the publication of Wagner's study, the non-quantitative view of foreign trade under depreciated paper rather dropped from sight. In the remaining years of the nineteenth century, as we have already seen, the dominant trend lay along the lines of thought derivable from the teachings of the English classical writers. With the opening of the present century, however, the non-quantitative explanation began to appear again. In the period since 1914, partly under the influence of nominalistic monetary theories and partly because of the desire to justify government action during and since the war, it has become characteristic of perhaps the larger part of German thought. In Austria, however, it has had less influence.

As far back as 1902 Spitzmüller, examining the recent monetary history of Austria-Hungary, concluded that the relation between the balance of international payments and the internal value of money was reciprocal. He found the explanation based on the quantity theory to be one-sided, for an inflationary increase in the paper currency is not the only event that can endanger the stability of the monetary circulation.[1] Spitzmüller concludes, after a rather thin historical and statistical investigation of a number of selected countries, that the balance of payments, and especially the balance of trade, may actually be the initial *cause* of protracted drains of specie. It may therefore be the ultimate source of a depreciation of the currency consequent on the issue of paper money — the issue being made, in the first instance, to replace the lost specie.[2] From these considerations, he is inevitably led to recommend various bank and government policies designed to maintain a "favorable" balance of payments.

In 1910 Lexis, discussing the general problem of paper money, adopted a somewhat different method of approach. He observed that the value of paper money has tended historically to have a certain stability of its own, an "independent" existence. He concluded that the maintenance of this stability is to be explained not by any quantitative limitation, but rather by the character of such money as legal tender, as a legal means of payment. While debtors profit by a fall in the value of money, creditors have an interest in keeping it up. In consequence, the prices of the totality of goods, services and revenues forms a system which is to some extent self-closing, and which tends to oppose the dislocation of

---

[1] A. Spitzmüller, *Die österreichisch-ungarische Wärungsreform* (Vienna and Leipzig, 1902), p. 101. See also F. Wieser, *Theorie der gesellschaftlichen Wirtschaft* (cited above), p. 434, for a clear suggestion that the foreign-exchange mechanism is far from self-equilibrating; and that, in the absence of intervention, it may bring about a corruption of the currency. See also his article, *Die Geldwert und seiner Veränderungen* (cited above), pp. 536–539.

[2] Spitzmüller, *op. cit.*, p. 70 (Russia); p. 82 (Roumania); p. 86 (Japan); etc.

individual prices from changes in the value of money.[1] This argument inevitably leads Lexis to the proposition that the internal value of a paper currency is wholly dissociated from its external value. The specie premium on such money is determined simply by the state of the balance of international payments, and its fluctuations therefore need produce no change whatsoever in *internal* prices. The premium simply settles at that point at which the total values of imports and exports (in the widest sense of these terms) are made equal. Finally, a depreciation of the exchanges does not give a true bounty to exportation from the paper country. It only allows the exporters to derive their usual profits from the business, despite the essentially unfavorable circumstances. A rise in world gold prices also results in no real gain, since the rise is offset by a corresponding fall in the premium.[2]

In a later work, however, Lexis adopted a much more refined position, which in effect contradicts these views. While again asserting the relative stability of the paper prices of those articles not directly affected by international trade, with respect to changes in the gold premium, he now finds that *because* of the relative stability of internal prices a rising premium stimulates exports, and checks imports. This phenomenon may make it possible for a paper country, even though it has no gold and no monopoly-product, to make payments in gold-standard countries, and perhaps to acquire gold itself. It is true that a decrease in the price of these exports in the foreign market is both a result of the rising premium and a necessary preliminary to increased export.

If, however, the export can be increased without sensibly affecting foreign prices, then the rising premium will also evoke a corresponding rise in the prices of the export commodities in the domestic markets. Under these favorable circumstances the premium would generally fall, without, however, a similar fall in the paper prices of the exports.[3]

---

[1] W. Lexis, article *Papiergeld* (*Handwörterbuch der Staatswissenschaften*, 3 ed., 1909–1911, vol. 6), pp. 987, 988. It is fair to add, however, that a limitation of sorts upon the quantity of paper money seems to be tacitly implied from the course of the argument, though such a limitation is not made an explicit condition of stability.

[2] *Ibid.*, pp. 988, 989.

[3] W. Lexis, *Allgemeine Volkswirtschaftslehre* (Berlin, 1910), p. 114. It is interesting to contrast the two positions here set forth with an intermediate position,

To this rather subtle analysis, it would be difficult to take exception. It may be pointed out, however, that Lexis still maintains here an ostensibly non-quantitative position. His results are in large part, it is true, those to which a pro-quantitative analysis would lead, but he himself does not tie his doctrines up with purely monetary conditions. He starts from the mere *fact* of depreciation, whatever its antecedent cause.

6. In the light of the two principal groups of theories already examined, the German and Austrian literature of trade under depreciated currencies published since 1914 presents little that is of especial difficulty, or of especial interest from the theoretical point of view. The non-quantitative, not to say agnostic teachings of the state theory of money have been applied to the problems of international exchange in a way that is only too obvious. Since the value of money is held to be not related to its quantity, the adherents of the theory assert that that quantity can have no particular bearing upon the level of the foreign exchanges — that is, upon the inter-currency quotation. The exchange rates, therefore, are determined simply by the balance of international payments.[1] There is nothing necessarily automatic about their maintenance, no "real" inter-currency parity.[2] In consequence there is ample room for state interference and control, designed to improve the position of the local currency in the world market.[3] This view, especially in Germany, gained a considerable influence during the war and post-war periods, and was probably responsible in no small degree for the apparently blind unwillingness of the government to recognize any connection between the quantity of paper money and its depreciation. The disastrous character of the results needs no comment.

A similar set of conclusions has also been advanced by a number

adopted by Lexis in an article that has already been discussed at another point: his essay on *The Agio on Gold and International Trade* (Economic Journal, 1895). See ch. vi, sect. 5, above.

[1] See for example G. F. Knapp, *Staatliche Theorie des Geldes* (3 ed., Munich, 1921), pp. 200–216.

[2] *Ibid.*, pp. 202 ff.

[3] *Ibid.*, pp. 236–252. See also J. Bonar, *Knapp's Theory of Money* (Economic Journal, 1922), pp. 40–42.

of writers who, while not basing their arguments directly on the state theory, have yet regarded the quantity of money as being at best a very secondary factor in the determination of its value. Thus Diehl declares that the chief cause of the depreciation of the German exchanges has been not the increase in the quantity of currency itself, but the position of the balance of trade and of payments.[1] Moreover, the chief cause of the rise in internal prices has lain on the commodity side, not on the monetary side.[2] With respect to both forms of depreciation, the quantity of money has had an effect so "secondary" as to be almost negligible. Hahn, too, refuses to recognize the fact of inflation. His general theory is that excess imports cause specie drains, and then, when the specie is exhausted, a drain of paper money. This drain results in a fall in the foreign value of money, and the fall is reflected, by a process not clearly indicated, in its internal value. In the particular case of Germany, however, he finds that the initial cause has been the unkind influence of malicious foreign speculation in German currency. This started the drain of German paper. The sequence of other results, including the adverse balance of trade, then followed.[3] In a word, it was not Germany's fault. Her own conduct was impeccably virtuous. She was imposed upon by the foreigner.

Taken as a whole, this post-war German and Austrian literature impresses one as a calamitous reversion to the stage of thought characteristic of England before the time of the Bullion Controversy. Most of the professedly "scientific" writers have started from a refusal to recognize any necessary relationship whatsoever between the quantity of money and its value, whether internal or external. They have then come out with proposals for exchange regulation and control, protective-compensating tariffs, and for state interference in general, of types that are almost archaic.[4] In Germany, a considerable part of the explanation

---

[1] K. Diehl, *Über Fragen des Geldwesens und der Valuta* (Jena, 1921), p. 48.

[2] *Ibid.*, pp. 59, 60.

[3] A. Hahn, *Statische und dynamische Weckselkurse* (*Archiv für Sozialwissenschaft*, 1922), pp. 761, 762, note 2. See also his earlier article, in the same Journal for 1921: *Handelsbilanz, Zahlungsbilanz, Valuta, Güterpreise.*

[4] A few voices were raised in protest and warning against the storm. An excellent review and criticism of the views just commented on is given by L. von Mises,

seems to have lain in a desire to justify the government's actions
at all costs, and if possible to transfer the blame to other countries. In Austria, as throughout Central Europe, the principal
motive has been a blind and fanatical nationalism, political and
economic and social, of the most distrustful and anti-solidaristic
type.

In these countries the purchasing-power-parity doctrine, whatever its defects, could have been of incalculable value in meeting
the practical problems of the day intelligently. Yet it is precisely
here that the doctrine has encountered the greatest indifference.
The hard-won experience of other nations and other generations
has been very largely ignored.

7. It remains to give some account of the general theory of international trade itself in Germany and Austria in the last sixty-
odd years, and of certain recent analyses of international price
structures. With respect to the theory of international trade, the
surface complexion of the literature closely resembles that of the
corresponding division of French thought. While the classical
theory of specie flows and price movements has found many adherents, and while Goschen's analyses of the foreign-exchange
mechanisms have been quite widely studied, the English theory
of international values itself has been entirely neglected by the
great majority of writers. Nor have those few who have paid attention to it been able to arouse any controversy, or any general
interest. Their propositions, like those of the corresponding
French economists, have remained undisputed not so much from
agreement as from indifference. International trade, from the
point of view of the general theory of value and prices, has not
been thought to present peculiarities which warrant its separation
from the theory of purely internal exchange.

Only three writers, Roscher, Mangoldt, and Földes, seem to
have dealt at all seriously with the classical English theory of in-

Zahlungsbilanz und Devisenkurse (Mitteilungen des Verbandes österreichen Banken
und Bankiers, 1919), pp. 39–46.

It is only fair to add that with the inception of the Dawes plan arrangements,
and of definite monetary stabilization, the German and Austrian literature has begun to take on a quite different complexion. What the new orientation will be, however, is not yet clear.

ternational values, and one of them with only a part of it. Roscher, recognizing the existence of serious obstacles to the international mobility of labor and capital, and perceiving that money costs of production can therefore remain permanently different as between countries, is led from these considerations to a rather obscure formulation of the law of comparative costs, and to various conclusions as to the possible extremely unequal division of the gain from foreign trade.[1] In this, he refers frequently to Ricardo and Mill. But Mill's apparatus, as distinct from Ricardo's, is not employed, and Mill's entire discussion of the equation of international demands is passed by. Nor does Roscher add any definite formula of his own to explain the determination of a particular ratio of exchange *within* the limits set by comparative costs.

Mangoldt, however, presents a much subtler elaboration of the classical doctrine. Were we concerned here with every aspect of the general theory of international trade itself, his analyses would require detailed study. Within any one market, he finds that any one article can have only a single price at a given time. General groups of such prices are established in proportion to the corresponding costs of production. Further, in closely adjacent markets prices and costs will not differ by more than the cost, per unit of product, of transplanting the given industry. But as between more distant markets, and especially in foreign trade, the cost of transplantation becomes prohibitive. It is therefore usually more advantageous to import the given article from the low-priced into the high-priced market. In this event costs of production cease to govern prices, except in so far as potential domestic production may set a maximum to the prices of the imports. The principle governing the exchange, therefore, is no longer absolute but comparative costs.[2]

Even if absolute costs of production be entirely the same, an exchange of the given article is still possible if only there be another article at hand which, in relation to the first, reveals different costs.[3]

[1] W. G. F. Roscher, *Grundlagen der Nationalökonomie* (17 ed., Stuttgart, 1883), sect. 126; *Nationalökonomik des Handels und Gewerbfleisses* (Stuttgart, 1881), sect. 38.

[2] J. C. E. von Mangoldt, *Grundriss der Volkswirtschaftslehre* (2 ed., by Kleinwächter, Stuttgart, 1871), pp. 97, 98. (First edition, 1863.)   [3] *Ibid.*, p. 98.

Under the operation of this principle of comparative costs, each country will gradually concentrate on the production of those articles in which it has a comparative advantage. This process, the redistribution of productive energies, will of course not be effected without difficulty.[1] But it will go on

until no more articles are left which can be exported with advantage; that is, until the exchange relationships of the totality of goods against one another is the same in both countries.[2]

This last proposition is suggestive, but somewhat incomplete.

The actual ratio of exchange, *within* the limits of comparative costs, will be determined by demand and supply. Further, the greater the increase in demand produced by a lowering of the price of the country's imports, the less will be its share of the advantage from the exchange. These two propositions Mangoldt then works out more or less simultaneously, with respect to conditions under which the quantity taken increases more, the same, or less than, in proportion to the decrease in price.[3] He also attempts to take account of varying conditions of supply, though with less closely defined results. The net conclusions he puts into a statement which reads much like Mill's equation of international demand, though it is less clearly formulated:

The exchange relationships, for those goods for which the relatively strongest demand exists in other countries, are determined according to the potentiality of the supply of different goods.[4]

An additional suggestion is then made, to explain the general structure of international exchange relationships:

Exchange values definitely tend so to regulate themselves that each article will be paid for in proportion to the relation of its value, in the country of origin, to those articles whose costliness is the same in the two countries.[5]

The costliness is to be measured in terms of an article which is produced in both of the countries. This useful standard of comparison was novel at the time.

He goes on to develop these propositions in somewhat greater detail, but without altering their general trend, and then turns to

[1] Mangoldt, *op. cit.*, pp. 203, 204.　　[2] *Ibid.*, p. 223.
[3] *Ibid.*, pp. 206–212. That is, under varying elasticities of demand.
[4] *Ibid.*, p. 209.　　　　　　　　[5] *Ibid.*, p. 212.

the conditions that determine the benefit from foreign trade. The problem at issue is not relevant here, but one general observation may be made. Throughout this latter part of his analysis — throughout the whole Appendix in which the theory of foreign trade is elaborated — Mangoldt speaks not of the Ricardian "amounts of labor," but of comparative *exchange values*. But in the text itself he used the term "costs of production" in the familiar Ricardian sense. Whether this very important inconsistency is due to a too unquestioning acceptance of the cost-of-production theory of value, or simply to "compartment-thinking," cannot be said. Its effect, at least, is undeniably to give a somewhat inconclusive surface complexion to the analysis.

The grasp and penetration of Mangoldt's work, which first appeared in 1863, deserves the highest praise. In it are found, obscurely expressed but none the less unmistakable, the specific application of a theory of varying elasticities of demand and supply to the determination of ratios of international exchange, and the elaboration of these considerations to provide a measure of the benefit from trade. The most recent writers of the English school itself have added nothing more in these directions. From the historical point of view, however, almost no importance can be attached to Mangoldt's doctrines. They seem to have remained entirely unnoticed in the later German and Austrian literature, and only in more recent years have been revived by a few foreign economists.[1]

The last important reflection of the English theory of international values, presented by Földes, appeared during the war.[2] Földes undertook no elaboration of the Ricardo-Mill theory, however, and a reference is sufficient. Like Mangoldt, he seems to

[1] See especially F. Y. Edgeworth, *The Theory of International Values* (Economic Journal, 1894), pp. 630–638.

[2] B. Földes, *Zur Theorie vom internationalen Handel* (*Jahrb. für Nationaloekonomie*, 1915), especially pp. 765–790.

Reference should also be made to two other works which, while having nothing to say of the classical theory, nevertheless afford interesting examples of the application of the mathematical method to the problem of international exchange. The books are: W. Launhardt, *Mathematische Begründung der Volkswirtschaftslehre* (Leipzig, 1885), especially pp. 157–164; and Auspitz and Lieben, *Untersuchungen über die Theorie des Preises* (Leipzig, 1889), especially pp. 408–429. The French transla-

have been wholly unsuccessful in arousing comment among other writers.

8. The remaining important aspect of the classical English theory of international trade, the theorem dealing with price movements, specie flows, and the world distribution of the precious metals, has met with a much wider and more favorable reception, as has the English theory of the foreign exchanges. The various treatments of these problems, however, do not in the main offer any important advances over the English models, and do not require detailed examination. Among the more important writers in the field have been Rau,[1] Roscher,[2] Mangoldt,[3] Fellmeth,[4] Hertzka,[5] and Heiligenstadt;[6] and, more recently, Petritsch,[7] Mises,[8] and Földes.[9] Only the last four writers, however, lay especial stress on the necessarily automatic character of the price-specie flow adjustment. In the others the mechanism itself is given, but the doctrine of a self-restoring equilibrium is usually ignored.

tion of the latter work (1914) has been mentioned elsewhere. The most interesting feature of Launhardt's discussion is an attempt to determine the possible ratios of exchange by the use of those equations which, in graphic form, are represented by elliptic curves (*op. cit.*, p. 157).

[1] K. H. Rau, *Grundsätze der Volkswirtschaftslehre* (6 ed., Leipzig, 1855), sects. 286–291, 418–423.

[2] W. G. F. Roscher, *Grundlagen* (cited above), sects. 125–126; *Nationalökonomik des Handels* (cited above), sects. 38, 59.

[3] Mangoldt, *op. cit.*, especially pp. 117–119.

[4] A. Fellmeth, *Zur Lehre von der internationale Zahlungsbilanz* (Heidelberg, 1877), *passim*.

[5] T. Hertzka, *Die Gesetze der Handels- und Sozialpolitik* (Leipzig, 1880), vol. 1, pp. 29–32, 44. A less clear exposition is given in an earlier book, *Währung und Handel* (Vienna, 1876), pp. 83–94. See also his *Das Wesen des Geldes* (Leipzig, 1887), pp. 44–46, 70–98; and his *Weckselkurs und Agio* (Vienna, 1894), pp. 6–12, 26–28.

[6] C. Heiligenstadt, *Beiträge zur Lehre von den auswärtigen Weckselkurse* (*Jahrb. für Nationaloekonomie*, 1892–1894); *Die internationalen Goldbewegungen* (*Jahrb. für Gesetzgebung*, 1894). In the second of these especially, an elaborate attempt is made at statistical investigation and partial verification.

[7] L. Petritsch, *Theorie von der sogenannten günstigen und ungünstigen Handelsbilanz* (Graz, 1902), especially pp. 118–131.

[8] L. von Mises, *Theorie des Geldes und der Umlaufsmittel* (Munich and Leipzig, 1912), pp. 203–207.

[9] B. Földes, *Zur Theorie vom internationalen Handel* (*Jahrb. für Nationaloekonomie*, 1915), especially pp. 793–801.

Petritsch, whose excellent book is a most illuminating study, even attempts to go beyond the Ricardo-Mill conception of the working of this equilibrium.

He finds that any analysis which makes commodity prices the sole intermediary between the balance of payments, the quantity of money, and the movements of commodities and gold is much too simple. A whole range of other factors also intervenes, such as discount rates, the exchanges, the cost of making payments, and so on. No one necessary relationship, therefore, can safely be affirmed. The exchange-market mechanism is the first thing to feel changes in the balance of payments, in the discount rates, or in the exchange rates. The corrective action set in motion by a relatively "favorable" or "unfavorable" balance of payments therefore proceeds, not directly through the commodity markets, but through arbitrage operations and the exchange market. It is these which exert the initial corrective, and which in the majority of cases are the principal agency, if not the only one, actually operating to maintain equilibrium.[1] For example, an alteration in discount rates consequent on the position of the balance of payments has but little influence upon the volume of commodity movements. In a similar way a change in the balance of trade, or in the quantity of money in circulation, does not necessarily produce a corresponding change in the balance of payments. Commodity prices are not the sole intermediary, and the disturbance may be absorbed in some other fashion.[2]

It might have been expected that the anti- and non-quantitative theorists in Germany and Austria would also select the price-specie flow analysis for critical attention, as the corresponding French writers have so forcefully done, but this question, on the contrary, they have rather neglected. Hildebrand entirely discards the classical mechanism, although he is left somewhat at a loss for an alternative explanation of the known phenomena.[3] Helfferich, in less unqualified terms, also rejects it on the ground

---

[1] Petritsch, *op. cit.*, pp. 124–126. See also pp. 94–96, 106, 107, 118–120.

[2] *Ibid.*, pp. 130, 131.

[3] R. Hildebrand, *Die Theorie des Geldes* (Jena, 1883), especially pp. 128–134; also pp. 115–127.

that an internal shortage of currency need not necessarily affect the balance of international payments. It can instead be met adequately by the issue of paper money, or by the creation of bank credit. But if these be insufficient, he concedes that there may be a "tendency" to satisfy the need by an international movement of the precious metals.[1] Finally, Knapp discards Ricardo's theory as being "amateurish," but he too is rather hard put to it to find a satisfactory substitute.[2]

Like many of the general treatises on money, as also on banking, these works are weak in their discussions of the international aspects of money, and rather tend to evade the problem of its world distribution. The existence of an automatic equilibrium tendency is denied, but the consequent necessity of relying upon the supposed action of artificial "policies" of various sorts, to explain the apparent course of events, fails to provide an independent and self-supporting position.

A more detailed and cogent criticism has been brought against the classical theory here, however, by Wieser. In addition to his denial, already noted, of a necessary equilibrium-tendency in the exchange markets, he strenuously combats the classical doctrine of the world equalization of the value of money. The principal points in his argument are these.[3] First, the proportion of goods entering international trade is small, and the obstacles to the free movement of even this portion are great. Second, international bill-speculation and differences in discount rates produce international movements of money quite as surely as do the prices and movements of commodities. Third, the importance of the "invisible items" is so great in modern commerce that goods no longer exchange against goods. A theory based on the barter assumption is therefore unreal. Fourth, the classical doctrine very much over-simplifies the problem by failing to perceive that trade is conducted between individuals, not between countries. Finally, as a corollary, Wieser declares that in consequence this doctrine is unable to explain *how* the balance of payments, which

---

[1] K. Helfferich, *Das Geld* (2 ed., Leipzig, 1910), pp. 507–509.

[2] Knapp, *Staatliche Theorie des Geldes* (2 ed., 1918), p. 245.

[3] F. Wieser, *Theorie der gesellschaftlichen Wirtschaft* (cited above), pp. 433–437.

is simply an aggregation of disconnected individual payments, is in point of fact equalized.[1]

From this diversified set of propositions, Wieser concludes that neither commodity prices nor the value of money can be regarded as "equal" between countries. The movements of money do not appear in response to changes in commodity prices alone. The value of money therefore cannot be regarded as being simply the reciprocal of those commodity values which are asserted to be uniform throughout the various markets. At the same time, the obstacles to the movements of commodities themselves usually prevent an actual equalization of such values in different countries.

Of these interesting suggestions, it can only be said here that they are not proven. Wieser also fails to offer a complete and self-maintaining theory to replace the one which he seeks to destroy.[2]

9. The last division of the German and Austrian thought which it is proposed to examine consists of some three or four rather isolated fragments that deal with national and international price structures, and with the problem of permanent differences in costs of production and prices. The writers in this group are Schüller, Lexis, Wieser, and on some points Mises. Except Mises, who is here a critic, each appears to have worked in complete independence of the results obtained by the others.

Schüller's concern, in the parts of his book relevant here, is with costs of production. He first asserts that such costs are permanently different as between one enterprise and another in any given industry, not only between countries but also within any one country, and in industry and commerce as well as in agriculture.[3] These cost-differences are due to differences in: (1) nat-

---

[1] Wieser's own explanation consists simply in the assertion that since the international balance is merely the sum of the individual balances, it must inevitably tend to equilibrium. That is, equality proceeds simply from the tendency of demand and supply to equalization. The doctrine is further supplemented by the not altogether consistent proposition that international capitals tend always to seek the best market, and by their movement facilitate the restoration of equilibrium (Wieser, op. cit., pp. 437–439).

[2] For a fuller discussion of Wieser's doctrines with respect to the historically-derived differences in national price structures, and the differences in prices that proceed from this source, see sect. 10, below.

[3] R. Schüller, Schutzzoll und Freihandel (Vienna and Leipzig, 1903), pp. 9, 10.

ural conditions; (2) the effectiveness of labor, in its widest sense, — the skill of the workers, the capacity of the managers, the standard of living, the price of the necessaries of life, and so on; (3) the facilities for obtaining capital and credit, with respect both to their price and to the amount available.[1] These three conditions, operating together, result in differences which are enduring.

But, granted the fact of such differences, why do the low-cost plants not drive the high-cost plants out of business, as the competitive assumption apparently requires? Schüller's answer is subtle, and interesting in the extreme. Essentially, it is simply that an increase in production does not necessarily result in a gain *to the plant undertaking the increase.* Increased output means increased costs of transportation, both for the raw materials, which must often be purchased at more distant sources, and for the finished product, which must be sold in new and less accessible markets.[2] Expansion beyond a certain point also usually necessitates using dearer or less skilled labor, and eventually bringing it from farther away. Aggregate labor costs then rise.[3] Finally, it entails either a less adequate equipment of capital and credit, or else the payment of a higher price for their possession.[4] All three of these forces work in such fashion that as output increases, and as the point of maximum utilization is approached, the influences tending to raise costs of production begin to offset those tending to decrease them, and soon outweigh the latter group. From that point onward, the advantage of the low-cost plant over the high steadily diminishes. Moreover, expansion also means lower prices. But the low-cost plants often prefer to keep prices high, by restricting output. They thus secure a higher rate of profit per unit, and undergo less risk.[5] In this way the apparent motive to an increase in production may be entirely removed. The situation, which Schüller finds more typical than abnormal, is evidently one of quasi-monopoly. Cost differences of the sort in question are also often perpetuated by the difficulty, especially

---

[1] Schüller, *op. cit.*, pp. 10–12.   [2] *Ibid.*, p. 16.
[3] *Ibid.*, pp. 16, 17.   [4] *Ibid.*, p. 17.
[5] *Ibid.*, pp. 19, 20.

where the plant makes a number of articles, of actually ascertaining the cost of any one type of commodity.[1]

He then examines in more detail the actual effects of the expansion of an industry. Such an expansion may result in driving out the high-cost plants, but usually, he says, it will not.[2] Under certain conditions, and within certain limits, increased production will also cause costs to fall. As a rule, however, they will rise. They will rise not only for the high-cost plants, but also for the low. But in the latter the rise will usually be slower, and the spread between maximum and minimum costs in the industry will therefore increase.[3] An interesting corollary to this last proposition is also presented. As between industries, those in which the spread between the maximum and minimum costs is least will show the least increase in costs as production grows. The spread is usually greatest in the extractive industries, and in them the rise in costs, with rising output, is therefore usually sharpest.[4] But Schüller finally concludes that over periods of time increased output usually *lowers* costs, because of the indirect effects of general increases in the scale of production, from technical advances, and so on.[5]

The relation of market prices to these varying levels of costs, in Schüller's exposition, is somewhat less definite. The lowest costs set the minimum below which prices cannot fall, but it does not follow that at any one time the highest costs (of the "necessary" supply) set the maximum. They may be above, or they may be below, though in either case a process of corrective adjustment is then set into rather cumbrous motion. The net result is a somewhat uncertain border zone, relative to the various levels of actual costs, within which prices fluctuate.[6] It does not appear, however, that Schüller has in mind that possible reflection of cost differences in prices, of which Wieser (see below) later made so

---

[1] Schüller, *op. cit.*, pp. 20, 21.
[2] *Ibid.*, pp. 25–30.
[3] *Ibid.*, pp. 30, 31.
[4] *Ibid.*, pp. 48–58; especially p. 56.
[5] *Ibid.*, pp. 31 ff.
[6] *Ibid.*, pp. 39–42. Schüller acknowledges a debt to Menger here.

much. His doctrine is the more familiar theory of price *equalization*, as between different markets.

Lexis, a few years later, presented somewhat different views, and indeed had in mind a somewhat different problem. He takes issue with the Ricardian theorem that prices will be determined at the limits of the highest costs of production, and that that portion of the total output which is produced under the most favorable conditions cannot be increased at will without a relative loss. He finds that this view does not coincide with reality, and says instead:

Enterprises operating under objectively unfavorable circumstances supply as a rule only a small part of the total production. When prices rise from increasing demand, production will be enlarged chiefly in its more favorably-conditioned levels, not by the addition of inferior enterprises. Under modern economic conditions, those branches of production are few and unimportant whereof the output cannot be increased in all its levels in proportion to the greater outlay of capital and labor, and especially in the higher levels.[1]

("Levels," it may be added, of course refers to levels of advantage in production.) Lexis admits, it is true, that there is a point at which diminishing returns will set in for agricultural products, but he finds that technical advances in point of fact keep on deferring this point indefinitely whenever it is approached on an important scale.[2] He does not, however, seem to recognize that problem which Schüller had made it a special point to solve. This is the question why, granted the fact of such cost differences and granted the possibility of increased output from the better-situated plants, these last do not drive the high-cost plants out of business.

With respect to the way in which such changes actually work, he finds that an initial rise in prices may be arrested and removed by an increase in supply. More usually, however, both prices and production increase, until a point is reached at which production is oppressively in excess. At this point both prices and production tend to fall again.[3] Except on the assumption that costs remain comparatively stable, however, the doctrine is open to the objec-

[1] W. Lexis, *Allgemeine Volkswirtschaftslehre* (Berlin, 1910), p. 83.
[2] *Ibid.*, pp. 83, 84.
[3] *Ibid.*, p. 84.

tion that no very definite stopping-point in the process of change is indicated. Lexis seems to adopt an agnostic view.

Finally, Lexis has something to say on the question of price structures and their changes. He finds that for articles of which the production is large, inter-plant differences in the conditions of production and transportation do *not* exert an influence upon the determination of prices. These prices are governed, on the one hand, simply by the total supply, and on the other by the total demand — that is, by the portion of the total national income available for the purchase of each article (or, in the case of producers' goods, by the portion of the total capital). The part played in prices by the charges of commerce varies in different industries, and is especially large for agricultural products, but these charges exert a relative rather than an absolute influence. With respect to agricultural products, for example, the *relative* scale of prices as between countries is determined by the costs of transportation, of distribution, and so on, but the *absolute* level is governed by the harvests. In this sense, therefore,

there is a constant tendency to an equalization of prices in the different markets, so that even with a general rise of prices their previous relationships, as determined by the world-economy relationships of the markets, are maintained within limits that at most are narrow.[1]

10. Almost the exact converse of this qualified doctrine of world price equalization was advanced at about the same time by Wieser. His views were first presented in partial form in 1910,[2] but were much elaborated in his treatise of 1914, and it is to this last that I shall refer here.[3] Wieser's general thesis is that the prices of a given article in different markets, both in and between countries, do not tend to equality, but fall into a graduated scale whose differences are maintained permanently. Some of the causes to which he ascribes these differences, such as costs of transportation, tariffs, and local legal regulations, are of an ob-

[1] Lexis, *op. cit.*, p. 85. See also pp. 86–88. These considerations, however, are not applied to non-agricultural classes of goods.

[2] F. Wieser, *Der Geldwert und seiner Veränderungen* (*Schriften des Vereins für Sozialpolitik*, vol. 132, Leipzig, 1910). See especially pp. 530–532.

[3] Wieser, *Theorie der gesellschaftlichen Wirtschaft* (cited above), especially pp. 429–433.

vious character, and would be granted by all writers. Others of them, however, would perhaps not be. There are two principal divisions in the argument, one seeking to show how and why such price differences appear, the other to show why they are not removed — why the classical doctrine of equalization-tendencies is wrong.

Apart from those just mentioned, the causes of price differences between countries are asserted to be twofold. The primary cause lies in the fact that the historical development or evolution of each national economy has in considerable measure taken place independently of the evolution of other economies. Its economic habits, its methods of production, its standards of living, its social structures, and all the other factors that go to make up the development of its total economic organization, are therefore unlike those of other nations.[1] As an inevitable consequence, its wage, cost, and price structures and levels are largely different. It is therefore beside the point to speak of an "equality" of prices as between nations, or conversely of an equality of the value of money. Such an equality simply does not and cannot exist. What we actually find is not an equalization of prices as between nations, but a more or less irregularly graduated *scale*, the differentials in which tend to endure.[2] The same phenomenon appears, though in less marked degree, within any one country.[3] The second cause lies in the fact that the national markets, taken as a whole, are not sub-markets within the world market. World markets exist for only a small fraction of the total number of products. There is no *general* world market for the majority of products, and hence there can be no tendency to price-equality in the world economy as a whole.[4]

The reasons for the endurance of these price differences lie first in the fact that, as just indicated, the proportion of goods which actually ente rinternational trade is extremely small; and second, in the fact that even for those articles which do enter, obstacles of a "socio-historical" character impede free movement.[5] The one fact leads to inter-local or international differences in the

---

[1] Wieser, *op. cit.*, pp. 426–429.   [3] *Ibid.*, pp. 429 ff.   [5] *Ibid.*, p. 433.
[2] *Ibid.*, pp. 431, 432.   [4] *Ibid.*, pp. 430, 433.

prices of particular articles, the other, to differences in the general value of money. Such differences, it is true, are reduced by decreases in the cost of transportation, but they are not thereby removed. Migratory movements of the population, far from producing equalization, simply raise the general level of prices.[1]

From this Wieser goes on to an attack upon the classical English theory of price-equalization.[2] The attack is based, apart from those objections to the mechanistic explanations of the theory which we have examined elsewhere, on its failure to take account of precisely the socio-historical considerations just set forth. He does not, however, add anything more to his general theory of price differences.

To some extent at least, Wieser is here engaged in combat with a windmill. The classical English writers have never maintained a doctrine of the equalization of *all* prices, nor of the equalization of the value of money with respect to all commodities. In so far as Wieser's propositions are relevant, they turn at bottom on two points. The first is the assertion that national peculiarities lead to different conditions of production, to different levels of costs, and therefore to different prices. The second is the assertion that the obstacles to free international economic movement — of goods and of capital, of money and of populations — are of such character that the tendency to price equalization cannot in point of fact be effective. Permanent differences can and must exist. With respect to the second point, however, Wieser does not seem to me to have advanced any propositions not already fully recognized and taken account of by the classical theorists. When the socio-historical and developmental wrappings are stripped from his argument, the concrete mechanisms remaining are not substantially different from the "obstacles to mobility" of classical theory. With respect to the first point, it may at once be granted that the conditions and costs of production, especially the levels of wages, are conspicuously different both in and between countries. But that these differences are reflected in permanent differences in prices is quite another proposition. There is nothing in Wieser's argument — again with the socio-historical wrappings

<hr>

[1] Wieser, *op. cit.*, p. 432.   [2] See especially, in *ibid.*, pp. 433, 434.

removed — which seems to justify the assertion. As Professor Mises has clearly pointed out, these conditions will affect the general price level of the given article, but there is no evidence in Wieser's discussion to show that inter-local price *differences* will emerge.[1] How far the quite different type of argument advanced by Schüller would justify the position, is a problem that will be examined in a later chapter.

Apart from the question of proof, however, it is evident that Wieser's doctrines are diametrically opposed to those of the other writers in this group. All of them recognize permanent differences in costs, but whereas Schüller, Lexis, and Mises adopt the more familiar theory of a substantial inter-local *price* equalization, Wieser maintains that the cost-differentials must inevitably be reflected in the comparative structures and levels of prices themselves.

11. Our survey of the recent German and Austrian literature dealing with the various component parts of the theory of international prices is now complete. In so far as it constitutes a coherent group of doctrines, this literature occupies a position midway between the corresponding body of French and Italian writings. It is far more original than the one, and partakes far more of the character of an independent body of thought, of purely indigenous origin. The foreign influence, especially in more recent years, has been notably weak. But it has been much less rich than the other in its contributions to the theory which is of interest here. Its most illuminating suggestions, lying principally in the fields of trade under depreciated currencies and of the theory of general cost and price structures, have in the main fallen outside of the central current of contemporary speculation, and have been correspondingly unsuccessful in provoking subsequent controversy or fruitful amplification. The explanation of this neglect is probably to be found largely in the character of the dominant trend in German monetary theory during the last half century. Concerned primarily with what we have called the "metaphysics" of money, in one form or another, it has inevi-

---

[1] L. von Mises, *Theorie des Geldes und der Umlaufsmittel* (cited above), pp. 193–195.

tably slighted and rather scorned the merely mechanistic aspects of monetary phenomena.

Finally, an observation with which we began this chapter may well be repeated here. Despite the elaboration, often extremely suggestive and valuable, of many of its principal constituents, a complete theory of international prices has never been evolved from that plentiful store of materials which the combined German and Austrian investigations contain.

PART III

A RESTATEMENT OF THE THEORY OF INTERNATIONAL PRICES

CHAPTER XIV

THE CLASSICAL ENGLISH THEORY: RECAPITULATION
AND FURTHER CRITICISM

1. In the preceding chapters we have traced the growth of the elements which contributed to the English classical theory of international trade, the formulation and elaboration of the theory itself in England, and finally its varying fortunes in other countries. On the Continent especially, we have seen it subjected to criticism at almost every point, and often flatly ignored as a gratuitous and barren complication in the general body of economic theory. What can be said of this fundamental antithesis between the English and the Continental positions? Is the numerical majority that favors the characteristic Continental view right, or does the truth lie with the classical minority? Or is there a tenable intermediary position? It will clarify the problem to begin by reviewing the principal tenets of the classical doctrine, and the principal lines of criticism which have been brought against it. One or two further objections to particular parts of the doctrine will also be suggested. With these elements in mind, more positive conclusions can then be reached, and a definitive formulation can be presented.

If we disregard the question of the tariff, and center attention on those problems of mechanism which make up the larger part of the theory of international prices, the classical theory of international trade presents only some four or five cardinal points. They are as follows. The first is the distinction between internal trade and international trade itself, which is based primarily on the asserted relative immobility of labor and capital as between countries. In consequence of the distinction, it is assumed that a theory of international values different from that for domestic trade is necessary. The second is the formulation of this theory in terms of the principle of comparative (labor) costs and of Mill's "equation of international demand." The third is the so-called price-specie flow analysis. From this analysis are derived, logically at least, the familiar doctrine concerning the world distribution of the precious metals, the classical theorem of equilibrium in international trade, the justification for the so-called "barter assumption," and the characteristic classical practice of regarding money as a colorless intermediary, itself virtually incapable of influencing the determination of international values. Finally, there is the classical explanation of international trade under disturbed monetary conditions. The explanation is based on the quantity theory of money, and proceeds from the value of money itself to the balance of payments and the movements of commodity trade.

These are the elements. It can fairly be said, however, that the classical writers never worked them into a complete theory of international *prices*, as such. Their chief interest lay in the problem of national gains or losses from foreign trade, and from the manner in which it is conducted. They dealt with international values as subsidiary to this more central theme, and therefore treated such values primarily from the point of view of national productive power, — days of labor, — not from that of money prices and price structures. Indeed, the whole classical theory of value itself tended to discourage the latter method of approach. The constant effort was to go behind the phenomena of money prices, and to explain the facts in other terms.

Nor is it altogether easy to say just what the strictly classical theory of international prices would have been. The position is not complete. It is true that certain elements had been worked out. These were an (intra-national) theory of money and prices, a theory of ratios of international exchange, and an at least partial doctrine of equilibrium. But with respect to the determination and maintenance of international money prices themselves surprisingly little was said, and that little was of a rather contradictory character. The Ricardian "equilibrium" in trade, for example, was in the first instance an equilibrium of mechanisms. It was based on the evident fact of equality in the balance of payments. Pursued somewhat farther, it seems to rest also on the assertion of a tendency to equality in the world value of money;

and it is in this sense that the classical theorem has been most commonly interpreted by other writers, both adherents and critics. But the conclusions of an earlier chapter show that what Ricardo had in mind was chiefly an equality in the value of specie *as measured in terms of the various currency units*, not in terms of goods. He explicitly denied that there is any necessary equalization in commodity prices, and of course did not make such an equalization a condition of his general conception of equilibrium.[1] Yet this leaves the place and character of international prices themselves rather indefinite.

A similar hiatus exists in Mill, and indeed Mill does not seem to have perceived the real nature of the problem at all. In Goschen the "equilibrium" described is one of the foreign exchanges and the balance of payments alone, not of prices. In later writers the whole question is rather glossed over.

It is true that the germs of a possible alternative answer to the problem are found in the doctrine developed by Senior, and recently repeated in much more refined form by Professor Taussig. If the relative efficiency or effectiveness of labor can be used as a working measurement, then it is evident that we have an adequate criterion for determining the relative scales of money incomes and prices as between countries. But this doctrine was never integrally tied up with the classical conceptions of equilibrium and of mechanisms. The interrelations of the two bodies of theory have not been completely worked out, and indeed the logical dependence of Senior's proposition upon a prior theorem of equality or inequality in *money prices* has usually escaped attention. Even from this point of view, therefore, the classical teaching does not itself offer a satisfactory theory of international prices.

2. Of these cardinal features in the general classical theory of international trade, there is not one that has escaped searching criticism, and not one but what has been rejected by at least a few writers of repute. The criticisms have of course come chiefly from the Continental economists, the majority of whom, indeed, have never recognized the claims of the English doctrine at all. Some

[1] See ch. iii, sects. 5 and 7, above.

of them, however, have come from English sources as well. I do not propose to repeat at this point the detail of each writer's argument, but the principal lines of attack may be brought together.

(1) To the distinction between international trade and internal trade, it has been objected that the differences are wholly quantitative, not qualitative; that they are not of kind, but only of degree. An example of such differences is provided by the greater costs of international transportation, and by tariffs. Tariffs and transportation costs are held to be simply legal obstacles, which do not alter the fundamental character of the trade itself. As to the immobility of labor and capital, it is pointed out that this immobility can be ascribed quite as correctly to internal as to international trade. The immobility is simply somewhat greater, as a rule, in the latter case. None of these essentially quantitative differences are admitted as a sufficient ground for a separate theory of international trade and values. If any distinction is to be made at all, it should be a distinction between different markets, whether in the same or in different countries.

This position is as far as the economists who choose to ignore the classical theory itself usually go. It is characteristic of most French and German thought.

(2) The classical practice of stating the problem in terms of quantities of labor, instead of in terms of ratios of exchange as between commodities, has been rejected by almost all of the writers of the mathematical school. They have not so much sought to criticize it, however, as simply to adopt the alternative method of approach. They find in the latter a more accurate device, better suited to their style of treatment. Pareto's doctrine, however, can be regarded as an attempted reconciliation of the two, while Nicholson has explicitly tried to base his interpretation on the use of both of them. Shadwell, on the other hand, asserts that the whole classical position rests on a confusion of "value" with "cost." The latter term is inapplicable in comparisons between partially closed markets.

(3) The classical statement of the principle of comparative costs itself has been attacked on a number of grounds. Pareto and his followers have asserted that it can be expressed accurately only

by the use of the mathematical apparatus. They have also shown that under certain conditions the operation of the principle (with its concomitant, an international division of labor) may lead not to a greater but to a *lesser* total product. In this conclusion Graham has concurred. Other Continental writers, overlooking the possible increase in the total product and the lack of equivalence in the value of a day's labor in different countries, have declared it absurd that a nation should be supposed to import those articles which it can itself produce with a smaller absolute quantity of labor. Still others, while not adopting quite so crude a position, have proceeded directly from comparative labor costs to comparative prices, and have pointed out the obvious error of holding that a nation will import an article of higher price than the domestic product. These last two groups of objections, however, are based on a misunderstanding of what the classical theorists were trying to express.

(4) Mill's equation of international demands has encountered two principal criticisms. In the first place, since the days of Thornton a series of men have pointed out the fact that the formula does not necessarily determine a definite ratio of exchange. Under certain conditions, an infinite number of ratios may satisfy the equation. They have also called attention to the unsatisfactory character of Mill's attempt to escape the difficulty. Indeed, Shadwell and Nogaro have maintained that the "equation," far from being an explanation of the problem, is only a restatement, and tells us nothing new. In the second place a few writers, of whom Musgrave and Nogaro furnish examples, have held that in modern money economies the pairing of a particular export transaction with a particular import is impossible in theory, and absurd in practice. In consequence, the conception of an "equation" of demands for such exports and imports is simply meaningless. International commodities are not directly exchanged against other similar commodities, but against money. The process of international exchange itself is therefore a series of unrelated and unilateral transactions, in which the only "equation" is that resulting from the equality of the totals of international payments.

Moreover, even if money is ruled out in order to generalize the analysis, a further difficulty is introduced by the existence of the so-called "invisible items," which are of growing importance. They make it literally impossible to offset commodity transactions against one another, and in the case of capital movements make impossible any complete offset of even the most broadly conceived exchanges of national products or services, except over considerable periods. To speak of an "equation," in Mill's sense, is then to assume a state of affairs that does not necessarily exist. Under these conditions, commodities are at best exchanged for other commodities which are to be received in the *future*, not in the present.

(5) The classical price-specie flow mechanism has offered an especially tempting target to opponents of the quantity theory of all complexions. Some, like Laughlin, have denied the necessary influence of specie flows upon prices, and especially that they produce uniform and regular changes. On this adequate ground they have rejected the whole mechanism. Others, like Nogaro, have further asserted that even should a change in general prices appear in one country, and affect the balance of its international payments, still there is no reason for holding that specie will necessarily flow to meet the deficit. The movement of other articles may, and usually does, restore equilibrium in the exchange markets without the assistance of specie flows. Even if specie should move it need not, in the anti-quantitative view, exert a corrective influence upon the relative levels of prices as *between* the given countries. Still other writers, especially in Germany, have declared that the world distribution of the precious metals themselves is governed by no sort of automatic and self-adjusting mechanism whatever. It is regarded as being the consequence of deliberate action taken by governments and central banks, in the form of discount rate policies, premium policies and so forth. A corollary of this view is the doctrine that an unfavorable balance of payments may drain out all the country's specie, and deteriorate its currency. Foreign-exchange policies are therefore not only desirable, but necessary to the national monetary stability. Finally, the whole classical treatment of money as an essentially

colorless and comparatively frictionless translating agency — a treatment dependent for success on the validity of the specie flow mechanism itself — has been questioned and condemned by such men as Musgrave and Nogaro.

(6) The classical explanation of the course of foreign trade under fluctuating monetary conditions has also been an obvious mark for anti-quantitative polemics. Especially in Germany and France, many writers have concluded that the original source of the disturbance usually lies in an initial unfavorable position of the balance of payments. They then proceed from this to the depreciation of the exchanges, the drain of specie, and eventually to the depreciation of the internal currency itself. The classical doctrine, of course, regards the balance of payments, specie drains, and the exchanges as being substantially self-corrective as long as the internal value of the currency is maintained. Only when the currency is allowed to go to a premium in terms of specie will the other elements be seriously affected; and even then its depreciation is treated as the dominating and controlling factor.

(7) Finally, the doctrine of international price equalization, which is so often erroneously attributed to the classical writers, has recently been subjected to a new examination by Schüller and by Wieser. Wieser rejects the doctrine entirely, but, unlike the other opponents of the classical teaching here, he does not confine himself to the operation of the exchange mechanisms involved. He goes back of these to the general character of the national price and cost structures themselves, and finds in the differences in the conditions of their historical development a sufficient ground for denying the thesis of equalization. But this and one or two other isolated studies are the only attempts that have been made by the anti-classical economists, except the writers of the mathematical school, to fill in the gap in the classical theory. This gap is the lack of a complete theory of international prices themselves, and of the relationships between national price structures.

3. These are the principal types of criticisms which have been brought against the general classical position. Some of the criticisms will be reaffirmed and elaborated in later chapters, and at certain points an attempt will be made to develop alternative solutions to the problems which the English theory sought to answer. It also seems to me, however, that this theory is open to two further objections of a positive character. One involves the distinction between internal trade and international trade, and its significance; the other, the value of the principle of comparative costs. It will suffice to outline these objections rather briefly.

The classical distinction between international and internal trade was based on the asserted relative immobility of labor and capital — especially labor — as between countries. From the fact of this immobility, it was inferred that the relation of quantities of labor to quantities of product is different in different countries; that comparable cost-of-production bases for the determination of value cannot be established between one country and another; and that, in consequence, a separate theory of international values themselves is required.

With the problem of value in general, as distinct from that of prices, we have not attempted to deal in these pages. Two *ex cathedra* suggestions, however, may be made. In the first place, it seems to me that the asserted differences between international trade and internal trade are quantitative rather than qualitative, when they are based on the fact of immobility. These differences appear quite as genuinely, though perhaps to a less degree, between different districts in the same country. In the second place, the immobility of labor and capital as between countries has comparatively little influence upon the determination of the *money prices* of the articles exchanged, in any one country. These prices have an at least general tendency either to international equality, or to a fairly definite scale of differentials, as will be shown later. Since the levels or scales are primarily determined by world conditions, except in the case of partly monopolized articles, the influence of conditions in any one country is therefore usually small.[1] Quite as probably, the fact of immobility takes effect solely in producing differences between countries in the rates of

---

[1] Except where, despite adequate competition between individual producers, the fact that it is the chief source of supply or the chief market for the article concerned gives a country a monopoly.

return to the labor involved, for each given grade of effectiveness or skill. That is, instead of its being true that costs control prices, *prices* very largely control *costs*, so far as concerns the internationally traded group of commodities. The fraction that the country's supply and demand make of the world total is usually small. To take over Professor Marshall's familiar metaphor, the demand blade of the shears is very long, but each country's supply blade is comparatively short. This is, however, an essentially long-time doctrine. In the immediate sense, costs probably govern prices.

The essential differences between international trade and internal, with respect to the process of price determination, are rather these. First, the greater costs of transportation in international trade, which is a purely quantitative difference; second, the presence of tariffs and other legal obstacles; and third, the fact that currencies are dissimilar, and that a foreign exchange mechanism is therefore necessary. The principal objective distinctions between the establishment of internal and of international prices can be explained very largely in terms of these three elements alone.

The other criticism concerns the principle of comparative costs. This principle has been one of the most firmly established theorems in the classical teaching, and at first glance seems one of the least assailable. Yet if we examine its meaning more closely, it seems to me that certain doubts must arise. What are we to understand by a "comparative" advantage in trade, and how are we to pass from a comparative advantage of this sort to that absolute advantage *in terms of prices* which is the indispensable requisite of nearly all commerce?

The classical theory was stated in terms of days of labor. If country A produces certain quantities of two articles, with 10 and 15 days' labor respectively, and if country B produces similar quantities of the same articles with 12 and 20 days' labor respectively, A is said to have an absolute advantage in both branches of production. But A's absolute advantage is less with respect to the first article — as is B's absolute disadvantage. B therefore has a *comparative advantage* in the production of the first article.

It will pay her to produce the first article alone, and to import the second; while it will pay A to produce the second alone, and to import the first. Gain to both countries will ensue from such an exchange. Trade therefore takes place.

Every proposition in this series may be granted except the last.[1] How can we possibly pass from quantities of labor in one country to quantities of labor in the other? And how proceed to those relative *prices* which actually determine the initiation of trade? As the statements just given stand, there is no visible reason why trade *should* take place, for no way of bridging the gap is indicated. Two things are needed. One is a link between the quantities of labor and the ratios of exchange (or market prices) in each country. The other is a link between ratios of exchange in the one country, and those in the other. The second link is provided by such articles as are actually common to both countries. The first the classical theorists found in their labor theory of value, when this is combined with the postulate of the international immobility of labor. Since the relation between quantities of labor and ratios of exchange is not necessarily the same in different countries, they regarded it as permissible to suppose that a comparative advantage in terms of labor (although perhaps an absolute disadvantage) may be reflected as an absolute advantage in terms of market prices.

But this result does not necessarily follow, at least in money economies. Let us reduce the situation to terms of the accompanying table, with reference to countries A and B and to commodities M and N. Suppose that (granting for convenience a labor theory of value) the relation of days of labor to the price of

	Days of labor	
	M	N
Country A	10	15
Country B	12	20

a given quantity of the product M is, in country B, as 12 is to 1. Assume that the price of the product is $1.00. If this same price-labor relation prevails in country A, the price of M there will be B's price times 10/12, or $0.83 1/3. In that event, instead of

---

[1] Pareto and Graham have also questioned the last statement but one, holding that a net gain does not necessarily result. See ch. iv, sect. 9, and ch. x, sect. 2, above.

its being true that A will import M and B export it, just the converse will be true. Country A will then have an absolute price advantage in *both* commodities. Country B can export M only if the price-labor ratio in B is *enough lower* than that in A to make B's price for M below A's price. Furthermore, it is evident that if country B's price-labor ratio continues to fall relative to the ratio in country A, a point may be reached at which B can export not only M but also N.

It is not a sufficient answer to this proposition to say that specie flows will take place, and will alter prices in such manner that the comparative advantages in terms of labor become absolute advantages in terms of money prices. That might be true where trade is composed of two articles alone, but where many enter, there is no *a priori* reason for holding that the *aggregate* balance of payments will be altered to the necessary extent. For some articles specie flows may convert the comparative labor advantage into an absolute price advantage, but for others just the opposite situation will quite certainly appear.

We need not pursue this argument further, for the demonstration just given has sufficiently emphasized the point which it is desired to bring out. That point is simply that comparative costs do not, *in themselves alone*, provide a sufficient *a priori* explanation of the course and terms of trade. Nor do they show why the trade itself should take place. However great the comparative advantage in terms of labor, market prices, whether expressed in terms of money or of some other commodity, may well be such that the exchange indicated on the basis of comparative labor costs is actually impossible. In other words the principle of comparative costs, if it is taken by itself, is indefinite and indeterminate. It becomes significant only through the essential mediation of market prices, of actual ratios of exchange. When it is made logically antecedent to market prices, the principle explains nothing. There is no way of passing from labor costs in one country to those in another *except* through relative prices. It is these last which are of primary importance, in the first instance. It is they which give rise to trade, and which govern its terms. The substitution of "units of productive power" for "quantities of labor" also fails to provide an escape, for the same objections hold good.

After trade has been set up we can "read back," and determine what the comparative labor costs in the selected case actually are, but if we are given only these costs, we can tell absolutely nothing about the course and terms of the ensuing trade.

If we know all the other statistical facts in the history of a given set of exchanges, we can also use comparative costs to tell us something of the size of the relative gains (in a general sense) of the countries concerned, and something of their relative effectiveness in production. But the principle seems to have no other independent value. When the attempt is made to treat it as the *a priori* determinant of ratios of inter-commodity exchange between countries, it becomes wholly indefinite.[1]

4. Such are, in general form, the principal propositions in the English theory that bear upon the problem of international prices, and such are the principal lines of criticism. Criticism and original theory are at most points fundamentally opposed. Not even the most ingenious eclecticism can altogether reconcile them. In the following chapters, therefore, we shall try to break the ground afresh, and to discover what results a somewhat different method of attack will yield. Although many of the necessary elements are already in existence, some of them require modification in the light of past criticism, and certain gaps must be filled. Nor have the elements ever been completely combined to provide a solution of the questions which a theory of international prices must answer.

The problems to be considered are, first, the character of the national price and income structures, and of the relationships between them; second, the nature of the actual mechanisms of international exchange appearing under similar and dissimilar monetary standards, and of the equilibrium tendencies resulting from their operation; and finally, the determination of international ratios of inter-commodity exchange. The various doctrines which will now be advanced to meet these problems, taken as a whole, constitute a general theory of international prices themselves.

---

[1] A similar view has been outlined by Landry. See ch. x, sect. 1, above.

CHAPTER XV

GENERAL RELATIONSHIPS BETWEEN NATIONAL
PRICE STRUCTURES

1. In order to understand the character of the relationships between prices and money incomes in different countries, it is first necessary to understand the composition of the national price structures themselves.

For many purposes, especially the handling of confused statistical data and the analysis of complex mechanisms, it is convenient to distinguish between international prices and domestic, and even to subdivide the first class into export and import. The three groups combined make up the aggregate price structure of the country. But this distinction is extremely misleading at times, and may result in conclusions which are quite erroneous. Despite the convenience of the phrase, there is in strict accuracy no such thing as an "international" price. What we actually find, of course, is that in the totality of *national* prices a certain group is composed of the prices of those articles which in point of fact usually do or may enter foreign trade. There is no such thing, for example, as an international or a world price of wheat, even at a given instant. There is, instead, a series of *national* prices for wheat in a series of different countries and markets. The more correct procedure, therefore, is to think of international prices as simply a rather loosely defined part of the national price structure. The term "international" is justified by the fact that these particular groups in the various general structures tend in given periods to maintain a fairly constant numerical relationship to one another as between countries, in terms of some common measure, and to fluctuate substantially together.

Nor is there a true generic distinction between domestic and international commodities. Any movable article whatsoever *may* enter international trade, and may be exported or imported or both, irrespective of its character.[1] The criterion as to whether it

---

[1] And so, under certain conditions at least, for such immovable economic goods as land or buildings or industrial plant in the same or adjacent districts, which are

will or will not in point of fact move between countries is wholly an empirical one, incapable of establishment except by inference from particular cases. The first requisite for movement is that the money prices receivable, translated through a common measure, shall be higher in one country than in the other; the second, that the difference shall at least cover costs of transportation of all sorts, including tariff charges. These two provide as a rule the "necessary" condition for the existence of trade. Yet even when this condition is fulfilled, as we shall see, and even when the "sufficient" condition is present — of possible sale at or above the usual rate of profit — an international movement may not take place; and the far from uncommon phenomenon of "dumping" often provides a case of trade where even the "necessary" condition is apparently absent. (Though this last is usually a short-run, rather than a long-run, phenomenon.) In other words, there is no hard and fast rule. It is obvious, of course, that the great majority of the articles in each country do not, and under extant conditions cannot, enter foreign trade. The prohibition arises either from the absolute levels of their money prices, or from exorbitant costs of transportation. But with the exception of a comparatively small number of staples, even the rough dual grouping that this condition suggests has nothing very definite about it. Many of the articles concerned pass continually from one category to the other; the direction of their international movement is not infrequently reversed; and the very character and composition of the articles themselves, in the aggregate, is always changing.[1] The recognition of these conditions provides

divided only by the accident of a political frontier. The transfer of titles to such property may be so easy, and the structure of the population so similar, that the immovable property *in effect* becomes mobile as between the two countries. The full competitive condition, with substantial equalization of prices and profits, may well prevail. A temporary difference in prices or profits, leading to an international movement of the corresponding capital, would thus produce results not dissimilar to those that would have ensued could the property itself have been actually moved across the border.

[1] For the staples, as various writers have suggested, there are import and export points quite as truly as for gold. But for less actively traded and less standardized commodities the "point" becomes a rather indefinite zone, and may virtually disappear.

perhaps the strongest argument for questioning the appropriateness of erecting a separate theory of international prices or values. If there is no necessary and generic distinction between the various classes of commodities themselves or their markets, how justify the use of different theories to deal with them? The conclusion may well be that international trade, like trade between two markets in the same country or even within the same market, is best regarded as simply a case of composite supply and composite demand. The actual adjustment is made less accurate than that in domestic commerce by the presence of certain obstacles and intermediaries, which retard the process, but it does not necessarily follow that they alter the essential character of the process itself.

With these considerations in mind, the general problem of international price relationships then offers two principal aspects. One is the question of international price equalization, with respect to particular commodities. The other is that of the relations between the aggregate price and income structures of different countries. In discussing these questions, it will be assumed throughout that the countries concerned maintain a common and stable metallic standard. The situation arising under dissimilar and depreciating currencies is of quite another order, and will be treated separately in a later chapter.

2. With respect to the first question, a recent report of the United States Tariff Commission presents an empirical classification of prices and commodities which seems to me extremely useful.[1] It is based on the strength of the tendency, in numerous specific cases, to an actual price equalization between countries. At one extreme are placed the actively and steadily traded articles that make up the backbone of all foreign trade. They are the great staple necessities, such as wheat and cotton and copper, of which certain countries control the supply, and of which other countries regularly need large quantities. For these staples, the data go to show that world prices tend always to maintain an approximate equality. The size and number of the alternative mar-

[1] United States Tariff Commission, *Depreciated Exchange and International Trade* (Washington, 1922), pp. 3 ff. (See ch. vii, sect. 5, above.)

kets makes for price stability in any one country at any one time, while the intensity and universality of competition makes for uniformity, and for quickness in adjustment. This equality, however, necessarily refers to the maintenance of a given *scale* of money prices, not to absolute equality in the prices themselves. The gradations in the scale, at a particular moment, are determined primarily by current costs of transportation, and by extant tariff regulations.

At the other extreme are those articles — the great actual majority in each country — which under extant circumstances are absolutely prohibited from entering foreign trade. The prohibition arises either from the state of relative prices themselves, or from costs of transportation, or from tariffs and similar restrictions; or from a combination of all three. With respect to these non-traded commodities, there is obviously no direct international competition, and hence no reason, as far as the immediate operations of the market go, for any equalization of prices at all. Whether or not such an equalization nevertheless tends to appear, in consequence of the general relations between national price and income structures, will be considered in a later section.

Finally, between the two extremes there is the large number of articles of which the international movement is dependent in chief degree upon the changing conditions of the moment. Of these the less common foodstuffs and the more highly manufactured industrial products afford examples. They are at or near the "margin of doubt." They may or may not flow between countries, as prices and costs of transportation and even exchange rates vary, and as a whole they are constantly passing back and forth from the "domestic" to the "international" category. They do not possess a world market, in any wide sense of the term. Competition here, while perhaps intense as between given pairs or small groups of countries, is usually not very effective with respect to the world markets as a whole. For this class of partially traded commodities in the aggregate, the (relative) equalization of international prices is at best only partial. In other words, differences greater than those justified solely by transportation costs or tariffs usually appear. These differences have no necessary corrective, and tend to become permanent.

3. The conclusion that for large classes of articles international price inequality is the typical situation is borne out by considerations of another order, based upon the character of industrial and commercial organization in general.[1] Suppose that a difference in price appears for a given article as between any two markets, which is much greater than the difference imposed by costs of transportation or by tariffs. At first glance, it seems natural to expect that producers for the low-price market will expand their field of activity, and by invading the high-price market will bring the two prices back to a maximum difference set by costs of transportation (in the widest sense). With respect to the actively and regularly traded staples, this is precisely what usually happens. But with respect to partially traded articles, the situation is less clear.

Certain obstacles tend to oppose the (relative) levelling of the prices of such articles, in the ordinary course of events. The first and most obvious obstacle is a lack of accurate information, in each market, as to the conditions of the moment in the *other* market. The second is a lack of sufficient initiative and enterprise, on the part of the manufacturers and dealers, to take advantage of the discrepancy. The third is the fact that selling in a new market requires the prior erection of trade connections, and of a distributive mechanism. Much trouble and no little expense are usually involved at the outset, and although eventually the gain might well more than offset the initial loss, it may be thought that the additional profit is simply "not worth the bother." This argument of course has no relevance where such trade connections already exist. But the very character of the "partially traded" commodities themselves make it seem certain that, in a group of countries dealing in these articles, such connections will not always be steadily maintained between each market and every other. Nothing more than the occasional cessation of trade, common for articles of the partially traded group, is itself sufficient to

---

[1] The following argument is adapted in part from R. Schüller, *Schutzzoll und Freihandel* (Vienna and Leipzig, 1905), especially pp. 88–93. (See ch. xiii, sect. 9, above.) In still larger part, however, it is taken from an amplification of his views which Dr. Schüller himself was kind enough to outline for me verbally in the spring of 1923.

impair the distributive organization abroad, and in consequence to diminish the sensitivity of the international adjustment.

The last and perhaps the most important obstacle to equalization is the relation between costs, prices, and the volume of output. If the low-price manufacturers expand into the high-price market, this expansion will ultimately mean an increase in the volume of their production. Up to the point of maximum utilization of the extant available plant and supplies, such an expansion will usually be accomplished by decreasing costs and greater profits. But beyond that point costs will begin to rise, profits will fall, and the advantage in production over less well situated manufacturers will decline.[1] Under the full competitive assumption, this last is precisely what is expected to happen. The high-cost producers should be driven out. But actual experience seems to provide a great many cases where, in point of fact, a different situation develops. Inter-market price differences distinctly in excess of costs of transportation or other charges are allowed to persist, without correction. The explanation apparently lies in the fact that the low-cost manufacturers often prefer, by keeping output down and by refraining from taking advantage of every price discrepancy and every consequent opportunity for expansion, to maintain a higher rate of profit per unit of product. Their risk of loss from fluctuations in market price is thus lessened, and their general position is made more stable. The effect on the process of price determination is analogous to that of a quasi-monopoly.

How widely the conditions suggested in the two preceding paragraphs prevail, can of course be determined only by a study of actual cases. There seems to be reason, however, for thinking them more nearly characteristic of industrial and commercial conditions at large than the classical competitive assumption is usually taken to imply. If they are at all true of trade within a country, they are doubly true of international exchange, for the incompleteness of information, and the difficulty and expense of setting up new trade connections, are much greater there.

[1] Factory space becomes inadequate; labor and raw materials must be brought from more distant points, at greater expense; a larger but less certain market must be sought for the products; and so on.

The conclusion to which we are led with respect to the problem of international price equalization is this. For the great staples, the relative price equalization is accurate and general; for partially traded articles the equalization is at best incompletely effective, while wide differences can appear without necessary correction; and for non-traded articles there is of course no direct equalization at all. The importance of the second group, relative to the total volume of international commodity exchange, is probably large.

The exactness of these propositions, however, depends in considerable degree upon the length of the time period held in mind. Other things equal, the shorter the period the greater will be the differences in price that can appear between countries, for any one article. In periods of a few days or weeks, for example, a sudden increase in local demands or an unexpected failure of local supplies may cause the prices of even the chief staples to pass well beyond the differentials set by the aggregated costs of transportation. On the other hand, if we take periods of perhaps several years the average prices of even the infrequently traded articles are not likely to exceed a fairly constant differential. This latter differential, however, will usually be greater than costs of transportation alone can account for. The excess is explained by, and in a sense measures, the forces of inertia already commented on.[1]

4. Before proceeding farther, something must be said of the tendency to international equalization in the prices of the other elements that enter the exchange between countries. We shall thus secure a complete picture of the separate items in the situation. These elements are three in number. One is the movement of long-term capital, one the quite different movement of short-term capital, and one the exchange of those services which give rise to the remaining "invisible" items — that is, ocean freight services, services to tourists, and so on.

[1] The inadequacy of the data makes it difficult to test these conclusions statistically without a great deal of labor. The U. S. Tariff Commission report, already referred to, is the only compilation of the kind that I know of, although several writers have called attention to discrepancies and apparent limits for particular groups of commodities. *The Federal Reserve Bulletin*, however, has for some years been computing separate index numbers for import commodities and for export commodities.

It requires no demonstration that the price of long-term capital is not the same in all countries, even assuming equal risks. If it were, the movement of international investment itself would necessarily cease. Nor is it even the same in different parts of the *same* country. The making of comparisons is therefore often difficult, and competition correspondingly incomplete. On the other hand, however, there is a far from negligible tendency to the establishment of a loose scale of international price differentials, not unlike that which has been shown to exist for the less actively traded commodities. The size of the various steps in the scale is determined by the degree of knowledge of conditions in foreign countries, by the risks thought to be involved, and by the strength of the predilection for domestic rather than for foreign investment. When the differential is exceeded, capital will go abroad. If the process is continued for some time, the price of capital will then fall in the receiving country and rise in the exporting country, until something approaching the previous difference — a *relative* equalization of prices — is reëstablished. There is, for example, a certain amount of evidence to show that European investment in the United States during the nineteenth century produced such an effect as this on American interest rates. But the equalization tendency is at best approximate, and works in only one direction in a given general period. A country will ordinarily not import large amounts of capital in one year, and export large amounts in the next.[1] Finally, the equalization is very distinctly a long-time rather than a short-time phenomenon. An exception is provided, it is true, by the undeniable equality (within narrow limits) in the prices of those securities which are actively traded between countries, and which therefore have a genuine world market. But this equality is itself a product of short-time forces. As

---

[1] A partial exception to this is provided by the history of the United States in the decades before the war. Taking a considerable number of years at a span, we were both receiving capital from Europe and ourselves making large investments abroad — chiefly in other American countries, and to some extent in the Far East. We were in effect a sort of reservoir, an *entrepôt*, connecting these last countries with Europe.

The great numerical majority of countries, however, fall in only one of the two categories in given eras. They are capital providers or capital receivers, but not both on any important scale.

already remarked, if it were carried over into long periods and for a wide range of securities, international investment would cease. It would give way to the temporary movements induced by discount and exchange rate fluctuations.

The prices of short-term capital likewise reveal not an absolute equality as between countries, but a scale of differentials. In various other respects, however, the two cases are dissimilar. The steps in the price scale for short-term capital are much smaller (from one half to two per cent, depending on the financial centers selected for comparison), and the adjustments are much more rapid.[1] Moreover, a country may at one time find the price of its short-term capital higher than anywhere else, and at other times lower. In other words, the scale of differentials is effective in *both* directions instead of in only one. A further dissimilarity arises from the fact that although the movements of such capital may be of great volume at a given time, over longer periods they are very largely self-returning. There is never a *permanent* export or import of short-term capital, except in so far as there is a change in the relation between the current balances which a country keeps abroad and the balances kept with it. The price-equalizing influence of such movements is therefore confined to periods of relatively brief duration. It is true that the available evidence strongly suggests that the larger and longer fluctuations of discount rates in different countries follow far from dissimilar paths, though sometimes inversely, and nearly always with a lag. This similarity is not primarily due, however, to the direct mechanical effects of the *movement* of short-term capital in response to price discrepancies. It is explained in part by seasonal influences that are common to the countries concerned, but chiefly by the tendency to a coincidence or a parallelism in their cyclical oscillations. To the latter point we shall return elsewhere.

Finally, the prices of those items which are neither merchandise nor capital — freight services, tourists' expenditures, and so on —

[1] See, for example, the recent study by E. G. Peake, *An Academic Study of some Money Market and other Statistics* (London, 1923).

The "price" of short-term capital, as between countries, is evidently the joint result of the position of the discount rates and the exchanges. Conceptually the two can be separated, but in dealing with actual data they are hopelessly intertwined.

reveal a confusion of tendencies. The international competition for ocean freight is keen, but with respect to the last two items mentioned it is almost impossible to secure any basis for effecting direct comparisons between countries. It is hence difficult even to conceive of an international "equality" in their prices. The quantitative importance of the whole group, however, is small.

If we take the non-commodity group in the aggregate, it is evident that, like the situation with respect to commodities, the tendencies to international price equality are neither universal nor always definite. For some elements in the group they are almost imperceptible. For others they are strong, yet only in the sense of keeping prices within certain fairly wide differentials. A closer relationship exists, it is true, with respect to the larger oscillations of discount rates, but this is the product of coincident seasonal or cyclical fluctuations in general business conditions, not directly of the movements of short-term capital itself between countries. In none of these cases, it may be added, is there much evidence to show that the partial tendencies in question will increase the degree of equalization in *commodity* prices.

5. The other major problem is that of the relationships between the aggregate price and money income *structures* of different countries. We shall examine here only the general qualitative character of the relationships, leaving until the next chapter the more difficult problem of how they are actually maintained.

To this problem, it will be remembered, an *a priori* answer has been worked out along classical lines by Professor Taussig.[1] Briefly put, the argument is simply that money wages in the export industries are governed, relative to the prices of the exported products, by the effectiveness of the labor concerned; that these wages in turn set the pace for the wages of similar grades of labor in other industries in the country — and are in part reciprocally governed by them; and that the general scale of wages thus established determines, relative to the effectiveness of labor in the various industries, the prices of the corresponding products.

It is possible to take this doctrine in a rather rigid and quick-acting sense. If this be done, a basis is provided for comparing

[1] See ch. iv, sect. 8, above.

the prices of all commodities in each country, whether traded or not, with those in other countries; and also the money wages of all labor. The requisite common terms for making the comparison would of course be the relative effectiveness of labor as *between* countries, measured in the competing export industries; and the relative effectiveness of labor *within* each country, measured in the latter's own different industries.[1]

Professor Taussig himself, however, does not adopt so extreme a position. In the first place, he applies his doctrine only in a rather loose and long-run sense, using it simply to explain the general price and income relationships which appear between various countries over a period of years. In the second place, he does not confine the basis of the international comparison to labor in the competing export industries alone. He adopts, rather, the pragmatic and *post facto* view suggested by the arguments of Senior and Mill. He holds that the rate of money wages in the export industries depends not only on the relative effectiveness of labor, but also on the conditions of international demand as they exist at the time. Of this last element, of course, no *a priori* determination is possible. It therefore follows that no general formula for international comparisons can be laid down, except with reference to empirically established conditions of the past or present.

The line of approach suggested by the classification of prices and commodities given above also fails to indicate that any very rigid relationship exists between the aggregate price and money income *structures* of one country and those of another, unless over periods of considerable length. In a static condition of affairs, and when trade is in equilibrium, it is true that the extreme inter-

[1] A fairly rigid relationship of this sort as between countries, even in the prices of non-traded articles, has been suggested on somewhat different grounds by Professor Pigou. The argument is based on the assumption that equilibrium rates of exchange, or norms, exist between any two commodities at a given time. On this assumption, it is easy to proceed from norms as between countries in traded articles, and from norms as between these and other articles in a given country, to effective norms between countries for articles which do not themselves enter international trade at all. But the argument of the preceding section of the present chapter, in so far as it is accepted, casts doubt on these propositions. Pigou's fundamental and rather tacit assumption, of effective competition and mobility, does not seem to be altogether borne out by the facts. (A. C. Pigou, *The Foreign Exchanges: 37 Quarterly Journal of Economics*, 1922. See ch. vii, sect. 3, above.)

pretation of Professor Taussig's theorem would undoubtedly tend to be realized as an actual fact. But under the changing and dynamic conditions of reality, it can hardly hold true in any exact sense. Where the exporting industries of two countries are in competition with one another, money wages, in so far as the tendency to international price equalization is operative, will undoubtedly be substantially in proportion to the relative effectiveness of their labor. It seems not only improbable but impossible, however, that a change in this relative effectiveness can of itself alter the general price and income scales of each country, except in long periods. Its immediate influence will be confined to the particular industries in which the change occurs. The importance of any one industry is too small, compared to the inert aggregate of economic activity in the entire country. What is much more likely to happen, at a given time, is just the opposite: that a change in the aggregate national scales of prices will alter prices *in the exporting and importing industries.* Only if the change in international conditions is important, general, and continued (as happened after 1914) will the national structures be substantially affected in any very short-run period.[1]

The general type of analysis which Professor Taussig has so skilfully elaborated is subject to one other fundamental difficulty, which may appropriately be pointed out here. The immediate validity of the analysis rests very largely on its treatment of "effectiveness of labor" as the origin of given relative rates of wages and prices in different countries, and as the measuring rod for making international comparisons. But what is "effectiveness of labor," and what determines its size in the given case?

There are at bottom really two agents of production, and only two. They are, men and natural resources. Other things equal, if the supply of labor is relatively small its marginal productivity, and therefore its "effectiveness," will be relatively high; and vice

---

[1] A certain rather loose tendency to an intra-national equalization of wage rates, for similar grades of labor, can probably also be granted. But for profits this tendency does not exist in any sense accurate enough to be significant. That is, the national distributive mechanism is not knit closely enough together to make possible any very rapid transmission of changes from one part to another.

versa. But certain other factors also influence this effectiveness. They are, the skill and inventiveness with which the labor is applied, the manner in which the whole process of production is organized, and the strength of the demand for the output. Under actual conditions the position of the first pair of factors, the relation between natural resources in use and the supply of labor, is much the most important determinant of the degree of relative effectiveness at a given time. Variations in the other factors may radically change the conditions of production for particular articles, but they will not greatly alter the level of effectiveness in the country as a whole, except over periods of considerable length. (And except in the case of such abnormal shifts in demand as were produced by the war.) It therefore follows that when we refer the problems of international wage and price relationships to the effectiveness of labor, as a standard of comparison, we have by no means gotten to the end of the story. When the attempt is made to establish the nature of the "causal" or sequential relations involved, it becomes necessary to resolve the standard itself into terms of other and antecedent elements which are more complex, and which are less easily handled. Moreover, one of these elements is the intensity of demand itself. Yet in dealing with the erection of international prices, demand must sometimes be treated as a factor coördinate with, and for purposes of exposition independent of, the effectiveness of labor — of which it is nevertheless itself a determinant. There is thus a very real danger of introducing circularity into the reasoning.[1]

These comments are in no sense intended to deny the usefulness of the sort of analysis which Professor Taussig has presented. That analysis is of the greatest importance and value. But, as Professor Taussig himself has pointed out, it is best regarded as a general and perhaps rather loose description of certain relationships, not as a complete causal or sequential explanation. It is an account of the fairly long-time course of those objective events which we may look to see worked out in response to significant general alterations in the conditions of international trade, not an

---

[1] Some further difficulties involved in using the term "effectiveness of labor" will be indicated later, in a footnote at the end of ch. xviii, sect. 6.

account of processes and changes that will appear in any very immediate or short-run period.[1]

6. The conclusions that have been reached to this point are as follows. First, the prices of the commodities exchanged between countries definitely tend to maintain a world equality within assignable limits, or a scale of fairly constant differentials, although the closeness of the equalization varies for different kinds of commodities. Second, there is a relationship of sorts, of a type that may be described as "organic," between the price and income structures of the various trading countries. On *a priori* grounds, it seems probable that this last relationship is strong enough to impart a substantial similarity to the movements of prices in different countries — although, like the tendency to price equalization, it will be less effective the shorter the period considered. But these propositions are necessarily rather loosely defined. Is it possible to secure more precise results?

If we turn from the materials of general reasoning to the materials provided by empirical evidence, one significant fact immediately stands out: namely, that the general price indices of at least the more advanced countries of the world have undoubtedly moved very intimately together in the past. Consider, for example, the comparison of prices in England and in the United States from 1800 to 1921, made recently by the Harvard Economic Service. When the two (annual) indices are reduced to a similar base, they show a remarkable degree of closeness in the time, the direction and even the amplitude of the larger oscillations; that is, of oscillations covering periods of three or four years or more.[2] The only important exceptions arise during the inter-

---

[1] Professor Taussig has been very guarded in assigning anything more than the surface meaning to his discussion.

On the other hand, the data he has presented in a recent article on *The Change in Great Britain's Foreign Trade Terms after 1900* (Economic Journal, 1925) indicate that there is a far from loose long-time relationship between the import – export ratio and the course of money wages. It is possible to interpret this as an empirical confirmation of the general theory presented in the text, which connects the levels and major movements of money incomes with the changing terms of foreign trade. (Also see a footnote in ch. vii, sect. 5, above.)

[2] Harvard Economic Service, *Weekly Letter:* June 10, 1922. What appear to be the cyclical fluctuations coincide usually, and the secular movements always (with the exceptions noted in the text).

vals when one country or the other was on an inconvertible paper basis, as from 1797 to 1820, 1862 to 1879, and since 1914. At these times, of course, the two groups of prices followed entirely different courses. On the other hand the short-time fluctuations, in so far as annual data can be regarded as indicative, were sometimes similar, but quite as frequently not. Barring the intervals of inconvertibility, however, the general paths of the two curves are almost identical. The long-time movements are virtually coincident. At most points, a zone not more than 10 per cent in width would include all of the deviations of one from the other. Nor is there any evidence whatsoever of a cumulative tendency to a long-time separation of the indices. Rather, each has to some extent the appearance of acting as a norm for the other.

Substantially similar results are indicated by another recent comparison of English, American and German prices from 1850 to 1910, although the degree of divergence is somewhat greater.[1] And so for other countries before 1914, where data are available. It is true that since the war the agreement has been much less close, because of the distortions imposed by currency depreciation and collapse, and some of the Continental price levels seem to have moved to permanently lower levels.[2] But there continues to be a general concordance in the time and direction of the larger movements, which is becoming increasingly pronounced as more normal conditions are restored. Indeed, Professor Fisher's plotting of English prices with American in the last two or three years indicates a remarkable degree of correlation in even the weekly oscillations. There is ground, however, for questioning the real significance of this.[3]

---

[1] W. T. Layton, *An Introduction to the Study of Prices* (London, 1920), pp. 150, 151.

[2] Expressed, that is, in terms of gold. See the compilations published in the *Federal Reserve Bulletin*, and in other sources.

[3] See Professor Fisher's comparisons of his index for the United States with Mr. Crump's for England, published weekly. There are two difficulties, however. In the first place, a considerable proportion of the commodities used in making up the indices do or may enter international trade, and are therefore common to both. This could be obviated only by constructing separate indices for "domestic" prices alone. Should they also show an intimate and very short-time relationship — which is not likely — the evidence would then be conclusive. In the second place, there is no pos-

The evidence thus strongly suggests, if it does not conclusively prove, that the movements of general prices in the leading countries of the world (I have no data available on the less advanced countries) are remarkably similar in their larger, long-time oscillations, and have at least a certain tendency to equivalence in shorter periods.[1] To put it in other terms, the various national price structures can be thought of not inaccurately as a series of solar systems, which maintain a fairly constant relationship in their movements through space. But the component parts of the systems — individual prices — are in a state of ceaseless change relative to the elements in both their own and other systems. Their places in the national structure may vary widely, although the place of the *aggregate* of such prices remains comparatively stable.

It is not possible to carry a strictly empirical analysis beyond this point with any assurance, however, for adequate data have not yet been worked up that cover a sufficient number of years in a sufficient number of countries.[2] The fascinating question of international cyclical relationships, for example, must be allowed to await the collection of further material. Instead, we shall try to

sible way of *explaining* such relationships: there is no connecting link. For correlations over longer periods, however, the situation is different. See a footnote near the beginning of the next section; and especially ch. xvi, sect. 5, below.

[1] If the various price indices on whose movements these propositions are based were indices of "domestic" prices alone, and hence really independent, the conclusiveness of the evidence would be virtually absolute. Unfortunately for the purposes here in hand, such index numbers have been constructed only in recent years. The older ones necessarily include a number of international prices that are common to the countries concerned, and that exaggerate the appearance of similarity in the fluctuations. The weight of this qualification, however, becomes less as the importance of international trade in the national economic life grows, while where its importance is small international prices will presumably assume a minor rôle in the general price index. I have therefore not undertaken to introduce these considerations into the discussion in the text.

The recorded similarity of the major price fluctuations in the leading countries, in the face of wide differences in many specific domestic prices and in money incomes, indicates that the general character of the economic structure, the technique of production, and the content of the economic life itself, must be fundamentally similar in these countries.

[2] See, however, N. J. Silberling, *British Prices and Business Cycles, 1779–1850* (*Review of Economic Statistics*, 1923), in which a quite intimate relationship of a *cyclical* character between English and American prices is suggested.

discover what further inferences can be drawn from the facts already available as to the real character of international price relationships, and as to the mechanism of their maintenance.

7. The use of index numbers in making international comparisons over any period of time involves one fundamental difficulty, or at least a fundamental assumption, on which attention has begun to center in recent years.[1] It has just been shown that the prices of internationally traded articles maintain, in the aggregate, a significant degree of at least relative equality as between different countries. The obvious corollary is that their oscillations must be substantially similar in these countries. But it has also been shown that at least the larger and more long-run movements of *general* prices have been quite closely coincident. One of two conclusions therefore necessarily follows. Either the relative position of the group of international prices, in each national price structure where this coincidence has appeared, has in the aggregate not changed substantially (despite pronounced variations with respect to individual prices); or else such changes as have actually taken place have on the whole been substantially the *same*, in the various countries. Suppose that the place of the international group had altered in one country, but not in the other, or had altered to a greater degree. Then international prices would continue to maintain their equality, but the various *general* price indices would necessarily draw apart. They would have shifted their positions relative to the international indices (which remain equal, within the limits already considered), and therefore relative to one another. But the available statistics indicate that this has not actually occurred, at least as between the leading countries of the world. The necessary further inference then is that their *domestic* prices must likewise have followed roughly similar paths of movement, taking these prices as a whole, since they are the remaining components of the general indices.[2]

[1] See ch. vii, sect. 5, above. This is simply another form of a difficulty long familiar: that, over periods of time, the composition and relative importance of the items entering a price index necessarily change, in ways that cannot be allowed for adequately by statistical methods.

[2] It may at once be objected that the concurrence in movement of general price indices, as between countries, results simply from the fact that a large number of

There is no direct mechanical relationship, however, between the prices of non-traded articles in different countries. If they nevertheless move together, even if only in the aggregate, it must therefore apparently be true that the movements of international prices dominate the movements of the prices of non-traded "domestic" goods. International prices are the only connecting link between the domestic prices of different countries that is certainly operative, except in rather long-run periods.[1] Yet at first glance it is not easy to understand their dominance. There are two possible lines of explanation.

First, there is a relationship between the various domestic price structures from the side of production and of costs. International commodities enter into the manufacture of certain domestic articles, and compete with others; and some tendency to an equalization in the prices of domestic products in different countries undoubtedly results. But the strength of this tendency must evidently be small at any one time, and its operation slow. It cannot be adequate to explain the comparatively quick adjustments that actually take place. Moreover, these adjustments are not ones necessarily involving the establishment of *equality* in the prices of domestic articles. They involve only a general parallelism in the

commodities—the international group—is common to them all. This was the objection brought above against the apparently close weekly correlation between American and English prices recently announced by Professor Fisher.

I think, to repeat, that the objection is valid with respect to very short-time correlations. In periods of one or two weeks, there is literally no possible connection between the movements of *domestic* prices in different countries (see ch. xvi, sect. 3), and an apparent relationship can be due only to the fact that the index numbers have a considerable proportion of common elements. But over longer periods this is not necessarily true. In the first place, as will be shown below and in the following chapter, a reasonable explanation of *long*-time relationships *can* be developed, that is independent of the character of the particular index numbers selected for comparison. In the second place, the importance of international trade in national economic life was of course much less in the nineteenth century than it is now. Consequently the extent to which interdependence could be asserted of the various national price indices in that period was likewise much smaller.

But these considerations apply, at least in the first instance, only to the interpretation to be placed on particular empirical data; data themselves admitted to be not entirely adequate. They do not affect the validity of the general argument developed in the text.

[1] When the influence of money wages, for example, might have some effect.

major movements of the aggregate of domestic prices. There is no evidence to show that particular individual articles are unmistakably held in such a relationship.

Second, it is possible that a disequilibrium between countries in the prices of international goods (presumably involving a parallel disequilibrium with respect to strictly domestic articles) brings corrective forces into play that affect not only international prices themselves, but also all the *other* prices in the total national structure. This is the sort of doctrine which was at the heart of the classical price-specie flow analysis, and of at least Mill's theory of international equilibrium. The specie flow analysis, at least in any short-time sense, is now discredited in the eyes of most writers. The underlying doctrine itself, however, I think remains essentially valid. No other type of explanation can adequately account for the known facts. Prices in different countries do not move together, over long periods of time, by sheer accident. There must evidently be some connecting link between them. But the influence exerted by international prices alone, on the various national price structures, is not great enough to provide this link. It is necessary to discover some condition or element that is capable of affecting the totality of prices indiscriminately, and fairly rapidly. This element is found in the mechanism by which the balance of international payments is kept in equilibrium.

But the questions here at issue are larger than those involved in the relations between commodity prices alone. They must be reserved for the next chapter, in which a substitute for the price-specie flow analysis will be developed. With this substitute as a tool, it will then be possible to present a complete picture of the general influences and specific mechanisms which connect the price structures of different countries.

8. Before leaving this general field, of the relationships between price and income structures in different countries, something must be said of the major sources of disturbance in the prices of international commodities themselves, and of the kinds of doctrine they make it necessary to incorporate into the general theory of international price relationships.

The most obvious source, in the short-time period, is of course seasonal fluctuations. But seasonal factors, in the first instance, operate on *particular* commodities and prices alone. Their effect on the *aggregate* of prices is much less pronounced and less regular.[1] It becomes smaller, the wider the distribution of types of seasonal influence. Moreover, other things equal, these oscillations are substantially self-returning, and do not shift the relative positions of international prices permanently.

Seasonal fluctuations apart, the disturbances are of three principal types. They may arise from a change in the conditions of demand or supply in one or more countries, with respect to the articles entering foreign trade. In this case the immediate effects are largely confined to the particular articles actually involved. Only after the lapse of a certain period of time will the course of the international exchanges as a whole be altered; and only if the movement is relatively large and enduring will general *domestic* conditions be affected. Or the disturbance may be due to a change in monetary conditions. That is, while what we may call "real" demand and supply schedules remain unchanged, the quantity and even the quality of the national currencies may vary. In that case the change in prices within the given country will be general. Either an absolute or at least a relative alteration in the prices of international articles as a whole will result directly, and the terms and course of trade will be altered. If the initial change be large, some repercussion on purely domestic money-price conditions may then be expected. Finally, the disturbance may be due to those general fluctuations in business and agriculture which combine changes in non-monetary demand and supply with changes in the quantity of money itself.

A study of the effects of variations in the general conditions of supply and demand [2] which occur apart from monetary disturbances involves, among other things, a theory of the variations in

---

[1] Although where a country's foreign trade is dominated by a few commodities that are subject to similar seasonal influences, the position of the aggregate of international prices in the national price structure will obviously be affected materially. So especially of the agricultural exporting countries.

[2] From the demand side, a recognition of the probability of different elasticities at different points in the demand schedule is sufficient.

money costs of production as quantities themselves vary. Here, however, usable explanations already exist. For virtually all competitive commodities, the "average" situation is probably such that at any given moment the extant facilities of production are not completely utilized. Stocks currently on hand also usually provide a further element of elasticity. At first, therefore, the total national output can usually be increased without an increase in costs, and costs may even fall. Beyond the point of maximum utilization, however, a further increase in the rate of output involves a rise in costs. Yet if the increase be large and continued, improvements in organization and in technical methods will in turn ordinarily cause them to fall again. The picture, over periods of time, is thus that of a series of waves. In manufacturing industry the general trend of the waves is typically downward, other things equal, while even in extractive enterprises it apparently does not rise in the long run.

A study of the effects of monetary changes, on the other hand, involves a theory of money and prices. Here the character of the generalized formula adopted must evidently depend on the type of situation held in mind. If the monetary standard itself is kept stable — if, in practice, the gold standard is maintained — the enduring changes in the quantity of money and credit that arise independently of seasonal or cyclical oscillations will be comparatively small and gradual. The resulting long-time changes in prices can then be explained chiefly in quantitative terms of a familiar order.[1] In shorter periods, however, the largest and most significant changes in money and credit are bound up with seasonal and especially cyclical oscillations — themselves to be examined again in a moment. It is of course beyond our province here to venture into the theory of business cycles, for too little is yet known about their origins and operation to make comprehensive conclusions possible. It seems clear, however, that the corresponding changes in money and credit are more results than

---

[1] The long-time *trend* of gold prices in the resultant, is each country, of changes in the volume of gold holdings and in the methods of economizing its use, on the one hand; and of changes in the volume of production on the other. The increasing urbanization of populations also makes necessary a larger volume of media of exchange to support a given general price level.

causes of the general cyclical oscillations. A doctrine of wider scope than that contemplated by the older theories of money and prices is therefore necessary.

If on the other hand the currency is depreciating, a quite different type of problem arises. When the depreciation is at all severe and rapid, the dominant factors become not so much the direct mechanical action of the quantity of money and credit itself, as the anticipation of future changes in this quantity, and the effects of movements of the foreign exchanges. The cyclical influence, and even the seasonal movements, are entirely buried. These matters, however, will occupy a later chapter.

Finally, there remains the question of the effects of the cyclical fluctuations themselves on the course of international prices. The data here are as yet too scanty, and cover too small a range of countries,[1] to permit the erection of even a tentative conclusion. Yet the problem is evidently of the greatest significance—unless, indeed, only periods longer than the duration of the cycle itself be considered. Under stable currency conditions these fluctuations are probably the most important single source of general changes in the prices within any country; and therefore, taking two or more countries together, in international prices. Changes in non-monetary demand and supply affect particular commodities alone, and those changes in the quantity of currency and credit which occur apart from cyclical variations are usually not important in short periods (exception of course being made for seasonal oscillations, which however affect the *total* of prices far less than they affect individual items). Cyclical fluctuations, on the other hand, involve changes not only in non-monetary demand and supply, but also in the quantity of money. There is no question as to the universality of their effects.

If the cycles in any two countries are moving together in direction and time, the corresponding international prices need not be altered except in their absolute levels. Their relative positions in

---

[1] For example, we know a good deal about the simultaneous or non-simultaneous occurrence of financial crises in different countries, but except for England and the United States we know almost nothing, as yet, about the equally important oscillations that have *not* led to such spectacular and conspicuous climaxes.

the national price structures, that is, will not be changed. But if the cycles are moving in different directions, or if one is clearly preceding the other, then both the absolute and the relative positions of the international group of prices will vary. The first hypothesis has been set forth with especial clarity by Hawtrey. A plausible partial alternative can be made to run in terms of *coincident* cycles with respect to the leading countries of the world, which can then be regarded as constituting a quite closely integrated economic unit; and of *inverse* cycles as between them and the economically less advanced countries. But there are evident difficulties; and, as already indicated, the definitive evidence as yet collected hardly does more than warrant a consideration of some of these possibilities.

9. The conclusions to which the present chapter have led are these. First, the prices of the articles that enter international trade maintain either a virtual equality between countries, or at least a limiting scale of maximum differentials, depending on the character of the commodities concerned and the activity with which they are exchanged. But permanent differences, greater than costs of transportation and all other charges, can appear. Second, the movements of *general* prices in different countries have usually been substantially similar with respect to long-run periods (of several years or more), and are sometimes coincident even in shorter periods. At least, this seems to be true of the leading countries. The situation of the less advanced countries is uncertain. Third, it follows that the place of the international group of prices, in the aggregate price structures of these leading countries, cannot have changed greatly in the periods for which data exist, or else have changed in roughly equal degree; and therefore that purely domestic prices have undergone substantially equivalent long-run movements. There is also a tendency, much less clearly defined, toward a long-run similarity in the direction of change in money incomes, though of course not in their absolute magnitudes. Finally, apart from monetary disturbances the most important single source of comparatively short-time changes in the aggregate of international prices is the cyclical fluctuations of business and agriculture. These cycles may or may not be coin-

cident. Changes in (non-monetary) demand and supply affect
only particular commodities, while the seasonal fluctuations are
also of limited effect.

On the other hand, it must be admitted that these propositions
are far more true of the period before the war than they are at
present. The discrepancies since 1914, however, can be explained
very largely in terms of currency depreciation and of the general
disruption of economic life. They are gradually but surely dis-
appearing, and are giving way to the pre-war types of relationship.

The next step in the general analysis is an explanation of what
the mechanisms actually are which keep the long-time (and to
some extent the short-time) movements of both international and
domestic prices in substantial harmony, as between different
countries. In this is involved the still larger problem of the maintenance of equilibrium in the balance of international payments.
When an account of that process has been given, it will then be
possible to turn back to the question of prices, and to show how
their major fluctuations are held together.

CHAPTER XVI

THE MAINTENANCE OF EQUILIBRIUM IN THE BALANCE OF INTERNATIONAL PAYMENTS

1. There are now in existence two principal doctrines, or two principal types of doctrine, which deal with the question of equilibrium in the balance of international payments. One declares that the forces put into motion by the attempt to liquidate the obligations currently coming due between countries are of such character that the balance maintains itself automatically. This doctrine, first clearly stated by Henry Thornton, and given general currency by Mill,[1] holds in substance that an otherwise uncorrected disequilibrium in the balance of payments will lead to specie flows; this to general price changes in the countries concerned; and this to an alteration in the commodity balance of trade sufficient to restore the balance of international payments itself to equilibrium. The other, on the contrary, denies this whole analysis. It finds that the equilibrium is far from self-maintaining; that if specie flows are not deliberately checked they will or may continue until the country's entire metallic stock is drained out; and that preventative measures, such as the raising of discount rates and the putting into operation of a deliberate foreign-exchange policy, are imperatively required. This view has on the whole been the one characteristic of Continental economists and bankers.

The question here is of course not that of the equality of the actual *payments* themselves, as between countries. With allowance for changes in the size of the net balances left abroad by bankers and traders, and for the occasional cancellation or repudiation of debts, the two totals of payments made and payments

---

[1] Ricardo, it will be remembered, denied that an initial disequilibrium in the balance of payments leads to specie flows and price changes. His own explanation, which is incomplete and unconvincing, ran in terms of the presumably consequent alterations in international demand, taken *apart* from monetary changes. See ch. iii, sect. 3, above; also sect. 5.

received always necessarily balance. This is true both of longer periods, and of intervals of even a few days. The alternative is evidently an accumulation of net debts on one side or the other which would soon reach impossible proportions, and which is of course not witnessed in actuality. The point really at issue is that of a persisting tendency of the antecedent obligations to pile up more rapidly in one country than in the other, and thus to make impossible a complete mutual offset under the familiar clearing principle. Should such a tendency continue long, it would be necessary for the debtor country to transmit additional media of international payment, such as gold, in larger volume than the general conditions of international exchange themselves (apart from the conditions of international *payment*) would have called for in the ordinary course of events. The further question then arises as to whether these drains of gold, and of such other media of payment as are available, are really self-corrective.

Of the two alternative doctrines referred to, the second seems to me to be flatly erroneous, provided that convertibility of the currency is maintained, and provided that the banks and the government of the country are both willing and able to apply what are now recognized as reasonable banking and monetary precautions. Granted these precautions, no further premeditated control over gold movements and the exchanges is necessary. The defense of this view will be found implicit in the later positive argument of the present chapter.

The first doctrine, if interpreted in any literal and short-time sense, is now rejected by all English and American economists of even the most orthodox type, except when they speak carelessly. It is perfectly obvious that neither the magnitudes nor the directions of the international flow of gold are adequate to explain those close and comparatively rapid adjustments of payment-disequilibria, and of price relationships, which were witnessed before the war, and to a somewhat less extent since. The magnitudes are too small, and the directions too apt to be largely offsetting even in rather brief periods.[1] Nor will the character of

---

[1] This is less true, however, of flows of silver to and from the silver standard countries. See ch. xvii, sect. 2, below.

modern banking permit the ascription of any very high degree of intimacy to the connection between a country's metallic stocks and its price level. Finally, gold is among the least sensitive of the media of international payment, one of the slowest to move. Many if not most of the less severe disequilibria are probably corrected without any substantial flow of gold at all. A theory which places its chief reliance upon the effects of such flows is therefore untenable.[1]

On the other hand, the hypothesis which underlay the classical doctrine itself — the hypothesis that the equilibrium of the balance of payments is in some way self-restoring — seems to me fundamentally sound. Indeed, it is impossible to account for the extraordinary similarity in the long-time movements of prices in different countries without resorting to a concept of this general type. There is no other way of providing a connecting link having sufficient strength. But it is evident that the *content* of the classical theory, the characteristic reliance upon the effects of specie movements, is in large part incorrect. Some substitute must be found.

One fundamental assumption, however, must again be made. Throughout the argument of the present chapter it will again be

---

[1] The media of international payment can be placed in a rather loose hierarchy, according to the degree of sensitivity of their international movements in response to fluctuations in the exchange rates — fluctuations which are the objective indices of disequilibrium. The most sensitive media are usually cable transfers, bankers' drafts, and commodity bills. Then come short-time borrowings between banks (finance bills, etc.); then those short- and long-time securities of which the international movements respond quickly to variations in the discount and exchange rates; and finally, the various commodities for which an open market exists. Of this last class specie is the most obvious representative, but the group also includes all those other commodities which are near enough to the "margin of doubt" so that exchange rate fluctuations can materially alter the volume, and even the direction, of their international movement. These groups, however, are by no means rigid and mutually exclusive. Drains may begin from one class long before the possibilities of the preceding class have been exhausted.

It is entirely evident, therefore, that specie flows have no great significance so far as concerns the process of international debt settlement itself. Any other of the media of international payment will serve just as well, and most of them will ordinarily be used in preference to gold. The significance of such flows arises, rather, in connection with their effects upon the general banking situation; a matter of which more will be said subsequently.

taken for granted that the countries concerned maintain the convertibility of their currencies into gold or silver, and that the same standard is employed by each. The presence of dissimilar standards, and especially of depreciating paper currencies, introduces conditions which make it impossible to speak of an "equilibrium" of payments in the sense here in mind. Under a common metallic standard, a failure of the total of international payments to balance can be corrected (except within the narrow limits set by the specie points) only through the actual transfer of additional media of payment, or through a destruction of the excess claims. Under paper, on the other hand, the existence of disequality will itself shift the current exchange rates. The shift will alter the relative values of the current totals of international debits and credits, in terms of one currency or the other, and may well go so far that it restores the payment-equilibrium by itself alone.[1] No change need then take place in the volume of the media of payment actually supplied by either country, as measured in terms of its *own* currency. Moreover, whether this perhaps hypothetical stage is ever reached or not, the connection between the balance of payments and internal conditions takes on a character quite different from that existing under stable currencies.

Assuming, then, that similar metallic standards prevail, what is the process by which equilibrium in the balance of international payments is maintained?

2. To take one of the least complicated sorts of case, let us suppose that a country has just bought a large quantity of newly-issued foreign securities. It is now under the necessity, therefore, of transmitting the proceeds abroad. Assuming that the balance

---

[1] If, under paper, country A's debt to country B is measured by 5 units of A's currency, and country B's debt to A by 1 unit of B's currency, the rate of exchange will be 5 to 1. If now A's debt doubles, while B's stays the same, the rate of exchange will (or may) move to the ratio 10 to 1. If prices do not alter, B then gets twice as many imports for the same quantity of exports.

These propositions are of course arbitrarily stated, and neglect the inevitable subsequent changes in prices in one or both countries. But they seem to find some confirmation in the effects of Germany's attempts to transfer Reparations payments in 1920 and 1921. The exchanges were forced up first, and only later were followed by general prices. In the interval, Germany must have lost heavily in terms of "real" values.

of its international payments has previously been in equilibrium, it must either increase the volume of the remittances it is currently making to foreign countries, or in some way decrease the volume it is currently receiving; or both. The process will go on until the country's current excess of credits over debits in the international account is equal to the sums which must be transmitted. How will these changes be brought about, and what will be their effects? To explain this, it is first necessary to say something of the relation between a country's holdings of foreign bills and the volume of its purchasing power.

The size of the banks' holdings of such bills,[1] at a given time, is itself the resultant of two sets of forces. On the one hand the banks are continually discounting bills, for exporters and for others who have acquired the right to receive foreign currencies. The making of the discounts increases the banks' holdings, and also increases the volume of their deposits. Or rather, deposits are increased in the first instance. Later, to the extent that they are drawn out in the form of cash, they will decline somewhat. But in any event the net effect of the discounts is to increase the *total volume of purchasing power in circulation* in the country — cash and deposits taken together — by the amount of the bills originally presented (less, of course, the discount charged). On the other hand, the banks are continually selling bills to importers, and to others who have payments to make abroad in foreign currencies. The sales decrease the banks' holdings, and they also decrease the volume of purchasing power in circulation in the country. If the bills are bought with checks on the selling banks, a corresponding volume of deposits is obviously wiped out. If they are bought with checks on other banks, the volume of purchasing power will decline in corresponding degree as soon as the inter-bank balances are liquidated. Finally, if they are bought with cash the money passes into the banks' reserves, and thus goes out of circulation.

---

[1] The bills may also, of course, be held by exchange dealers who are not bankers. But this possibility simply introduces an additional step into the analysis, without changing its character, and for the purposes of exposition can be disregarded. The exchange dealers must evidently draw their funds either from the banks or from the general monetary circulation.

These two sets of forces, of increase and of decrease, of course do not offset one another exactly; and the total volume of purchasing power in circulation (so far as it is governed by them) is never long constant except by accident. But in the absence of outside interference the relation between the demand and supply for foreign bills, and also the volume of purchasing power in circulation, follow paths which we may describe as "normal." The "normal" evolution is that which would appear if the only forces affecting the course of events were those recurrent and cyclical oscillations in each country, and those secular movements of general growth, which can be regarded as being of primarily domestic origin. The volume of purchasing power, and the size of the country's bill holdings, would then fluctuate in a manner which could be explained with substantial accuracy and even predicted, given adequate statistical data and technique. So also of the changing course of foreign trade itself. But the introduction of the "invisible" items into international exchange, especially capital movements, produces disturbances which are not regular or recurrent, and which therefore cannot be foreseen. Yet they are important. The use of the purely conceptual device of a "normal" development makes it possible to measure these disturbances in terms of their deviation from the normal, and to orient them on (conceptually) known points of reference; a possibility which itself justifies the partial fiction inherent in the idea of a "norm." [1]

To return now to the international borrowing operation, it is evident that such transactions are an example of precisely the sort of disturbances just spoken of. When the new securities are sold in the lending country, in return for its currency, the local agents of the borrowing country will go to the banks (or to other exchange dealers) and endeavor to buy up the desired quantity of

---

[1] The actual course of events, and actual data, of course never correspond exactly to the presumably "normal" situation. Unpredictable and non-recurring disturbances constantly intervene. There is hence ground for holding, as a general proposition, that the "norm" should not be employed at all in the sense of a point or curve or condition to which actual deviations tend to return, but rather in the sense suggested in the text — simply as an arbitrary point of mental reference, to provide a convenient conceptual measure of such deviations.

foreign bills. This new demand for bills will accelerate the rate at which the banks' holdings are depleted. But there has been no increase in the rate of supply, except in so far as it is temporarily increased by the drawing of finance bills, and the average size of the holdings will therefore fall.[1] Or rather, it will fall *relative* to the point at which it would normally have been, in the sense defined above. In absolute terms it may remain constant, or even rise. This relative fall, as we have just seen, will bring with it a corresponding relative decline in the volume of purchasing power in circulation — in bank deposits, or cash, or both.

Evidently the process, potentially at least, can go on until the market is stripped, and bills are sold to those having payments to make abroad as fast as they are bought from exporters and their like. The banks' current holdings would then fall to practically nothing. But in point of fact any such shortage of bills soon brings corrective forces into play, which in some measure check the decline. The increase in the demand leads to an increase in the supply. These corrective forces are of two principal sorts. One, essentially short-time in character, avails to adjust only rather small disturbances. The other continues to operate over longer periods, and in the face of larger maladjustments.

In the first place, the increase in the demand for bills will necessarily find expression in an advance in the prices offered for them. That is, the foreign-exchange rates will move in a sense "unfavorable" to the lending country.[2] This will in itself speed up the rate at which bills are supplied to the market. It will also encourage the drawing of finance bills, already commented on, and will in general stimulate speculative operations based on the expectation of a later return movement of the exchanges. Moreover, it will increase the number and quantity of things which the country can export, and decrease the number and quantity of those which it can import. Under stable monetary conditions, it

---

[1] The drawing of finance bills by the lending country may postpone this fall for a time, but cannot prevent it, since the loans involved must be repaid later.

[2] The "prices" of bills are a composite, chiefly, of discount rates and foreign exchange rates. But no change in discount rates is as yet supposed to have taken place. The rise in price can therefore be regarded as concentrated on the exchanges.

is true, the possible range of the exchange fluctuations is too narrow to have a really marked effect on the international movements of any commodities except gold and silver, but the effect on the movement of securities can evidently be very great. All of these expedients, however, afford a relief which is only temporary. In large part, their possibilities will soon be exhausted. If the disequilibrium in the balance of payments, which has resulted here from the flow of new investment, is enduring and of significant size, other offsets must be sought.

In the second place, the relative shortage of bills of exchange will embarrass at least certain of the bankers who have contracted to make payments abroad. Unable to purchase bills at what they regard as a reasonable price, they will then export gold. The movement will be independent of (though a consequence of) the flows directly induced by the mere position of the exchange rates. If protracted, the gold exports will have far-reaching effects. Time is required, however, for their appearance. The immediate quantitative importance of the gold movements with respect to the adjustment of the balance of payments itself is not very great, simply because the supply of gold available at a given time is ordinarily rather small.

In the third place, if the disturbance is on a large scale it is almost inevitable that discount rates will be forced up in the lending country. This will help to correct the balance of payments, not by increasing the supply of bills but by checking the demand, and if pushed far enough will lead to a counterflow. It will also induce the return of gold.

The rise in discount rates will be the result of two conditions. One is that tendency to a drain of gold which has just been examined; a drain which cannot be allowed to continue indefinitely without danger. The other is the effect of the diminution in the country's supply of purchasing power, produced by the decline in bill holdings. The decline, which we shall come to again in a moment, will cause some distress if it is protracted, and will create a demand for more bank credit to replace that part of the country's purchasing power which has (in effect) been exported. But to yield to these demands would be tantamount to inflating credit.

The physical volume of business in the country has not increased, and there is hence no legitimate excuse for an expansion of loans. The root of the difficulty lies not in the fact that the quantity of bank credit currently supplied is too small, but in the fact that a part of the purchasing power already in existence is being sent abroad. To resist this pressure, if it is on any significant scale, the banks will be compelled to raise their discount rates until such time as a new adjustment is reached. That this will in point of fact be done seems the more probable because, other things equal, international borrowing is especially attractive at times when discount rates are relatively low in the lending country.

3. The various correctives of the exchange market situation hitherto examined, however, are of limited effect, and will exhaust their influence comparatively soon. To account for the adjustment of a large and persisting disturbance, some other explanation must be sought. This explanation lies in the direct effects produced by the decline in the total volume of purchasing power itself.

The decline, to repeat, is the result of that relative or even absolute fall in the country's bill holdings to which, other things equal, the attempt to export capital leads. If it be assumed that the decline is large and enduring, a reaction upon prices is inevitable, although the process may take some time to work out — perhaps a number of months. The decline in purchasing power is in the first instance made at the expense of those who buy the new foreign securities. In virtue of their investments they have less purchasing power left available for domestic purposes, and will buy less. As the effects of this decrease spread, a marked depressing influence will be exerted on general prices, for there has been no corresponding decrease in the quantity of things offered for sale. It does not require a quantity-theory polemic to establish the validity of this conclusion. The change in prices *may* also be accelerated in so far as the metallic reserves and long-term security holdings of the banks have been diminished by the exchange-market situation, and in so far as discount rates have been raised. This depends on the position of the country at the time in the business cycle. The effect will be pronounced in the upper phase of the cycle, but in periods of depression may quite fail to appear.[1]

Two qualifications, however, are necessary. In the first place, the decline in prices need not be *absolute*. It will only be relative; relative, that is, to the levels which would "normally" have been attained. If it occurs near the peak of the business cycle, absolute prices will continue to move upward, but will rise less rapidly than they otherwise would. If it occurs in a time of crisis, on the other hand, the absolute decline in prices will be aggravated. In the second place, not all classes of prices will be affected in equal degree. Import prices are in the first instance fixed primarily in the world markets, and will therefore react comparatively little, if at all. Domestic prices, on the other hand, are largely free from this influence, and will feel the full effect of the depressing influence. Export prices, finally, occupy a middle position. The exports are sold in foreign markets, where prices have presumably not fallen; but they are manufactured from domestic materials, of which the costs are going down.

These differential price changes will have a marked effect on the commodity balance of trade. The effect may be of very wide extent, and provides the ultimate explanation of the adjustment of the balance of *payments* after other correctives have been proved inadequate. Export prices, though they have fallen, have not fallen as far as domestic prices, and the manufacture of articles for the export trade will become relatively profitable. This stimulates exportation, and consequently increases the supply of bills coming into the exchange market. On the other hand import prices have fallen very little. But the decline in domestic prices will make imported articles seem relatively expensive,[2] and will

---

[1] It may be remarked in passing that the attempt is sometimes made to explain capital movements themselves — the case here selected to illustrate the mechanism of the balance of payments — in terms of differences in the cyclical oscillations as between countries. The evidence available does not seem to support such a thesis, and *a priori* reasoning does not lead to any definitive conclusion. The question will be discussed in more detail in Appendix B, sect. 9.

[2] Corresponding though much more gradual changes will occur in the various groups of money wages. The exporting industries will become more prosperous than the general domestic average; the importing industries, and those dependent in any considerable degree on imported materials, less prosperous.

impose a check on importation. The demand for bills in the exchange market will therefore fall off.[1]

How far will the changes in the balance of trade go? Evidently as far as is necessary in order to restore the balance of international payments itself to equilibrium.[2] Suppose that the annual volume of new foreign investment (net) is five hundred million dollars. Then the balance of trade will shift until the country's exports have increased, relative to the volume of importation, by substantially the same sum of five hundred millions a year. To some extent, it is true, changes in other items will occur, but historically these have not been of great quantitative importance. For practical purposes, it is accurate to say that the balance of trade will alter until it can account for all or nearly all of the volume of new capital exportation. That is, it will alter until the capital movements are effected primarily in the form of commodity movements. Any smaller change than this in the balance of trade will leave the balance of payments still in disequilibrium. A further decline in the volume of purchasing power in circulation and in prices will then result, and another shift in the balance of trade will occur. Too large a change, on the other hand, will produce just the opposite results. Finally, it is evident that an alteration in the annual volume of foreign investment itself will lead to a corresponding adjustment in the balance of trade, although an interval of some length may be required for the process.

The validity of this general analysis is borne out, on the whole, surprisingly well, by such empirical data as are available. Con-

---

[1] In point of fact, of course, these changes in the balance of trade and in the bill market will be relative rather than absolute; relative, that is, to the changes which would *otherwise* have taken place.

[2] If a country is willing to pay the necessary price, in the form of high discount rates, abstention from currency inflation, falling prices and wages, and general business depression during the period of transition, there is virtually no limit on the size of the credit surplus which it can acquire in the international account. At least, there is no limit as far as its own situation is concerned. At a given time, the demand of foreign markets for its commodities and services is limited, but over longer periods this check can very largely be made to disappear.

The country's exportable surplus can even be greater than the current excess of production over the minimum consumption if it fails to make the necessary renewals in the productive equipment. But this is tantamount to an exportation of the equipment itself, and must eventually lead to total national prostration.

siderations of space make it seem advisable to place these data in an Appendix [1] rather than here, but the principal conclusions to which they lead can be summarized briefly. They are based on the history of the United States from 1866 to 1879, and of Canada from 1900 to 1913. The periods are ones in which both countries were borrowing heavily from Europe, although the American borrowing became unimportant after 1873. These are cases of capital *importation*, it is true, whereas the case hitherto borne in mind is that of capital *exportation*, but the one is (with essentially minor qualifications) simply the converse of the other.

If we take the *net* movement of capital to and from these countries, in each year, the following relationships are indicated with some definiteness. First, whenever the net import of capital exceeded the net import of "final" means of international payment (that is, when it exceeded the excess of imports of commodities and of all other items over the corresponding exports), a roughly equivalent increase in the volume of bank deposits took place. The situation meant that the supply of foreign bills was in excess of the demand for them (a demand created by the importation of non-capital items), and therefore that the volume of domestic purchasing power was being built up.[2] Of this volume, bank deposits are the most convenient index which the data available provide.[3] Whenever the net import of capital fell below the net

[1] Appendix B, especially sects. 1 and 2. The data are in large part annual only, and of course were influenced by other factors as well as by the capital movements. But explanations can be made of the principal discrepancies revealed, and the relationships indicated are sufficiently close to be regarded as significant.

The two studies from which the data referred to in the text have been taken are F. D. Graham, *International Trade under Depreciated Paper* (36 Quarterly Journal of Economics, 1922); and J. Viner, *Canada's Balance of International Indebtedness, 1900–1913* (Cambridge, 1924). The conclusions I have drawn from the data differ in a number of respects, however, from the ones reached by these writers.

[2] The importation of capital, to repeat, ordinarily increases the supply of bills of exchange sent to the capital-receiving country for rediscount. If this increased supply is not offset by a surplus demand, resulting from an excess of non-capital imports over non-capital exports, the bill holdings of the banks must evidently be increased also.

[3] Bank deposits are of course not an accurate index of the general volume of purchasing power in circulation for short periods, since the proportion between them

import of "final" means of payment, on the other hand, bank deposits declined. Here, the demand for bills exceeded the supply. Second, changes in bank deposits were accompanied by changes of the character that we would expect in the commodity balance of trade. An increase in deposits was later followed by an increase in the surplus of imports, a decline by a fall. The capital movement — bank deposit — balance of trade sequence, however, involved a lag that runs up to a year in length, so far as the data show. Finally, the changes in prices were more gradual, but also substantially those which would be anticipated.[1] Export prices rose relative to import prices, and domestic prices rose relative to both groups. These changes were in largest part the immediate instrument which brought about the necessary alterations in the trade balance.

It is of course true that these data, and the general reasoning which they have here been called upon to support, deal only with one particular form of disturbance in the balance of payments: namely, that which is created by the continued export or import of capital on a large scale. But precisely the same sort of analysis can be applied to the correction of any other sort of disturbance. The critical condition in a disequilibrium, the condition that reacts upon prices and the balance of trade, is not the fact that "too much" capital or "too many" commodities are being exported relative to the volume of importation (or vice versa). It is the fact that the relation between the demand for bills of exchange and their supply has altered, and that, in consequence, the total volume of purchasing power in circulation has been changed from that presumably "normal" level which at each given time it would otherwise have attained. The condition is generalized in character, and is usually not directly affected by the nature of the particular transactions in which it originates — whether move-

and money in circulation varies constantly. The data here used, however, are annual only. With respect to periods of a year or more in length, bank deposits are a sufficiently accurate index, for the fluctuations in the distribution of purchasing power between them and money in circulation tend to be smoothed over with respect to such periods.

[1] As were the movements of the various groups of wages, although the data are not very satisfactory here.

ments of commodities, of capital, or of the other "invisible" items.[1]

One further qualification must be made. The analysis of the relation between a change in the volume of internal purchasing power and the consequent change in the commodity balance of trade evidently rests on one major assumption. This is the assumption that an alteration in the general level of internal prices will carry the international group with it. If the international group entirely fails to react, no corrective influence on the course of foreign trade will be exerted. The analysis will then break down. But in point of fact this never happens, except momentarily.[2] The international group is always affected, to some extent at least, and the correction here postulated comes into play. It is true that it may not move as far as the general aggregate. In that event the national price levels of the different countries involved will draw apart. But while this divergence may retard the operation of the mechanisms of adjustment, it will not impair the validity of the general analysis itself.

4. The general conclusions to which we are therefore led, on the question of the maintenance of equilibrium in the balance of international payments, are as follows.[3]

When a disequilibrium occurs in the balance of payments, a

---

[1] The drawing of finance bills, however, and other forms of explicitly short-term international borrowing, provides an exception. A given movement in one direction in these cases is necessarily soon followed by an equal movement in the opposite direction.

[2] It will be remembered that a common gold standard is assumed here. When the trading countries are under inconvertible paper a movement of general prices in one of them will carry international prices with it, and yet may produce no other effect than a displacement of the foreign exchange rates. If the exchanges move exactly with prices, no corrective whatsoever will appear. These questions, however, are reserved for the next chapter.

[3] The general type of analysis presented in the preceding section was suggested by the writer in two chapters contributed to a recent study by the National Industrial Conference Board, *The Inter-Ally Debts and the United States* (New York, 1925): chs. 5 and 6.

Professor F. D. Graham has also reached essentially similar conclusions as to final results, in an article published after these pages were first written: *Germany's Capacity to Pay and the Reparation Plan* (*American Economic Review*, 1925). He says nothing, however, of the *intermediary* mechanisms and relationships stressed here.

series of forces are successively called into play which exert a corrective influence, and which will eventually restore equilibrium no matter how severe the initial disturbance. In the first instance, the disturbance leads to a movement of the foreign exchanges. If it is small and temporary, this adjustment alone may suffice, for it will accelerate or retard the rate at which bills of exchange are currently offered in the market. If that is inadequate, gold will flow; and discount rates, especially in the gold-exporting country, will be affected. If even this fails to correct the situation, finally, an alteration will take place in the underlying conditions that govern the general course of international exchange itself. The volume of purchasing power in circulation in the creditor country will be built up, in consequence of the increase in the banks' holdings of bills. In the other country it will be reduced, through the decline there in bill holdings. These changes, in turn, will operate upon the corresponding general price levels. The latter effect is often, though not always, strengthened by alterations in the discount rates. The movements in prices will then influence the commodity balance of trade, in ways long familiar, and will continue to do so until the change in the commodity trade has become great enough to offset and correct the original disturbance in the balance of international payments.

In a word, temporary disturbances are adjusted by essentially immediate and short-time influences, but a large and enduring disturbance, such as is created by the exportation of capital, can be corrected only through an alteration in the commodity balance of trade itself. This is a slower process, and will carry over into the so-called long-time period. There is no sharp and necessary distinction, however, between the two processes. They go on more or less concurrently, and their effects are intertwined. When the attempt is made to verify them in terms of concrete empirical data, also, it must be borne in mind that the changes involved are all *relative*, not absolute. They are to be measured, that is, in terms of variations from some sort of "normal" development of events, in which the international situation plays no significant and controlling part.

It is evident that these propositions have a fundamental anal-

ogy to the classical theory [1] of international adjustments, an
analogy resting on the hypothesis and conclusion that the balance
of payments is in some way self-equilibrating. But the classical
theory took little account of what have here been described as the
short-time influences, except for the rather limited effect of exchange rate fluctuations on commodity movements. It also gave
a quite different description of the way in which price movements
and changes in the balance of trade are brought about. The process was made to turn on the asserted fact that disturbances in the
balance of payments give rise to gold flows, and that these in turn
exercise a direct influence upon prices. Moreover, it was usually ·
implied that the changes in question take place rather quickly.
The doctrine which has been set up here, on the other hand, regards gold flows as an essentially short-run phenomenon, usually
of temporary importance alone. It bases its more long-run conclusions on the effects which significant changes in the relation
between the demand and supply of *bills of exchange* produce upon
the total volume of purchasing power in circulation. It rejoins
the classical line of analysis only at the point where general price
changes begin to appear.

5. The preceding sections have been concerned in the first instance with the balance of international payments alone, and have
considered price movements only in their relation to the correction of disequilibria originating in this general balance. It now
remains to say something of the reverse process: of the connection that runs *from* prices *to* the balance of payments. This leads
back to the problems of the last chapter, and will enable us to
complete the tentative conclusions there reached.

Suppose that a substantial credit expansion takes place in one
of two trading countries, while conditions in the other country remain unchanged. Prices in the first country will rise, and will no
longer be in line with those in the other. What will happen? Evidently the commodity importation of the first country will be
increased, and its exportation checked. Its international payments will therefore cease to balance. The processes already dis-

---

[1] That is, to the doctrine of Thornton and Mill, but not at all points to that of
Ricardo. The differences have been elaborated at sufficient length elsewhere.

Surely the external value would fall more
than the internal and the reverse of what
Angell suggests would result. As in any
county which inflated to balance its budget after 1918

cussed will then be set into motion. The country's holdings of bills of foreign exchange will be diminished, the total volume of purchasing power in circulation will fall, prices will decline, the course of foreign trade will be affected, and the balance of payments will move back towards equilibrium. Apparently, at least, the series of changes will continue until prices at large in the one country and the other are restored to their previous relationship.

Allowance being made for the somewhat unreal rigidity and exactness of this analysis, introduced for the sake of brief exposition, we thus seem to be led to the conclusion that the movements of general prices in different countries are kept in a high degree of intimacy, through the direct effects of the maintenance of equilibrium in the balance of international payments. But this conclusion is in point of fact true only if one important condition exists: namely, if the place of "international" prices in the various national price structures does not change, or at least changes equally in different countries. The organic connection between each pair of these structures is at bottom found only in the prices that are common to both of them. Suppose that the place of the international group of prices can alter easily, and can alter more in one country than in another. Then it is evident that a rise in the general price level in one country need not carry the international prices of other countries with it, and may therefore fail to set up forces tending to keep the level in harmony with those elsewhere. From the international point of view, the net effect of the disturbance will simply be a decline in the prices of international commodities *relative* to prices at large, in the country concerned, or else a rise in the other countries.

But the empirical evidence submitted in the preceding chapter, although not entirely conclusive, strongly indicates that at least the major movements of prices in the leading countries actually do keep fairly well together. As already suggested, it must then follow that the position of the international group of prices in the national structures does not change, except temporarily and in short periods, or else changes in equal degree in each of them; and that the domestic groups similarly follow roughly parallel courses. The explanation of the relationships between these structures is therefore substantially that outlined a page or two above. It runs in terms of the effect of differences in their movements upon the balance of payments.

The relationship, however, is probably weak and often ineffective in the short-time period. An interval is required before general price changes can influence the balance of trade materially, and a further interval before the resulting disturbances in the balance of payments will react upon prices themselves. How long this process takes can hardly be determined in advance of the collection of adequate data for a number of countries. But a lag in the machinery of correction will certainly develop, and may, to judge from the evidence available, be as great as a year or more in length. The appearance of any intimate correlation in the very short-time fluctuations of prices must assuredly be due either to some peculiarity in the case selected, or to the interdependence of the price indices used.[1] In periods of longer duration, on the other hand, the explanation here advanced evidently makes it entirely possible to account for such relationships as the empirical data show to exist. Before the war, the secular movements of prices in certain leading countries revealed a very high degree of correlation. The cyclical oscillations also revealed one which was extremely significant, if not quite so definitely established. Since the war, on the other hand, the relationships have been much less close. As stable conditions are restored, however, the discrepancies are becoming less pronounced, and in one or two countries have largely disappeared. But the position of international prices in certain of the national structures has very clearly altered. It is therefore probable that although the direction and magnitude of fluctuation in the price indices of these countries will soon coincide fairly well (in the comparatively long-run sense), their *absolute levels* will not be equal until the indices themselves are readjusted to a base placed in the post-war period.

6. The general problem of the maintenance of equilibrium in the balance of international payments thus presents two principal aspects. One involves the correction of those disturbances that originate in the balance of payments itself. If the disturbances

[1] See ch. xv, sect. 6, above.

are comparatively small, the operation of essentially short-time forces will suffice. If they are large and enduring, however, they can be completely corrected only through the effects of changes in the general level of prices. These price changes are evidently themselves *results* of the international situation. The other involves the correction of discrepancies between the movements of general prices in different countries. Here the adjustment can be effected only through changes in the balance of international payments. The balance then in turn becomes a resultant.

On both of these questions we have reached conclusions which are at bottom in harmony with the teachings of the classical theory as it left Mill's hands, if not always as it left Ricardo's. But it has been necessary to alter the *content* of the classical theory quite radically, and to make it more explicit in certain directions. The principal modifications involved are two in number.

The first turns on the question of the relation between general prices in different countries. This relation can be interpreted in either of two senses. It can be taken as meaning that prices are *equalized* — that the price of an article in one currency is equivalent to its price in another, times the current rate of foreign exchange. Such an equalization, however, we found to be true of only a very limited range of commodities. This conclusion is entirely in harmony with the classical view. Indeed, the classical writers usually denied the existence of such an equalization at all, in any very exact sense. Or the relation can be taken as meaning that, irrespective of the position of particular prices, the movements of national prices *as a whole* are harmonious: that the various general price indices, for example, tend to agree in their oscillations. The empirical evidence indicates that this view is substantially correct, as applied to the larger and more enduring changes. The secular trends, and most of the cyclical fluctuations, seem to correspond very closely as between the leading countries, though a pronounced lag often appears, if not usually. The short-time movements, however, are much less clearly related, and it is not easy to show on *a priori* grounds why they should be. The coincidence of the larger oscillations, on the other hand, can be accounted for in terms of the effects of changes in the volume of purchasing power and in general prices.

It is not easy to find these last conclusions explicitly stated in the classical theory. They are entirely consistent with that theory, and indeed are latent in it, but they were not worked out in any such detail. Ricardo, for example, spoke of "redundancies" of the currency and of their correction, but did not further define the relation between those general price changes by which such redundancies must actually be measured.[1]

The second modification required in the classical doctrine is more fundamental. We have agreed that the equilibrium of the balance of payments is self-restoring, but it has been necessary to work out a quite different explanation of the intermediary mechanisms involved. The essential feature of the older analysis of mechanisms lies in the rôle assigned to specie flows. These flows were regarded as both certain to occur, and as being fairly rapid in their effects. Here, on the contrary, they have been relegated to a minor place. In the short-time period they are only one of a number of possible correctives, and exert their principal influence on discount rates, while in the long-time period they do not have much significance. The ultimate key to the maintenance of equilibrium in the balance of payments in the face of enduring disturbances, and the key to the problem of international equilibrium at large, must be sought in another direction. It lies in the effects that a persisting change in the relation between the demand and supply of bills of foreign exchange produces upon the volume of purchasing power in circulation, and through it upon the general level of prices.

The analysis to this point has rested on the assumption that the countries concerned maintained common metallic standards of money. The presence of dissimilar and depreciating currencies, however, introduces problems of quite another order, and makes it impossible to speak of an international "equilibrium" in any very exact sense. To these problems we shall now turn.

---

[1] That is, taking his position as a whole. At certain points he gave what seem to be more explicit statements, only to contradict them or otherwise invalidate them somewhere else. (See ch. iii, sects. 3 and 5, above.)

Mill's doctrines here, designedly patterned after Ricardo, are similarly incomplete, and indeed Mill does not seem to have perceived the nature of the problem very clearly. (See ch. iv, sect. 3, above.)

CHAPTER XVII

DISSIMILAR CURRENCIES AND THE EFFECTS OF DEPRECIATION

1. When the countries participating in international trade maintain similar metallic standards, and permit free coinage, the possible disturbances in the currency and in the exchanges are small, and their effects are comparatively unimportant. It is true that the various national price aggregates may move in different degrees, and even in different directions. But no departure from the monetary standard is involved in such divergences, and they usually prove self-corrective after a time. When the standards are dissimilar, on the other hand, currency and foreign exchange disturbances are always significant, and often come to dominate the whole course of the international exchange itself. Although many of the mechanisms appearing under a common metallic standard continue in operation, the link connecting the several price systems is no longer rigid. The oscillations of the ratios of exchange between currencies cease to be held within definite limits, unless momentarily, and may fluctuate very widely. In consequence, the relationships that would otherwise appear are often entirely broken, and are always distorted. The character of the mechanisms involved is also altered in some degree, and in extreme cases becomes entirely different.

There are two principal types of monetary dissimilarity. First, one of the countries engaged in trade may be under a gold standard, and one under silver. Second, one or both countries may be under inconvertible paper. Of these types the first has been much the less important in the last ten years, and can be dismissed rather briefly. The second, which leads into the extraordinary conditions produced by the war, will require more detailed study.

2. At any one time, the character of the trade between a gold-standard and a silver-standard country is like that between countries in which the metallic standard is the same. Granted free coinage, a true par of exchange will appear, and the familiar machinery of the specie points on either side of it is operative. The peculiarity of the case develops only when the gold-silver ratio itself alters. This alteration compels the exchange rates to move permanently away from the previous parity, and entails a more or less protracted series of disturbances in the previous price relationships. The causes of such alterations, and the precise character of the effects that they produce, have been matters of controversy ever since the fall in the gold value of silver began to be a matter for general concern, some fifty years ago.

The common explanation of the fall in the value of silver dwells primarily on the depressing effects of the numerous demonetizations witnessed after 1870. Indeed, without much attempt at a more precise definition of terms, the fall is often cited as an example of the working of the "law" of demand and supply. The difficulty with stopping here, however, is that under this "law" the fall should have taken place once for all (barring the effects of improvements in the actual processes of production), instead of being more or less continuous. Moreover, it might well have been followed by a rise, in consequence of the diminution in current production. The question of why the demonetizations themselves occurred also remains unanswered.

An alternative explanation has been advanced recently by Professor Nogaro.[1] Nogaro accounts for the movements of the gold-silver ratio in the first three quarters of the nineteenth century in terms of the balance of payments between the gold-standard countries, especially England, on the one hand; and the silver-standard countries, largely in the Far East, on the other. The bimetallic countries, of whom France was the chief, served during this period as an intermediary reservoir, — or, more accurately, as a currency-exchange bureau. Until 1873 the bimetallic countries allowed free coinage of both metals. It therefore followed that whenever England, for example, needed silver to remit to India, she had only to send gold to France and exchange it for French silver, while India used her silver to purchase French gold for the settlement of balances due England. Until after the mid-

---

[1] B. Nogaro, *La Monnaie* (Paris, 1924), especially pp. 34, 44–46.

dle of the century, Professor Nogaro finds, the sums thus due and receivable came out substantially equal. No large permanent transfers in either direction were necessary. But about 1867 the international situation began to turn definitely against the silver countries, taken as a whole,[1] and the price of silver fell off. When the bimetallic countries successively suspended the *free* coinage of silver, after 1873, the fall became permanent, for there was no longer any center in which unlimited quantities of silver could be exchanged for gold at a fixed price. This second phenomenon, the suspension of free coinage, is often asserted to have been the chief cause of the fall of silver itself. But Nogaro declares that it was distinct from the latter, and was subsequent to it. It merely permitted forces already at work to find unrestricted expression in the gold-silver ratio, although it undoubtedly increased their influence.

The truth of the case probably lies somewhere between these two interpretations. One difficulty in the first view has already been pointed out. The objection to Professor Nogaro's position is that the net excess of payments due from the silver-standard to the gold-standard countries was in all likelihood not *big* enough, except for brief periods, to be a sufficient explanation in itself alone of the fall in the gold value of silver. But that it played an important part — granting the fact of its existence [2] — seems certain.

In general terms, the fall was probably accounted for by the increase in the production of silver (relative to gold), on the one hand, and on the other by the fact that improvements in monetary and banking technique steadily diminished the demand for so cumbrous a currency. The various demonetizations merely emphasized, and for the time being increased, a fall which was in any event inevitable.[3] That they came just when they did, rather

---

[1] Especially for India. Nogaro points out that the termination of the Civil War relieved the abnormal demand placed upon India for cotton, thus greatly diminishing the volume of her exportation. At the same time she had to pay considerable sums as interest and profits on the investments in cotton plantations made with her, during the Civil War, by England and other European countries.

[2] It is hardly possible to reconstruct the actual balances now. Professor Nogaro does not himself give consecutive data.

[3] Unless the leading countries had all gone over to full bimetallism.

than sooner or later, is explained partly by the international balance of payments situation, which Nogaro stresses, and partly by the great silver discoveries of the 1870's in the United States. Once the movement toward the gold standard was well under way the psychological and perhaps the political pressure to join in it, to which the remaining bimetallic countries were subjected, was undoubtedly great.

The position of silver since 1914 is a study in itself, and cannot be entered into here. Taken as a whole, however, the short-time movements in the gold-silver ratio have been dominated by the changing volume of remittances which it has been necessary to make to the Far East — that is, by the balance of international payments. Here the principal *fluctuations* in the gold-silver ratio have been traceable to the side of demand rather than of supply, and to demands for international-payment purposes rather than for monetary purposes. But the rise in the general *level* of this ratio has been due chiefly to the depreciation, in terms of commodities, of gold itself.

The question of the effects of a change in the value of silver relative to gold is less debated, and less difficult. If the levels of prices and of costs of production in the silver-standard country move with changes in the gold-silver ratio, all at the same time and in equal degree, then the course of international exchange will not be affected.[1] But this is almost certain not to occur. A lag of some sort will develop, and perhaps an enduring discrepancy.

International prices may evidently lag behind the foreign exchanges. Except temporarily, this is improbable with respect to the actively traded staples, but with respect to the commodities in which competition is less keen the lag is very likely to develop. In the latter case, the discrepancy will not disappear unless it is great enough to overcome the forces originally making for international inequality in the prices of such articles. If it endures, however, the course of trade will still not be necessarily affected. The only immediate result will be an increase or a decrease in the profits accruing to the exporters and importers concerned, in the

---

[1] The same result will appear if precisely the opposite movements take place in the gold-standard country.

one country or the other.[1] The commoner and more important lag, however, is that of money costs of production behind *both* international prices and the exchanges. If the latter rise more rapidly, for example, commodity exportation will evidently be stimulated by the increased spread between prices and costs, while importation will be checked. This condition will continue until the gradual diffusion of the relative depreciation of silver, within the silver country, has brought the aggregate of prices and costs there up to the new level. The process of adjustment is by no means necessarily rapid.

At the same time, international prices in the gold countries will feel a depressing influence in response to the price movements in the silver countries.[2] The fall of prices in the gold countries may even become generalized, and will then cause widespread distress. This is precisely what happened in Europe toward the close of the nineteenth century, especially in the last decade. The extent to which such a decline in the gold-silver ratio actually causes gold prices to fall, or silver prices to rise, depends on the trading strength of the respective dealers. If the silver country is the chief market or chief source of supply for the gold country, prices in the latter will fall considerably. There is some evidence to show that, due to such conditions, the depreciation of silver in the forty years before the war caused the prices of the articles exchanged with silver countries to move to a permanently lower level, in the gold-country price structures.

One other observation may be added here: namely, that in a generalized analysis much more importance must be assigned to flows of silver than to flows of gold. The changes in the value of silver relative to commodities at large, in which such flows ultimately originate, have been much greater historically than the

---

[1] Depending on which currency the goods are invoiced in. If the silver-country exports and imports are invoiced in the gold currency, for example, its exporters will gain by a declining gold value of silver (a "depreciation"), and its importers will lose. If invoiced in silver, the *foreign* exporter *loses*, and the foreign importer gains. The exchange risk, that is, is borne by the country which invoices in the other currency.

[2] The gold-country imports will increase, and their exports decline. This is, of course, the reverse of the changes in the silver countries.

changes in the value of gold, and the net flows themselves have been correspondingly larger. The direct effect upon prices has therefore also been more marked, because the proportion that the silver movements bore to the total currency supply of the countries concerned has been higher. The objections made in the previous chapter to the classical price-specie flow doctrine lose a considerable part of their force when they are taken as applied to at least the larger movements of silver that have actually occurred in the past. On the other hand, however, the silver flow is not infrequently accompanied by a parallel and uncorrected movement of capital. A decline in the value of silver causes the value of all obligations payable in that metal to fall in terms of gold. The foreign (and often the domestic) holders of such obligations then seek to liquidate them as quickly as possible, lest a still greater fall appear. A "flight from the currency" develops, on a moderate scale, and the disturbances arising from the international payment situation give way to those created by incipient depreciation.[1] These consequences, of course, do not accompany the flow of gold except as the prelude to a régime of inconvertibility.

3. The other type of monetary dissimilarity is that appearing when one or more of the trading countries is under inconvertible paper. Before 1914 this situation was regarded as something of an economic curiosity, and as being an evidence, in modern times, of weak government. But during and after the war it became so nearly universal that discussions of the conditions prevailing under a common gold standard have in turn seemed, until recently, almost academic.

It is not the fact of inconvertibility itself, however, that gives international exchange under such conditions its peculiar character. It is the fact of instability. There are at least two instances, and probably more, in which the currency quotation was kept within what were substantially specie points over considerable periods, yet at levels very much below the par value, and in the

---

[1] Very much this sort of thing appeared repeatedly in Spain, for example, in the years before and after 1900. See the brief account in ch. xi, sect. 4, and in ch. xiii, sect. 4, above; also the references at each point.

face of real inconvertibility. This occurred several times in Russia in the second half of the nineteenth century, and towards its close in Austria-Hungary.[1] For foreign-exchange purposes the currency was then equivalent to gold, and no important disturbance appeared. In the great majority of cases, however, and especially since 1914, the paper currencies have been not only inconvertible but also more or less violently fluctuating in value. These fluctuations have disrupted the course of international exchange, have sometimes brought it to a standstill, and have usually caused it to take on a quite new aspect.

The history of the paper-currency depreciations witnessed before the war need not be recapitulated here, although the lessons and conclusions to which they point should be borne in mind. An account of a number of them has been given in earlier chapters of the present volume. Instead, we shall turn at once to the events of the past ten years, especially since 1918.

Even the most cursory examination of recent history shows that the precise nature of the effects produced by a fluctuating paper currency depends very largely on whether the currency and the exchanges are moving upward or downward, and on the rapidity with which the change is taking place. The general analysis of the situation produced by monetary dissimilarity must therefore give way, in the first instance, to a study of the successive phases of depreciation and of their characteristics. The relationships and apparent "causations" involved in one phase are frequently entirely unlike those appearing in another. The experience of Europe since the war suggests that these phases are some four in number: moderate depreciation, severe depreciation, ex-

---

[1] Through the purchase and sale of bills of exchange by the government or the central banks. The operation was strictly analogous to the *method* by which the more familiar gold-exchange standard is maintained. But the base was not gold: it was *foreign currency units*. The power to acquire gold in foreign centers at a virtually fixed price was an incidental result, but in no sense essential to the working of the (informal) exchange control. The statement in the text above, that the currencies were inconvertible, is literally and legally correct.

The control remained effective as long as there was no general distrust of the currencies either at home or abroad, except for short intervals, and hence no tendency to a cumulative bear movement against them. But whenever these conditions began to appear, it inevitably broke down.

treme depreciation and collapse, and finally — a stage which may happily intervene at any point in the cycle — recovery and stabilization. England provides an example of the first phase, France of the second, Germany and Austria of the third, and the last has now appeared in all of the countries named except France. The other countries of the world can easily be assigned to their proper positions in the grouping.

It is not proposed to undertake here a complete statistical or even descriptive study of any one of these phases. The labor involved is enormous, and by no means all of the data are as yet accessible. But it is possible to reach several quite definite conclusions, for which a reasonable amount of statistical corroboration can be provided.[1]

4. The origin of the world's recent currency difficulties has lain in one thing, and only one: the imperative need of the belligerent governments for far greater sums of money than it was within the capacity of taxation to yield. From this all else followed as night follows day. The issuing of paper currency, increasing taxation, the floating of internal and external loans, were but different aspects of the same central phenomenon. Similarly, the permanent correction of currency and exchange depreciation has proved to be possible only after budgetary equilibrium had at last been restored.

Yet the depreciation directly traceable to government finance may only be the first stage. There is a second stage, from which all but a few countries have been spared, but which is far worse. It appears when the great majority of people, at home and abroad, have completely lost confidence in the national currency and the national finances. The bear movement then grows rapidly, soon becomes viciously cumulative, and can apparently be stopped only by a resort to outside assistance in one form or another. The action of the government here ceases to be a significant factor in the situation, for its printing presses literally cannot keep up with the rise in prices. It is speculation, in the widest sense of the term, which is dominant.

---

[1] A good many of the relevant facts have already been presented as an incident to the discussions, in other chapters, of recent theories. See especially chs. vii and xi.

Of the first stage, a depreciation which remained moderate and which is explained in the first instance by the government's need for funds, an illustration is afforded by England. Even a cursory examination of the data, however, shows that the actual sequence of events did not run *directly* from government finance to prices and the exchanges.[1] Another element was injected, and one which dominated the surface course of events in the critical period if not their underlying character. This element was the inflation and contraction of private credit.

Certain features in the progress of the English depreciation are shown in Chart I.[2] It is quite evident that the sequence of events at the turning point, in 1920, was exchanges — prices — money, not the reverse. Exchange rates reached their peak in February, 1920, prices two months later,[3] and the note circulation not until July. (The apparent note-circulation peak of December simply reflects the end-of-the-year settlements, and is not significant.) Thereafter all three fell rapidly, though the exchanges subsequently rose again. But how account for the initial improvement in the exchanges themselves?

The answer is not to be found in Government borrowing, at least in so far as its operations at the Bank of England are concerned. Public deposits reached their peak in March of 1920, not in February, and the Bank's holdings of Government securities not until June. The answer lies, rather, in the movements of *private* borrowing. Private deposits at the Bank [4] reached their

[1] The data used here, for constructing the charts presented below and for other purposes, are either taken directly or computed from the compilation in the U. S. Senate Commission of Gold and Silver Inquiry report, entitled *Foreign Exchange and Currency Investigation* (Washington, 1925), Serial 9, vol. 1. The figures used in constructing the charts will be found in Appendix C, below, but it has not seemed worth while to present the others here. They are perfectly accessible.

[2] The data are given in Appendix C, Table I.

[3] The fact that the exchanges fell so much less than prices is explained by the contemporary movements in American prices. The exchanges are quoted in terms of the dollar, and when allowance is made for the American price fluctuations most of the discrepancy disappears. See Chart II, below, which shows the magnitudes of the exchange oscillations to have been nearly the same as those of the price *parities*.

[4] Monthly figures for other London banks are not available, in compiled form, until 1921.

highest point in December of 1919 (partly a seasonal influence), and another peak in February, 1920. This was the result of the post-war boom and inflation, seen in every country. But they then declined prodigiously,[1] in consequence of the severe advance in the Bank rate, and with two exceptions never again rose to anything like the same level.

The correction of the exchanges coincided with this fall in private deposits at the Bank, and is explained by it. *In the first instance*, the improvement in the exchanges and prices and the note circulation were therefore entirely due to the rigorous contraction of private credit which the Bank enforced.

But it requires no demonstration that this explanation lies only on the surface, is only the immediate one. If the Government had then proved unable to balance its budget — what happened, as we shall see, in France — it would necessarily have had to resort to new inflation, either by note issue or by borrowing. Prices and the exchanges must inevitably have reacted, and the process of depreciation would have begun again. The underlying reason for the British currency restoration, the condition that made it possible, is therefore to be found in the fact that the budget was definitely restored to equilibrium after 1920, and that the threat of further inflation was thus definitely removed. That the exchange recovery came just when it did was due to the contemporary deflation of private credit, but without the fundamental control exerted by budget equilibrium the recovery could only have been temporary. The exchanges would have depreciated again, and prices would have followed. Although prices are less sensitive than the exchanges when the depreciation is only moderate, they too reflect quite accurately the current degree of general confidence.

Evidently no strictly mechanical explanation will account for these changes. It is totally impossible, for example, to pass from the degree of credit contraction, whether private or public, to the degree of exchange improvement, or from exchange improvement to prices. As can be seen clearly from Chart I, the magnitudes involved are entirely dissimilar. It is true that a rough quantita-

---

[1] In March, 1920, to 60 per cent of the February figure.

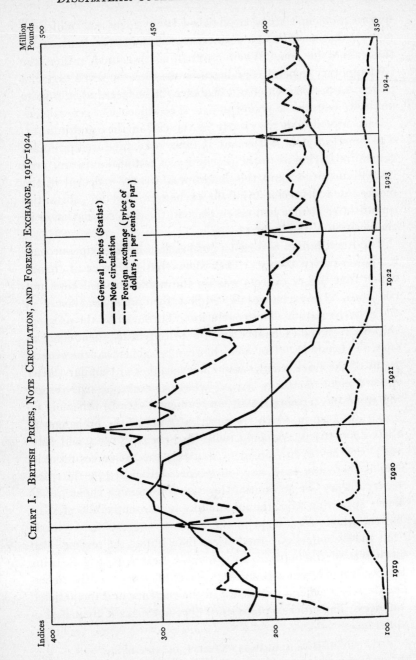

CHART I. BRITISH PRICES, NOTE CIRCULATION, AND FOREIGN EXCHANGE, 1919–1924

——— General prices (Statist)
– – – Note circulation
–·–·– Foreign exchange (price of dollars, in per cents of par)

tive relationship can be established between prices, credit and note circulation, although very loosely, but for the exchanges even this cannot be done. Their fluctuations measured, rather, the contemporary general confidence in the Government's financial policy: at first in its ability to balance the budget, and later in its ability to restore the pound to par. The influence of general confidence was also shown clearly at the end of 1923 and in 1924. The American debt settlement of June, 1923, produced profound general misgiving as to the possibility of restoration in any very immediate future, and this doubt was at once reflected in the marked new depreciation of the exchanges. Yet no substantial quantitative change had taken place in the note circulation or in the position of the budget.

The English data also cast a good deal of light on the purchasing-power-parity theory. They show that the order of change which that theory expects was on the whole reversed here, not confirmed. The exchanges moved first, then prices, and last of all the note circulation. This conclusion is borne out by the relationship between the exchanges and the price parities themselves, as shown in Chart II.[1] The most that can be said is that the general paths of the price parities and the exchanges are similar. After the first eight months of 1919 — when the exchanges were reacting from the termination of government control — there is no important case in which the parities preceded the exchanges in their fluctuations, and only twice (in February, 1920, and July, 1921) do they even coincide. As a rule the exchanges precede. Nor is there any easy way, on grounds recognized by the price-parity theory, of accounting for the considerable difference in levels appearing from the middle of 1922 to the middle of 1924. On the whole, the weight of the evidence suggests more clearly that the exchanges governed prices than it does the reverse. But both sets of fluctuations are probably best regarded as being simply two different aspects of a central phenomenon, the changing degree of general confidence in the currency and the national finances. The order of precedence does not make a great deal of difference.

[1] The data are given in Appendix C, Table I, and are computed from the U. S. Senate *Foreign Exchange and Currency Investigation* (cited above).

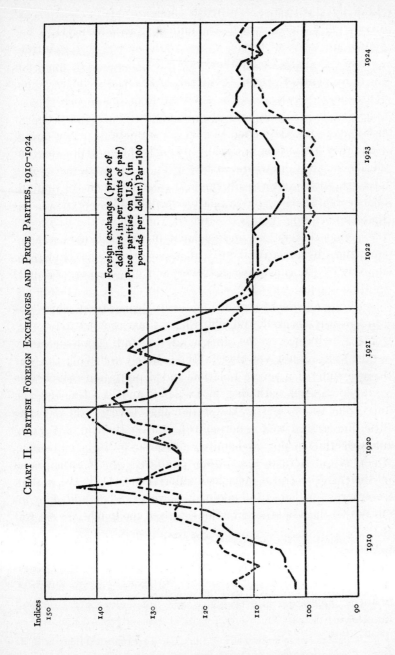

CHART II. BRITISH FOREIGN EXCHANGES AND PRICE PARITIES, 1919–1924

Indices

Foreign exchange (price of
dollars, in per cents of par)
Price parities on U.S. (in
pounds per dollar.) Par=100

Finally, the course of British foreign trade presents some interesting features which are indicated in Chart III.[1] The figures are for total money values (data on physical quantities were not available), and allowance must therefore be made for the movements of prices. It is clear, however, that in the period of exchange depreciation the total value of the British exports increased more rapidly than that of imports, and continued their rise longer.[2] In the period of severe contraction, to the end of 1921, they *declined* more rapidly. This is substantially the conclusion reached elsewhere with respect to the trade between a silver-standard and a gold-standard country: namely, that exchange depreciation gives a relative stimulus to exportation, and that appreciation retards it. Indeed, throughout the balance of the period the gradual improvement in the exchanges was accompanied by a relative increase in importation. The changes are too small to be conclusive, however, and may well be explained in other ways.[3]

5. England offers a case of a moderate depreciation, which was courageously checked, and which has at last been entirely overcome. In France, on the other hand — as in Belgium and Italy — the story is not yet closed. Immediately following the war France suffered a severe inflation and depreciation, which was contemporaneous with that in England, and like England she faced the task of currency restoration aggressively. But after the situation seemed well under control — after the end of 1921 — the Government proved definitely unable to balance the budget. In default of German Reparations payments, and in anticipation of their later receipt, France had undertaken to begin the work of reconstruction herself. This load, however, when added to increased outlays in other directions, proved too much. Resort was

[1] The data are given in Appendix C, Table I, and are copied from the U. S. *Foreign Exchange and Currency Investigation* (cited above).

[2] With allowance for price changes, the "real" value of exports fell off, but the real value of the imports fell still farther. It has not seemed worth while to make the long computations necessary to show this graphically.

[3] Such as the decline in productive capacity consequent on severe business depression, and the relatively greater inability of domestic production to meet domestic needs.

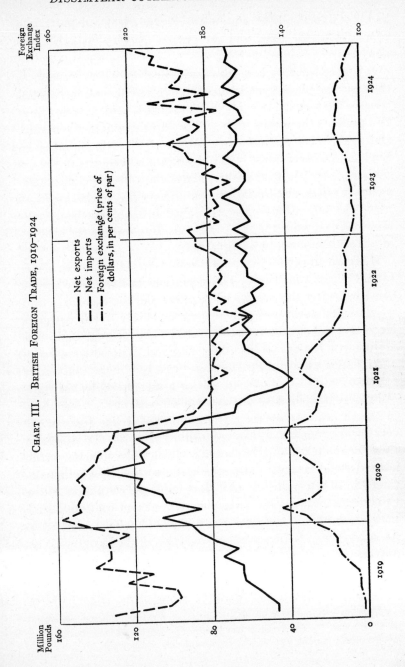

CHART III. BRITISH FOREIGN TRADE, 1919-1924

——— Net exports
— — — Net imports
—·—·— Foreign exchange (price of
dollars, in per cents of par)

had to still further borrowing, a good deal of which was apparently concealed at the time, and the process of depreciation was renewed.

It is even less easy here than in the English case to account for the resulting phenomena in quantitative and directly mechanical terms. The course of events in France, as is evident from Chart IV,[1] presents three chief phases. They are depreciation, recovery, and again more gradual depreciation. Unlike the situation in England, however, most of the significant movements of the exchanges *follow*, instead of preceding, the corresponding movements of prices, and the latter seem to have played the dominant rôle. The only exceptions are the peak in 1920 and the fluctuations of 1924, when the two coincided. But how are the changes in prices themselves to be explained?

It is clear from the chart that the note circulation, taken alone, cannot account for them. The alterations in its volume always came well after the alterations in prices and the exchanges, and were results, not causes. They operated chiefly to support price levels that had already been established. The explanation, rather, is similar to the one advanced for England. The post-war boom and inflation were in the first instance checked by the contraction of *private* credit, in consequence of pressure applied by the Bank of France. The Bank's [2] private deposits were at their maximum in March, 1920. They then fell rapidly, the decline being 20 per cent in five months. Prices reached a peak a month later, and then likewise fell, as did the exchanges (which here followed prices, instead of moving first). Minor oscillations aside, this decline continued until the spring of 1923. But the Bank's advances to the Government did not fall on any important and continued scale until much later — not until the middle of the next year, 1921. As in England, the immediate explanation of the recovery therefore lay in the deflation of private credit, not of Government credit. On the other hand, however, the deflation of private credit could not have exerted a more than temporary corrective

---

[1] The data are given in Appendix C, Table II, and are copied or computed from the U. S. Senate *Foreign Exchange and Currency Investigation* (cited above).

[2] Combined monthly data for the other banks are not available.

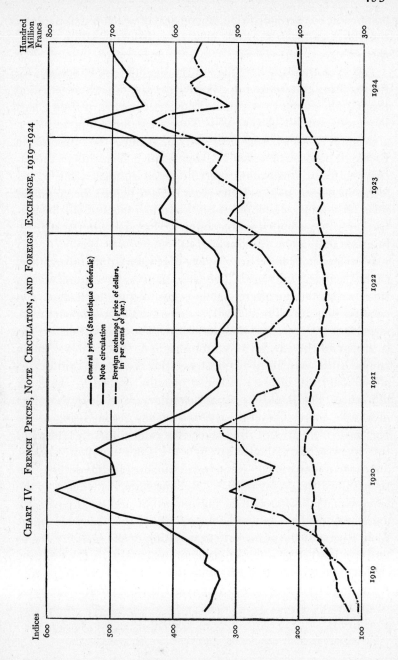

CHART IV. FRENCH PRICES, NOTE CIRCULATION, AND FOREIGN EXCHANGE, 1919–1924

influence if it had not been generally expected that the budget would be balanced. It is true that an actual equilibrium was not then achieved, but at that time — in the latter part of 1920 and in 1921 — equilibrium seemed not far distant. Government borrowing was diminishing, and the budget deficit growing less. Had this expectation not existed a general bear movement must have developed, in anticipation of the effects of renewed inflation.

The improvement continued for a year and a half, but in the spring of 1922 a new depreciation began. This cannot be explained by the movement of private credit, however, for the volume of private credit continued to decline until near the end of the year. The note circulation also remained substantially stable. Rather, it is accounted for by an increase in Government borrowing, especially from the Bank. The low point in this borrowing was reached in March, 1922. Thereafter it increased rapidly, and probably far more than the published figures show. The increase was the signal for a renewed and uncontrollable rise in prices and the exchanges. At this point it was no longer general speculation, the *anticipation* of a given state of the budget, that induced the new collapse, but the actual appearance of an increased disequilibrium. Until then the general expectation had been optimistic.[1] Prices and the exchanges had fallen steadily, despite the existence of a budget deficit. But in the spring of 1922 it had at last become clear that the Government could not master the situation; that the reconstruction and other additional expenditures could not be met without renewed inflation. Whether this inflation would take the form of increased note issues or of further borrowing made but little difference. Prices and the exchanges at once reacted unfavorably. The movement has not yet been checked (November, 1925), and will not be until the budget situation is once more in hand. An actual budget surplus is not necessary, but it must be entirely clear that the Government can and will prevent new deficits, and consequent new inflation.

[1] Probably very much too optimistic. The admissions made by the French Government in the spring of 1925 indicate that for a number of years the published Bank returns have been, to say the least, incomplete.

The nature of the relation between price movements and exchange movements is less clear for France than it was in England. As already observed, if the exchanges are compared directly with prices the latter have a clear though not invariable tendency to precede, and in no case do they follow (see Chart IV, above). But when the exchanges are compared with the price *parities*, the principal movements tend rather to coincide. This is shown in Chart V.[1] At certain points, it is true, the price parities precede, and a rather weak case can be made out to show that at these times they controlled the exchanges. But the safest conclusion is that prices and the exchanges were substantially equivalent measures, in direction of change if not always in magnitude, of the same thing; that is, of the degree of trust in the future of the currency, in the first instance, and ultimately in the future of the Government finances. This confidence was usually greater within France itself than in the exchange markets, for the price parities were as a rule below the exchanges.

Finally, the course of French foreign trade is indicated in Chart VI.[2] It was here possible to get figures for the physical volume of the movements, and thus to avoid the distortion produced by price movements, but on the other hand the figures present a true picture only if it can be assumed that the *composition* of the exports and imports remained unchanged. Granting this assumption, however, it is evident that the exchange fluctuations had surprisingly little effect. The necessary inference is that the exchange and price movements were so nearly simultaneous, and so nearly equivalent, that no important discrepancy appeared. In consequence, there was neither stimulus nor check to the course of trade. This is unlike the situation in England, where the lag of prices in the first years after the war seems to have had a marked influence. It is true that the trend of French importation was slowly but steadily upward throughout the period, whereas exportation, on the average, declined after 1920. But we are hardly

---

[1] The data are given in Appendix C, Table II, and are computed from the U. S. Senate *Foreign Exchange and Currency Investigation* (cited above).

[2] *Ibid.* These figures are simply copied.

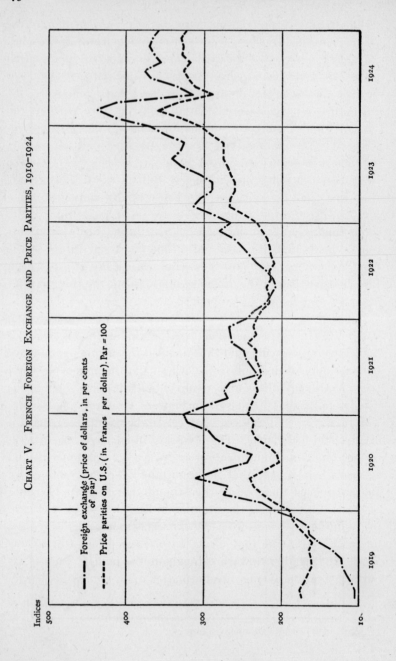

CHART V. FRENCH FOREIGN EXCHANGE AND PRICE PARITIES, 1919–1924

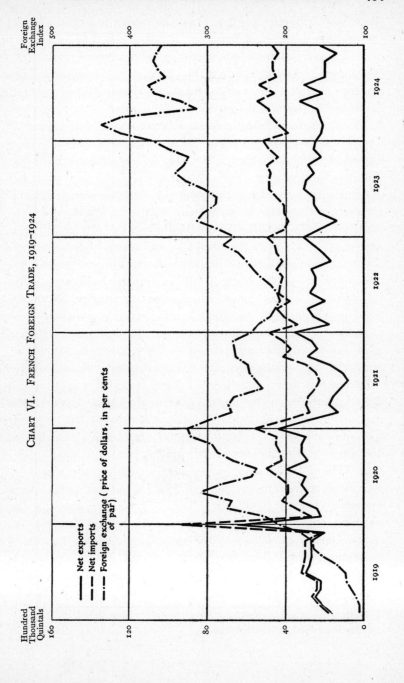

CHART VI. FRENCH FOREIGN TRADE, 1919–1924

Net exports
Net imports
Foreign exchange (price of dollars, in per cents
of par)

justified in trying to relate so small and long-run a divergence to the position of the exchanges.

6. There remains the last phase in the downward movement: the phase of extreme depreciation and ultimate collapse. This extreme depreciation, which France and England were spared, developed in Germany after the middle of 1921. No attempt will be made to present continuous data here, except on the course of foreign trade, for the grotesque size of the figures makes it almost impossible to handle them.[1] Nevertheless certain general conclusions can be reached.

Until July, 1921, the depreciation in Germany remained in the same general universe of phenomena as those in France and England, and can be explained in not dissimilar ways. It was far more severe (the price index, for example, was nearly twice as high as the maximum reached in France), but was still not beyond the possibility of control. Then, largely in response to adverse political events, it began to grow with cumulative velocity. Not only the depreciation itself, but the *rate* of its progress increased to an incredible extent. This stage lasted until April, 1923. It then gave way to an absolute collapse, which was terminated in December of 1923. Since then the currency has been virtually stable.

Except for two months in 1923, the exchange depreciation was always greater than the internal price depreciation. In part, this was because the mark inspired somewhat more confidence at home than abroad, but in the later stages one may suspect that it was due simply to the inability of the printing presses to keep up the pace. The fluctuations of prices were virtually coincident with the exchange movements, however, and indeed after 1921 were commonly quoted directly in a foreign currency. Mechanically speaking, the beginning of the more severe stage of depreciation clearly came from the side of the exchanges, not from the side of money and prices. The increase in the note circulation, though rapid enough, was far slower than that of the exchanges themselves. From January of 1919 to December of 1921 it had in-

---

[1] See the invaluable compilations of data in the U. S. Senate *Foreign Exchange and Currency Investigation* (cited above).

creased only five fold, while the exchange depreciation had increased 25 times, and prices 14 times. From January, 1922, to July, 1923, the further increases were respectively 375, 1,800 and 2,000. Thereafter, it is true, the note circulation made up much of the lost ground, but its major accelerations nearly always came one to two months *after* the corresponding movements in prices and the exchanges. It continued to rise in the first half of 1924, despite the existence of exchange stabilization.

The lag of money behind prices and the exchanges can evidently be explained only in terms of velocity of circulation. During the period of collapse, especially in the later stages, the effort to get rid of marks as soon as they were received led to an enormous increase in this velocity, and thus enabled the country to get on with a much smaller total gold value of the currency than before.[1] But after exchange stability seemed definitely assured, the cumulative and widespread bear movement turned in the other direction. The velocity of circulation of the currency fell rapidly, and the continued increase in the note issue did no more than fill up the gap, without affecting prices.[2]

Taking the German history as a whole, the sequence of events seems to have been this. The prime mover in the depreciation, the "original cause," was budget disequilibrium. This dated back to the early part of the war. To it were added, after 1918, a series of ominous political events, and later the threat of catastrophic Reparations payments. As the disrupting influence of these factors became increasingly pronounced, distrust in the future of the German finances and currency grew both at home and abroad, and gave rise to a long series of bear movements — that is, to universal and pessimistic "speculation," in the widest sense. To this speculation the exchanges responded perhaps more easily than prices, but not more certainly. The increase in the note circulation lagged far behind, but was virtually offset by a great rise in

[1] In November, 1922, it was less than one thirty-eighth of the value in January, 1919. This was the lowest point reached. The ratios fluctuated widely, however.

[2] A similar series of events had been witnessed in Austria in the previous year. There, however, the depreciation was infinitely less severe. See ch. vii, sect. 8, above.

the velocity of circulation of money. Finally, stabilization proved impossible to accomplish until after budgetary equilibrium had been definitely restored. Given this, the exchanges ceased to depreciate, and prices and the note circulation adjusted themselves very nearly automatically.

Attention may also be called to one other aspect of the situation, the effect of the depreciation on German foreign trade from 1921 to 1924. This is shown in Chart VII.[1] The data are for physical quantities only. The qualification indicated in that connection with respect to France is even more important here, for it is certain that the composition of the German exports and imports did *not* remain unchanged. Nevertheless the figures are significant. Exports maintained a surprisingly even level, but on the whole declined until the beginning of the stabilization, when they rose. Imports, on the other hand, increased rapidly until the final collapse began. Then they fell off badly, but recovered somewhat under the stabilization. The decline in the volume of exports is in part accounted for by the fact that the currency collapse was often so rapid that before the payments received could be converted into something tangible, much of their value had been lost. Exportation, despite all attempts at avoiding the exchange risk, therefore became unprofitable. But this explanation is admittedly uncertain. The relative increase in importation is even less easy to account for. Had the imports been paid for in marks alone, the nature of the stimulus to importation would be obvious, but in point of fact this was not usually the practice. It seems probable that the changes in both exports and imports were primarily due to conditions other than the exchange depreciation itself, such as the need for foreign raw materials, the severe control over exporting and importing operations, and so forth.

7. It is not necessary to push the study of concrete cases beyond this point. The range covered has been wide enough to include the more important types and phases of monetary

---

[1] The data are given in Appendix C, Table III, and are copied from the U. S. Senate *Foreign Exchange and Currency Investigation* (cited above). Data before May, 1921, are not available in this form.

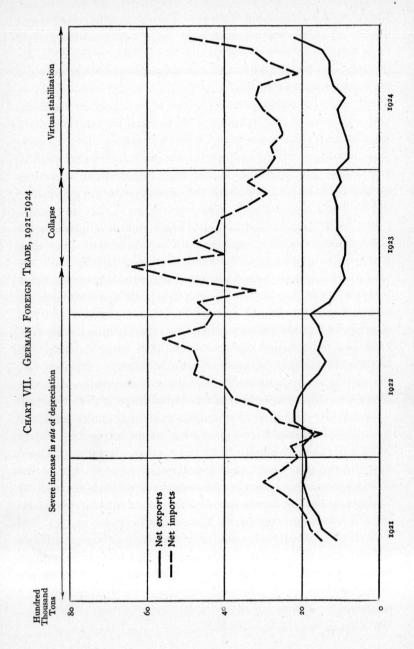

CHART VII. GERMAN FOREIGN TRADE, 1921–1924

dissimilarity as between countries, and to bring out the characteristics of each. The various results reached may now be brought together.

When the dissimilarity involved is produced by the existence of a gold standard in one country and a silver standard in the other, the case is comparatively simple. At any one time, the situation is precisely analogous to that appearing under common metallic standards. Over longer periods, however, the gold-silver ratio inevitably shifts, and carries the par of exchange with it. Differential movements of prices then appear, both in and between the countries concerned, and the course of foreign trade is affected as long as the discrepancies endure. The stimulus or check arises in part from the lag of certain groups of international prices behind the exchange rates, but chiefly from the lag of domestic costs of production behind both. These lags, however, will eventually be overcome, except in so far as the international group of prices moves to a permanently different place in the various national price structures.

When the dissimilarity is produced by the existence of a régime of inconvertible paper, the situation is vastly more complex. An inconvertible paper currency is usually (always since 1914) a fluctuating one as well, and the problem of the effects of dissimilarity therefore gives way to the problem of depreciation and appreciation. Moreover, the changes potentially involved are on a far larger scale than is ever possible when the currencies, though different, are both metallic. These conditions are studied most easily in the history of Europe since 1914.

Taking Europe as a whole, the origin of the recent currency depreciations has lain in the financial needs of the belligerent countries. From them it spread to most of the neutral countries,[1] and soon came to cover the larger part of the civilized world. But this is self-evident. The critical questions are just where and how the movement started, in each country, what the controlling factors were, and how it was checked. To answer these questions, it is necessary to distinguish between the various phases of the cycle

[1] Sweden, however, suffered for a time from an *appreciating* currency.

of depreciation. These are moderate, severe, and extreme depreciation, and stabilization.

The general process of depreciation since 1914, to repeat, has always originated in the needs of government finance. Vastly larger sums were required by the belligerent countries than could possibly be secured from taxation. The inevitable result was the issuing of additional paper currency, and the floating of long- and short-term loans. The latter, since the securities could always be discounted at the central banks for cash, had an inflationary effect almost as great as that proceeding from the outright issue of paper money. But once the post-war depreciations had gotten well under way, government inflation ceased to exert so direct and immediate an influence. Inflation underlay the situation, of course, but the degree of the depreciation at a given time — the level of the exchanges, and in the more severe cases the level of prices — was largely determined by another element. This new element was the degree of confidence, at home and abroad, in the future ability of the government to balance the budget and to stabilize the currency. It was determined in the first instance by the immediate financial policy of the governments involved, but was also influenced by the course of political events in general. Nothing other than confidence, or the lack of it, can account for the movements that actually took place in the later years of the various depreciations. The fluctuations of prices and the exchanges had absolutely no direct mechanical or quantitative relationship to *antecedent* fluctuations in the volume of public and private credit, or in the note circulation. They greatly exceeded the degree of change in these elements, and often preceded them.

To put it in general terms, the controlling factor in the later stages of depreciation, at given moments, was "speculation" or "anticipation" in the widest sense. The importance of this factor was in substantially direct ratio to the severity of the depreciation itself. Where the depreciation was moderate, as in England, it did not play a dominant rôle except at particular moments. The dominating condition, rather, was the actual degree of governmental and private inflation. Speculation accounted only for the waves on the surface of the general movement.

Where the depreciation was severe, as in France, speculation was much more significant, and to some extent explained the general movement as well as the surface oscillations. As in the first case, however, it seems on the whole to have taken an over-optimistic view of the situation, and often kept the currency and exchange fluctuations at lower levels than strictly quantitative considerations would apparently have justified. Finally, in the later stages of the German experience speculation was the sole determinant. Here the degree of the depreciation had absolutely no immediate relationship to government finance, and was far greater than could be explained by the quantitative position of the note circulation or the budget.[1]

The beginning of recovery, on the other hand, has had a somewhat different immediate explanation. In England and France the first step was neither a restoration of confidence nor the establishment of budgetary equilibrium. It was the severe contraction of private credit consequent on the application of pressure by the central banks. In Germany, on the other hand, it was accomplished only through the repudiation of the government's debts, together with the assistance of foreign-exchange support.[2] In none of these cases, however, could the improvement have become permanent if the budget had not either been balanced or at least placed unmistakably on the road to equilibrium. Otherwise general confidence could not have been secured, and widespread bear speculation would soon have started a new and worse depreciation. It is only necessary, for proof of this, to call attention

[1] The effect of speculation has been especially stressed by Professor Allyn A. Young, in a paper on *War Debts, External and Internal (Foreign Affairs*, 1924). His position was examined in ch. vii, sect. 7, above.

I have adopted the broad use of the term "speculation" from Professor Young's discussion.

[2] In Austria and Czecho-Slovakia, similarly, an initial outside point of support proved necessary. This was secured in Austria by the use of foreign loans. In Czecho-Slovakia it was consequent on the heavy importation of capital from Austria itself and from Germany, where the contemporary currency depreciations were far more acute. But the really critical factor was the definite guarantee of budget equilibrium. When this was assured, the exchange depreciation stopped of itself, and prices and the quantity of money then adjusted themselves almost automatically. See ch. vii, sect. 8, and ch. xi, sect. 9, above.

to the disastrous experience of France since 1923. When the promise of budget equilibrium was seen to be definitely beyond the possibility of immediate fulfillment, speculation almost instantaneously induced a new upward movement of the French exchanges and prices. The movement had absolutely no mechanical relation to the actually small changes in the position of the government's finances which were taking place at the time.[1]

In view of these considerations, the long-debated question of the relation between prices and the foreign exchanges — the question of the accuracy or inaccuracy of the purchasing-power-parity doctrine, and of alternative theories — seems almost beside the point. Neither prices nor the exchanges can properly be regarded as having been the "cause" of the general movement in any specific case. Nor was the level of either, except in a very immediate sense, ever the "result" of the other's fluctuations. Rather, both price and exchange movements were common products of a common antecedent condition. In the earlier and less severe stages of depreciation this antecedent condition was the existence of inflation, partly in private credit but chiefly that produced by government financial operations. Here a loose mechanical and even quantitative relationship existed between the degree of inflation on the one hand, and the levels of prices and the exchanges on the other. But the relationship soon began to break down, for with the progress of the depreciation itself the degree of inflation ceased to be the controlling factor. This factor became, instead, speculation in the widest sense. Speculation was the origin of the later exchange and price movements, the condition that determined them, and they in turn served as almost equivalent measures of its character and direction.

It can fairly be said that prices and the exchanges tend to maintain a sort of short-time equilibrium as between themselves. They never get very far apart, for too great a differential soon brings corrective forces into play, through the influence of the commodity balance of trade or through foreign-exchange specula-

---

[1] The dominant importance of budgetary equilibrium was vigorously demonstrated by Professor Charles Rist in his most recent book, *La Déflation* (Paris, 1923). He seems to have been the first to amplify this thesis. He says little, however, about the more general effects of speculation. See ch. xi, sect. 9, above.

tion itself.[1] It is impossible and useless, however, to try to determine which one acts as the norm for the other. Their effects are reciprocal. Nor can any other genuine "causal" relationship between them, in the short-time period, be deduced from general reasoning, except where — as in cases of extreme depreciation and collapse — internal prices are explicitly quoted in terms of a foreign currency. The "causal" relation runs, rather, from antecedent conditions to both prices and the exchanges themselves.

It is of course true that if a country has a large net excess of actual payments to make abroad, this will affect the exchanges, and a consequent rise in prices will appear which would not have taken place otherwise. Such seems to have been, at one time, the consequence of Germany's attempts to transfer her Reparations payments. But that type of situation is rare in the history of the recent depreciations. The more characteristic state of affairs has been that in which exchanges and prices were both common measures of a common antecedent element: of the internal inflation in the country, or of the direction and intensity of the speculation in its currency.

In the latest formulations of the purchasing-power-parity theory, however, the doctrine of the short-time equilibrium has dropped into the background, and the principal stress has been placed on long-time relationships. It is now asserted that the price parities act simply as the long-time norm for fluctuations of the exchanges. The difficulties in this view have been commented on elsewhere.[2] Under inconvertible paper, the relations between the price structures of different countries are almost entirely severed. A price movement in one country will simply alter its exchange rates, and will have no necessary effect whatsoever on the price levels of other countries. The exchange rates may, it is true, become effective quotients between the various general price levels, but this relation is not an equilibrium in any true sense of

---

[1] The cases reviewed in the present chapter indicate that where the depreciation is moderate, the correction is exerted through the commodity balance of trade. Where it is severe, however, the fluctuations of prices and the exchanges are too nearly coincident for this, and are adjusted to one another's movements too rapidly. They are then held together, rather, by the effects of speculative operations.

[2] See ch. vii, sect. 5, above.

the word. A divergence of the exchanges from the price parities may be corrected in time, but a divergence of the parities from the exchanges need not be. The "equilibrium," that is, is strictly empirical, and exerts little or no control over its component elements. Moreover, even this empirical relationship may quite fail to work out. With the passage of time, the places of "international" prices in the various national structures will change, the "real" terms of international exchange will shift, and the ratio between general price indices will cease to reflect accurately the ratio between the prices (expressed in the one currency and the other) of the articles actually entering foreign trade. Yet it is these last which control the general levels of the exchanges. The price parities and the exchanges may therefore diverge more or less permanently, without setting up any definitely corrective forces. It seems fairly clear that such divergences have actually taken place since 1914, and on an important scale. It is difficult to explain the situation shown in Charts II and V, above, in any other terms.

The effect of depreciation on the course of foreign trade is not uniform, and not always definite. Where the depreciation has been moderate, as in England, the trade movements were substantially those outlined for the gold-silver case. Exports were stimulated by rising exchanges, and imports checked, while improving exchanges produced the opposite effects. Where the depreciation was severe, however, as in France, it seems to have had surprisingly little influence. The explanation is that the exchange and internal price movements were so nearly simultaneous that no substantial lag of one behind the other could appear, and hence no stimulus or check. The trade movements were probably determined largely by other conditions. In Germany, finally, *importation* was increasing relatively until the ultimate collapse. This fact too presumably finds its chief explanation in conditions other than the direct mechanical effect of depreciation on foreign trade.

One other observation may be made. The two preceding chapters were concerned with the character and extent of the equilibrium tendencies appearing in international exchange under common metallic standards, and with the processes by which equilibrium is maintained. In the present chapter, these questions have received comparatively little attention. As already remarked, the phenomena of depreciation make it almost impossible to speak of any constant relationships between countries whatsoever, except in the most general and self-evident terms. There is ample room for a description of the processes and sequences of events which these conditions involve, but the analysis cannot be pushed through to the grander concepts of equilibrium. The content and even the form of the theory of international prices here are therefore quite different from the doctrines appropriate to trade under common monetary standards.

CHAPTER XVIII

THE DETERMINATION OF RATIOS OF INTER-
NATIONAL EXCHANGE

1. We have been concerned to this point only with the general structural and mechanical aspects of international exchange in the aggregate. The existence of the exchange itself has been taken for granted, as have its terms. Evidently there are important questions here, however, which cannot be dismissed casually.

To these questions the classical theory of international trade offers a logically complete and self-consistent answer. It holds that the ratios of international exchange — international values — are determined in general by comparative labor costs in the one country and the other, and that within the limits set by these costs they are determined by the relative strength of the demands for the various products. But detailed objections have been brought, in earlier chapters, against both the principle of comparative costs and the classical application of reciprocal demand.[1] Reciprocal demand does not suffice to establish a *single* ratio of exchange, since an indefinite number of ratios may satisfy the given conditions. Moreover, it is in practice impossible to apply reciprocal demand except where the international exchange is made up almost entirely of commodities. There is no acceptable way, for example, of relating the demand for commodities to a corresponding opposite demand for capital. A true "equation" cannot be secured. And although comparative labor costs, in the classical sense of the term, can be used to "read back" from the facts of a known exchange to its underlying elements, they are incapable of determining the exchange *in advance* of the erection of actual money prices and money wages. The relation between labor costs and money prices is not the same in different countries, nor does the relation in one country bear a constant proportion to that in others.

[1] See especially ch. xiv, sects. 2 and 3.

In the present chapter we shall try to work out an alternative approach to the problem.[1] We shall be concerned primarily with actual ratios of exchange, whether expressed in money or in commodities, and shall deal only incidentally with labor costs or other non-pecuniary sacrifices. The conclusions thus reached can be applied equally well to purely internal trade, for they make the distinction between it and international trade quantitative alone. The first part of the argument is really nothing more than an application of the general methodology long familiar in the mathematical literature. The explicitly mathematical verbiage and apparatus have been removed, however, except with respect to the simple graphic devices used, and somewhat different results are obtained.

2. It is convenient to begin, in the traditional manner, by assuming a barter trade in only two commodities, each of which is produced in only one of the two countries. Let the countries be A and B; and the commodities Ma, produced in A, and Nb, produced in B. Supposing first that trade in these commodities actually exists, what are the terms and conditions of the trade? In country A, the import Nb has at the moment a certain value in terms of Ma, the article given in exchange for it, while in country B the import Ma has a certain value in terms of the export Nb. It is evident that, since trade is actually taking place, the value of Nb in terms of Ma must be less in B, the country of origin, than it is in A, the importing country. Similarly the value of Ma, in terms of Nb, must be less in country A than it is in country B. In other words the ratios of exchange between the two commodities, in the one country and the other, are not mutually exclusive. On the contrary, they include one another, and trade is therefore possible. These ratios, however, are ratios *in* the one

----

[1] It should be pointed out that the classical analysis of ratios of international exchange was really an introduction to the larger problem of the nature and determination of the benefits derived from foreign trade. That question lies beyond our province here, partly from considerations of space and partly because the matters involved are in some respects of a different nature from those hitherto dealt with. An illuminating example of the trend taken by certain recent discussions in this field is presented in a note by Professor Allyn A. Young, *Marshall on Consumers' Surplus in International Trade* (39 *Quarterly Journal of Economics*, 1924).

country and the other. They are what we may call the "limiting" ratios of the *international* exchange. Any rate of international exchange which exceeds both, or lies below both, will be unprofitable to the traders of one country or the other; but any rate which lies between these limits will be profitable to each group. The determination of the rate is thus indefinite. Any rate falling within the indicated limits will satisfy all the conditions.

As the quantities exported and imported in a given period increase, however, the relative values of the commodities will change. As country A gets more and more of the import Nb, the value of Nb in terms of the export Ma will tend to fall in A. Conversely, the value of Ma in country B, which imports it, will tend to fall in terms of the export Nb. In other words the limiting ratios, *in the one country and the other*, will begin to draw together. The range within which the actual rates of *international* exchange may vary will then narrow.

This last situation is shown in Diagram I. Curve O–A represents the limiting value, decreasing as quantities increase, of the import Nb in country A. It is measured in terms of the export Ma. Curve O–B represents the limiting value, decreasing as quantities increase, of the import Ma in country B. It is measured in terms of the export Nb. Any rate of international exchange such that, for a given quantity of Ma, more of Nb is received than the quantity indicated by the curve O–A will obviously be profitable to the traders of country A; while a rate such that for a given amount of Nb, more of Ma is received than the quantity indicated by the curve O–B will be profitable to the traders of Country B. In other words, all rates within the zone bounded by the curves will be profitable to both groups of traders, and are possible ratios of exchange. But any ratio which lies outside the zone, such as that represented by the point P′, will impose a positive loss on one country or the other. Finally, it is clear that a limit also exists on the possible increase of the quantities exchanged in the given period. This is the limit set by their intersection, P. Any increase beyond this point will necessarily produce a ratio unfavorable to one country or the other, or to both.[1]

This type of composite curve has long been familiar in the mathematical literature.[2] I do not propose to deal here with the sometimes tortured refinements which the mathematical economists place upon it, nor to carry out its implications very far. Some two or three points alone need be mentioned.

First, the assumptions on which the curves are based, and the limitations to which they are subject, are precisely the same as

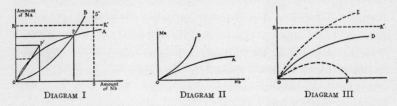

DIAGRAM I   DIAGRAM II   DIAGRAM III

for composite demand and supply curves of the more familiar sort. The preference for them is based simply on their greater advantage, for certain purposes, as a graphic device. I shall use them here to represent only those "normal" types of demand for which every increase in quantity is accompanied by the same or a lower demand price. The abnormal types, the curves for which

[1] Should the limiting ratios in the one country and the other be mutually exclusive from the outset, and trade hence impossible, the situation would be that represented in Diagram II. This situation is, presumably, actually characteristic of the relations between the great numerical majority of the articles in any one country and those in another.

[2] It seems to have been first applied in the mathematical economics by Professor Marshall, in his unpublished essay on *The Pure Theory of International Values* (1879). It was not presented to the general body of students, however, until ten years later, when Professor Pantaleoni repeated it in his *Principii di Economia pura* (1 ed., 1889; 2 ed., 1894; English translation by T. B. Bruce, London, 1898). See also Marshall's own recent presentation, in his *Money Credit and Commerce* (London, 1922), Appendix J. The credit for independent discovery, however, must be shared with Auspitz and Lieben, whose *Theorie des Preises* appeared in the same year as Pantaleoni's work.

See also F. Y. Edgeworth, *International Values* (*Economic Journal*, 1894); Pareto's works, *passim*; Henry H. Cunynghame, *A Geometrical Political Economy* (Oxford, 1904), especially ch. 10; and various other works. Cunynghame's analysis of international trade runs in terms of relative *money* costs and prices alone, and entirely disregards the classical theory.

are self-returning, have a considerable theoretical interest, but their significance in the great majority of exchanges seems doubtful. In consequence, the curves of Diagram I will be assumed to approach limits. Curve O–A approaches the horizontal projected from the assumed point R, as R–R′, and O–B the vertical from S, as S–S′.

Second, each curve is necessarily determined not only by the effect of increased importation upon the demand price for the import, but also by the effect of increased exportation upon the supply price of the corresponding export. In other words, they measure simultaneously both the elasticity of demand for the import, and the "elasticity" of supply of the export, in each country. The two forces are combined in the maximum (or minimum) limiting ratios. Thus if curve O–A in Diagram I be supposed to have been drawn with constant costs for the export Ma, then under increasing costs the curve would run somewhat below O–A (the divergence becoming greater, the greater the quantity), and under decreasing costs would run somewhat above. This condition, indeed, may entirely destroy the tendency of the curves to approach real limits, and may make them in effect self-returning. Thus in Diagram III let O–D represent the demand schedule alone. Under constant costs it will be unaffected by the supply price of the export, but under decreasing costs it may rise to the position O–E, and under increasing costs fall to O–F. The theoretical complexities which may ensue, however, I shall arbitrarily pass by here. The mathematical writers have indicated them at sufficient length.

Finally, it is usually assumed that the exchanges will be pushed to their maximum possible limit; that is, that the quantities imported and exported will be increased until the limiting ratios in each country become the same. Point P, at the intersection of the curves in Diagram I, then becomes a point of stable equilibrium. Under conditions of perfect competition, mobility and information, this assumption may be granted, and it is in practice probably true of the great staples of commerce. But for other classes of goods it is by no means necessarily valid. Indeed, in so far as the argument of Chapter XV is correct, the probability is that it is wrong. Pushing the exchange to the maximum possible limit evidently means reducing the margin of possible profit on each transaction, and thus increasing the risk from market fluctuations, while the elasticities of demands and costs may well be such that the total net return is less than from some intermediary ratio. For perhaps the majority of commodities, therefore, the ratio of international exchange is probably indeterminate. It will lie somewhere between the origin and the maximum limit, and somewhere between the limiting ratios, but just where cannot be discovered in advance. Under monopoly, although the exchange is ordinarily not extended to the point P, it will usually be pushed until the demand-curve limit is reached. But under partial or full competition, even this quasi-equilibrium need not be attained. The ratio will lie somewhere between the two limits. Presumably the relative bargaining powers of the traders concerned will suffice to establish it fairly definitely at any given moment, but subsequent changes will ensue. Many if not most of the commodities entering foreign trade are not standardized, and not actively traded. The lack of a sure tendency to international price equalization is itself an evidence of the indefiniteness of their ratios of exchange, within the indicated limits.

Curves of the type here used also offer an easy way of showing the effects of costs of transportation. These costs will narrow the possible zone of profitable exchange, and if sufficiently great may make it entirely impossible. Their relative distribution, as between one country and the other, will likewise affect the position of the zone itself. Diagram IV shows an even distribution of these costs (indicated by the dotted lines), Diagram V an unequal distribution, and Diagram VI the effective prohibition of trade.[1] The curves also permit an easy measurement of the direct bene-

---

[1] The possible variable distribution of costs of transportation leads to a further difficulty in sustaining the argument for any specific equilibrium in the rates of exchange. In Diagram VII (p. 459), let the dotted curve OH show the situation when all the costs are borne by country A; OK when they are borne by Country B; and OL, OL', when they are equally divided. In these three cases, the "equilibrium" points are respectively P^1, P^2 and P^3. Equilibrium therefore comes to be represented not by a specific point, but by a curve, — the locus of P^1, P^2, P^3. It is therefore indefinite, and except at a given moment need not be stable.

fits from trade, but with that problem we are not concerned here. Finally, the *direct* effects of a tariff upon the ratios of exchange are precisely the same as those appearing when all the costs of transportation are borne by the given country. It decreases the amount of the import that can be obtained for each given quantity of the export, and narrows the width and length of the zone of possible exchange. It also, of course, shifts the position of the zone in a sense less favorable to the taxing country.

3. The second type of situation is that of barter trade in two commodities, one or both of which is produced in both countries.

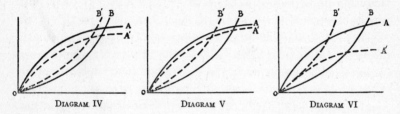

DIAGRAM IV   DIAGRAM V   DIAGRAM VI

This situation will arise in only four principal cases: (1) where the domestic article is produced under increasing costs, and the imported article can therefore be sold more cheaply than the domestic, after a certain level of domestic output and costs is reached; (2) where, despite constant or even decreasing costs in the production of the domestic article, costs of transportation *within* the country are so high as to make the importation of a part of the supply profitable, with respect to certain regions in the the country; (3) where a tariff permits the continuation of the domestic production of an article, which would otherwise be driven out by foreign competition; (4) where the imported product is itself in process of driving the domestic producers out of the market, or vice versa.

The diagrammatic representation of these various alternatives is difficult, and it seems wiser not to attempt it here. The graphs become too confused to be useful. The general theory of the problem is nevertheless not complex. Essentially, the condition is simply one of composite supply or composite demand; or, not infrequently, of both. When, either from increasing local costs of production or from tariffs, transportation charges or other causes, the price that can be gotten for the foreign product in the local market is greater than that currently secured in the market of origin, then importation becomes possible. Under the argument of Chapter XV above, however, this need not take place unless the article is one of the actively traded staples. If the importation *is* undertaken, three factors set a limit to its possible expansion. One is the effect on the markets of the country of origin. If the import is secured by a diversion of supplies from the foreign market, prices there will rise. If, on the other hand, it is secured by a substantial increase in the volume of production, increasing costs will probably set in, in the short-time period at least. The second limitation is the effect on the importing market. An increase in the total supply will force down prices there, and thus lessen the international price differential. Finally, in so far as the importation simply replaces the domestic supply, the price of the domestic product will usually fall. This too will decrease the international differential. If the importation is then increased steadily, a limit will be reached beyond which it becomes unprofitable, and beyond which further increases cannot be made. It by no means follows, however, that importation will necessarily be pushed to this point.

The argument of the preceding paragraph has been stated in terms of the prices or exchange ratios of the market. It was suggested in an earlier section, however, that these market prices may lie anywhere within the "zone of profitable exchange" defined by the limiting curves. Now this same analysis of limiting ratios of exchange, which we have used for trade as *between* countries, is equally valid for trade *within* a country. In other words, for at least many classes of commodities market price is within limits indefinite, since the exchange need not be pushed to that maximum at which a stable equilibrium is alone possible.[1] This

[1] For the purpose of representing internal exchanges, the two curves must be given meanings somewhat different from those hitherto assigned. Thus in Diagram VIII, curve O–A represents the limiting demand price alone, for each given quantity, and curve O–B the limiting supply price, under *increasing* costs. Under constant costs the supply curve would be a straight line, like the dotted curve O–B[1]. and under decreasing costs would incline downward, like the dotted curve O–B[2]. The position and shape of the zone of profitable exchange, and the point of intersection, are correspondingly altered.

situation makes the determination of the actual volume of importation or exportation, and of the point at which a limit will be reached, likewise rather indefinite.

To demonstrate this, let us examine the situation *within* the importing country. For each given quantity of the selected commodity, let curve O–A in Diagram IX represent only the limiting demand price; and curve O–B only the limiting supply price for the domestic output — thus giving the curves meanings somewhat different from those assigned in the preceding diagrams.

If, for example, the market price in the importing country were at first somewhere in the zone between the limiting ratios in

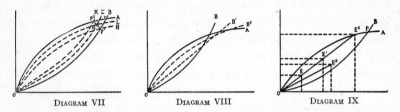

DIAGRAM VII   DIAGRAM VIII   DIAGRAM IX

that country — as at point E, in Diagram IX — then importation might result in the maintenance of the price OE, but with an *increase* in the total quantity sold. The increased volume of exchanges would then be represented by the prolongation of OE to OE^1. Only when the line of market price cuts the limiting demand curve, O–A, will market price itself fall. Thus if point E^2 is reached, any further increase in quantity must be accompanied by a decline in market price (represented graphically by a rotation of the line OE^2 to the right, on the pivot O). Or the importation might cause market price to fall, as to a point E^3. As long as E^3 remains above the limiting cost curve O–B, however, the domestic producers will not be hurt. Their profits will decrease, but they will not be driven out of business. Importation itself need not cease until the import-cost curve (not shown) cuts the local demand curve. This may occur either before the curve of *domestic* costs cuts the local demand curve, or at the same time, or afterwards. There is no *a priori* way of telling. Nor is accurate graphic representation possible, at least on two-dimensional diagrams, for the demand curve must be considered with respect to *both* sources of possible supply. There are three independent variables. Finally, it is necessary to allow for the fact of differences as between countries in the elasticities of the demand and supply curves. The limiting points in the exporting and importing operations will be correspondingly affected.

The third principal type of case is that met with in actuality, trade in a number of commodities some of which are produced in only one country, and some in both. But under the barter assumption, however large the number of commodities exchanged the general character of the analysis remains the same as when only two are involved. Each import must be accompanied by a corresponding and equivalent export, or vice versa, and the exchange therefore reduces to a series of pairs of independent operations. For each pair the apparatus of limiting ratios and curves may be set up, and the same conditions obtain as those already outlined. The principal qualifications arise simply from the greater complexity of the case, and are essentially quantitative alone. Any one commodity may, and usually will, enter into more than one transaction in a given period. The limiting curves of each operation, therefore, are affected by the quantity of the commodity already exchanged in the period, and during the period as a whole they may shift their position and shape very considerably. Some sort of composite curve (perhaps multidimensional) for the aggregate time area, however, could presumably be erected by the use of the familiar demand- and supply-curve assumptions.

These are the principal types of barter exchange between countries. Our analysis of them has been made to run solely in terms of the demand and supply schedules for the articles concerned, in each country. Given such schedules, we have then found it possible to establish the character and limits of the trade. The practice of dealing only with current ratios of exchange and the factors immediately controlling them, however, is evidently at marked variance with that of the classical writers. The classical theorems here paid relatively little attention to the phenomena of ratios of exchange, — prices, — and sought instead to go back of them to factors exerting a more fundamental control over international trade. These factors were held to find their expression in comparative labor costs. Should we not now, therefore, similarly extend our analysis to include the presumably dominant though less conspicuous conditions with which the older doctrine was concerned?

Unequivocally, no. It is unnecessary to repeat here the criticisms brought at another point against the classical principle of comparative costs, but the positive result of those criticisms may be recalled to mind. This is the conclusion that the so-called underlying factors in international exchange — whether comparative labor costs, effectiveness of labor, or rates of wages — cannot of themselves alone provide an adequate *a priori* basis for establishing the terms of the exchange. If we are given *only* them, we have no way of comparing conditions in one country with those in another, and hence no way of knowing what the nature of the trade between them will be. A connecting link is needed: namely, the actual ratios of exchange current at given times within each country. Such ratios provide the starting point of concrete trading operations, and must fulfill a similar function in any theoretical analysis. The further problems involved in comparative labor costs, the effectiveness of labor, and so on, are therefore of great importance, but they are not immediately relevant to the determination of ratios of *international* exchange.

In attacking this last problem the only directly relevant factors are the demand and supply schedules, and the ratios of exchange, which actually or hypothetically prevail in the countries concerned. The problem itself therefore reduces to the relatively simple one of showing how these factors operate, and how they control the course of trade. It is impossible to go back of them to a single more "fundamental" set of factors, and futile to try. They are themselves — to borrow from the vocabulary of algebra — the lowest common terms to which the situation can be reduced. Any further reduction leads, instead, to complexity and incompleteness. No one of the elements which go to make up the demand and supply schedules in each country is adequate, of itself alone, to explain these schedules. Still less can any one of them be adequate, therefore, to explain the ratios of international exchange which are derived from the schedules. In analyzing the process by which such ratios are established, it is in the first instance necessary to take the conditions of cost and demand within each country for granted — to treat them as original data in the problem. Only after the ratios have been determined can we go back to these conditions themselves, antecedent though they are, and make significant international comparisons.

To this point we have been concerned only with the rather unreal case of barter trade. It now remains to examine the more complex conditions of trade as it is actually conducted among the leading nations, and to discover how far the conclusions found valid in the one situation can be applied to the other.

4. Under barter the only determinants of international exchange, or at least of its possible limits, are the demand and supply schedules in each country for the particular commodities concerned. A change in these schedules will affect the course of international exchange, but (except within the limiting ratios) it can be affected by nothing else. There is a direct connection between demands and costs and the ratios of exchange of traded goods in either country, on the one hand, and the similar elements in the remaining country on the other. When we pass from the assumed case of barter to the conditions of modern commerce, however, two intermediaries are introduced, and two new sources of disturbance appear. One is the presence of money; the other, the presence of the foreign exchange markets and of the quoted exchange rate. The demand and supply schedules for the various articles concerned continue to dominate the course of trade, and they function in precisely the same way as under barter, but changes in one or both of the two intermediaries may entirely alter the manner and degree in which given schedules in one country (expressed in its own currency) operate upon conditions in another.

The general modifications introduced into trade by the presence of money are fairly evident. The values of the articles exchanged cease to be expressed in terms of one another, and become expressed in terms of the common measure, money. The consequence is a much wider and quicker tendency to price equalization, since it is now possible to compare prices in different places with a fair assurance that the standard of measurement is the same. But two other consequences also follow, and are due to the fact that the value of the common measure itself is variable. Within any one country, the absolute level of this value is of course of no significance. But the differences in the effects produced by changes in the value of money upon different classes of commodities and services are important. These differences are ones of rapidity in response — lags in time — and also, frequently, of degree, for permanent changes in relative values may follow from a change in the absolute levels of prices. As *between* countries, however, not only these relative differences but also the absolute levels of prices themselves (or of the value of the various currencies) are significant. A change in the general level of prices in one country, unaccompanied by an equivalent movement of the exchange rates, will have precisely the same effect upon a foreign country as though demand and cost schedules had themselves changed. When to these considerations is added the influence of possible changes in relative prices *within* any one country, it becomes evident that the presence of money may have a very marked effect upon the course and terms of international exchange. How great the effect actually is in practice, will be considered in a moment.

The general modifications introduced by the presence of a foreign exchange mechanism are also of a self-evident character. Articles produced in one country cease to be exchanged directly for those produced in another country. They are exchanged for the *currency* of the country of origin; this is exchanged for claims to the currency of the other country; and these claims, in turn, are directly or indirectly exchanged for goods there. (Or the order may be reversed.) International exchange continues, it is true, to be essentially an exchange of one country's goods (in the widest sense) against the other's. But the character of the mechanism involved is fundamentally altered. The exchange ceases to consist of a series of pairs of operations, in which each export is accompanied by the equivalent import. It becomes a great double flow of importation and exportation, in which any one transaction is lost. Here the offsetting of a particular import operation against a particular export is impossible in practice, and would be meaningless if achieved. Both types of operation go on more or less simultaneously, but they are related to one another only by their effects upon the total current balance of imports and exports (again in the widest sense); that is, upon the balance of international payments.

This fact also brings out another peculiarity of the situation. Under barter, each transaction is entirely devoid of direct mechanical connection with any other transaction, unless it be those in the particular article concerned. But where a foreign exchange mechanism exists, each transaction is intimately related to *all* the others taking place at the same time, through the agency of the exchange rate. Each is primarily dominated by the aggregate of the others, but it also contributes its small share towards determining the aggregate itself.

Under actual conditions, therefore, three intermediaries intervene between the cost and demand schedules of one country and those of another, and may distort their interaction. They are, first, the levels of money prices in one country, and their changes; second, the exchange rates; and third, the levels and changes of money prices in the *other* country. It is possible that the changes in these intermediaries will exactly offset one another. In that event, the terms of trade will be what they would have been under barter (except in so far as money, by facilitating trade, makes wider and quicker exchanges possible, and increases the closeness of the adjustments). This is the essence of the classical view. But if the fluctuations in the intermediaries do not offset one another, then the terms of the international exchange must evidently be different from those prevailing under barter. By examining the three principal types of monetary situation that appear in trade, we can determine which of the two conclusions is correct.

5. The most important case is that of countries under similar metallic standards. Here the exchange rate fluctuations are confined within such narrow limits as to be negligible, with respect to

commodities as a whole. The problem then is, do or do not prices in different countries tend to move in harmony? The possibility of correction from exchange rate fluctuations being in large measure ruled out, will the movements of money prices be such that the terms of trade continue to be those of barter? It is extremely difficult to support the affirmative position, except with respect to periods of some length. Suppose trade and prices to be in a given position of equilibrium. Then further suppose that the aggregate of prices in one of the countries rises twenty or thirty per cent. The prices of international goods may rise with the rest, in which case prices in the *other* country will be affected; or they may stay the same, in which case their relative position in their own national structure will alter; or, more probably, an intermediary position will emerge. But whatever the character of the adjustment made, the immediate result will be a change in the *relative* position, in one or both countries, of international prices in the national structure. This change in turn, by causing a partial redistribution of incomes and of the objects of the aggregate national expenditure, and by altering relative *money* costs of production, will produce effects similar to those proceeding from an original change in cost and demand schedules. It will thus alter the limiting terms of international exchange.[1] These effects

---

[1] With reference to a particular commodity, the effect of a rise in prices in one country unaccompanied by a similar rise in the other would be to raise the position of the limiting supply curves in the importing country. This is exemplified, in Diagram X, by the shift from OB to OB'. (These curves are like those of Diagram VIII above. OA represents the limiting demand curve, OB the limiting supply curve.) If the shift were great enough, the exchange would become entirely impossible.

Moreover, as suggested in the text above, even if prices in the second country rose so that its demand schedules for foreign products were the same in terms of money, it will almost necessarily be true for a considerable period that its cost schedules will have altered *relatively*, for they will not rise so rapidly. A change in the terms of international exchange, taken as a whole, must ensue. Finally, the redistribution of incomes and of productive forces caused by a general and important change in prices is fairly certain to be such that, even if the terms of international exchange themselves should chance to remain unaltered in the long run, the position of international prices and commodities in the national structures will be different.

The case of partially traded commodities also offers some interesting possibilities. If the change is not too great, either demand or supply schedules may alter without necessarily affecting market price. Thus, in Diagram XI, let OA and OB be the former limiting demand and supply curves for a given import, and OE market price.

will be further accentuated, in the case of particular commodities, in so far as *relative* prices within each group are disturbed in either country.

This is the situation which will appear immediately, in the short-run period. Over longer periods, on the other hand, the discrepancies will in considerable part be smoothed out. It was shown in another chapter that the long-run movements of prices, at least in the leading countries, tend to coincide (though often with a lag); and that the international group of prices maintains

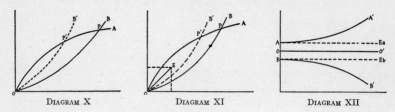

| DIAGRAM X | DIAGRAM XI | DIAGRAM XII |

a position in the various national price structures which is either fairly constant, or at least changes only gradually. Yet a large fraction of the commodities exchanged are not traded very actively, and the international equalization of their prices is far from exact. A movement of general prices may therefore permanently alter their relative position, and with it alter the demand and supply schedules based on them.

On all of these counts it seems clear that the terms of trade under money, even granted common metallic standards, are *not* the same as those appearing under barter. Changes in general prices — in the value of money — will change the conditions that determine the course of trade very greatly in the short-run period, and despite the subsequent partial correction may leave the demand and supply schedules for particular articles in permanently new positions. The classical hypothesis, that the introduction of

(Increasing costs are assumed.) Then suppose prices in the foreign country to have risen, so that OB moves to OB'; and suppose prices in the importing country to have moved in sympathy, though somewhat less. OE still remains inside both curves, and will not *necessarily* move. The foreign producers still make some profit at the extant price, and may fear to lose their market by increasing prices — though in the case here assumed the fear is unjustified.

money imposes no substantial modification on the terms of barter trade, is at the least incomplete, and is probably erroneous.

The discussion of the immediately preceding paragraphs has been primarily concerned with commodities alone. For them, as a rule, the fluctuations of the exchange rates under a common standard are too small to affect prices or quantities materially. This is not entirely true, however, of commodities which are near the "margin of doubt," and it is not at all true of securities and short-time capital. For the last two especially, an important exchange rate fluctuation is equivalent to an alteration in the limiting supply schedule. Since these items are traded in a highly competitive and highly organized market, they are usually at or near the point of maximum quantities. Or rather, to put it more accurately, they are at the maximum relative to the prices currently prevailing. Even a small oscillation of the exchange rates therefore produces a marked effect upon the quantities traded.

The international movement of securities and short-time capital is further unlike the movement of the great majority of commodities in that the *direction* of the movement may be reversed quite rapidly, as exchange and discount rates alter their position. The quantities that can flow are also more rigorously limited at given times. The current "supplies" available are not large, and the effect of changes on both discount and exchange rates is immediate. Thus, in Diagram XII, let the line O–O' represent absolute price equality, and the difference between it and line A–Ea or line B–Eb the minimum amount by which prices in one country must differ from those in the other to induce any movement at all.[1] Then let curve A–A', measured above O–O', represent the

---

[1] The size of this difference will evidently vary at different points in the business cycle. If money is tight in both countries, it will be relatively large; if easy, small. A period of strain in the exchange market, such as that induced by seasonal food importation, will also increase it.

Nor need it be the same in each direction, either at a given time or permanently. Before the war, for example, a relatively small rise in the London discount rate produced as much quantitative effect, on the average, as a relatively large one in the less important money centers. The more highly organized the market, the smaller is the difference necessary to produce an *inward* movement. The opposite difference required to produce an outward movement, on the other hand, depends on the foreign center held in mind.

successively greater quantities that will flow to country A as A's prices rise above country B's; and curve B–B', measured below O–O', the quantities that will flow to B as B's prices rise above A's. It will be observed that each curve tends to reach a vertical limit, at which no further movements can be induced, but this is of course true only with respect to particular time periods.

The second chief type of monetary situation — to return to our main argument — is that of trade between a gold-standard and a silver-standard country. Here, at any one time, the situation is the same as that appearing in trade between countries under similar standards, and the same considerations apply. Over longer periods, as we have seen in another chapter, the gold-silver ratio can vary, and by its movement cause discrepancies between the exchanges, prices, and costs of production in the silver country. A change in the terms of international exchange is inevitable, and it does not seem likely that a given previous set of relationships will ever be entirely regained.

The third and last principal case is that of trade with a country which is under inconvertible paper. Here again, after what has been said in the last chapter above, no especial comment is necessary. The exchange rates can fluctuate without limit, and in so far as they reflect the current levels of prices and costs, the "real" terms of international exchange need not be affected. In a rather loose sense, this requirement probably does tend to be realized to a considerable extent. In so far as discrepancies appear, however, the exchange rate fluctuations will in effect alter the demand or supply schedules or both, as between countries. The graphic representation of the situation is essentially the same as that shown in Diagram X, though the adjustment will usually be much less close. It may be added, however, that the rapidity and violence of the fluctuations under paper are often so great as to make even this very summary sort of analysis quite beside the point. The limiting ratios often become virtually inoperative, and no general rule can be applied.

These cases of trade under dissimilar currencies simply serve to emphasize the conclusion reached with respect to trade under a common metallic standard. Whatever the situation, the intervention of money and of the foreign exchange mechanisms leads to permanent and unpredictable alterations in the conditions and terms of trade, relative to the conditions which would appear in a state of barter. These alterations are independent of antecedent changes in the demand and supply schedules themselves, and are a separate factor in the situation. The ratios of international inter-commodity exchange are therefore determined not only by the non-monetary demand and supply schedules for the given articles in each country, at given levels of general prices, but by the effective variations in these schedules imposed by the movements of general prices and the foreign exchanges themselves. They are the product of the combined action of three sets of variables, not of two. This reveals, incidentally, the error in the familiar classical assumption that the terms of trade under money are substantially the same as those prevailing under barter — that money is in effect a colorless transmitting medium, except with respect to very short-time relationships.

6. It now remains to bring together these rather formal conclusions with respect to the determination of ratios of international exchange, and to indicate their relation to the older classical theory. For the purpose in mind, we can assume that the countries concerned are under a stable monetary régime, since the cases of dissimilar and depreciating currencies present problems of a quite different order.

The position here reached is substantially as follows. At any given time, the ratios of international exchange — the relations between the prices of traded articles — are governed simply by the current relation between market demand and market supply. For the great majority of commodities, these ratios are indeterminate within a certain range, and do not focus around any one point of stable equilibrium. The limits on their fluctuations are set by the schedule of maximum demand prices for the particular commodity concerned, in the one country, and by the schedule of minimum costs of production in the other country.[1] The schedules define a "zone" of possible exchange, within which any ratio

---

[1] And in the importing country when the commodity is also produced at home.

will be profitable to the countries involved. Except for the most actively traded commodities, however, there is no necessary tendency to push the exchange through to the point of maximum quantities. Inertia, imperfect competition and similar factors will usually prevent. In consequence, market prices are usually indeterminate inside of the possible zone, and will respond without impediment to changes in the current relation between demand and supply.

Such is the immediate and very short-time situation. Over longer periods, however, the limiting ratios may themselves be altered. In ways that are entirely familiar, persisting changes in demand will react upon costs of production, while a general change in these costs will alter the character and intensity of the demand itself. Moreover, quite apart from changes related to particular commodities, the larger movements of general prices lead to marked and often enduring discrepancies as between countries, and will alter the various non-monetary or "real" demand and cost schedules. In some cases a subsequent correction appears, but in others it does not. In these longer periods, therefore, the situation is one of continual change. Any normative or self-equilibrating tendency is at best only partially effective. At given times, it is true, a real equilibrium will appear within the limits set by current cost and demand schedules, but eventually the limits themselves will almost certainly change. It is therefore difficult, and perhaps impossible, to arrive at a satisfactory generalized formulation of the long-run relationships involved. Nor is it possible, at least in making international comparisons, to go behind the cost and demand schedules themselves to any more "fundamental" determinants of the course of the exchange. These schedules are the lowest factors to which the situation can be reduced.[1]

This type of doctrine is in essence an application of the principle of reciprocal demand, although in a sense quite different — and less precise — than that involved in Mill's celebrated Equa-

---

[1] It will be observed that the general conclusions here reached can be applied, with obvious modifications, to internal trade as well. The differences, at bottom, are very largely quantitative alone. See ch. xiv, sect. 3, above.

tion. When it is combined with the conclusions reached in Chapter XVI, above, it enables us to form a reasonably complete picture of international exchange. Taking that exchange *in the aggregate*, it is evident not only that the demands of the various countries for one another's products and services are reciprocal, but that they substantially offset one another; and that they do explicitly determine the course of international exchange at given times.[1] This equation of demands is itself the consequence of the equilibrium of the balance of international payments, which is ultimately maintained through the effects of general price changes upon the commodity balance of trade. There is also another equilibrium tendency of sorts, less exact and strictly empirical, which results from the fact that the movements of general prices themselves in different countries appear to be substantially harmonious over periods of time. But when we pass from these general relationships to particular groups of prices and particular groups of commodities, the tendency to any necessary equalization disappears. It becomes impossible to speak of "reciprocal" demands at all. In the operations of the actual markets commodities are not exchanged for commodities, nor for any other specific *product* of the foreign country. They are exchanged for currency, or for claims to currency: that is, for generalized purchasing power. The force of this consideration appears with especial clarity when a large import or export of capital is taking place.

The classical theory, however, had two aspects or divisions, of which reciprocal demand was only one. Reciprocal demand was used to explain the phenomena of the relatively immediate or short-time period. This explanation is entirely acceptable when it is confined to the course of international exchange in the aggregate, as just indicated, although it is invalid with respect to particular transactions or groups of transactions. To account for long-time relationships, recourse was had to the principle of comparative costs.

Comparative costs were made to provide the limits within which reciprocal (short-time) demand works. Given them, as be-

---

[1] Over periods of time, it will be remembered, particular demands not only vary unpredictably, but are themselves altered by such influences as the movement of general prices.

tween any two or more commodities and any two or more countries, the course of the exchange was held to be determined. But it was shown in an earlier chapter [1] that this view is not correct. It is impossible to proceed directly from labor costs to the terms of international exchange, under actual conditions, for there is another variable still to be accounted for: namely, money prices and money wages. If we know these, we can then "read back" to comparative costs, and determine what they really are in a particular case, but comparative costs are not *in themselves alone* a sufficient determinant. The relation between such costs and money prices is not the same in different countries, nor does the relation in one country bear a constant proportion to that in others.[2]

Yet although the principle of comparative costs must be rejected with respect to particular pairs of commodities, it nevertheless retains a certain value, a value similar to that assigned to the principle of reciprocal demand. If we take international exchange in the aggregate and over periods of time, it is evidently quite true that the course and character of the exchange is determined by a certain kind of comparative cost. But these costs must themselves be interpreted with respect to entire countries, not with respect to specific products or even specific branches of production.[3] If one country is relatively richer than another in natural resources, for example, while it is inadequately supplied with labor, the general character of the trade between the two is established.[4] Moreover, the trade will alter in proportion as these relationships are altered. In this sense, comparative costs are clearly the controlling factor. The meaning of the term here in-

[1] Ch. xiv, sect. 3.

[2] A further difficulty in attempting to apply comparative costs to particular commodities arises from the fact that, except in the short-run period (where the principle was not applied), labor and capital are fairly mobile between countries. This alters the costs themselves, and makes their relationship of uncertain significance as a *determinant* of international exchange. The relationship can almost as well be considered a *result*.

[3] Except in given brief periods. Over longer periods the relationship between similar industries in different countries changes.

[4] The trade between the United States and western Europe, especially in the nineteenth century, is a conspicuous example. The United States had natural resources, but relatively little labor and capital. Europe was in the opposite situation.

volved, however, is far removed from the meaning the classical writers had in mind. The "costs" involved are really not so much labor costs for particular articles as general productive costs. They might equally well be measured — if it is desired to express the volume of the total product in terms of one factor of production alone — by amounts of capital, or by quantities of raw materials.[1]

7. It is not proposed to carry the present study beyond this point. A word may be added, however, as to the position in which it leaves the general classical theory of international trade.

The conclusions reached here and in the preceding chapters have sought to make serious inroads upon that theory, so long regarded as the one unassailable part of the older English teaching, and have arrived at a quite different general view. In some directions, although the main framework of the theory remains valid, the nature of present-day banking and financial conditions, necessitates great alterations in its actual content. In other directions the theory itself, both in its specific tenets and in the general relationships which it postulates, has been shown to be erroneous. The principal modifications indicated are three in number. First, the classical doctrine of international values, which was oriented primarily on the principle of comparative labor costs, is not tenable when it is interpreted in any sense immediate enough or exact enough to be significant. An alternative analysis has therefore been worked out, which is based on actual money costs and money prices. Second, the doctrine of equilibrium in the mechanisms of international exchange is sound in its underlying principle, but

We exported food stuffs and raw materials, and took manufactures in payment. Indeed, because of the investment of European capital here we often got far more commodities than we gave, in particular periods.

[1] So also of the "effectiveness" of labor, in any sense wider than the skill and industriousness of the individuals concerned. It is quite as reasonable to speak of the "effectiveness" of capital or of natural resources. The measure of relative effectiveness is simply relative volume of output — which is the joint product of all three factors.

Other difficulties in speaking of the effectiveness of labor were suggested above, at the end of ch. xv, sect. 5. It may also be remarked that a greater "effectiveness" in one country than in another, at least for periods of some length, may result solely in producing a higher level of money incomes. In that event neither prices nor the course of foreign trade will be affected.

has practical value only when the specie-flow analysis is replaced by another and more complex explanation. This explanation rests on the effects which changes in the demand and supply of bills of exchange produce in the volume of bank deposits, and in the levels of general prices. Finally, the classical account of the phenomena appearing under dissimilar and depreciating currencies, which ran in terms of changes in the quantity of money and of the resulting effect upon prices and the foreign exchanges, has been shown to have only a very general and non-quantitative application to any such conditions as those witnessed since 1914. A whole range of factors which it never contemplated, turning on the effects of widespread speculation in the currency and the exchanges, must also be included.

Defenders of the classical theory may object that the treatment offered in these pages does not go deep enough, that it does not explain the conditions which at bottom govern the course of trade and determine the superiority of one country or another in particular branches of production. In answer to this objection, it is only possible to repeat the observation made at other points. Comparisons between countries, and even between districts, can safely be effected only by the use of relative money prices. It is necessary to let all presumably antecedent theories of "value," as distinct from theories of the proximate determination of market prices, go by the board. Propositions can of course be formulated which go behind the phenomena of market price, and which undertake to explain their underlying determinants, but only in such general terms that they have little significance for the concrete problems of international exchange.

APPENDICES

APPENDIX A

THE BANK RESTRICTION PERIOD IN ENGLAND, 1797–1821

1. Recent studies of the Bank Restriction period in English financial history, especially those of Professor Silberling, have made it possible to form a much more complete picture than before of the essential facts in the situation.[1] These facts, in so far as they are relevant to the problems involved in the theory of international prices, are presented in the tables and charts that follow. They cast new light on the doctrines that were advanced in the course of the Bullion Controversy, and make necessary a considerable revision of the older view of their merits.

The principal conclusions to which the new facts lead may well be presented in advance of the somewhat laborious data themselves. The reasoning on which these conclusions rest will then be explained in more detail by an examination of certain selected groups of facts, brought together in the form of a series of charts and accompanying notes. Finally, the basic data themselves are given in tables at the end of this Appendix. The conclusions are as follows:

First, the course of the foreign exchanges, and of the premium on silver, were intimately governed by the balance of international payments, but — directly at least — by little else. The dominant factor in the exchange market was the imperative need of the British government for making continued remittances to the Continent: remittances to support the British armies, for direct or indirect subsidies to other countries allied against France, and for all the other expenditures involved in carrying on a war abroad. To this constant pressure was also added the occasional strain of abnormal grain imports, in times of harvest dearth at home. The close relationship between these extraordinary and primarily military remittances, the exchanges, and the specie premium is indicated in Chart VIII.[2] The *inverse* relationship

---

[1] N. J. Silberling, *Financial and Monetary Policy of Great Britain during the Napoleonic Wars* (*38 Quarterly Journal of Economics*, February and May, 1924); *British Prices and Business Cycles, 1779–1850* (*Review of Economic Statistics*, October, 1923, Supplement). On the development of contemporary opinion, see ch. iii, above.

[2] Also see Chart XIII, for a study of the causal connection between the remittances and the exchanges.

between the remittances and the reserves of the Bank of England — the latter showing a distinct lag — is indicated in Chart IX. England made every effort to keep up her foreign exchanges by exporting specie, and the specie, directly or indirectly, was largely taken from the Bank.

Second, there was a very general and loose relationship between the premium and the exchanges on the one hand, and the course of general prices on the other. But the relationship is far too uncertain to permit the assertion that either set of changes *caused* the other set, or to permit of their being attributed directly to a common cause. This is shown in Chart X. So far as there was any common cause at all, it is to be found in the exigencies of government war-time finance. To anticipate somewhat, the government's need for means of making foreign remittances led to exchange depreciation; and its need for domestic funds contributed, through the advances made by the Bank, to currency inflation and to the rise in domestic prices. But between the foreign exchanges and domestic inflation, between internal and external "depreciation," there was no direct short-time connection at all. The general fact that the exchanges actually were depreciated, and stayed so for over twenty years, is of course in part explainable by the existence of inflation. But all of the critical *fluctuations* in the exchanges are traceable to the balance of payments, not to changes in the quantity of money.

The recently resurrected purchasing-power-parity doctrine hence cannot explain the situation, at least so far as the fluctuations in English prices are concerned (data on Continental prices are not obtainable). Nor can the opposed doctrine, which proceeds from the balance of payments and the exchanges *to* internal prices, and the volume of currency, be convincingly applied.

Third, the most probable explanation of the actual fluctuations in prices turns on the fluctuations in the volume of domestic currency and credit. To 1806–1807, the explanation is difficult to make, because of the lack of statistics. The only data obtainable, those for the Bank of England, can at best be made to account for a third of the rise. We are compelled to fall back on general inferences as to the character of the missing elements. Of these the uncontrolled inflation of country note issues and credits seems, on the basis of the known data of later years, to be in all probability the most important. The price peak of 1801, however, was due to agricultural dearth rather than to strictly monetary conditions. After 1806, the explanation is simpler, if the calculations here presented are correct, and if the interpretation placed upon them is justified. The fluctuations in prices correspond, on the whole very closely, to the deviations of the combined country and Bank of England note circulations as measured from an estimated norm of growth. The corresponding data, original and computed, are set forth in Charts XI and XII respectively.

Fourth, the principal causes of the increase in the note circulation itself were two-fold: the action of the country banks, and the needs of the government. The innumerable and weed-like country banks were virtually free from any sort of control, either by governmental examination or by an effective requirement of convertibility, even into Bank of England notes. The consequence was extravagant expansion just before and during prosperity, and ruinous contraction before and during crises. The numerically larger part of the banking system had thus become essentially speculative. The other source of increase was the action of the government, which was constantly in need of domestic funds to supply the domestic needs of war. These funds, directly or indirectly, it obtained very largely from the Bank; and the Bank, compelled to grant larger and larger credits in the face of all its sound misgivings, became the apparent agent of inflation. Yet there is little evidence that the Bank inflated *private* credit. Rather, its private advances were kept moderate in times of rising prices, and expanded when prices fell. As far as its own deliberate and intended policy went, it should be exonerated from virtually all blame.

Fifth, these last conclusions place the Bullionist writers, and especially the authors of the Bullion Report, in a new light. Far from being the inspired expounders of sound monetary analysis and policy, they were at least two thirds wrong, and probably more — some from pecuniary interest, the majority from simple ignorance of the facts. The "high price of bullion" had no direct connection at all with the operations of the Bank. The high price of things in general — inflation — was due to the policies of government financiers (uncriticized by the Bullionists), and to the exonerated country banks. Inflation, though unavoidable in any event, was greatly and needlessly exaggerated by the country banks. And it took place not because of, but in spite of, the voluntary operations of the Bank of England. The Bank alone remained the refuge of sound policy. At least one writer has well remarked that, had the recommendations of the Bullion Committee been put into effect, there would probably be no British Empire to-day. Contraction, by paralyzing government financing, would have lost the war.

Finally, there remains the question of why the exchanges returned to a substantial parity after 1816, and why prices fell to a permanently lower level. It is not easy to answer this question in quantitative terms. The return of the exchanges was in the first instance due to the removal of the chief disturbing cause, abnormal governmental payments abroad. (See Chart VIII.) Ultimately, however, the psychological effect of the stabilization of British finances must have exerted a strong influence. The fall of prices was similarly related in part to the financial situation of the government, but also to the general condition of private credit. That is, prices were a direct function of the current volume of credit as a whole, both private and governmental. The reduction and ultimate cessation of the pressure of government borrowing, especially short-time, and the gradual correction of the inflationary tendencies of the country banks, combined to bring about the reduction of prices to a very much lower level after 1814. This is shown clearly in Chart XII.

2. The conclusions just presented are based on the character of the relationships that exist between various measurable factors in the situation. These relationships it is now proposed to examine in more detail, by graphic methods. No statistical refinements, however, will be attempted. So far as the data available permit such refinements at all, they have in large part been made already in those studies by Professor Silberling which have been referred to above.

I. EXTRAORDINARY FOREIGN PAYMENTS, THE EXCHANGES, AND THE SILVER PREMIUM

These data are presented in Chart VIII. The curves are plotted from columns 1, 2, and 3 of the Statistical Tables. The foreign exchange quotations are those on Hamburg. The Paris quotations are substantially the same in their movements (except 1804–1805, and 1815–1816), but they are less complete and less sensitive.

The coincidence of these curves in the general direction of their movement is on the whole very close. The only important discrepancy is that between the peaks of 1811 and 1813. It is in general close enough to suggest very strongly a causal relationship, *from* the volume of foreign payments *to* the silver premium and the exchanges. To 1808 the exchanges followed the payments more closely than did the premium. This was presumably due to an actual scarcity of metallic currency in England, which forced the premium up independently of the situation of the exchange market: coins were drawn from circulation by exportation, and to some extent by hoarding. Thereafter the premium followed the payments as closely as did the exchanges. The relatively high level of both exchanges and premium in 1811–1812 — with the exchanges showing a characteristic tendency to anticipate and exaggerate the movements of the payments — was due to the adverse trade balance with Northern Europe, caused largely by the blockade measures. (See N. J. Silberling, "Financial and Monetary Policy," *loc. cit.*, pp. 231–233.) The difference in the apparent levels of the exchanges and the volume of extraordinary payments is due, not only to the obvious explanation of a difference in the scales and methods of measurement, but to the fact that complete data on the volume of payments are lacking. The apparently excessive depreciation of the exchanges from 1808 to 1816 (that is, beyond what the volume of extraordinary payments seem to justify) was probably due — speculation apart — to a falling off in the total of *other* remittances payable abroad: the government remittances became relatively more important in the total of the payment operations. On this see Chart XIII.

It will be remembered that the quotation on gold, when obtainable, moved closely with that on silver. (See column 20, and note.)

Finally, it is evident that the removal of the pressure for governmental remittances was directly responsible, in the first instance at least, for the return of the exchanges to substantial parity after 1816.

II. Extraordinary Foreign Payments and Bank of England Reserves

The data are presented in Chart IX. The curves are plotted from columns 1 and 6 of the Statistical Tables.

The relationship of the curves is clear. Each increase in the volume of extraordinary remittances led to a subsequent decline in the Bank's reserves, while every slackening of the pressure allowed them to be built up again. This shows conclusively the source from which England's war-time payments to the Continent were as far as possible taken. England was making every effort to pay her way abroad, and to keep up the exchanges by using specie directly, thus decreasing the pressure for drafts on London. (See N. J. Silberling, "Financial and Monetary Policy," *loc. cit.*, pp. 231–233.) The lag of fluctuations in the reserves behind fluctuations in the volume of payments, which appears to run as high as a year or more, would be much diminished had it been feasible to present the *quarterly* figures for reserves. In part, also, it is probably accounted for by the delay in the transmission of effects

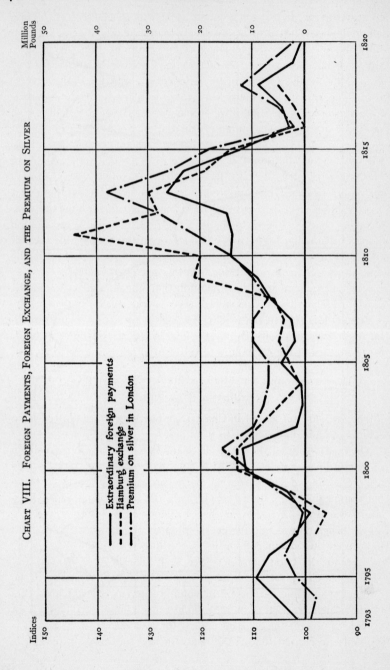

CHART VIII. FOREIGN PAYMENTS, FOREIGN EXCHANGE, AND THE PREMIUM ON SILVER

Extraordinary foreign payments
Hamburg exchange
Premium on silver in London

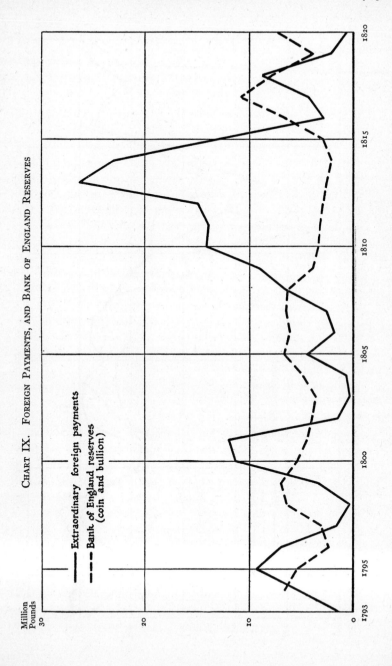

CHART IX. FOREIGN PAYMENTS, AND BANK OF ENGLAND RESERVES

Extraordinary foreign payments
Bank of England reserves
(coin and bullion)

from the exchange market to the money market and the Bank. By no means all of the payments, even on government account, were drawn *directly* from the Bank's reserves.

III. Prices, Exchange Rates, and the Premium on Silver

The data are presented in Chart X. The curves are plotted from columns 2, 3, and 11 of the Statistical Tables.

These curves show that there was a general and rather loose relationship between the major movements of the exchanges and the silver premium, on the one hand, and the course of general prices on the other. But the coincidence is not very close, and is especially doubtful for the critical years 1810–1815. It cannot be claimed, by the adherents of the purchasing-power-parity doctrine, that the rise in prices altogether accounts for the depreciation of the exchanges. (At least, in so far as British prices are an index: data on Continental price movements are missing.) Nor can the adherents of the opposite view claim that the depreciation of the exchanges entirely explains the rise in prices. There is undoubtedly a general coincidence of movements. But it is not close enough to justify either an assertion that the two elements were causally related, in one direction or the other, or that they were mutually dependent on a joint *antecedent* source of disturbance. As will be seen from the charts that follow, the addition of another independent element is necessary for a complete explanation. This element is largely provided by the fluctuations in the volume of domestic media of exchange.

It may also be pointed out that, contrary to the opinion of most contemporary writers, neither the specie premium nor the rise in the foreign exchanges were correct measures of the depreciation, if this last be measured by commodity prices. Both were much too low. Furthermore, both were tied up directly with the balance of payments, but *not*, in the first instance at least, with increases in the quantity of money. The characteristic Bullionist thesis was true, if at all, only very loosely. (Also see note to Chart XII.)

IV. Prices, Bank Advances, and Note Circulations

The data are presented in Chart XI. The curves are plotted from columns 5, 7, 9, 11, and 14 of the Statistical Tables. The first three and the last provide various partial indices of fluctuations in the volume of domestic currency and credit.

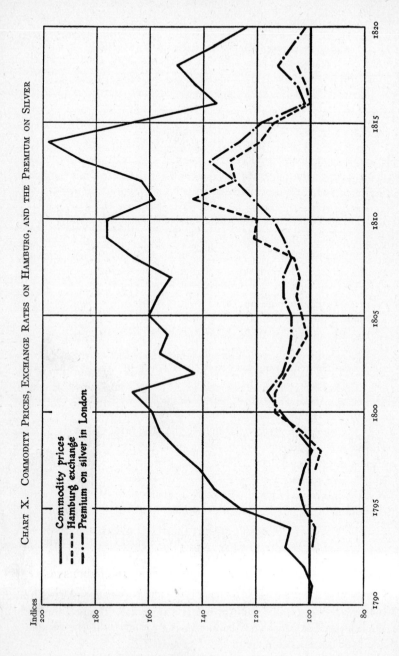

CHART X. COMMODITY PRICES, EXCHANGE RATES ON HAMBURG, AND THE PREMIUM ON SILVER

The greatest fluctuations were those in the Bank's total advances, and this seems to support the conclusions of the Bullionist writers. But the item is a composite. It is made up both of loans (direct or indirect) to the government, and loans to the market — of which the item commercial discounts is here taken as an index. It is evident that while the movements of the Bank's note issues were fairly well synchronized with the movements of prices, its total advances were not, and its advances to the market still less so. These last reached a peak in 1810, not 1814, and their fluctuations tended to be just *opposite* to those of prices. When prices were rising — especially after 1805 — discounts were held moderate or even contracted; when prices were falling they were usually increased, relatively if not always absolutely. In other words the Bank, in that part of the credit extensions over which it had independent control, exercised a *moderating* policy, of restraint in boom times and of assistance in stringency. (For a more detailed demonstration of this see Silberling, "British Prices," *loc. cit.*, pp. 240–241.) The inflationary element in its credit expansions was primarily due, rather, to the insistent pressure of the government for continued accommodation; an accommodation which the Bank was compelled to grant, despite its constant protests.

The Bank *note* circulation was a comparatively stable element, increasing steadily but moderately to 1817, then declining more abruptly. The great element of fluctuation in the volume of currency was, rather, the issues of the country banks. These issues usually expanded greatly before and during a rise in prices, while they contracted even more abruptly before and during a fall.

It therefore seems safe to conclude that the principal sources of the rise in prices — of inflation — were, first, the demand of the government for loans, as reflected in the volume of the Bank's total advances, and to a less extent in its note issues; and second, the operations of the greatly increased number of practically unregulated country banks. The Bank of England, *in so far as its independent and uncontrolled loan-extensions were concerned*, was largely blameless. (See Silberling, "British Prices," *loc. cit.*, p. 246; and note to the next chart following.)

V. Prices and Note-Circulation Deviations

The data are presented in Chart XII. The curves are plotted from columns 8, 10, and 11 of the Statistical Tables. The composition of the note-deviation curves is explained in the notes to the corresponding

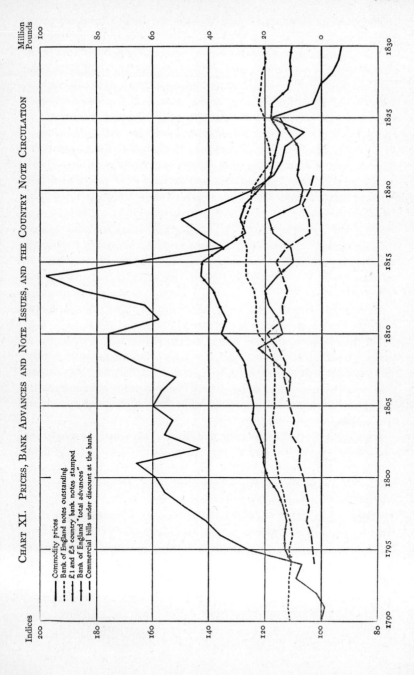

CHART XI. PRICES, BANK ADVANCES AND NOTE ISSUES, AND THE COUNTRY NOTE CIRCULATION

Commodity prices
Bank of England notes outstanding
£1 and £5 country bank notes stamped
Bank of England "total advances"
Commercial bills under discount at the bank

columns. They represent deviations from an estimated (and straight-line) norm of growth.

These curves are an attempt to discover how far the variations in the volume of internal currency and credit can explain the variations in general prices. The reasons for selecting the indices of internal circulation here used, instead of some other, are given in the note to column 10. The indices of course do not take direct account of variations in bank credit in *excess* of that represented by outstanding note issues. The assumption must therefore be made that such excesses fluctuated substantially in proportion to the note issues themselves. The results obtained, however, make this assumption seem not unreasonable. The assumption is conspicuously *not* true for the Bank of England during the restoration period. But the fluctuations in the excess of the Bank's total advances above its note issues were due primarily to the demands of government war-time finance, not to strictly commercial operations (see below, and also the note to column 5); and the *relative* changes in advances were out of all proportion to the fluctuations in prices. (See Chart XI.)

It is at once evident that the data available by no means tell the whole story for the earlier period, up to 1807–1808; while in 1817 and 1818 they seem to tell too much. In the period from 1807 to 1815–1816, however, the coincidence of the price curve and the combined note-deviation curve is convincingly close. The general range is similar, and the price curve follows the other with a reasonable lag (which would be considerably diminished had it been practicable to present the quarterly figures here).

The period to 1806–1807 is the least easy to explain, for the available data account, at best, for less than a third of the actual rise in prices. There is good ground for thinking (see Silberling, "British Prices," *loc. cit.*, p. 246) that the missing element is largely to be found in the fluctuations of country bank notes and country credit — a conclusion which is supported by the known facts of the years subsequent to 1806. But certain other factors must also be considered: (1) The "psychological" impetus given to prices by the outbreak of war. There is no other way of explaining the abrupt rise of 1794 and 1795, after the slight check of 1793–1794. The Bank circulation, for example, was on the whole, *decreasing*. (2) An actual shortage of certain commodities, due to the ordinary war-time interruptions to trade, and later to the various blockades. (3) The depreciation of the exchanges produced by the position of the balance of payments — leading directly to higher

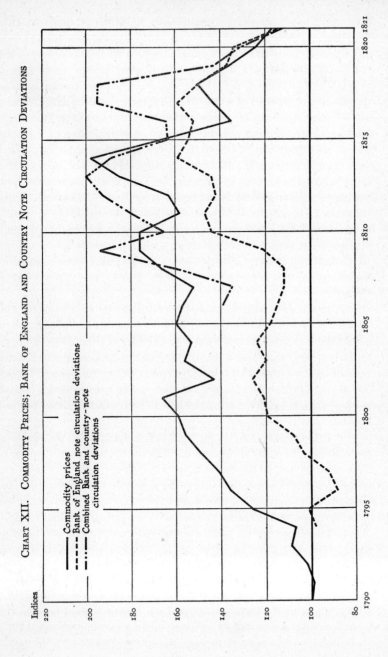

CHART XII. COMMODITY PRICES; BANK OF ENGLAND AND COUNTRY NOTE CIRCULATION DEVIATIONS

Indices

Commodity prices
Bank of England note circulation deviations
Combined Bank and country-note circulation deviations

import prices, and indirectly, by domestic competition, to higher export prices. That this element was not especially important in the Restriction period *as a whole*, however, is shown by Charts VIII and X: the exchanges and the silver premium are intimately related to the balance of payments, but only very loosely to the course of prices. (4) Working in the opposite direction, toward a *fall* in prices, there was a decrease in the metallic circulation from exportation and from hoarding, which was not offset by the increase in paper money for some years — judging from the Bank circulation at least.

In the period from 1807–1808 to 1815–1816, the effects of the statistically unascertainable factors seem to have been fairly well offset by the increase in the Bank and country circulations: the price curve and the combined deviations-curve are satisfyingly similar. (The average deviation from the "normal" is, for the combined Bank and country note issues from 1806 to 1816 inclusive, 171.1; for prices, 166.5.) It will be observed, however, that the curve for the deviations of Bank of England notes taken alone appears to *follow* rather than to precede the price curve, and to be relatively stable when the *combined* curve was most variable. The critical fluctuations in the total volume of paper currency were due, rather, to the uncontrolled country issues — further evidence of the error in charging the Bank with the entire responsibility for inflation. The country issues seem to have anticipated and exaggerated the changing fortunes of business at every turn, whereas the Bank circulation was relatively stable — as in the crises of 1810–1811 and 1814–1815. (Also see Silberling, "British Prices," *loc. cit.*, pp. 237–238.)

In the period after 1816, the country issues again soared. Prices responded, but much less than in proportion (here they moved more closely with the Bank circulation alone) and soon resumed their drastic post-war collapse. The crisis of 1819–1820 ensued.

A further conclusion can also be drawn from this and the preceding chart: namely, that the Bullionists in general, and the framers of the "Bullion Report" especially, were apparently somewhat less than one third right in their condemnation of the Bank. It is true that the Bank's excessive issues of currency and credit were one of the two chief sources of inflation. But, in the first place, the responsibility for the excess lay primarily with the government, not with the Bank itself. In the second place, the more violent and more disastrous fluctuations in the total volume of media of exchange were due to the operations of the uncontrolled country institutions, not of the Bank. Finally, in the only part of its loan-extensions over which it retained full control — its advances to the market — the Bank gives evidence at almost every stage of having followed a *non*-inflationary and commendable policy. The government and the country banks were to blame for inflation and for "the high price of bullion," not the Bank of England. The curves of Chart XI indicate clearly that the volume of commercial discounts moved *after* prices rather than before, and with a moderating influence. This is shown still more clearly by the quarterly data Professor Silberling has collected, although the data are too voluminous to reproduce here. The Bank's *total* advances, on the other hand, were fairly well synchronized with prices. Now commercial discounts made up only 35 per cent of the Bank's total advances for the whole period 1794–1821, and only 24 per cent for the period 1811–1821. (See note to column 15 of the Tables, below.) The balance of the item was in part made up of loans on commercial collateral, but the greatest part of it almost certainly represented the direct or indirect carrying of government obligations, especially short-time. This conclusion is partly verified by the fact that, until after 1815, the difference between discounts and advances was nearly always larger than, and fluctuated roughly with, the excess of governmental outlay over revenue. (See column 16 of the Tables.) It therefore seems highly probable that while government borrowings were an important factor in the rise of prices, the commercial operations of the Bank were not. The Bank was not to blame. (Also see Cannan, *op. cit.*, p. xlvi; Silberling, "Financial and Monetary Policy," *loc. cit.*, pp. 221–222 and following; and idem, "British Prices," *loc. cit.*, pp. 240–242.)

VI. GOVERNMENT REMITTANCES AND THE FOREIGN
EXCHANGES AGAIN

The data collected by Professor Silberling have made it possible to draw a further tentative conclusion, of considerable theoretical interest, as to the quantitative relation between the abnormal government remittances to the Continent and the course of the exchanges. In his article on "Financial and Monetary Policy," already referred to, he presents figures for the total commodity imports and commodity exports of England during this period. I have taken the figures for commodity imports, and added to them the figures for government remittances, in order to get the total volume of payments due by England to other countries. (The figures for government remittances are secured by subtracting those for excess grain imports, shown in column

19 of the Tables below, from those for the totals of extraordinary foreign payments in column 1.) These totals were then divided into the volume of government remittances alone, in order to estimate the importance of the government-payment item in the total balance of payments. A similar operation was performed with exports as the base, instead of imports. These various figures are given in full in Table V. (There are no import and export figures for 1813.)

The ratios showing the relative importance of government remittances were then compared with the course of the exchange on Hamburg. The correlation between the remittance ratios and the exchange is extraordinarily close, with the ratios on the whole preceding somewhat. It seems impossible not to conclude that the immediate cause of the exchange depreciation and fluctuation was the pressure for government remittances; and that the exchanges moved only just far enough, on the whole, to equate the total volume of payments due *to* England (measured in foreign currencies) with the total volume of payments due *from* England. The relations on which these conclusions are based are presented graphically in Chart XIII. In the chart, the ratio derived from exports is used instead of that derived from imports, because it gives a closer correlation. This last fact is presumably due simply to the existence of unrecorded non-commodity debit items other than government remittances, which also entered the balance of payments. The curves begin with 1797, since before then the gold standard was operative. On the chart, a par rate of exchange is plotted as 100, a depreciation of 25% as 125, and so on. To make the curves comparable, therefore, a remittance ratio of 0 is similarly plotted as 100; a ratio of 25% is plotted as 125; and so on.

But a fundamental difficulty is involved in the original data, which makes the significance of these correlations uncertain. The figures for imports and exports are based on "official" valuations, themselves derived from prices current toward the close of the seventeenth century. The movements of the import and export figures are therefore only indices of changes in the physical volume (at fixed prices) of imports and exports, not of changes in the total sums of money due or receivable. The actual close correlation between the remittance ratios based on them, and the course of the exchanges, seems to show that the physical volume of goods, and the volume of total money payments due or receivable for them, moved fairly closely together. If prices moved upward, however, and thus increased the volume of payments more than in proportion to the increase in physical quantities, this ought to make

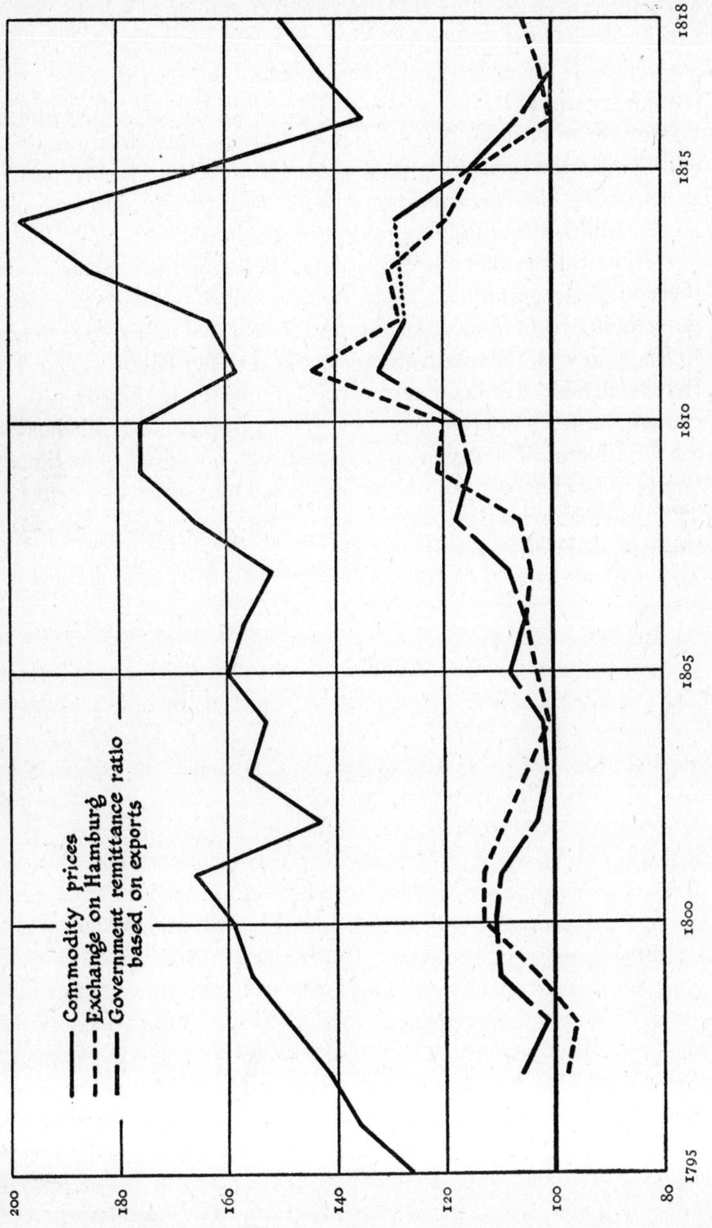

CHART XIII. THE VOLUME OF GOVERNMENTAL FOREIGN REMITTANCES AND THE EXCHANGES

the remittance ratios, as here calculated, too high. For the denominator in the ratios, physical volume, would be too small. If on the contrary prices moved upward, the opposite ought to be true: the denominator would be too large, and the resulting ratios too small. It is interesting to observe that those expectations are substantially borne out by the relationships shown on Chart XIII. During periods of rising prices, the remittance ratio was *above* the actual exchanges, as a rule, while during falling prices it was below.

Despite the peculiarities of the data, therefore, the conclusions of the preceding paragraph are on the whole justified — that the exchanges moved only just far enough to equate the total of money payments due to England with the total volume due by her. The balance of payments, that is, would have been very near equilibrium at the par rate of exchange, had the government not been compelled to remit heavily to the Continent. The exchanges depreciated enough to allow these payments to be effected, and when they ceased moved back to near parity. The general theoretical significance of the substantial verification of this proposition is evidently great.

3. The statistical data on which the conclusions of this Appendix are based are presented in the following pages. Their source and composition are indicated in notes placed after the tables.

TABLE I. THE FOREIGN EXCHANGE SITUATION

Year	1 Extraordinary for- eign payments. In million pounds	2 Per cent premium on silver in London. Par = 100	3 Deviations of ex- change on Hamburg. Par = 100	4 Deviations of ex- change on Paris. Par = 100
1791	...	...	...	...
1792	...	...	...	...
1793	1.4	99	...	...
1794	5.3	98	...	...
1795	9.4	102	...	...
1796	7.0	104	...	...
1797	1.6	102	98	...
1798	0.3	99	96	...
1799	3.4	105	103	...
1800	11.3	111	113	...
1801	12.0	116	113	...
1802	1.5	110	109	106
1803	0.3	108	105	103
1804	0.7	107	101	100
1805	4.5	107	103	99
1806	1.8	110	105	103
1807	2.6	110	104	104
1808	6.6	107	106	108
1809	9.1	110	121	123
1810	14.1	114	120	125
1811	13.8	121	144	139
1812	14.8	128	128	131
1813	26.3	138	130	127
1814	23.1	126	119	116
1815	11.9	118	114	117
1816	2.9	102	100	100
1817	4.4	105	102	102
1818	8.9	112	105	104
1819	2.2	107	...	...
1820	0.7	102	...	...

TABLE II. THE BANK OF ENGLAND; COUNTRY NOTES

Year	5 "Total advances" of the B. of E. In million pounds	6 B. of E. reserves: coin and bullion. In million pounds	7 B. of E. notes outstanding. In million pounds [1]	8 Deviations of B. of E. circulation from a "norm." In per cents	9 £1 and £5 country notes stamped. In million pounds	10 Deviations of B. of E. *plus* country circulations. In per cents
1791	...	...	11.8	...	...	...
1792	...	...	11.5	...	...	...
1793	...	...	11.6	...	...	...
1794	10.5	6.7	10.8	98	...	...
1795	13.0	5.4	11.5	101	...	...
1796	13.1	2.3	10.2	88	...	...
1797	12.4	3.1	11.0	92	...	...
1798	13.6	6.4	12.6	103	...	...
1799	15.4	7.0	13.5	108	...	...
1800	19.0	5.4	15.2	119	...	...
1801	20.6	4.5	15.8	121	...	...
1802	20.5	4.0	16.9	126	...	...
1803	22.1	3.6	16.5	120	...	...
1804	24.5	4.8	17.4	124	...	...
1805	24.0	6.7	16.9	118	...	...
1806	25.0	6.1	16.8	115	11.6	139
1807	26.6	6.5	16.7	112	11.1	135
1808	27.3	6.4	17.1	112	16.4	160
1809	30.3	4.0	18.7	121	22.4	194
1810	35.7	3.4	22.5	144	13.9	165
1811	33.9	3.3	23.5	147	15.4	180
1812	36.4	3.0	23.2	142	18.9	193
1813	38.5	2.6	24.0	144	20.2	200
1814	42.9	2.2	26.9	159	15.9	189
1815	42.5	3.0	26.9	154	10.1	163
1816	34.6	6.6	26.6	152	11.0	164
1817	27.0	10.8	28.3	159	17.3	195
1818	29.0	7.8	27.2	150	18.9	195
1819	27.2	3.9	25.1	137	7.9	143
1820	22.2	7.3	24.9	134	6.7	131
1821	18.0	...	21.6	114	8.7	113
1822	17.1	...	17.9	...	8.0	...
1823	16.0	...	18.6	...	8.4	...
1824	14.8	...	20.1	...	11.8	...
1825	17.9	...	20.1	...	14.9	...
1826	17.6	...	22.3	...	...	...
1827	12.0	...	21.5	...	...	...
1828	10.8	...	21.1	...	...	...
1829	11.2	...	19.7	...	...	...
1830	10.6	...	20.5	...	...	...

[1] The figure for 1790 is 11.1.

TABLE III. COMMODITY PRICES

Year	11 Silberling's index of commodity prices. 1790 = 100	12 "Residual" prices: silver premium removed. 1790 = 100	13 Jevons's index of commodity prices. 1782 = 100
1791	99	...	...
1792	102	...	93
1793	109	110	99
1794	107	108	98
1795	126	123	117
1796	136	131	125
1797	141	139	110
1798	149	151	118
1799	156	149	130
1800	159	143	141
1801	166	144	153
1802	143	131	119
1803	156	145	128
1804	153	143	122
1805	160	150	136
1806	157	143	133
1807	152	139	132
1808	166	155	149
1809	176	160	161
1810	176	154	164
1811	158	132	147
1812	163	128	148
1813	185	134	149
1814	198	157	153
1815	166	140	152
1816	135	132	109
1817	143	136	120
1818	150	135	135
1819	136	127	117
1820	124	123	106
1821	117	...	94
1822	114	...	...
1823	113	...	...
1824	106	...	...
1825	118	...	...
1826	103	...	...
1827	101	...	...
1828	97	...	...
1829	94	...	...
1830	93	...	...

TABLE IV. STATISTICS SUPPLEMENTARY TO TABLES I, II, III

Year	14 Commercial bills under discount at the B. of E. In million pounds	15 Percentage of Bank's commercial discounts to total advances	16 Excess of government outlay over revenue. In million pounds [1]	17 Unfunded governmental borrowing. In million pounds	18 Funded governmental borrowing. In million pounds	19 Grain imports above two million pounds. In million pounds	20 Premium on gold in London. Par = 100.
1791	...	...	...	10.5	...	...	...
1792	...	...	−1.9	8.5	...	...	...
1793	...	...	4.4	8.5	3.9	...	...
1794	2.5	24	9.4	10.0	12.9	...	...
1795	3.0	23	31.8	13.7	18.8	...	...
1796	3.5	27	36.2	7.0	28.6	2.5	...
1797	5.2	42	27.4	10.2	42.8	...	100
1798	4.4	33	19.9	14.3	22.8	...	100
1799	5.5	36	19.8	27.2	16.4	...	...
1800	6.3	23	22.4	26.0	20.5	6.8	107
1801	8.0	39	26.5	23.6	36.1	8.2	109
1802	7.6	37	13.1	16.5	26.1	0.2	...
1803	10.8	49	10.4	18.9	12.0	...	...
1804	9.8	40	12.4	18.7	14.2	...	103
1805	11.3	47	16.0	27.7	25.3	1.8	103
1806	12.1	48	12.7	30.9	20.1	...	...
1807	13.3	50	8.0	34.5	15.5	...	...
1808	12.9	47	10.0	45.1	14.2	...	...
1809	15.3	51	12.8	36.1	22.6	0.7	...
1810	19.5	55	9.7	37.7	21.6	5.1	...
1811	13.7	40	18.4	41.2	23.8	...	124
1812	14.0	39	21.2	45.8	34.9	...	130
1813	12.3	32	36.7	54.2	51.1	0.2	136
1814	14.0	32	35.2	52.3	36.6	0.8	124
1815	16.2	38	19.9	44.8	50.7	...	119
1816	12.3	36	2.5	46.6	9.3	...	103
1817	4.3	16	1.5	...	...	4.4	102
1818	4.6	16	−2.0	...	...	8.9	105
1819	6.9	25	−0.4	...	...	2.2	...
1820	4.2	19	−1.9	...	...	0.7	...
1821	2.9	16	−2.8	...	...	...	...

[1] Minus sign: excess of revenue.

TABLE V. THE RATIO OF GOVERNMENT REMITTANCES TO THE TOTAL
BRITISH BALANCE OF INTERNATIONAL PAYMENTS

Year	21 Com- modity exports. In million pounds	22 Com- modity imports. In million pounds	23 Government remittances (col. 1 minus col. 19). In million pounds	24 Exports plus government remittances. In million pounds	25 Imports plus government remittances In million pounds	26 Ratio of govt. remit- tances to total credit payments. (Based on exports.) In per cents	27 Ratio of govt. remit- tances to total debit payments. (Based on imports.) In per cents
1791	20	17	...	...	...	...	...
1792	22	17	...	...	...	...	...
1793	18	16	1.4	19.4	17.4	...	...
1794	23	19	5.3	28.3	24.3	...	...
1795	23	20	9.4	32.4	29.4	...	...
1796	26	21	4.5	30.5	25.5	...	...
1797	24	18	1.6	25.6	19.6	6	8
1798	28	26	0.3	28.3	26.3	1	1
1799	30	24	3.4	33.4	27.4	10	12
1800	36	28	4.5	40.5	32.5	11	14
1801	37	31	3.9	40.9	34.9	10	11
1802	40	30	1.4	41.4	31.4	3	4
1803	29	27	0.3	29.3	27.3	1	1
1804	32	28	0.7	32.7	28.7	2	2
1805	31	29	2.7	33.7	31.7	8	8
1806	34	27	1.8	35.8	28.8	5	6
1807	31	27	2.6	33.6	29.6	8	9
1808	30	27	6.6	36.6	33.6	18	20
1809	48	31	8.4	56.4	39.4	15	21
1810	45	40	9.1	54.1	49.1	17	18
1811	29	27	13.8	42.8	40.8	32	34
1812	40	27	14.8	54.8	41.8	27	35
1813	...	...	26.1	...	...	...	...
1814	55	34	22.3	77.3	56.7	29	39
1815	60	33	11.9	76.9	44.9	15	27
1816	49	27	2.9	51.9	30.0	6	9
1817	52	31	negligible	52.0	31.0	0	0
1818	56	37	after 1816	56.0	37.0	0	0
1819	43	30	...	43.0	30.0	0	0
1820	49	32	...	49.0	32.0	0	0
1821	52	30	...	52.0	30.0	0	0

4. Notes to statistical tables.

Column 1. Extraordinary foreign payments. — Taken from N. J. Silberling, "Financial and Monetary Policy of Great Britain during the Napoleonic Wars" (38 *Quarterly Journal of Economics*, February and May, 1924), p. 227. This item includes bills drawn and specie remitted for: (1) the British armies in Europe; (2) British subsidies, loans, etc., to foreign states and to diplomatic agents; (3) the estimated excess value of British grain imports from the Continent *above* £2,000,000. (This last figure is taken as the maximum that would be imported in normal years of no especial crop deficiency. The item of excess grain imports is spasmodic: see column 19.) The data were computed by Professor Silberling from government accounts, documents, etc.

Column 2. Per cent premium on silver in London. — Taken from N. J. Silberling, "Financial and Monetary Policy," *loc. cit.*, p. 227. The quotation is for Spanish silver dollars, to the nearest per cent.

Column 3. Deviations of exchange on Hamburg. — Taken from R. G. Hawtrey, "The Bank Restriction of 1797" (*Economic Journal*, March, 1918), p. 64.

Column 4. Deviations of exchange on Paris. — Taken from R. G. Hawtrey, "The Bank Restriction of 1797," *loc. cit.*, p. 64. Despite the existence of a state of war with France during most of this period, exchange on Paris continued to be quoted: Paris and Hamburg remained the chief Continental exchange markets.

Column 5. "Total advances" of the Bank of England. — Taken from N. J. Silberling, "British Prices and Business Cycles, 1779–1850," (*Review of Economic Statistics*, October, 1923, Supplement), p. 255. Silberling gives quarterly figures, from which the annual ones here presented were obtained by a simple averaging. They include both advances to the money market, and advances to the state.

Column 6. Bank of England reserves: coin and bullion. — Taken from N. J. Silberling, "Financial and Monetary Policy," *loc. cit.*, p. 225.

Column 7. Bank of England notes outstanding. — Taken from N. J. Silberling, "British Prices," *loc. cit.*, p. 255. Silberling gives quarterly figures, from which the annual ones here presented were obtained by a simple averaging.

Column 8. Deviations of Bank of England circulation from a "norm." — These figures are calculated from the preceding column. The "norm," from which they represent the percentage deviations of the actual circulation, is the annual increase in the circulation which it is estimated would have taken place, without war or inflation, because of the normal growth of the country. To obtain this norm, the mean of the actual circulation from 1792 to 1796 was subtracted from the mean of the period 1822 to 1826 (respectively, in million pounds, 11.1 and 19.8), and the difference was distributed over the intervening years as an equal annual increment (of 0.29). The resulting norm is of course rectilinear.

Column 9. £1 and £5 country notes stamped. — Taken from N. J. Silberling, "British Prices," *loc. cit.*, p. 258. Silberling gives quarterly figures, from which the annual figures here presented were obtained by a simple averaging. They cover a limited period, but are the only index of the country note circulations and credit obtainable that is suited to the present purpose.

Column 10. Deviations of Bank of England *plus* country circulations. — These figures are calculated from columns 7 and 9, by a process essentially similar to that employed in computing the figures of column 8. The country circulation, taken alone, showed no definite trend either of increase or of decrease. To obtain a basis for calculation, therefore, the following procedure was used. The average country circulation, in the part of the Restriction period for which data were available (taking this period to extend to 1821, to get the widest possible base), was compared with the average Bank of England circulation in the same period (1806–1821). The averages, in million pounds, were respectively 14.6 and 23.1. Country notes alone, that is, made up 38.7 per cent of the average combined circulation. 38.7 per cent of the average country circulation, therefore (or 5.65 million pounds), was added to the "norm of increase" for Bank of England notes alone (as calculated for column 8 above). In this way a composite straight-line "norm" of growth was secured; and from it is calculated the deviations of the sum of the actual Bank and country circulation.

The resulting figures are by no means entirely satisfactory (as see Chart XII, and the note to it). But on the other hand they provide (together with the figures of column 8 alone, to 1806) a much better index of the volume of internal currency and credit than any of the other statistics available. Use of different bases for the Bank index (column 8), such as 1790–1794 and 1826–1830, gives practically the same combined deviation-index, at most 2 or 3 per cent lower. Use of the Bank's "total advances" (column 5), or of its commercial bills alone (column 14), produces either grotesque distortion, or insensitivity to critical general changes. The influence of loans to the government upon "total advances," for example, is far too great, relative to the influence of loans to the money market and relative to the apparent effect upon prices. (See, however, Silberling, "British Prices," *loc. cit.*, p. 240.)

Column 11. Average commodity prices. — Taken from N. J. Silberling, "British Prices," *loc. cit.*, p. 232. Silberling gives quarterly figures, from which the annual figures here presented were obtained by a simple averaging. The index, an original computation by Professor Silberling, is made up from 17 commodities of high value relative to freightage charges, and 18 of low. It differs considerably at important points from the index ordinarily used for this period, that computed by Jevons from Tooke's data. (See column 13.) The defects of Jevons's index are indicated by Silberling in the text accompanying his table. For an account of the events that accompanied the principal fluctuations in these prices, see *ibid.*, pp. 237–238.

Column 12. "Residual" prices: silver premium removed. — These figures were calculated by dividing the general price index (column 11) by the silver premium (column 2), with the object of estimating the amount of the fluctuations in prices due to causes other than those bound up with the appreciation of silver. Silver is used as a base rather than gold, because the gold quotations are not continuous. The value of gold in terms of silver, however, does not seem to have varied sufficiently to produce an important change in the residual price calculations. (See column 19, and note.) It should be remarked, however, that this elimination of the silver premium does not seem to lead to conclusive results. Various attempts to compare the corresponding curve with other series failed to reveal significant relationships.

Column 13. Jevons's index of commodity prices. — Taken from E. Cannan, "The Paper Pound of 1797–1821" (London, 1919), pp. xliii–xliv. This index, though not used in the calculations here, is presented for purposes of comparison. (See note to column 11.)

Column 14. Commercial bills under discount at the Bank of England. — Taken from N. J. Silberling, "British Prices," *loc. cit.*, p. 256. Silberling gives quarterly figures, from which the ones here presented were obtained by a simple averaging.

Column 15. Percentage of the Bank's commercial discounts to total advances. — Computed from the data of columns 5 and 14. These percentages are on the whole surprisingly low. For the whole period 1794–1821 the average is 35 per cent; while for the critical later years, 1811–1821, it is only 24 per cent.

Column 16. Excess of government outlay over revenue. — Taken from Cannan, *loc. cit.* A *surplus* is indicated by a minus sign. Also see Silberling, "Financial and Monetary Policy," *loc. cit.*, for further data on the way in which this deficit was made up; and columns 17 and 18.

Column 17. Unfunded governmental borrowing. In million pounds. — Taken from N. J. Silberling, "Financial and Monetary Policy," *loc. cit.*, p. 217.

Column 18. Funded governmental borrowing. In million pounds. — Taken from N. J. Silberling, "Financial and Monetary Policy," *loc. cit.*, p. 217. The figures for this and the preceding column are here confined to the war period.

Column 19. Grain imports in excess of two million pounds. In million pounds. — Taken from N. J. Silberling, "Financial and Monetary Policy," *loc. cit.*, p. 227. See note to column 1, above.

Column 20. Premium on gold in London. Par = 100. — Taken from R. G. Hawtrey, "The Bank Restriction of 1797," *loc. cit.*, p. 64. These figures, when they are obtainable, correspond fairly closely with the quotations for silver. (See column 2.) The ratio of gold to silver at Hamburg stayed within the range 15.11–16.11, and more than half of the quotations fall within the range 15.41–15.79. (See table, in *ibid.*)

Columns 21 and 22. Commodity exports and imports. In million pounds. — Taken from N. J. Silberling, "Financial and Monetary Policy," *loc. cit.*, pp. 228–229.

Columns 23 to 27 are self-explanatory.

Supplementary Bibliography. In addition to the publications already referred to here, and the more familiar general works dealing with the period, see H. S. Foxwell's preface to A. Andréadès's "History of the Bank of England" (2 ed., London, 1924); N. J. Silberling, "British Theories of Money and Credit," 1776–1848 (unpublished Ph.D. thesis, dated 1919, in the Harvard University Library), which contains a wealth of doctrinal as well as statistical material; and R. G. Hawtrey, "Currency and Credit" (2 ed., London, 1923), chap. 16—largely a reprint of his article in the "Economic Journal" for 1918, already referred to. Hawtrey attributes the drain of specie from England to the return of France to a metallic basis after the collapse of the assignats, rather than to remittances by the British government. (*Loc. cit.*, pp. 266 ff.) Silberling, who maintains the opposite thesis ("Financial and Monetary Policy," *loc. cit.*, pp. 231–233), admits some truth in this, but is puzzled as to why the flow of gold should have been so large, if this is to be the chief explanation. (*Ibid.*, p. 232, n. 3.) Silberling's data seem to support his view rather than Hawtrey's, as see Chart VIII above.

APPENDIX B

A NOTE ON THE INTERNATIONAL TRANSFER OF CAPITAL

The general form in which capital is transferred from one country to another has been quite definitely established. Both the writers who employ deductive methods and those who have undertaken inductive investigations are agreed that the transfers are effected primarily by means of changes in the commodity balance of trade. But it is not always quite clear just how the changes in the balance of trade are brought about, nor what are the effects of the capital transfers themselves. Much light has been cast on these questions by the considerable volume of statistical material that has been compiled in recent years. It is the purpose here to bring together the principal conclusions to which the study of this material has led, and to see what further inferences can be drawn from it. The bearing of such a discussion on the problems that are involved in the general theory of international prices requires no demonstration. The transfer of capital is evidently, from the point of view of that theory, simply one major source from which may come both changes in the ratios of commodity exchange between countries, and changes in the levels of international prices themselves.

The treatment of these questions, however, must necessarily be brief, and the details be left to the works cited. Moreover, in most of the cases it will be possible to examine the situation only with respect to the country which *receives* the capital. This limitation results from the character of the available data. Finally, nothing can be said about international transfers of capital other than those giving rise to the movement of securities or of other recorded obligations, for no comprehensive statistics dealing with such transfers have as yet been compiled. We shall consider only certain cases of private borrowing, in which the transfer of securities was involved; and certain cases of inter-governmental payments. In brief, they are: Canada, 1900–1913; the United States, 1860–1878; Argentina, 1881–1900; England, 1880–1913; France and Germany, 1871–1873; again England, 1793–1816; and the United States, 1919–1924.[1]

---

[1] Most of the material given in this note was used by the present writer in preparing a chapter for a recent publication of the National Industrial Conference Board entitled *The Inter-Ally Debts and the United States* (New York, 1925).

1. Canadian Borrowings, 1900–1913.[1]

During the years from 1900 to 1913, Canada was borrowing steadily and in increasing volume from foreign countries, especially from England. The borrowing was relatively moderate until 1908, but then expanded rapidly, reaching a high point of $547,000,000 in 1913. For the period as a whole, the total exceeded $2,500,000,000. The money was used for all sorts of industrial, commercial and even agricultural purposes, and was apparently a principal cause of the remarkable economic growth of Canada in the decade before the war. The period was one of rising prices and wages, and evidences of rapidly increasing prosperity were to be found in every direction.

The main features of the situation have already been indicated at another point in the present study (ch. vi, sect. 9, above; see also ch. xvi, sect. 3). The case is so good an example of the first phase in a borrowing operation, however, that it seems worth while to present the significant data in more detail.

An examination of the Canadian balance of international payments for the period as a whole shows that the new borrowings, amounting to $2,546,000,000, were received in these ways:

	%
Debits on capital account	42
Net commodity imports	49
Non-loan debit balances	7
Unaccounted for	2
Total	100

The debits on capital account represent interest and amortization charges payable, which were in effect cancelled by the new borrowings, and also a small volume of foreign lending by Canada herself. They form a surprisingly large fraction of the total.

The *net* import of capital was of course much smaller than the total new borrowings, since these borrowings were in part offset by the debits on capital account just referred to. It amounted to $1,538,000,000, and was received in these ways:

	%
Net commodity imports	83
Non-loan debit balances	14
Unaccounted for	3
Total	100

[1] The data on which this section is based are taken from Professor Viner's book, already referred to, on *Canada's Balance of International Indebtedness, 1900–1913* (Cambridge, 1924).

It is thus clear that the net imports of capital were received primarily in the form of an excess of commodity imports over commodity exports.[1] This conclusion is confirmed by the close correlation between the annual fluctuations in the volume of net capital import and those in the balance of trade, shown in Chart XIV. The trade balance, however, appears to follow with a lag of a year. This is probably due to

CHART XIV. CANADIAN COMMODITY AND CAPITAL IMPORTS
1900–1913

In million dollars

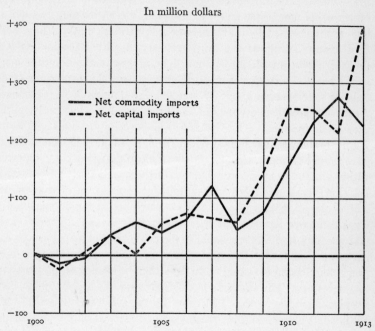

two things: first, to the interval between the announcement of each new loan (at which time it was usually credited to Canada) and its actual flotation; and second, to the lag between the accumulation of the capital abroad and the appearance of the resulting changes in the commodity balance.

Furthermore, the movements of the various groups of prices within Canada were those which would be necessary to make possible the transmission of the net capital imports primarily in the form of goods;

---

[1] The other debit items in the total Canadian balance of international payments were comparatively stable and insensitive.

that is, such as to increase commodity importation relative to exportation. This is shown by the data in Table I, below. Strictly domestic prices rose steadily to a level of 161.7 at the end of the period (with 1900 = 100). Import prices, on the other hand, rose to only 114.1, and their average for the period was only 102. Import prices are established primarily in the world markets, and the world average did not go up in anything like the same degree as Canadian domestic prices. This caused the prices of imports to fall *relative* to the general level of prices within Canada, and thus stimulated importation. Export prices, on the other hand, rose more than import prices, to 133.9, but not as high as domestic prices. This narrowed the foreign markets for Canadian exports, while at the same time making their production less profitable than the production of articles for the purely domestic market. Thus the necessary semi-permanent general changes in the trade balance were brought about. Were data also obtainable for the movements of the various groups of wages, they would undoubtedly reflect these price changes.

But this leaves unanswered the question of *how* the changes in prices were brought about; that is, of how the capital imports so operated within Canada as to alter the balance of trade to the necessary extent. Despite Professor Viner's rather different interpretation (see ch. vi, sect. 9, above), I think the solution is to be found in the fluctuations of Canadian bank deposits.[1] If in any given year the net volume of capital to be imported was just equal to the net volume of "final" means of payment available — the net volume of commodity imports, plus freight-service imports, and so forth — then no change in the situation was necessary. The sums made currently due to Canada by her borrowings abroad were then just offset by the sums she had to pay for her imports of commodities, freight services, etc. If on the other hand the net volume of capital to be imported materially *exceeded* these final means of payment, what apparently happened was that Canadian bank deposits were increased, in consequence of the increased offer for

---

[1] Bank deposits are taken as the most convenient available index of the total volume of purchasing power in circulation. In short periods this index is of course made inaccurate by changes in the distribution of currency as between bank reserves and active circulation. But in handling annual data — that is, over periods of some length — the effects of these changes tend to be smoothed over, while the general *trends* of the movements of deposits and currency in circulation are usually consistent. Moreover, the total amount of money in circulation is much smaller than the total volume of bank deposits, so that its fluctuations are, in a sense, of the second order of importance.

discount (relative to the demand) of bills of foreign exchange. If this increase in deposits was large and of some duration (statistical evidence on short-time adjustments is almost impossible to get), it led to a further rise in Canadian prices, and to a consequent further increase in commodity imports relative to exports. A considerable lag, however, usually appeared. When, finally, the net imports of capital fell *below* the final means of payment available, the opposite sequence of events occurred, though again with a lag. Taking the period as a whole, these changes in the balance of trade were on the average of such size as to enable the changing volume of borrowings to be transmitted primarily in the form of goods. The general *a priori* analysis of this process has been presented at sufficient length elsewhere (see ch. xvi, sects. 2 and 3), and need not be repeated.

The substantial validity of the explanation here advanced is clearly suggested, if not conclusively proved, by the correlations indicated in Charts XV and XVI. Chart XV shows that the changes in bank deposits *followed*, with a lag up to a year, the changes in the excess of net capital imports over final means of payment; and that the magnitudes involved were roughly similar when the lag is allowed for. Now the increase in bank deposits of course arose from general economic growth, as well as from the effects of the borrowing operations, and was hence greater than the excess of net capital imports. But this growth was fairly even, as indicated by the movements of the various price groups, whereas the volume of net capital imports fluctuated widely. It is therefore significant that the fluctuations in deposits tend to coincide with the capital-import fluctuations, after allowance is made for a year's lag. The latter set of fluctuations evidently dominate the first set. The only exception is in 1910, when deposits reacted after their too-abrupt rise in 1909. The lag is accounted for by the delay, already commented on, between the announcement of each loan and its transmission.

Finally, the fluctuations in deposits show a fairly good general correlation with those in the balance of trade. The latter has, however, a characteristic tendency to a lag of about a year. Their relationship can be inferred from the corresponding curves, as shown in Chart XVI.

The sequence of events therefore seems to have been substantially as follows: increase in volume of borrowing, excess of capital imports over final means of payment, increase in bank deposits, rise in prices, increased excess of commodity imports over exports, and final transmission of the capital imports primarily in the form of commodities.

CHART XV. NET CANADIAN CAPITAL IMPORTS AND BANK DEPOSITS
1900–1913

In million dollars

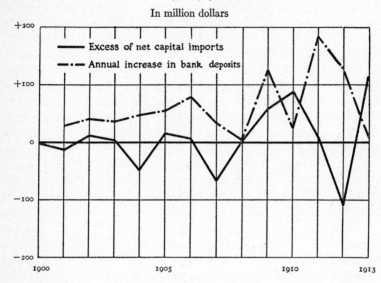

CHART XVI. CANADIAN BANK DEPOSITS AND THE BALANCE OF TRADE
1900–1913

In million dollars

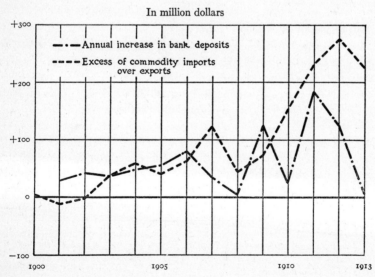

TABLE I. Canadian Foreign Borrowing, 1900–1913, and its Effects

Year	Capital and Trade Movements. In million dollars				Prices. (1900 = 100)			
	1 Net commodity imports [1]	2 Net capital imports [1]	3 Excess of capital imports [2]	4 Increase in bank deposits	5 General wholesale prices	6 Domestic prices	7 Import prices	8 Export prices
1900	4	3	− 2	...	100	100	100	100
1901	−12	−25	− 13	29	100	112	95	101
1902	− 3	5	11	42	104	119	93	103
1903	38	36	3	37	104	119	98	103
1904	59	2	− 49	48	105	119	94	104
1905	40	55	15	56	108	121	98	108
1906	62	72	7	80	114	123	107	115
1907	122	65	− 67	33	122	136	114	124
1908	45	59	− 2	3	118	134	100	120
1909	73	143	58	126	119	141	102	124
1910	154	257	89	24	121	146	105	126
1911	232	253	− 8	184	124	151	104	129
1912	275	213	−112	125	136	162	113	139
1913	223	400	113	6	132	162	114	134

[1] Minus sign: net export.
[2] Minus sign: net capital imports are *less* than the combined total of "final" means of payment (net commodity imports plus other net non-loan imports).

2. American Borrowings, 1860–1878.[1]

The principal features of the foreign borrowings by the United States from 1860 to 1878, like those of the Canadian case, have been presented elsewhere in the present study (see ch. vi, sect. 7). In their essentials the two cases are much the same. In the period of net capital importation, 1860–1873, 51 per cent of the total new American borrowings, which amounted to $1,065,000,000, was received in the form of an effective cancellation of interest and amortization payments on outstanding loans. Of the balance, 72 per cent was received as commodity imports, and 28 per cent as imports of freight services. In the period of net capital exportation, however, from 1874 to 1878, the net payments of $512,000,000 were transmitted entirely as commodity exports, since the service items all showed debit balances.

[1] The data used here are taken from F. D. Graham, *International Trade under Depreciated Paper: the United States, 1862–1879* (36 *Quarterly Journal of Economics*, 1922), unless otherwise indicated.

The relative movements of the various groups of prices were also what we should expect. In the first period (with the exception of one or two years) export prices were higher than import prices, and domestic prices higher than either group. In the second period, when capital was flowing out, the situation was reversed. Export prices became *lower* than import prices by the end of the period, and domestic prices lower than either. This operated to stimulate exportation, while checking importation. Furthermore, the movements of wages were of the character which these price changes would lead us to look for — a type of data, incidentally, not available for the Canadian case. In the period of capital importation, wages in the purely domestic industries were well above those in the industries competing with foreign products, indicating that the latter class of industry was unprosperous relative to the general American average. In the period of capital exportation domestic wages, it is true, had not fallen to the level of the other group at the end of the period for which data are available, but the difference was rapidly diminishing. This indicates that the prosperity of the industries which competed with foreign products was *rising*, relative to the general standard. The data on which these conclusions are based are presented in Table II, below. On the other hand in England, the principal lending country, just the opposite price movements tended to appear. The prices of exports were relatively *higher* in the borrowing period, and lower in the repayment period, than the general English level. Thus it became possible for England too to transmit and receive the capital primarily in the form of goods.

Finally, the intermediary process by which these changes in prices, and hence in the balance of trade, were effected, seems to have been the same as that suggested in the Canadian case: namely, by fluctuations in bank deposits. The data on which this conclusion rests are also presented in Table II. The correlation between the excess of capital imports above final means of payment and fluctuations in bank deposits is shown in Chart XVII. It was especially close in the period of net capital importation, but the similarity in the direction of change is marked throughout. That between bank deposits and the balance of trade is shown in Chart XVIII. It too was close to about 1874–1875, with the balance of trade showing a lag of about a year. After 1875, however, it looks as if the excess of commodity exports were increasing in the face of a nearly constant volume of deposits, whereas we should expect a *decrease* in deposits because of the growing volume of capital exportation. The explanation probably is that the country at

large was growing rapidly, and needed an increasing volume of bank
credit merely to *maintain* any one level of prices. The substantial con-
stancy in the volume of deposits was in effect equivalent to a *relative* decline — relative, that is, to the needs of the country. This last conclusion is confirmed by the fact that the general price level was falling

CHART XVII. AMERICAN CAPITAL MOVEMENTS AND BANK DEPOSITS
1866–1876

In million dollars

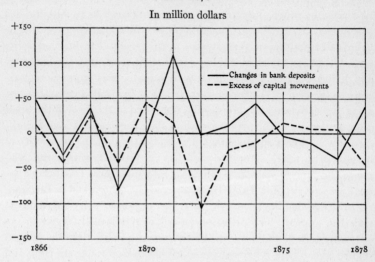

CHART XVIII. AMERICAN BANK DEPOSITS AND THE COMMODITY
BALANCE OF TRADE, 1866–1878

In million dollars

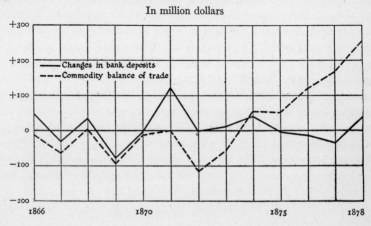

much more rapidly than the gold premium, which indicates that there was an actual shortage of bank credit at the then-current levels of prices.

The study of the American situation at this time is also complicated by the contemporary depreciation of the currency. If the reasoning presented above is correct, however, this depreciation had comparatively little effect on the essential features of the borrowing operations. Allowance must be made for it, but the important factors were the *relative* changes in the different groups of prices and wages, and the relative changes in bank deposits. Not much more stress should be placed on the gold premium in this connection, for example, than on the paper price of any other "international" commodity. It had no greater influence than any one of them in facilitating the capital movements, and was in turn no more affected. Nor does the relation between the exchanges on the one hand, and the ratio between the American and foreign prices on the other — the "price parities" — seem to have played a controlling part. Discrepancies between the price parities and the exchanges, so far as they were related to the capital-transfer operations, were results rather than causes. Nor do they appear to have exerted, of themselves alone, a corrective effect upon the situation.

The data of Table II are not begun until 1866, even where available before then, in order to avoid the confusions of the war period.

3. Argentine Borrowings, 1881–1900.[1]

The history of the foreign borrowing by Argentina from 1881 to 1900 is enough like that of the American case to make a detailed review unnecessary. Its main outlines have also been presented elsewhere (ch. vi, sect. 8). The data available cover both of the two chief phases involved in such operations, one of net capital import and one of net export due to the growing volume of interest payments on prior loans. In the first phase, nearly 35 per cent of the total new borrowing was offset by interest payments. Of the balance, 41 per cent was received in the form of net commodity imports, while 59 per cent was "unaccounted for." The size of this last item is due to the fragmentary character of the usable data. A very large part of it was probably composed of imports of freight services. In the second period, of net capital exportation, the figures for gross imports and exports themselves are

---

[1] The data used here are taken from J. H. Williams, *Argentine International Trade* (Cambridge, 1920). See Table III, below (p. 516).

Table II. American Capital Movements, 1866–1878, and Their Effects

Year	Capital movements. In million dollars			Prices. (1860 = 100)				Wages. (1860 = 100)	
	1 Excess of net capital movements [1]	2 Changes in bank deposits[2]	3 Commodity balance of trade[3]	4 Premium on gold	5 Domestic prices	6 Export prices	7 Import prices	8 Wages in "domestic" industries	9 Wages in "international" industries
1866	+ 12	+ 48	− 11	141	182	181	175	165	150
1867	− 42	− 31	− 63	138	173	165	163	171	151
1868	+ 26	+ 36	+ 4	140	173	167	161	174	151
1869	− 42	− 79	− 94	133	164	162	161	180	152
1870	+ 45	− 3	− 10	115	146	144	153	181	154
1871	+ 15	+121	+ 1	112	144	134	138	182	152
1872	−106	− 2	−116	112	147	137	136	183	154
1873	− 23	+ 11	− 57	114	146	134	132	182	153
1874	− 23	+ 43	+ 57	111	139	140	124	177	151
1875	+ 15	− 4	+ 52	115	130	135	119	168	148
1876	+ 7	− 13	+120	112	116	123	113	160	144
1877	+ 6	− 36	+167	105	110	118	120	147	141
1878	− 44	+ 38	+254	101	99	100	108	142	137

[1] Plus sign: excess of net capital movements over net means of final payment. Minus sign: excess of means of payment over capital movements.

[2] Original data from the annual Reports of the Comptroller of the Currency. Figures are for a day in the first week of October.

[3] Plus sign: net export. Minus sign: net import.

incomplete. Of the *net* export of capital, 96 per cent was accounted for by the net export of commodities. It is interesting to observe, incidentally, that this export excess was secured not so much by an actual increase in the volume of exportation, as by a *decrease* in importation. Finally, for the period as a whole the commodity balance of trade accounts for only 57 per cent of the total net capital movements. But, as shown in Chart XIX, the fluctuations in the latter item correspond very closely with those in the former. This clearly suggests that the trade balance was the chief means by which *changes* in the volume of net capital movements were effected. The other elements in the Argentine balance of payments, that is, were comparatively insensitive.

Data are missing to show statistically *how* the shifts in the trade balance were brought about, and we can only speculate as to the nature of the process. The data on price and wage movements are also fragmen-

CHART XIX. THE ARGENTINE BALANCE OF TRADE AND CAPITAL
MOVEMENTS, 1881–1900

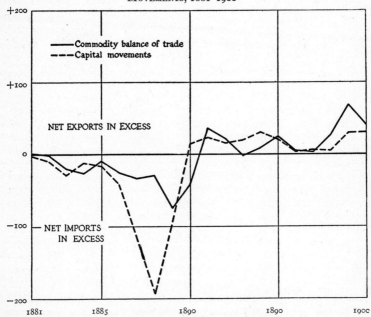

tary. These movements seem, however, to have been dominated chiefly by the internal depreciation of the currency. The effects of the borrowing operations on them were largely covered over.

4. The Export of Capital from England, 1880–1913.

A study which has been made recently by Professor Taussig [1] casts a good deal of light on what happens during a period of international borrowing from the point of view of the *lending* country. Its results are necessarily tentative, in the absence of complete data on the British balance of international payments, but they are entirely in line with the conclusions drawn from other quantitative investigations.

From 1880 to 1900, England was constantly making new foreign loans — such as those to Argentina, already discussed. The available evidence goes to show, however, that these loans were on the average much more than offset in each given year by the interest and amortization payments on *prior* loans. Such was the case with respect to Ameri-

[1] F. W. Taussig, *The Change in Great Britain's Foreign Trade Terms after 1900* (*Economic Journal*, 1925). I shall not present Professor Taussig's statistics here.

TABLE III. NET BALANCES OF ARGENTINE COMMODITY AND
CAPITAL MOVEMENTS, 1881–1900 [1]

(*In million gold pesos*)

Year	Period of Net Capital Importation		Year	Period of Net Capital Exportation	
	Commodity trade	Capital movements		Commodity trade	Capital movements
			1890	−41	+15
1881	+ 2	− 2	1891	+36	+24
1882	− 1	− 9	1892	+22	+16
1883	−20	− 28	1893	− 2	+20
1884	−26	− 12	1894	+ 9	+31
1885	− 8	− 16	1895	+25	+21
1886	−25	− 41	1896	+ 5	+ 3
1887	−33	−116	1897	+ 3	+ 6
1888	−28	−193	1898	+27	+ 5
1889	−75	− 94	1899	+68	+30
			1900	+42	+31

[1] Plus sign: net export. Minus sign: net import.

can borrowings, it will be remembered, after 1873. In other words, the net movement of capital was probably *into* England, and on a considerable scale. This conclusion both is borne out by, and helps to explain, the fact that British commodity imports were heavily in excess of exports during the period, by £100,000,000 to £150,000,000 a year on the average. Furthermore, the ratio between physical *quantities* of exports and physical quantities of imports — what Professor Taussig calls the "gross barter terms of trade"—was falling steadily. That is, a decreasing quantity of exports was being given for the same quantity of imports. This clearly suggests, if it does not definitely prove, that Great Britain was receiving the net income from her outstanding foreign investments (her net import of capital) primarily in the form of commodities; a conclusion which harmonizes with the results of the investigations made for other countries. The index of money wages was also rising, which shows that the general prosperity of the country was growing. This was presumably as the result, in considerable part, of the net payments being currently received from abroad.

From 1900 to 1913, however, a new flood of capital exportation developed. Commodity imports still exceeded commodity exports, but of the two, exports were increasing much more rapidly. Furthermore, the ratio of physical quantities of exports to physical quantities of imports was *rising*, and rising far more rapidly than it had in the earlier period. This indicates that although the net movement of capital was still into England rather than away from it, the amount of the net importation was declining. Furthermore, the upward movement of the money wage index almost ceased. From 1900 to 1911 there was virtually no change. This, again, was probably due in large part to the decrease in the net volume of payments currently received from abroad.

These data, as far as they go, serve to confirm the main conclusion we have sought to draw from other investigations — that the *net* movements of capital between countries are effected primarily through the agency of the commodity balance of trade. Furthermore, they indicate that there is a relation of sorts between such capital movements and the level of money wages, and of money incomes in general. Net capital importation means more "favorable" terms of commodity trade (fewer exports, per physical unit of imports) and a larger volume of spendable national income, measured in money, than would otherwise have existed. Individual money incomes, that is, will rise. Net capital exportation, on the other hand, means just the reverse: less favorable terms of trade, a smaller volume of national money income (because some of it is being invested abroad), and comparatively stationary individual money incomes. But these last propositions, in the absence of more conclusive quantitative data, must be regarded as tentative.

5. The French Indemnity Payments, 1871–1873.[1]

The various international transfers of capital hitherto discussed have all been cases involving borrowing and repayment operations; operations in which the lenders, if not always the borrowers, were private individuals or enterprises. The French indemnity payments to Germany after the Franco-Prussian War provide an example of transfers exclusively between governments, in which no subsequent counterflow of capital was involved.

The indemnity amounted to about five billion francs. It was paid *legally*, or proximately, in the following ways:

---

[1] The data used here, unless otherwise indicated, are taken from an article by A. E. Monroe, *The French Indemnity of 1871 and Its Effects* (*Review of Economic Statistics*, 1919).

	Million francs
Transfer of Alsace-Lorraine railroad..................	325
French gold and silver.............................	512
Foreign bank notes and coin........................	230
Bills of exchange, acquired by:	
Subscription to loans.........................	1,773
Bankers' syndicate	700
Purchases in the market......................	1,774
Total bills...............................	4,247
Total payments......................	5,314

Of this total, 500,000,000 francs were transferred within a few weeks of the signing of the agreement, in 1871. In the last twelve months of the period, in 1872 and to September, 1873, the payments were made at the rate of about 250,000,000 francs a month. In consequence, roughly 2,250,000,000 francs must have been paid in each of the years 1872 and 1873.

The source of the *economic* payments — that is, the funds from which these means of legal payment were secured — seems to have lain largely in a diversion to Germany of French credits in the international capital account. This diversion accounts for about two thirds of the total, as follows:

	Million francs
Sale of government securities abroad, and of foreign securities held in France...	1,400
Estimated sacrifice of income from outstanding foreign investments...	1,500
Net excess of commodity exports........................	420
Coin and notes...	1,000
Unaccounted for.......................................	600
Total...	4,920

The item "coin and notes" is larger here than that shown in the preceding table, because it includes an additional 250,000,000 francs in gold sent abroad by French bankers to cover their foreign-exchange transactions. The basis for estimation of the item "sacrifice of income" will be explained below.

There still remains, however, the problem of showing how the diversion of credits in the international capital account was itself effected, and what form it took. In the absence of more extensive data than we now possess, this cannot be done with much definiteness, but a suggestion may be ventured. Let us assume that by 1878 or 1879 French foreign-trade relationships had been restored to their ordinary terms, and that by then the effects of the indemnity payments had been worked out. The excess of imports over exports in 1879 was 1,365,-000,000 francs. For the five years before the war the average annual excess was 300,000,000. The difference is 1,065,000,000. If we arbitrarily distribute this sum over the period 1868–1879, as an equal annual increment of roughly 95,000,000, we then have the "normal" balance of trade which would presumably have appeared as the average condition, in the absence of the indemnity operations. This "normal" balance represents the volume of payments that France would otherwise have received, as the income from her foreign investments. If it be compared with the actual trade balance, the difference can be taken as indicating the amount of her foreign income in each year which France sacrificed. This difference constitutes the "effective" French balance of trade. The comparisons involved are made in Table IV.

TABLE IV. THE FRENCH BALANCE OF TRADE, 1871–1879

(In million francs)

Year	Actual balance [1]	Estimated "normal" balance [1]	"Effective" balance [2]
1871	− 695	− 590	− 105
1872	+ 190	− 685	+ 875
1873	+ 230	− 780	+1,010
1874	+ 195	− 880	+1,075
1875	+ 335	− 975	+1,305
1876	− 410	−1,075	+ 665
1877	− 235	−1,170	+ 935
1878	− 995	−1,265	+ 270
1879	−1,365	−1,365	0

[1] Plus sign: excess of exports. Minus sign: excess of imports.
[2] Plus sign: absolute amount by which the actual balance was less "unfavorable" than the estimated normal balance. Minus sign: amount by which the actual balance was more "unfavorable."

The total of the "effective" balances from 1871 to 1879 is 5,900,-000,000 francs, which is a little more than the total of the indemnity payments. This suggests that even the secondary effects of the indemnity on French foreign trade were exhausted by 1878 or 1879, and justifies the selection of 1879 as a "normal" year. For 1872 and the first three quarters of 1873, the total is roughly 1,500,000,000 francs, which is the figure used above for the estimated sacrifice of income from abroad in those two years.

The conclusion to be drawn from these calculations, however tentatively, is as follows. By 1878 or 1879, France had bought back the foreign securities which she had previously sold to help pay the indemnity; she had bought back her government bonds sold abroad, or their equivalent, and her former holdings of coin and notes; and she had recouped herself for the diversion to Germany, from 1871 to 1873, of income from her foreign investments. She did this through her commodity balance of trade, in some part by acquiring an actual excess of exports over imports, but chiefly by abstaining from taking the large excess of *imports* which her prior foreign investments entitled her to receive currently. That is to say, the indemnity was *ultimately* paid, though over a number of years, by a diversion of French credits in the international capital account. At the time the indemnity payments were actually made, France sacrificed much of both the income and the principal of her foreign holdings. But in the following five or six years she bought them back again, primarily with the income from the holdings she had retained. With that income she was also able to pay off her own governmental borrowings abroad. This diversion of credits was effected through changes in the commodity balance of trade from the levels at which it would otherwise have been established.

Presumably the changes in the trade balance itself were brought about, as in the other cases examined, by differential changes in the various groups of French prices, but data on this point have not been compiled. French prices as a whole were distinctly below the German level until 1876.

The data on the receipt of the indemnity by Germany are scanty. "Legally," they were received in the manner already pointed out in connection with the payments by France. "Economically," they were received in three principal ways; by a net excess of commodity imports over exports, by the discharge of foreign debts contracted to carry on the war, and by an increase in German foreign investment. Germany also received some 500,000,000 marks in new gold, but this addition proved to be for the most part temporary. It is not worth while to go into the further details of the case here, because of the lack of usable statistics. At a rough estimate, however, 75 per cent of the indemnity was received "economically" in the form of an excess of commodity imports, and 25 per cent as gold bullion and foreign currencies. The subsequent loss of most of the latter item was offset by new German investment abroad. The situation is complicated, however, by the fact that from 1871 to 1873 German private enterprises borrowed very large sums, perhaps 2,000,000,000 marks or more, from foreign markets.

The nature of the general economic effects produced within Germany by the indemnity receipts is not easy to determine. The surface facts are these. From 1871 until the middle of 1873 Germany had a financial and industrial boom of unusual size and intensity; then a catastrophic collapse; and then a long period of severe depression and recurring smaller crises, which lasted until the end of the decade. To some it has seemed obvious to attribute these events to the artificial stimulation of the indemnity. But many writers, among them Wagner, have denied this. They point out that the crisis of 1873 was world-wide, not confined to Germany alone; and that it began in Vienna rather than in any German center. At most, they admit that the periodic (rather than continuous) receipt of the payments had a temporarily disadvantageous effect, especially in the money markets; and that the retirement of a considerable part of the national debt released capital for use in business enterprises — which were necessarily somewhat speculative. On the other hand, the boom was admittedly much greater in Germany than in other countries, while the depression was both more acute and more prolonged.

The correct explanation of the situation — although lack of adequate statistical data makes any positive conclusion uncertain — probably lies somewhere between the two interpretations just outlined. In 1872 and 1873, all of the leading commercial countries were in the upward phase of the business cycle, so that some sort of crisis and depression were ultimately inevitable. In Germany, this "normal" upward swing was greatly accentuated by — though it was not exclusively due to — the inflationary effects of the *sudden* receipt of the indemnity, and by the general optimism consequent on the successful termination of the war. The crisis and later depression were correspondingly more acute, although again they did not originate solely in the indemnity receipts. Moreover, it made little difference where the actual crisis began. If it had not begun in Vienna, the structure of speculation and inflated values and over-investment, which was characteristic of other countries as well as of Germany, must surely have cracked elsewhere. A severe readjustment of some sort was inevitable. In a word, the effects of the indemnity receipts were simply superimposed, in Germany, upon the relatively "normal" development of the business cycle. They greatly exaggerated the upward and downward swings of this cycle, but did not "cause" them.

It seems likely, however, that Germany could have avoided suffering materially more than other countries at the time, had she received the payments as a continuous small flow, spread out over a considerable interval. The resulting stimulus would then have been gradual, instead of being impossibly abrupt, and German finance and industry would have had time to make the necessary readjustments. It was not so much the *fact* that payments were received, as the *manner* in which the receipts themselves were taken, that produced a greater financial disaster in Germany than in the rest of Europe.[1]

6. British Government Remittances during the Napoleonic Wars.

The remittances of the British government to the Continent, from 1793 to 1816, have been discussed at length in Appendix A. Attention is again called to them here because they present a case in which the necessary relative changes in the various groups of prices, requisite to alter the commodity balance of trade, were brought about in a way not hitherto encountered. In the other cases examined, whenever the data were adequate, it appeared that the price changes were produced by changes in the volume of domestic currency and credit. Here they seem to have been produced by the effects of the depreciation of the foreign exchanges.

In the Appendix already referred to (see especially Charts VIII and XIII therein presented), it was shown that the exchanges were dominated by the pressure of the government for foreign bills. When the pressure was great the exchanges depreciated roughly in proportion, since England was in effect under inconvertible paper. When it relaxed, they moved back towards par. Now a depreciation of the exchanges, other things equal, operates to increase the price (in the domestic currency) that importers in the depreciated country must pay for bills. It also increases the sums that its exporters receive. Other things again equal, this will stimulate exportation and check importation. When the exchanges improve, the opposite tendencies appear.

---

[1] For more detailed discussions of these problems see, in addition to the article by Professor Monroe already referred to, the following: A. Wagner, *Das Reichsfinanzwesen* (Schmoller's Jahrbuch, 1874); H. H. O'Farrell, *The Franco-German War Indemnity* (London, 1913: Garton Foundation Publications), which has an extended bibliography; a British Foreign Office handbook, *Indemnities of War* (London, 1920); G. Carano-Donvito, *Indennità di guerra e debiti interalleati* (*Riforma Sociale*, 1925); and a chapter by the present writer in the National Industrial Conference Board report, *The Inter-Ally Debts and the United States* (New York, 1925).

There is hence good ground for holding that the government remittances were in effect transferred by means of changes in the commodity balance of trade, but that these changes were produced by exchange depreciations *themselves* caused by the government demand for foreign bills.

It is of course true that exchange depreciation tends to produce corresponding alterations in the prices of commodity exports and imports in the country concerned, and when this adjustment is completed the direct mechanical influence of the depreciation on the course of foreign trade disappears. But the statistics and charts submitted in the previous Appendix show that there was no very intimate connection between the fluctuations of the exchanges and the movements of prices. These last were, rather, dominated by the severe and largely independent depreciation of the English currency itself, and indeed went to much higher levels than the exchanges. On the whole, therefore, the exchange fluctuations can therefore be regarded as having exerted their full effects on foreign trade, *without* having given rise to corrective price changes of substantial size.

7. The Export of Capital from the United States, 1919–1924.

In the six years after the war the United States exported an enormous volume of capital, over $8,500,000,000 in amount at the least. Of this sum roughly $2,700,000,000 represents advances made by the American government, chiefly in 1919, for reconstruction and relief, but the remainder is almost entirely private investment. On the other hand the United States imported nearly $4,000,000,000, the largest item being the repayment of foreign loans, so that the *net* export was only some $4,600,000,000.

The statistics are so biased by the post-war inflation in this country, and by the depreciation of the European currencies, that it is almost impossible to show in any detail what the processes involved really were. So far as the data go, however, they bear out the conclusions reached in other cases. Net capital movements and the commodity balance of trade maintained a close relationship, as is shown in Chart XX, and the capital exports can reasonably be regarded as having been effected primarily in the form of commodities. The difference in the levels of the two curves is accounted for by net debits in the other items of the balance of payments, debits which were a moderately stable element in the situation. Beyond this, however, it does not as yet seem worth while to try to go.

The relevant data are presented in Table V. They are taken from the estimates published by the U. S. Department of Commerce.[1] It may be remarked that the "unaccounted for" item is explained very

CHART XX. THE AMERICAN BALANCE OF TRADE AND THE
NET MOVEMENT OF CAPITAL, 1919–1924

In million dollars

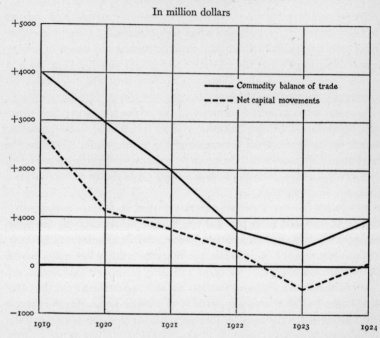

largely by bankers' and traders' balances, left abroad either voluntarily or involuntarily after the war and later gradually withdrawn.

8. Summary of Conclusions.

The principal conclusions to which this review of the available continuous data on the international transfer of capital leads may now be summarized. They apply, however, only to comparatively long-time

[1] *Trade Information Bulletins*, Nos. 144, 215, and 340.

A more elaborate study of the situation has been made by the present writer in a chapter on *The Debts and American Finance*, in the report of the National Industrial Conference Board on *The Inter-Ally Debts and the United States* (New York, 1925). Such additional conclusions as are there reached, however, rest on data which are too elaborate to be presented here, and which are less certain. Sufficient time has not yet elapsed since the war, for example, to warrant the drawing of definitive inferences from price and bank deposit statistics.

TABLE V. NET BALANCES OF AMERICAN INTERNATIONAL
PAYMENTS, 1919–1924

(*In million dollars*)

Plus sign: Net export. Minus sign: Net import

Year	1 Merchandise	2 Gold, silver, and other currency	3 Other non-capital items [1]	4 Total "final" means of payment, net (1+2+3)	5 Capital movements	6 Un-accounted for (5−4) [2]
1919	+4,016	+403	−557	+3,862	+2,780	−1,082
1920	+2,950	+ 79	−757	+2,272	+1,129	−1,143
1921	+1,976	−778	−667	+ 531	+ 759	+ 228
1922	+ 754	−246	−693	− 185	+ 303	+ 448
1923	+ 389	−246	−768	− 625	− 473	+ 152
1924	+ 970	−272	−847	− 149	+ 63	+ 212

[1] Net balance of freight charges, plus immigrants' remittances and relief, plus tourists' expenditures.
[2] I. e., the annual credit (+) or debit (−) balances unaccounted for.

relationships — to periods of at least a year in length, and usually more. It does not seem possible to get satisfactory data on the processes of short-time adjustment. These conclusions are most conveniently presented in an order the reverse of the actual sequence of changes.

(1) The *net* transfers [1] are eventually effected primarily in the form of changes in the commodity balance of trade. This balance is much the biggest single item in the net movements of those "final" means of payment which are to be offset against the capital movements, and is also much the most sensitive to changes in the latter. If the capital transfers are large and sudden, however, as in the case of the French indemnity, they are apt to be effected in the first instance through the transfer of *other* kinds or forms of capital. The movement of securities provides an example. But ultimately these latter alternative capital movements are reversed, and are replaced by corresponding movements in the balance of trade.

[1] In the case of borrowing and repayment operations from 35 per cent to 50 per cent or more of the dominant capital movement, in the cases here examined, was offset by a counter-flow of capital — either of interest payments, or of new investments, according to the case. At any one time, in advanced countries, the situation always shows a complex network of capital movements simultaneously proceeding in opposite directions. This is precisely like the course of the strictly commodity trade.

(2) The changes in the balance of trade itself, at least under stable metallic standards, are brought about by changes in the various groups of prices within the countries concerned. In a country importing capital, for example, export prices will move above import prices, and domestic prices above both. Similar changes appear in the corresponding classes of wages, and in the relative prosperity of the corresponding classes of industry.

(3) The movements in prices, in turn (again assuming stable monetary standards), are produced by changes in the total volume of purchasing power in circulation. These changes are themselves the consequence of a shift in the relation between the demand and the supply of bills of exchange. In a country importing capital, for example, an excess of net capital importation above the quantity of "final" means of payment available increases the rate at which bills of exchange are currently supplied to the exchange market. Since no change has taken place in the demand, the banks' holdings of such bills, and therefore their deposits, will expand. A part of the increased deposits may subsequently be transformed into cash, but the net result will be an augmentation in the country's total supply of purchasing power in circulation. This will operate to raise the general level of prices, and also to increase the divergence between the various price groups. It will thus alter the balance of trade to the necessary extent. But these various relationships, it must be repeated, take time to work out. They are not to be interpreted in any short-run or very immediate sense.

In a country exporting capital, or importing it at a less rapid rate than before, the opposite changes presumably appear, although this is less clearly established by the data available. The demand for bills of exchange is increased, relative to the supply; the total volume of purchasing power in circulation declines; and prices fall. The differential movements of the various price groups are also reversed, and the balance of trade changes in the opposite direction. If the capital-exporting country is under inconvertible paper, however, there is some evidence to show that the changes in prices and the balance of trade are produced simply through the effects of a depreciation of the foreign exchanges, itself a consequence of the increased demand for bills. But this takes place only in so far as the general price level *fails* to reflect the movements of the exchanges.

(4) The importation of capital on any important scale leads to general prosperity and expansion during the continuance of the importation, or at least during the time its rate is increasing, and probably for

some time afterward. It also leads to rising money incomes. The exportation of capital, on the other hand, does not necessarily induce depression and falling incomes. But it does cause the country's general economic advance to be less rapid than it would presumably have been otherwise.

9. Rejection of the Cyclical Hypothesis.

The existence of a fairly intimate (though not a short-time) connection between capital movements and the commodity balance of trade thus seems clearly established by the available statistical data. It is tempting to try to relate both the movements of capital and the fluctuations of the trade balance to an antecedent common cause, the cyclical oscillations of business at large.

Evidently if the cycles in two different countries are coincident, and of roughly equal magnitude, their influence will not materially affect the situation. But if they are not, discrepancies of various sorts will arise, and will affect the international movement of goods and capital. Suppose, for example, that one country is in the midst of a boom period, while the other is in a less active phase of the cycle or even in a depression. In the first country, prices are relatively high. This stimulates commodity importation relative to exportation. Profits and interest rates are also high, thus stimulating the import of capital for investment in fixed-yield securities (the prices of which are low), and checking its export. On the other hand, however, the capitalized value of businesses and of shares of stock is high too. This will *check* the import of capital for investment in them. In the other country, prices are low, and commodity exportation from it will be relatively increased. Profits and interest rates are also low. This will check the import of capital for investment in fixed-yield securities (the prices of which are now high), and stimulate its export. On the other hand, the low capitalized value of businesses and of stocks will stimulate the *importation* of capital for investment in them.

Now the great bulk of the securities that move between countries is of the fixed-yield type. As far as they are concerned, therefore, the cyclical hypothesis is borne out. The import of capital and the import of goods, or vice versa, will move together, and be jointly due to the cyclical fluctuations of business. But a very large part of the international investment of capital, almost as large a part perhaps, takes the form of the purchase of ownership, not of fixed-yield debts; that is, the purchase of stocks, and of direct titles (such as the acquisition of real estate, etc.). This type of capital moves in just the opposite direction. It is *exported*, for example, at times when the position of the business cycle is stimulating commodity *importation;* and vice versa.

A priori reasoning thus leaves us in some doubt as to the correctness of the hypothesis. Its validity seems to depend on whether the purchase of fixed-yield securities predominates over other types of foreign investment. Moreover, it deals only with new *investment*. The commodity balance of trade, however, responds rather to changes in the *net* movement of capital, which is made up of interest and profits payments as well as of investment itself. But the volume of interest payments is of course not related to the cyclical fluctuations of business. At any one time it is comparatively constant, and it may therefore upset that relation which might otherwise appear between capital movements and the trade balance. The payment of profits to foreigners, also, will be large in a boom period, yet at this same time the low price of fixed-yield securities is stimulating their sale abroad.

Taking the situation as a whole, therefore, it is evident that there can be no uniform and invariable relation between the *net* movement of capital and the business cycle, for each phase of the cycle induces important capital flows in *both* directions. Depending on the international investment situation in the particular case, and on the precise form the investment itself takes, cyclical fluctuations may produce a flow in *either* direction.

Nor does the statistical evidence in the cases examined above here seem to support a cyclical theory. It is of course true that the available data are annual only, and therefore tend to cover over rather than to accentuate any cyclical influences that may actually exist. But the fluctuations in the net movements of capital and in the trade balances take place too frequently, and in too nearly a constant relationship, to suggest clearly a common cyclical origin. At different points in non-coincident cycles, we should expect quite different degrees of effect and of connection. The distribution of the peaks and valleys also fails to indicate a recurring cycle.

Finally, the cyclical hypothesis is of little or no direct use in accounting for the appearance and correction of changes in the *other* items in the balance of international payments — in freight charges, tourists' expenditures, and so forth. Yet they too exert an important influence on the trade balance. With respect to these adjustments, the explanation advanced at another point alone seems adequate. This is the explanation which turns on the effects of changes in the supply and demand for foreign bills of exchange upon the volume of purchasing power in circulation.

APPENDIX C

BRITISH, FRENCH AND GERMAN STATISTICS, 1919–1924

The figures here presented are the data used in constructing the charts of Chapter XVII. They are copied or computed from the elaborate and valuable compilations contained in the U. S. Senate Commission of Gold and Silver Inquiry report, entitled Foreign Currency and Exchange Investigation, Serial 9, vol. 1 (Washington, 1925).

No attempt has been made in the present study to draw up charts or tables for Germany, except those dealing with the physical volume of foreign trade. The statistical work involved is very laborious, because of the enormous size of the figures, and the grotesque distortion imposed by the ultimate complete collapse makes it almost impossible to derive useful conclusions different from those obtainable from the more easily handled data for other countries. After the end of 1922, prices, exchanges and note circulation all rose with skyrocket velocity, but the relative order and magnitudes of the movements seem to have had little significance. Each was simply a different aspect of the same phenomenon: the "flight from the mark." The flight itself was induced, in the first instance, by events of a political rather than a primarily economic character.

An interesting study of these movements, however, is made in the Senate report just mentioned. To this the reader may be referred.

TABLE I. BRITISH STATISTICS, 1919–1924

Year and Month	1 Foreign exchange: price of dollars in per cents of par.[1] Par = 100	2 Price parities on U. S. (In pounds per dollar).[2] Par = 100	3 Total note circulation (£ millions)	4 Price index [3]	5 Net imports (£ millions) [4]	6 Net exports (£ millions) [4]
1919 — I...	102	112	377	224	130	47
II...	102	114	385	220	102	47
III...	103	111	402	217	97	53
IV...	104	109	426	217	99	58
V...	104	113	421	229	124	64
VI...	105	116	421	235	111	65
VII...	110	117	418	243	141	65
VIII...	114	116	411	250	133	75
IX...	116	120	413	252	133	67
X...	116	125	419	264	134	79
XI...	119	125	423	271	123	87
XII...	128	124	444	276	143	91
1920 — I...	132	124	414	288	158	106
II...	144	132	417	306	148	86
III...	130	131	435	307	150	104
IV...	124	128	439	313	147	106
V...	124	124	452	305	146	119
VI...	124	124	464	300	150	116
VII...	126	125	469	299	145	137
VIII...	132	129	462	298	140	115
IX...	138	125	463	282	139	117
X...	140	133	465	282	133	112
XI...	142	134	458	263	131	119
XII...	140	135	481	243	130	97
1921 — I...	130	137	452	232	107	93
II...	126	134	444	215	89	68
III...	125	134	454	208	85	67
IV...	124	134	447	199	81	60
V...	122	132	442	191	79	43
VI...	129	129	443	183	81	38
VII...	134	132	434	186	71	43
VIII...	132	128	427	181	79	51
IX...	130	124	420	175	78	55
X...	126	115	416	163	74	62
XI...	122	114	418	161	79	63
XII...	117	112	433	157	76	59

TABLE I. — (*Continued*)

Year and Month	1 Foreign exchange: price of dollars in per cents of par.[1] Par = 100	2 Price parities on U. S. (In pounds per dollar).[2] Par = 100	3 Total note circulation (£ millions)	4 Price index [3]	5 Net imports (£ millions) [4]	6 Net exports (£ millions) [4]
1922 — I...	115	113	408	156	68	63
II...	112	110	400	155	59	58
III...	111	111	404	157	78	65
IV...	110	111	402	158	71	56
V...	109	107	400	159	80	58
VI...	109	106	399	159	76	52
VII...	109	102	400	157	73	60
VIII...	109	99	396	152	75	60
IX...	109	99	390	150	70	63
X...	110	100	387	153	77	60
XI...	108	99	390	153	86	66
XII...	106	98	405	152	86	59
1923 — I...	105	99	381	153	90	67
II...	104	99	391	155	74	58
III...	104	99	388	156	81	61
IV...	105	99	384	157	74	63
V...	105	100	390	155	77	72
VI...	105	99	389	150	78	63
VII...	106	98	392	147	68	60
VIII...	106	99	387	147	82	60
IX...	107	98	384	150	75	64
X...	108	99	383	150	89	71
XI...	111	103	384	156	91	66
XII...	112	104	405	156	99	64
1924 — I...	114	107	384	161	88	64
II...	113	108	381	163	83	68
III...	113	108	384	161	91	61
IV...	112	109	393	161	74	63
V...	112	110	389	161	109	70
VI...	113	110	394	160	78	62
VII...	112	111	400	163	98	71
VIII...	108	108	392	162	93	66
IX...	109	112	387	166	91	63
X...	108	113	386	172	108	69
XI...	106	112	386	171	106	68
XII...	104	111	396	174	120	69

[1] Monthly average for cables.
[2] Monthly average. *Statist* index for England, *Bureau of Labor Statistics* index for United States.
[3] Monthly average. *Statist* index.   [4] Excluding gold and silver.

TABLE II. FRENCH STATISTICS, 1919-1924

Year and Month	1 Foreign exchange: price of dollars, in per cents of par.[1] Par = 100	2 Price parities on U. S. (In francs per dollar).[2] Par = 100	3 Total note circulation (In hundred million francs)	4 Price index[3]	5 Net imports (100,000 quintals)[4]	6 Net exports (100,000 quintals)[4]
1919 — I...	105	174	320	348	18	16
II...	105	177	327	340	23	21
III...	109	171	334	336	27	25
IV...	116	167	340	332	24	22
V...	122	161	340	325	24	22
VI...	123	162	344	329	32	30
VII...	134	165	350	349	31	28
VIII...	152	160	351	347	30	27
IX...	164	170	358	360	30	27
X...	166	180	370	382	30	27
XI...	182	187	374	405	22	20
XII...	208	190	373	423	93	65
1920 — I...	227	209	376	487	27	22
II...	274	225	378	522	34	24
III...	269	237	376	555	42	33
IV...	310	241	377	588	39	29
V...	282	223	379	550	39	32
VI...	244	203	375	493	44	30
VII...	238	206	377	496	50	40
VIII...	268	217	379	501	42	29
IX...	287	233	392	526	43	32
X...	295	238	391	502	45	32
XI...	322	236	388	461	45	30
XII...	326	243	379	435	56	44
1921 — I...	300	240	379	407	41	29
II...	269	236	378	377	28	13
III...	274	232	384	360	30	18
IV...	267	234	382	347	29	16
V...	231	227	382	329	25	12
VI...	238	229	374	325	23	8
VII...	247	234	369	330	25	11
VIII...	249	233	368	331	30	18
IX...	265	244	371	344	42	29
X...	267	233	371	331	38	24
XI...	268	237	363	332	42	27
XII...	246	233	365	326	49	35

TABLE II. (*Continued*)

Year and Month	1 Foreign exchange: price of dollars, in per cents of par.[1] Par = 100	2 Price parities on U. S. (In francs per dollar).[2] Par = 100	3 Total note circulation (In hundred million francs)	4 Price index [3]	5 Net imports (100,000 quintals)[4]	6 Net exports (100,000 quintals)[4]
1922 — I...	237	227	364	314	34	18
II...	221	217	362	306	41	26
III...	214	216	355	307	45	29
IV...	208	220	358	314	38	20
V...	212	214	357	317	44	28
VI...	220	217	360	325	43	25
VII...	233	210	360	325	42	25
VIII...	243	214	364	331	45	27
IX...	252	216	366	329	42	17
X...	262	219	367	337	45	21
XI...	281	226	361	352	46	26
XII...	267	232	364	362	50	31
1923 — I...	288	248	368	387	41	22
II...	314	268	371	422	39	14
III...	306	267	372	424	41	23
IV...	290	261	365	415	41	26
V...	289	261	367	407	45	26
VI...	305	267	367	409	49	31
VII...	328	270	369	407	49	30
VIII...	342	276	364	413	48	26
IX...	330	276	376	424	50	29
X...	325	276	377	421	44	22
XI...	350	291	373	443	49	26
XII...	368	304	379	459	52	25
1924 — I...	413	328	388	495	39	22
II...	437	359	393	544	44	21
III...	412	333	395	499	48	23
IV...	314	289	398	450	49	24
V...	334	312	396	459	55	33
VI...	368	321	396	465	46	21
VII...	377	327	403	481	54	31
VIII...	355	318	400	477	45	20
IX...	364	328	403	486	47	20
X...	370	327	405	497	47	20
XI...	366	329	404	503	44	14
XII...	358	323	406	507	47	22

[1] Monthly average for cables.
[2] Monthly average. Index of *Statistique Générale* for France, *Bureau of Labor Statistics* index for United States.
[3] Monthly average. Index of *Statistique Générale*.　　　　[4] Excluding gold and silver.

TABLE III. GERMAN FOREIGN TRADE, 1921–1924 [1]

In hundred thousand metric tons

Year and Month	1 Imports	2 Exports	Year and Month	1 Imports	2 Exports
1921 — V......	15	11	1923 — III......	52	9
VI......	18	15	IV......	64	10
VII......	19	16	V......	40	9
VIII......	21	18	VI......	48	9
IX......	25	19	VII......	42	11
X......	30	20	VIII......	41	11
XI......	25	19	IX......	34	11
XII......	21	19	X......	29	12
1922 — I......	23	20	XI......	34	10
II......	15	17	XII......	29	11
III......	26	22	1924 — I......	27	8
IV......	29	22	II......	28	8
V......	38	21	III......	25	9
VI......	40	19	IV......	26	10
VII......	48	16	V......	30	11
VIII......	47	14	VI......	32	9
IX......	48	16	VII......	31	12
X......	56	15	VIII......	21	13
XI......	45	16	IX......	29	13
XII......	43	18	X......	33	15
1923 — I......	47	13	XI......	49	22
II......	32	11	XII......	50	30

[1] Data earlier than May, 1921, not available.

APPENDIX D

BIBLIOGRAPHY

In the following bibliography, secondary works dealing with the *doctrines* of given periods are classified according to the date of the subject-matter, not of publication. Recent studies of the English Bullion Controversy, for example, are placed in the division 1800–1850. The purpose is to make each division a guide to both the content and the subsequent interpretation of each principal group of ideas.

The bibliography is admittedly incomplete with respect to Continental publications since 1914, especially those of the last two or three years. I have had considerable difficulty in obtaining access to them.

I. ENGLISH AND AMERICAN THOUGHT

Titles of Principal Periodicals

American Economic Review. 1911 ff.
Annals of the American Academy of Political and Social Science. 1890 ff.
Economic Journal. 1891 ff.
Journal of Political Economy. 1893 ff.
Publications of the American Economic Association. 1886–1910.
Quarterly Journal of Economics. 1886 ff.

1. The period before 1800

Ashley, Sir W. J.: *The Tory Origin of Free Trade Policy.* 11 Quar. Jour. Econ., 1897.
Barbon, N.: *A Discourse concerning Coining.* London, 1696.
——: *A Discourse of Trade.* London, 1690.
Cantillon, Philip: *The Analysis of Trade.* London, 1759.
Cantillon, Richard: *Essai sur la nature du commerce en général.* Probably written in 1730–1734; first printed in 1755. Reprinted for Harvard University, 1892.
Child, Sir Josiah: *New Discourse of Trade.* London, 1693.
Clark, Walter E.: *Josiah Tucker.* New York, 1903.
Clement, S.: *The General Notions of Money, Trade and Exchange.* London, 1695.
Cossa, Emilio: *L'Interpretazione Scientifica del Mercantilismo.* Messina 1907.
Cossa, Luigi: *Introduction to the Study of Political Economy,* translated by L. Dyer. London, 1893.
Cunningham, W.: *Growth of English Industry and Commerce in Modern Times.* London, 1882; later editions in 2 vols., paged continuously; 4 ed., 1905–1907.

Davenant, Charles: *An Essay on the Probable Methods of making a People Gainers in the Balance of Trade.* London, 1699; 2 ed., 1700.

Douglass, William: *A Discourse concerning the Currencies of the British Plantations in America.* 1740. Reprinted: in *Tracts on Paper Currency and Banking* (J. R. MacCulloch, editor, London, 1857); in *Colonial Currency Reprints* (Prince Society, Boston, 1910–1911: 4 vols.), vol. 3; and by C. J. Bullock, editor (New York, 1897).

Franklin, Benjamin: *Remarks and Facts relative to the American Paper Money.* London, 1765. Reprinted in his *Works* (J. Sparks, editor, Boston, 1836), vol. 2.

Furniss, E. S.: *The Position of the Laborer in a System of Nationalism.* New York, 1920.

Gee, Sir Joshua: *The Trade and Navigation of Great Britain.* London, 1729; 4 ed., 1738.

Great Britain. H. M. Council of Trade: *Advice concerning the Exportation of Gold and Silver.* London, 1660. Reprinted in *Tracts on Money* (J. R. MacCulloch, editor, London, 1856).

Hales, John: *A Discourse of the Common Weal.* 1581. Reprinted by E. Lamond, editor (Cambridge, 1893).

Harris, W.: *Essays upon Money and Coins.* London, 1757–1758: 2 vols.

Hewins, W.: *English Trade and Finance, chiefly in the Seventeenth Century.* London, 1892.

Higgs, A.: *The Physiocrats.* London, 1898.

Hollander, J. H.: *A Reprint of Economic Tracts.* Baltimore, 1903–1914.

Horrocks, J. W.: *A Short History of Mercantilism.* London, 1925.

Hume, David: *Essays, Moral, Political and Literary.* 1741. (Edition used: London, 1860.)

Ingram, J. K. A.: *A History of Political Economy.* London, 1897; new edition, with a supplementary chapter by W. A. Scott: London, 1919.

Jevons, W. S.: *Richard Cantillon and 'he Nationality of Political Economy.* 49 Contemporary Review, 1881.

Law, John: *Money and Trade Considered.* Glasgow, 1705.

Liebnecht, W.: *Zur Geschichte der Werttheorie in England.* Jena, 1902.

Locke, John: *Some Considerations of the Consequences of the Lowering of Interest.* London, 1691; 1692; 1695.

MacCulloch, J. R., ed.: *Tracts on Money.* London, 1856.

——: *Tracts on Paper Currency and Banking.* London, 1857.

——: *Early English Tracts on Commerce.* London, 1856.

——: *Scarce Tracts on Commerce.* London, 1859.

Malynes, G. de: *On the Maintenance of Free Trade.* London, 1622.

Mildmay, Sir W.: *The Laws and Policy of England.* London, 1765.

Monroe, A. E.: *Monetary Theory before Adam Smith.* Cambridge, 1923.

Mun, Thomas: *A Discourse of Trade.* London, 1621.

——: *England's Treasure by Foreign Trade.* London, 1664.

North, Dudley: *Discourses of Trade.* London, 1691.

Packard, Lawrence B.: *International Rivalry and Free-Trade Origins, 1661–1678.* 37 Quar. Jour. Econ., 1923.

Petty, Sir William: *The Economic Writings of Sir William Petty.* C. H. Hull, editor. Cambridge, 1899: 2 vols.

Pollexfen, Sir Henry: *A Discourse of Trade.* London, 1697.

Prince Society: *Colonial Currency Reprints, 1682–1751.* Boston, 1910–1911: 4 vols.

Schmoller, Gustav: *The Mercantile System.* New York, 1902.

Smith, Adam: *Lectures on Justice, Police, Revenue and Arms.* 1763. E. Cannan, editor, Oxford, 1896.

——: *Wealth of Nations.* London, 1776. E. Cannan, editor, London, 1904: 2 vols.; 3 ed., 1922.

Steuart, Sir James D.: *Principles of Political Economy.* London, 1767: 2 vols.

Unwin, George: *Industrial Organization in the Sixteenth and Seventeenth Centuries.* Oxford, 1904.

Usher, Abbott P.: *The History of the Grain Trade in France, 1400–1710.* Cambridge, 1913.

Vanderlint, Jacob: *Money Answers All Things.* London, 1734.

Whitaker, A. C.: *History and Criticism of the Labor Theory of Value in English Political Economy.* New York, 1904.

2. 1800–1849

Baring, Sir Francis: *Observations on the Publication of Walter Boyd.* London 1801.

Blake, W.: *Observations on the Effects produced by the Expenditure of Government during the Restriction of Cash Payments.* London, 1823.

——: *Observations on the Principles which regulate the Course of Exchange.* London, 1810.

Bosanquet, C. W.: *Practical Observations on the Report of the Bullion Committee.* London, 1810.

Boyd, Walter: *Letter to . . . William Pitt, on the Influence of the Stoppage of Issues in Specie at the Bank of England.* London, 1801.

Cannan, E.: *The Paper Pound of 1797–1821.* London, 1919. A reprint of the Bullion Report of 1810, with comments.

Foxwell, H. S.: *Preface* to A. Andréadès's *History of the Bank of England.* London, 1909; 2 ed., 1924.

Fullarton, John: *On the Regulation of Currencies.* London, 1844; 2 ed., 1845.

Great Britain (Parliament, 1810). Committee on the High Price of Gold Bullion: *Report.* London, 1810. (This is the Bullion Report of 1810.)

——: *Parliamentary Debates.* Cobbett, editor, to 1803; Hansard, 1803 ff.

——: *Sessional Papers.* (Including reports from committees.)

Hawtrey, R. G.: *The Bank Restriction of 1797.* 28 Econ. Jour., 1918.

Hollander, J. H.: *A Reprint of Economic Tracts.* Baltimore, 1903–1914.

——: *The Development of the Theory of Money from Adam Smith to David Ricardo.* 25 Quar. Jour. Econ., 1911.

Horner, Francis: *An Inquiry into the Nature and Effects of the Paper Credit of Great Britain.* By Henry Thornton, M.P. 1 Edinburgh Review, 1802. (The review is unsigned.)

——: *Thoughts on the Restriction of Payments in Specie at the Banks of England and Ireland.* By Lord King. 2 Edinburgh Review, 1803. (The review is unsigned.)

Huskisson, W.: *The Question concerning the Depreciation of our Currency.* London, 1810. Reprinted in *Tracts on Paper Currency and Banking* (J. R. MacCulloch, editor, London, 1857).

King, Lord Peter: *Thoughts on the Restriction of Payments in Specie at the Banks of England and Ireland.* London, 1803; 2 ed., 1804.

Lauderdale, Earl: *The Depreciation of the Paper Currency of Great Britain Proved.* London, 1812.

——: *Further Considerations on the State of the Currency.* Edinburgh, 1813.

Liverpool, Lord: *Treatise on the Coins of the Realm.* London, 1805.

MacCulloch, J. R., ed.: *Tracts on Paper Currency and Banking.* London, 1857.

——: *Principles of Political Economy.* London, 1825.

——: *A Treatise on the Circumstances which determine the Course of Exchange.* London, 1820.

Malthus, Thomas R.: *The Measure of Value.* London, 1823.

——: *Publications on the Depreciation of Paper Currency.* 17 Edinburgh Review, 1811. (A review of Mushet, Ricardo, Blake, Huskisson, Bosanquet.)

Mill, James: *Elements of Political Economy.* London, 1821; 3 ed., 1826.

Mill, John Stuart: *Essays on some Unsettled Questions of Political Economy.* London, 1844; 2 ed., 1874.

——: *Principles of Political Economy.* London, 1848. W. J. Ashley, editor. London, 1909, 1920.

Miller, H. E.: *Banking Theories in the United States before 1860* (unpublished Ph.D. thesis, in the Harvard University Library; dated 1923).

——: *Earlier Theories of Crises and Cycles in the United States.* 38 Quar. Jour. Econ., 1924.

Mushet, R.: *The Effects produced . . . by the Bank Restriction Bill.* London, 1810.

Overstone, Lord: *Tracts and other Publications on Metallic and Paper Currency.* London, 1858.

Ricardo, David: *Economic Essays by David Ricardo,* E. C. K. Gonner, editor. London, 1923.

——: *The High Price of Bullion.* London, 1810; 4 ed., 1811.

——: *Letters of David Ricardo to Thomas Robert Malthus, 1810–1823,* J. Bonar, editor. Oxford, 1887.

——: *Letters of David Ricardo to John Ramsay MacCulloch, 1816–1823,* J. H. Hollander, editor. 10 Publ. Am. Econ. Assoc., 1895.

——: *Letters of David Ricardo to Hutches Trower, 1811–1823,* J. Bonar and J. H. Hollander, editors. Oxford, 1899.

——: *Observations on the Depreciation of Paper Currency.* London, 1811.

——: *Principles of Political Economy and Taxation.* London, 1817. E. C. K. Gonner, editor, London, 1891, 1924. (Also see the convenient edition in the Everyman Library.)

——: *Proposals for an Economical and Secure Currency.* London, 1816; 3 ed., 1819.

——: *Reply to Mr. Bosanquet's Observations.* London, 1810.

——: *Three Letters on the Price of Gold* (to the Morning Chronicle, London: Aug. 29, Sept. 20, Nov. 23, 1809). Reprinted in *A Reprint of Economic Tracts,* J. H. Hollander, editor. Baltimore, 1903.

Senior, N. W.: *Three Lectures on the Value of Money* (delivered in 1829; privately printed in 1840).

——: *Three Lectures on the Transmission of the Precious Metals.* London, 1827.

——: *Three Lectures on the Cost of Obtaining Money, etc.* London, 1830.

Silberling, N. J.: *British Prices and Business Cycles, 1779–1850.* Review of Economic Statistics, 1923.

——: *British Theories of Money and Credit, 1776–1848.* (Unpublished Ph.D. thesis, in the Harvard University Library; dated 1919).

——: *Financial and Monetary Policy in Great Britain during the Napoleonic Wars.* 38 Quar. Jour. Econ., 1924.

Sinclair, Sir John: *Observations on the Report of the Bullion Committee.* London, 1810.

Smith, Thomas: *The Bullion Question.* London, 1812.

——: *The Theory of Money and Exchange.* London, 1807; 2 ed., 1811.

Thornton, Henry: *The Nature and Effects of the Paper Credit of Great Britain.* London, 1802; 2 ed., 1810. Reprinted in *Tracts on Paper Currency and Banking,* J. R. MacCulloch, editor. London, 1857.

Tooke, T.: *An Inquiry into the Currency Principle.* London, 1844.

——: *Considerations on the State of the Currency.* London, 1826.

——: *On the Currency in connection with the Corn Trade.* London, 1829.

——: *Thoughts and Details on the High and Low Prices of the Last Thirty Years.* London, 1823; 2 ed., 1824.

Torrens, Col. Robert: *A Comparative Estimate of the Effects of Removing the Restriction on Cash Payments.* London, 1819.

——: *The Budget.* London, 1844.

——: *The Economists Refuted.* London, 1808.

——: *Essay on Money and Paper Currency.* London, 1812.

——: *Essay on the Production of Wealth.* London, 1821.

——: *The Principles and Practical Operation of Sir Robert Peel's Act.* London, 1848; 2 ed., 1857. (The second edition contains a reprint of *The Economists Refuted.*)

Trotter, Coutts: *The Principle of Currency and Exchanges.* London, 1810.

Wheatley, John: *An Essay on the Theory of Money and Principles of Commerce.* Vol. 1: London, 1807.

——: *Remarks on Currency and Commerce.* London, 1803.

3. 1850–1913

(a) *Books*

Andréadès, A.: *History of the Bank of England.* London, 1909; 2 ed., 1924.

Barbour, Sir David: *The Standard of Value.* London, 1912.

Bastable, C. F.: *Commerce of Nations*. London, 1892; 5 ed., London, 1911.

——: *The Theory of International Trade*. London, 1893; 4 ed., 1903.

Cairnes, J. E.: *Essays in Political Economy*. London, 1873.

——: *Leading Principles of Political Economy*. London, 1874.

——: *The Principles of Currency involved in the Bank Charter Act of 1844*. London, 1854.

Carlile, W. W.: *The Evolution of Modern Money*. London, 1901.

——: *Monetary Economics*. London, 1912.

Clare, G.: *A Money Market Primer*. London, 1891.

Cournot, A. A.: *Researches into the Mathematical Principles of the Theory of Wealth*, N. T. Bacon, translator. New York, 1897.

Cunynghame, Henry H.: *A Geometrical Political Economy*. Oxford, 1904.

Elliot, Hugh: *Letters of John Stuart Mill*. London, 1910: 2 vols.

Farrer, Baron T. H.: *Studies in Currency*. London, 1898.

Fisher, Irving: *The Purchasing Power of Money*. New York, 1911.

——: *Mathematical Investigations in the Theory of Value and Prices*. New Haven, 1892; reprinted, 1925.

Flux, A. W.: *Economic Principles*. London, 1904; 2 ed., 1923.

Giffen, Sir Robert: *Essays in Finance*. First Series: London, 1879; 5 ed., 1890; Second Series: London, 1886; 3 ed., 1890.

——: *Stock Exchange Securities*. London, 1877.

Goschen, Viscount G. J.: *Foreign Exchange*. London, 1861. (Many reprints.)

Great Britain. Gold and Silver Commission of 1888: *First Report:* 1887 Parl. Papers, xxii; *Second and Final Reports:* 1888 Parl. Papers, xlv.

——: Indian Currency Committee of 1893: *Report:* 1893–1894 Parl. Papers, lxv.

——: Indian Currency Committee of 1898: *Reports:* Part I, 1898 Parl. Papers, lxi; Part II, 1899 Parl. Papers, xxxi.

——: Indian Currency Commission, 1913–1914: *Interim Report:* 1914 Parl. Papers, xix; *Final Report:* 1914 Parl. Papers, xx.

Hobson, C. K.: *The Export of Capital*. London, 1912.

Hobson, J. A.: *Gold, Prices, and Wages*. London, 1913.

——: *International Trade*. London, 1904.

Jevons, W. S.: *Money and the Mechanism of Exchange*. London, 1875.

——: *Investigations in Currency and Finance*, H. S. Foxwell, editor. London, 1884; new ed., 1909.

Kemmerer, E. W.: *Money and Credit Instruments in their Relations to General Prices*. Ithaca, 1907; 2 ed., New York, 1909.

Keynes, J. M.: *Indian Currency and Finance*. London, 1913.

Kinley, D.: *Money*. New York, 1904.

Laughlin, J. L.: *The Principles of Money*. New York, 1903.

MacLeod, H. D.: *Banking and Currency*. London, 1855–1856; 5 ed., 1893.

——: *The Principles of Economic Philosophy*. 2 ed., vol. 1 and vol. 2, Part I: London, 1872–1875.

Marshall, A.: *The Fiscal Policy of International Trade*. London, 1908. (Memorandum to the House of Commons).

——: *Principles of Economics.* London, 1890; 8 ed., 1920.

——: *Pure Theory of Foreign Trade* (privately printed, 1879).

——: *Evidence,* given before the Gold and Silver Commission of 1888. 1888 Parl. Papers, xlv.

——: *Memorandum on the Effects of Differences in Currencies.* Submitted to the Gold and Silver Commission of 1888. 1888 Parl. Papers, xlv.

——: *Testimony,* given before the Indian Currency Committee of 1898. 1898 Parl. Papers, lxi; 1899 Parl. Papers, xxxi.

Mitchell, W. C.: *Business Cycles.* Berkeley, 1913.

——: *Gold, Prices and Wages under the Greenback Standard.* Berkeley, 1908.

——: *A History of the Greenbacks.* Chicago, 1903.

Musgrave, A.: *Studies in Political Economy.* London, 1875.

Nicholson, J. S.: *A Treatise on Money.* London, 1888; 5 ed., 1901.

——: *Principles of Political Economy.* London, 1893–1901: 3 vols.

O'Farrell, H. H.: *The Franco-German War Indemnity.* London, 1913. (Garton Foundation Publications.)

Pantaleoni, M.: *Pure Economics,* T. B. Bruce, translator. London, 1898.

Patten, Simon N.: *The Economic Basis of Protection.* Philadelphia, 1890.

Pigou, A. C.: *Wealth and Welfare.* London, 1912.

Price, L. L.: *Money and Its Relations to Prices.* London, 1896.

Scott, W. A.: *Money and Banking.* New York, 1903.

Shadwell, J. L.: *A System of Political Economy.* London, 1877.

Sidgwick, H.: *Principles of Political Economy.* London, 1883. (3 ed., bv J. N. Keynes, London, 1901.)

Taussig, F. W.: *Principles of Economics.* New York, 1911; 3 ed., 1922.

——: *The Silver Situation.* 2 ed., New York, 1893.

Walker, F. A.: *Money.* New York, 1878.

(b) *Periodical Articles*

Andrew, A. P.: *Credit and the Value of Money.* Publ. Am. Econ. Assoc., Series III, vi: 1905.

Atkinson, F. J.: *Silver Prices in India.* Journal of the Royal Statistical Society, 1897.

Bastable, C. F.: *The Incidence and Effects of Import and Export Duties.* Report of the British Association, 1889.

——: *On Some Applications of the Theory of International Trade.* 4 Quar. Jour. Econ., 1889.

——: *On Some Disputed Points in the Theory of International Trade.* 11 Econ. Jour., 1901.

Bell, S.: *A Statistical Point in Ricardian Theory of Gold Movements* [sic.]. 15 Jour. Pol. Econ., 1907.

Carver, T. N.: *Some Theoretical Possibilities of a Protective Tariff.* Publ. Am. Econ. Assoc., Series III, vol. iii: 1902.

Clow, F. R.: *The Quantity Theory and Its Critics.* 11 Jour. Pol. Econ., 1903.

Conant, C. A.: *The Distribution of Money.* 9 Jour. Pol. Econ., 1901.

Edgeworth, F. Y.: *Disputed Points in the Theory of International Trade.* 11 Econ. Jour., 1901.

——: *On a Point in the Theory of International Trade.* 9 Econ. Jour., 1899.

——: *The Theory of International Values.* 4 Econ. Jour., 1894.

Fisher, Irving.: *Cournot and Mathematical Economics.* 12 Quar. Jour. Econ., 1898.

Giffen, Sir Robert: *The Excess of Imports.* Journal of the Royal Statistical Society, 1899.

Hardy, S. Maclean: *The Quantity of Money and Prices, 1860–1891.* 3 Jour. Pol. Econ., 1895.

Hourwich, I. A.: *The Production and Consumption of the Precious Metals.* 10 and 11 Jour. Pol. Econ., 1902 and 1903.

Jevons, W. S.: *Richard Cantillon and the Nationality of Political Economy.* 49 Contemporary Review, 1881.

Kinley, D.: *The Relation of the Credit System to the Value of Money.* Publ. Am. Econ. Assoc., Series III, vi: 1905.

Laughlin, J. L.: *Gold and Prices, 1890–1907.* 17 Jour. Pol. Econ., 1909.

——: *Prices and the International Movement of Specie.* 10 Jour. Pol. Econ., 1902.

Leslie, T. E. C.: *The Known and the Unknown in the Economic World.* Fortnightly Review, 1879.

Lexis, W.: *The Agio on Gold and International Trade.* 5 Econ. Jour., 1895.

Loria, A.: *Notes on the Theory of International Trade.* 11 Econ. Jour., 1901.

Magee, J. D.: *Money and Prices.* 21 Jour. Pol. Econ., 1913.

Mitchell, W. C.: *The Quantity Theory of the Value of Money.* 4 Jour. Pol. Econ., 1896.

——: *The Real Issues in the Quantity-Theory Controversy.* 12 Jour. Pol. Econ., 1904.

Nicholson, J. S.: *The Effects of the Depreciation of Silver.* 4 Econ. Jour. 1895.

Persons, W. M.: *The Quantity Theory as Tested by Kemmerer.* 22 Quar. Jour. Econ., 1908.

Scott, W. A.: *The Quantity Theory of Money.* Am. Econ. Assoc. Studies, vol. 2: 1897.

Sprague, O. M. W.: *The Distribution of Money between the Banks and the People since 1893.* 18 Quar. Jour. Econ., 1904.

Taussig, F. W.: *Wages and Prices in Relation to International Trade.* 20 Quar. Jour. Econ., 1906.

Walker, F. A.: *The Quantity Theory of Money.* 9 Quar. Jour. Econ., 1895.

——: *Value of Money.* 8 Quar. Jour. Econ., 1893.

Walker, Francis: *Increasing and Diminishing Costs in International Trade.* 12 Yale Review, 1903.

Whitaker, A. C.: *The Ricardian Theory of Gold Movements and Professor Laughlin's Views of Money.* 18 Quar. Jour. Econ., 1904.

Whitelaw, T. N.: *Professor Nicholson on "The Causes of Movements in General Prices."* 14 Econ. Jour., 1904.

Willis, H. P.: *Credit Devices and the Quantity Theory.* 4 Jour. Pol. Econ., 1896.

4. The period since 1914

(a) *Books*

Anderson, B. M.: *The Value of Money.* New York, 1917.

Bordes, J. van Walré de: *The Austrian Crown.* London, 1924.

Brussels International Financial Conference, 1919: *Proceedings, Reports, etc.* London, 1920.

Cassel, G.: *Money and Foreign Exchange after 1914.* London, 1922.

——: *The World's Monetary Problems.* London, 1921.

Flux, A. W.: *The Foreign Exchanges.* London, 1924.

Furniss, E. S.: *Foreign Exchange.* New York, 1922.

Graham, F. D.: *International Trade of the United States, 1862–1879* (unpublished Ph.D. thesis, in the Harvard University Library; dated 1919).

Great Britain. Committee on Currency and Foreign Exchanges after the War: *First Interim Report:* 1918 Parl. Papers, vii; *Final Report:* 1919 Parl. Papers, xiii.

——. Foreign Office, Historical Section: *Indemnities of War; Subsidies and Loans.* London, 1920. (Peace Handbooks, no. 158.)

Gregory, T. E.: *Foreign Exchange.* London, 1922.

Hawtrey, R. G.: *Currency and Credit.* London, 1919; 2 ed., 1923.

——: *Monetary Reconstruction.* London, 1923.

Keynes, J. M.: *A Revision of the Treaty.* London, 1922.

——: *Monetary Reform.* London, 1924.

Laughlin, J. L.: *Money and Prices.* New York, 1919.

Layton, W. T.: *An Introduction to the Study of Prices.* London, 1922.

Lehfeldt, R. A.: *Gold, Prices and the Witwatersrand.* London, 1919.

Marshall, A.: *Money Credit and Commerce.* London, 1922.

Mitchell, W. C.: *International Price Comparisons.* Washington, 1919.

National Industrial Conference Board: *The Inter-Ally Debts and the United States.* New York, 1925.

Nicholson, J. S.: *Inflation.* London, 1919.

Peake, E. G.: *An Academic Study of some Money Market and other Statistics.* London, 1923.

Rasin, Aloys: *Financial Policy of Czecho-Slovakia.* Oxford, 1923.

Robertson, D. H.: *Money.* London, 1922.

Taussig, F. W.: *Free Trade, the Tariff and Reciprocity.* New York, 1920.

——: *Some Aspects of the Tariff Question.* Cambridge, 1915.

U. S. Federal Reserve Board: *Prices in the United States and Abroad: 1919–1923.* Special Bulletin, Washington, 1924.

U. S. Senate Commission of Gold and Silver Inquiry: *Foreign Exchange and Currency Investigation.* Washington, 1925: Serial 9, vol. 1.

U. S. Tariff Commission: *Depreciated Exchange and International Trade.* Washington, 1922.

Viner, Jacob: *Canada's Balance of International Indebtedness, 1900–1913.* Cambridge, 1924.

Whitaker, A. C.: *Foreign Exchange.* New York, 1919.

Williams, J. H.: *Argentine International Trade, 1880–1900.* Cambridge, 1920.

(b) *Periodical articles*

Anderson, B. M.: *Cheap Money, Gold, and Federal Reserve Bank Policy.* Chase Economic Bulletin, 1924.

——: *The Gold Standard versus "A Managed Currency."* Chase Economic Bulletin, 1925.

——: *The Report of the Dawes Committee.* Chase Economic Bulletin, 1924.

Angell, J. W.: *International Trade under Inconvertible Paper.* 36 Quar. Jour. Econ., 1922.

——: *Monetary Theory and Monetary Policy.* 39 Quar. Jour. Econ., 1925.

Bickerdike, C. F.: *Internal and External Purchasing Power of Paper Currencies.* 32 Econ. Jour., 1922.

Bonar, J.: *Knapp's Theory of Money.* 32 Econ. Jour., 1922.

Bonn, M. J.: *The Fall in German Exchange.* 31 Quar. Jour. Econ., 1916.

Bullock, Williams and Tucker: *The Balance of Trade of the United States.* Review of Economic Statistics, 1919.

Burgess, W. R.: *The Velocity of Bank Deposits.* Journal of the American Statistical Association, 1923.

Cannan, E.: *The Application of the Theoretical Apparatus of Supply and Demand to Units of Currency.* 31 Econ. Jour., 1921.

Cassel, G.: *Abnormal Deviations in International Exchanges.* 28 Econ. Jour., 1918.

——: *Depreciation of Gold.* 27 Econ. Jour., 1917.

——: *Depreciation of the Mark.* 29 Econ. Jour., 1919.

——: *The Present Position of the Foreign Exchanges.* 26 Econ. Jour., 1916.

——: *World's Monetary Problem.* 30 Econ. Jour., 1920.

Chandler, H. A. E.: *Discussion of Some Fundamental Factors in Foreign Exchange Fluctuations.* Commerce Monthly, 1921.

Copland, D. B.: *Currency Inflation and Price Movements in Australia.* 30 Econ. Jour., 1920.

Crump, N. B.: *A Review of Recent Foreign Exchange Fluctuations.* Journal of the Royal Statistical Society, 1921.

Davies, J. M.: *The Quantity Theory and Recent Statistical Studies.* 29 Jour. Pol. Econ., 1921.

Elsas, M.: *The Internal Purchasing Power of the German Mark.* 31 and 32 Econ. Jour., 1921 and 1922.

Emery, H. C.: *The Tariff and the Ultimate Consumer.* 5 Am. Econ. Rev., 1915.

Feis, H.: *What Determines the Volume of a Country's International Trade.* 12 Am. Econ. Rev., 1922.

Graham, F. D.: *Germany's Capacity to Pay and the Reparation Plan.* 25 Am. Econ. Rev., 1925.

——: *International Trade under Depreciated Paper: the United States, 1862–1879.* 36 Quar. Jour. Econ., 1922.

——: *Some Aspects of Protection Further Considered.* 37 Quar. Jour. Econ., 1923.

——: *The Theory of International Values Re-examined.* 38 Quar. Jour. Econ., 1923.

Harvard Economic Service: *Commodity Prices during the Present Decade.* Weekly Letter, June 10, 1922.

Hollander, J. H.: *International Trade under Depreciated Paper.* 32 Quar. Jour. Econ., 1918.

Keynes, J. M.: *Alfred Marshall, 1842–1924.* 34 Econ. Jour., 1924.

Laughlin, J. L.: *The Quantity-Theory of Money.* 32 Jour. Pol. Econ., 1924.

Monroe, A. E.: *The French Indemnity of 1871 and Its Effects.* Review of Economic Statistics, 1919.

Nicholson, J. S.: *Inflation of the Currency and the Rise in Prices.* 26 Econ. Jour., 1916.

Peake, E. G.: *The Relationship between the American and French Exchanges and the Rates of Interest and Discount.* 112 Bankers' Magazine, 1921.

Penson, J. H.: *The Polish Mark in 1921.* 32 Econ. Jour., 1922.

Persons, Warren M.: *Indices of General Business Conditions.* Review of Economic Statistics, 1919.

Pigou, A. C.: *The Foreign Exchanges.* 37 Quar. Jour. Econ., 1922.

——: *Some Problems of Foreign Exchange.* 30 Econ. Jour., 1920.

——: *The Value of Money.* 32 Quar. Jour. Econ., 1917.

Shirras, G. F.: *Some Effects of the War on Gold and Silver.* Journal of the Royal Statistical Society, 1920.

Snyder, Carl: *A New Index of Business Activity.* Journal of the American Statistical Association, 1924.

——: *A New Index of the General Price Level from 1875.* Journal of the American Statistical Association, 1924.

——: *New Measures in the Equation of Exchange.* Am. Econ. Rev., 1924.

Stewart, W.: *Social Value and the Theory of Money.* 25 Jour. Pol. Econ., 1917.

Taussig, F. W.: *International Trade under Depreciated Paper.* 31 Quar. Jour. Econ., 1917.

——: *The Change in Great Britain's Trade Terms after 1900.* 35 Econ. Jour., 1925.

Van Dorp, E. C.: *Abnormal Deviations in International Exchanges.* 30 Econ. Jour., 1920.

——: *The Deviation of Exchanges.* 29 Econ. Jour., 1919.

Wicksell, K.: *Gold, Inflation and the Exchange.* 28 Econ. Jour., 1918.

——: *International Freights and Prices.* 37 Quar. Jour. Econ., 1918.

Williams, J. H.: *Foreign Exchange under Depreciated Paper.* Journal of the American Bankers' Association, 1922.

——: *Foreign Exchange, Prices and International Trade.* Annals, 1920.

——: *German Foreign Trade and the Reparations Payments.* 37 Quar. Jour. Econ., 1922.

——: *Latin American Foreign Exchange and International Balances during the War.* 33 Quar. Jour. Econ., 1919.

Working, H.: *Prices and the Quantity of Circulating Medium, 1890–1921.* 37 Quar. Jour. Econ., 1923.

World's Monetary Problem: a symposium. Annals, 1920.

Young, Allyn A.: *Marshall on Consumers' Surplus in International Trade.* 39 Quar. Jour. Econ., 1924.

——: *War Debts, External and Internal.* Foreign Affairs, 1924.

II. FRENCH THOUGHT

Titles of Principal Periodicals and Collections

Collection des Principaux Économistes (edited by E. Daire, Paris, 1843–1847: 15 vols.; not numbered).

Journal des Économistes. 1842 ff.

Revue d'Économie Politique. 1887 ff.

Revue Économique Internationale. 1904–July 1914; May 1920 ff.

Revue d'Histoire des Doctrines Économiques et Sociales. 1908–1912: 5 vols. Continued as: Revue d'Histoire Économique et Sociale. 1913 ff.

1. The period before 1800

Arias, G.: *Les idées économiques d'Antonio Serra.* Jour. des Écon., 1922.

——: *Les précurseurs de l'économie monétaire en Italie. Davenzati et Montanari.* Rev. d'écon. pol., 1922.

Bacalan, Isaac de: *Paradoxes philosophiques sur la liberté du commerce entre les nations.* Bordeaux, 1764. (Reprinted, with comments, by F. Sauvaire-Jourdain, in *Isaac de Bacalan.* Paris, 1903.)

Bodin, Jean: *Réponses aux Paradoxes du Sieur de Malestroit.* 1568. (Reprinted in a single volume, together with the *Six Livres de la République* (1576), and other works. Lyon, 1593, Vincent.)

Boisguilbert, Pierre de: *Détail de la France.* 1697.

——: *Factum de la France.* 1707. (Both this volume and the *Détail* are reprinted in the Coll. Prin. Écon., 1843.)

Bridrey, E.: *La théorie de la monnaie au XIV siècle. Nicole Oresme.* Paris, 1906.

Cantillon, Richard: *Essai sur la nature du commerce en général.* (Probably written in 1730–1734: printed 1755. Reprinted for Harvard University. Boston, 1892.)

Condillac, Etienne B. de: *Le commerce et le gouvernement.* 1776. (Reprinted in the Coll. Prin. Écon., 1847.)

Cossa, Luigi: *Histoire des doctrines économiques* (translated by A. Bonnet, from the third Italian edition: Paris, 1899.)

Deschamps, Auguste: *Le métallisme et la politique mercantile.* Paris, 1920. (Reprinted from Rev. d'hist. écon., 1920.)

Dubois, A.: *Précis d'histoire des doctrines économiques.* Paris, 1903.

——: *Un rapport d'Isaac de Bacalan.* Rev. d'hist. des doct. écon., 1908.

Forbonnais, François V. de: *Principes Économiques.* Amsterdam, 1767. (Reprinted in Coll. Prin. Écon., 1847.)

Gonnard, René: *Histoire des doctrines économiques.* Paris, 1921–1922: 3 vols.

Guyot, Yves: *Quesnay et la physiocratie.* Paris, 1896.

Hume, D.: *Essais sur le commerce, etc.* (Incompletely translated in 1754, 1767, etc.; reprinted in Coll. Prin. Écon., 1847.)

Laffemas, B.: *Comme l'on doit permettre la liberté du transport de l'or.* Paris, 1602.

Legrand, R.: *Richard Cantillon.* Paris, 1900.

Martin, G.: *La monnaie et le crédit privé en France aux xvi°–xvii° siècles; les faits et les théories (1550–1664)*. Rev. d'hist. des doct. écon., 1909.

Melon, J. F.: *Essai politique sur le commerce*. 1734; 2 ed., 1736. (Reprinted in Coll. Prin. Écon., 1843.)

Montchrétien, Antoyne de: *Traicté de l'œconomie politique*. 1615. (Edited by Funck-Brentano, Paris, 1889.)

Montesquieu, Charles de: *L'esprit des lois*. Geneva, 1748: 2 vols.

Quesnay, F.: *Œuvres economiques et philosophiques*. (Edited by Oncken, Frankfort and Paris, 1888. Also see the reprints in the volume "Physiocrates" in Coll. Prin. Écon., 1846.)

Rivière, Mercier de la: *L'ordre naturel*. Paris and London, 1767. (Reprinted in Coll. Prin. Écon., 1846.)

Rouxel, M.: *Un précurseur des Physiocrates: Cantillon*. Jour. des Écon., 1891.

Sauvaire-Jourdain, F.: *Isaac de Bacalan*. Paris, 1903.

Schatz, A.: L'individualisme économique et social. Paris, 1907.

Sully, Maximilien duc de: *Économies Royales*. 1598. (Edited by J. Chailley, Paris, 1889.)

Vene, A.: Montchrétien et le nationalisme économique. Paris, 1923.

Weulersse, G.: *Le mouvement physiocratique en France*. Paris, 1910: 2 vols.

2. 1800–1899

Allard, Alphonse: *Les changes fossoyeurs du libre-échange*. Paris, 1890.

——: *La crise, la baisse des prix, la monnaie*. Brussels, 1895.

——: *La crise en Angleterre*. Brussels, 1888.

Aubry, Jules: *Quelques observations sur la valeur de la monnaie*. Rev. d'écon. pol., 1887.

Barrault, H. E.: *Les doctrines de Cournot sur le commerce international*. Rev. d'hist. des doct. écon., 1912.

Bastiat, F.: *Harmonies économiques*. Brussels, 1850.

Block, M.: *Les progrès de la science économique depuis Adam Smith*. Paris, 1890: 2 vols.; 2 ed., 1897.

Bourguin, M: *La mesure de la valeur et la monnaie*. Paris, 1896.

Cauwès, P.: *Précis du cours d'économie politique*. Paris, 1878–1880: 2 vols. (Third and later editions bear the title, *Cours d'économie politique*.)

Cherbuliez, A. E.: *Précis de la science économique*. Paris, 1862; 2 vols.

Chevalier, M.: *Cours d'économie politique*. Paris, 1841–1850: 3 vols.; 2 ed., 1855–1866.

Clare, G.: *Le marché monétaire anglais* (translated by G. Giraud, from the second English edition, Paris, 1894).

Coullet et Juglar, editors: *Extraits des enquêtes parlementaires anglaises*. Paris, 1865: 8 vols.

Courcelle-Seneuil, J. G.: *Traité théorique et pratique d'économie politique*. Paris, 1857: 2 vols.; 3 ed., 1891.

Cournot, A. A.: *Principes de la théorie des richesses*. Paris, 1863.

——: *Recherches sur les principes mathématiques de la théorie des richesses*. Paris, 1838.

——: *Revue sommaire des doctrines économiques*. Paris, 1877.

Essars, Pierre de: *La vitesse de la circulation de la monnaie.* Paris, 1895.

Foville, A. de: *La théorie quantitative et les prix* L'Économiste français, 1895: vol 1.

Gide, C.: *Principes d'économie politique.* Paris, 1884. (Editions after 1908 continued with title, *Cours d'économie politique.*)

Gide et Rist: *Histoire des doctrines économiques.* Paris, 1909; 4 ed., 1922.

Goschen, G. J.: *Théorie des changes étrangers* (translated by L. Say, from the fifth English edition, Paris, 1866. The second (1875) and later French editions also contain Say's report on the French Indemnity payments of 1871–1873).

Juglar, Clement: *Du change et de la liberté d'emission.* Paris, 1868.

Laveleye, Émile de: *Le marché monétaire et ses crises.* Paris, 1865.

——: *La liberté commerciale.* Paris, 1857.

——: *La monnaie et le bimétallisme international.* 2 ed., Paris, 1891.

Leroy-Beaulieu, Paul: *Traité théorique et pratique d'économie politique.* 2 ed., Paris, 1896: 4 vols.; 4 ed., Paris, 1905.

Mawas, A.: *Le "Bullion Report" anglais de 1810.* Rev. d'écon. pol., 1920.

Milet, H. A.: *D'un aphorisme orthodoxe mais inexact sur la monnaie.* Rev. d'écon. pol., 1890.

Mill, John Stuart: *Principes d'économie politique* (translated by Dussard and Courcelle-Seneuil, from the third English edition, Paris, 1873: 2 vols.).

Mongin, M.: *Des changements de valeur de la monnaie.* Rev. d'écon. pol., 1887.

——: *La monnaie et la mesure des valeurs.* Rev. d'écon. pol., 1897. (See other similar articles by Mongin.)

Pareto, V.: *Cours d'économie politique.* Lausanne, 1896–1897: 2 vols.

Ricardo, David: *Des principes de l'économie politique et de l'impôt* (translated by S. S. Constancio, Paris, 1819: 2 vols.).

——: *Œuvres complètes* (translated by Constancio et Fonteyraud, Paris, 1847).

Say, J. B.: *Cours complet d'économie politique pratique.* Paris, 1828–1829: 6 vols.; 2 ed., by H. Say, 1840: 2 vols.

——: *Traité d'économie politique.* Paris, 1803; 2 vols.; 6 ed., by H. Say, 1841: 1 vol.

Smith, Adam: *Recherches sur la nature et les causes de la richesse des nations* (translated by G. Garnier, Paris, 1843: 2 vols.).

Théry, Edmond: *La crise des changes.* 4 ed., Paris, 1894.

——: *Les finances et le change du Brésil.* Paris, 1898.

Walras, Léon: *Éléments d'économie politique pure.* Lausanne, 1874.

——: *Théorie du libre échange.* Rev. d'écon. pol., 1897.

Wolowski, L.: *Le change.* Jour. des Écon., 1866.

——: *Le change et la circulation.* Paris, 1869.

3. The period since 1900

(a) *Books*

Ansiaux, Maurice: *Principes de la politique regulatrice des changes.* Brussels, 1910.

Antonelli, E.: *Principes d'économie pure.* Paris, 1914.

Arnauné, A.: *La monnaie, le crédit, et le change.* Paris, 1902; 6 ed., 1922–1923: 2 vols.

Aupetit, A.: *Théorie générale de la monnaie.* Paris, 1901.

Auspitz and Lieben: *Recherches sur la théorie des prix* (translated by L. Suret, Paris, 1914).

Bastable, C. F.: *La théorie du commerce international* (translated by F. Sauvaire-Jourdain, from the second English edition, Paris, 1900).

Bonnet, G. E.: *La politique anglaise d'assainissement monétaire, 1918–1922.* Paris, 1923.

Cassel, G.: *La monnaie et le change depuis 1914* (translated by G. Lachapelle, Paris, 1923).

Colson, C.: *Cours d'économie politique.* Paris, 1901–1907: 3 vols.; 3 ed., 1910–1921: 6 vols.

Damiris, C. J.: *Le système monétaire grec et le change.* Paris, 1920: 3 vols.

Decamps, J.: *Les changes étrangers.* Paris, 1922.

Dolléans, Ed.: *La monnaie et les prix.* Paris, 1905.

Favre, Jean: *Les changes dépréciés.* Paris, 1906.

Fontana-Russo, Luigi: *Traité de politique commerciale* (translated by F. Poli, Paris, 1908).

Foville, A. de: *La monnaie.* Paris, 1907.

Guyot et Raffalovitch: *Inflation et déflation.* Paris, 1921.

Landry, A.: *Manuel d'économique.* Paris, 1908.

Masson-Forestier, L.: *Les caisses de conversion et la réforme monétaire en Argentine et au Brésil.* Paris, 1913.

Mawas, A.: *Le système monétaire et le change anglais depuis la guerre.* Paris, 1921.

Mitjavile, H.: *La crise du change en Espagne.* Bordeaux, 1904.

Nogaro, B.: *Éléments d'économie politique.* Paris, 1913–1914: 2 vols. (The second edition, dated 1921, bears the title, *Traité élémentaire d'économie politique.*)

——: *La monnaie.* Paris, 1924.

——: *Le rôle de la monnaie dans le commerce international.* Paris, 1904.

——: *Réparations, dettes interalliés, et restauration monétaire.* Paris, 1922.

Pallain, J.: *Des rapports entre les variations du change et les prix.* Paris, 1905.

Pareto, V.: *Économie mathématique* (article in Encyclopédie des sciences mathématiques, Paris, 1911 ff.)

——: *Manuel d'économie politique* (translated by A. Bonnet, Paris, 1909).

Questions monétaires contemporaines. Paris, 1905. (By a symposium of writers.)

Reboud, P.: *Essai sur les changes étrangers.* Paris, 1900.

Rist, Charles: *La déflation en pratique.* Paris, 1924.

——: *Les finances de guerre de l'Allemagne.* Paris, 1921.

Roux, G.: *Le change espagnol et son amélioration actuelle.* Montpellier, 1911.

Subercaseaux, G.: *Le papier-monnaie.* Paris, 1920. (Translated from the Spanish original of 1912.)

Théry, Ed.: *Un grave danger monétaire pour les pays prêteurs.* Paris, 1913.

——: *Le problème du change en Espagne.* Paris, 1901. (See a number of similar works by Théry, published from 1903 to 1914, on Greece, Japan, Russia, Italy, etc.)

Théry, René: *Rapports des changes avariés et des règlements extérieurs.* Paris, 1912.

Valaoritis, J. A.: *La question du cours forcé et du change en Grèce.* Athens, 1902–1903: 2 vols.

Viollet, E.: *Le problème de l'argent et l'étalon d'or au Mexique.* Paris, 1907.

(b) *Periodical articles*

Aftalion, A.: *La circulation, les changes et les prix.* Rev. écon. int., 1924.

——: *Les variations du change tiennent-elles aux cycles économiques?* Rev. écon. int., 1925.

Arnauné, A.: *Le bimétallisme français et le bimétallisme indien.* Comptes-rendus de l'Académie des Sciences morales et politiques, 1903.

Barrault, H. E.: *Le sens et la portée des théories antiquantitatives de la monnaie.* Rev. d'hist. des doct. écon., 1910.

Barré, M.: *La circulation fiduciare.* Rev. d'écon. pol., 1918.

Baudin, L.: *L'or du Transvaal.* Rev. d'écon. pol., 1922.

Dechesne, L.: *Influence de la monnaie et du crédit sur les prix.* Rev. d'écon. pol., 1904.

——: *Pour la théorie quantitative de la monnaie et du crédit.* Rev. d'écon. pol., 1914.

De Miguel, A.: *La crise des changes.* Rev. écon. int., 1924.

Gide, C.: *L'or et le change.* Rev. d'écon. pol., 1915.

——: *De l'influence de la guerre sur les prix.* Rev. d'écon. pol., 1916.

Gignoux, C.-J.: *Le problème monétaire mondiale et la théorie du professeur Cassel.* Rev. d'écon. pol., 1922.

G.-M.——: *Dépréciation de l'or dans les pays scandinaves.* Rev. d'écon. pol., 1916.

Guyot, Yves: *La production de l'or et les prix.* Jour. des Econ., 1911.

——: *Le professeur Cassel et la dépréciation systématique de la monnaie.* Rev. écon. int., 1923.

Lachapelle, G.: *Les théories du professeur Cassel sur la monnaie et le change.* Rev. d'écon. pol., 1923.

Landry, A.: *La rapidité de la circulation monétaire.* Rev. d'écon. pol., 1905.

Lescure, Jean: *L'accroissement de la production de l'or et la hausse générale des prix.* Rev. d'écon. pol., 1911.

——: *Hausses et baisses générales des prix.* Rev. d'écon. pol., 1912.

Mourre, Baron Charles: *Les causes de la hausse des prix.* Rev. d'écon. pol., 1919.

Nogaro, B.: *Contribution à une théorie réaliste de la monnaie.* Rev. d'écon. pol., 1906.

——: *Les dernières expériences monétaires et la théorie de la dépréciation.* Rev. écon. int., 1908.

——: *L'expérience bimétalliste du xixe siècle et la théorie générale de la monnaie.* Rev. d'écon. pol., 1908.

——: *Les phénomènes monétaires et la théorie de la monnaie.* Rev. écon. int. 1920.

——: *Le problème du change espagnol.* Rev. écon. int., 1910.

———: *Le problème national des échanges avec l'extérieur.* Rev. écon. int., 1911.
———: *La signification de l'expérience monétaire Tcheco-Slovaque.* Rev. écon. int., 1924.
Olivier, M.: *Le change et les prix.* Rev. d'écon. pol., 1922.
Pinard, A.: *Ricardo.* Jour. des Écon., 1901.
Pupin, R.: *L'or, les prix, la guerre.* Jour. des Écon., 1917.
Rist, C.: *La circulation monétaire française et le mouvement des prix.* Rev. d'écon. pol., 1914.

III. RECENT ITALIAN THOUGHT

TITLES OF PRINCIPAL COLLECTIONS AND PERIODICALS

Biblioteca dell' Economista. Turin, 1850 ff.
Giornale degli Economisti. 1875–1878, 1886 ff.
Riforma Sociale. 1894 ff.

1. Books

Amoroso, Luigi: *Lezioni di economia matematica.* Bologna, 1921.
Barone, E.: *Principii di economia politica.* Rome, 1908.
Bastable, C. F.: *Teoria del commercio internazionale* (translated in the Bibl. d. Econ., Series V: 1921).
Berardi, D.: *La moneta nei suoi rapporti quantitativi.* Turin, 1912.
Buzzetti, A.: *Teoria del commercio internazionale.* Milan, 1877.
Cairnes, J. E.: *Alcuni principii fondamentali di economia politica* (translated in the Bibl. d. Econ., Series III, iv: 1878).
Cossa, E.: *L'interpretazione scientifica del Mercantlismo,* Messina, 1907.
Cossa, L.: *Introduzione allo studio dell' economia politica.* 3 ed., Milan 1892.
———: *Primi elementi di economia sociale.* 1875; 13 ed., by A. Graziani, Milan, 1914.
De Viti De Marco, A.: *Moneta e pressi.* Citta di Castella, 1885.
Fanno, M: *La Moneta.* Turin, 1908.
Ferraris, C. F.: *Moneta e corso forzoso.* Milan, 1879.
Fontana-Russo, Luigi: *Trattato di politica commerciale.* Rome, 1906.
Goschen, G. J.: *Teoria del corso dei cambi esteri* (translated in the Bibl. d. Econ., Series IV, ii; 1899).
Graziani, A.: *Istituzioni di economia politica.* Turin, 1904; 3 ed., 1917.
———: *La moneta nei pagamenti internazionali.* (In *Studi giuridici in onore di Carlo Fadda.* Naples, 1906, vol. v.)
———: *Sulle relazioni fra gli studi economici in Italia e in Germania nel secolo XIX.* (In G. Schmoller, *Entwicklung der deutschen Volkswirtschaftslehre.* Leipzig, 1908, vol. i.)
Leone, E.: *Lineamenti di economia politica.* Rome, 1914.
Loria, A.: *Corso completo di economia politica.* Turin, 1910; 2 ed., 1919.
———: *Il valore della moneta.* Turin, 1905. (In: Bibl. d. Econ., Series IV, vi: 1905.)
———: *Le peripezie monetarie della guerra.* Milan, 1920.

——: *Studi sul valore della moneta.* Turin, 1891; 2 ed., 1901.

Lorini, E.: *La moneta e il principio del costo comparativo.* Turin and Rome, 1896.

——: *La questione della valuta in Austria-Ungheria.* Turin and Rome, 1893. (See other similar studies published by Lorini from 1893 to 1904.)

Luzzatti, G.: *La teorica del commercio internazionale e il costi di reprodusione.* (In *In Onore di Tullio Martello.* Bari, 1917).

——: *Valore e prezzi.* Padua, 1914.

Martello, T.: *La moneta.* Florence, 1883.

Messedaglia, A.: *La moneta.* Florence, 1883.

Mill, John Stuart: *Principii di economia politica* (translated in the Bibl. d. Econ., Series I, xii: 1851).

Pantaleoni, M.: *Principii di economia pure.* Florence, 1889; 2 ed., 1894.

Papi, J. U.: *Prestiti esteri e commercio internazionale.* Rome, 1923.

Pareto, V.: *Manuale di economia politica.* Milan, 1906.

——: *L'Aggio e il cambio.* (In *In Onore di Tullio Martello.* Bari, 1917.)

Ricardo, D.: *Principii dell' economia politica* (translated in Bibl. d. Econ.: Series I, xi: 1856).

Smith, A.: *Ricerche sopra la natura e le cause della ricchezza delle nazioni* (translated in Bibl. d. Econ., Series I, ii: 1851).

Straulino, G.: *Il commercio internazionale e la circulazione monetaria nello stato.* Rome, 1891.

Supino, C.: *La carta moneta in Italia.* Turin, 1921.

——: *Il mercato monetario internazionale.* Milan, 1910.

——: *Principii di economia politica.* 2 ed., Naples, 1905; 5 ed,, 1920.

2. Periodical articles

Bresciani-Turroni, C.: *Considerazioni su alcune recenti esperienze monetarie.* Giorn. d. Econ., 1925.

——: *Oscillazioni dello sconto e dei prezzi.* Giorn. d. Econ., 1916.

——: *Relazioni fra sconto e prezzi durante i cicli economici.* Giorn. d. Econ., 1916.

Carano-Donvito, G.: *Indennità di guerra e debiti interalleati.* Rif. Soc., 1925.

Cossa and Bertolini: *Bibliografia economica.* Giorn. d. Econ., 1891–1895, *passim.* Also rebound separately.

C. R. ——: *Keynes sulla riforma monetaria.* Rif. Soc., 1924.

Del Vecchio, G.: *Contributi alle dottrine della circolazione.* Giorn. d. Econ., 1914.

——: *I principii della teoria economica della moneta.* Giorn. d. Econ., 1909.

——: *Questioni fondamentali sui valore della moneta.* Giorn. d. Econ., 1917.

——: *Teoria della esportazione del capitale.* Giorn. d. Econ., 1910.

Einaudi, L.: *Corso dei cambi, sbilancio commerciale, e circolazione cartacea.* Rif. Soc., 1918.

Fanno, M.: *Inflazione monetaria e corso dei cambi.* Giorn. d. Econ., 1922 and 1923.

Graziani, A.: *La moneta nei pagamenti internazionali.* Rif. Soc., 1906.

Jannacone, P.: *Il "dumping" e la discriminazione dei prezzi.* Rif. Soc., 1914.

——: *Relazioni fra commercio internazionale, cambi esteri, e circolazione monetaria in Italia nel quarantennio 1871–1913.* Rif. Soc., 1918.
Murray, R. A.: *Sulla teoria dei costi comparati.* Giorn. d. Econ., 1914.
Pareto, V.: *Teoria matematica dei cambi forestieri.* Giorn. d. Econ., 1894.
——: *Teoria matematica del commercio internazionale.* Giorn. d. Econ., 1895.
Ricci, U.: *Travisamenti della teoria degli scambi internazionale.* Giorn. d. Econ., 1907.
Sensini, G.: *Teoria dei cambi esteri.* Giorn. d. Econ., 1907.
Supino, C.: *Moneta e prezzi.* Rif. Soc., 1917.
Zagnoni, A.: *Una teoria protezionista dei cambi esteri.* Giorn. d. Econ., 1894.
——: *Moneta e costi comparati.* Giorn. d. Econ., 1896.

IV. RECENT GERMAN AND AUSTRIAN THOUGHT

PRINCIPAL DICTIONARIES AND PERIODICALS

Handbuch der politische Ökonomie. Edited by Schonberg and others (1 ed., 1882; 4 ed., 1896–1898).
Handwörterbuch der Staatswissenschaften. Edited by Conrad and others (1 ed., 1890–1897; 3 ed., 1909–1911).
Archiv für soziale Gesetzgebung und Statistik (1888–1903). Continued under title: Archiv für Sozialwissenschaft und Sozialpolitik.
Jahrbuch für Gesetzgebung, Verwaltung und Rechtspflege. Edited by Holkendorff (1871–1876). Continued as a new series under title: Jahrbuch für Gesetzgebung, Verwaltung und Volkswirtschaft. Edited by Schmoller and others (1877 ff.).
Jahrbücher für Nationaloekonomie und Statistik. Edited by Hildebrand, Conrad, and others (1863 ff.)
Zeitschrift für Volkswirtschaft, Sozialpolitik und Verwaltung. Edited by Böhm-Bawerk, Wieser, and others (1892–1918, 1921 ff.).

1. Books

Altmann, S. P.: *Zur deutschen Geldlehre des 19. Jahrhunderts.* (In G. Schmoller, *Die Entwicklung der deutschen Volkswirtschaftslehre.* Leipzig, 1908, vol. i.)
Auspitz and Lieben: *Untersuchungen über die Theorie des Preises.* Leipzig, 1889.
Bendixen, F.: *Das Wesen des Geldes.* Munich, 1908; 2 ed., 1918.
——: *Geld und Kapital.* Jena, 1912; 3 ed., 1922.
——: *Währungspolitik und Geldtheorie im Lichte der Weltkrieges.* Munich, 1916; 2 ed., 1919.
Conrad, J.: *Grundriss zum Studium der politische Ökonomie.* Jena, 1896–1900: 4 vols.; 8 ed., 1920.
Diehl, K.: *Die Entwicklung der Wert- und Preistheorie im 19. Jahrhundert.* (In G. Schmoller, *Die Entwicklung der deutschen Volkswirtschaftslehre* Leipzig, 1908, vol i.)
——: *Über Fragen des Geldwesens und der Valuta.* Jena, 1921.
Döring, H.: *Die Geldtheorien seit Knapp.* 2 ed., Griefswald, 1922.

Fellmeth, A.: *Zur Lehre von der internationale Zahlungsbilanz.* Heidelberg, 1877.

Földes, Bela: *Der Einfluss des Agio's auf den Aussenhandel.* Vienna, 1877.

Goschen, G. J.: *Theorie des auswärtigen Weckselkurse* (translated by F. Stöpel from the second French edition, Frankfurt, 1875).

Grundriss der Sozialökonomik. Tübingen, 1914 ff. By a symposium of writers.

Grunzel, J.: *Der internationale Wirtschaftsverkehr und seine Bilanz.* Leipzig, 1896.

——: *Handels-, Zahlungs-, und Wirtschaftsbilanz.* Vienna, 1914.

Hagen, K. H.: *Die Nothwendigkeit der Handelsfreiheit.* Königsberg, 1844.

Helferrich, K.: *Das Geld.* Leipzig, 1903; 4 ed., 1919.

——: *Studien über Geld- und Bankwesen.* Berlin, 1900.

Hennicke, G.: *Die Entwicklung der spanischen Währung (1868–1906).* Stuttgart, 1907.

Hertzka, T.: *Die Gesetze der Handels- und Sozialpolitik.* Leipzig, 1880.

——: *Währung und Handel.* Vienna, 1876.

——: *Weckselkurs und Agio.* Vienna, 1894.

——: *Das Wesen des Geldes.* Leipzig, 1887.

Hildebrand, R.: *Die Theorie des Geldes.* Jena, 1883.

Hilferding, R.: *Das Finanzkapital.* Vienna, 1910.

Hirsch, Julius: *Die deutsche Wahrungsfrage.* Jena, 1924.

Hoffman, F.: *Kritische Dogmengeschichte der Geldwerttheorien.* Leipzig, 1907.

Knapp, G. F.: *Staatliche Theorie des Geldes.* Munich, 1905; 3 ed., 1921.

Knies, Karl G. A.: *Geld und Kredit.* Berlin, 1873–1879: 2 vols.; vol. i: 2 ed., 1885.

Launhardt, W.: *Mathematische Begründung der Volkswirtschaftslehre.* Leipzig, 1885.

Lexis, W.: *Allgemeine Volkswirtschaftslehre.* Berlin, 1910.

——: *Papiergeld.* (Article in Handw. d. Staatsw.)

Mangoldt, J. C. E. von: *Grundriss der Volkswirtschaftslehre.* Stuttgart, 1863; 2 ed. (posthumous, by F. Kleinwächter), 1871.

Menger, Carl: *Geld.* (Article in Handw. d. Staatsw.)

——: *Beiträge zur Währungsfrage in Österreich-Ungarn.* Jena, 1892. (Reprinted from Hildebrand's Jahrb., Series 3, vol. 3.)

Mill, John Stuart: *Grundsätze der politischen Oekonomie* (translated by A. Soetbeer, Hamburg, 1852: 2 vols.)

Mises, Ludwig von: *Theorie des Geldes und der Umlaufsmittel.* Munich, 1912; 2 ed. in progress.

Petritsch, Leo: *Die Theorie von der sogenannten günstigen und ungünstigen Handelsbilanz.* Graz, 1902.

Philippovich, Eugen von: *Grundriss der politischen Oekonomie.* Freiburg, 1893–1907: 2 vols. (Later editions by parts.)

Rau, K. H.: *Lehrbuch der politischen Ökonomie.* Heidelberg, 1826. (Later editions, by parts, down to 1869.)

Ricardo, D.: *Grundsätze der politische Oekonomie* (translated by Pfundt, Weimar, 1821. There are also a number of later translations).

Roscher, W. G. F.: *System der Volkswirtschaft.* Stuttgart, 1854 ff.: 5 vols. (Later editions by parts.)

Rühe, F.: *Das Geldwesen Spaniens seit dem Jahre 1772.* Strassburg, 1912.

Schlesinger, Karl: *Theorie der Geld- und Kreditwirtschaft.* Munich, 1914.

Schmoller, G.: *Die Entwicklung der deutschen Volkswirtschaftslehre im neunzehnten Jahrhundert.* Leipzig, 1908. (A commemorative volume, by a symposium of writers.)

——: *Grundriss der allegemeinen Volkswirtschaftslehre.* Leipzig, 1900–1904: 2 vols.; revised ed., by L. Schmoller, 1920.

Schüller, R.: *Schutzzoll und Freihandel.* Leipzig and Vienna, 1905.

Schumpeter, J.: *Das Wesen und der Hauptinhalt der Theoretischen Nationalökonomie.* Leipzig, 1908.

Smith, Adam: (*Wealth of Nations:* many translations, under various titles, beginning in 1776–1778).

Soetbeer, G. A.: *Materielen zur Erläuterung . . . der wirtschaftliche Edelmetallverhältnisse.* Berlin, 1885; 2 ed., 1886.

Spiethoff, A.: *Die Quantitätstheorie.* (In *Festgaben für Adolph Wagner.* Leipzig, 1905.)

Spitzmüller, A.: *Die österreichisch-ungarish Währungsreform.* Vienna and Leipzig, 1902.

Wagner, A.: *Die russische Papierwährung.* Riga, 1868.

——: *Theoretische Sozialökonomik.* Leipzig, 1907–1909: 2 vols.

Wieser, F. von: *Theorie der gesellschaftlichen Wirtschaft.* Tübingen, 1914. (In *Grundriss der Sozialökonomik*, by a symposium of writers: vol. i, pt. 3.)

Wolter, Johannes: *Das staatliche Geldwesen Englands zur zeit der Bank-Restriction, 1797–1821.* Strassburg, 1917.

Zuckerkandl, R.: *Zur Theorie des Preises.* Leipzig, 1889.

2. Periodical articles

Amonn, Alfred: *Das Ziel der Wahrungspolitik.* Zeitschrift f. Volksw., 1921.

Budge, S.: *Zur Frage der Bankrate und des Geldwertes.* Arch. f. Soz., 1917–1918.

Elster, K.: *Die "Grundgleichung" der Geldtheorie.* Hildebrand's Jahrb., 1920.

Földes, B.: *Ursachen und Wirkungen des Agios.* Hildebrand's Jahrb., 1882.

——: *Zur Theorie vom internationalen Handel.* Hildebrand's Jahrb., 1915.

Haberler, G.: *Kritische Bemerkungen zu Schumpeters Geldtheorie.* Zeitschrift f. Volksw., 1925.

Hahn, A.: *Statische und dynamische Weckselkurse.* Arch. f. Soz., 1922.

Heiligenstadt, Carl: *Beiträge zur Lehre von den auswärtigen Weckselkursen.* Hildebrand's Jahrb., 1892-1894.

——: *Die internationalen Goldbewegungen.* Schmoller's Jahrb., 1894.

Helferrich, K.: *Aussenhandel und Valutaschwankungen.* Schmoller's Jahrb., 1897. (Reprinted later in his own *Studien:* see supra.)

Kerschagl, Richard: *Überblick über das Schriftum des Geldwesens von 1914 bis 1920.* Zeitschrift f. Volksw., 1921.

Marschak, Jacob: *Die Verkehrsgleichung.* Arch. f. Soz., 1924.

Menger, Carl: *Die Valutaregulierung in Österreich-Ungarn.* Hildebrand's Jahrb., 1892.

Mises, Ludwig von: *Die Quantitätstheorie.* Mitteilungen des Verbandes österreichen Banken und Bankiers, 1918.

——: *Zahlungsbilanz und Devisenkurse.* Mitteilungen des Verbandes österreichen Banken und Bankiers, 1919.

——: *Zur Klassifikation der Geldtheorien.* Arch. f. Soz., 1917–1918.

Sachs, L.: *Die italienische Valutaregulierung.* Hildebrand's Jahrb., 1892.

Schönfeld, Leo: *Über Joseph Schumpeters Lösung des ökonomischen Zurechnungsproblems.* Zeitschrift f. Volksw., 1924.

Schumpeter, J.: *Das Sozialproduct und die Rechenpfennige.* Arch. f. Soz., 1917–1918.

Vogel, Emmanuel Hugo: *Stabilisierung oder Valutahebung als Ziel der Wahrungsreform.* Zeitschrift f. Volksw., 1921.

Waffenschmidt, Walter G.: *Studien zu einer quantitativen Geldtheorie.* Arch. f. Soz., 1924.

Wagner, A.: *Das Reichsfinanzwesen.* Schmoller's Jahrb., 1874.

Wieser, F. von: *Der Geldwert und seine geschichtlichen Veränderungen.* Zeitschrift f. Volksw., 1904.

——: *Der Geldwert und seiner Veränderungen.* Schriften des Vereins f. Sozialpolitik, 1910.

INDEX

INDEX

Adams, C. F., 118 n.
Aftalion, A., 293, 550.
Allard, A., 282, 547.
Altmann, S. P., 324 n., 326 n., 336 n.,
   553.
Amonn, A., 555.
Amoroso, L., 551.
Anderson, B. M., 160, 179, 192; works,
   543, 544.
Andréadès, A., 40 n., 503, 539.
Andrew, A. P., 127 n., 541.
Ansiaux, M., 141 n., 251 n., 269 n.,
   285 n., 548.
Antonelli, E., 548.
Argentina, 167 ff., 284, 513 ff.; in bibli-
   ography, 543, 549.
Arias, G., 206 n., 210 n., 546.
Arnauné, A., 251 n., 549, 550.
Ashley, Sir W. J., 11 n., 535.
Asymmetrical markets, 243 ff.
Atkinson, F. J., 541.
Aubry, J., 279 n., 547.
Aupetit, A., 258, 279, 549.
Auspitz, R., 259 n., 279 n., 347 n., 454 n.;
   works, 549, 553.
Australia, 94 n., 130, 144 ff., 154 n., 269.
Austria (-Hungary), 332, 340, 425; after
   1914, 196 ff., 293, 296, 316 n., 344,
   441 n., 446 n.; in bibliography, 552,
   554, 555, 556.

Bacalan, I. de, 223 ff., 546.
Bagehot, W., 313.
Balance of bargains school, of Mercantilism, 12 n.
Balance of payments, Torrens's theories,
   62; disequilibrium in, as source of
   depreciation, 188 n., 189 n., 193, 195,
   284 ff., 290 ff., 295 n., 334, 338, 340 ff.,
   368, 420 ff., 448, 523; maintenance of
   equilibrium in, ch. xvi; kept in equilibrium by exchange rate movements,
   402, 412 n., 522; and equilibrium in
   international demands, 471; the determinant of the foreign exchanges,
   477 ff., 491 ff.; and bank reserves, 478,
   481; and see Currency depreciation,

Foreign exchange depreciation, Price-
   specie flow analysis.
Balance of trade, determines the value
   of money, 28 n.; relation to exchange
   rates, 317, 319, 481; to the currency
   circulation, 319; the ultimate corrective of international disequilibria,
   408 ff., 413; and see International
   capital movements, Price movements,
   Price-specie flow analysis.
Balance of trade theory, in Mercantilism, 11, 14, 207 n., 210, 211; attacked
   by Barbon, 23; in Cantillon, 212,
   Forbonnais, 217; and see Specie flows.
Bank Charter Act of 1844, 75, 137.
Bank Charter Controversy, 75, 116.
Bank deposits, the determinant of prices
   in Fullarton and Tooke, 76; rôle in
   adjustment of balance of payments,
   172, 403 ff., 507, 508, 511, 526; and
   see Bank reserves.
Bank of England, ch. iii passim; during
   the Restriction period, 40 ff., App. A
   passim; attacked by the Bullionists,
   41, 61, Boyd, 44, Ricardo, 55; the
   attacks unjustified, 43, 65 n., 479, 486,
   490; defended by Thornton, 46,
   Wheatley, 52; position since 1918,
   117, 426 ff.
Bank of France, 434, 436 n.
Bank rate, see Discount rate.
Bank reserves, related to prices by Sidg-
   wick, 117, Giffen, 119, Nicholson, 122,
   Marshall, 123, Lexis, 125, Sprague,
   130; this view attacked by Laughlin,
   160; effect of international payments,
   478, 481; and see Bank deposits.
Banking principle, 75; anticipated by
   Torrens, 63 n.
Barbon, N., 23, 535.
Barbour, Sir D., 539.
Baring, Sir F., 44 n., 537.
Barone, E., 308 n., 551.
Barrault, H. E., 240 n., 268 n., 280 n.,
   291 n.; works, 547, 550.
Barré, M., 279 n., 550.
Barter assumption, see Barter trade.

of criticisms, 367, 451; final evaluation, 471; and *see* International values.
Equilibrium, in international exchange,
in Ricardo, 69, 364, Mill, 88, Pareto,
253; absent under depreciated conditions, 402, 418, 449; in ratios of international exchange, 455 ff., 470; in internal exchange, 458; final estimate
of its character, 471; and *see* Balance
of payments, International price equality, Value of money.
Essars, P. de, 279 n., 548.
Europe, since 1914, 178 ff., 186 ff., 194,
291 ff., 342 ff., ch. xvii *passim;* effects
of gold discoveries, *see* Discoveries.
Export prices, *see* International prices.

Fanno, M., 310, 313, 316 n., 551, 552.
Farrer, Baron T. H., 127 n., 540.
Favre, J., 549.
Feis, H., 544.
Fellmeth, A., 348, 554.
Ferrara, F., 303 n.
Ferraris, C. F., 551.
Finance bills, and the balance of pay-
ments, 405, 412 n.
Finland, 294.
Fisher, I., 26 n., 131 ff., 178 ff., 186 n.,
193, 196; on Cournot, 238 n., 243 n.;
his position in Italy, 310, Germany
and Austria, 328; his international
price comparisons, 389, 391 n.; works,
540, 542.
Flux, A. W., 103 n., 540, 543.
Földes, B., 332 n., 347, 348, 554, 555.
Fontana-Russo, L., 305 n., 549, 551.
Forbonnais, F., 216 ff., 229 n., 277, 546.
Foreign exchange depreciation, in Argentina, 167 ff., 284, 515, Austria, 196 ff.,
332, 340, Brazil, 290, Czecho-Slovakia,
293, 296, 299, 446 n., France, 299,
432 ff., Germany, 194, 440 ff., Great
Britain, 41, 299, 427 ff., App. A.,
Greece, 286 n., Italy, 316 ff., Russia,
284, 336 ff., Spain, 283, 286 n., 290,
334, United States, 161 ff., 511; effect
on international trade, in Boyd,
46, Goschen, 140 ff., Marshall, 149,
Bastable, 154, Lexis, 155, Taussig,
161, 167, Graham, 161 ff., Williams,
194, in early French writers, 220,
Bourguin, 283, Subercaseaux, 287,
Jannacone, 319, Földes, 332, Hennicke,

334, Wagner, 336 ff., Lexis, 155 ff.,
340; differential effect on prices, 161 ff.,
167 ff., 287, 337, 522, 526; as source
of currency depreciation, 197, 293,
295, 478, 484; compensating tariffs
against, 281, 343; and *see* Balance of
payments, Budget equilibrium, Currency depreciation.
Foreign exchange mechanism, effect,
463.
Foreign exchanges, theory of under
stable conditions, in Mercantilists,
20, 21, 25, Blake, 61, Macleod, 138,
Goschen, 139 ff., Bourguin, 283; relation to the balance of trade, in Hume,
27, Ricardo, 70; to discount rates, in
Macleod, 138, Goschen, 139; and international capital movements, 467;
under depreciated conditions, *see*
Foreign exchange depreciation.
Foreign trade, in antiquity, 3.
Foville, A. de, 279, 548, 549.
Foxwell, H. S., 40 n., 61 n., 503, 537.
France, after 1918, 293, 295, 299, 426,
432 ff.; under bimetallism, 420; in-
demnity payments to Germany, 517 ff.;
in bibliography, 541, 545, 548.
Franklin, B., 28 n., 536.
Free-trade doctrines, in North, 16,
Smith, 35, the Physiocrats, 221, Baca-
lan, 223.
Fullarton, J., 75 ff., 85, 87 n., 116, 537.
Function-index, in Pareto, 253 n.
Furniss, E. S., 11 n., 12 n., 18 n., 32,
212 n.; works, 536, 543.

Gee, Sir J., 211, 536.
Germany, after 1918, 194, 197, 293, 296,
299 n., 316 n., 330, 343, 402 n., 426,
440 ff.; price movements since 1850,
389; effect of indemnity payments by
France, 520 ff.; in bibliography, 544,
545, 549, 554.
Gide, C., 222 n., 229 n., 250, 313 n., 548,
550.
Giffen, Sir R., 118 ff., 309 n., 320; works,
540, 542.
Gold, *see* Discoveries, Specie flows.
Gold exchange standard, 167, 284 n.,
425 n.
Gold-silver ratio, effect of changes in,
143, 148, 150, 283, 420, 422 ff., 444,
468.